Parties, Politics, and Democracy in the New Southern Europe

The New Southern Europe

P. Nikiforos Diamandouros and Richard Gunther

General Series Editors

Parties, Politics, and Democracy in the New Southern Europe

Edited by P. Nikiforos Diamandouros and Richard Gunther

The Johns Hopkins University Press
Baltimore and London

Sponsored by the Subcommittee on the Nature and Consequences of Democracy in the New Southern Europe of the Joint Committee on Western Europe (1975–96) of the American Council of Learned Societies and the Social Science Research Council

This book was brought to publication with the generous assistance of the Mershon Center, the Ohio State University.

Printed in the United States of America on acid-free paper
9 8 7 6 5 4 3 2 1

The Johns Hopkins University Press
2715 North Charles Street
Baltimore, Maryland 21218-4363
www.press.jhu.edu

Library of Congress Cataloging-in-Publication Data

Parties, politics, and democracy in the new Southern Europe / edited by P. Nikiforos Diamandouros and Richard Gunther.
p. cm.
"Sponsored by the Subcommittee on the Nature and Consequences of Democracy in the New Southern Europe of the Joint Committee on Western Europe (1975–96) of the American Council of Learned Societies and the Social Science Research Council"—T.p. verso.
Includes bibliographical references (p.) and index.
ISBN 0-8018-6517-4 (alk. paper) — ISBN 0-8018-6518-2 (pbk. : alk. paper)
1. Europe, Southern—Politics and government. 2. Political parties—Europe, Southern. 3. Democracy—Europe, Southern. 4. European Economic Community—Europe, Southern. 5. Socialism—Europe, Southern. I. Diamandouros, P. Nikiforos. II. Gunther, Richard. III. Social Science Research Council (U.S.). Subcommittee on the Nature and Consequences of Democracy in the New Southern Europe. IV. American Council of Learned Societies. V. Title.
JN94 .P37 2001
320.94—dc21 00-008848

A catalog record for this book is available from the British Library.

Contents

Tables and Figures

Tables

Figure

Preface and Acknowledgments

The preface to *The Politics of Democratic Consolidation: Southern Europe in Comparative Perspective,* edited by Richard Gunther, P. Nikiforos Diamandouros, and Hans-Jürgen Puhle, the first in a series of volumes, systematically presented the intellectual rationale for, and background to, this project on the new southern Europe, undertaken in the context of the renewed interest in the nature and dynamics of modern democratic regimes prompted by such major contributions as *The Breakdown of Democratic Regimes,* edited by Juan Linz and Alfred Stepan, and *Transitions from Authoritarian Rule,* edited by Guillermo O'Donnell, Philippe C. Schmitter, and Laurence Whitehead.

The agenda of that first volume was to move the frontier of inquiry beyond transitions from nondemocratic rule and to engage in a systematic examination of the requisites of democratic consolidation, using insights and lessons derived from the study of southern Europe, conceptualized, for reasons extensively discussed in Edward Malefakis's contribution to *The Politics of Democratic Consolidation,* as comprising Greece, Italy, Portugal, and Spain. The rationale for such a conceptualization goes well beyond the obvious similarities stemming from socioeconomic modernization in the post–World War II period and democratization since the 1970s. It reflects, rather, deeper structural and historical parallels. The most salient among these are linked to the four countries' similarities in (a) physical characteristics—namely, Mediterranean climate, a pronounced mountainous topography, and a dearth of coal and iron deposits, but a relative abundance of nonferrous minerals; (b) agricultural patterns—namely, prevalence of luxury crops, such as wine, olives, and fruit, that require marketing, preclude subsistence farming, and are labor-intensive, thus resisting modernization and retarding the rural exodus to urban centers that it implies; (c) the salience of regionalism (itself a by-product of mountainous topography), the antagonism between highlanders and plains people that this breeds, and the social banditry naturally issuing from such antagonism; (d) a strong maritime tradition resulting from proximity to the sea and nearby islands; and (e) the early development and persistence over time of complex urban structures linked to some of the factors just mentioned (crop diversity, maritime tradition), but also to easy access to the complex civilizations of the ancient Middle East.

Put otherwise, the initial object was to identify the long-term and short-term conditions that either promoted or acted as confining conditions for the consolidation of new democratic regimes. In pursuit of that goal, the contributors to *The Politics of Democratic Consolidation* systematically examined the impact on consolidation of socioeconomic modernization, the character of the predecessor nondemocratic regime, civil-military relations, international factors, collective actors, institutions, organized interests, and political parties.

The Politics of Democratic Consolidation also sought to place democratic consolidation in the broader context of the overall process of democratization, and to point to its links with phases causally or temporally anterior or posterior to it. In this context, we identified a period of "democratic persistence" as a phase in the democratization process subsequent to consolidation, in which political arrangements, crafted during the transitions and institutionalized during consolidation, acquire further roots and contribute to the deepening of democracy and to the improvement of its quality, or, conversely, to its erosion and possible deconsolidation or reequilibration.

The major conclusion of *The Politics of Democratic Consolidation,* which serves as an underpinning for the more specific inquiries undertaken in each subsequent volume, is that, in at least two major areas, those of socioeconomic development and politics, southern Europe has, over the past few decades, undergone a fundamental structural transformation, as a result of which it irreversibly crossed a critical threshold in its transition to modernity. More specifically, the region's spectacular socioeconomic modernization, initially observed in Italy, beginning in the 1950s, and amply reproduced in the other three countries since the 1970s, has enabled it effectively to leave behind a legacy of socioeconomic decline and delayed development dating back to the seventeenth and eighteenth centuries. Succinctly put, southern Europe has, in the course of the past four decades, ceased to be part of the semiperiphery of the world system and become part of its center.

A similar qualitative change has taken place at the level of politics. The region's successful democratization over the past half century, and the consolidation, since the 1970s, of democratic regimes in the four countries comprising it has freed it from a legacy of right-wing authoritarianism that had plagued it since the Napoleonic period, and had stood at the root of its abortive democratic experiments over the past century and a half. As a result, its political fortunes have taken on a distinctly modern quality and have allowed for its incorporation into the universe of democratic regimes, heretofore inhabited by advanced industrial democracies. Taken together, these two structural transformations lend substance to the central claim of the intellectual project that gave rise to this series, concerning the emergence, in recent decades, of a new southern Europe, qualitatively different from its "old" incarnation, that has successfully leapfrogged into socioeconomic and political modernity.

The aim of this project is to explore the various dimensions of democratic persistence by attempting to answer one general question: does democracy make a difference? Put otherwise, our research agenda takes democratic consolidation as its starting point and explores its impact on, or significance for, politics (in the present volume), economics, the state, and the interplay between culture and politics, systematically highlighting the changes that have taken place in southern Europe over the past thirty years or so by juxtaposing preauthoritarian with postauthoritarian arrangements and experiences. We also seek to place the experience of democratization in southern Europe in a broader context by means of comparisons with both advanced industrial democracies in northwestern Europe and, to a lesser extent, democratic experiments in selected countries of Latin America and eastern Europe.

Parties, Politics, and Democracy in the New Southern Europe first of all explores the proposition that, rather than remaining frozen or hostage to inertia, democratic regimes evolve following democratic consolidation. A subsidiary goal is to test the distinction made in *The Politics of Democratic Consolidation* between consolidation of democracy *qua* regime, on the one hand, and consolidation of its component subsystems, or "partial regimes," on the other. We conclude that the two processes of consolidation need not analytically coincide, and that the consolidation of partial regimes is not a precondition for democratic consolidation. A third major goal of this volume is to inquire into the validity of the notion of "leapfrogging" development, conceptualized as a heuristic device capable of adequately conveying the rapidity with which socioeconomic and political change occurred in southern European countries, catapulting them into the qualitatively different world of modern politics, economies, and cultures. These central questions are explored by the contributors to the volume in chapters dealing with the nature and evolution of the political systems in the region, the anchors of partisanship in each country, the advent of a new campaign politics intimately linked to leapfrogging, the antiparty phenomenon in Italy, and the manner in which conservative, socialist, and communist parties adjusted to and, in turn, helped shape the dynamics of the region's party systems.

The Intellectual History of This Project

The intellectual history of the various initiatives that eventually gave rise to this project is perhaps worth recounting briefly. The initial stimulus for the creation of a committee of social scientists interested in studying the evolution of southern European transitions to democracy was provided by the events that toppled the authoritarian regimes of Greece and Portugal in 1974. Following a series of formal and informal meetings over the ensuing two years, a research group was formed, called the Committee on Southern Europe (COSE), whose purpose was to promote the systematic study of the region over the period from the end of the Napoleonic Wars to the present. Initial participants in this effort were Douglas A. Chalmers, P. Nikiforos Diamandouros, Giuseppe DiPalma, James R. Kurth, Juan J. Linz, Edward E. Malefakis, Joyce F. Riegelhaupt, and Philippe C. Schmitter. The eventual product of this initiative was the creation of an informal, interdisciplinary network of scholars interested both in southern Europe as a region and in the particular historical or political processes it exemplifies best, such as rapid and profound socioeconomic transformation in late-developing societies and successfully negotiated transitions to democracy. This coordinate research effort helped raise the visibility of the southern European region in meetings of professional associations at the national level (in particular, political science and sociological associations in Europe and the United States, including the Council of European Studies in the latter), the regional level (e.g., the European Consortium for Political Research, where a separate Southern European Study Group was set up in the early 1980s), and the international level (e.g., the International Political Science Association and the International Sociological Association). The result was a significant accumulation of knowledge on various dimensions of the polities, economies, and cultures of southern European societies, with significant spillover effects for both area studies and comparative analysis.

This process reached happy fruition in 1987–88. Two informal meetings served as the immediate stimulus for a new round of activity: the first took place in the context of a conference on transition and consolidation in Latin America and southern Europe, organized by Guillermo O'Donnell and Philippe Schmitter at the Kellogg Institute of the University of Notre Dame, in April 1987. There, a small group consisting of Maria Carrilho, P. Nikiforos Diamandouros, Richard Gunther, Juan Linz, and Philippe Schmitter explored available options for a new initiative and extensively deliberated the requisites and content of its agenda. This was followed by a second crucial planning session, made possible through Schmitter's energies and capacity to secure the required financial support, which brought together a larger number of European and American specialists on southern Europe in the magnificent setting of the European University Institute, in San Domenico di Fiesole, near Florence, in September 1987. It was on the sedate and austere premises of the institute that the central themes informing this project were initially articulated and widespread consensus was reached on the desirability of focusing not on transition but on consolidation, whose qualitatively different attributes and properties had yet to be seriously studied and analyzed.

This culminated in a decision to approach the Joint Committee on Western Europe of the American Council of Learned Societies (ACLS) and the Social Science Research Council (SSRC) with the idea of their sponsoring this activity. The joint committee's prior interest in democratization and regime transition in southern Europe made it an appropriate vehicle for a larger undertaking centered on democratic consolidation. Endorsing the idea for such an initiative, in December 1987, the joint committee proposed to the boards of the ACLS and SSRC the establishment of the Subcommittee on the Nature and Consequences of Democracy in Southern Europe, which, following approval, formally came into being in April 1988. Cochaired by P. Nikiforos Diamandouros (University of Athens) and Richard Gunther (Ohio State University), the subcommittee consisted of the following members, drawn from Greece, Italy, the Federal Republic of Germany, France, Portugal, Spain, the United Kingdom, and the United States: Manuel Villaverde Cabral (University of Lisbon), Maria Carrilho (Advanced Institute of Labor and Enterprise Sciences, Lisbon), Juan J. Linz (Yale University), Carmelo Lisón

Tolosana (University of Madrid-Complutense), Edward E. Malefakis (Columbia University), George Th. Mavrogordatos (University of Athens), Yves Mény (Institut d'Etudes politiques, Paris), José Ramón Montero (Autonomous University of Madrid), Leonardo Morlino (University of Florence), Gianfranco Pasquino (University of Bologna), Víctor Pérez-Díaz (Juan March Center for Advanced Study in the Social Sciences, Madrid), Hans-Jürgen Puhle (University of Bielefeld), Sidney Tarrow (Cornell University), and Loukas Tsoukalis (St. Antony's College, Oxford). Hans-Jürgen Puhle played a particularly important role over the following decade, steering the subcommittee's project through the German foundation world and providing sage advice at crucial intervals.

The subcommittee's charge was dual: "(1) to engage in a systematic study of the nature of democratic consolidation in Greece, Portugal, Spain, and postfascist Italy, by exploring its cultural, economic, political, and social dimensions; and (2) to use the insights derived from this regional case study to contribute to the emergent, more general, theoretical debate concerning the properties of, and processes involved in, the consolidation of democracy." There were five interrelated dimensions of change in the new southern Europe that the subcommittee was to explore: processes of democratic consolidation, the nature of democratic politics, economic and social relations in the region, the changing functions of the state in the post-Keynesian era, and the dynamics of cultural change.

The final step toward the realization of what had, for more than a decade, been an elusive goal came in May 1988. At that time, the Stiftung Volkswagenwerk, underscoring its role as a preeminent European institution committed to the fostering of social science across national borders, agreed to provide generous support for a five-year program of research, conferences, and publication activities, designed to produce five and possibly six collective volumes dealing with the five interconnected dimensions of change mentioned above and drawing together the major theoretical findings issuing from the project. With additional support from the Werner-Reimers Stiftung and the German Social Science Study Group on Spain and Portugal, the project was informally launched in Bad Homburg, Germany, in July 1989, where specific conference and publication plans were made.

The first volume of the series, *The Politics of Democratic Consolidation,* was the product of a conference held in Madrid at the Juan March Center for Advanced Study in the Social Sciences in July 1990, and of a follow-up authors' meeting hosted by the Department of Sociology, University of Rome, in December of the same year. This second volume was made possible by an initial meeting held at the European Cultural Center in Delphi, Greece, in July 1991, and a follow-up authors' conference, sponsored by the Institute Clingendael, in The Hague in March 1992. A third volume will also be based on a twin set of conferences, the first held in Sintra, Portugal, in July 1992, and a follow-up session hosted by the Levi Foundation in Venice in April 1993. The initial conference leading to a fourth volume in the series was hosted by the Zentrum für interdisziplinäre Forschung of the University of Bielefeld, Germany, in July 1993, and the authors' meeting was held at Boğaziçi University in Istanbul in July 1994. A final volume is to be based on an initial meeting (also the last formal meeting of the Subcommittee on Southern Europe) in the magnificent setting of Elounda, in eastern Crete, Greece, in July 1995, and a follow-up authors' conference in Majorca, Spain, in July 1996. It is hoped that these conferences and resulting published volumes will fulfill the subcommittee's mandate, which was to more fully integrate southern Europe into the mainstream of comparative social science research and to derive from the study of its experience insights capable of contributing to the fast-growing body of theoretical literature on democratization.

Acknowledgments

The numerous intellectual debts accumulated over the years in connection with the intellectual, organizational, financial, and administrative aspects of the overall project of which this volume forms a part have already been gratefully recorded in the acknowledgments section of *The Politics of Democratic Consolidation.* Here, we shall confine ourselves to thanking all those individuals and institutions who contributed to the birth of this volume, *Parties, Politics, and Democracy in the New Southern Europe.* We should like to begin by thanking the European Cultural Centre in Delphi and the Clingendael Institute in The Hague for having hosted the two conferences that gave rise to the volume. If the mental associations generated by Delphi sufficed to make our meeting there a success, our visit to The Hague was, in many ways, rendered memorable by Hans Daalder's generous hospitality and untiring concern with both organizational detail and intellectual substance.

Thanks are due as well to Paul Allen Beck, Hans Daalder, Jane Jensen, and Peter Mair, who commented on the various contributions to the two conferences leading up to this volume and provided a comparative context in which they could be assessed and subsequently improved. The encouragement and advice these scholars provided, both at the conference and subsequently, have contributed much to the quality of this book.

We should also like to express our deep appreciation to Dr. Helga Junkers of the Volkswagen Stiftung for supporting our efforts and ensuring the continuous flow of the financial support that have made both this volume and the larger project of which it is a part possible. Thanks are also due to Kenton Worcester, the program director at the Social Science Research Council, and Elizabeth O'Brien, the staff assistant, who provided steady and reassuring administrative support and guidance to the subcommittee's activities relating to this volume. Finally, we should like to express our sincere appreciation to the Johns Hopkins University Press and, especially, the executive editor, Henry Tom, for having agreed to make the intellectual products issuing from this project, including this volume, part of its broader commitment to the study of democracy. Thanks, too, go to Peter Dreyer for his copyediting of our collective product and for the gracious and professional manner in which he handled the many complicated questions that inevitably arose in the process of seeing the manuscript to press. Finally, we are extremely appreciative of the generous financial support from the Mershon Center of the Ohio State University that has helped make possible the publication of a paperback edition of this volume.

P. Nikiforos Diamandouros and Richard Gunther
General Series Editors

Acronyms and Abbreviations

AN	Alleanza Nazionale (former MSI) (Italy)
AP	Alianza Popular (later PP) (Spain)
ASP	Acção Socialista Portuguêsa
CCD	Centro Cristiano Democratico (Italy)
CD	Coalición Democrática (Democratic Coalition) (Spain)
CDS	Centro Democrático y Social (Social and Democratic Center) (Spain)
CDS	Partido do Centro Democrático Social (Portugal)
CDU	Coligação Democrática Unitária (Unitary Democratic Coalition) (Portugal)
CIS	Centro de Investigaciones Sociológicas
CiU	Convergència i Unió (Spain)
CNEP	Comparative National Elections Project
DC	Democrazia Cristiana (Italy)
DIANA	Demokratike Ananeosse (Democratic Renewal) (Greece)
DIKKI	Demokratiko Koinoniko Kinema (Democratic Social Movement) (Greece)
DS	Democratici della Sinistra (Democrats of the Left) (Italy)
E. Ar.	Ellenike Aristera (Greek Left) (formerly KKE-Es)
EDA	Eniaia Demokratike Aristera (United Democratic Left) (Greece)
EDE	Ethnike Demokratike Enosis (Greece)
EDIK	Enose Demokratikou Kentrou (Union of the Democratic Center) (Greece)

EK	Enosis Kentrou (Center Union) (Greece)
EMU	European Monetary Union
EP	Ethnike Parataxis (National Front) (Greece)
EPEN	Ethnike Politike Enosis (National Political Union) (Greece)
ERE	Ethnike Rizospastike Enosis (National Radical Union) (Greece)
ETA	Euskadi ta Askatasuna (Basque separatist organization, Spain)
EU	European Union
FI	Forza Italia!
IU	Izquierda Unida (United Left) (Spain)
KKE	Kommounistiko Komma Elladas (Greece)
KKE-Es	KKE-Esoterikou (Greek Communist Party of the Interior) (later E. Ar.)
KP	Komma Proodeftikon (Party of the Progressives) (Greece)
Lega	Lega Nord (Italy)
MDP	Movimento Democrático Português (Portugal)
MFA	Movimento das Forças Armadas (Portugal)
MS-FM	Movimento Sociale–Fiamma Tricolore (Italy)
MSI	Movimento Sociale Italiano (later AN)
ND	Nea Demokratia (Greece)
ÖVP	Österreichische Volkspartei (Austrian People's Party)
P. Seg.	Patto Segni (Italy)
PASOC	Partido de Acción Socialista (Spain)
PASOK	Panellinio Sosialistiko Kinema (Panhellenic Socialist Movement) (Greece)
PCE	Partido Comunista de España
PCI	Partito Comunista Italiano
PCP	Partido Comunista Português
PDC	Pacte Democràtic per Catalunya (Spain)
PDCI	Partito dei Comunisti Italiani
PDS	Partito Democratico della Sinistra (Democratic Party of the Left) (Italy)
PLI	Partito Liberale Italiano
PNV	Partido Nacionalista Vasco (Spain)
POLAN	Politike Anoixe (Political Spring) (Greece)
PP	Partido Popular (originally AP) (Spain
PP	Partido Popular (originally CDS) (Portugal)

PPD	Partido Popular Democrático (later PSD) (Portugal)
PPI	Partito Popolare Italiano
PPM	Partido Popular Monárquico (Portugal)
PRD	Partido Renovador Democrático (Democratic Renewal Party) (Portugal)
PRI	Partito Repubblicano Italiano
PS	Partido Socialista (Portugal)
PSD	Partido Social-Democrata (originally PPD) (Portugal)
PSDI	Partito Socialista Democratico Italiano
PSI	Partito Socialista Italiano
PSIUP	Partito Socialista di Unità Proletaria (Italy)
PSOE	Partido Socialista Obrero Español (Spanish Socialist Workers' Party)
PSP	Partido Socialista Popular (merged with PSOE in 1978) (Spain)
PSUC	Partit Socialista Unificat de Catalunya (Spain)
RC	Partito della Rifondazione Comunista (Party of Communist Refoundation) (Italy)
SYN	Synaspismos tes Aristeras kai tes Proodou (Coalition of the Left and Progress) (Greece)
UCD	Unión de Centro Democrático (Union of the Democratic Center) (Spain)
UDC	Unione Cristiana Democratica (Italy)
UDP	União Democrático Popular (Portugal)
UDR	Unione Democratica per la Repubblica (Italy)
UGT	União Geral dos Trabalhadores (Portugal)
UGT	Unión General de Trabajadores (Spain)

Parties, Politics, and Democracy in the New Southern Europe

1 Introduction

P. Nikiforos Diamandouros and Richard Gunther

Greece, Italy, Portugal, and Spain warrant the label "The New Southern Europe" because they are "new" countries in two distinct albeit interrelated senses: (1) their relatively affluent, modern social structures are qualitatively different from the premodern societies found in this region until recently; and (2) in sharp contrast to southern Europe's past inability to sustain stable democratic regimes, they all are consolidated democracies. Accordingly, the interaction between socioeconomic modernization and democratization is a leitmotif of this volume, which not only describes the basic characteristics of key political institutions and patterns of political behavior in these countries but seeks to explain them in terms of these two intertwined and interacting transformations.

In *The Politics of Democratic Consolidation: Southern Europe in Comparative Perspective* (Gunther, Diamandouros, and Puhle 1995), we examined the processes by which democratic regimes were established in these four countries and concluded that all four democracies had been consolidated by the early to mid 1980s. A number of crucial questions that have traditionally been the foci of enquiries in comparative politics were, however, beyond the scope of that book. These include the nature and interrelationships among the key governmental institutions of these democratic systems, the structure and dynamics of their respective party systems, the linkages, in each country, between parties and social structure, the basic characteristics of electoral politics, and the ideologies, organizational features, and overall strategies of the major political parties. In this volume, we intend to examine these dimensions of democratic politics by addressing a series of related questions. How, for example, has democratic consolidation affected politics in these four countries? How did the establishment of new, democratic rules of the game affect the strategies and orientations of key actors in the political system? Did democratic consolidation set off a series of institutional and strategic adaptations that, in a cumulative and recursive fashion, served to further strengthen democracy itself?

We also address a similar set of theoretically interrelated questions about the relationship between socioeconomic development and democracy. How have socioeconomic modernization, as reflected in the emergence of a large, affluent middle class, and technological innovation, exemplified by the increasing dominance of television as the primary medium for political communication, affected the conduct of election campaigns, the changing electoral fortunes of different types of parties, and the programmatic stands and basic organizational features of political parties? Have social and technological change affected politics in a uniform, linear, and incremental manner, or do differing trajectories of political change—uneven, subterranean, circuitous, or abrupt—suggest that other, less uniform or less universal forces exert significant influence?

Our central aim here is thus to examine the ways in which democratic consolidation has influenced democratic politics in the new southern Europe. In so doing, we examine several broader issues of considerable theoretical significance. The first set of issues concerns the link between "democratic consolidation" and the following phase of "democratic persistence" that we identified in *The Politics of Democratic Consolidation.* Does the consolidation of democratic regimes imply that democratic institutions and practices are effectively frozen, potentially unresponsive to altered circumstances, new challenges, and pressures for change, or do parties and governmental institutions retain the potential to evolve after their democratic regimes have been consolidated? Some scholars have suggested, for example, that democratic regimes that achieve consolidation through "pacts" or "elite settlements" are more rigid and exclusionary, and less adaptable, than those involving a more substantial and autonomous input from the masses (see, e.g., Karl 1990). Reversing the temporal ordering, others have suggested that a democratic regime cannot be regarded as consolidated until its component subsystems or "partial regimes"—including party systems, interest intermediation processes, and governmental structures—become stable and consolidated.

Questions concerning regime consolidation and the institutionalization of democratic politics are particularly important in the specific context of these four southern European countries. The political histories of these countries in the twentieth century have featured extended authoritarian interludes. Indeed, three of the four (Greece, Portugal, and Spain) emerged from their latest and most protracted encounter with authoritarian rule only in the mid 1970s and had never previously experienced extended periods of democratic stability. And although Italy has been democratic for over five decades, its highly fragmented party system, "polarized pluralism," entrenched clientelism (degenerating into widespread corruption by the 1980s), cabinet instability, complete absence of alternation in government, and governmental inefficacy have hardly been desirable characteristics of democratic governance. Indeed, public dissatisfaction with this state of affairs led in the mid 1990s to the complete disappearance of Italy's traditional political parties, a vigorous purge of its political class, and, in the view of some observers, the founding of a "Second Republic." Questions regarding the nature of these partisan and governmental institutions are thus of considerable salience in this region.

A second set of theoretical issues relating to democratic consolidation derives from the notion of "path dependency." In *The Politics of Democratic Consolidation,* we analyzed the trajectories followed by these political systems, from the breakdown of the former authoritarian regime through the consolidation of the new democracies. We concluded that the processes of consolidation in these four countries were profoundly affected by the particular trajectory followed in each instance. Indeed, these trajectories varied greatly. In the case of Italy, defeat in World War II triggered the demise of authoritarian rule and initiated a democratization process dominated by two sets of antifascist forces (Christian Democrats and the left), whose suspicions of one another were intensified with the outbreak of the Cold War. As a result of the polarized conflict between the two camps, democratic consolidation was delayed for decades, as the electorally very significant left and the much smaller but certainly not insignificant far right were excluded from sharing in power throughout the forty years of the "First Republic." In Portugal, the first phase of the post–Estado Novo period saw a military coup, followed by a social revolution, which appeared initially to propel that country toward a nondemocratic form of government. Instead, a second military coup reversed this situation, but for some time the emerging democratic regime remained under military tutelage. As a result, Portugal did not become a fully consolidated democracy until the 1980s. The Spanish case stands at the opposite end of the continuum. Democratization in Spain followed an evolutionary trajectory and unfolded within an institutional context established by General Franco himself, and both the transition to a fully democratic system and the consolidation of that new regime took place rather quickly (with the former completed in 1979 and the latter by or shortly before 1982). In Greece, too, a democratic system came into being very quickly, but the rise of PASOK, the Panhellenic Socialist Movement, an apparently radical and seemingly only semiloyal opposition party, led to doubts about the prospects for democratic consolidation. After storming to power in 1981, however, PASOK significantly moderated its stance and embraced the new democratic regime, signaling its consolidation. The coming to power in 1989 of a coalition of communists and conservatives—former opponents in the Greek Civil War of the 1940s—provided additional confirmation of the extent to which consolidation had been secured. These varying transition trajectories, we argue, affected the timing and the processes of regime consolidation, facilitating rapid consolidation in two cases but complicating and protracting those processes in others. In this volume we examine to what extent these legacies of the preauthoritarian or authoritarian past, and of the transition, continue to affect the basic character of democratic politics in these consolidated democratic systems. Do the "birth defects" of the transition continue to act as a constraint on relations among parties or the performance of governmental institutions, or are these subsystems able to evolve in such a manner as to adjust to changing circumstances?

Political scientists have long studied the stabilization—as contrasted with the evolution and fluidity—of electoral politics in new democracies. Following Seymour Martin Lipset and Stein Rokkan's classic *Party Systems and Voter Alignments* (1967), it has been noted that the alignment of party systems with key groups and cleavages in a given society tends to stabilize at a particular period, such that voting patterns may continue well into a period when the initial cleavages that gave rise to the alignment of partisan forces have faded or been superseded altogether. At what point and through what processes would the new party systems of southern Europe stabilize? And what kinds of cleavages would be reflected in the structure of partisan competition in each country? Would partisan alignments precisely reflect the varying cleavage structures present when the new parties were founded (implying a socioeconomic determinist process of partisan alignment), or would the stabilization of voting patterns occur later, as a result of evolutionary processes more complex than considerations of cleavage salience alone would suggest? In other words, does the phase of democratic persistence allow for change, whether incremental or abrupt, that can affect the politics of an already consolidated democracy?

How would the legacies of the preauthoritarian past affect contemporary electoral behavior or the basic ideological orientations and behavioral styles of the major parties? These legacies were almost without exception negative in their implications for the prospects of establishing stable democratic competition. The political regimes of Greece, Italy, Portugal, and Spain in the late nineteenth and early twentieth centuries can be called "limited democracies" (Burton, Gunther, and Higley 1992, 5–7). Although these regimes provided for the election of both representative and governing elites, they fall short of our criteria for democracy, particularly insofar as the dominant groups used intimidation, deference to local notables in patron-client networks, bribes, outright fraud, and restricted suffrage, among other tactics, to perpetuate their rule. In the case of Italy, there was the added complication that Catholics were forbidden by the Church to participate in the politics of the regime throughout the "liberal era." Efforts by excluded sectors of the population to participate more fully in the politics of these restrictive "limited democracies" caused instability and conflict that eventually brought about the demise of these regimes and paved the way for authoritarian seizures of power by the antidemocratic right. When democratic interludes were present in the preauthoritarian histories of these countries (such as the Spanish Second Republic and the Italian system between 1919 and Mussolini's seizure of power), they were marked by extreme political polarization, instability, and extraparliamentary mass mobilizations that often involved violence. The ideologies or basic orientations of the major parties of both the left and the right in these earlier historical periods were often also characterized by semiloyal or antisystem stands. Thus, at the time the current democratic regimes were being established, salient questions came to the fore concerning the extent of ideological polarization among parties, as well as their orientations toward democracy. (This was especially the case with parties of the right, which were often associated in the minds of many voters, fairly or unfairly, with the former right-wing authoritarian regimes.)

Given strong polarization and the weakness of moderate political forces that characterized earlier democratic experiments in the region, a further question that preoccupied the authors in this volume was the extent to which democratic consolidation in the new southern Europe could be expected to result in a move away from centrifugalism and the politics of exclusion, and to inject into the new political systems a logic of moderation and of centripetalism, very often observable in long-established democratic political systems. Put otherwise, would the dynamics of a consolidated and stable democracy help structure opportunities that could serve as incentives for new political forces to adopt a moderate style of politics?

Similarly, the selection of governmental institutions for the new democracies, and their capacity to function efficiently and adapt in the face of new demands were important questions. Would electoral systems allow for the fair representation in democratic arenas of all significant political forces, and, at the same time, provide for the formation of stable governments? Would executives have sufficient power to govern efficiently, or would excessive intervention by parliaments on behalf of particularistic veto groups lead to democratic stalemate? Would demands for decentralization of the state in Spain, and subsequently Italy, be adequately addressed, or would conflicts over this issue give rise to challenges to the democratic regime itself? The experiences of previous democratic interludes were not promising in this regard. The Spanish Second Republic, for example, combined many of the worst features of various institutional alternatives: its electoral law had grotesque majoritarian biases, fragmented the party system, and made formation of stable governments difficult; and disputes over the basic form of the state (centralized vs. decentralized, monarchy vs. republic) led to the alienation of important sectors of society.

A third set of important theoretical concerns that preoccupied the authors of this volume relates to the concept of "leapfrogging" development, introduced in *The Politics of Democratic Consolidation.* Would the basic characteristics of political parties and electoral politics conform to the standard models that developed elsewhere in western Europe in the late nineteenth and early twentieth centuries (falling into the cadre or mass-based categories as defined in the classic literature)? Or would they leapfrog over the developmental stages that gave birth to those classic party models and assume new organizational forms and voter-mobilization strategies? Would election campaigns be conducted along the lines established in older democratic systems or would they be characterized by a "new campaign politics" relying heavily on the careful crafting and broadcasting over television of the most attractive personal characteristics of the parties' national leaders, at the expense of mass organizational efforts by party militants and the parties' ideological precepts or electoral programs?

Finally, a fourth set of questions concerns the similarities among the four countries—an issue addressed at length in *The Politics of Democratic Consolidation,* particularly in the historical overview by Edward Malefakis, and in a more summary fashion, in the preface to this volume. Malefakis identified a number of common elements in their histories and social structures: the conflicting legacies issuing from protracted struggles between liberalism and absolutism; the "precocious" introduction of electoral democracy into premodern social settings; relatively recent experiences with right-wing authoritarian rule; lagging socioeconomic development; and, in the cases of Italy, Portugal, and Spain, extreme economic inequality in southern regions characterized by latifundia and economic underdevelopment. To what extent are these social-structural and historical parallels reflected in similarities in current democratic structures and practices? The four countries were often previously regarded as constituting a semiperiphery of the better developed, more affluent and more democratic northern portions of western Europe. Can this conceptualization be extended to include a southern European model of democratic politics in the current era?

The chapters that follow attempt to address many of these questions, guided by a number of working hypotheses, which need to be briefly spelled out here. One of these is that socioeconomic development and democratic consolidation are closely linked and relate to each other in a mutually reinforcing and, hence, recursive manner. Put otherwise, we wish to test the proposition that democratic consolidation and the institutionalization of the rules of the game that it implies enhance the capacity of politics to shape outcomes and to influence developmental trajectories. A closely related proposition we wish to test is that consolidated democracies create institutional environments conducive to the primacy of politics. More broadly put, the open-ended logic informing democracies in general finds favorable ground for advancement and further development in consolidated democratic regimes and contributes to the deepening of democracy and enlargement of its scope.

We also wish to explore the working hypothesis that the phase of democratic persistence with which this volume is primarily concerned can accommodate change, whether of the slow, evolutionary type reminiscent of the hard-to-discern, subterranean movement of tectonic plates or of the more sudden and abrupt variety more closely resembling seismic activity. Confirmation of such a hypothesis would also provide evidence in support of the proposition that consolidated democracies are endowed with sufficiently resilient institutional arrangements to withstand even abrupt change, such as the collapse of one of their partial regimes, without endangering their stability.

A third working hypothesis suggests that the combined outcome of socioeconomic development and democratic consolidation in southern Europe has been an "approximation" of a number of features and dimensions of politics long identified with western European democracies. Implicit in this approximation is the absence of a southern European model of democracy, distinct from that of industrial democracies in western Europe. Indeed, our expectation is that, notwithstanding this approximation, the evolution of politics within the region has, in a number of ways, been marked by divergence rather than convergence among Greece, Italy, Portugal, and Spain. We seek to identify and highlight the factors underlying this apparent diversity.

A fourth working hypothesis relates to the nature and dynamics of the political systems spawned by democratic consolidation in the region. Our assumption is that the dynamics of consolidated democracies favor the emergence and consolidation of partial regimes of electoral, political, and party systems that are driven by centripetal logics. In turn, such systems tend to foster moderate and inclusive, as opposed to divisive and exclusive, types of politics, and to avoid the pathologies of polarization and the threat of deconsolidation implicitly associated with it. Put otherwise, the logic of interaction in this relationship is recursive and mutually reinforcing, as democratic consolidation favors the emergence of centripetalism, which in turn contributes to the deepening of democracy and, through the promotion of consensual mechanisms of conflict regulation, substantively enhances its quality.

A final working hypothesis concerns political parties. It is our assumption that, in a twist of history replete with irony, political parties born in and reaching maturity in recent decades, during a period distinguished by the dominance of the electronic media (and, above all, television) on the conduct of politics (especially electoral politics) have a competitive advantage over class-based parties typical of the mass era of politics. Being less encumbered by strong links and attachments to powerful institutions associated with the class model of mass politics, these latecomers would appear to be better equipped than their older counterparts to cope with the multifaceted challenges posed by the logic of "catch-allism," so perspicaciously analyzed by Otto Kirchheimer (1966) over three decades ago.

Taken together, these hypotheses inform the analyses that follow, and lend support to our central claim concerning the significance of the new southern Europe as an object of social-scientific inquiry capable of yielding important insights for the comparative study of democratization.

The Contents of This Volume

The following eight chapters systematically examine democratic politics in the new southern Europe with an eye to addressing the aforementioned substantive and theoretical questions. In Chapter 2, Thomas Bruneau, Nikiforos Diamandouros, Richard Gunther, Arend Lijphart, and Leonardo Morlino (in collaboration with Risa Brooks) employ Lijphart's typology of "majoritarian" versus "consensual" democracies to identify the defining characteristics of the types of democracy that have been established. This makes it possible to standardize and quantify institutional features regarding two fundamental dimensions of democratic politics: an "executives/parties" cluster, based upon indicators of cabinet durability, formation of "oversized" versus "minimum-winning-coalition" governments, party-system fragmentation, the disproportionality of representation in electoral systems, and the number of salient issue areas over which conflict is waged, on the one hand; and a "federal versus centralized" dimension, which includes measures of the distribution of fiscal resources between central and local/regional government bodies, the presence or absence of a balanced bicameralism, and the existence of a written constitution that includes strong guarantees of the interests of minorities, on the other. This framework enables us to compare the democracies of Greece, Italy, Portugal, and Spain with other democratic systems to determine whether these four countries do in fact align in a distinct southern European model of democracy. In order to answer other questions about the evolution of these democratic systems over time, we go beyond Lijphart's standard treatment of these quantitative measures by presenting data from each individual component of the two broader dimensions at three distinct points in time. In this manner, we can determine the extent to which change has taken place since these regimes were consolidated, as well as the extent to which they might be converging on some common model of democracy.

In Chapter 3, Richard Gunther and José Ramón Montero present a detailed analysis of the nature and evolution of support for the principal political parties of Greece, Italy, Portugal, and Spain. They begin with the observation that average electoral volatility scores for these four countries are much higher than in other democratic systems. Indeed, the Spanish party-system realignment of 1982 and the collapse of the traditional Italian party system in 1994 were the two most volatile European elections of the twentieth century. Given this volume's concern with the adequate functioning of key democratic institutions and interest in patterns of stability or change since the consolidation of democracy in Greece, Italy, Portugal, and Spain, the authors undertake a comparative analysis of several alternative sources of electoral stability in these countries (in comparison with a number of other democratic systems): the psychological attachment of voters to political parties ("party identification"); the development of supportive organizational structures for voter mobilization (i.e., political parties and allied secondary organizations); the social-structural anchoring of electoral support (or "cleavage encapsulation"); and the linkage in the minds of voters of specific political parties with the abstract categories of "left" and "right." The core of this analysis takes the form of multivariate Probit analyses of voting in these countries in several elections over the past two decades, using as a comparative baseline parallel analyses of electoral behavior in five other democracies. Given the increasing prominence of the "leadership factor" as a determinant of the vote in "the new campaign politics," the impact of this variable is assessed as the last step in a stepwise analysis of electoral behavior. The collapse and reconfiguration of the Italian party system in the 1990s has given added salience to this systematic assessment of "the anchors of partisanship" in southern Europe.

This development has been so significant in the postwar political history of western Europe that we devote an entire chapter to analyzing its origins and consequences. In Chapter 4, Giacomo Sani and Paolo Segatti examine the collapse of the Italian First Republic's traditional parties. A number of factors, ranging from long-term features of Italian political culture to short-term, elite-driven crises, are found to be responsible for this phenomenon, whose implications for the future evolution of the Italian party system are briefly addressed. The authors then focus their attention on a paradoxical feature of Italian politics that has particular salience in explaining the evolution of the party system in that country: the coexistence of strong parties with widespread, intense distrust of party politics. They attribute this paradox to a number of factors peculiar to postwar Italian political development and, above all, to the dynamics of party institutionalization immediately after World War II, when Italy was still a country marked by low socioeconomic development and when religion and the Cold War underpinned powerful cleavages. A central feature of the party system established at the time was the coexistence of a strong commitment to democracy with a profound distrust of political parties. The latter was as much the legacy of Fascism, which identified the (single) party with the nation, as it was reflective of an aversion to social division—a typical feature of underdevelopment. The attenuation, during the past two decades, of the traditional cleavages based on class, religion, and the Cold War eroded the foundations upon which the postwar party system had been anchored, opening the way for the emergence in the 1990s of heretofore quiescent lines of conflict and of a political environment decidedly less propitious for stable party anchoring.

In Chapter 5, Gianfranco Pasquino explores the distinguishing features of "The New Campaign Politics" and assesses the extent to which they have become distinguishing characteristics of electoral campaigning in Greece, Italy, Portugal, and Spain. Pasquino rejects the simplistic notion that this recent development is the product of little more than social-structural change and the introduction of television. Instead, the presence or absence of this style of conducting election campaigns is the product of the interaction of a number of factors, including basic features of governmental institutions in these countries. The presence or absence of these traits enables us to address the "leapfrogging" hypothesis: if these characteristics are more prevalent in new democracies than they are in more established party systems, this could be regarded as an indication that these newly established parties did, indeed, leapfrog over developmental stages followed by older parties, and more clearly reflect the new than they do the old style of campaign politics. The case of Italy in the 1990s is particularly interesting from this perspective, since the individual who owned most of the private television channels and networks in the country entered politics when the old parties were collapsing and, although a novice with no prior experience in government, was elected prime minister.

Chapters 6, 7, and 8 examine the evolution of individual parties in the region that fall within the general categories of conservative, socialist, and communist. Takis Pappas analyzes the historical evolution of the parties of the right and center-right. Starting from the recognition that conservative parties in southern Europe have in the past often been ambivalent about, or only semiloyal to, democracy, and, in some instances, outright antidemocratic, he focuses his analysis on the evolution of these parties since the founding of the current democracies. He also explores their efforts to become more appealing to the moderate majority of voters in these countries. Although the democratic credentials and ideological moderation of Italy's Democrazia Cristiana were never in doubt, this has clearly not been the case with right-wing parties in Greece, Portugal, and Spain. Thus, acceptability as loyal democratic competitors and as parties whose basic ideas and programmatic commitments are not too divergent from those of the moderate majority of voters in these countries has been absolutely crucial in their efforts to establish sufficient support for electoral victory. But while all of these parties, including the once neofascist Movimento Sociale Italiano (MSI), have all moved toward the democratic center, the trajectories they followed were remarkably different. Constantine Karamanlis's Nea Demokratia and Adolfo Suárez's Unión de Centro Democrático had a much easier time in securing electoral support because their parties' founders had been the principal bringers of democracy to Greece and Spain. (This was not enough, however, to ensure the continuing electoral appeal, and even organizational survival of Spain's UCD, as we shall see.) In the case of Portugal, the exigencies of the revolutionary period and the struggle to rescue the transition from the grasp of an authoritarian military government intimately linked to the extreme left meant that all parties, including the forerunners of the current Partido Social-Democrata and the Partido Popular (the Partido Popular Democrático and the so-called Partido do Centro Democrático Social respectively), were forced to take up positions much farther left than would otherwise have been preferred by their conservative and religious electorates. Thus, even though the long-term evolution of the Portuguese right was toward the democratic center, in the aftermath of the revolution, right-wing parties in Portugal shifted back toward more conservative images and stands. Finally, the more recent reconstruction of right-wing and centrist parties in Italy following the collapse of Democrazia Cristiana illustrates party building on the right of center.

Hans-Jürgen Puhle's study of socialist and social democratic parties in Greece, Italy, Portugal, and Spain analyzes the varying degrees to which they have succeeded in pursuing the four "historic" objectives of democratization, modernization, Europeanization, and development of the welfare state. Each of these is crucial, given the long-term trajectories of these southern European countries—three of which were until quite recently late modernizers on the "semiperiphery" of Europe, with undemocratic or unstable democratic regimes—whose provision of welfare services has lagged substantially behind the rest of the industrialized world. Of these, the socialist parties of southern Europe gave highest priority to, and experienced the greatest success in achieving, democratization and the consolidation of their respective regimes. In giving "primacy" to politics, Puhle argues, the other three objectives were substantially affected. Democratic consolidation transformed the dynamics of politics, which (along with the modernization of their respective economies and societies) created a centripetal dynamic of partisan competition. And that in turn had a considerable impact on the conversion of the socialist parties (no matter how radical their rhetoric may have been at the onset of the democratic transition) into moderate catch-all parties. In the end, all of the socialist parties emerged as modern catch-all parties and have even experienced some of the difficulties characteristic of the "crisis of catch-all parties" in Western democracies. They have varied considerably, however, in their developmental trajectories, with the Portuguese Partido Socialista remaining a faction-ridden and personalistic party (dominated by Mário Soares until the mid 1980s, and only overcoming these institutional weaknesses beginning in the early 1990s), and PASOK in Greece remaining heavily reliant on a populist, centralized-bureaucratic clientelism until the demise of its creator, Andreas Papandreou, in the 1990s. Only the Spanish Partido Socialista Obrero Español (PSOE) undertook its transformation and internal modernization at an early stage (with the most decisive steps taken in 1979), and only the PSOE used its protracted period in government to implement policies (unpopular over the short term) designed to modernize Spanish society and make it economically more competitive. Pursuit of moderate voters near the center of the left-right spectrum and its vigorous modernization policies in government, however, fractured the "socialist family" that had characterized the party for over a century, alienating its traditional trade union ally. The Greek socialists, meanwhile, did not choose to adopt policies that would advance the cause of societal modernization until the mid 1990s, preferring to practice the politics of populism, personalism, and clientelism. While they thereby avoided the kinds of intraparty stresses that divided the Spanish socialists, their tenure in government has been regarded by some as a decade of missed opportunities to modernize the country. In the case of the Portuguese socialists, sharing power with a dizzying array of coalition partners in the first decade of democracy and exclusion from government for the second decade did not provide opportunities to implement modernization policies, even if they had been higher on the party's agenda. Under the leadership of new, modernizing elites, however, single-party socialist governments in both Greece and Portugal have a chance to make up for lost time.

Anna Bosco's analysis of the communist parties of southern Europe in Chapter 8 also focuses on efforts by parties whose commitment to democracy was initially questioned to appeal to a broader segment of the voters in the context of consolidated democracy. Although the

Partito Comunista Italiano (PCI) and Partido Comunista de España (PCE) had long been conscious of the need to adapt to the altered circumstances of a modern and relatively affluent southern Europe, the collapse of the Soviet Bloc in 1989 quickly gave an added urgency to this quest throughout the region. The resulting adaptation, however, was neither uniform nor uneventful. Faced with the dual challenge emanating from the structural transformation of their domestic and international environments (i.e., consolidated democracies at home and the end of the Cold War abroad), the communist parties in the region undertook what turned out to be a remarkable change in their identities and profiles. The end result was full integration into the democratic rules of the game prevailing in their respective political systems and the deepening of democratic consolidation in each country. In the process, meanwhile, the PCI had ceased to exist, having been replaced by a new, consciously left-of-center party, the Partito Democratico della Sinistra (PDS), which held onto most former PCI voters. In a stunning affirmation of the fundamental changes in the Italian party system in the 1990s, the PDS became the major partner in the governing coalition brought to power in the elections of 1996, thereby ending the legacy of exclusion of the left from power and confirming its democratic legitimation. To be sure, the price of this reversal was another split, as a sizable number of erstwhile PCI voters and cadres who remained loyal to more orthodox communist stands chose to create a splinter party, the Rifondazione Comunista (RC). In Spain, the Partido Comunista de España adopted a strikingly different strategy. Having initially presented itself as a moderate, Eurocommunist party (and playing a very important role in the consolidation of Spain's democracy), the PCE suffered a series of schisms, eventually emerging as a more orthodox Communist party. Rather than seeking to enhance its electoral appeal through ideological moderation, it attempted to attract new voters by forging a sometimes-uneasy electoral alliance with a number of small new-left groups. Finally, confirming the different trajectories toward integration in the new democratic systems in southern Europe, the communist left in Greece and Portugal followed a much slower and more circuitous route. Holding fast to their more orthodox beliefs, both the Kommounistiko Komma Elladas (KKE) in Greece and the Partido Comunista Português (PCP) in Portugal adjusted very slowly, in reactive fashion, and only after their electoral appeal had declined significantly.

Finally, in Chapter 9, we reflect on the empirical findings set forth in the earlier chapters, use them address the working hypotheses outlined above, and attempt to draw broader, comparative implications from them.

The questions posed and analyses provided in this book serve two analytically distinct but closely intertwined goals. First, they aim to enhance our understanding of parties and politics in the new southern Europe, a region until recently considered a semiperiphery or backwater of the more advanced industrial democracies to its north that has undergone rapid and fundamental socioeconomic and political change in the course of recent decades. Second, they seek to make use of insights derived from the southern European experience to highlight processes of change and sources of continuity in democracies more generally. Our hope is that lessons with "transfer potential" for other democracies, both new and old, may be learned from the capacity of these late-developing southern European societies to leapfrog into socioeconomic and political modernity.

2 Democracy, Southern European Style

Thomas C. Bruneau, P. Nikiforos Diamandouros, Richard Gunther, Arend Lijphart, Leonardo Morlino, and Risa A. Brooks

The Politics of Democratic Consolidation (1995), the volume that preceded this book, presented the intellectual rationale for the concept of southern Europe, and concluded that democracy in Greece, Italy, Spain, and Portugal had been consolidated by the early to mid 1980s. Beyond the scope of that volume, there remained, however, a large number of questions concerning the nature of the political systems that took shape in the course of these democratization processes. Among them, two sets of questions seem paramount and serve as the principal foci of the analysis in this chapter. The first involves the basic features of the core political institutions of these regimes. To what extent are they sufficiently similar to allow us to speak of a "southern European model" of democracy? What accounts for any distinguishing features of those political systems? What are the implications of such features for the basic character of democratic politics? The second set of issues involves the notion of "democratic persistence," introduced in Chapter 1. Does the consolidation of a democratic regime effectively "freeze" a political system, or does it allow for continued evolution in accordance with changing domestic or international circumstances? Which institutionalized features are more stable, and which structures or fundamental behavioral patterns remain somewhat malleable and adaptable?

Lijphart et al. 1988, a preliminary assessment of some of the fundamental structural characteristics of the Greek, Portuguese, and Spanish political systems, concluded that, despite many similarities in social structure and historical experiences, by the mid 1980s, these countries had developed democratic systems that varied quite considerably, such that one could not speak of a "Mediterranean model of democracy." That initial assessment did not, however, explore all aspects of the differences among the four countries. Based upon a single snapshot of political-system characteristics, taken in 1986, it did not attempt to determine whether these differences resulted from variations in the trajectories from authoritarianism to democracy followed by these countries or whether they were the products of older traits of these societies. Similarly, it did not consider the extent to which these democratic systems had evolved since the time of their consolidation. This prevented the authors from attempting to answer several of the crucial questions outlined above and in the preceding chapter. Accordingly, in this chapter we assess the similarities and differences among these systems over time. This enables us not only to reexamine the tentative conclusion of Lijphart et al. 1988 but also to categorize and analyze any patterns of change that might imply some subsequent convergence, on the one hand, or increasing distinctiveness, on the other. Since the publication of Lijphart et al. 1988, moreover, the Italian political system has undergone a major crisis and reequilibration, which, among other things, culminated in a profound transformation of its parties and a partial change of the party system. These dramatic developments have meant that after over four decades of stability (if not stagnation), Italy's democratic system is in need of a systematic reassessment.

In this chapter, we describe key characteristics of these four southern European democracies by placing them in a common analytical framework alongside a broad array of democratic systems, using Arend Lijphart's (1984) empirical scheme for classifying political systems as "majoritarian" or "consensual." Given our interest in analyzing the evolution of these political systems over time, we depart here in two ways from the manner in which data were presented in Lijphart et al. 1988. One change is that, in addition to presenting the standard cumulative scores on these indicators for all the countries listed (since the establishment of democracy in the 1970s for Greece, Portugal, and Spain, and since World War II for all other countries), we also present the scores for the four southern European countries for specific periods, corresponding to important phases of their institutional development. In a second departure from the practice followed by Lijphart et al. 1988, we also present a separate and detailed analysis of each of the variables that make up the aggregate "executive/parties" and "federal/unitary" dimensions of these models, making possible a more detailed monitoring of institutional changes. If only the aggregate indices were presented, substantial change in one particular institutional feature (e.g., cabinet durability, or decentralization of the state) might not be readily apparent. By aggregating data from between three and five different variables, a major change in one indicator may be mitigated or entirely offset by continuity or contrary shifts in others. There was no change, for example, in either "constitutional flexibility" or "bicameralism" in our four southern European countries, thereby suppressing the apparent extent of a substantial decentralization of the Spanish state. Similarly, the extent of a marked shift toward a more majoritarian electoral law and style of government in Italy is more than offset, in terms of the aggregate "executives/parties" dimension (see below), by an increase in the fragmentation of the Italian party system.

The first of the periods to be examined spans the late 1970s (but 1946–79 in the case of Italy), by which time the basic institutional configurations of the new Greek, Portuguese, and Spanish political systems had been established, although not yet consolidated. The second period includes most of the 1980s (but 1979–92 in the case of Italy) and ends, in each case, with noteworthy changes in the partisan composition and basic nature of the government (i.e., the formation of the "catharsis" government in Greece in 1989, the end of unstable multiparty government in Portugal in 1987, and the end of the PSOE's absolute majority in the Spanish elections of 1989). The third period takes us up to the most recent elections in each country—1996 in Italy, 1999 in Portugal, and 2000 in Greece and Spain. This division into periods enables us to monitor the evolution of these democratic institutions during key periods of democratic transition and consolidation more closely, thereby making possible an assessment of their resilience in the face of numerous exogenous and endogenous challenges.

Southern European Democracies in Comparative Perspective

Our system for categorizing democratic regimes as either majoritarian or consensual combines two dimensions. The "executives/parties" dimension distinguishes between political institutions and practices that have the effect of manufacturing parliamentary majorities so as to enable a party (or very small number of parties) to form a powerful government and remain in office over an extended period of time, on the one hand, and those that result in parliamentary party systems and/or governments that accurately reflect the diversity of the electorate's political preferences, perhaps at the expense of government stability, on the other. This latter category also involves government policy-making processes based upon broad interparty consultation and consensus. The second, the federal/unitary dimension, seeks to distinguish between political systems that concentrate power, economic resources, and the ability to effectively modify the constitutional order in the hands of a centralized governing elite, at one end of the continuum, and, at the opposite extreme, those that devolve significant decision-making authority and resources to subnational governmental units, provide for checks and balances through a bicameral system, and function within a clearly established constitutional framework that provides strong protection for minority rights.

One feature of majoritarian government is the formation of governments supported by only *a minimum winning coalition of* parliamentary parties. Its polar opposite is the formation of "oversized" coalition governments that include significantly more parties than are strictly necessary for cabinet stability and the enactment of legislation but allow interparty consultation and consensus-building more scope in formulating government policy. Somewhere between these two extremes are minority governments, which sometimes depend in a stable and predictable manner on parliamentary support from a single party, or two (analogous to a minimum-winning-coalition government), but sometimes shift from one party to another in search of a supportive consensus. *Cabinet durability* is a second indicator within this executives/parties dimension. In order to distinguish between mere personnel adjustments, on the one hand, and true shifts in the partisan makeup, dominant ideology, and programmatic preferences of the government, on the other, the number of months in office of a single partisan configuration of the government is used to indicate continuity and durability, even if new elections are held and a new parliament is seated. The third indicator in this dimension is the *effective number of parties* in parliament, which counts the number of parties weighted by party size (see Laakso and Taagepera 1979). The degree of fragmentation of a parliamentary party system is, in turn, the product of the extent to which the electorate is divided by deep cleavages, as well as the degree to which the electoral system accurately reflects the partisan preferences of citizens in translating popular votes into parliamentary seats, on the one hand, or introduces representational biases as a by-product of pursuing its often explicit objective of manufacturing government majorities, on the other. Hence, the final two indicators are the number of *issue dimensions* that divide the electorate and the degree of *disproportionality* of the electoral system.

The federal/unitary dimension is somewhat simpler, and is based on three indicators. The first distinguishes between those systems that have a *balanced and incongruent bicameral* legislature (that is, two houses with roughly equal powers but different membership compositions), at one end of the continuum, and unicameral systems, at the other. Falling between these two extremes are those systems in which one legislative chamber is clearly dominant over the other or the two chambers are similar in composition. The second involves the extent of *decentralization* of control over fiscal resources and is measured by the combined share of spending by local, regional, provincial, and/or state governments as a percentage of total expenditures by all levels of government (excluding social security). Finally, the extent to which a regime has an elaborate and relatively *rigid constitution* whose provisions are protected from undue alteration by requiring extraordinary majorities for amendment and defended by an independent judiciary serves as the third indicator making up the federal/unitary dimension. Great Britain, with its unwritten constitution, anchors the unitary end of this continuum, and the United States the federal end.

The positions occupied by our four southern European countries when rank-ordered with a number of other democracies on the executives/parties dimension are shown in Table 2.1. As can be seen, the four southern European countries do not cluster together. Spain and Greece are among the more majoritarian countries in this sample, while Italy lies near the consensual end of the continuum. Some signs of change are also visible: Spain and, especially, Portugal became more majoritarian during this period, while Greece became somewhat less so. Italy, meanwhile, has shifted even farther toward the consensual end of the continuum over the course of the past five decades, although, on closer inspection, sharply divergent trends are apparent beginning in the early 1990s among the individual components that make up this aggregate dimension, with some moving toward majoritarianism and others pushing Italy even farther toward the consensual end of the continuum.

These southern European countries also vary considerably with regard to the second aggregate dimension, as can be seen in Table 2.2. Greece and Portugal emerge as highly unitary democracies, while Spain and Italy are closer to the federal pole. These aggregate figures also give an inkling of Spain's transformation from a unitary to a more federal system over the course of the three periods under examination.

These figures, however, underrepresent the actual extent of change that was taking place with regard to certain key institutional structures and relationships. For this reason, we present data from each of these indicators separately. Table 2.3 presents data for each country indicating the percentage of time when a minimum-winning-coalition government was in office. These figures reveal both a wide range of variation among the four countries and some substantial changes over time. Greece emerges as by far the most majoritarian of the four countries, while Italy is, by a wide margin, the most consensual. Spain's position shifted significantly over time. In the first period (1977–82), it was under a minority UCD (Unión de Centro Democrático) government; in the second (1982–89), the socialist PSOE (Partido Socialista Obrero Español) governed with the support of an absolute majority in parliament; and in the third (1989–96), the PSOE initially governed with an effective majority only because of the boycott of parliament by the four deputies representing the Basque separatist, antisystem Herri Batasuna, and between 1993 and 1996, it ruled through a single-party minority government. Spain remained in this minority government category in the aftermath of the electoral victory of the Partido Popular (PP) in 1996, but shifted to the majoritarian pattern after the PP secured an absolute majority in parliament in the 2000 elections. Similarly, Italy's shift from consensual centrism to alternation between majoritarian blocs of left and right following the 1994 election represented a substantial change in the format of government. This shift toward majoritarianism is not readily apparent in the data presented in Table 2.3, in part because this period includes the final two years of what some have called the "First Republic" and the first two years of the new style of government, and in part because of the counting rules that we must employ for the sake of consistency. The Berlusconi government of May 1994 to January 1995 is counted as an "oversized" coalition because it included more parties than necessary to form a government, largely because the conservative coalition of parties somewhat overshot the electoral level of support necessary to form a minimum winning coalition. If the Polo delle Libertà had been counted as one party, rather than as an electoral and governmental coalition, this would have been categorized as a minimum-winning-coalition government, and the aggregate score for this period would have been 42, rather than 16. By far the most dramatic shift, however, is that of Portugal, which abruptly departed from its previous pattern of fragmented multiparty governments in 1987 by entering into a period (which continued to at least 2000) of single-party governments, first under the center-right leadership of Aníbal Cavaco Silva (outright majorities), then under the socialists (large pluralities).

One of the most dramatic changes that we analyze in this chapter

Table 2.1 Majoritarian and Consensual Democracies: The Executives/Parties Dimension (high = majoritarian, low = consensual)

1st Period		2d Period		3d Period		1945–96	
						New Zealand	1.55
						Canada	1.45
						United Kingdom	1.45
Greece (1974–81)	1.29			Portugal (1987–95)	1.24	Australia	1.41
		Greece (1981–89)	1.00			United States	.78
						Spain (1977–96)	**.72**
		Spain (1982–89)	.64			**Greece** (1974–96)	**.66**
				Spain (1989–96)	.53	Austria	.53
				Greece (1989–96)	.43	Ireland	.34
						Luxembourg	.29
						France, Vth Rep.	.28
						Japan	.20
Spain (1977–82)	.06					Iceland	−.04
						Portugal (1976–95)	**−.14**
						Germany	−.15
						Norway	−.20
						Sweden	−.25
						Denmark	−.76

Portugal (1976–80)	−.81	Portugal (1980-87)	−.90			Belgium	−.92
Italy (1946–79)	−.98					Netherlands	−1.06
						Italy (1946–96)	**−1.16**
		Italy (1979–92)	−1.35			Finland	−1.42
				Italy (1992–96)	−1.56	Switzerland	−1.59
						France, IVth Rep.	−1.80

Note: Scored by type (minimum-winning-coalition, "oversized" coalition, or minority) of government, cabinet durability, the effective number of parties in parliament, issue dimensions, and the disproportionality of the electoral system. Minimum-winning-coalition governments are scored as 1, oversized coalitions are scored as 0, and minority governments are scored as .5 for each period under consideration. The number of issue dimensions is based upon subjective judgments by scholars with expert knowledge of each country: 1 point was allocated if a cleavage was of great importance and highly divisive, 0 points if it was of low salience, and half a point if it was of intermediate importance/divisiveness. The potential cleavages judges were asked to assess were: socioeconomic, religious, ethnic-cultural, urban-rural, pro/anti-system, foreign policy, and postmaterialist. The "least-squares" index of disproportionality, initially designed by Michael Gallagher (1991) and subsequently modified by Arend Lijphart (1994), is the square root of the sum of the difference between the percentages of votes received and seats won by each party, squared and divided by two. Israel was included in the sample of countries examined in Lijphart 1984, but it has been omitted here because, among other things, it is not a member of the OECD, and therefore one important indicator would have to be omitted from this survey.

Table 2.2 Federal and Unitary Democracies (high = unitary, low = federal)

1st Period		2d Period		3d Period		1945–96	
						United Kingdom	1.50
						Iceland	1.45
						Luxembourg	1.22
Portugal (1976–80)	1.01	Portugal (1980–87)	1.13			**Portugal** (1976–95)	**1.00**
Greece (1974–81)	.89	Greece (1981–89)	.89	Greece (1989–96)	.93	**Greece** (1974–96)	**.90**
				Portugal (1987–95)	.88	France, IVth Rep.	.78
						Sweden	.54
						Finland	.47
						France, Vth Rep.	.45
						Belgium	.40
						Ireland	.34
						Norway	.34
Spain (1977–82)	.22					Denmark	.23
						Austria	−.10
		Spain (1982–89)	−.27	Italy (1992–96)	−.28	**Spain** (1977–96)	**−.23**
		Italy (1979–92)	−.32			**Italy** (1946–96)	**−.35**
Italy (1946–79)	−.38			Spain (1989–96)	−.50	Netherlands	−.38
						Canada	−.97
						Australia	−1.33
						Switzerland	−1.39
						Germany	−1.50
						Japan	−1.52
						United States	−1.93

Note: Scored by dominance of legislative chamber, decentralization of control over fiscal resources, and rigidity of constitution. See also note to Table 2.1.

Table 2.3 Percentage of Time Under Minimum-Winning-Coalition Government: Four Southern European Democracies in Comparative Perspective

1st Period		2d Period		3d Period		1945–96	
Greece (1974–81)	100	Greece (1981–89)	100	Portugal (1987–95)	100	New Zealand	100
		Spain (1982–89)	100				
						Greece (1974–96)	**99**
				Greece (1989–96)	97	Luxembourg	97
						United Kingdom	96
						Iceland	90
						Australia	90
						Canada	90
						Ireland	87
						Japan	86
						Norway	75
						Portugal (1976–95)	**74**
						Spain (1977–96)	**73**
						Belgium	70
						Germany	70
Portugal (1976–80)	64			Spain (1989–96)	64	Sweden	63
						Denmark	63
						Austria	58
Spain (1977–82)	50					Netherlands	50
		Portugal (1980–87)	48			France, Vth Rep.	48
Italy (1946–79)	36					**Italy** (1946–96)	**26**
						Finland	27
				Italy (1992–96)	16*	France, IVth Rep.	20
		Italy (1979–92)	4			Switzerland	0

*If our counting rules were modified to reflect the qualitative change in coalition behavior beginning in 1994, this score would have been 42.

Table 2.4 Number of Months Between Changes of Government: Four Southern European Democracies in Comparative Perspective

1st Period		2d Period		3d Period		1945–96	
						Australia	119
						Spain (1977–96)	**114***
				Portugal (1987–95)	98	Austria	100
						Canada	96
		Greece (1981–89)	93			United Kingdom	94
Greece (1974–81)	83	Spain (1982–89)	83*	Spain (1989–96)	78*	New Zealand	74
Spain (1977–82)	66					Luxembourg	65
						Sweden	61
						Germany	60
						Ireland	49
						Norway	48
						Greece (1974–96)	**44**
						Netherlands	36
						Portugal (1976–95)	**36**
						Iceland	34
						Denmark	34
		Portugal (1980–87)	23			Belgium	27
Italy (1945–79)	17	Italy (1979–92)	17	Greece (1989–96)	22	**Italy** (1945–96)	**17**
Portugal (1976–80)	12			Italy (1992–96)	10	France, IVth Rep.	9

*The cumulative figure is longer than any of those for the three separate periods because there was no change in the partisan composition of government between 1982 and 1996, which spans the two periods presented separately in columns two and three.

is revealed in Table 2.4, which shows the number of months that elapsed between changes of government. While it should be noted at the outset that it is somewhat misleading to compare the duration of southern European governments during short periods of time with the cabinet durability averages of other democratic systems over five decades, these figures accurately reflect important changes in Greece, Portugal, and Spain. Most remarkable is the case of Portugal, which had one of the sorriest records for government instability in Europe throughout the first twelve years of its democratic history. An apparently lasting change that completely reversed this pattern occurred in 1987, however, when Cavaco Silva's Partido Social-Democrata (PSD) was elected to office with an outright parliamentary majority (see Appendix Table A.4). The PSD's success was repeated in the 1991 elections, allowing Silva to retain government power for eight years. In the 1995 and 1999 elections, it was the opposition Partido Socialista (PS) that secured a substantial plurality of parliamentary seats and was able to form a single-party government. An even more impressive record for longevity in government was that of Spain's Felipe González, who served as prime minister from November 1982 until March 1996. While this did not represent as dramatic a reversal vis-à-vis the intermediate score for González's UCD predecessors, it was nonetheless a remarkable achievement in a country whose previous democratic regime (the Second Republic of 1931–36) had featured a cabinet crisis on average once every three months. In sharp contrast, Spain's current democracy has had governments that are among the most stable of any democratic system. The cases of Greece and Italy are less clearcut. Although Constantine Karamanlis and Andreas Papandreou enjoyed long tenures in office during the first fourteen years of Greece's restored democracy, a series of corruption scandals beset Papandreou and his PASOK government throughout the late 1980s, leading all the major parties in opposition (from the communist KKE to the right-wing Nea Demokratia) to join forces in an effort to clean up the mess, forming the so-called catharsis government. Not surprisingly, this highly unorthodox combination of parties was inherently incompatible, ushering in a short period of cabinet instability and the convening of three elections in 1989–90. Even though Greek democracy reverted to its familiar pattern of majoritarianism after 1990, this episode has had the effect of substantially reducing Greece's average score for cabinet durability. Finally, the case of Italy is one whose ultimate outcome is unclear at the time of this writing. Although the partisan infighting and abrupt collapse of Silvio Berlusconi's center-right government was consistent with the cabinet instability of the first five decades of Italian democracy, the 29-month lifespan of the center-left coalition under Romano Prodi (1996–98), the third-longest-serving government in postwar Italian history, suggests that the general trend toward majoritarianism and bipolarity that the 1993 electoral-law-reform referendum was intended to promote may have had some positive impact.

One of the most important institutional underpinnings of stable governments is the existence of an electoral law that translates popular votes into parliamentary seats in such a fashion as to manufacture a majority or large plurality in support of a governing party. Indeed, as we can infer from Table 2.5, one factor that helps to explain the durability of governments in Greece and Spain is that their electoral systems have strong majoritarian biases. In the Spanish case, the UCD was able to form reasonably stable single-party minority governments in 1977 and 1979, even though it had received just over a third of the popular votes cast in those elections, and the PSOE enjoyed outright parliamentary majorities from 1982 to 1989 without ever receiving a majority of votes cast (see Appendix Table A.5). Conversely, the perennial instability of Italian governments for nearly five decades was at least partly due to Italy's highly proportional electoral system. The adoption in 1993 of a new electoral law with significant majoritarian biases (resulting from its first-past-the-post allocation of seats on the first round) helps to account for the transformation of the Italian party system. But this institutional factor fails completely to account for the radical alteration of the nature of parliamentary government in Portugal beginning in 1987 (see Appendix Table A.4). Not only was its remarkable increase in cabinet durability not preceded by any change in the electoral law, but Portugal's is a relatively proportional electoral system. Given the large number of deputies elected from each district, this electoral law does not substantially magnify popular vote pluralities into parliamentary majorities and therefore cannot account for the predominance of single-party majority governments since that time.

The degree of fragmentation of parliamentary party systems is reflected in the figures appearing in Table 2.6. As can be seen, Greece has had a two-dominant party system ever since its democracy was restored in 1974. Given the strong majoritarian biases in its electoral law, this has enabled the left-of-center PASOK and the conservative Nea Demokratia to alternate in power in single-party majority governments for all but a short (and exceptional) period of time. The Spanish system has also been dominated at the national level by two parties that have alternated in power: in 1982, the center-left PSOE

Table 2.5 Electoral Disproportionality: Four Southern European Democracies in Comparative Perspective (high = strong majoritarian biases, low = proportional)

1st Period		2d Period		3d Period		1945–96	
Greece (1974–81)	14.69					France, Vth Rep.	11.84
						Canada	11.72
						New Zealand	11.11
Spain (1977–82)	10.27					United Kingdom	10.33
						Australia	8.94
						Spain (1977–96)	**8.15**
		Greece (1981–89)	7.74			**Greece** (1974–96)	**8.08**
		Spain (1982–89)	7.47	Spain (1989–96)	7.19		
				Italy (1992–96)	6.11		
						United States	5.33
				Portugal (1987–95)	5.40	Japan	5.30
				Greece (1989–96)	4.94	Norway	4.93
						France, IVth Rep.	4.38
						Iceland	4.25
						Portugal (1976–95)	**4.04**
						Italy (1946–96)	**3.49**
						Ireland	3.45
Portugal (1976–80)	3.28					Luxembourg	3.26
		Portugal (1980–87)	3.19			Belgium	3.24
Italy (1946–79)	2.84					Finland	2.93
		Italy (1979–92)	2.58			Germany	2.58
						Switzerland	2.53
						Austria	2.47
						Sweden	2.09
						Denmark	1.83
						Netherlands	1.30

Table 2.6 Effective Number of Parties: Four Southern European Democracies in Comparative Perspective

1st Period		2d Period		3d Period		1945–96	
				Italy (1992–96)	6.13		
						Switzerland	5.24
						Belgium	5.05
						Finland	5.03
						France, IVth Rep.	4.87
						Netherlands	4.65
						Denmark	4.51
						Italy (1946–96)	**4.16**
		Portugal (1980–87)	3.97				
Portugal (1976–80)	3.80	Italy (1979–92)	3.89			Iceland	3.72
Italy (1946–79)	3.53					France, Vth Rep.	3.43
						Luxembourg	3.36
						Norway	3.35
						Sweden	3.33
						Portugal (1976–95)	**3.33**
						Japan	3.08
Spain (1977–82)	2.86					Ireland	2.84
				Spain (1989–96)	2.75	**Spain** (1977–96)	**2.76**
		Spain (1982–89)	2.68			Germany	2.64
						Australia	2.50
						Austria	2.48
				Portugal (1987–96)	2.38	Canada	2.37
				Greece (1989–96)	2.32		
						Greece (1974–96)	**2.20**
Greece (1974–81)	2.04	Greece (1981–89)	2.12			United Kingdom	2.11
						New Zealand	1.96
						United States	1.93

replaced the center-right UCD (which had governed since 1977), and in 1996, the PSOE was itself replaced as the governing party by the center-right Partido Popular. Given the significant number of regional parties, however, the Spanish party system is characterized by moderate pluralism. From 1975 until 1985, the Portuguese party system featured four significant parliamentary parties, which formed a series of shifting and unstable coalition governments. In the 1985 election, the party system became even more fragmented, with the appearance of President Ramalho Eanes's Partido Renovador Democrático (Democratic Renewal Party), or PRD. Then, quite abruptly, Portuguese voters concentrated their electoral support on two parties, the center-right PSD and the center-left PS. By 1995, these two parties were attracting a combined total of over 79 percent of valid votes cast (up from 58 percent in 1985). These gains came at the expense of the Partido Comunista Português (PCP), whose electoral support declined from between 17 and 19 percent in the early 1980s to less than 9 percent in 1995, the conservative Partido do Centro Democrático Social (CDS), which declined during this period from 12–16 percent to 9 percent, and the PRD, which disappeared altogether. The Italian party system served as the very model for the concept of "polarized pluralism." Throughout the 1970s and 1980s, there were always at least seven to nine parties with parliamentary representation, and no party ever held more than 42 percent of the seats in the 1970s or 37 percent in the 1980s. Frustrated with the stagnation that paradoxically accompanied high levels of cabinet instability, and pushed by scandals and criminal investigations of party corruption, Italian voters imposed an electoral law reform in 1993 whose objective was to introduce majoritarian biases that might facilitate the formation of stable governments. Again paradoxically, the result was an increase in the effective number of parties, from just under four during the First Republic to over six in the mid 1990s. Considerable regional variations in support for parties, in combination with interparty alliances in single-member district elections, have served to defeat the purpose of the electoral reform. So, too, has the allocation of a quarter of the seats through a modified proportional system. The net result is that Italy's electoral system has resulted in the worst features of available electoral systems: its majoritarian biases have distorted the representation of partisan options in parliament, while party-system fragmentation has increased.

The number of issue areas that serve as salient political cleavages in each country is a further indicator included in the majoritarian/consensual dimension. While this numerical listing of issue dimensions does not reflect the intensity or potential for disruptive conflict of any particular cleavage, it is a useful indicator of the number of conflictual matters on the political agenda that posed challenges to these democratic systems at various points in time. As can be seen in Table 2.7, Greece, Portugal, and Spain ranked near the top of this list in the late 1970s, when all three were struggling through the processes of democratic consolidation. In Spain, this issue (scored as "medium," given the lingering nondemocratic values of many military officers) stood alongside those of class, religious, and ethnic-cultural cleavages. Democratic consolidation was achieved by the mid 1980s, so the anti-system issue was replaced by one regarding foreign policy, which resulted from conflict growing out of an election promise by the PSOE to lead Spain out of NATO. By the mid 1990s, however, there were no divisive foreign-policy issues on the Spanish political agenda. In addition, secularization of the society and the continued restraint of political elites in dealing with religious issues had substantially diminished the salience of the religious cleavage in Spanish society. In Greece and Portugal, the earlier periods prominently featured questions about regime support, as well as salient cleavages over foreign policy. With the consolidation of the two regimes and the normalization of these countries' relations with NATO (and, in the case of Portugal, completion of the decolonization process), the number of divisive issue areas decreased. In Italy, the socioeconomic issue dimension remained constant throughout the three periods under examination, as did some conflict over foreign policy. One major change, however, has been the virtual disappearance of partisan division over religious issues, and its replacement as a substantial cleavage by a center-periphery cleavage, resulting from demands for increased autonomy (if not outright independence) by the Northern League. Indeed, the Northern League's radicalism over this issue raises new questions about regime support (discussed below). Finally, there have been increased mobilizations over environmental issues, adding this as a less potentially disruptive area of conflict to the agenda of the Italian political system.

The final indicator that we shall examine involves the degree of centralization of the state. The indicator used in Lijphart et al. 1988 was the share of tax revenues collected by the central government. However, a measure based on tax collection can substantially under-represent the extent to which subnational levels of government (region, state, province, municipality) have been entrusted with the authority to formulate and implement government policy, because in many countries the central government collects revenues and subse-

Table 2.7 Number of Issue Dimensions: Four Southern European Democracies in Comparative Perspective

1st Period		2d Period		3d Period		1945–96	
						France, IVth Rep.	4.5
Spain (1977–82)	4.0						
						Finland	3.5
						Belgium	3.0
						Germany	3.0
Italy (1946–79)	3.0	Italy (1979–92)	3.0	Italy (1992–96)	3.0	**Italy** (1946–96)	**3.0**
Portugal (1976–80)	3.0	Portugal (1980–87)	3.0			Netherlands	3.0
		Spain (1982–89)	3.0			Norway	3.0
Greece (1974–81)	3.0					Switzerland	3.0
						Spain (1977–96)	**2.9**
						Sweden	2.5
		Greece (1981–89)	2.5			Denmark	2.5
						France, Vth Rep.	2.5
						Japan	2.5
						Greece (1974–96)	**2.3**
						Portugal (1976–95)	**2.2**
				Spain (1989–96)	2.0	Iceland	2.0
						Luxembourg	2.0
						Australia	1.5
				Greece (1989–96)	1.5	Austria	1.5
						Canada	1.5
						Ireland	1.5
						United Kingdom	1.5
				Portugal (1987–96)	1.0	New Zealand	1.0
						United States	1.0

quently transfers a portion of them to states and localities as (in U.S. terminology) "block grants." This is particularly true of Spain, where the use of a "revenue collection" indicator would be completely misleading. Accordingly, we have shifted to a new index based on the percentage of total government spending (excluding social security) attributable to the local and regional levels of government.

Two striking results emerged from this reanalysis, as can be seen in Table 2.8. The first is that, at the beginning of this period, Spain, Greece, and Portugal were by far the most centralized states among the OECD countries. Italy did not occupy quite as extreme a position, but it was also substantially more centralized than the average. The second finding is that a profound devolution of government authority, from the center to regional governments, occurred in Spain in a remarkably short period of time. Spain abandoned its status as the third most centralized state among Western industrialized countries and moved to a position near the middle of the pack.

While allowing for comparisons with more established political systems, the preceding discussion does not exhaust the noteworthy dimensions of governmental and political institutions in these southern European democracies. The position of the head of state, for example, has at times been of exceptional importance in the political development of Greece, Portugal, and Spain, as has the relationship between the military and elected civilian elites. Moreover, while our analysis dealt with some important features of majoritarian versus consensual forms of governance, other nonquantifiable institutional characteristics (such as patterns of recruitment to key government posts and state agencies) have remained unexplored. We therefore turn to a country-by-country overview of important institutional characteristics and their evolution over time.

Portugal

Portugal underwent a remarkable evolution toward democratic stability during the timespan under examination in this chapter. Indeed, in 1980, its political system could not even be regarded as fully democratic: even though the military junta that took power in the immediate aftermath of the revolution had been deposed, the military retained strong reserve powers and continued to play significant political roles through the Council of the Revolution and a strong presidency in this semipresidential system. The constitution enacted in 1976 was also divergent from those of other democratic countries insofar as it included substantive commitments of a programmatic and

Table 2.8 Decentralization: Local and Regional Government Spending as a Percentage of Total Government Spending, Excluding Social Security

1st Period		2d Period		3d Period		1955–92	
						Switzerland	72.6
						Japan	67.8
						Canada	59.3
						Denmark	59.2
						Germany	56.1
						United States	50.8
						Finland	50.8
						Australia	49.9
						Netherlands	47.6
						Sweden	47.2
				Spain (1992)	44.0	Norway	45.2
						Austria	39.4
Italy (1980)	37.3	Italy (1985)	35.4			**Italy** (1955–92)	**36.5**
		Spain (1985)	34.3	Italy (1992)	34.0	Ireland	34.2
						Spain (1980–92)	**32.9**
						United Kingdom	32.6
						France, Vth Rep.	29.4
						France, IVth Rep.	27.8
						Iceland	26.2
						Belgium	19.8
Spain (1980)	17.1						
Greece (1980)	15.4	Greece (1985)	15.4	Portugal (1989)	16.2	**Greece** (1980–93)	**14.9**
				Greece (1993)	12.4		
Portugal (1980)	11.0	Portugal (1985)	6.8			**Portugal** (1980–89)	**11.4**

Source: OECD, *National Accounts,* vol. 2, detailed tables, 1977–89 and 1981–93. These data do not include social security spending. Figures represent the total of local and regional government spending (tables 6.3 for most countries; tables 6.2 plus 6.3 for Austria, Canada, Germany, and Switzerland) as a percentage of the sum of local and regional government spending plus central government spending (table 6.1). Except for Greece and Switzerland (lacking a published capital accumulation account), these expenditures represented the sum of lines 22, 23, 26, 27, and 36, minus line 29, of the income and outlay account, plus the sum of lines 9, 10, 13, 14, and 15, minus line 16, from the capital accumulation account. They thus represent the sum of final consumption expenditure, property income, subsidies, transfers (excluding transfers to other government subsectors), increase in stocks, gross fixed capital formation, net purchases of land and intangible assets, and capital transfers (excluding transfers to other government subsectors).

Note: This indicator combines both municipal and regional governments into one category and therefore underrepresents the extent to which power has been devolved to the regional level in Spain. One study revealed that there was very little change in the share of spending by Spanish municipal governments (which increased from 10.5 percent to 11.5 percent of all government spending) between 1980 and 1994; during that same period, the share of overall government expenditures under the control of the regional governments increased from 0 to 21.2 percent, which exceeds the 21.0 percent of German public spending by the *Länder.* See *Anuario El País, 1998* (Madrid: Ediciones El Pais, 1998), 93.

ideological nature. Thus, the highly "conditioned" situation of the Portuguese regime in 1980 meant that politics was greatly constrained by the events of recent history and tutelage under nondemocratic actors and institutions. Sharp ideological cleavages also posed a threat to democratic stability, with the PCP retaining a Marxist-Leninist program and an antisystem stance until the early 1990s (see Chapter 8 below). And the parliamentary party system was sufficiently fragmented to impede the formation of stable, responsible governments.

Over the following decade, however, substantial change altered each of these characteristics (see Haltzel 1990; Opello 1991). Civil-military relations were regularized and made to conform to principles of civilian control fundamental to our procedural definition of democracy. A series of constitutional reforms abolished the undemocratic Council of the Revolution, reduced the powers of the president, and eliminated from the constitution substantive commitments to defend the "conquests of the revolution." The PCP abandoned its antisystem stance and declined significantly as an electoral force. Membership in the European Union and the collapse of the Soviet Union cemented Portugal's position within the community of Western democratic nations. And the highly unstable coalition governments of the first decade of Portuguese democracy gave way to alternation in power between stable, single-party governments. In the aggregate, a substantial "sorting out" of actors, institutions, and issues had taken place, which helped to consolidate a fully democratic regime.

Although the collapse of the corporatist Estado Novo, headed for almost five decades (1928–74) by Antônio de Oliveira Salazar and Marcello Caetano, had been rapid and unpredictable, democratic consolidation and the redefinition of the roles of political institutions was slow, heavily negotiated, and legalistic. A number of factors made for the protracted nature of the transformation: the initially sweeping scope of socioeconomic and political change during the revolution; concern over polarization of society and the prospect of civil war; the reassertion of the country's legalistic tradition; severe social and economic problems accompanying the repatriation of over 600,000 refugees fleeing Portugal's former colonies; and the challenge of finding a new national mission after 500 years of colonialism. The forces driving this political change are to be found in the original configuration of relations among actors and institutions that emerged from the revolutionary period. An adequate understanding of this evolution requires, therefore, that we set these developments in the context of that era.

Transition

The military coup of April 25, 1974, that ended the Estado Novo did not initially result in the establishment of a democratic regime: instead, Portugal was governed by a military junta headed by left-wing military officers affiliated with the previously clandestine Movimento das Forças Armadas (Armed Forces Movement), or MFA. Democratization in Portugal should thus properly be regarded as the ultimate outcome of *two* transitions: one that quickly liquidated the right-wing authoritarian Salazar/Caetano regime and installed a revolutionary left-wing military junta in its place; and a second that gradually removed the military from power and substantive revolutionary commitments from the constitution.

Any attempt to understand the nature and implications of the Portuguese transition must take into account the fact that it occurred during a countertrend *toward* authoritarian regimes in South America and South Asia and before any of the so-called negotiated transitions were initiated. It was the first of what Samuel Huntington (1991) has called the "third wave" of democratic transitions. As such, there were no established models to follow and no understanding of what to expect. Neither domestic elites nor foreign observers were confident that the Portuguese revolution would ultimately result in a democracy. There were concerns that the newly empowered military government would be unwilling to surrender political power. Concerns over the direction of the Portuguese transition were heightened as well by the fact that it took place during a particularly troubling phase of the Cold War. Thus, the prominent role played by the orthodox, pro-Moscow PCP not only pushed the political spectrum to the left within Portugal, but also attracted much foreign attention to Portugal, a member of NATO with important bases and facilities. The net result of these aspects of political change was that the emergence of Portugal as a stable liberal democracy was regarded as questionable, if not unlikely.

In many respects, the political evolution that unfolded over the following decade and a half can be regarded as aimed at undoing the excesses of the revolution and moving Portugal closer to the mainstream of "procedural" democracies. But political change also involved correction of some dysfunctional aspects of Portuguese democracy not necessarily related to these "birth defects." Three different stages of change can be identified: the first (1976–82) was characterized by governmental instability (with seven governments in five years), a predominant role for the armed forces in politics, a strong president in a strong presidency, and an extremely confining constitution. The second (1982–87) began with constitutional reforms that diminished the role of the armed forces in politics and reduced the powers of the president, but was also characterized by continuing governmental instability (three governments and four prime ministers), and retention in the constitution of the earlier period's programmatic economic commitments. The third period began in 1987 with the formation of the first of a series of stable single-party majority governments.

Civil-Military Relations

The coup that brought down the Estado Novo was carried out by left-wing middle-level officers (captains, majors, and colonels) belonging to the MFA (see Medeiros Ferreira 1992; Graham 1993; Maxwell 1991). Overturning the armed forces hierarchy, it placed relatively inexperienced junior officers in charge not only of what was, relatively speaking, a huge military apparatus—Portugal had the second-highest ratio between soldiers and total population in the world (Porch 1977)—but of the state itself. During the following two years, the military was the single most important actor in Portuguese politics. Political parties not only had to compete with one another but had to struggle to establish a political system in which democratically responsible parties and elections would decide who held power.

Even after the election in 1976 of the first popularly elected president and parliament, the military remained a central actor. In negotiating its partial extrication from power with political parties in February 1976, it enshrined in the constitution a self-appointed Council of the Revolution (CR), with exclusive jurisdiction over all aspects of military affairs. The CR also functioned as a constitutional court and advisory council for the president. Thus, in creating the CR, the military not only refused to acknowledge the supremacy of elected civilian governments over military affairs but continued to exert a powerful influence over domestic politics.

Military power and political influence also derived from the semi-presidential system established in 1976, which endowed the presidency with extensive powers, including the right to veto legislation approved by the Assembly and considerable freedom of decision concerning the appointment and dismissal of governments and the dissolution of parliament. General Eanes, elected president in 1976 and 1981, also served as commander in chief of the armed forces and chief of the general staff.

The armed forces operated largely autonomously as a separate, self-governing branch of government beyond the control of parliament and the elected civilian government. The military's autonomy was also enhanced by the instability of civilian governments, not to mention their lack of expertise in security matters (see Bruneau 1991–92). Given this military tutelage, Portugal could not be considered fully democratic (see Linz, Stepan, and Gunther 1995, 86).

This situation began to change only in the early 1980s. For the first time since 1926, the cabinet formed in January 1980 included no representative of the armed forces. (Subsequently, the defense minister has always been a civilian.) In addition, the powers of the president were reduced, when, in exchange for the Partido Socialista's support for his reelection bid in 1980, President Eanes agreed to give up the position of chief of the general staff. The next, and most important, step was the agreement among the CDS, PSD, and PS in 1982 to enact constitutional reforms that would not only reduce the powers of the president but also abolish the Council of the Revolution. Without the Council of the Revolution, the armed forces no longer had an institutional vehicle through which they could govern themselves. In its place, new institutions created to oversee the military—the Council of State, Constitutional Court, and Higher Council for National Defense—are dominated by representatives of political parties. These reforms represented bold steps by civilian elected officials to define and delimit the roles and prerogatives of the armed forces. Another sign of change was that none of the candidates for president in 1986 was a military officer. Indeed, that year Mário Soares became the first civilian president since 1926.

Until 1987, however, the service chiefs continued to enjoy considerable autonomy, and the general staff retained considerable power over budgets and personnel policy, thus rendering effective civilian control of the armed forces elusive. With the 1987 election of a PSD majority government, this picture began to change. The most decisive steps in this direction were taken between 1990 and 1994 by Fernando Nogueira, defense minister and minister of the presidency, whose reforms substantially strengthened civilian control over the armed forces and the basic outlines of Portuguese defense policy. It is important to note that, in contrast to the predominantly majoritarian policy-making style of the Cavaco Silva governments regarding nonmilitary issues, policy change in this area was secured through extensive deliberations among political parties, military officials, and representatives of interested sectors of academia, business, and government in general over more than three years, culminating in a broad-based consensus. These reforms revised fundamental military strategy, downsized the armed forces (from 282,000 in 1974 to 42,000 in 1996), and reduced the jurisdiction of the general staff primarily to operational issues and personnel management. Thus, civil/military relations in Portugal came to resemble those found in other European democracies.

Political Parties

Under Salazar and Caetano, political parties were banned and suppressed. The regime relied upon its official movement, Acção Nacional Popular (National Popular Action), or ANP, for control and legitimation. The opposition was periodically allowed to "contest" elections to the National Assembly, but not as political parties. In any case, neither the National Assembly nor the Corporative Chamber had any real power, which was effectively concentrated in the hands of Salazar or Caetano and their councils of ministers.

Only the PCP succeeded in maintaining an organizational presence, operating clandestinely within Portugal, with bases of support in the Lisbon and Alentejo regions and in the largely underground trade union movement. Other parties formed very rapidly immediately after the coup, but, given the Communist Party's organizational strength and centrality (it was linked, for a time, to an important faction of the MFA), the PCP exerted a disproportionate influence over the course of politics, economy, and society, sustaining the momentum of revolutionary change throughout the mid 1970s. Indeed, because of pent-up demands for change that had accumulated under the authoritarian regime and the revolutionary atmosphere created and sustained by the PCP/MFA alliance, most of the four dozen parties and movements that formed after the coup were positioned on the left or far left of the political spectrum. During this initial period, the entire political system was skewed to the left, and radical, if not revolutionary, rhetoric and program proposals were predominant. In the Constituent Assembly elections of April 25, 1975 (in which an astounding 92 percent of voters participated), 54 percent of the vote went to parties defining themselves as of the socialist left or beyond, and an additional 6 percent cast blank ballots in a vote of confidence in Portugal's nondemocratic revolutionary government, as advocated by a radical faction of the MFA. Even the names of the four major parties were indicative of the temporary leftist slant that characterized this period. Although the PCP remained true to its name throughout the 1970s and 1980s, however, the socialist PS subsequently behaved more like a social democratic party; the Partido Social-Democrata

(PSD) was closer to a European liberal or even conservative party; and the Partido do Centro Democrático Social (CDS), despite its name, was neither social democratic nor centrist but rather conservative or Christian Democrat. It was not until the early 1980s that the last three of these parties would shed these trappings of leftism and more clearly represent the preferences of the most conservative electorate in southern Europe.

The environment of the mid 1970s was most problematic for the prospects for democracy. The MFA was itself divided among several radical factions, and land and property seizures by individuals and groups acting on their own created a situation of revolutionary chaos. At one point, it appeared that the Constituent Assembly might not be allowed to complete its work: for two days in the fall of 1975, its members were prevented from leaving the chamber by striking workers barring the doors. In addition, the Assembly's work was constrained by pacts negotiated (in April 1975 and February 1976) between the main parties and the MFA that sought to ensure a continuing role for the MFA through the Council of the Revolution, thereby conditioning the future role of parties in the political system.

The socialists, communists, and allies of the PCP held a parliamentary majority, and formulated a constitution in line with their respective approaches to socialism. Accordingly, the constitution promulgated in April 1976 was laced with references to socialism, a socialist economic system, and extensive rights for workers. The third longest constitution in the world (with 312 articles), it included a number of programmatic principles that sought to constrain subsequent political action through detailed articles dealing with every imaginable topic and granting great power to the nonelected Council of the Revolution (see Maxwell and Monje 1991; Bruneau and Macleod 1986, ch. 6). In effect, it sought to constitutionally enshrine the "conquests of the revolution." In response, the conservative CDS did not vote in favor of the constitution.

The 1976 constitution and the electoral law of 1979 included features designed to strike a balance between, on the one hand, concerns over the prospects of excessive party-system fragmentation and government instability, which had characterized the First Republic (1910–26; see Linz 1978, 111–12), and, on the other, the desire to give all serious parties parliamentary representation, in an effort to reverse the excesses both of the Estado Novo (1928–74) and of the more recent revolutionary period of 1974–75 (as stipulated in the First Party Pact of April 11, 1975). The result was a system of proportional representation with large electoral districts and no minimum threshold (see Lijphart 1994, 23). In the aggregate, the Portuguese electoral system, while not unduly distorting the popular mandate in translating votes into parliamentary seats, has effectively reduced the number of parties represented in the Assembly; has slightly magnified the larger parties' shares of seats; has, over the long term, induced parties to adopt electoral strategies designed to take advantage of these representational biases; and has somewhat overrepresented the country's more populous, urban areas at the expense of rural districts. The net result was that in the October 1995 parliamentary elections, the PS and PSD together received 10.4 percent more seats than their share of popular votes, the CDS/PP and PCP together won 4.7 percent fewer seats than votes, and the other parties, with 4.4 percent of the votes, received no seats at all. The same trend persisted in the 1999 elections.

The constitution of 1976 also defined extensive roles for political parties in a series of articles dealing with the public enterprise sector, labor, research institutes, and the media. It sought to guarantee the centrality of political parties in political life by precluding amendment of certain "reserved" articles dealing with political pluralism, political parties, and proportional representation as the electoral system. This highly detailed and specific document thus sought to secure the prominent position of parties and to protect pluralism in Portuguese politics for the foreseeable future.

With the end of the revolutionary period and the normalization of partisan politics, a shift toward the right led to pressures for constitutional reform. In 1982, the PSD/CDS Democratic Alliance government reached agreement with the Partido Socialista to amend the constitution, tilting the balance of power from the presidency to parliament. The president's ability to dismiss the government was decreased, the pocket veto abolished, and the "*political* responsibility" of the government to the president was reduced to simple "responsibility." The socialist economic commitments in the constitution were spared, however, given opposition from the left wing of the PS. These reforms were passed over the opposition of President Eanes, who had, however, no legal option other than to promulgate them. The constitutional revision made Portugal's democratic system more semiparliamentary and less semipresidential. The revision reinforced the government's dependence on the Assembly and, in turn, on the political parties. Still, the system is only semiparliamentary, insofar as there remains a separation of powers between the parliament and the presidency. Its actual functioning is captured by Premier Cavaco

Silva's statement that "the president presides and the government governs" (cited in Frain 1995, 669).

The third period began in 1987 with the PSD winning what no political party until that time had achieved—a majority of votes and seats in parliament. It must be stressed that these results (repeated in 1991) did not reflect a fundamental shift in Portuguese electoral behavior. Rather than a reversal, they were the long-term product of electoral trends, in combination with certain short-term factors (especially relating to the economic situation and the personalities who dominated electoral politics). Perhaps the most important cause of this development was a negative reaction by voters against the high level of instability that had characterized Portuguese governments in the late 1970s and early 1980s. Indeed, the public's distaste for unstable governments during this period led to a collective image of irresponsibility on the part of politicians, and even undermined support for the democratic regime itself.[1] While some signs of a shift toward bipolar competition between the PS and the PSD were apparent in 1983, it was the emergence of President Eanes's PRD in 1985 that signaled the beginning of the end of fragmented multipartyism. The PRD failed to realize Eanes's ambitions of serving as a pivotal party of the center, but it succeeded in shifting a number of voters from the left to the "electorally available" center. In 1987, the PSD, which had participated in every government since 1980, was able to capitalize on strategic errors and internal splits within the PS and PRD, contrasting their shortcomings with its own strong, unquestioned leadership under Cavaco Silva. The PSD also succeeded in convincing the electorate that it had an attractive plan for Portugal, based on accession to the European Community and improvement in the economic situation (see Bruneau 1997, esp. chs. 1, 4, and 5). This inaugurated a period of government stability that stands in contrast with the frequent cabinet crises of the preceding decade. Indeed, the increase in cabinet durability and the shift to single-party governments have remained lasting features of Portuguese government (see Corkill 1996).

Another change that became clearly apparent during this period was the electoral decline of the PCP, which dropped from a high of nearly 19 percent of the votes in 1979 to less than 9 percent in the 1995 and 1999 elections (see Chapter 8 and Appendix Table A.4 below; Cunha 1997). The reasons for this decline are not hard to identify. The appeal of the orthodox line of the PCP was seriously undercut by the collapse of the Soviet Union. The effect was all the greater because of the PCP's inability to rejuvenate its leadership until the early 1990s (and even then, the veteran PCP leader Álvaro Cunhal continued to exert influence behind the scenes). The PCP continued to oppose European integration even while literally billions of dollars flowed annually into Portugal from Brussels. Although the PCP remains one of the four major parties in Portugal, its role and its relevance today are only faint echoes of its position during the revolutionary period of the mid 1970s.

Given these domestic political changes, the progressive economic integration of Portugal into the European Community, and a surge of economic growth in the late 1980s, the stage was set for one final round of reforms of the 1976 constitution. Given the progressive decline of the PCP, the PS was no longer so concerned about the electoral challenge from the left and was therefore willing to join with the PSD government and the conservative CDS to eliminate the constitution's protections of "the conquests of the revolution." Accordingly, in the 1989 revision, all references to socialism as the goal of society disappeared, and the government began to reprivatize many of the firms that had been nationalized in the mid 1970s (see Maxwell and Monje 1991).

Continuity and Change

As we have seen, much changed during the two decades following the Portuguese revolution: the heavy political intervention of the armed forces (so extensive as to prevent us from regarding Portugal as democratic until 1982) was terminated, and the military was confined to playing a role virtually indistinguishable from that found in established democratic systems; the political authority of a once powerful president was substantially reduced, and the undemocratic Council of the Revolution was abolished; the constitution's commitments to a socialist economy were eliminated in 1989, meaning that no policy domains were effectively "off limits" for democratically elected governments; and unstable multiparty governments have given way to stable single-party governments. In addition, the sharp ideological polarization that characterized the 1970s, skewing partisan politics toward the far left, was followed by a shift in both political climate and the composition of governments toward the center-right—significantly to the right of the other three southern European democracies examined in this series.

At the same time, there have been important continuities in the key actors and institutions of Portuguese politics, most notably in the party system. Although all parties (even the once orthodox Marxist-

Leninist PCP) have substantially modified their rhetoric and programmatic appeals away from leftist, if not revolutionary, stands of the 1970s, the identity and the nature of popular support for those parties have remained unchanged. Portuguese democracy emerged initially as a predominantly four-party system, and it remains so today. New parties have not successfully emerged to challenge the established four parties. And the same four parties that established their dominant positions in the 1970s remain dominant today, more than two-and-a-half decades later. The short-term and ultimately unsuccessful challenge by President Eanes's PRD in 1985 was a temporary aberration. In addition, survey data indicate that the vast majority of Portuguese voters are quite content with their parties. There are no signs of a decline of parties or of alienation of voters from the electoral process. And although levels of voting turnout have declined since the first elections, this largely reflected a shift toward democratic normalcy and away from the polarized mobilization of the revolutionary era (Bacalhau 1994, 131–34).

Clearly, the magnitude and direction of these changes suggest that Portuguese democracy and its electoral institutions have been fully consolidated, and that the system has been quite adaptable. When the dysfunctional features of institutional arrangements inherited from the past became apparent, they were eliminated—albeit one by one, and over a protracted period of time. In this respect, we cannot conclude that democratic consolidation impedes institutional adaptability. Indeed, in the Portuguese case, substantial institutional change was a prerequisite to democratic consolidation: as long as institutions like the Council of the Revolution existed, the system could not be regarded as fully democratic; and as long as substantive commitments to socialism were enshrined in the constitution, that legal-institutional framework could not be regarded as fully legitimate, and the system could not be consolidated.

Spain

The basic characteristics of Spain's democratic regime are quite different from those of Portugal, as was the trajectory of political development that created its institutional framework. In contrast to the revolutionary transition to democracy in Portugal, Spain's political evolution (in the end no less extensive) unfolded within the institutions and according to procedures established under Francisco Franco. Spanish democracy was relatively quickly consolidated (within about five years after the first democratic elections), whereas consolidation in Portugal was quite protracted and complex. Unlike in Portugal (where extrication of the military from powerful government posts and the establishment of civilian control over the armed forces posed a serious challenge to the democratization process), the principle of civilian government was taken for granted throughout the Spanish transition. In contrast to Portugal's powerful, partisan, and somewhat controversial head of state, Spain's King Juan Carlos I very quickly emerged as an overwhelmingly popular, nonpartisan, but politically important figurehead. High levels of cabinet instability beset Portugal's multiparty coalition governments for more than a decade, whereas Spain's uninterrupted string of single-party governments have been among the most durable in western Europe. The Portuguese state is highly centralized. Spain has been undergoing a profound process of decentralization since 1980. One final difference is that stable and well-institutionalized parties emerged in Portugal (perhaps as a by-product of the high levels of political mobilization of the revolutionary period), whereas Spanish parties have been characterized by low levels of membership and party identification by voters, and the party system underwent a radical transformation just five years after coming into being (perhaps as a by-product of tactical demobilization, which characterized the most crucial stages of the transition).

In some other respects, however, Portugal and Spain are alike. In both countries, institutions have evolved over time and were not "frozen" as a by-product of regime consolidation; and that evolution has unfolded in a path-dependent fashion, in which the process of institutional change was strongly influenced by key events and decisions from earlier stages in the transition. This is not to say that this evolution has always had positive results, or that Spain has a flawless political system. Indeed, some of the political choices made during the transition may have helped to consolidate the new political regime, but they have also given rise to significant problems over the long term. The ad hoc, one-by-one decision-making processes that decentralized the state may have been the only way to contain the explosive potential of Basque and Catalan nationalism during the critical early stages of democratization, but over the long term they have culminated in the emergence of an uneven and confusing distribution of policy jurisdictions among central and regional government bodies and have given rise to considerable waste and inefficiency. Similarly, while the tactical demobilization of opposition party and trade union organizations may have contributed greatly to the stabilization of the political environment during a potentially chaotic period of change (see Gunther 1992), it also undermined the capacity of key secondary associations to become institutionalized during the highly malleable environment of the mid to late 1970s, thereby culminating in a relatively weak and disorganized civil society, with some negative implications for the quality of Spanish democracy (see Tarrow 1995, 228–30).

The Monarchy and the Military

Two institutional inheritances from the authoritarian Franquist regime proved to be most beneficial for Spain's transition to democracy: the monarchy of Juan Carlos I, and the relationship between the military and the government. At a key point in the democratization process, these two became very closely interrelated.

Francisco Franco came to power by overthrowing the Second Republic (1931–36), which, in turn, had come into being in the aftermath of the abdication of King Alfonso XIII. By the mid 1960s, the aging dictator and his inner circle of friends and advisors became preoccupied with the question of succession. His decision, ratified in a referendum in 1967, was that Prince Juan Carlos would be crowned king of Spain following Franco's death. Franco was careful to point out that this was an instauration of the Borbón monarchy, rather than a restoration: the new head of state was to be the grandson of Alfonso XIII, rather than his son, Don Juan, who had alienated Franco by calling for his overthrow following the Allied victory in World War II. Nonetheless, even though Juan Carlos was handpicked by Franco, and his education carefully scrutinized, the new king played a decisive role in dismantling the Franquist regime and establishing a new democracy. The presence of the reformist Juan Carlos as head of state meant that the processes of change would unfold under an individual perceived by Franquist loyalists as fully possessing legitimate authority. Similarly, Prime Minister Adolfo Suárez's decision to use the institutions and procedures established by Franco (specifically, the Cortes and the referendum process) as the vehicle for dismantling the authoritarian regime further contributed to what Giuseppe Di Palma has referred to as the "backward legitimation" of the democratic transition (see Di Palma 1980; Podolny 1993). This institutional continuity played an important role in securing the support or, at least, acquiescence of those loyal to *franquismo* (see Linz 1982, 37). More broadly, this continuity meant that change would take place within a relatively stable institutional framework, and not in a chaotic political vacuum, as in Portugal.

The role of the king was particularly important given his position as commander in chief of the armed forces. Even though Franco had come to power as head of the armed forces at the end of the Civil War (1936–39), and his early governments featured significant numbers of military officers heading civilian ministries, by the 1970s, government departments were headed exclusively by civilians, except for the military ministries themselves. Nonetheless, the stance of the armed forces vis-à-vis the new democratic regime was a subject of great concern. All officers had been educated in military academies that disseminated explicitly antidemocratic propaganda, and a detailed study of the attitudes and behavior of the Spanish military found that, as late as the early 1980s, a substantial number of prominent military leaders continued to hold undemocratic or antidemocratic attitudes and values (see Agüero 1995). Respect for Juan Carlos's legitimate authority as commander in chief proved to be crucial for the survival of Spain's fledgling democracy, particularly at one dramatic moment during the consolidation process. On February 23, 1981, at a time when virtually all of Spain's top-ranking party leaders were seated in the Congress of Deputies (the "lower house" in this highly unbalanced bicameral system) to vote on the investiture of Leopoldo Calvo Sotelo as Adolfo Suárez's successor as prime minister, a well-armed group of paramilitary rebels (linked in a complex antidemocratic conspiracy to important sectors of the military) burst into the chamber to initiate what they hoped would be a coup d'état, and one captain-general proclaimed martial law in his region. Despite its initial tactical success, the attempted coup collapsed overnight as the result of decisive action in defense of democracy by the king. Juan Carlos moved swiftly to isolate those who had taken an active stand, and (through an extensive series of personal telephone conversations) to order the captains-general to remain loyal to the regime. Those orders were obeyed by all but one, who quickly stood down. Thus, the legitimacy of the king was absolutely decisive in preserving the new regime at a moment of great crisis.

Despite his importance as commander in chief and defender of Spanish democracy, Juan Carlos has behaved in an impeccably nonpartisan manner. His constitutional prerogatives as head of state, moreover, were sharply limited as a result of historic compromises. On the one hand, the parties of the left were obliged (despite their traditional republicanism) to accept the "parliamentary monarchy" as the political form of the state (article 1.3 of the 1978 constitution), and the Communist PCE acknowledged Juan Carlos as Spain's legitimate head of state, in part in order to acquire status as a legal political party. On the other hand, the parties of the left were concerned that restoration of the monarchy would lead to the crown's interference in partisan politics—fears heightened by the fact that both Juan Carlos's grandfather (Alfonso XIII) and brother-in-law (the former King Constantine of Greece) had seriously undermined their respective democratic regimes through frequent meddling in partisan-political matters. As a result, the Spanish constitution requires that all decrees and other "acts" of the king, as well as dissolution of parliament, must be countersigned by the prime minister or by the relevant government minister. Similarly, the nomination and designation of the prime minister (which is effectively determined by parliament) must be countersigned by the president of the Congress of Deputies.

Overall, then, the importance of Juan Carlos as a legitimate symbol and defender of Spanish democracy cannot be overstated. In terms of his influence over everyday politics, however, the king is a powerless figurehead who has behaved in a strictly nonpartisan manner.

Majoritarian and Consensual Governance

Throughout its first two decades of existence, Spain's democratic government has featured elements of both majoritarianism and consensualism. In the process of establishing the basic political institutions of the new democracy, a consensual style of decision making was employed, which at crucial moments involved the broad participation of nearly all politically significant groups. Also in keeping with the consensual model of democracy, majoritarian winner-take-all rules were abandoned in favor of a kind of "mutual veto": as described by one of the authors of the first draft of the constitution, there was the widespread understanding that the objective of decision makers was not to be "in agreement with everything, but that the constitution would not contain any aspect that would be absolutely unacceptable to any political group."[2] Nonetheless, while consensual rules of the game played a crucial role in the transition and consolidation processes, consensualism has not been a permanent or consistent feature of either elite recruitment or decision-making practices in Spain.

Majoritarianism has always been adopted in the formation of governments in post-Franco Spain, which have been one-party governments even when the governing party has lacked a parliamentary majority, as in the 1977, 1979, 1993, and 1996 legislatures. It has also been prevalent in the staffing of ministerial positions, which, while varying somewhat from one ministry to another, typically involves partisan, single-party appointments to all posts at the level of director-general and above. Whenever a government has had an absolute majority in parliament, a restrained form of majoritarianism has prevailed in the policy-making process as well, although even when the PSOE government commanded an absolute majority in the 1982 and 1986 legislatures, it usually sought parliamentary support for its legislative proposals from at least one other party (see Capo Giol 1990; Maurer 1995). It remains to be seen whether the PP absolute majority government issuing from the 2000 elections will conform to this practice.

Governmental majoritarianism derives from several institutional features of the regime. The first is the electoral law, which magnifies electoral pluralities into parliamentary majorities or near majorities. As can be seen in Appendix Table A.5, the main effect of the electoral law is to overrepresent the two largest parties and greatly underrepresent smaller parties with geographically dispersed bases of electoral support. Over time, small nationwide parties have been progressively eliminated. This same electoral law, however, because it uses the province as the principal electoral district, allows smaller parties (such as Basque and Catalan nationalist parties) to be fairly represented in the Congress of Deputies. Indeed, purely regional parties have persisted as a significant feature of the Spanish party system.

The second source of majoritarianism is the inclusion in the constitution (article 113) of a German-style "constructive" vote of no confidence. Once a government has been installed in office, it can only be removed through approval of a motion of no confidence by an absolute majority vote, which would simultaneously install a successor government. In the 1979 legislature, for example, this would have meant that opposition parties could only remove the UCD from office if virtually all of them (from the Communist Party on the left to the Alianza Popular on the right, and including the major Basque and Catalan nationalist parties) were able to agree on the composition of a new government. The difficulty of meeting this requirement can be seen in the fact that governing parties have had the support of an absolute majority of the Congress of Deputies in only three of the seven legislatures under the 1978 constitution, and yet there has never been a successful no-confidence vote against Spain's numerous single-party minority governments. The combined effects of the majoritarian biases of the electoral law and the constructive motion of no confidence provide an institutional incentive toward the formation of stable governments: over the course of the first two decades of post-Franco Spanish democracy, there were only two changes in the partisan composition of government, giving Spain an average cabinet durability score of 114 months for the period 1977–96 (see Table 2.4), one of the longest among all the democratic systems considered. Given the reelection of a PP government in 2000 (this time supported by an absolute majority in parliament), this pattern of governmental longevity is likely to continue well into the twenty-first century.

The dominant position of the government vis-à-vis parliament is further reinforced by other constitutional provisions that greatly strengthen the hand of the prime minister. Unlike in many other parliamentary systems, only the prime minister is subject to parliamentary votes of investiture or no confidence. The Congress of Deputies has neither the authority to vote in favor of individual members of the government (or the cabinet as a whole) nor the ability to remove them from office, leaving the prime minister free to appoint or dismiss individual ministers without parliamentary approval. The prime minister is also largely autonomous in deciding upon the dissolution of parliament, as well as in calling for consultative referenda. Even the rules governing the investiture of the prime minister help to reinforce the power of the executive vis-à-vis the opposition parties in parliament. An absolute majority of all of the members of the Congress is required on the first ballot of the investiture process, but if a candidate fails to muster a majority on the first ballot, a prime minister can be elected with the support of merely a plurality of those voting in the second round.[3] Thus, the institutional framework of the current regime decisively stacks the deck in favor of government stability and executive dominance.[4]

A counterpart to the institutional provisions that concentrate power in the hands of the executive are other factors that undermine the ability of individual members of parliament to play important roles in the policy process. A rigorous study of the role of parliament in the legislative process found that the most important determinants of the independent impact of members of parliament on policy were the relative size of the government's parliamentary delegation; the level of party discipline within that group; whether the establishment of key institutions or ordinary legislation was the object of parliamentary activity; and various aspects of the structure of parliament itself (Maurer 1995). Specifically, the absence of a parliamentary majority, weak party discipline, and the special requirements of "the politics of consensus" made it possible for ordinary backbenchers to have considerable influence over the course of legislation. These circumstances were most clearly apparent under the UCD governments of 1977–82, when enactment of every piece of legislation required considerable bargaining with opposition parties and even UCD backbenchers. At the other end of the continuum were the PSOE governments of 1982 and 1986, when the executive was supported by an absolute majority in the Congress of Deputies. By this time, all parties had been so alarmed by the collapse and complete disappearance of the UCD that the imposition of party discipline was paramount (and in the case of the PSOE rigidly enforced). In addition, these phenomena occurred after consolidation of the regime had been achieved and political elites had concluded that the broad, interparty negotiations and mutual veto that characterized the "politics of consensus" were no longer necessary, and, indeed, that the economic crisis and the need for long-term restructuring required bold policy initiatives by a strong government. In this sense, it is important to note that, far from "freezing" the policy options available to governments, democratic consolidation actually freed the Spanish government from the restraints it had imposed upon itself during the more uncertain and tenuous periods of political change.

Following its loss of an absolute parliamentary majority in 1989, the PSOE again depended on the support of other parties in order to pass its legislation, but its bargaining strategies were much closer to the majoritarian than to the consensual model, tending to secure ad hoc minimum-winning coalitions with other parties in parliament. Falling to minority status after the 1993 election, the PSOE again altered its government format by forging a coalition agreement with the Catalan nationalist Convergència i Unió (CiU). While the CiU rejected an offer of cabinet seats, it gave stable parliamentary support to the minority PSOE government, in exchange for which the Catalan leader Jordi Pujol acquired considerable influence over government policy. This pattern was continued following the 1996 victory of the conservative Partido Popular. Also lacking a parliamentary majority, the PP negotiated a pact with the center-right regional parties of Catalonia, Euskadi, and the Canary Islands in which they would support a minority PP government in exchange for influence over policy priorities. A simpler form of majoritarianism returned in 2000, following an election that produced an absolute majority in parliament for the PP. Although it formed a single-party government without having previously negotiated pacts with minority regional parties, however, it remains to be seen whether the PP will seek to secure the support of other parties in enacting legislation.

Parliamentary structures and procedures further weaken the position of individual deputies. Support services (secretarial and research assistance) are fully under the control of the heads of the parliamentary parties and are not available to individual members. High turnover on parliamentary committees prevents members from acquiring the expertise regarding specific policy areas that is usually a prerequisite for being an effective legislator (see Morán 1989; Maurer 1995). Only parliamentary groups (formation of which is restricted to parties represented by fifteen or more deputies in the Congress) may introduce *proposiciones de ley* ("private members' bills"), and amendments to bills may only be introduced with the approval of the *portavoz* (spokesperson) of the parliamentary delegation (Colomer 1995, 220). Parliamentary regulations clearly subordinate the individual member to the leaders of his or her parliamentary group. This does not mean, however, that the Congress of Deputies was irrelevant to the policy process, even in those legislatures when the PSOE held an absolute majority. While government bills were rarely modified through votes in committee or plenary sessions, "ministers reported that they often took opposition views into account either through negotiations or unilateral concessions when drafting bills" (Maurer 1995). Nonetheless, in comparative terms, the Spanish government, and especially its prime minister, must be regarded as extraordinarily powerful and dominant in the policy process.

Majoritarian, ma non troppo

Spanish-style majoritarianism, even following consolidation of the democratic regime and the coming to power of a PSOE majority government in 1982, is different from the pure variety of majoritarianism found in Great Britain and in the executive branch of the U.S. government. While ministerial posts are partisan appointments, consensualism applies to the staffing of certain government bodies that are regarded as above partisan politics because of their fundamental roles as guarantors of fair play, basic civil or political rights, and the nonpartisanship of key state institutions. These "arbiter" institutions include the Constitutional Court, the Supreme Court, the Junta Electoral Central (which oversees the electoral process), the Tribunal de Cuentas (Court of Accounts), the Consejo General del Poder Judicial (which appoints judges and oversees the court system), the ombudsman (*defensor del pueblo*), and the boards that oversee the public broadcasting and university systems. The importance of maintaining some minimal level of partisan balance is reflected in the legal frameworks regulating these institutions (either the various organic laws or the constitution itself), which require that appointments be ratified by qualified majorities in parliament (by votes of at least 60 percent). Inasmuch as no parliamentary party has ever controlled that number of seats, interparty agreements must be reached concerning all such appointments. It is interesting to note, however, that the scope of interparty consensus has increasingly gone well beyond minimal compliance with these oversized-majority requirements. In 1994, for instance, the PSOE could have met the 60 percent minimum requirement by reaching agreement with just one other party, the PP. Instead, it also included a number of nominations by Basque and Catalan nationalist parties, as well as by Izquierda Unida (United Left, a coalition that includes the PCE). Consensual norms have even applied to some government bodies, such as the Council of State (which provides the government with legal opinions regarding a number of policy issues), where appointments do not have to be ratified by oversized majorities. Finally, the presidencies of the various committees in the Congress of Deputies and the Senate are parceled out proportionally among the various parliamentary parties. These limitations on the scope of partisan politics stand in sharp contrast to the extreme majoritarianism practiced by the executive branch at the local, state, and national levels in the United States, where the majority party controls all legislative committees, where partisan "packing" of the Supreme Court has often occurred, and where partisanship can extend to the appointment or election of county engineers and coroners.

With regard to the type of democracy to have emerged in Spain, the most important general conclusion is that the central government institutions created in the mid to late 1970s have proven flexible and adaptable enough to fit the political demands of consolidating and effectively governing a new democratic regime. Gianfranco Pasquino has argued that consensual forms of government are most appropriate for the transition to democracy and for the early phases of the consolidation process (when the competing demands of politically significant groups must be articulated and taken into consideration in establishing a new regime), but that once this malleable, formative stage has passed, more decisive, majoritarian government may be necessary in order to formulate policies capable of addressing serious social, economic or political problems (Pasquino 1995). The case of Spain is a clear example of how this shift from one style of democracy to another can be functional both for the consolidation of democracy and for its capacity to act decisively over the long term. The institutions we have examined in this chapter (the electoral law, the constructive vote of no confidence, and the extraordinary powers of the prime minister) predispose the Spanish government toward majoritarianism. The restraint and good judgment of Spanish elites during crucial phases of the transition and consolidation, however, led them to adopt consensual decision-making principles that, as we have argued, contributed greatly to the resolution or successful regulation of traditionally divisive issues, and to virtually universal acceptance of the new regime's central institutions as the only legitimate framework for political contestation. Once the consolidation of Spanish democracy had been achieved, however, consensualism was no longer seen as necessary, except with respect to those institutions regarded as arbiters and guarantors of fair play in the game of democratic politics. Accordingly, more majoritarian decision-making principles were employed in addressing such critical issues as restructuring the inefficient and uncompetitive parastate sector of the economy.

The ad hoc, one-by-one procedures that were so essential for securing Basque and Catalan acceptance of the new regime culminated, however, in the institutionalization of an unbalanced and complex decentralized state structure. In most federal systems, governmental functions are allocated to all states, provinces, or *Länder* through specific constitutional provisions. The 1978 Spanish constitution established procedures for the transfer of governmental functions from the central government to new Autonomous Communities and enumerated the kinds of functions that could be devolved to the regions. But the actual devolution of authority from the central government to each individual region was determined through a protracted series of bilateral negotiations between the Spanish government, on the one hand, and the Basques, then the Catalans, then the Gallegos, then the Andalusians, then the remaining regions, on the other. This has resulted in an uneven distribution of powers among the regions and an extremely conflictual process of determining the levels of revenues given the regions to support their government functions.[5] While some have argued that the simplicity and uniform distribution of functions that characterize other federal systems,[6] as well as the fiscal autonomy of their central and subnational governments, are preferable to the complexity and inherently conflictual budgetary processes of the Spanish system, these options were effectively precluded by the necessity of taking prompt action to secure Basque and Catalan support for Spain's new democracy in the late 1970s.

Spain thus confirms Pasquino's hypothesis: institutional arrangements that are most suitable for one particular set of circumstances (e.g., the transition to democracy) may prove to be quite dysfunctional over the long term, having adverse consequences for the quality of democracy.

Greece

Of the four southern European political systems examined in this chapter, the Greek case is undoubtedly the one that reveals the greatest amount of continuity in its evolution over the past two decades. There is nothing in Greece's postauthoritarian experience similar to the painful and protracted adjustment to the norms of democracy that characterized Portugal and delayed the consolidation of its democratic regime until 1982, if not 1989. Nor, for that matter, did Greece witness a phenomenon comparable to the qualitative shift from consensual to majoritarian politics that characterized Spanish politics after 1979. Finally, the impressive continuity of the Greek party system stands in sharp contrast to the major transformation of its Italian counterpart during the 1990s.

The single most important structural characteristic distinguishing the Greek political system from the others is its pronounced majoritarianism. Indeed, compared to the three other countries in the region and measured by Lijphart's various indices, Greece emerges as a prototypical case of majoritarianism, a trait that has been remarkably persistent and stands as a defining characteristic of Greek politics.

On closer examination, however, significant evolution and change become apparent. The most important of these changes has been a gradual shift away from polarized, exclusivist, and centrifugal forms of majoritarian rule toward the moderate, inclusive, and centripetal type of politics that has increasingly characterized the other southern European political systems discussed here and brought them closer to their western and northern European counterparts. This interplay between continuity and change will constitute the main focus of the analysis that follows.

Majoritarianism has been a salient characteristic of the Greek political system practically throughout the half century since the end of the Greek Civil War (1946–49). With the exception of three brief periods (March 1950 to November 1952, November 1963 to February 1964, and June 1989 to April 1990), all post–Civil War elections have produced single-party governments. The strongest factor accounting for the low number of "effective parties" in Greece (see Table 2.6) is the electoral system of "reinforced" proportional representation. This strongly majoritarian system is a variant of proportional representation expressly designed to discourage multipartyism, to foster the emergence and persistence of large parties, to facilitate the formation of minimal-winning-cabinets based on a single party enjoying majority support in parliament, and to penalize smaller ones. Its more dominant version has, with slight variations, been in use since 1958. The sole exception was the June 1989–April 1990 period, in which an electoral system approximating simple proportional representation was adopted and quickly abandoned.[7]

Strongly influenced by the logic of this electoral system, the Greek political landscape was, in the years leading up to the authoritarian interlude of 1967–74, dominated by two large parties, the Ethnike Rizospastike Enosis (National Radical Union), or ERE, on the right of the political spectrum, and the Enosis Kentrou (Center Union), or EK, near the center. During the 1960s, the share of the vote received by these two parties ranged between 81.4 percent and 88.0 percent. In the postauthoritarian period, the adoption of virtually the same electoral system served as the foundation upon which two new large parties, Nea Demokratia (New Democracy) and the Panellinio Sosialistiko Kinema (Panhellenic Socialist Movement), or PASOK, founded in 1974 by Constantine Karamanlis and Andreas Papandreou respectively, built their undisputed dominance of the country's first genuinely democratic political system.[8] Between them, they have garnered between 79.6 and 86.9 percent of the vote during the 1980s and 1990s, and their average joint share of the total vote (84.6 percent) has been almost identical to that of ERE and EK in the preauthoritarian period (see Diamandouros 1998).

The strongly majoritarian nature of the Greek political system is borne out by all of the indicators for measuring majoritarianism employed by Lijphart 1984. Despite the fact that between 1989 and 1990, three elections were held under systems approximating simple proportional representation, the average index of disproportionality for the seven parliamentary elections held in Greece between 1981 and 1996 is 8.08, which is much higher than for most other democracies.

Cabinet durability has been a standard feature of the Greek postauthoritarian system. With the exception, once again, of the ten-month period of coalition government between June 1989 and April 1990, all Greek cabinets since 1974 have been based on a single majority party. The executive dominance over the legislature that this implies is further evidenced by a series of additional indicators, including the virtual omnipotence of the party leadership relative to backbenchers, and the strict majoritarianism governing the operation of parliamentary committees, where the government of the day routinely secures adoption of its proposals.[9]

With regard to the issue dimensions of partisan conflict, Greece has, over the past decades, moved increasingly in the direction of straight majoritarianism. The number of issue dimensions dividing the major parties has gradually but steadily declined over the years. By the mid 1990s, with one partial exception, to be mentioned later, the left-right issue was by far the most salient issue dimension separating parties. The regime support dimension has also steadily declined in salience, as the country's communist left moved from illegality (1947–74) to legality (1974 on), and, as Anna Bosco shows in Chapter 8 of this volume, its more orthodox variant, the Communist Party of Greece (KKE), gradually accommodated itself to, and in practice accepted, the democratic rules of the game.

Finally, Greece's majoritarianism is also confirmed when measured by indicators relating to Lijphart's federal/unitary dimension. Throughout the postwar period, Greece has had a strongly unicameral parliament and completely rigid constitutions. Notwithstanding recent legislation introducing two tiers of decentralization—brought about, above all, by increasing integration into the structures of the European Union—the country's centralist tradition, dating from the modern Greek state's inception, has survived virtually intact to date.[10]

Greek majoritarianism also has a cultural dimension. In many ways, this is a reflection of the zero-sum logic that historically underpins many social arrangements in modern Greece. The valorization of winner-take-all approaches to conflict resolution that such a logic implies has imparted to Greek political culture a distinct propensity for polarization and a commensurate tendency to privilege political arrangements and strategies geared to exclusion, while exhibiting a weak interest in more moderate, inclusivist, and consensual alternatives (see Mavrogordatos 1990). Polarization and the centrifugal logic underpinning it were preeminent traits of Greece's preauthoritarian political system (1950–67). As many analysts of the country's political system have pointed out, they were largely responsible for that system's incapacity to attain consolidation, as well as its rapid destabilization and demise within the short span of six years, from 1961 to 1967 (see Alivizatos 1979; Meynaud 1965; Diamandouros 1986).

These multiple manifestations of majoritarianism notwithstanding, we contend that what above all distinguishes Greece's unstable, preauthoritarian political system from its democratic successor regime (1974–) is a gradual but distinct decrease in the salience of polarization in Greek politics. In turn, this change has introduced into Greek majoritarianism a propensity for moderation, inclusion, and centripetalism that has substantively altered the character and dynamics of the Greek political system and decisively contributed to the consolidation of Greek democracy.

Variations on the Theme of Majoritarianism

For purposes of this analysis, we should like to distinguish between two phases in the evolution of Greek majoritarianism since 1974. To draw a clear distinction between the preauthoritarian and postauthoritarian variants, we shall refer to the former as "majoritarianism-1," or M1. To underscore the continuing salience and evolving nature of majoritarianism in the Greek political system, we shall label that of the first postauthoritarian phase "majoritarianism-2," or M2, and the most recent variant "majoritarianism-3," or M3. M2 extends from the new democratic regime's inauguration in 1974 to the end of PASOK's first term in office in 1985. M3 covers the period from PASOK's reelection to another term in office in June 1985 and continues to date.

Given the continuing dominance of reinforced proportional representation as the electoral system of choice since 1958, what accounts for this change in the dynamics of Greek majoritarianism? One set of explanatory factors is inherent in the democratization process itself and the ensuing evolution of the dynamics of politics. Three specific changes intimately linked to the advent of full political democracy merit attention in connection with the transition from M1 to M2. The first concerns the decision taken in the summer of 1974, in the early days of the transition to democracy, to formally rescind all legal constraints on the free operation of political parties. The legalization of the communist left, which this decision effectively implied, removed a major parameter that had decisively contributed to the preauthoritarian regime's exclusivist character and to the polarizing and, above all, centrifugal dynamics of its profoundly anticommunist political system. Put otherwise, this development helped invest the new system with a logic of inclusion that was to have profoundly beneficial results for the eventual consolidation of democracy in Greece (see Gunther, Diamandouros, and Puhle 1995; Diamandouros 1984).

The legalization of the communist left had an additional byproduct that positively affected the dynamics of M2 in Greece's postauthoritarian political system. The legitimation of the communist left essentially opened up the center-left area of the left-right spectrum, which the centrifugal logic of the preauthoritarian system had effectively kept off-limits to potential occupants, declaring it to be too close to the ideologically polluted pole occupied by the Eniaia Demokratike Aristera (United Democratic Left), or EDA, which, in the absence of the outlawed Kommounistiko Komma Elladas (Communist Party of Greece), or KKE, was the surrogate party of the far left. The opening up of the center-left space created the preconditions for the emergence both of a center-left party in Greek politics and, more broadly, a moderating, centripetal dynamic in the new political system.

In a narrow sense, the third change was the mirror image of the first. It concerned the delegitimation of the far right of the Greek political spectrum, which, in the preauthoritarian period, had served as the pivotal point of reference and central pole of legitimation for the political system and, more generally, for the post–Civil War regime of circumscribed parliamentarianism constructed by the victors in that internecine struggle. A number of factors account for this reversal: (1) the profound delegitimation of anticommunism, brought about, inter alia, by the patent failure of the military regime established by George Papadopoulos and his fellow right-wing colonels after their coup d'état on April 21, 1967, to produce any convincing evidence of a communist threat in Greece, both at the time of its advent to power in 1967 and throughout its seven years' rule, and thus to justify its existence; (2) the direct implication of the armed forces in the overthrow of a popularly elected regime in Cyprus and their manifest inability effectively to deal with the Turkish invasion of that island brought about by a Greek-led coup d'état; and (3) the elimination, through an impeccably held referendum, of the monarchy, which had served as a powerful legitimating pillar of the anticommunist political system of the post–Civil War era and, more generally, of the forces opposed to democratization in Greece.

The net result of the delegitimation of the far right, the relegitimation of the far left and, above all, the legitimation of the center-left was a massive repositioning of the Greek political system's center of gravity away from the extreme points of the left-right spectrum and toward the center. The centripetal dynamic with which the new system was accordingly endowed manifested itself most clearly in two complementary ways: first, in Karamanlis's conscious attempt to position his new party, Nea Demokratia, in the center-right space of the left-right spectrum and to invest it with the pertinent ideological mantle; second, in the success with which Greece's first-ever major noncommunist party of the left, PASOK, was able to occupy the center-left space of the political spectrum and to use it as the springboard for its meteoric rise to power within a mere seven years of its founding.[11] The ultimate outcome of all these developments was a political system that, although strongly majoritarian, lacked the polarizing and centrifugal qualities that had so heavily contributed to its preauthoritarian predecessor's undoing. Hence our inclination to consider this a distinct phase in the evolution of Greek majoritarianism, M2.

This having been said, postauthoritarian Greek majoritarianism, although clearly much less geared to polarization than its centrifugal, preauthoritarian counterpart, nonetheless retained distinct elements of polarization. The lingering animosities that were a legacy of the

Civil War helped make the left-right cleavage by far the most salient issue in Greek politics. Further contributing to the intensity of this cleavage were memories of the colonels' authoritarian regime and of the fanatical anticommunism it had espoused.

Left-right polarization also stemmed from a partly unanticipated consequence of democratization. The dismantling of the post–Civil War state brought about by democratization effectively restored the political rights of citizenship to extensive social strata that had been subjected to systematic discrimination, marginalization, and exclusion during the preauthoritarian period because of their real or alleged association with the vanquished side in the Civil War. Their political enfranchisement was manifested in the emergence of a solid block of voters defining themselves, above all else, as "antiright" and seeking to reap the benefits arising out of the newfound democratic legitimacy accorded to the left. In practical terms, this search for "benefits" took the form of demands for compensation, real or symbolic, for wrongs (actual or perceived) suffered in the preauthoritarian period. These demands reached their apogee after 1981, when, propelled in great part by the massive support it received from these very strata, PASOK completed its meteoric rise to power and assumed the reins of government in the name of the "nonprivileged Greeks," in order to bring about the much touted structural change, or *allaghi* (Diamandouros 1997).

In this sense, then, as the self-styled expression of the "nonprivileged Greeks," PASOK was, from the very beginning, intimately linked to the type of polarization associated with the centripetal majoritarianism of the postauthoritarian Greek political system. In great part, the inclination toward polarization stemmed from PASOK's self-image as the agent of structural change and of a "radical rupture with the past." This self-image and the desire to establish beyond doubt its credentials as a totally novel political formation, with an identity that was qualitatively different from that of "traditional" political parties, led PASOK to opt for a style of politics emphasizing its commitment to radical change and its disdain for continuity with the past (depicted in uniformly negative terms). Driven forward by its charismatic leader, Andreas Papandreou, and unencumbered, during the critical initial years of its existence, by the constraining realities of office, the party called for a third road to socialism capable of eschewing the failures associated with its extant or social democratic variants; exit from NATO and the European Economic Community; the separation of Church and state in Greece; and an overhauling of a series of existing institutional arrangements. The manichean populist discourse consciously adopted by Papandreou and the party elite proved ideally suited to attract to the new party the large part of the Greek population radicalized by the experience of the authoritarian regime, by the newfound freedoms of the democratic game, and by inchoate yearnings for a "new Greece." The polarization of politics that these factors produced was somewhat inevitable and gave M2 its basic content.

The high point of polarization of Greece's postauthoritarian political system occurred between 1981 and 1985. Once in office, PASOK pursued policies and adopted a discourse that both overtly and covertly subscribed to the unarticulated principle of "compensatory justice." The guiding logic of that principle was the satisfaction of as many as possible of the particularistic demands put forward by its supporters seeking compensation for wrongs, real or perceived, suffered under the anticommunist, post–Civil War state. Somewhat inevitably, the systematic distribution of benefits by the state and the wider public sector (banks, public utilities, etc.) through such fiercely narrow, partisan "compensatory" criteria contributed to increased polarization.

Developments within the Nea Demokratia camp led in the same direction. Shaken by the loss of political power, to which it had been accustomed since its founding in 1974, and deprived of the moderating influence of its founder, Constantine Karamanlis, and of his immediate successor, George Rallis, that party lapsed into a defensive and increasingly confrontational type of politics. The resulting polarization was exacerbated by the rise to party leadership of the liberal centrist Constantine Mitsotakis, whose profound (and fully reciprocated) antipathy for Andreas Papandreou dated back to the 1960s and their struggle to succeed George Papandreou at the helm of the EK, as well as their deep involvement in the political and constitutional crisis that led to the breakdown of parliamentary rule in 1967.

Polarization reached its peak in the 1985 election. PASOK opted for an electoral discourse effectively invoking the imagery of the "two [political] worlds," into which ostensibly Greece was divided. Nea Demokratia was identified with the "forces of darkness," the "accursed Right," the anticommunist, post–Civil War past, and the traditional political forces, whose democratic credentials were either deemed suspect or directly questioned. The "forces of light" were represented by PASOK and the "other progressive or democratic forces," an elliptical formulation designed to include all political parties making up the "antiright" bloc, whose democratic legitimacy was a priori regarded as given.[12]

It is not easy to ascertain the exact point in time when polarization became attenuated and the latest phase of majoritarianism, M3, began. The coalition governments of 1989–90 seem to be a reasonable point of demarcation, given the unprecedented decision of the political and intellectual heirs to the two sides of the Civil War, Nea Demokratia and the communist left (both orthodox and Eurocommunist), to form a coalition government. Indeed, this development has been widely regarded as signaling the symbolic end of that great conflict. Reinforcing the temptation to identify 1989 as marking a transition to a more consensual style of politics in Greece is the fact that a more strictly proportional electoral system was used in all three electoral contests held during this ten-month period (see Pridham and Verney 1991). Alternatively, Andreas Papandreou's last administration, beginning in October 1993, and the rise of Costas Simitis as the new PASOK leader in 1996 should also be seen as important milestones.

Nevertheless, our own inclination is to look to the period immediately following the 1985 elections and PASOK's reelection to a second term in office as the *terminus post quem* for a trajectory leading away from M2 and toward the increasingly more moderate and pragmatic politics of M3. While not denying the symbolic importance of the events of 1989, we base this choice on the adoption of a distinctly more conciliatory public discourse and set of policies by PASOK immediately following its 1985 electoral victory.

The adoption of this more moderate form of majoritarianism appears to be the product of three factors relating (in varying degrees) to structural changes in Greece's international environment. The first stems from the country's deepening involvement in the process of European integration. At multiple levels, the logic of European integration pushes member states in the direction of moderate policies, especially in the realm of economics and, increasingly, politics. Ironically, Greece's failure to meet the criteria for entry into the European Monetary Union alongside the initial group of EU member-states in 1999 means that the pressure for a continuing demonstration of its political commitment to the goals of convergence prescribed by the Single European Act, the Treaty of Maastricht, and the Treaty of Amsterdam, and to the restructuring of state and market that these imply, will continue unabated until 2001, when, it is widely expected, Greece will enter the EMU. The increasing internationalization of the Greek economy and its growing integration into the world economy is a second factor pushing in the direction of convergence with the general practices and policies of the advanced industrial societies. Finally, the end of the certainties and rigidities associated with the Cold

War has meant that Greece must adapt to the greater fluidity of the post–Cold War era and, thus, align its international policies with those of its partners at the European and international levels. The net impact of these international developments is the adoption of increasingly moderate and pragmatic sets of policies.[13]

Thus, while retaining its strong majoritarian characteristics, the Greek political system has undergone an attenuation of the polarizing dynamics that characterized previous periods, and the intensity of the left-right cleavage has declined. To be sure, this cleavage still constitutes the most important issue in Greek politics. Its salience, however, is clearly lower than it was both in its heyday, during the post–Civil War years (M1), and in its improved version (M2) during the first decade or so following the transition to democracy in Greece.

Although the old left-right cleavage has moderated, a new issue dimension directly associated with the structural changes Greece is currently undergoing has emerged, pitting the potential or actual losers against the winners resulting from these adjustments. This emerging cleavage "cross-cuts" existing social and political alignments and divides sectors within the same political parties. In general, those individuals or groups who are better endowed with skills and access to capital and advanced technology—who are therefore more likely to compete successfully in the newly emerging environment—are more likely to favor structural change in state-society relations. These changes entail, inter alia, the strengthening of Greece's historically weak civil society and a shift in the state's basic orientation away from overprotection and overregulation to more flexible and selective intervention, designed to provide the legal and institutional framework facilitating the growth of a more empowered and competitive civil society. Conversely, individuals and groups poorly endowed with these three attributes are more likely to fail in this more competitive environment, and thus are likely to identify with what Diamandouros has called the "underdog culture." This orientation favors a highly protectionist and interventionist state, concerned more with addressing the needs of the less competitive and dynamic segments of Greek society than with rendering them (and Greek society as a whole) better capable of confronting European and international competitors. Time will tell how the growing salience of this cleavage will affect the left-right cleavage that has dominated Greek society and politics for almost half a century. One possible turn of events could entail the further attenuation of that cleavage, while retaining intact the structure of the postauthoritarian party and political systems. Another outcome would involve a reconceptualization of left and right in a manner reflecting the dynamics of the new social and political realities associated with this new cleavage and, in extremis, affecting the structure of the postauthoritarian party and political systems (Diamandouros 1994). Some tentative signs of this development appeared in the 1990s, with the emergence of two new parties, Politike Anoixe (Political Spring), or POLAN, on the center-right, and the Demokratiko Koinoniko Kinema (Democratic Social Movement), or DIKKI, in virtually the same space occupied by PASOK. Both parties (as well as the KKE) cater to those segments of the underdog coalition most adversely affected by the restructuring and rationalization of economic and political arrangements. Despite this development, however, the party system continues to be dominated by the country's two largest parties. Their combined total of the popular vote was 86.2 percent in 1993, when POLAN first contested an election, and 79.6 percent in 1996, when both breakaway parties participated in that year's electoral consultation.[14]

The trend toward majoritarianism and two-party dominance was further strengthened in the closely contested 2000 elections, in which the political system's centripetalist logic was clearer than ever before. The two major parties' combined share of the popular vote reached 86.53 percent, with PASOK receiving 43.80 percent and Nea Demokratia 42.73. Squeezed by the two dominant contestants, smaller parties fared worse in these elections. POLAN chose not to run at all, DIKKI received 2.69 percent of the vote and was excluded from parliament (entry into which requires a minimum 3 percent of the vote, the Synaspismos saw its share of the vote drop to 3.20 percent (as opposed to 5.52 for the KKE), and the tiny Liberal Party, a newcomer on the Greek electoral scene, secured parliamentary representation by its leader and one deputy only as a result of an electoral alliance with Nea Demokratia.

Overall, Greek political institutions have shown a remarkable continuity, and majoritarianism remains strongly entrenched. This notwithstanding, the restructuring of the country's political system in the wake of democratization, the exigencies of European integration, the growing ascendancy of the social and political forces favoring reform, and the resulting turn toward greater moderation and pragmatism have unquestionably imparted an increasingly centripetal dynamic to Greek politics. In the process, the latter has undergone a subtle but unmistakable change in character and has evolved toward, and converged with, its southern and western European counterparts.

Italy

The case of Italy is significantly different from those of Greece, Portugal, and Spain. Our exploration of these other southern European cases generated three different stories of institutional stabilization and consolidation: of a general lack of institutional change in the case of Greece; of steady, incremental evolution and subsequent stabilization in the case of Spain; and of institutionalization of procedural democracy in Portugal, following an initial period of revolutionary turmoil. In contrast, following a long period of institutional stability in Italy, from the 1950s through the 1980s, major changes were set in motion whose ultimate outcomes are still not entirely clear. This substantial restructuring of relationships among key democratic institutions was accompanied by a shift from a highly consensual type of democracy to a still-evolving system that is decidedly different in several ways. Our overview of institutional evolution in Italy, therefore, begins with a description of the most salient features of the consensual system that existed for over three decades. We then examine both those features that have undergone substantial change and those characterized by considerable continuity with the past.

Consensual Democracy, Italian Style

One of the defining characteristics of Italian democracy during its first four decades was the large number of political parties. As we have seen in Table 2.6, the Italian party system was highly fragmented. Throughout this period, there were at least seven significant parties, ranging from the far right to the left: the Movimento Sociale Italiano (MSI); Democrazia Cristiana (DC); Partito Liberale Italiano (PLI); Partito Repubblicano Italiano (PRI); Partito Socialista Democratico Italiano (PSDI); Partito Socialista Italiano (PSI); and Partito Comunista Italiano (PCI). A number of new minor parties also appeared on the scene (e.g., the Radicals and the Greens), albeit some of them only temporarily (e.g., fragments that split off from the PSI in the 1960s). In this party system, Christian Democracy always had a prominent position, leading many observers to speak of a dominant or quasi-dominant party system (see Tarrow 1990). Also characteristic of this highly fragmented party system were a high level of ideological polarization and widely divergent policy positions, making it the classic case of "polarized pluralism" (see Sartori 1976).

As we have seen in Table 2.7, these differing stands were rooted in three basic social cleavages—involving socioeconomic differences, religiosity, and foreign policy (although the latter declined in salience over time). These interacted in such a manner as to give rise to complex patterns of competition among parties within each major bloc—with the domestic translation of the Cold War, for example, dividing parties of the left, and the religious cleavage separating parties within the large center bloc. While these cleavages were significant in their own right, they were perpetuated (even well past their respective periods of maximum salience) by party traditions and well-developed party organizations. As we shall see Chapter 3, these remained as bases of partisan mobilization until well into the 1990s.

Thus, during this first period, Italian democracy was characterized by a high degree of party-system fragmentation, polarization between left and right, permanent exclusion of significant parties on both the left and the right from government, and the protracted incumbency of a center party. Countering the tensions inherent in such a polarized party system, however, and consistent with the rationale of a besieged democracy underpinning Italian politics, were quasi-consociational arrangements geared to the promotion of consensual practices. One of these was the formation of oversized coalition governments throughout most of this period (see Table 2.3). This practice dates from a decision made in 1948 by Prime Minister Alcide De Gasperi, who chose to invite social democrats, liberals, and republicans into the government rather than form a minimum winning cabinet supported only by his party, the DC. The inclusion of socialists in governments beginning in the 1960s, and, more important, the cabinet of "national solidarity" of the second half of 1970s (which received "external" support from the PCI, although the communists were not given government posts) were also consistent with the rationale of a besieged democracy that regarded the adoption of consensual practices as necessary.

Another noteworthy feature of Italian democracy is that it has a symmetrical bicameral system, in which the two chambers have the same legislative powers. Indeed, the parliamentary party systems in the two houses were similar throughout the first four decades, in part because both chambers were the products of highly proportional electoral systems, and of similar representational patterns, which reflected the population at large and did not overrepresent specific minorities.

Italy's highly proportional electoral laws, even at the municipal and provincial levels, were neutral vis-à-vis the parties: lacking significant majoritarian biases, they simply allowed parliamentary representation to mirror the cleavages and conflicts existing in civil society. Given the limited legitimacy enjoyed by democratic institutions, openness and neutrality were important: these fundamental "rules of the game" simply granted parliamentary representation to every relevant political force, thereby making the political system more acceptable to all groups. Indeed, an attempt by the DC in 1953 to shift to a more majoritarian system triggered massive mobilizations against the so-called *legge-truffa* (swindle law).

Decision-making processes adopted by the national government were also characterized by features designed to allow for the representation of the maximum array of interests. Both decision-making rules and informal norms—allowing for numerous amendments to every legislative proposal—gave parliament the real ability (vis-à-vis the cabinet) to influence public policies. Parliament's leverage was further strengthened by the special role of several powerful standing committees, within which parties represented a broad range of interests, and whose deliberations took place behind closed doors. These institutional features permitted the opposition to perform an active and influential role in the policy-making process. More broadly, the fragmented and diversified arena within which the legislative process took place provided opportunities for virtually every interest group to bargain in support of its demands. This generated complex networks of interactions between parties and interest groups, leading to an overwhelming volume of policy proposals and amendments, but, at the same time, establishing an open legislative process that performed an integrative function that contributed significantly to democratic consolidation.[15] This was particularly important with regard to the inclusion within the standing committees of parliament of parties of the left, which were otherwise marginalized and excluded from power at the national level. Intense involvement in parliamentary activity played an important symbolic role as a manifestation of integration within the political system and a mechanism allowing parties to establish their respective images vis-à-vis the groups they represented. Parliamentary committee involvement also allowed parties of the left to work for legislative solutions to the problems of their working-class and peasant supporters (see Cazzola 1972; Morisi 1991). Thus, parliament was vital not only for the interests represented and protected by the dominant party (DC) and its coalition partners (PLI and PRI), but also for the very survival of the organizations of the left during this particularly difficult period.

This first period was one of strong party government, in which parties exercised tight control over civil society and functioned as the principal channels for the articulation of demands. The DC, in particular, was most capable of performing this task, not only in a wide array of organized sectors of society—in agriculture, industry, and trade—but also for many diffuse, disorganized interests, as indicated by the large number of bills introduced in parliament involving small-scale, particularistic interests. Indeed, party factions reinforced these ties to various sectors of society and facilitated the parties' control of access to decision making in parliament.

In the aftermath of the worker, youth, and civil rights mobilizations of the late 1960s, the consensual elements of the model were further strengthened by two institutional adaptations: referenda and the implementation of previously frozen constitutional provisions concerning the regions. Regional decentralization gave control over some Italian regions, such as Emilia, Tuscany, and Umbria, to leftist forces, symbolically offsetting their exclusion from government at the national level. The integrative, legitimizing impact of this reform was particularly significant in altering the governmental role of the PCI in the 1970s and in mobilizing communist support for democracy during the years of terrorism that followed.

By the 1980s, when terrorism seemed defeated and the communists returned to the opposition, the problem of democratic legitimacy had been greatly reduced: the democratic loyalty of the left had been largely proven in the most difficult moments of Italian democratic history. At this same time, however, the problem of decision-making inefficacy became increasingly acute (particularly under the Spadolini and Craxi governments of 1981–87), aggravated by intense conflict within the cabinet between the DC and PSI. In several respects, inefficacy or stagnation can be regarded as a negative side-effect of consensualism.

Beginning in the 1970s, referenda were increasingly utilized to give voice to civil society and marginalized political groups, and to settle conflicts over policy that could not be resolved by parties and parliamentary procedures. It is generally accepted that the referendum is, by its very nature, a majoritarian instrument. The Italian constitution imposes limits on its use, only permitting the repeal of previous parliamentary decisions. As such, the referendum is a control mechanism in the hands of citizens, and referenda were actually used to resolve conflicts over the most controversial issues, such as divorce, abortion, and the electoral law, as well as to end stalemates brought about by partisan conflicts. In effect, the use of referenda (54 of them from 1974 through 2000) enlisted the electorate as arbiter and allowed civil society to redress its grievances.[16] Thus, it also helped the political system to overcome policy impasses that might have threatened the old consensual order. Ironically, then, the use of the referendum had a consensual rather than majoritarian impact overall.

Changes

The model began to change in the late 1980s and early 1990s, particularly with regard to the electoral system and the parties. Modification of Italy's electoral law in 1993–94, in an attempt to introduce a more effective majoritarian model, was a key precipitating development. Although this reform effort can be regarded as a partial failure (resulting in an actual increase in partisan fragmentation), some positive accomplishments can be identified. Cabinet stability appears to have increased as a result of the establishment of a weak bipolarism, whose centerpiece is the formation of two broad and durable electoral/governmental coalitions. Closely related to this is the inclusion in national governments of formerly marginalized parties of the right and the left, which has strengthened democratic legitimacy. Some increased governmental effectiveness has also been achieved, largely as a result of the imposition of policy constraints by the European Union, rather than as a product of the shift toward a more majoritarian model of government.

To better understand the changes of the late 1980s and early 1990s, a more encompassing analysis is necessary. As Giacomo Sani and Paolo Segatti more fully argue in Chapter 4, a "window of opportunity" for expressing discontent with the old order was opened by the disappearance of several significant constraints (the fading of the collective memory of Fascism and World War II, the end of the Cold War and the anticommunism of the moderate parties, and the gradual weakening of clientelism and other partisan ties) and the emergence of new facilitating conditions (the delegitimating impact of the *mani pulite* ["clean hands"] investigations of corruption by high-ranking politicians, the economic crisis, the April 1993 referendum on the electoral law, and the subsequent change of electoral laws for parliament [see Morlino and Tarchi 1996]). Among these factors, the April 1993 referendum deserves special attention.

Long-frustrated demands for an increase in decision-making efficacy and an end to partisan stalemate culminated in a referendum on the electoral law for the Senate. By repealing only ten words of article 17, the old law was shifted toward greater majoritarianism. In stark contrast with the relatively pure proportional representation system applied during the preceding four decades, the new law allocates three-quarters of the seats in both Houses (475 seats for the Chamber of Deputies, out of a total of 630, and 232 of 315 seats for the Senate) on the basis of a plurality (single-member) electoral system. The remaining quarter of the seats (155 and 83 respectively) are allocated on the basis of proportional representation to partially compensate those parties denied representation through the first (plurality) segment. The complicated electoral system associated with these changes came into effect at the general elections for the Senate and the Chamber of Deputies held on March 27–28, 1994.[17]

Since the introduction of this electoral system, Italian democracy has shifted toward a more bipolar party system featuring an entirely new set of political parties. This was, in part, the product of elite-level decisions in interaction with the mechanical effects of the electoral system. One factor accounting for the disappearance of the traditional parties and the emergence of new ones is the reshaping of the most salient issues. An initial indication of the changes to come emerged in the late 1980s, when local lists first started to flourish and the predecessors of the Northern League first appeared. A more dramatic manifestation of the transformation of Italian parties involved the principal party of the left, the Partito Comunista Italiano. Having experienced significant erosion in its electoral support during the preceding decade (down from 34 percent in 1976 to 27 percent in 1987), the party was confronted with the crisis triggered by the fall of the Berlin Wall in November 1989 (see Chapter 8 below). A new party, the Partito Democratico della Sinistra (Democratic Party of the Left), or PDS, was created in February 1991, with a new logo. A segment of the old PCI with more orthodox communist views created a splinter party, the Rifondazione Comunista (RC), whose electoral support is between one-quarter and one-third of that of the PDS (5.6 percent vs. 16.1 percent for the PDS in 1992; 6.1 percent vs. 20.4 percent in 1994; and 8.6 vs. 21.1 percent in 1996). In early 1998, the PDS changed its name (but not its organizational substance) again in an effort to attract all fragments of the new and traditional left (except for the RC), christening itself the Democratici della Sinistra (Democrats of the Left), or DS.

The other key development in the first phase of party-system change was the emergence and success of the Lega Nord (Northern League), whose first party conference was held in February 1991. The party is the result of an association of various leagues and other local lists, especially from Veneto, Lombardy, and Piedmont, which all together had won about 6 percent of the vote in the regional and municipal elections of 1990. The Lega Nord received 8.7 percent of the vote in 1992, then surged to 19.4 percent in 1994, before declining to 10.1 percent in the 1996 elections.

The next phase of this transformation occurred during the summer of 1993, when the DC, already internally divided, split into several groups. Following the replacement of its party secretary and a long intraparty struggle, a new Partito Popolare Italiano (PPI) was born in January 1994. This was accompanied by schisms from both the left and right wings of the DC: some leaders entered the right-wing Alleanza Nazionale (AN), formerly the MSI, while others formed the Centro Cristiano Democratico (CCD), becoming part of a center-right electoral coalition, the Polo delle Libertà (Freedom Pole), in the 1994 elections; others followed the former DC politician Mario Segni into his Patto Segni; still others entered the leftist PDS-led coalition under the name of Cristiani Sociali or joined la Rete (the Network), a tiny leftist group that was also close to the PDS; and, finally, a few entered the new Forza Italia! (Go Italy!), or FI.

The crisis and breakdown of the Partito Socialista Italiano resulted from the *mani pulite* investigation of the PSI's leaders for widespread corruption. A second contributing factor was the political immobility of its leaders, particularly Bettino Craxi, who had sealed a pact with the two main DC leaders of the time (Giulio Andreotti, as prime minister, and Arnaldo Forlani, as party secretary since 1989). In early 1993, signs of crisis could be seen in a struggle for control of the party secretariat, and the first of a series of defections to the short-lived Alleanza Democratica and, later, to Forza Italia! After the party's electoral defeat in 1994, it fragmented into numerous splinters. Similarly, the PLI and PRI suffered schisms and have virtually disappeared. And the PSDI was virtually eliminated by the majoritarian bias of the new electoral law.

As for the right, partly as a result of its strong performance in the local by-elections in 1993, the MSI seized the political initiative by maintaining and softening its rightist positions. Its secretary, Gianfranco Fini, was very careful to convey a clearly defined democratic image to the general public (some small, vociferous extremist groups notwithstanding). Moderation of the party's image was also helped by the recruitment of conservative democratic intellectuals. Two further decisive steps in the direction of democratic integration were inclusion in the Berlusconi cabinet of the MSI-AN, as the staunchest ally of Forza Italia! in a heterogeneous coalition, after the 1994 election,[18] and the transformation of MSI in 1995 into the new Alleanza Nazionale, whose image was further enhanced following the departure in 1996 of some nostalgic neofascists to form the tiny Movimento Sociale–Fiamma Tricolore (MS-FM).

The founding of Forza Italia! was the most important development during the second phase of this transformation (1992–94). The delegitimation of the DC, PSI, and their smaller allies (PLI, PRI, and PSDI) left the vast moderate segment of the electorate in a void. Within a few weeks of its establishment in January 1994 by the television magnate Silvio Berlusconi, opinion polls indicated that Forza Italia! would become the largest party in the new parliament. This dramatic advance was made possible by the massive use of television propaganda by the party's founder, who owned three national television networks and several local channels. Taking advantage of loopholes in the law regulating electoral propaganda, and basing his campaign appeals on opinion-poll data, Berlusconi was able to target an audience near the center and center-right with a skillful advertising message about a "new product" likely to appeal to voters longing for change (Diamanti 1994).

Berlusconi's victory signaled the end of the old style of consensual politics. In contrast to the incremental shifts among centrist, center-left, and center-right coalitions of the First Republic, all of which remained well in the moderate middle of the ideological continuum, it brought to power a coalition that was decidedly right of center and included the formerly marginalized successor of the MSI. In addition, quasi-consociational practices such as the *lottizzazione* (in which all politically significant parties were given their respective shares of control over segments of the state administration) abruptly gave way to majoritarian appointments to important state positions, such as the oversight board regulating the RAI television networks (see Marletti and Roncarolo 2000).

The electoral victory of the center-right coalition did not, however, usher in a new period of political stability. Despite its parliamentary majority, the Berlusconi government collapsed even more quickly than the average government in the First Republic, and there were schisms and instability in a number of parties, including splits in the Northern League and the PPI. Even Rifondazione Comunista suffered defections, eventually leading to the formation of "Communists for Unity." Most important, however, the progressive segments of the PPI joined forces in support of Romano Prodi, eventually forging an electoral coalition that straddled the historical divide between the so-called *rosso* and *bianco* camps, including former DC leaders in the PPI alongside former communists of the PDS, Greens, Laburisti, and Rinnovamento Italiano. This coalition between post-DC and postcommunist elites and organizations, which formed the government after winning the 1996 election, is of historic significance not only because it overcame a once seemingly unbridgeable cleavage in Italian society but also because it appears to have inaugurated a period of government stability: the coalition remained in office longer than any postwar Italian government save one.

There has also been considerable change in the salience of once divisive issues. As can be inferred from the above (and confirmed by an analysis of survey data in Chapter 3), the religious cleavage has virtually disappeared in Italy. It has been replaced, however, by a growing conflict over center-periphery relations. A radical, antisystem challenge to the Italian state has been mounted by a strong organization of militants, with substantial financial resources, under the leadership of the Northern League. This has somewhat altered the "regime-support" issue that had characterized the postfascist and Cold War eras in Italian politics. Another issue dimension, which is much less salient and potentially disruptive, involves the environment. In part, its low salience derives from the weak organization of the Greens, which remain more a federation of groups and movements than a party.

Finally, there has been a profound change in the nature and structure of party linkages with civil society and, especially, interest groups. In part stimulated by the party changes described above, by European Union membership, and by new economic policies, trade unions and business groups have been motivated to assume a more direct role in the political process. To some degree, the prominent position of business elites like Berlusconi and many other Forza Italia! candidates illustrate this change. Even the leading business association, Confindustria, has become more active, playing a more directly political role in Italian politics than it traditionally did, and on occasion even outbidding political parties.

Continuities

Ironically, despite the magnitude of the changes noted above, the basic contours of the Italian party system remain largely unchanged. Even though the electoral law now has majoritarian biases (see Table 2.5), the effective number of parties (see Table 2.6) and the level of vote fragmentation have both *increased*. Most of this increase in party-system fragmentation is attributable to the breakup of the DC, as well as to the splitting of Rifondazione Comunista from the rest of the PCI when it became the PDS. Given that cabinet formation is usually easier when there is a dominant party (particularly when it is near the center of the political spectrum), the disappearance of the powerful DC made government formation according to the old formula impossible. Initially, government instability continued to characterize the party system. Partly because of its smaller parliamentary size, Forza Italia! could not assume the crucial unifying role of the DC: in the earlier center-left cabinets, a crisis could only be precipitated by the withdrawal of the socialists, whereas withdrawal of either the MSI-AN or the Northern League could precipitate the collapse of the Berlusconi cabinet, as actually occurred in December 1994 with the departure of the League. The same could be said of the center-left coalition that took over after the April 1996 election. Even though the Prodi government survived much longer than the average postwar government, it was eventually toppled by the withdrawal of parliamentary support by Rifondazione Comunista. In this sense, the increased fragmentation of the party system and the collapse of the center pose a considerable threat of renewed cabinet instability, significantly increasing the "blackmail potential" of other parties. Indeed, given the more even distribution of the vote among the major parties, such party-system pluralism is even more extreme: previously, the DC was so large that it could maneuver to the left or right to pick up support from one or a combination of small parties; since 1994, no party has similarly been in the "driver's seat," and the bargaining power of medium-sized parties like FI, AN, the League, and the PDS is much greater than that enjoyed by the smaller parties in the traditional governing coalitions of the previous era, especially because substantial ideological space separates the parties that are the most likely coalition partners.

Overall, however, the challenge to Italy's democratic regime has diminished because of democratic consolidation and the reduced threat (real or perceived) posed by antisystem parties. By 1994, all of the traditional parties had been integrated into the system, as most clearly signaled by the transformation of the Partito Comunista Italiano into the PDS in February 1991 and of the Movimento Sociale Italiano into the Alleanza Nazionale in January 1995. Even Rifondazione Comunista cannot help but recognize the legitimacy of Italy's democratic institutions, which have been in existence for half a century. The dynamics of competition in the party system have also been transformed, insofar as its governments no longer confront a bilateral structure of opposition. The inclusion of the Alleanza Nazionale in the Berlusconi cabinet of 1994 meant that opposition could come only from one end of the political spectrum—from the center and left. Similarly, under the Prodi government, opposition could only come from the right. And in sharp contrast to the exclusion of the PCI from governments in the past, the coalition capacity of the DS (former PDS) may now be taken for granted. Given the fragmentation of the once-dominant center, the disappearance of bilateral opposition, the actual possibility of alternation in power (as occurred in 1996), the legitimation and moderation of formerly marginalized antisystem parties, and the disappearance of polarizing traditional issues and ideological orientations, the deradicalization of Italian political parties (except for the League) has been set in motion.

At the same time, however, a new set of factors conducive to polarization has emerged. Although the current party system lacks antisystem parties of the traditional variety, a new antisystem party has emerged. The Northern League underwent a significant radicalization following its departure from the Berlusconi government in 1994, in part because of a schism in its ranks and the need to reestablish its hegemony as the principal protagonist in the center-periphery conflict, and in part as a result of its strategy of attracting support from the sizable sector of dissatisfied voters in the north protesting economic and other conditions. For about five years (until 1999), the League's leader, Umberto Bossi, supported secession from Italy, and his movement has engaged increasingly in activities that are on the very edge of legality.

Other new factors were also conducive to intensified conflict. The need to reform welfare, pension provisions, and budgetary policies (in part to meet the Maastricht criteria) has raised the stakes inherent in economic policy disputes. Parties of the right and center-right attempted to recreate an artificial cleavage between communists and anticommunists in an effort to strengthen their hold over centrist and conservative voters. Although this terminology is obsolete, it still conjures up animosities in the collective memory of Italians. The low institutionalization of parties, their shallow penetration into society, and their internal divisions and conflicts also have destabilizing (or at least unsettling) implications for the parties themselves. Another factor exerting a polarizing influence in the new Italian politics is an accentuated verbal violence in political discourse, which was especially intense throughout 1994 and 1995, when the very institutions of Italian democracy (including the most basic of governmental institutions and the electoral law) were objects of political conflict. An accentuated territorial pluralism, in which different parties have come to dominate different regions (with the right and Forza Italia! strongest in the south, the parties of the left controlling the center, and the

League and FI the dominant parties in parts of the north), has superimposed regional differences on the left-right cleavage, intensifying conflict and polarizing parties over the League's challenge to the traditional structure of the state.

The net result is that centrifugal drives that had almost disappeared during the 1980s have reemerged in a somewhat different form within a "neopolarized system," characterized by a new antisystem party rooted in a newly salient political cleavage, by alternation between left and right in lieu of centrist stagnation, by an often rancorous style of elite conflict, and by an even more fragmented party system—consisting of two large parties (FI and DS), three middle-sized parties (AN, PPI, and the League), and several small parties whose support is crucial for coalition formation (CCD-CDU, Rinnovamento Italiano, the Greens and, above all, Rifondazione Comunista [see Morlino 1996]). Fragmentation of the party system has been reinforced by a growing territorialization of electoral support.

The party system is, however, only one dimension of the democratic model, albeit an important dimension in the Italian case. Another important element of continuity must be recalled: Italy was and still is the most extreme case of parliamentary dominance, in which policies emerge as the product of both parliamentary and government initiatives. Ever since the second legislature (1953–58), between one-quarter and one-third of legislative output has been introduced by members of parliament. Parliamentary dominance grew dramatically in the 1994–96 legislature: less than 6 percent of the 5,254 legislative proposals in that short parliamentary session had been introduced by the government, and only 11 percent of the measures passed had been government initiatives (see Morlino 1998, 62–63). Overall decision-making efficacy, moreover, collapsed during that parliament: only 9 percent of the government's legislative proposals, and less than 5 percent of private members' bills were enacted into law. In addition, the use of decree-laws (which had been employed very successfully and with increasing frequency by the government between 1948 and 1979, and with relative success between 1979 and 1992) to circumvent parliamentary stalemate also collapsed as an effective means of passing legislation: during the 1992–94 legislature, only 118 of the government's 522 decree-law proposals were ratified, and between 1994 and 1996, only 113 out of 690 were enacted (Morlino 1998, 67). Access to this legislative alternative was further reduced in summer 1996, when the Constitutional Court forbade the reiterated introduction of the same bill, once the period of validity (sixty days) had been expired without parliamentary ratification.[19] By way of comparison, in Greece during the 1974–95 period, all of the approximately 150 decree-laws introduced by the government were ratified (Morlino 1998, 67). In the late 1990s, efforts were made to strengthen the role of the cabinet vis-à-vis the parliament and to enhance its decision-making capacities. The governments of Romano Prodi (1996–98) and Massimo D'Alema (1998–2000) streamlined legislative procedures in an effort to overcome the previous sources of paralysis and stagnation.

In the end, the Italian story is one of a failed attempt to install a majoritarian style of government. Not only is the party system even more fragmented than before, but new sources of conflict and potential instability have emerged. Although electoral-law changes were enacted, more far-reaching constitutional reforms have been blocked by many actors and vested interests. Nonetheless, some rationalization of the old consensual model has taken place. The old system based on bilateral oppositions, the absence of alternation in government, and center-dominated coalitions has been replaced by a new one, whose most salient features include weak bipolarity and the alternation of left and right in power. To some extent, this was the product of deliberate choice by political elites to establish electoral alliances and maintain durable parliamentary coalitions. Beginning in 1996, this appears to have culminated in greater government stability and increased decision-making efficiency. To be sure, these new political-system characteristics were partly motivated by powerful international incentives to improve decision-making efficiency: the implications of the Maastricht Treaty, and the specific budgetary and economic requirements imposed as a precondition for entry into the European Monetary Union have glossed over the weaknesses in the Italian model of democracy and brought trade unions and business entrepreneurs to cooperate with the government in implementing neocorporatist agreements. Nonetheless, the primary forces that led to this transformation had their origins in Italian society and domestic politics.

Conclusions

A number of general observations issue from the preceding analysis. To begin with, southern European democracies have exhibited a remarkable capacity to evolve after having become consolidated. Put otherwise, the experience of the new southern European polities lends strong support to the idea, articulated in *The Politics of Democratic Consolidation,* that democratic persistence, the phase of the overall democratization process that follows consolidation, is not static. Far from implying the "end of politics," or the "freezing" of institutional arrangements in patterns that will militate against future change, democratic persistence amply allows for change, whether evolutionary or abrupt. Once their democracies were consolidated, Greece, Italy, Spain, and Portugal all experienced significant evolution in their political or party systems. To be sure, they did not evolve identically. Greece showed most continuity. But even in this case, evolution was unmistakable. In the other three cases, however, significant changes occurred. This is observable at both the level of institutions and that of the regimes themselves. In Spain, the consensualism that was so pronounced during the transition to democracy gave way to a much more majoritarian pattern of politics. At the same time, the Spanish state underwent a profound process of decentralization and a veritable transformation of some of its basic structures. In Portugal, waves of change swept the basic institutions of government, particularly in the early stages of the transition, as the country lurched from the prospect of an uncertain and potentially undemocratic future to a consolidated democratic regime. Since consolidation, the scope of change has been much reduced, largely involving the emergence of stable, single-party governments. Italy, on the other hand, stands out as an example of a democratic polity that has been able to absorb abrupt, far-reaching change without endangering or damaging the legitimacy of the democratic regime itself.

The manner in which the democratic regimes in southern Europe have evolved over the longer term leads to our second general observation, which has to do with the path-dependent nature of political change. Implicit in the heuristic device of path dependency is the notion that the structure of opportunities in a given historical conjuncture can have a profound impact on the manner in which subsequent events unfold. This, however, does not imply lack of room for human action and for the capacity of human agency to modify the thrust of events, or even to alter their course. In short, path dependency does not imply determinism. Rather, it bears a closer conceptual affinity to Otto Kirchheimer's "confining conditions" that have to be overcome in order for a new situation, order, or regime to emerge. Both Portugal and Italy would seem to bear out this observation. The particular circumstances surrounding the birth of Italian democracy in the immediate aftermath of World War II undoubtedly had a profound impact on that country's political system and institutions, allowing analysts to point to the Italian experience as bearing out the logic of path dependency. The events of the mid and late 1990s, on the other hand, provided powerful confirmation of the capacity of human actors, and especially of political elites, to break out of that logic and, through a process of abrupt discontinuity, to establish new political parties and a substantially restructured party system. In Portugal, too, the unfolding of events following the revolution of 1974 and the institutionalized presence of the military moved the emerging political system in a direction in which a democratic outcome was hardly a foregone conclusion. And yet, within less than five years, the democratic forces in that country were able to break with the revolutionary logic of the "first transition" and steer Portugal in the direction of democratic consolidation. An additional point worth making is that, whereas the capacity of human agency to bring about change manifested itself in Portugal in the course of the transition, in the case of Italy, change occurred long after consolidation had occurred. The examples of Greece and Spain, on the other hand, provide support for the importance of path dependency. In both countries, the developmental trajectory followed by their democratic regimes flowed out of the structure of opportunities that emerged at the time of the transition and subscribed to the logic of continuity and evolution.

The third general observation issuing from this chapter relates to the theoretical point raised by Philippe Schmitter's contribution to *The Politics of Democratic Consolidation* and concerns the distinction between democratic regimes and partial regimes. Here, the Italian experience of the 1990s provides the most compelling example. The disintegration of that country's party system brought about by the 1994 and 1996 elections in no way affected the legitimacy of democracy as the political regime of choice for the overwhelming majority of Italians. Nor, for that matter, has the ongoing restructuring of the Italian political system adversely affected the legitimacy of the democratic regime. On the contrary, the radical restructuring of these partial regimes made it possible to supersede some of the most intractable features of the old arrangements—most notably the inability to provide for alternation in government. This has arguably had a virtuous impact on the legitimacy and the quality of the democratic regime and facilitated the transition from what is often referred to as the First Republic to the emerging Second Republic. The radical restructuring of the Spanish state constitutes a further example of a partial regime that has undergone profound change without adversely affecting the consolidated nature of the democratic regime itself. The shift from one of the most rigidly centralized political systems in Europe, under Franco, to one marked by a high degree of decentralization is one of the most remarkable achievements in that country's democratic experience and, indeed, its history. Finally, the Italian (and to a lesser extent, the Spanish) cases bear out a further conclusion issuing from *The Politics of Democratic Consolidation:* the enhanced capacity of consolidated democracies to accommodate structural change without experiencing deconsolidation. In an important way, the greater stability observable in consolidated democracies is a by-product of path-dependency and of the virtuous-cycle logic of cumulation implicit in it.

A fourth general observation is that democracy makes a difference. Put otherwise, the consolidation of democracy in southern Europe has helped bring about modern political systems that bear little resemblance to their preauthoritarian predecessors. The high levels of party-system fragmentation, of government instability, and of centrifugalism that constituted salient characteristics of these countries' political systems in the past have been replaced by modern political and party systems, revolving primarily around two predominant parties or, in the emerging Italian system, coalitions of parties, subscribing to a centripetal, moderate logic, and producing stable governments.

A fifth general observation issuing from the preceding analysis is that the cumulative effect of the changes in the structure of politics in Greece, Italy, Spain, and Portugal brought about by the consolidation of democracy in the four countries and by the evolution of their political systems has been that these southern European democracies have converged to a significant degree with the more advanced industrial democracies in northern and western Europe. This confirms the conclusions of Lijphart et al. 1988 regarding the absence of a "model" of democracy peculiar to southern Europe as a region and different in its structural characteristics from that encountered in other advanced industrial societies.

The absence of a clear model notwithstanding, it is possible to discern a perceptible trend toward majoritarianism in southern Europe that imparts a certain distinctiveness to the region. This trend is especially salient in Greece, but it is also quite obvious in the other three countries and seems to acquire momentum with the passage of time. Its roots can be traced to the quest for governability and to the desire to avoid the problems associated with the type of polarized politics that in the past plagued many of the region's democratic experiments and often led to their deconsolidation and collapse. At another level, the trend toward majoritarianism can also be linked to the gradual emergence in all four countries of moderate electorates clustering around the center of the left-right spectrum and exhibiting a distinct aversion for polarized politics.

In either case, they tend to confirm the absence of the southern European exceptionalism that until recently plagued the comparative study of the region. This underlines the intellectual cogency of the concept of a new southern Europe and the convergence within the broader universe of advanced industrial democracies that it implies.

3 The Anchors of Partisanship

A Comparative Analysis of Voting Behavior in Four Southern European Democracies

Richard Gunther and José R. Montero

A comparative analysis of the social-structural and organizational bases of support for the political parties of southern Europe, defined for purposes of this study as Greece, Italy, Portugal, and Spain, is of direct relevance to three crucial sets of questions central to democratic theory. The first has implications for one important dimension of the quality of democracy in each country. A principal function of all political parties is the representation of the interests of the electorate and of the key organized groups. To what extent do parties have organizational linkages to, or solid bases of electoral support in, their respective social or ideological constituencies? If parties are to play the role of transmission belt between the electorate and governing elites, then the nature of these linkages and of the parties' electoral support are of obvious relevance. In recent years, with the increasing importance of catch-all or other more purely electoralist party types, these representational ties have been blurred in many countries. Accordingly, there is some evidence that party elites may be seen by the public as primarily concerned with winning and staying in office, at the expense of representing and advancing the interests of those sectors of society that elect them; that the programmatic commitments of parties are becoming weaker, more poorly defined, and more ephemeral; and that electoral campaigns are tending to focus more on the personal merits of candidates and on trivial issues of only temporary salience, rather than on more fundamental issues relevant to the adoption of alternative public policies. There is also evidence that these developments may be contributing to an alienation from or cynicism toward parties and party elites on the part of mass publics. Thus, it could be argued that too weak a linkage with specific sectors of society and key social groups might be detrimental to the performance of the representation function and the overall quality of democracy.

On the other hand, an excessively tight linkage between parties and the social groups that support them might be detrimental, not only to the parties' ability to adapt to changing social conditions and flexibility in maneuvering to maximize votes and win elections, but also to the stability of a democratic regime. A rigid compartmentalization of social/partisan groups—a division of society into mutually antagonistic camps—has often been found to be conducive to a polarization of electoral competition and eventually of the polity itself (cf. Powell 1970). These kinds of concerns are particularly relevant to two of the countries of southern Europe, Spain and Italy. The drastic polarization of the Spanish political system brought the country's previous democratic regime to a violent end, and it was plunged into civil war. In postwar Italy, the outcome of this kind of polarization was less dramatic, but nonetheless detrimental to the quality of democracy. The deep division of the country into "red" and "white" camps effectively led to the permanent exclusion of a sizable segment of Italian society from power at the national level throughout the more than four decades of the so-called First Republic. This would suggest that, just as the absence of social roots of political parties can be detrimental to the quality of democracy, so, too, can an excessively rigid segmentation of society into rival partisan camps.

The third crucial set of questions involves the stability of party systems. Alternation of parties in power may be essential for the health of a democracy, but excessively high levels of electoral volatility (that is, the net shifts in shares of the total valid vote among all parties in the party system) can have detrimental consequences for a party system. The extensive literature on electoral stability distinguishes between "intrabloc volatility," or shifts in vote shares among parties within the same bloc on the left-right continuum, and "interbloc volatility," or more fundamental shifts in voting that bridge significant class or left-right cleavages (see Bartolini and Mair 1990; Bartolini 1986). In our view, both types of volatility are significant, both theoretically and in terms of their actual impact on the performance of political systems. Frequent shifts from parties of the left to parties of the right, and vice versa, can cause policy instability (Weaver and Rockman 1993), undermining the coherence of governmental policies over time. More radical shifts of this kind can also contribute to a polarization of politics when divisive issues, rather than being resolved incrementally, are reinvigorated by policy reversals as the pendulum swings from one end of the spectrum to the other: this was clearly one of the origins of the progressive polarization of political conflict that eventually led to the collapse of the Spanish Second Republic and the outbreak of the Spanish Civil War. But even shifts from one party to another within the same basic ideological segment can have negative implications for a party system if they are frequent and sufficiently extreme. High levels of turnover may remove skilled, experienced politicians, and they may be replaced by individuals lacking the knowledge and expertise necessary for effective government.[1]

While these theoretical and empirical concerns are of relevance to all democracies, they are particularly significant for newly emerging parties and party systems. The stabilization of electoral competition, and the nature of the social bases on which that anchoring takes place, can have a significant impact on the performance of representative and governmental institutions, as well as on the quality of democracy itself. At the time when the first draft of this chapter was written (in 1991), we were particularly concerned over high levels of electoral volatility in the new democracies of Greece, Portugal, and Spain. Before this edited volume could be completed, however, this analytical effort took on an added urgency as the result of a dramatic development: the complete collapse of the Italian party system. Although that event delayed the publication of this book for several years (since every chapter had to be substantially rewritten to take these profound changes into consideration), it has provided us with the best possible example of why the issues under examination here are of importance, both theoretically and for the real world of democratic politics.

The starting point for this analysis is an examination of the nature and extent of electoral volatility in the southern European democracies in comparison with a sample of more established democracies. In effect, this exercise defines a "dependent variable," to be analyzed in the first part of this chapter. In short, we seek to explain cross-national and temporal variations in the degree of electoral stability, or, conversely, electoral volatility. The centerpiece of our analysis takes the form of a detailed multivariate study of the social-structural anchors of party preferences.[2] Added to this multivariate analysis of social-structural determinants of the vote are two additional factors commonly found to be powerful predictors of the vote—the proximity of respondents to the various parties of the left-right continuum, and their positive or negative evaluations of the leader of each respective party. In many respects, our findings raise more questions than they resolve. As we shall see, in southern Europe and elsewhere, there has been a general tendency over time for religion and social class to decline as determinants of the vote. At the same time that these social-structural anchors are weakening, however, the proximity of respondents to parties on the left-right scale is increasing in importance. Similarly, the significant role of party leaders in determining the votes cast for catch-all parties will be identified, but the implications of this development for the quality of democracy remain an issue pending further study.

Finally, we set forth an argument attempting to account for these differing patterns. In sharp contrast to the social-structural-determinist and universal-culture-change hypotheses set forth in several major works in the literature on the changing social bases of partisanship, we find that the four southern European party systems have followed remarkably different developmental paths, which defy simple attempts at explanation focusing on changes in social structure or modal cultural values. Our explanation, instead, involves complex interactions among mass-level social-structural factors, the historical legacies of the major partisan traditions in each country, the electoral mobilization strategies of elites, and a variety of constraining exogenous factors, including the nature of the international environment. After setting forth the theoretical core of this explanation, we apply it to a historical analysis of the processes that led to the establishment of these patterns of partisanship and, in the Italian case, their disruption and reestablishment along different lines.

The survey data used in the analysis of the southern European electorates were collected by the Four Nation Study coordinated by Giacomo Sani and Julián Santamaría in the mid 1980s; the Comparative National Election Project's surveys of the Greek, Italian, and Spanish elections of 1993 and 1996; a 1993 survey of Portuguese public opinion; and three studies of the Spanish electorate (in 1979, 1982, and 1993). For comparative purposes, data from Austria, Finland, Great Britain, the United States, and West Germany (at two different times over the past three decades for the last three nations) have also been included in this analysis.[3]

Electoral Volatility and Partisanship

Perhaps the simplest measure of the extent to which partisan preferences are anchored is the level of volatility of the vote from one election to the next. Other things being equal, firmly anchored electorates should be more stable and predictable in their electoral preferences than those in which partisanship is ephemeral. An initial indication of the extent to which this set of questions is particularly relevant to the four southern European political systems discussed here can be seen in Table 3.1, which presents data concerning the

Table 3.1 The Most Volatile European Elections, 1945–2000

Years	Country	Total Volatility
1979–82	**Spain**	42.3
1992–94	**Italy**	41.9
1977–81	**Greece**	26.7
1956–58	France	26.7
1985–87	**Portugal**	23.4
1946–48	**Italy**	22.8
1983–85	**Portugal**	22.5
1974–77	**Greece**	22.3
1949–53	West Germany	21.2
1971–73	Denmark	21.2

Years	Country	Interbloc Volatility
1977–81	**Greece**	23.5
1985–87	**Portugal**	15.4
1991–95	**Portugal**	13.8
1974–77	**Greece**	13.7
1946–48	**Italy**	12.9
1988–94	Sweden	10.8
1992–97	Great Britain	10.3
1990–94	Germany	8.1
1994–96	**Italy**	7.5
1996–2000	**Spain**	7.4
1991–95	Finland	7.2
1945–49	Belgium	7.2
1949–53	West Germany	6.8
1979–82	**Spain**	6.7
1975–76	Portugal	6.6
1994–96	**Italy**	6.6
1978–76	France	6.3
1945–49	Austria	6.0
1992–94	**Italy**	5.8
1987–92	**Italy**	5.2
1945–48	Netherlands	5.3
1972–76	**Italy**	4.5

Sources: For Greece (1974–93), Italy (1976–94) and Portugal (1975–91), Morlino 1995, 318 and 320. For other countries up to 1983, Bartolini and Mair 1990; for all other years, our own calculations (using the Bartolini and Mair system—see the appendix to their book), based upon data published in Mackie and Rose 1991; various issues of the *European Journal of Political Research* and *Keesings Contemporary History.*

most volatile European elections of the postwar era. It is noteworthy that the four southern European democracies produced seven of the eight most volatile electoral turnovers in western Europe since 1945. In terms of total volatility, the Spanish election of 1982 and the Italian election of 1994 were by far the most extreme. Indeed, of 303 elections held since 1885 surveyed by Bartolini and Mair, only the Weimar election of 1920 and the French election of 1906 come close, with volatility scores of 32.1 and 31.1 respectively (Bartolini and Mair 1990, 70). Although somewhat less extreme, the Greek and Portuguese party systems have each undergone two high-volatility elections that are rivaled only by the French election of 1958 (held in the course of a full-blown regime crisis and transformation).

How are the high levels of volatility of southern European electorates to be interpreted? Clearly, one explanation has to do with the age of the party system. If, as Philip Converse (1969; see also Niemi et al. 1985) has suggested, it may require a generation or more before stable psychological attachments to parties take root among voters in a new democracy, then it could be argued that the higher levels of volatility experienced by the Portuguese, Spanish, and Greek party systems are at least in part a reflection of the recent reestablishment of electoral politics in those systems. From a different theoretical perspective, Stefano Bartolini and Peter Mair reached a similar conclusion: the process of cleavage encapsulation in new democracies requires some time for its completion; thus, the cleavage-anchoring of electoral support should increase over time (Bartolini and Mair 1990, 96). The data presented in Table 3.1 give credence to such speculations. As can be seen, the volatility experienced by the recently reestablished Greek and Portuguese party systems was roughly comparable to that in the newly installed postwar democracies of Italy and West Germany (as well as in Japan, where the total volatility score for the 1949 election was 26.0). The Spanish and Italian electoral earthquakes of 1982 and 1994, however, are so extreme that they stand apart from all the rest.

If these high volatility scores are nothing more than a reflection of the recent reintroduction of electoral politics in Portugal, Spain, Greece, and postwar Italy, then a detailed investigation of the origins and underpinnings of partisanship in these countries would not be very interesting. It would only be a matter of time before partisan attachments would be forged in a manner and to a degree comparable with the postwar experiences of the very stable German, Italian, and Japanese party systems. The data presented in Table 3.2 do reveal that all four southern European party systems appear to have stabilized within ten to fifteen years following their creation (Morlino 1995, 317–28). Greece and (in the immediate aftermath of World War II) Italy experienced high levels of volatility in the first elections following the restoration of democracy, but they then appear to have stabilized over the course of subsequent elections. Even more noteworthy, the Spanish party system became remarkably stable (in terms both of total volatility and, especially, interbloc volatility) following the massive party-system realignment of 1982. In the four elections following that realignment, both its average intrabloc and interbloc volatility scores (6.8 and 1.9 respectively) were below the western European averages (8.2 and 2.9).

In several respects, however, the varying evolutionary trajectories of these four party systems since the reestablishment of democracy raise questions of considerable interest and theoretical relevance, and suggest that the process of party-system consolidation is much more complex than could be explained by reference to the examples at any given point in time of Portugal and Greece.

Why did electoral volatility *increase* a full decade after the establishment of the new democratic regime in Portugal and nearly two decades following the rebirth of Greek democracy? Even more dramatically, why did the Italian party system collapse completely following decades of stability? Clearly something more complicated than the mere passage of time is involved in stabilizing electoral support in new party systems. Second, it was never previously possible to explore the processes by which stabilizing anchors for partisan competition are embedded in a newly democratized society, utilizing the full array of social-science research techniques currently available. Analyses of the establishment of older party systems were restricted to aggregate data and occasional insights derived from the study of documents and memoirs of the relevant elites. Never before has it been possible to conduct research on the establishment of partisanship using tools and resources relevant to all aspects of these formative processes, including several waves of nationwide surveys of voters over the course of several decades.

Table 3.2 also reveals a pattern differentiating the cases of Greece and Portugal from those of Italy and Spain. A very sizable portion of the total volatility exhibited by the Greek and Portuguese party systems in these elections was interbloc volatility. That is, not only was there a substantial reallocation of votes among parties, but many voters shifted their electoral support to parties on the other side of the left-right cleavage (about which much more will be said later in this chapter). The Greek elections of 1981 and 1977 (with interbloc volatil-

Table 3.2 Electoral Volatility in Greece, Italy, Portugal, and Spain

	Total Volatility	Intrabloc Volatility	Interbloc Volatility	Interbloc Volatility as a Percentage of Total Volatility
Greece				
1974–77	22.3	8.6	13.7	61.4%
1977–81	26.7	3.2	23.5	88.0
1981–85	6.3	3.2	3.4	53.9
1985–89	6.9	2.2	4.7	68.1
1989–89	4.3	3.8	0.5	11.6
1989–90	3.3	1.2	2.1	63.6
1990–93	17.1	13.4	3.7	21.6
1993–96	7.2	5.4	1.8	25.0
1996–2000	6.9	5.3	1.6	77.2
Mean	11.8	5.1	6.7	49.2
Italy				
1946–48	22.8	9.9	12.9	56.6%
1948–53	13.3	8.7	4.6	34.6
1953–58	4.5	3.6	0.9	20.0
1958–63	7.9	6.6	1.3	16.4
1963–68	3.4	2.0	1.4	41.2
1968–72	4.9	3.8	1.1	22.4
1972–76	8.2	2.8	5.4	65.8
1976–79	5.3	4.6	0.7	13.2
1979–83	8.5	8.2	0.3	3.5
1983–87	8.4	6.8	1.6	19.0
1987–92	16.2	11.0	5.2	32.1
1992–94	41.9	36.1	5.8	13.8
1994–96	17.3	9.8	7.5	43.4
Mean	12.5	8.8	3.7	29.4
Portugal				
1975–76	11.3	4.7	6.6	58.4%
1976–79	10.5	7.3	3.2	30.5
1979–80	4.6	2.9	1.7	36.9
1980–83	11.2	3.5	7.7	68.7
1983–85	22.5	22.0	0.5	2.2
1985–87	23.2	7.8	15.4	66.4
1987–91	9.5	8.3	1.2	12.6
1991–95	18.2	14.5	3.7	20.3
1995–99	3.9	1.8	2.2	56.1
Mean	13.9	8.9	5.0	37.0
Spain				
1977–79	10.8	8.6	2.2	20.4%
1979–82	42.3	35.6	6.7	15.8
1982–86	11.9	9.5	2.4	20.2
1986–89	8.9	7.2	1.7	19.1
1989–93	9.5	7.8	1.7	17.9
1993–96	4.4	2.7	1.7	38.6
1996–2000	10.1	2.7	7.4	52.9
Mean	14.6	11.9	2.7	22.0

Sources: For Greece (1974–93), Italy (1976–94) and Portugal (1975–91), Morlino 1995, 318 and 320. For other countries up to 1983, Bartolini and Mair 1990; for all other years, our own calculations (using the Bartolini and Mair system—see the appendix to their book), based upon data published in Mackie and Rose 1991; various issues of the *European Journal of Political Research* and *Keesings Contemporary History*.

ity scores of 23.5 and 13.7), the 1987 Portuguese election (15.4), and the Italian election of 1948 (with an interbloc volatility score of 12.9) greatly exceeded the European average of 2.9 (1911–85) and were among the most volatile elections among the 303 studied by Bartolini and Mair. Only the Swiss election of 1917 (21.5) and the Swedish election of 1911 (13.9) exceeded an interbloc volatility score of 10, thereby approximating these southern European elections (Bartolini and Mair 1990, 75).

In sharp contrast, despite the fact that the total volatility scores for the Spanish election of 1982 and the Italian elections of 1994 and 1996 were extraordinarily high, their respective interbloc volatility scores (6.7 percent and 5.8 percent) were surprisingly low. That is, despite the enormous magnitude of total electoral turnover, most Spanish and Italian voters simply shifted their support to a different party *within the same bloc.* This qualitative difference in the nature of electoral change is the central question addressed in the final section of this chapter. Why is it that despite the general propensity of these southern European electorates to change their partisan support from one election to the next, Italian and Spanish voters were loathe to shift their votes to parties outside of their preferred bloc?

Meanwhile, the Portuguese party system, after undergoing a very substantial restructuring in 1987, reemerged as a system in which the two largest parties on either side of the left-right cleavage became dominant and have alternated in power twice in less than a decade. Accordingly, its interbloc volatility score for the 1987 election is very high. It is also noteworthy that Spanish voters significantly altered their electoral behavior in the 2000 elections. After having maintained a high level of bloc stability of the vote in the three previous elections (with interbloc volatility scores at an extraordinarily low level of 1.7 percent), a surprisingly high net shift from parties of the left to parties of the center and right occurred in 2000.[4] Thus, even though the total volatility experienced in that election (9 percent) did not indicate that any destablization of the party system had occurred, the level of interbloc volatility was the highest ever recorded in a post-Franco election.

The Italian case further reveals that processes of party-system stabilization are neither unilinear nor irreversible. After over three decades of extraordinary electoral stability (1953–87), when both its average total volatility score (6.4) and its average interbloc volatility score (1.6) were significantly below the northern European average (8.1 and 2.9 respectively), the Italian party system underwent a process of deconsolidation and virtually total realignment. Indeed, none of the parties that had dominated Italian parliamentary politics over the previous three decades survived the 1994 election without at least substantial restructuring and a change of party name. And the governing centrist coalition, led without interruption for over four decades by Democrazia Cristiana, was displaced from power, first by a right-wing coalition of postfascists, northern federalists, and a media tycoon without a party, and subsequently by a government supported by a parliamentary alliance among progressive former Christian Democrats and both of the parties that emerged from the once permanently excluded PCI—the post-Eurocommunist Partito Democratico della Sinistra (PDS) and the unreformed Partito della Rifondazione Comunista (RC). Nonetheless, despite the magnitude of this electoral earthquake, it is remarkable that only 5.8 percent of Italian voters crossed over the barrier separating the traditional *rosso* and *bianco* camps in 1994, and just 6.6 percent did so in the 1996 election that brought the left to power. This is particularly surprising insofar as the post-Eurocommunist PDS—which had thoroughly revamped its ideological tenets and programmatic commitments in a manner designed to appeal to moderate Italian voters and was virtually the only mainstream party not to have been soiled by the scandals of the late 1980s and early 1990s—received no larger a share of the votes cast than the PCI had received in previous elections under the First Republic.

Party Identification and Organizational Penetration

One possible explanation of these patterns of stability and change involves the psychological anchoring of partisanship or party identification, the classic conceptualization of which was set forth by Campbell et al. 1960. Although the concept of party identification has been the subject of considerable debate for over three decades in a very extensive literature (too voluminous to be cited here), the relative strength within an electorate of psychological ties to political parties is widely regarded as an important component of the dynamics of electoral competition. Strong psychological anchoring of partisanship has often been regarded as stabilizing an electorate, while a dealigned, prealigned, or nonaligned electorate may be potentially volatile.

Somewhat surprisingly, a simple examination of "marginals" from Eurobarometer surveys, in conjunction with the levels of electoral volatility exhibited at the very next election, fails to reveal any apparent relationship that would suggest that these varying levels of volatility are explained by cross-national differences in aggregate levels of party identification. Greece, Italy, Portugal, and Spain have been arrayed in rank order in Table 3.3, alongside other European Union countries, in terms of the percentages of their electorates self-identified as "not close" to any political party. The Portuguese and Italians are relatively high in their aggregate levels of identification with parties, with only about a third of those interviewed in these surveys claiming not to be close to any political party in the mid 1980s. To be sure, the share of Italians falling into this category increased somewhat over the following decade, by the end of which the old party system collapsed. By 1993, in the midst of the corruption scandals and on the eve of a massive party-system realignment, the percentage of Italians claiming that they were not close to any party had increased to 46.9 percent. Other survey data reveal the same pattern: the percentage of respondents claiming to identify with a party declined from 87 percent in 1968 to 55 percent in 1990, indicating that some "dealignment" was taking place (Bellucci, Maraffi, and Segatti 1998, table 3). While this trend indicates that support for the traditional parties was weakening, its magnitude is clearly insufficient to account for the electoral earthquake that took place in 1994 or its "aftershock" in 1996. There is, however, no apparent relationship across this sample of countries between aggregate levels of party ID and electoral stability. Portugal and the Netherlands in the mid 1990s had by far the largest percentage of voters who identified to some degree with a po-

Table 3.3 Party Identification and Electoral Volatility Among EU Electorates: Percentage Not Close to any Party, 1986 and 1996, and Volatility in Next Election

Country	Not Close 1986	Volatility	Not Close 1996	Volatility
Portugal	31.2	23.2 (1985–87)	25.3	18.2 (1991–95)
Netherlands	20.6	4.4 (1986–89)	28.0	14.3 (1994–98)
Denmark	32.8	6.8 (1984–87)	36.0	8.9 (1990–95)
Italy	32.6	8.0 (1983–87)	39.5	17.3 (1994–96)
France	41.8	16.1 (1981–86)	39.5	11.7 (1993–97)
Greece	29.8	4.3 (1985–89)	44.7	7.2 (1993–96)
Belgium	50.1	3.6 (1985–87)	47.0	4.3 (1991–95)
Germany	33.9	5.3 (1983–87)	47.8	8.1 (1990–94)
Spain	61.9	8.9 (1986–89)	49.2	4.4 (1993–96)
Great Britain	59.5	3.2 (1983–87)	53.5	10.3 (1992–97)
Ireland	59.0	15.3 (1982–87)	60.2	7.6 (1992–97)

Sources: Party identification data from *Eurobarometer,* #34 and #44. For sources of electoral volatility data, see Table 3.1.

litical party, and yet they had rates of electoral volatility significantly above average. Conversely, even though the number of Spaniards identifying with a political party increased between the mid 1980s and mid 1990s, Spain still had one of the lowest aggregate levels of party identification, and yet, as we have seen, its party system had undergone an impressive process of stabilization.

This simplistic comparison of aggregate levels of party identification with electoral volatility by no means suggests that, at the individual level, psychological attachments to a political party do not serve as a powerful determinant of the vote, but the lack of any apparent relationship in Table 3.3 certainly implies that cross-national differences in overall levels of party identification cannot be regarded as a sufficient explanation of differences in electoral volatility.

Party Membership and Organizational Penetration of Society

A second overtly partisan factor directly relevant to the stabilization of electoral support is the extent to which parties have established an organizational presence in a society. Insofar as a principal function of parties is to mobilize sectors of a society in support of their candidates, the capacity of parties to establish a stable organizational presence in a society should be closely related to their ability to maintain stable levels of electoral support over time. Table 3.4 presents data for 1970 through 1990 reported by parties themselves, standardized by the size of each country's electorate, and survey data for Greece, Italy, and Spain from the mid 1990s. The first pattern apparent is that, in accordance with general tendencies in most western European democracies, there has been a decline in levels of affiliation with political parties. Among all of the countries surveyed in Katz et al. 1992 (not all of which are listed in this table), the average number of party members as a percentage of the entire electorate declined from 14.6 percent in the 1970s to 10.5 percent in the 1980s. The second principal finding is that there is an enormous range of variation with regard to the levels of affiliation with parties in these countries. At one end of the continuum are the political parties of Austria and Finland, which, despite suffering some declines, were able to maintain high levels of affiliation. At the other extreme, Spanish and Portuguese parties were remarkably unsuccessful in attracting mass-membership bases, even two decades after the reestablishment of competitive party politics. By the mid 1980s, the parties of Greece and Italy had managed to build mass bases of intermediate size. These data are remarkably consistent

Table 3.4 Party Membership Rates in Selected European Countries, 1970–1996

Country	1970	1975	1983	1990	1993/96
Austria	25.9%	25.6%	24.1%	21.8%	
Finland	17.1	15.3	14.0	12.9	
Italy	12.3	10.5	9.4	9.6	6.2 (1996)
Great Britain	8.0	5.9	3.9	3.3	
West Germany	3.1	4.5	4.5	4.2	
Greece	—	1.7	7.5	7.0	6.6 (1996)
Portugal	—	3.5	6.0	4.5	
Spain	—	1.7	1.9	2.0	1.7 (1993)

Sources: For Greece, Italy, and Spain, 1993 and 1996, Comparative National Elections Project surveys, and other years, Morlino 1995, 332–38; for other countries, Katz, Mair, et al. 1992.

with those derived from the Eight Nation and Four Nation surveys.

Overall, the most striking conclusion to be derived from these data involves the extraordinarily low level of affiliation of Spanish parties—a finding that is perfectly parallel with the low levels of attitudinal support for parties in Spain reported above and elsewhere (see Morlino 1998; Montero 1981). The shallow organizational penetration of Spanish society by political parties greatly limits their ability to mobilize and stabilize supportive clienteles. A contextual analysis of Spanish voting behavior lends credence to this assertion. In a Probit analysis of voting behavior in 1979 and 1982, Richard Gunther incorporated into an equation, along with the best-predicting individual-level data (derived from postelection surveys), a measure of party affiliation within each province, standardized as a percentage of each province's electorate. For only one party in 1979, the Partido Comunista de España, was there a statistically significant relationship between the organizational presence of the party in the province and propensity to vote for that party. PCE affiliation in the province in that year "explained" about 1 percent of the vote above and beyond that which was explained by the individual-level variables. In 1982, however, following a profound crisis and organizational decline of the PCE, this contextual variable failed to have a statistically significant impact on the vote. But in that year, too, another party's organizational strength began to have some impact on mobilization of the vote: the level of affiliation with the Alianza Popular emerged as a determinant of an additional 1 percent of the vote for that party. By and large, it can be said that party organizational strength at the provincial level played little or no role in mobilizing the electorate in Spain.

Social Structure and the Institutionalization of Partisanship

One alternative to party identification and party organizational penetration into society, as stabilizing "anchors" of the vote, is "social partisanship." As Barnes et al. 1985 argues, "Trade union, religious and class cues, and possible other factors, have seemed to encourage stable voting in Germany, Austria and Italy, for example, without correspondingly high levels of party attachment." Bartolini and Mair 1990 also places great emphasis on the social structuration or "cleavage encapsulation" of partisanship in its analysis of electoral volatility in western European democracies over the past century, as do the contributors to the more detailed analyses of sixteen democratic electorates in Franklin et al. 1992 and Rose 1974. We argue that the extent of cleavage encapsulation that serves as an anchor for partisanship will be a function of several different factors at several different levels of analysis. First, the nature and the depth of the mass-level cleavages themselves will obviously help to determine the extent to which partisan preferences reflect and are rooted in social divisions. Other things being equal, class polarization of partisan politics is more likely in a society deeply riven by socioeconomic cleavages. (But other things are not always equal, as we shall see.) A second factor affecting the translation of objective mass-level cleavages into prominent features of partisanship is the extent to which these social differences are reflected in and articulated by politicized secondary organizations. As the following data reveal, there are considerable differences among these countries with regard to the extent of such organization. This, in turn, varies according to the extent to which political elites choose to clearly articulate conflicting positions relating to these social-structural differences at crucial, formative phases of the party-building process and, in effect, to "freeze" them into lasting patterns of partisan conflict. We explore each of these determinants of the encapsulation of social cleavages by political parties below.

The Depth of Social Cleavages

There are significant differences among Greece, Italy, Portugal, and Spain with regard to the depth and polarizing potential of social cleavages that are often relevant to partisan politics, particularly those related to social class, religion, and left/right ideological or attitudinal orientations. In the mid 1970s, for example, income was distributed more unequally in Portugal, Italy, and Spain than it was in most other

Table 3.5 Income Inequality in Southern Europe in Comparative Perspective

	Percentage of Total Household Income Received by		
Country	Top 20%	Bottom 20%	Gini Index
Portugal	49.1%	5.2%	.396
France	46.9	4.3	.392
Italy	46.5	5.1	.376
West Germany	46.1	6.5	.363
Spain	44.0	5.7	.352
Greece (1974)	41.9	7.1	.342
United Kingdom	38.7	6.3	.304
Greece (1982)	39.1	8.0	.304
Sweden	37.0	6.6	.290
Netherlands	37.1	8.5	.266

Source: Figures for all countries except Greece from Hoover 1989. These data are from the mid 1970s. Greek data from Tsakloglou 1993.

Table 3.6 Percentage of Labor Force Employed in Agriculture, 1960–1997

Year	OECD Average	Italy	Spain	Portugal	Greece
1960	21.6%	32.6%	38.7%	43.9%	57.1%
1968	15.3	22.9	29.0	33.1	44.5
1974	11.8	17.5	23.2	34.9	36.0
1980	9.6	14.3	19.2	27.3	30.3
1988	7.9	9.8	14.4	20.7	26.6
1997	—	6.1	7.1	13.0	20.8*

Sources: For 1960–88, OECD 1990. For 1994–97, EIU (The Economist Intelligence Unit) 1998a, 28; EIU 1998b, 47; EIU 1998c, 12; EIU 1998d, 27.

*1994.

European countries, and Portugal had the most inegalitarian income distribution of any European country for which we have been able to collect data. The magnitude of these differences can be seen in Table 3.5.

In part, this reflects the relatively recent socioeconomic development of these countries as compared with others in western Europe. Two standard indicators of economic development both clearly reveal that the four southern European countries lagged significantly behind most industrialized societies at the beginning of the 1960s. Table 3.6 shows that, at that time, the segment of labor force active in the primary sector was 50 percent larger in Italy than in the hypothetical "average" OECD country, while in the other three countries it was between two and three times as large. The four southern European economies began to modernize rapidly in the 1960s and early 1970s, however, narrowing the gap separating them from the rest of the industrialized world quite significantly. By the 1980s and 1990s, Spain and, especially, Italy had moved quite close to the OECD average, while Greece and Portugal continued to lag.

These same patterns can be seen in Table 3.7, which presents per capita GDP figures for the four southern European countries (in Purchasing Power Parity units, designed to compensate for fluctuating exchange rates and differences in domestic price structures), in comparison with two affluent industrialized societies—Britain and the United States—and three large Latin American countries. Indeed, in the early 1950s, all four of the southern European economies not only lagged behind those of the industrialized world but were substantially behind Argentina in terms of economic output per capita, and Spain, Portugal, and Greece were behind Mexico as well. By the 1980s and 1990s, however, they had undergone substantial economic growth, surpassing all of the Latin American societies in terms of per capita wealth and approximating the levels of affluence of the rest of western Europe. Indeed, by this time Italy had caught up with Britain, while Spain had also narrowed the gap significantly.

One could argue that lagging development at least partly explains the greater inequality in income distribution than is found in other western European countries: in effect, delayed modernization placed these later industrializers at a lower point on the "Kuznets curve"

Table 3.7 Per Capita GDP in Purchasing Power Parity, International 1985 Dollars

Country	1951	1960	1970	1980	1990
United States	$9,121	$9,908	$12,969	$15,311	$18,087
Great Britain	5,613	6,808	8,527	10,161	13,223
Italy	2,964	4,580	7,558	10,316	12,486
Spain	2,205	3,128	5,861	7,391	9,576
Portugal	1,314	1,857	3,316	4,982	7,487
Greece	1,480	2,086	4,223	5,897	6,768
Mexico	2,317	2,825	3,985	6,051	5,825
Argentina	4,184	4,481	5,642	6,505	4,708
Brazil	1,269	1,780	2,427	4,297	4,043

Source: Penn World Tables, Release 5.6.

Note: Purchasing Power Parity units are designed to compensate for fluctuating exchange rates and differences in domestic price structures.

(Kuznets 1979) than those countries that had undergone their most substantial economic transformations in the nineteenth and early twentieth centuries. As the two data points for Greece in Table 3.5 indicate, other things being equal, economic growth over the long term is generally conducive to a more equal distribution of wealth.

But this economic-reductionist argument cannot be carried too far. Wealth is distributed much more equally in Greece than it is in Italy, Portugal, or Spain, despite the fact that it is economically the least developed of the four southern European countries. This anomaly suggests that other factors contribute to an explanation of the depth of socioeconomic cleavages. We contend that economic and social structures inherited from earlier (and often very distant) stages in a country's history can have a marked impact on income distribution and the nature of social relations over the course of several centuries, despite subsequent economic modernization. Specifically, policies adopted by governments in the early stages of state-building clearly differentiated the socioeconomic structures of Portugal, Spain, and Italy from those of Greece.

In both Portugal and Spain, state-building and the development of important social and economic relationships occurred as part of the reconquest of the Iberian Peninsula from the Moors, who had invaded in the early eighth century. Initially, confiscated lands were rather evenly redistributed among the conquering Christian populations, but changes in royal policy led to greatly different landownership patterns in territories that were seized in the later stages of the reconquest. In the end, the northern two-thirds of Portugal and the kingdom of Castilla-León were characterized by small to medium-sized family-owned farms, while latifundia predominated in New Castile, Extremadura, Andalusia, and the Portuguese Alentejo. Thus, wealth was (and continues to be) distributed more equally in the northern portions of these two countries, while the south was characterized by extreme inequality between aristocratic (often absentee) landlords and impoverished peasants employed as day laborers with no job security. As a result, the predominantly landowning rural populations in the north tended to adopt moderate or conservative political stands and social outlooks. In the south, however, extreme class polarization provided fertile ground for the growth of radical political movements.[5] Throughout the Franco and Salazar eras, the problems of inequality in the south remained totally unresolved and were alleviated only by massive migration.

State and societal development in Italy were quite different, but culminated in the same social-structural differences between the affluent north and the underdeveloped, inegalitarian, and largely impoverished south. In the south, the origins of extreme social inequality can be traced back to the mid thirteenth century (see Putnam 1993, 123–24). This inegalitarian, latifundist social order survived over the following seven centuries despite the disappearance of feudalism, the Risorgimento, and post–World War II economic development. In the north, in contrast, political and economic development followed a very different course, opening up a wide social, economic, and cultural cleavage separating the poorer, backward Mezzogiorno from the affluent north.

The case of Greece is very different. Egalitarian patterns of land ownership in "Old Greece" resulted from redistribution of agricultural lands seized from the Ottoman Turks in the course of the war of independence in the early to mid nineteenth century, as well as in Macedonia and Epirus following territorial gains in the Balkan Wars preceding the outbreak of World War I. Perhaps most important, aggressive land-reform policies under the governments of Eleftherios Venizelos following the National Schism of 1916–17, and especially accompanying the massive influx of Greek refugees from Asia Minor resulting from the post–World War I war with Turkey, led to nearly universal land-ownership among the rural population of Greece (see Mavrogordatos 1983c, 119, 145–68). Greece differs from its southern European counterparts with regard to the nonagricultural sector of its economy as well, resulting in an absence of class polarization (ibid., 145). Overall, 64 percent of the labor force in 1928 either owned their own businesses or agricultural land or were working for other family members, while just over 9 percent of the labor force were employed as manual workers in the industrial sector (ibid., 199).

Spanish and Italian economic development by that time, in contrast, had followed the more typical northern European pattern, in which heavy industry was the engine driving the processes of economic and social change. In the north of Italy, and in the Basque, Catalan, and Asturian regions of Spain, the early stages of economic development entailed a high level of class polarization, accompanied by the emergence of radical and militant working-class movements. By the 1950s in Italy and the 1960s in Spain, however, rapid economic growth led to the emergence of much more affluent mass-consumption societies in both countries, particularly in northern urban areas.

Portugal, meanwhile, simply failed to develop a thriving economy until well into the 1980s. At the time of the Portuguese revolution, it had the highest illiteracy rate in Europe outside of the Balkans, a still predominantly rural and agrarian population, by far the lowest per capita income in western Europe, and a small industrial sector, characterized by a high concentration of ownership and income inequality (Payne 1973, 673–80).

Religious cleavage. These four countries also vary substantially with regard to the nature and extent of religious practice, as well as the extent to which a potentially polarizing religious cleavage is present.[6] As can be seen in Table 3.8, survey data from the mid 1970s and mid 1980s reveal substantial variation in the frequency of religious practice. Several patterns can be observed in these data. The first is that with the exception of Italy in the 1970s, southern Europeans were substantially less religious than Americans. Second, among northern European societies, Austria stands out as a country where religious practice greatly exceeded the levels found elsewhere. Third, a significant secularization of Italian society is apparent in these figures. When the intensity of religious sentiment is measured by the percentage of Italians who attend mass at least once every week, this decline appears to be even sharper: from 53 percent in 1968 to 40 percent in 1975 to 30 percent in 1988 (Mackie, Mannheimer, and Sani 1993, 39). It is im-

Table 3.8 Frequency of Church Attendance

Country	Once a Month or More	Never
United States (1974)	58.2%	13.8%
United States (1993)	55.0	17.4
Italy (1975)	52.7	17.9
Austria (1974)	50.3	16.4
Portugal (1985)	44.8	30.0
Italy (1985)	43.8	23.0
Spain (1994)	44.0	32.0
Spain (1985)	41.2	36.1
Greece (1985)	36.5	14.5
Greece (1996)	35.8	8.8
West Germany (1974)	35.6	22.4
United Kingdom (1974)	22.0	29.9
Finland (1975)	9.7	5.8

Sources: For 1970s and 1980s data, the Eight Nation and Four Nation data sets; for Greece 1996, the Comparative National Elections Project (CNEP) survey of Greece; for Spain, 1994, Montero 1996.

Note: The response categories from the Eight Nation Study combined to create column one of this table include "every week," "almost every week," and "once or twice a month." The corresponding Four Nation response categories were "more than once a week," "every Sunday," and "two or three times a month."

portant to note that time-series data reveal that most of this secularization process had run its course by the mid 1980s: after 1985, the level of self-reported church attendance remained roughly constant (Bellucci, Maraffi, and Segatti 1998, fig. 4). Spanish society has undergone an even more dramatic secularization: between 1975 and 1985, the percentage of Spaniards who attended religious services once a month or more declined from 75 percent to 53 percent in 1981 to 41 percent in 1985, when this secularization process appears to have bottomed-out.[7] These behavioral data are paralleled by attitudinal data revealing that the percentage of Spaniards describing themselves as "very good Catholics" or "practicing Catholics" plummeted from 80 percent in 1965 to 31 percent in 1983, whereas those describing themselves as "nonpracticing," "indifferent," or "atheist" increased from 17 percent in 1976 to 45 percent in 1983 (Montero 1997; Sani 1991).

Seen from a somewhat different perspective, these data provide indirect evidence that the potential for polarization over the religious cleavage was greater in Spain than in any of the other countries, while the prospects for polarization over religious issues in Greece were very slight. While the percentage of respondents in Spain who reject religious practice altogether is significantly higher than in other southern European countries, the percentage of truly devout practitioners (who attend church once a week or more frequently) is also higher than in Italy or Greece; the Portuguese are the most devout as measured by this indicator. At the other end of this continuum, Greeks appear to be most homogeneous in their frequency of religious attendance. The percentages of Greeks who are either intensely devout or nonreligious are about half of the comparable levels for the other countries,[8] while nearly half the population "sometimes" attend church services.

More direct measures of the extent of polarization over religion can be seen in feeling thermometer evaluations of the Church. Survey data from the 1985 Four Nation Study reveal that Spaniards are divided and polarized in their attitudes toward the Church: 36 percent of Spanish respondents placed the Church in positions 1 through 4 on the feeling thermometer (reflecting hostility), while an identical 36 percent regarded the Church favorably (positions 7 through 10). These data suggest that potential political polarization along the religious dimension in Spain was substantially greater than in the other four southern European countries, a conclusion that accords with the sometimes violent and divisive religious conflicts over the past century. Levels of hostility toward the Church in Greece, Portugal, and

Italy were about half the Spanish figure (18, 18, and 20 percent respectively), while positive affect was much more widespread. Indeed, the 70 percent favorable rating by Greek respondents is most striking and exceeds favorable evaluations by Italians and Portuguese (57 and 54 percent) by a significant margin. The moderation of Greeks in religious matters is consistent with the absence of politically relevant religious conflict in Greece since the end of the war with Turkey and the final delineation of national boundaries in 1922. By the end of the Greek nation-building process, 94 percent of the Greek population was Orthodox, and there were few instances when the Orthodox population was divided over religious issues in a manner relevant to politics (see Macridis 1981, 6). Rather than serving as a source of polarization in Greek society, the Orthodox Church has historically functioned as a focus of national identity and an important common agent of political socialization (Prodromou 1994; Diamandouros 1983, 57–58).

An examination of other survey data from the Four Nation Study suggests that although the degree of polarization of Spaniards over religious issues was the highest among the four southern European countries, the overall impact of religion on politics and society in Spain was declining considerably. By the end of the 1980s, Spaniards had become more secularized than other southern Europeans: in one Eurobarometer poll, only 68 percent of Spaniards stated that they regarded themselves as "religious"; this is significantly less than the 86 percent of Portuguese respondents, the 85 percent of Greeks, and the 82 percent of Italians interviewed in that same poll who described themselves as religious.[9] Spaniards also expressed less confidence in the Church than did Portuguese and, especially, Italians. Their responses were also substantially lower in the importance they attached to religion, the frequency of religious practice, adherence to basic religious beliefs, and other indicators. Although the political impact of religion in Spain was historically one of polarizing conflict throughout much of the late nineteenth and early twentieth centuries, the strategies of both Church and party elites to avoid politicization and polarization of the religious cleavage, as well as substantial secularization from the 1960s through the 1980s, would thus seem to suggest that the disruptive potential of religious issues will decline over time.

The left-right cleavage. The final mass-level cleavage pertinent to our analysis is the left-right dimension. While the precise meaning of this attitudinal/cultural/evaluative/perceptual dimension is not entirely clear—and has been the object of considerable scholarly debate—numerous studies of continental European politics have repeatedly

Table 3.9 Self-Placement of Respondents on Ten-Point Left-Right Continuum

	Greece		Italy		Portugal		Spain		
	1985	1996	1985	1996	1985	1993	1985	1993	2000
1–2 Left	18%	7%	22%	23%	8%	5%	8%	16%	9%
3–4 Center-left	22	24	22	29	20	24	39	30	29
5–6 Center	35	40	40	14	48	43	35	37	44
7–8 Center-right	10	17	9	22	17	19	15	13	14
9–10 Right	14	12	6	12	7	8	4	5	4
Mean	5.1	5.6	4.6	4.9	5.3	5.5	4.8	4.7	4.9
(Don't know/ No answer)	(9%)	(11%)	(23%)	(9%)	(29%)	(20%)	(26%)	(10%)	(21%)

Source: For 1985, the Four Nation Study; for Greece, Italy, and Spain in 1993 and 1996, the Comparative National Election Project data sets. For Portugal, 1993, survey conducted by Mário Bacalhau. For Spain 2000, CIS pre-election survey.

Note: These figures are percentages of valid responses.

demonstrated its significance as a determinant of partisan political behavior.[10] As can be seen in Table 3.9, there are important differences among the four southern European cases with regard to this political cleavage.

Despite the relative absence of deep socioeconomic and religious cleavages in Greece, Greek respondents in the mid 1980s were much more polarized on the left-right dimension than other southern Europeans. In contrast with the unimodal distributions of respondents on the left-right continuum characteristic of Italians, Spaniards, and Portuguese, Greek respondents clustered in three groups, spanning the full range of the scale. Although as many Italians as Greeks can be found at the far left end of the scale, Greece is unique among these cases in that it also had an almost equal number at the far right end of the continuum.[11] Over the following decade, however, significant change took place, as the percentage of Greeks placing themselves on the far left declined and the share of those near the center increased appreciably. A second notable difference among these countries involves the location of the "center of gravity" of each electorate. Italians and Spaniards appear to be predominantly center-left, whereas Portuguese and (by 1996) Greeks are clearly more conservative in their political and social outlooks. This finding will take on added significance toward the end of this chapter, when we discuss the history of the Portuguese party system and the evolution of Greek parties. Finally, the overall moderation of Portuguese and Spaniards and their relative lack of left-right polarization is most striking. Indeed, only 8.5 percent of Spaniards and 8.9 percent of Portuguese respondents interviewed in 1985 placed themselves on either the far left or far right ends of the left-right continuum (positions 1 and 10)—a figure substantially less than the 21.9 percent of Italians and the 29.3 percent of Greeks who opted for extreme positions on this scale.

Left-right self-designations, in conjunction with the perceived locations of political parties on this ideological continuum, have been shown in numerous studies to be important determinants of the vote, particularly among respondents who lack psychological ties to specific political parties. In short, voters channel their support toward parties that are (in their perceptions) the "least distance" from their own self-placements on the left-right continuum (Sani 1974a). Insofar as both self- and party-placements on the scale are stable over time, this could help to stabilize voting patterns. This kind of anchoring would not preclude electoral volatility per se, but it would tend to reduce its magnitude by restricting shifts in electoral support to other parties within a given ideological space. In other words, intrabloc or total volatility may be considerable, but interbloc shifts of votes might be minimal.[12] We shall assess the extent to which the left/right dimension serves as an anchor of partisanship later in this chapter.

The Organizational Dimension of Politics

Given our interest in the extent to which class, religious, and left-right cleavages are embedded in patterns of partisan behavior, three different kinds of organization are clearly relevant: trade unions, religious associations, and political parties themselves. Let us briefly survey the extent to which trade unions and religious organizations are institutionalized in southern Europe, and the extent to which parties are linked to or reflective of class, religious, and left-right cleavages.

Parties and the Left-Right Cleavage

The extent to which the party systems of Greece, Italy, Portugal, and Spain reflect the left-right divisions described above can be seen in Table 3.10, which presents the mean placement of each party on the ten-point left-right continuum, as well as the share of the vote received by that party in the previous election. These placements are remarkably stable. As can be seen, perceptions of some parties' positions changed somewhat over time: in particular, PASOK (which had emerged in the 1970s as a party prone to rhetorical radicalism and anti-Americanism) shifted toward the center of the Greek political spectrum; both Izquierda Unida and the Partido Socialista Obrero Español in Spain shifted closer to the center-left of the continuum. Respondents' perceptions of certain other parties, however, remained stubbornly resistant to change, despite real change in both the personnel and the ideological/programmatic commitments of parties. At the time of its founding, for example, the PDS abandoned all pretense of being a communist party and shed all ties to those former PCI members with more orthodox communist values (who defected to Rifondazione Comunista); nonetheless, it was still placed near the left end of the Italian political spectrum, fully 2.5 points from the average self-placement of the Italian electorate. Similarly, the neofascist Movimento Sociale Italiana (MSI) remained at the far right end of the Italian party system despite its conversion into the postfascist Alleanza Nazionale under the leadership of the relatively attractive Gianfranco Fini. More strikingly, Spain's Partido Popular experienced great difficulty in moving closer to the modal center of the Spanish electorate, as perceived by voters, despite its consistent adherence to center-right positions over more than a decade and a complete demographic turnover since its first incarnation as Alianza Popular in 1977 (when it included among its leadership several prominent former ministers of the Franco regime). Throughout the 1980s and early 1990s, the party was located slightly to the right of 8.0 on the ten-point left-right scale. By 2000, it had succeeded in shifting its position somewhat toward the center (to 7.6 on that scale), as revealed in a preelection poll conducted by the Centro de Investigaciones Sociológicas.

A second notable aspect of these party systems involves the patterns of interrelationships among parties. For nearly five decades, the Italian party system was characterized by an extreme multipartyism and by a center occupied by a large number of parties. Despite the change in Italy's electoral law that launched the so-called Second Republic, fragmentation of the party system was not at all reduced (in fact, it slightly increased). Permanent incumbency by DC-dominated centrist coalitions has given way to alternation in power between blocs of parties on the left and right. The Spanish party system also underwent a considerable realignment: between 1979 and 1982, a moderate multiparty system (which balanced a moderate center-right party against a moderate center-left rival) was replaced by a predominant-party system, which was dominated for fourteen years by a socialist party of the moderate center-left, whose only serious challenger for power was perceived by voters to be on the right wing of the ideological continuum. Cabinet instability and polarization also initially characterized

Table 3.10 Placement of Major Southern European Parties on the Left-Right Continuum, 1980s and 1990s

	Greece		Italy		Portugal		Spain	
	1985	1996	1985	1996	1985	1993	1985	1993
Left	KKE 1.6 (9.9%)	KKE 1.6 (5.6%)		RC 1.4 (8.6%)		PCP 1.7 (8.6%)		
			PCI 2.1 (29.9%)		PCP 2.1 (18.7%)		IU 2.1 (4.0%)	
	KKE-Es 2.8 (1.8%)	LEFT 2.7 (5.1%)		PDS 2.4 (21.1%)				IU 2.7 (9.6%)
			PSI 3.9 (11.4%)				PSOE 3.9 (48.4%)	
	PAS 4.4 (45.8%)	D. Soc. 4.4 (4.4%)						PSOE 4.3 (38.8%)
						PS 4.6 (43.8%)		
		PAS 5.0 (41.5%)		PPI 4.9 (6.8%)	PS 5.0 (37.3%)			
			PRI 5.6 (5.1%)					CDS 5.5 (1.8%)
			DC 6.1 (32.9%)	CCD 6.3 (5.8%)			CDS 6.4 (2.9%)	
			PLI 6.5 (2.9%)	Lega 6.9 (10.1%)	PSD 6.9 (27.8%)			
		Pol. A. 7.6 (2.9%)				PSD 7.7 (34.1%)		
				FI 7.9 (21.0%)				
					CDS 8.1 (12.7%)	PP 8.1 (9.1%)	AP 8.1 (26.5%)	PP 8.2 (34.8%)
Right	ND 8.7 (40.9%)	ND 8.6 (38.1%)	MSI 8.7 (6.8%)	AN 9.1 (15.7%)				

Sources: For 1985, Four Nation Study; for 1993 and 1996, Comparative National Election Project surveys.

Note: Numbers in parentheses represent the share of the vote received by each party in the previous election; for the 1980s, these are the Greek election of 1985, the Italian election of 1983, the Portuguese election of 1983, and the Spanish election of 1982.

the Portuguese party system, with a large ideological gap separating the misnamed right-wing, Christian Democratic Centro Democrático y Social (CDS) from the orthodox communist PCP. Since 1987, however, the dynamics of competition in that system have been profoundly altered, with a centrist socialist party pitted against the center-right social democratic party, and with single-party majority governments replacing unstable multiparty coalitions.

Trade Unions

An economic or class variable strongly impinging on electoral politics is the extent of unionization of the labor force.[13] Affiliation with trade unions is relevant to electoral stability, however, only insofar as those labor organizations are tied to or otherwise systematically support specific political parties. Hence a few words describing the nature of party-union relationships are in order. Greece is the most unusual, in that left-right polarization and PASOK's attempted colonization of secondary associations has led to an odd party penetration of union structures based upon proportional representation of parties (see Chapter 7 below). More typically continental European patterns of union-party relationships are found in the other three countries. In Italy, the CGIL (Confederazione Generale Italiana del Lavoro) at the time of the Eight Nation survey had closer relations with the PCI than with other parties, the UIL (Unione Italiana del Lavoro) with the PSI, and the CISL (Confederazione Italiana dei Sindicati dei Lavoratori) with the DC. In Portugal, the CGTP (Confederação Geral dos Trabalhadores) is close to the Portuguese Communist Party (PCP), and the UGT (União Geral dos Trabalhadores) has a special relationship with the Socialist Party (PS). The Spanish Communist Party, and, hence, its broader electoral coalition, Izquierda Unida, has had strong ties with the Comisiones Obreras (CCOO) for decades, whereas until the mid to late 1980s, the socialist PSOE could rely upon the UGT (Unión General de Trabajadores) for electoral support. In general, it can be said that the relationships between southern European socialist parties are distinct from those linking trade unions to social democratic or labor parties elsewhere in Europe. Some party/union conflicts notwithstanding, in Austria, Germany, Norway, and Sweden, these two kinds of socialist organizations have tended to cooperate with each other in a very balanced manner. In Finland, the party appears to exercise a marked preeminence over the union, whereas British trade unions have exercised considerable control over the party (see Astudillo 1997). In contrast, in Greece, Italy, Portugal, and Spain, cooperation is less common or consistent and is disrupted by competition among various trade unions. As a result, labor relations in Greece, Portugal, and Spain are more conflictual and more fragmented than in northern Europe (see Ferner and Hyman 1992). The weakness of the party-union linkage is particularly notable in the case of Spain.[14]

Table 3.11 shows trade union membership as a percentage of the economically active population (excluding members of the armed forces). These data suggest that Greece, Italy, and Portugal are roughly comparable to other advanced industrialized societies in terms of the extent of trade union membership, while Spain lagged far behind, except for a brief period of euphoria following the legalization of trade unions in 1977. Indeed, Spain and France have the lowest trade union membership densities in all of Europe. It is interesting to note, however, that the intensification of conflict between unions and Felipe González's socialist government in the mid to late 1980s appears to have stimulated a revival of trade union affiliation (see Jordana 1996). The bonds that linked the UGT to the governing party became frayed and eventually snapped. Party-union relations degenerated to such an extent that the UGT actively cooperated with other trade unions in a successful general strike against the economic and social policies of the PSOE government in December 1988 and

Table 3.11 Trade Union Membership in Selected European Countries, 1950–1994 (as % of the economically active population)*

Country	1950	1975	1985	1990	1994
Sweden	66.7%	74.5%		82.5%	
Finland	33.6	67.4		72.0	
Denmark	53.2	67.4		71.4	
Norway	47.9	52.7		56.0	
Ireland	37.3	55.2		50.8	
Austria	61.3	56.1		46.2	
Great Britain	39.7	48.3		39.1	
Germany	36.4	36.6		32.9	
Switzerland	39.7	32.9		26.7	
Netherlands	43.1	38.4		25.5	
Italy	45.4	47.2		38.8	
Portugal		52.4		31.8	
Spain		26.0[a]	10.8	14.5	17.2
France	32.5	22.8		10.8	

Sources: For all countries except Spain, Ebbinghaus and Visser 1999; data for Spain from Jordana 1996. The more detailed data presented by Jordana are quite close to the Ebbinghaus/Visser figures for Spain for the years in which they overlap.

*Excluding members of the armed forces.

[a]1978.

helped organize a series of nationwide transportation strikes (affecting trains, airlines, and gasoline stations) in May 1991, at least in part to embarrass the PSOE government on the eve of municipal elections (Astudillo 1997).

Religious Organizations

Low levels of affiliation are also characteristic of religious organizations throughout the region. In the mid 1990s, the percentages of respondents to a Comparative National Elections Project (CNEP) survey claiming to belong to a religious organization ranged from 5 percent in Italy to just 1 percent in Greece. In earlier decades, Catholic Action had played important social and political roles in both Italy and Spain, but secularization and institutional crises (see Payne 1984) had greatly weakened the Church's organizational penetration of these societies. The net result, when combined with the aforementioned weakness of trade union organizations and the more general tendency of southern Europeans not to join organized groups, is that channels for intermediation between citizens and the state are weak and underinstitutionalized in these countries. Aside from its implications for the stabilization of partisanship, this can have a negative impact, not only on the nature of political action within a regime, but on political attitudes and the quality of democracy itself (Linz 1990, 659).

Social Structure and Partisanship

The overall picture that emerges from this brief overview is that in the 1980s and 1990s, there was no such thing as a "southern European model" of social structure or common pattern of "social partisanship." Wealth appears to have been most unequally distributed in Portugal and most evenly spread among Greeks. The potential religious cleavage was deeper in Spain and, to a lesser extent, Italy and Portugal in the 1970s and 1980s than it was in Greece. Spanish and Italian societies, however, were undergoing processes of secularization (particularly pronounced in Spain) that, we argue, have diminished the impact of the religious cleavage on politics over the long term.

In terms of ideological cleavages, a very different picture emerges. Despite the absence of deep class or religious cleavages, Greek society was most drastically polarized along the left-right dimension, although a notable shift toward the center appears to have taken place by the mid 1990s. Conversely, Spaniards were the most moderate in political matters. Finally, in terms of politically relevant secondary associations, we find that Italians in the 1970s and 1980s had the highest levels of affiliation with parties and trade unions, while Spaniards had by far the lowest levels of association with such groups. Greeks also tended to be relatively high in affiliation with parties and trade unions, but had the lowest level of membership in religious organizations. The Portuguese were very low in party membership, low-to-intermediate in trade union affiliation, and the highest among the four nations in terms of association with religious groups. Indeed, overall, Portugal had the most conservative and religious population among the four countries—a finding strikingly inconsistent with Portugal's left-leaning party system in the first years following the revolution.

A Multivariate Analysis of Voting Behavior

How have these varying features of Portuguese, Spanish, Italian, and Greek society affected voting behavior in each country? Is partisanship linked to social-class cleavages in any of these countries to such an extent that elections can appropriately be regarded as "the democratic expression of the class struggle"? How have differing levels of polarization along the religious and left-right dimensions been reflected in partisan loyalties? In general, to what extent have the democracies of southern Europe "encapsulated" social cleavages? Conversely, to what extent have the cleavage-based parties that emerged in western Europe in the late nineteenth and early twentieth centuries given way to "catch-all" or other electoralist party types characterized by thin organizational structures and shallow social roots?

We shall attempt to answer these questions through a multivariate analysis of electoral behavior in the four southern European democracies and, for comparative purposes, in a handful of "older" democracies for which comparable survey data are available. These survey data were collected at different times, ranging from the mid 1970s through the mid 1990s. In most cases (such as Greece, Italy, Portugal, Spain, Germany, Britain, and the United States), this enables us to compare data over time in an effort to measure change in the anchoring of partisanship, enabling us to make both cross-national and longitudinal comparisons.[15]

Before examining the results of this analysis, a few methodological observations are in order. This analysis is based on a series of parallel Probit equations for each country. The dependent variable in these analyses of survey data is self-reporting of vote in the previous election (except for the case of Portugal in 1993, which uses vote intention instead).[16] Independent variables included in this analysis include several measures of class position, affiliation with trade unions, religiosity, proximity to the party on the left-right continuum, and (for the southern European cases) feeling-thermometer evaluations of the party's leader. In order to simplify the presentation of data regarding the impact of eleven independent variables on electoral support for thirty-nine political parties in nine countries over seventeen different elections, we have chosen to eschew the conventional practice of presenting all of the more than 4,000 MLE coefficients for each of the 528 equations whose results appear in the following tables. These multivariate relationships (not to mention an even more extensive analysis of each individual bivariate relationship among all of these variables) have been thoroughly explored, but we believe that a more parsimonious summary presentation is more appropriate here. Tables 3.12–3.20 thus present only the McKelvey-Zavoina "pseudo-R^2" resulting from each Probit equation. As described by its creators, the pseudo-R^2 "represents the portion of the variance explained by the model if we could have measured the dependent variable on its underlying interval level."[17] Accordingly, the figures presented in the following tables for each individual party estimate the percentage of variance explained by the combined impact of all of the independent variables included in each equation. The first equation, for example, included all objective economic/class variables (occupational status, income, and status as employed or self-employed, and/or [when available or when one or more of the other three class variables were missing or made unusable by too many missing data] the interviewer's assessment of the respondent's house and/or neighborhood, ranging from "luxury" to "hovel" or "shack").[18] The reported R^2 thus measures the extent to which these objective class variables contribute to an overall explanation of the vote for each party. Subsequently, additional variables were added to this base equation in stepwise fashion. Thus, the "incremental R^2 (the difference between the R^2 from the initial equation and the next one in the series, which added trade union membership to the original class variables) measures the extent to which our ability to predict the vote for a particular party is increased by adding trade union membership to that initial equation—that is, it represents the incremental contribution of trade union membership to an explanation of the vote. It should be noted that in all of the following tables, the results of this analysis were statistically significant to the .001 level, unless otherwise indicated by a superscript number representing the level of statistical significance of that equation; relationships that were not significant at the .10 level were not presented in these tables.

Cross-national applications of this technique could be distorted in two ways, both of which have been addressed in the following analysis. One source of distortion derives from differences in the number of parties in each party system. Obviously, it is easier to predict the vote for a specific party in a two-party system (where random chance would correctly predict the vote up to 50 percent of the time) than in a fragmented multiparty system with, for example, eight significant parties (where the probability of success in randomly selecting a party would average only 12.5 percent). Other things being equal, this would tend to produce higher R^2 figures for two-party systems than for multiparty systems. We have corrected for this in the following manner. Each party system was divided into parties of the left and parties of the right. In running the analysis for a party of the left, votes for all other parties of the left were excluded from the sample. Thus, the equation effectively predicts votes for that particular party of the left versus all parties of the center and right. Similarly, when the equations for a party of the right were run, voters who supported other parties of the right were excluded from the sample. Accordingly, these data are a measure of the extent of *bloc-anchoring* of the vote, or, in other words, of the barrier between left and right that ought to be expected to result in lower *interbloc volatility.* It should be noted that this analysis goes beyond those in some similar studies (e.g., Rose 1974; Franklin et al. 1992) insofar as it presents the results of this analysis of bloc-anchoring *for each political party,* rather than simply presenting one aggregate measure for "all parties of the left" versus "all parties of the right"—which we also present, as a summary measure of the impact of a particular cluster of variables on the party system as a whole. The more detailed party-by-party analysis has the advantage of making it possible to convey, in relatively parsimonious terms, crucial characteristics distinguishing parties with a relatively homogeneous social-class base of support from parties with interclass, "catch-all" electorates; or parties with more-or-less uniformly religious or (conversely) nonreligious or anticlerical electorates versus parties whose electorates are drawn from both religious and nonreligious sectors of society.

One source of distortion that cannot be eliminated from this analysis derives from the fact that, insofar as there is any multicolinearity among independent variables included in "stepwise" fashion in either multivariate OLS or Probit equations, the order in which variables are entered into the series of equations will affect the apparent strength of each hypothesized causal relationship. Specifically, those variables entered into earlier equations will appear to be stronger than those entered in later steps in the analysis, because the variance apparently explained by any "overlap" between two correlated independent variables will have been captured entirely by the first variable to be entered into the series of equations. There is no way to definitively correct for this source of distortion. We have responded to this potential problem by entering *the same variables in the same order* for all countries, beginning with class variables, then moving on to religiosity, and finally to left-right proximity. This uniform ordering of the steps in the analysis means that each independent variable will be affected by this source of distortion in the same way in each country, so that no cross-national differences will appear to emerge solely as an artifact of stepwise ordering. In the case of the four southern European electorates, for which a more detailed analysis is desirable, the final step in the analysis was to add the feeling-thermometer evaluation of the leader of each respective party. It should be noted that this particular stepwise ordering inherently favors the class variables over all the others, and social-structural variables (relating to class and religion) over the attitudinal variables—left-right proximity and affect toward each party's leader.

Class, Trade Unions, and the Vote

The initial phase of this analysis is an examination of the strength of the relationship between objective measures of the *economic-class position* of each respondent and the propensity to vote for a particular party. The first equation included as independent variables occupational status, income, and the employed/self-employed dichotomy (the quintessential operationalization of Marx's primary measure of class, ownership of the means of production). As the data presented in Table 3.12 reveal, objective indicators of social class are much weaker as predictors of the vote in Greece and Italy than they are in the other western European countries.[19] In Italy, the percentage of the vote explained by these variables ranged from 3 to 7 percent, and in both Greek elections, they explained less than 1 percent of the variance. Even among the communist parties, the effect was surprisingly weak, explaining only 10 and 11 percent of the vote for the PCI in 1972 and 1983 respectively, and significantly less following the breakup of the PCI into Rifondazione Comunista and the PDS. In Greece, no more than 7 percent of the vote for the orthodox com-

Table 3.12 Objective Economic Class: Cumulative Pseudo-R^2

Country/Year	Parties: Left → Right							Left Parties vs. Right
Austria, 1971	SPö .25	FPö .13	ÖVP .24					.248
Finland, 1972	SKDL .31	SDP .26	LKP 23	KEK .34	KOK .20			.243
Spain, 1982	PCE .19	PSOE .19	AP .23					.196
Great Britain, 1987	Lab. .16	SDP/Lib. .12	Cons. .21					.163
Great Britain, 1970	Lab. .12	Lib.$^{.01}$ .06	Cons. .12					.120
Portugal, 1983	PCP .14	PS .11	PSD .09	CDS .11				.110
West Germany, 1972	SPD .07	FDP .08	CDU/CSU .07					.073
Italy, 1983	PCI .11	PSI .04	PSDI$^{.05}$ .09	PRI .24	DC .04	PLI$^{.01}$ .14	MSI*	.071
Spain, 1979	PCE .06	PSOE .06	UCD .06	AP .19				.058
Spain, 1993	IU *	PSOE .06	PP .06					.056
Italy, 1972	PCI .10	PSI*	PSDI$^{.02}$ .08	PRI*	DC .04	PLI*	MSI*	.044
Portugal, 1991	PCP .08	PS .03	PSD .03	PP .05$^{.01}$				.035
Italy, 1996	RC .07	PDS .02	PPI$^{.01}$ .04	Lega .07	FI$^{.01}$ .02	AN .03		.027
United States, 1992	Dem. .01	Rep. .01						.012
Greece, 1981	KKE *	PASOK$^{.10}$ .01	ND$^{.05}$ .01					.006*
United States, 1972	Dem.*	Rep.*						*
Greece, 1996	KKE$^{.01}$ .07	Left *	PASOK *	ND *				*

Note: All data are significant at the .001 level unless otherwise noted; * denotes that they are not significant at .10 level.

munist KKE was explained by objective indicators of social class. This is not surprising in the case of Greece, where, as we saw earlier, income is more evenly distributed and the class structure is less polarized than elsewhere in southern Europe. In the case of Italy, the weakness of this relationship is most likely the result of the often-cited cross-cutting of class distinctions by the more powerful religious cleavage (to be discussed below).

In Spain, this relationship varied greatly over time, and in a nonlinear fashion. In the 1979 election, the power of socioeconomic variables as determinants of the vote was much below that found in northern Europe. The three largest parties had markedly interclassist electorates: this is not surprising in the case of the catch-all Unión de Centro Democrático and its principal rival, the Partido Socialista Obrero Español, but even in the case of the Partido Comunista de España, these socioeconomic variables explained only 6 percent of the vote. The 1982 Spanish election, however, produced a substantial class crystallization of the vote. The class basis of electoral support was substantially strengthened for all major Spanish parties, and in the case of the Alianza Popular (renamed the Partido Popular in 1989), this class polarization was even stronger than that separating the British Labour and Conservative parties. Only Austrian and Finnish parties have a stronger objective class base. With the collapse of the UCD in 1982 and the massive increase in support for the AP (rising to 26 percent, from 8 percent of the vote in 1979), the Spanish party system underwent a significant class polarization as a by-product of that realigning election. With the passing of eleven years, however, the class basis of Spanish voting faded substantially, falling to the same level as in the 1979 election. As we shall contend, this is most likely the product of a sustained interclassist electoral strategy pursued by the Partido Popular ever since its "refounding" in 1989, in combination with considerable economic growth and social-structural modernization since the mid 1980s.

Trade union membership. To what extent does the "organizational dimension" of class conflict affect voting preferences? Parties often rely upon allied or otherwise sympathetic trade unions to mobilize voters. How might the addition of trade union membership to this equation add to the class basis of politics in southern Europe? Table 3.13 presents the incremental increase in R^2 resulting from the addition of the respondent's trade union membership to the equation including the aforementioned objective indicators of class position. It should be noted that, wherever appropriate, the particular trade union with which a party was linked (e.g., CGIL-PCI, CCOO-PCE) was used in

Table 3.13 Trade Union Membership: Incremental R^2

Country/Year	Parties: Left → Right							Left Parties vs. Right
Spain, 1979	PCE .21	PSOE .11	UCD .14	AP .14				.128
West Germany, 1972	SPD .08	FDP .04	CDU/CSU .09					.076
Great Britain, 1970	Lab. .07	Lib. .02	Cons. .08					.071
United States, 1972	Dem. .07	Rep. .07						.071
United States, 1992	Dem. .07	Rep. .07						.067
Portugal, 1983	PCP .13	PS .02	PSD .04	CDS .07				.058
Italy, 1996	RC .05	PDS .12	PPI .02	Lega .02	FI$^{.01}$ .06	AN .09		.057
Spain, 1993	IU .03	PSOE .02	PP .05					.047
Spain, 1982	PCE .17	PSOE .06	AP .03					.040
Italy, 1972	PCI .05	PSI*	PSDI*	PRI*	DC .04	PLI*	MSI*	.039
Great Britain, 1987	Lab. .08	SDP/Lib. .01	Cons. .05					.037
Portugal, 1991	PCP .08	PS*	PSD .03	PP .01$^{.01}$				.025
Finland, 1972	SKDL .01	SDP .04	LKP .02	KEK*	KOK .02			.018
Italy, 1983	PCI .08	PSI*	PSDI*	PRI .00	DC .01	PLI*	MSI*	.011
Greece, 1981	KKE .04	PASOK*	ND*					.008
Greece, 1996	KKE*	Left*	PASOK*	ND*				*

Note: All data are significant at the .001 level unless otherwise noted; * denotes that they are not significant at .10 level.

lieu of the more generic measure of trade union membership.

As can be seen in these data, trade union membership most significantly enhanced the ability of the PCE to attract Spanish voters, increasing its R^2 by 21 percent in 1979 and by 17 percent in 1982. Only the Portuguese PCP in 1983 and the Italian PDS came close, picking up an additional 13 and 12 percent, respectively, from the activities of their allied trade unions. The strength of the negative relationship between trade union membership and a vote for either of the two parties of right in the Spanish 1979 election is almost equally impressive. It would appear that in addition to functioning as "transmission belts" of electoral support for their respective allied parties, trade unions can establish a climate of opinion or a flow of formal political communications (or both) discouraging electoral support for parties regarded as antithetical to workers' interests.

The general weakness of these relationships in other countries is also striking, particularly in Greece (where the extreme partisan fragmentation of trade union organizations makes it difficult to test this relationship empirically) and in Italy, where communists, socialists, and Christian Democrats all attempted to use union organizations to mobilize support from workers. More broadly, the weakness of these relationships lends credence to interpretations of party-system "dealignment" within older democratic systems based upon the erosion or breakdown of "working-class solidarity" and the general decline of membership in politicized secondary associations. In Spain, as well, these party/trade union linkages weakened very substantially over time. In part, this may reflect the fact that the 1979 election took place near the high point of trade union membership, which declined substantially over the following decade. In the particular case of the PSOE, it is also likely that the breakdown of its previously close ties to the UGT in the mid 1980s has had a very negative impact on its ability to mobilize working-class support.

The cumulative impact of class variables. Table 3.14 presents the cumulative R^2 resulting from the inclusion of all class-related variables in the Probit equations for each party. One noteworthy finding is that class has an extraordinarily weak impact on the vote in Greece. Given the absence of latifundia and the widespread ownership of property in both the agrarian and urban sectors of Greek society, this seems quite understandable. It is nonetheless striking that class is a weaker predictor of the vote in Greece than it is in the United States. These class-related variables are also quite weak as predictors of the vote in Italy, explaining less than 9 percent of the vote from 1972 through 1996. Somewhat surprisingly, given the inegalitarian distribution of

Table 3.14 All Social Class Variables: Cumulative Pseudo-R^2

Country/Year	Parties: Left						Right	Weighted Ave. R^2
Finland, 1972	SKDL .32	SDP .30	LKP .25	KEK .34	KOK .22			.261
Austria, 1971	SPö .25	FPö .13	ÖVP .24					.248
Spain, 1982	PCE .36	PSOE .25	AP .27					.236
Great Britain, 1987	Lab. .20	SDP/Lib. .13	Cons. .27					.200
Great Britain, 1970	Lab. .19	Lib. .08	Cons. .20					.191
Spain, 1979	PCE .27	PSOE .17	UCD .18	AP .33				.186
Portugal, 1983	PCP .27	PS .13	PSD .13	CDS .18				.157
West Germany, 1972	SPD .15	FDP .12	CDU/CSU .16					.149
Spain, 1993	IU .04	PSOE .08	PP .10					.103
Italy, 1996	RC .13	PDS .14	PPI .06	Lega .10	FI$^{.01}$ .07	AN .13		.084
Italy, 1972	PCI .15	PSI .06	PSDI .09	DC .08	MSI$^{.10}$ .11			.083
Italy, 1983	PCI .19	PSI .05	PSDI*	PRI .27	DC .05	PLI .15	MSI *	.082
United States, 1992	Dem .08	Rep. .08						.082
United States, 1972	Dem. .07	Rep. .07						.067
Portugal, 1991	PCP .16	PS .03	PSD .05	PP .07				.060
Greece, 1981	KKE .05	PASOK .01	ND .01					.014
Greece, 1996	KKE .22	Left*	PASOK*	ND*				*

Note: All data are significant at the .001 level unless otherwise noted; * denotes that they are not significant at .10 level.

wealth in Portugal, the class basis of Portuguese electoral behavior was only of intermediate strength in 1983. Less surprisingly, the rapid economic development experienced by Portugal in the 1980s and early 1990s (Gibson 2000) appears to have contributed to a substantial decline in the impact of the class cleavage on voting: by 1991, these class variables explained an average of only 6 percent of the variance in electoral preferences, placing Portugal below even the United States.

The most interesting relationship between class and electoral preferences is to be seen in Spain. While the electorates of the PCE and AP were sharply polarized along class lines, the catch-all electoral strategies of the two largest parties meant that the overall class polarization of the Spanish party system was of notable but generally moderate. In 1982, however, a substantial class polarization of voting patterns took place, in large part as a consequence of the displacement of the catch-all UCD by the much more homogeneously middle- and upper-class AP as the largest party on the right of center. At the same time, the crisis of the PCE provoked the defection of much of its moderate middle-class electorate, largely reducing its support to a more homogeneous working-class constituency. By 1993, however, this class polarization had abated, in large measure because of the success of the rechristened Partido Popular in broadening its electoral appeal. Even more striking, by forming the Izquierda Unida electoral coalition, the PCE succeeded remarkably in transforming its base of support to include young, better-educated "postmaterialists" (see Montero and Torcal 1994), to the extent that all class variables combined explained only 9 percent of the vote.

More generally, these patterns over time are consistent with an *embourgeoisement* hypothesis for two of the four southern European countries. In Portugal, class declined in strength substantially, from explaining 16 percent in 1983 to about 6 percent in 1993, while in Spain, class variables also weakened, from 19 percent of variance explained in 1979 to 10 percent fourteen years later. And both Greece and Italy, the relationship between class and voting remained weak throughout the decades under examination here. These findings accord with those reported for most of the countries included in Franklin et al. 1992, in which socioeconomic variables were found to have declined in their predictive power over two decades in Australia, Belgium, Canada, Denmark, Great Britain, Ireland, the Netherlands, New Zealand, Norway, and Sweden. We are tempted to conclude, therefore, that socioeconomic change has contributed to the erosion of the class basis of politics in southern Europe, as it has in most other industrialized regions.

Both our data and theirs, however, also suggest that change in electoral behavior cannot be explained simply as the product of socioeconomic modernization. While it is clear that electorates in most countries, over the long term, have evolved in a manner consistent with the predictions of a socioeconomic-modernization or *embourgeoisement* hypothesis, not all countries do so, and certainly not necessarily over the short or medium term. Indeed, some countries, including the United States and the United Kingdom, experienced increases in class polarization in the 1980s.[20] The most substantial change, however, occurred in Spain between 1979 and 1982, where the objectively definable class basis of voting polarized quite suddenly and, despite the collapse of trade union membership from its high point in 1978, the effect of all class variables on the vote strengthened notably.

Religiosity

The second major social-structural factor whose impact on politics we shall examine is religiosity. Table 3.15 presents the incremental contribution to R^2 resulting from the addition to the preceding all-inclusive social class equation of variables relating to the religious involvement of the respondent: self-reports of frequency of attendance at religious services or of the intensity of religious devotion (except for Britain, where a different measure was used).[21] These data clearly reveal that religion had its strongest impact on voting behavior in Italy and Spain in the 1970s and 1980s, followed by Austria and West Germany. Whereas the electoral impact of religiosity was of intermediate strength in Portugal in the 1980s and 1990s, it was weaker than one might have expected on the basis of data presented earlier that reveal a potential religious cleavage in Portuguese society and illustrate the importance of religion for a substantial segment of the Portuguese population. Religion had a very weak impact on voting choice in Greece, Finland, and the United States in 1972. The weakness of this relationship was to be expected in Finland and Greece (where there is no religious cleavage to speak of) and the United States in 1972.

A closer inspection of these data reveals that a dramatic and revolutionary change took place in Italian electoral politics in the earlier 1990s. It had long been noted that religion was, throughout the so-called First Republic, a vastly stronger predictor of the vote than was social class. Even for the Communist Party (whose formal ideology placed great stress upon class), religiosity was more strongly related to partisan preference than was class. This is not surprising, since the

Table 3.15 Religiosity: Incremental Pseudo-R^2

Country/Year	Parties (Left → Right)	Weighted Ave. R^2
Italy, 1972	PCI .29; PSI .17; PSDI*; DC .35; MSI .02	.257
Spain, 1982	PCE .24; PSOE .21; AP .24	.255
Italy, 1983	PCI .19; PSI .10; PSDI$^{.10}$ .09; PRI .03; DC .29; PLI .04; MSI$^{.01}$ .02	.230
Spain, 1979	PCE .25; PSOE .19; UCD .23; AP .21	.225
Austria, 1971	SPö .15; FPö .04; ÖVP .18	.148
West Germany, 1972	SPD .13; FDP*; CDU/CSU .18	.132
Portugal, 1991	PCP .21; PS .06; PSD .08; PP .17	.099
Spain, 1993	IU .17; PSOE .00; PP .10	.095
Greece, 1981	KKE* .24; PASOK .04; ND .06	.062
Portugal, 1983	PCP .19; PS .03; PSD .05; CDS .07	.058
United States, 1992	Dem. .06; Rep. .06	.058
Great Britain, 1970	Lab. .05; Lib. .06; Cons. .04	.048
Great Britain, 1987	Lab. .04; SDP/Lib. .02; Cons. .04	.035
Italy, 1996	RC .16; PDS .05; PPI .05; Lega .03; FI .04; AN .02	.030
Finland, 1972	SKDL .02; SDP .03; LKP .06; KEK .03; KOK .03	.019
United States, 1972	Dem. .02; Rep. .02	.015
Greece, 1996	KKE .02; Left .11; PASOK*; ND$^{.01}$ .02	.010$^{.10}$

Note: All data are significant at the .001 level unless otherwise noted; * denotes that they are not significant at .10 level.

main rival of the PCI was the Christian Democratic Party, and these two parties for many years served as the principal electoral channels for the respective subcultures within which they were rooted. Indeed, it has often been argued that a significant cause of the weakness of class as a divisive force in Italian politics is that the class cleavage is cross-cut by religion (see, e.g., Barnes 1974; Sani 1974b; DiPalma 1970). Despite the secularization that took place in Italy in the 1960s, 1970s, and 1980s, there was very little weakening of the relationship between religious belief and electoral preferences throughout this period. "In contrast to the sort of decline seen elsewhere, the reduction in variance explained in 1988 is very slight, leaving Italian party choice still dominated by apparently powerful effects of social structure (particularly religion)," Mackie, Mannheimer, and Sani 1992 comments on this surprising stability (253). All of this changed dramatically in the course of the "electoral earthquake" of 1994 and its aftershock in 1996. By that time, the portion of variance in party choice had fallen from 23 percent in 1983 to just 3 percent. This latter figure placed Italy below even Great Britain, the United States (in 1992), and Greece (in 1981) in terms of its anchoring of the vote in the religious cleavage. Although the direction of change corresponds with that suggested by the secularization of Italian society, the timing and the abrupt and radical nature of this shift defies simple explanation in accordance with a social-structural reductionist argument: it should be recalled, for example, that most of the secularization of Italian society had taken place prior to the mid 1980s, and that various measures of indicate that the aggregate level of the Italian electorate's religiousness has remained roughly constant since 1985. The drastic decline of religion as a basis for the left-right anchoring of the Italian electorate did not occur until a decade later, and when it did, it appeared abruptly.

The case of Spain is also worthy of some discussion. Despite the absence of an explicitly Christian Democratic party and the general avoidance of religious issues by all parties in the 1979 and 1982 election campaigns, the religious cleavage significantly affected voting in the 1970s and 1980s. Indeed, in 1979, support for the UCD was as strongly rooted in the religious cleavage, as was support for the Christian Democratic Union (CDU/CSU) in West Germany and the Österreichische Volkspartei (ÖVP) in Austria. With the collapse of the catch-all UCD and its displacement from the political spectrum by the more clearly right-wing Alianza Popular, a sharper religious differentiation of voters on either side of the left/right divide emerged. Over the long term, however, the impact of religion as a divisive force in Spanish voting behavior declined substantially (in sharp contrast to the United States, where a significant politicization of religion had taken place prior to the 1992 election). This weakened link between politics and religion is almost certainly related to the secularization of Spanish society that many studies have documented (see Montero 1986 and 1993), but in some respects, the depoliticization of religion in Spain has gone further than one might have predicted on the basis of public opinion data alone. That same 1993 postelection survey revealed sharp polarization over such potentially salient issues as abortion: when asked to describe their attitudes toward abortion using a ten-point scale (with the complete legality of abortion under all circumstances represented by a score of 10, a complete ban on abortion under all circumstances indicated by a score of 1, and intermediate positions represented by numerical scores between these extremes), 39.4 percent of Spanish respondents placed themselves in one or the other of the most extreme positions on the scale. Why religion never realized its polarizing potential in Spain is a question whose answer cannot be extrapolated from mass-level opinion alone. A more complete answer, as we shall argue, involves the extent to which political elites and parties choose to ignore or intentionally depoliticize religious differences.

All Social-Structural Variables Combined

Table 3.16 presents a summary of the impact of all social-structural variables combined—religion and class, all objective, subjective, and associational measures included—on electoral behavior. It can be regarded as a grand summary of the extent of social-structural anchoring of partisanship in this sample of modern democracies. It is noteworthy that in the 1970s and 1980s, the party systems of Italy and Spain ranked among the highest in our sample of countries in terms of the social-structural anchoring of interbloc electoral stability. In contrast, the Portuguese electorate had relatively shallow roots in that country's class and religious cleavages, while that of Greece was hardly anchored at all. The case of Greece is not surprising, given the absence of a significant religious cleavage and the apparent shallowness of economic cleavages, but the Portuguese case certainly represents an anomaly deserving of further consideration, particularly in light of the depth of both class and religious cleavages in Portuguese society.

What is most striking in the Italian and Spanish cases is the extent to which this social-structural anchoring has weakened in the 1990s. The percentage of variance explained in the 1993 Spanish election

Table 3.16 All Social Structural Variables: Cumulative Pseudo-R^2

Country/Year	Parties (Left → Right)	Weighted Ave. R^2
Spain, 1982	PCE .59; PSOE .46; AP .51	.491
Spain, 1979	PCE .52; PSOE .36; UCD .41; AP .54	.411
Austria, 1971	SPö .40; FPö .17; ÖVP .42	.396
Italy, 1972	PCI .43; PSI .23; DC .43; MSI .06	.340
Italy, 1983	PCI .47; PSI .14; PSDI .09; PRI .27; DC .34; PLI .19; MSI$^{.01}$ .05	.312
West Germany, 1972	SPD .28; FDP .12; CDU/CSU .34	.281
Finland, 1972	SKDL .30; SDP .33; LKP .31; KEK .37; KOK .25	.280
Great Britain, 1970	Lab. .24; Lib. .13; Cons. .25	.239
Great Britain, 1987	Lab. .24; SDP/Lib .15; Cons. .31	.235
Portugal, 1983	PCP .46; PS .16; PSD .18; CDS .25	.215
Spain, 1993	IU .20; PSOE .08; PP .20	.198
Portugal, 1991	PCP .37; PS .09; PSD .13; PP .24	.159
United States, 1992	Dem. .14; Rep. .14	.140
Italy, 1996	RC .29; PDS .19; PPI .11; Lega .13; FI .11; AN .15	.114
United States, 1972	Dem. .08; Rep. .08	.080
Greece, 1981	KKE .29; PASOK .05; ND .08	.076
Greece, 1996	KKE .24; Left .13; PASOK*; ND$^{.01}$ .04	.022$^{.05}$

Note: All data are significant at the .001 level unless otherwise noted; * denotes that they are not significant at .10 level.

was less than half of that predicted by the same variables just nine years earlier, while Italian social-structural factors in 1996 explained only about one-third of the variance that they had accounted for in the 1970s and 1980s. This decline in the social-structural anchoring of the vote is strikingly consistent with the increasing tendency of both electorates to shift their support between parties of the left and right throughout the 1990s, in contrast to the extraordinarily high level of bloc loyalty exhibited by Spanish and Italian voters throughout the 1970s and 1980s. This was apparent with the progressive transfer of votes from the PSOE to the PP in 1993, 1996, and 2000, and with the shifts from right to left and back to right in the Italian general elections of 1996 and regional elections of 2000. Indeed, all four southern European countries reveal a weakening of this social structuration of partisanship during the period under study. Conversely, it should be noted that electoral competition in the United States has become more polarized along both class and religious lines over the past two decades.

The Left-Right Anchoring of Electoral Support

An additional source of stability in electoral behavior derives from the proximity between voters' self-identifications with the camps of left and right and their perceptions of the ideological orientations of the various parties. If such perceptions are widespread, stable, and salient in terms of voting choice, then it might be argued that support for parties might remain stable over time even in the absence of substantial social-structural anchoring of partisanship. Accordingly, the next step in our analysis is to add a measure of left-right proximity to the Probit equation including all social-structural variables combined to determine the extent to which left-right distance contributes to our ability to accurately predict the vote. Unfortunately, the Eight Nation study, CNEP's 1992 U.S. National Election Study, and the 1987 British General Election Study (see n. 3) did not include variables measuring the location of political parties on the left-right continuum. Thus, it is not possible to construct a simple "least-distance" model linking respondents with parties for these other democracies, and they cannot be included in the following analysis.

As can be seen in Table 3.17, the three Spanish surveys, data for Greece, Italy, and Portugal from the 1985 Four Nation Study, from the 1993 Bruneau and Bacalhau survey of Portugal, and from the 1996 Greek and Italian CNEP surveys reveal a broad range of variation in terms of the incremental impact on voting choice of this left-right

Table 3.17 Left-Right: Incremental Pseudo-R^2

Country/Year	Parties: Left						Right
Greece, 1996	KKE .40	Left .42	D. Soc. .39	PASOK .58	Pol. An. .40	ND .56	
Italy, 1996	RC .48	PDS .53	PPI .31	Lega .41	FI .63	AN .59	
Greece, 1981	KKE .53	PASOK .44	ND .57				
Portugal, 1991	PCP .45	PS .35	PSD .56	PP .43			
Spain, 1993	IU .35	PSOE .42	PP .49				
Italy, 1983	PCI .31	PSI .27	PSDI*	PRI .32	DC .32	PLI .19	MSI .57
Portugal, 1983	PCP .32	PS .27	PSD .42	CDS .40			
Spain, 1982	PCE .24	PSOE .25	AP .29				
Spain, 1979	PCE .22	PSOE .14	UCD .22	AP*			

Note: All data are significant at the .001; * denotes equation did not converge.

least-distance variable (the absolute value of the respondent's self-placement on the left/right continuum minus his/her placement of the relevant party). The most striking finding from this step of the analysis is that despite the absence of partisan polarization along social cleavage lines (economic position and religiosity), the Greek electorate was clearly crystallized along ideological or left-right lines. To a lesser extent, the simple least-distance model also partly explains the behavior of Italian and Portuguese voters. It is particularly noteworthy that support for the neofascist MSI is explained almost totally by this ideological factor, and is largely unlinked with social-structural variables. It is also noteworthy that the strength of this variable is inversely related to the strength of the social-structural factors analyzed above. Indeed, in the case of Italy, in particular, it appears that this left/right factor has rushed in to fill the gap left by the collapsing social-structural supports for partisanship. This finding is quite consistent with those from studies of Belgium, Denmark, the Netherlands, New Zealand, Norway, and Sweden that also found that left/right anchoring has increased as the social structuration of partisanship has declined.[22]

Table 3.18 presents the results of a "grand summary" measure of

Table 3.18 Left-Right plus Social Structural Variables: Cumulative Pseudo-R^2

	Parties								
Country/Year	Left								Right
Spain, 1982		PCE .83		PSOE .71				AP .80	
Italy, 1996	RC .77	PDS .72		PPI .43			Lega .54	FI .74	AN .74
Spain, 1993		IU .56		PSOE .50				PP .69	
Italy, 1983		PCI .78	PSI .41		PRI .59	DC .66	PLI .38		MSI .63
Greece, 1981	KKE .81			PASOK .50					ND .66
Spain, 1979		PCE .73	PSOE .50			UCD .63		AP*	
Greece, 1996	KKE .64	Left .56		D. Soc. .59	PASOK .44		Pol. An. .42		ND .60
Portugal, 1991	PCP .82			PS .44		PSD .69	PP .67		
Portugal, 1983		PCP .78		PS .43		PSD .60		CDS .60	

Note: * denotes that equation did not converge.

the extent of social-structural and left-right anchoring of partisanship. These data measure the percentage of variance in voting behavior (relevant to bloc-anchoring) that is "explained" by the relatively stable social-structural and ideological factors. The range of the differences among the southern European party systems in this respect is quite large. At one extreme, we find Portugal and, in 1996, Greece: except for the orthodox Marxist-Leninist communist parties in these two countries, in these cases, between 33 percent and 58 percent of the vote is *unexplained* by these stabilizing features, or, in other words, was "available" for capture by rival parties. At the other extreme are most of the parties of Spain (during the 1980s and early 1990s) and Italy, whose electorates are or were firmly anchored in these social-structural and ideological cleavages. It is noteworthy that these patterns are completely consistent with the levels of intra- and interbloc volatility in each of the southern European democracies. The massive party-system realignment in Spain in 1982 (but with low interbloc volatility), as well as the relatively high levels of both total volatility and interbloc volatility experienced repeatedly in Greece and Portugal are parallel to these patterns of cleavage anchoring, as is the stabilization of voting in Spain following the 1982 realignment. Indeed, the reluctance of Spanish voters to abandon the scandal-plagued PSOE in 1993 in favor of the Partido Popular does not appear surprising in light of these data. Indeed, it was only when the Partido Popular finally succeeded in shifting voters' perceptions of its ideological stance somewhat closer to the center (from 8.2 on the ten-point scale in 1993 to 7.6 in 2000), at the same time that a number of voters had migrated from the center-left to the center of the political spectrum (increasing the share of those placing themselves at positions 5 or 6 on that scale from 37 percent in 1993 to 44 percent in 2000), that the PP was able to secure a parliamentary majority. What is somewhat surprising is the extent to which the increase in left/right anchoring in Italy completely offset the collapse of social structuration of partisanship noted in Table 3.16. The net effect of the increases in left/right stabilization of the vote in both Spain and Italy appears to have been to compensate for the decline of social-structural anchoring in both countries by the 1990s.

Another Determinant of the Vote: Party Leadership

Earlier studies of Spanish voting behavior have found that voters' feelings about party leaders are a powerful predictor of electoral behavior (see Gunther, Sani, and Shabad 1986, ch. 8). The exact causal role of this factor is difficult to determine, however, because one might be tempted to overestimate the unique influence of party leadership if other important variables are not taken into consideration. Simple "zero order" measures of association between affect toward the party leader and votes might suggest that most of the variance in electoral support is explained by that factor alone. For example, when the respondents' attitudes toward the leader were included as the only independent variable in a Probit analysis of the vote for each Spanish party, the resulting R^2 suggested that this factor alone "explained" between half and two-thirds of the variance. Numerous empirical studies have found, however, that sentiments about party leaders are themselves partly "explained" by other factors, such as voters' ideological stances, religiosity, class identification, and so on. In other words, one's attitude toward Manuel Fraga Iribarne, Ronald Reagan, or Margaret Thatcher is at least in part a function of whether or not one is conservative. Thus, in order to better understand the significance of this party leadership variable, it is necessary to construct a complex causal model, in which attitudes toward the party's leader are themselves partly "explained" by other variables. For our purposes, it is sufficient to simply control for these other causal factors by entering the party-leadership evaluation as the last step in a multivariate Probit equation, as we have done throughout this chapter. In doing so, we can be reasonably certain that affect toward the party leader is not "standing in" for some other factor, such as ideological orientation, religiosity, or class. The results of this analysis can be seen in Table 3.19.

The impact of affect toward the party leader varies enormously from party to party and from one election to the next. The increase in the percentage of variance explained by adding this leadership variable ranges from 1 to 23 percent. A more detailed examination of the data for each party provides important insights into the nature of parties and the role of leadership as a potential "anchor" of partisanship. First, it should be noted that the incremental contribution of affect toward the party leader varies inversely with the strength of the relationship between the vote and our standard social-structural and left-right variables: the more deeply anchored the electorate in those cleavage-based blocs, the less of an independent contribution the party leadership factor makes to voters' choices. Conversely, the more weakly rooted a party's electoral support in distinct social or ideological blocs, the greater the extent to which voters' attitudes toward individual party leaders can affect voting decisions.

To some extent, this represents an important difference between traditional cleavage-based parties (whose constituencies are distinguished by class or religious differences) and "catch-all" parties. As Otto Kirchheimer noted long ago, such parties can be distinguished from traditional cleavage-based parties by their deemphasis or abandonment of a *classe gardée,* and their willingness to attract support from a variety of groups; by the drastic reduction of the party's ideological commitments; and by the strengthening of top leadership groups (Kirchheimer 1966). The data presented in the preceding tables provide clear evidence that this syndrome involves a tight linkage among each of its elements. Support for traditional "cleavage" parties such as the Portuguese, Italian, and Spanish communist parties was rooted in class, religious, and ideological divisions in these societies, and feelings about party leaders made little difference to most voters. Conversely, as the defense of group interests and ideological agendas weaken, attention shifts to the characteristics of party leaders as the foci of election campaigns and determinants of the vote. In our survey, we found that quintessentially catch-all parties such as the UCD, PASOK, and the Portuguese and Spanish socialist parties had shallow social-structural roots and had softened or abandoned their prior ide-

Table 3.19 The Incremental Contribution of Affect Toward Party Leader

Country/Year	Cumulative R^2 (Social Structure plus Left/Right)	Incremental R^2 (Affect Toward Party Leader)	Cumulative R^2 (All Variables Combined)
Greece, 1981			
KKE	.81	.08	.90
PASOK	.50	.08	.57
ND	.65	.04	.69
Greece, 1996			
KKE	.64	**.15**	.79
PASOK	.44	**<u>.20</u>**	.79
ND	.60	.08	.68
Italy, 1983			
PCI	.78	.02	.80
PSI	.41	.06	.48
PRI	.59	.07	.66
DC	.66	.02	.68
PLI	.38	.09	.46
MSI	.63	.06	.69
Italy, 1996			
RC	.77	.03	.79
PDS	.72	**.10**	.82
PPI	.43	**<u>.23</u>**	.66
Lega	.54	**<u>.20</u>**	.74
FI	.74	**.10**	.84
AN	.74	**.10**	.83
Portugal, 1993			
PCP	.82	.05	.87
PS	.44	**.14**	.58
PSD	.69	**.13**	.82
PP (CDS)	.67	.04	.71
Spain, 1979			
PCE	.73	**.11**	.84
PSOE	.50	**.18**	.67
UCD	.63	.09	.73
Spain, 1982			
PCE	.83	.01	.85
PSOE	.71	.09	.80
AP	.80	.07	.87
Spain, 1993			
IU	.56	**.12**	.68
PSOE	.50	**.19**	.69
PP	.69	.08	.77

ological appeals. Almost as a corollary, their electoral fortunes depended significantly on the attractiveness of their respective party leaders.

More broadly, a general shift over the course of the past three decades away from cleavage-based parties and toward "modern" catch-all or other more purely electoralist party types is apparent in southern Europe (a theme more fully explored in the following chapters). As Gianfranco Pasquino argues in Chapter 5 of this volume, the shift to the "new campaign politics" is nowhere clearer than in Italy. All of the parties in the First Republic had been founded in earlier decades (most of them in the 1940s); hence, they institutionalized the distinguishing characteristics of traditional cleavage parties, retarding the emergence of the new leadership-focused style of campaigning that had emerged elsewhere. Indeed, as Pasquino points out, prior to the 1990s, virtually all Italian parties studiously avoided emphasizing the personal qualities of their candidates for prime minister, even (as in the case of the PCI's Enrico Berlinguer) when the party was headed by a generally attractive figure. In sharp contrast, campaign politics in the Second Republic has been dominated by larger-than-life figures such as Silvio Berlusconi, Umberto Bossi, and Romano Prodi. This qualitative change is clearly reflected in the data presented in Table 3.19.

An even more substantial role of party leadership as a determinant of the vote can be seen *within* each bloc. In order to explore this relationship, another series of Probit equations were run in which all supporters of parties outside of the voter's bloc were excluded from the sample. Thus, this wave of analysis simulated head-to-head competition for the support of leftist voters between the PSOE and PCE/IU in Spain, the PCP and PS in Portugal, and Rifondazione Comunista and the PDS in Italy. On the right, it tapped into the competition among the Lega Nord, Forza Italia! and the Alleanza Nazionale in Italy, between the PSD and PP (formerly the CDS) in Portugal, and between the UCD and AP in Spain in 1979. The results of the final three steps of that analysis are presented in Table 3.20.

As can be seen from these data, social-structural variables (class position, class identification, trade union membership, religiousness and membership in religious organizations) are very poor predictors of which party within a bloc a voter will support. Indeed, with the exception of the PCE in 1982 (by which time a series of schisms and defections had largely reduced the once-interclassist catch-all party to the traditional working-class core of support for communist parties), in no case did all of these social-structural variables com-

Table 3.20 Competition Within Each Bloc: Cumulative and Incremental Pseudo-R^2

	Spain						
	PCE 79	PCE 82	IU 93	PSOE 79	PSOE 93	UCD 79	AP 79
All social structure combined (cumulative R^2)	.23	.33	.24	.23	.22	.18	.14
Left/right proximity (incremental R^2)	.02	.23	.10	.05	.20	.12	.24
Party leader evaluation (incremental R^2)	.21	.06	.20	.12	.15	.23	.17
All variables combined (cumulative R^2)	.46	.62	.54	.40	.57	.53	.55

	Portugal 1993			
	PCP	PS	PSD	PP
All social structure combined (cumulative R^2)	.23	.20	*	*
Left/right proximity (incremental R^2)	.28	.18	.16	.15
Party leader evaluation (incremental R^2)	.13	.00[1]	.14	.24
All variables combined (cumulative R^2)	.64	.38	.30	.39

	Italy 1996					
	RC	PDS	PPI	Lega	FI	AN
All class variables (cumulative R^2)	.04	.04	.05	.08	.02	.03
Religiosity (incremental R^2)	.11	.02	.18	.03	.00	.00
All social structure variables (cumulative R^2)	.16	.06	.23	.11	.02	.03
Left/right proximity (incremental R^2)	.17	.09	.15	.18	.13	.17
Party leader evaluation (incremental R^2)	.16	.19	.00	.36	.24	.17
All variables combined (cumulative R^2)	.49	.34	.38	.65	.39	.37

[1] R^2 increased by .10 when the name of the longtime PS leader (and former president of Portugal) Mário Soares was substituted for that of the PS's current leader, Antonio Guterres.

bined explain more than one-quarter of the vote. The most interesting barrier between parties within the same bloc separates the generally religious supporters of the Italian PPI (one of the groups formed in the aftermath of the DC's collapse) from the nonreligious or anticlerical supporters of Rifondazione Comunista. The variables representing religiosity (measured by frequency of church attendance and membership in religious organizations) explained between 11 and 18 percent of the variance separating the two. Thus, the religious cleavage that previously separated the parties of the left from those of the right now largely runs through the coalition of parties on the left and has disappeared as a basis of bloc-anchoring of partisanship.

The incremental improvement in predicting the vote within each bloc resulting from the addition of a simple least-distance left-right variable to the equation was also relatively modest. Left-right proximity added over 20 percent to the variance explained in Spanish voters' preference for the Alianza Popular over its more centrist rivals in 1982; in their choices between the PCE/IU and PSOE in both 1982 and 1993; and in differentiating supporters of the PCP in Portugal from those of the Partido Socialista in 1993. These relationships were weaker with regard to other parties. The incremental contribution made by the party-leadership variables is somewhat inconsistent: they were generally low in those cases where social-structural and left/right variables clearly differentiated between parties (e.g., the PCE in 1982, the Portuguese socialists in 1993, and the PPI in 1996), but for other parties they tended to be significant determinants of partisan preference. Particularly noteworthy is the great strength of the relationships linking votes for Italian conservative parties and feelings about their leaders. Fully 36 percent of the vote for the Lega was "explained" by attitudes toward Umberto Bossi (although it must be noted that one potentially powerful variable, region, was not included in these analyses), while nearly a quarter of the support within the conservative bloc for Forza Italia! is explained by the respondents' feelings about Silvio Berlusconi.

If social and ideological cleavages are declining as anchors of partisanship among catch-all parties in many democratic systems, what can we say about the "anchoring" of partisanship in attitudes toward party leaders? One obvious expectation is that the ability of party leaders to attract voters will be quite variable and dependent on a number of exogenous factors. Except in those cases where an individual serves as party leader over an extended period (e.g., Felipe González, Andreas Papandreou, Mário Soares, or Helmut Kohl), the personal attractiveness of the party's top candidate can vary considerably over time, with obvious implications for the party's electoral success (as the leadership of the German SPD and the British Labour Party throughout the 1980s amply demonstrated). Attitudes toward party leaders who head national governments are also very much a function of current economic and social circumstances, largely irrespective of the extent to which those individuals are responsible for creating those circumstances (as the hapless Jimmy Carter found in 1980, victimized by a mob of Iranian fundamentalists and the simultaneous occurrence of a "second oil shock" that devastated the world economy). In short, this variability suggests that countries whose electorates are relatively unanchored may be subject to higher levels of volatility, and the increased role of party leaders as the foci of election campaigns and determinants of the vote may do little to stabilize voting support. Indeed, under conditions of instability at the elite level, this heightened role of party leaders can serve to increase that volatility, as the fate of the Unión de Centro Democrático in Spain (discussed below) clearly attests.

The implications for the quality of democracy of the increasing importance of party leadership, as opposed to more traditional partisan preferences, are significant, but as yet a subject of dispute. Some scholars (see, e.g., van der Eijk and Niemöller 1993) have looked favorably upon this development, insofar as it frees voters from social constraints and enhances their freedom of electoral choice. Similarly, scholars who see increased "cognitive mobilization" as characteristics of modern electorates wax eloquent about dramatic improvements in the quality of citizen participation (see, e.g., Dalton, Beck, and Flanagan 1984, 18). Other observers, however, are less sanguine about the shift toward candidate-centered politics, which has been accompanied by a "dumbing down" of broadcast and print journalism and a personalization and trivialization of news coverage (see, e.g., Patterson 1993; Gunther and Mughan 2000). They are less than optimistic about the ability of citizens to base their electoral decisions on a substantial volume of unbiased and relevant information. Still others speculate that the decline of parties and mass-based secondary organizations as informed intermediaries, translating and channeling otherwise complex and incomprehensible political information to voters, may make informed participation difficult for most citizens faced with manipulative partisan messages channeled through the media in a largely unmediated fashion. Finally, the decline of parties and other politically relevant, broad-based organizations may be undermining the aggregation of interests and leading to a fragmented variety of political competition based on narrow, particularistic single issues (see van der Eijk et al. 1993).

Also worthy of future study are the nature and implications of the increasing importance of the left-right dimension as a basis of electoral anchoring. As we saw in the earlier analyses, social-structural determinants of partisan preference have either declined appreciably (as in Spain and, especially, Italy) or have always been weak (especially in Greece). Nonetheless, partisanship has continued to be structured in a surprisingly durable manner by the increasingly important division between parties of the left and right, both in these countries and elsewhere in western Europe. But what does the left/right cleavage represent? Should it be regarded as the "scar tissue" left behind in the aftermath of the disappearance of the traditional social-structural cleavages? Clearly, in an era of decline of parties based on stable cleavages (whose basic characteristics largely defined the difference between left and right) and an increase in some countries of more transitory factors (e.g., leadership rivalries and "single-issue politics"), a rigorous cross-national analysis of the evolving meanings of left and right is timely.

Toward an Explanation

This study has suggested that the bases of partisan support in elections are affected by a confluence of several factors. These certainly include the fundamental socioeconomic and cultural characteristics of a society. If deep social cleavages are not present in a society, for example, parties will have a difficult time "encapsulating" segments of the electorate based on social cleavages. Accordingly, the absence of deep religious or class cleavages in Greece is clearly reflected in the very small percentage of variance in electoral support explained by social-structural variables. At the other extreme is the Italian First Republic, born in a society riven by traditional cleavages between Catholic and socialist subcultures and anchoring bloc loyalties so effectively as to produce DC-dominated centrist governments throughout more than four decades of its existence.

The findings of this study also suggest, however, that the relationship between social structure and partisanship is far from deterministic. The bases of partisanship in Spain in 1979 and Portugal until the late 1980s, for example, significantly depart from what might have been predicted on the basis of social structure alone. In both of these countries there was a wider potential gap between religious believers and nonbelievers than in Italy, and Portugal had the most inegalitarian distribution of income in western Europe, and yet social-structural variables were much less powerful as determinants of support for the two main rival parties. Why did the anchoring of partisanship become so much deeper in Spain following the 1982 election—in essence "freezing" the Spanish party system into a highly unbalanced two-party rivalry for over a decade? And, most dramatically, why did the Italian party system, which had been so well anchored in Italian social cleavages, and, as a result, so stable for so long, abruptly collapse, to be replaced by a party system largely unaffected by the once-dominant religious cleavage?

We contend that these developments are related to "institutionalized historical legacies," to the behavior of party elites, and, in some degree, to the peculiar circumstances surrounding their respective transitions to democracy. In short, the manner in which political elites made strategic decisions translating latent or potential social cleavages into overt, institutionalized political divisions had a lasting effect on the underpinnings of partisanship in these countries (see Przeworski and Sprague 1986). Similarly, the abrupt and radical transformations of the Spanish party system in 1982 and the Italian party system in 1994 were produced by developments at the elite level. In short, while mass-level social characteristics are important determinants of patterns of partisanship, these relationships are established through an interactive process in which voters react to stimuli presented to them by elites. In the early stages of establishment of these party systems, elites help to structure party systems by developing and implementing social mobilization strategies, taking into account the contours of the societies within which they operate. The destruction of party systems, however, is more commonly the product of a reaction against party elites by a disgusted electorate.

Italy

Among the four southern European countries, Italy is the clearest case of cleavage or conflict encapsulation by political parties. The party system that existed until 1994 was founded in the aftermath of World War II, with many of its key organizational features strongly affected by the Catholic mobilization against the left in the early stages of the Cold War. But the roots of partisanship in Italy considerably predate that period, reaching all the way back to the Risorgimento, when two subcultures—one *rossa* and the other *bianca*—emerged as byproducts of the founding of the Italian nation-state. Since that process involved an assault on the political power and economic base of the Catholic Church in certain regions, it is not surprising to find that a deep religious cleavage quickly emerged in the new polity. This cleavage was, in fact, formalized with the issuance of the *non expedit* by the Church directly challenging the legitimacy of the new state and ordering Catholics to refuse to participate in the electoral politics of the new regime (see Cotta 1992a; Sasoon 1988, 220–21; Pombeni 1985). This directive had a considerable and lasting impact on the political orientations of rural Catholics, in particular, especially as the Church chose to address the "religious question" through development of extraparliamentary forms of protest and organization under the guidance of the Opera dei Congressi (formed in 1874 as a federation of Catholic organizations with a strong social presence and under the supervision of the Church hierarchy [see Kalyvas 1996]). The "red" subculture also emerged in reaction against certain aspects of the Risorgimento and the early governments of the newly united Italy, particularly the economic liberalism that characterized the new state, coupled with effective exclusion of the working classes from conventional political participation through the sharply restricted suffrage and *trasformismo*. Working-class alienation was channeled through the Italian Socialist Party (PSI) and affiliated secondary associations. The granting of universal suffrage in 1919, the opening up of the legislative arena through a shift to proportional representation, and formation of the Catholic Partito Popolare converted these social cleavages into organized partisan divisions.

Despite the brevity of full democracy in Italy and a fascist interlude of over two decades, this political cleavage was clearly reflected by parties that reemerged in the postwar era. Continuities between the electoral results of 1946 and those of 1919 and 1921 meant that these historical cleavages would continue to affect Italian partisan competition, and that networks of secondary organizations that had survived Mussolini's authoritarian regime would serve as supportive infrastructures for the remobilization of Italian voters.[23] It was, however, the strategy of the political leaders of the postwar era, particularly Alcide De Gasperi, that most firmly anchored Italian partisanship in these associational networks. De Gasperi felt that the establishment of democratic legitimacy and the assertion of political authority over traditionally dominant elites (unrepentant monarchists among them) required a deeper social basis than would have been provided by a parliamentary majority alone (Pombeni 1985, 373). And the outbreak of the Cold War created an environment highly consistent with his efforts to create a powerful political party with a strong base in the

Catholic subculture. The decision by the Vatican (under the militantly anticommunist Pope Pius XII) to collaborate actively with this strategy was crucial. Indeed, in terms of providing an infrastructure for a new political party, the mobilization of 25,000 priests (under the direction of Luigi Gedda and Catholic Action) must be regarded as decisive in encapsulating a large and (for some time) dominant segment of the electorate within a party of the center and right, which emerged as a bulwark against communism. The result was an enduring polarization between the two subcultures—now led by the two largest parties in Italy, one communist and the other Catholic and anticommunist—even decades later, when the cultural and social-structural basis that had given birth to this structure of competition had begun to erode away.

One final, less dramatic aspect of this politicization of secondary organizations shifts our attention from the electoral arena to the interest-articulation process. Far from being neutral, open, and universalistic, channels of access to governmental decision makers were highly politicized, often conforming to the classic *clientela* and *parentela* models described by Joseph LaPalombara and others (see LaPalombara 1964; Menapace 1974). The institutional penetration of the DC into Italian society was thus strengthened, insofar as individuals found political advantage in working through the DC's links with Catholic Action, Confindustria, the Coltivattore Diretti, and so on (Morlino 1998). Patterns of clientelism and favoritism spilled over into outright corruption, however, popular revulsion against which eventually triggered the collapse of the old party system.

In short, in Italy, the social-structuration of partisanship was hardly an accident; but neither was it an automatic outgrowth of social structure per se. It was the deliberate product of the party-building and institutionalization strategies of elites at a crucial formative stage in the reemergence of competitive politics. By the beginning of the 1990s, however, several important social and political changes had occurred. The socioeconomic development of the preceding decades greatly softened the class polarization that had characterized the immediate postwar years, when the First Republic's party system took shape. A far-reaching process of secularization had taken place, making the traditional religious cleavage in Italian society less relevant to everyday politics, and reducing the capacity of the Church to mobilize its electorate. And the collapse of communism in eastern Europe appeared to make the divide between left and right a less salient division in Italian society (Mannheimer and Sani 1987, 137).

Some political elites responded to these altered circumstances by reconfiguring their party organizations and programs. The first to do so was the Partito Comunista Italiano. In an effort to bring the PCI, its programs, and its ideology into closer accord with the realities of a modern, affluent Italy in the post-Soviet era, thereby enhancing its appeal to a broader segment of the Italian electorate, the majority faction of the party (under the leadership of Achille Occhetto) established the Partito Democratico della Sinistra. The founding of the post-Eurocommunist PDS had the unintentional effect of triggering a schism. More orthodox communists in the PCI split from the majority and gave their support to the new Rifondazione Comunista. Not only did this mean that the former PCI vote would now be divided between two parties, but it also created a sort of synergy in reverse, in which the organizational bases of the parties emerging out of the PCI together were weaker than the former party had been, declining from 1.3 million members in 1990 to a combined total of just 811,000 in 1993 (see Table 8.1 in this volume). Nonetheless, the new PDS appeared to be well positioned to take advantage of the scandals and crises that beset the traditional governing parties in the early 1990s and emerge from the ghetto of seemingly permanent opposition in which it had been trapped for over four decades as the bête noire of the Cold War era.

At the same time, the governing DC was experiencing a process of organizational decline, with its membership falling from 2.1 million in 1990 to 814,000 just three years later (Leonardo Morlino, personal communication). The real cause for alarm, however, was the outbreak of corruption scandals of startling magnitude, which affected all of the parties of the traditional DC-dominated centrist coalitions. Faced with the impending wrath of voters, and following a long intraparty struggle and replacement of its party secretary in 1993, the DC sought to transform its program and organization. As we saw in Chapter 2, this led to the fragmentation of the once-dominant centrist party into several different parties and factions. The organizational strength of the DC was shattered, and its once-unified "political offering" to Italian voters disappeared on the eve of the 1994 elections. Similar developments fragmented the elites and organizational resources of the socialist, republican, and liberal parties, leading to their disappearance or rebirth with different names and coalition partners. Thus, in the 1994 election, voters were presented with a new set of political parties and new leaderships competing under a new electoral law that led them to adopt new strategies for mobilizing votes.

A widespread electoral rebellion against the established elites (the origins of which are analyzed by Giacomo Sani and Paolo Segatti in

Chapter 4 of this volume) culminated in eradication of the old partisan political order and the coming to power as prime minister of a political novice, Silvio Berlusconi, who had campaigned against parties and the old style of politics, and who based his own campaign on saturation coverage of his candidacy by private television networks (which he owned) and by political mobilization of his business enterprises and his network of soccer clubs. As we saw earlier in this chapter, the 1994 Italian election produced the second-highest total volatility score of any European election in the twentieth century. It also represented a revolutionary change in both the nature of Italian campaign politics and of the structure of interelite coalitions. For the first time, the postfascist right wing of Italian politics was allowed to enter the governing coalition, as did representatives of the Lega Nord, a regional social movement (rather than a party) demanding autonomy (if not independence) from the rest of Italy. These governing parties articulated programs and visions of the future significantly different from those that had accompanied the establishment of the first Italian party system of the postwar era.

We have also seen how the social bases of partisanship were thoroughly altered. The social-structuration of partisan differences weakened considerably, as did religious cleavage. It is important to note that although the direction of change is compatible with a model of electoral change driven by social modernization (with the long-term secularization of Italian society eventually reflected in patterns of partisanship, and with *embourgeoisement* leading to a reduction in the electoral importance of class variables), the process by which this adjustment took place is not explicable in this way. Rather than incrementally diminishing in accordance with the gradual transformation of Italian society, voting remained anchored in the traditional cleavages for decades. When change took place, it was abrupt, dramatic, and triggered by events whose origins were to be found at the elite level of the polity.[24] In many respects, the Italian party system transformation of 1994 can be regarded as an "earthquake": pressure built up for decades as the tectonic plates of social change pushed inexorably, but the plates remained stuck in place until the scandals of the early 1990s abruptly shattered the old party structures.

Despite the magnitude of this transformation, the bloc-anchoring of the Italian electorate persisted, this time defined primarily along the ideological or attitudinal lines of left versus right. Despite the opportunity presented by the collapse of the traditionally governing parties, and by its efforts to organizationally and programmatically adapt to the circumstances of modern Italy, this newly reconstituted barrier prevented the PDS from significantly surpassing its traditional share of votes and becoming a party of government at the national level.

This situation was altered only following a new set of developments at the elite level. Conflict among the governing elites (particularly pitting the Lega's Umberto Bossi against Prime Minister Silvio Berlusconi) led to the collapse of the conservative coalition and, eventually, to new elections. This time, the PDS significantly altered its strategy, forging an alliance, l'Ulivo ("The Olive Tree") with the progressive faction that had splintered off from the DC, the Partito Popolare Italiano, and supporting Romano Prodi (not a member of the party) as its candidate for prime minister. This alliance between the postcommunist left and progressive Catholics succeeded in bringing the left to power for the first time in postwar history. Given the alliance's dependence on the deputies of Rifondazione Communista, it also meant that the "religious cleavage" would run within the coalition of the left, and would no longer serve as the principal source of differentiation of the left from the right.

Portugal

Portugal is an anomalous case. Despite the fact that its population is the most conservative and religious among the four southern European countries we have surveyed, until 1987 postrevolutionary Portuguese politics was largely dominated by parties of the left. And despite the fact that the survey data presented in the opening section of this chapter reveal a high level of potential polarization along the class and religious cleavages, social-structural variables are much less powerful as determinants of partisanship than in Italy. To be sure, the PCP is well rooted among the working classes of Lisbon and the latifundist Alentejo, but the other parties had very shallow social-structural anchors at the time of the 1985 survey. The barrier between the PS and PSD was so low as to allow for substantial cross-cleavage flows of votes from one election to the next.

In an effort to explain these anomalies, we would simply hypothesize that the circumstances of the Portuguese revolution constrained political elites—particularly those on the right—at the crucial period when parties were being organized. In the early stages of the revolution, largely dominated by forces on the extreme left, no party dared present itself as truly conservative. Indeed, in this early phase, both the CDS and PPD (precursor of the PSD) were harassed by leftists in parts of the country, and the more conservative Christian Democratic Party (PDC) was outlawed following António de Spínola's attempted coup of March 11, 1975. These disruptions both impeded organizational development and campaign activities and, presumably, contributed to the much poorer showing by the CDS and PPD than in any subsequent election. Second, both the PPD and CDS presented themselves during the first election campaign as parties much farther to the left than their subsequent behavior would justify, and than the relatively religious and conservative Portuguese electorate might have preferred. Accordingly, the PPD remained within the government in coalition with the PCP and PS until mid July 1975; it applied unsuccessfully for membership in the Socialist International; and it issued explicitly social democratic programmatic appeals. Similarly, the CDS posed as a centrist party, supporting worker participation in industry, expanded welfare services, and state intervention in the economy. Over time, both parties would drift toward the right: the PPD (despite renaming itself the Partido Social-Democrata in 1976) would emerge as a center-to-center-right party, and the CDS would be regarded as a party of the right. But at the crucial formative period in their respective histories, they abstained from establishing overtly conservative bases of support and institutional ties such as those that linked the DC to Catholic organizations in Italy (Lewis and Williams 1984; Gunther 1988).

It should be noted that from at least one perspective, the absence of deep interbloc-anchoring can serve a useful purposes. Indeed, "stabilization" of the party system is not very far conceptually from "stagnation," and too deep an anchoring of partisanship can preclude a healthy alternation in power between parties on opposite sides of the left-right barrier. Conversely, opposition parties of the center-left or center-right may gain more electorally if the barrier dividing the two sides of the political spectrum is relatively low. In this respect, one could argue that the great electoral victories of the center-right PSD in 1987 and 1991 had been facilitated by the fact that the party itself had shifted from its superficial stance on the left in the 1970s to the right side of the political continuum, thereby blurring the dividing line between left and right and reducing the salience of this division in the electorate. This low barrier also meant that the Socialist Party would more easily come to power in 1995, thus initiating a pattern of alternation in power between single-party governments of the center-right and center-left. It can be argued that alternation in power between moderate parties like these is healthy for democratic systems. Thus, the moderately higher levels of interbloc volatility that have characterized Portuguese electoral politics can be regarded as a positive development.

Spain

In Spain, since a civil war had relatively recently been fought over social-cleavage issues, it was perhaps inevitable that social cleavages would be imprinted into partisanship, even after nearly four decades of authoritarian rule. Juan Linz and José María Maravall, for example, have pointed to a strong ecological correlation between the vote in 1977 and electoral support in 1936 (the last democratic election before the Spanish Civil War), and have also documented the extent to which bloc loyalties were transmitted intergenerationally (Maravall 1978 and 1981, 39; Linz 1980). Nonetheless, the founding party elites of the new democratic era adopted strategies to mitigate class and religious divisions, and they consequently did not establish institutional linkages with secondary organizations (with the exception of ties between the socialist and communist parties and trade unions). These strategies were motivated by two different sets of concerns. The first was electoral in nature. All four nationwide parties bought into the "catch-all" model, and eschewed close institutionalized links with other groups (see Gunther, Sani, and Shabad 1986, esp. 113–77). Believing that most Spanish voters were moderate if not centrist in their ideological stands and programmatic preferences, they all adopted moderate—if not bland, copycat—electoral positions. This shift toward the center provoked severe crises within the two parties of the left (contributing to the eventual rupture of close relations between the UGT and the PSOE), partly alienating them from their traditional clienteles. Avoidance of polarization along traditionally explosive cleavage lines was also motivated by concerns over the survival and consolidation of the new democratic regimes. In contrast with the rancorous, polarizing birth of the Second Republic, elites of all four nationwide parties in the 1970s chose to enter into "the politics of consensus" (see Gunther 1992; Linz 1993) and to adopt markedly moderate stands. Partisan loyalties among Spanish voters may have been weakened by these consensus-building and conciliatory interactions among party elites, which were such central elements in Spain's transition to democracy. "Non-divisive issues that do not involve an exclusive appeal to distinct social groups are less likely to activate primary groups and mobilize strong partisanship," Ivor Crewe has suggested (1976, 58; see also Barnes, McDonough, and López Pina 1985, 715–16). In short, while "the politics of consensus" may have facilitated democratic consolidation by leading competing party elites to seek to resolve divisive issues (rather than articulating them for partisan purposes), to avoid rancorous interparty clashes, and to demobilize their respective blocs of supporters, it also may have lessened intergroup hostilities to a degree that undermined the development of stable partisan loyalties. In this respect, the extremely high total electoral volatility that characterized the 1982 party-system realignment, and the absence of strong attachments to political parties over an even longer term, may be regarded as one of the costs of the consensual path to democratic consolidation.

Although ideological and programmatic moderation would continue to characterize Spanish parties in the 1980s and 1990s, "the politics of consensus" clearly ended in 1979. The new democratic order having been set in place and enshrined in a new constitution and autonomy statutes for the Basque and Catalan regions, Adolfo Súarez, the leading centrist politician, came under intense personal attack from the PSOE, the main opposition party, and particularly from other UCD elites. These attacks had the dual effect of terminating Suárez's leadership (and destroying one of the UCD's principal electoral assets in the process), as well as of recasting the electoral dialogue in Spain in such a manner as to much more clearly articulate the choice between the left (PSOE) and right (AP). The resulting party-system realignment of 1982 brought voting behavior into much clearer alignment with the traditionally divisive cleavages in Spanish society. With the replacement of the centrist, vigorously interclassist, catch-all UCD by the AP, a profound social-structural crystallization and anchoring of the Spanish party system took place. At a time when the majority of Spanish voters were of the center-left and the AP/PP was perceived as a decidedly right-wing party, this created a highly unbalanced two-party competition that effectively isolated the AP/PP on the opposition benches of parliament for over a decade. At the same time, it should be noted that the firm social-structural and ideological anchoring of support for the AP/PP enabled it to undergo three changes in party leadership (Manuel Fraga Iribarne to Hernández Mancha, then back to Fraga, and then Fraga to José María Aznar in a period of three years) and a number of dramatic changes in its organizational format (especially its "refounding" as the Partido Popular in 1989) without suffering any significant electoral decline.

What is particularly noteworthy in the case of Spain is that this cleavage structure has undergone significant changes since 1982: subsequently, a process of dealignment has taken place as the social-structural bases of support for parties began to erode. The PSOE government increasingly found itself in conflict with its allied trade union, the UGT, and these rancorous relations eventually culminated in a rather nasty divorce. The PSOE government's pursuit of moderate (if not downright neoliberal) fiscal and monetary policies and its restructuring of parastate industries led to dissatisfaction over persistently high levels of unemployment, which were only partially ameliorated by its expansion of welfare policies (Maravall 1997; Boix 1998a). The secularization of Spanish society, the party strategies of not building political identities on the religious cleavage, and the scrupulous avoidance of public debate over potentially divisive issues relating to religious beliefs (such as abortion) greatly reduced the religious divisions between left and right (Montero and Calvo 1999). And the entry of an entirely new cohort of voters into the electorate further muddled the relationship between social-structural factors and partisanship.

Did this culminate in an unanchored electorate, as an exclusive focus on social cleavages might imply? No, because by 1993 the division between the PP and PSOE had largely been translated into ideological identities expressed in left-right terms. Indeed, what we may be observing is a manifestation of the "freezing" of partisanship noted long ago in Lipset and Rokkan 1967. In this respect, the cleavage that currently divides the Spanish party system may be regarded as not so much a reflection of the *present* class positions and religious orientations of Spanish voters as it is a reconfiguration of the competition between Spanish parties that resulted from an earlier critical election—that of 1982. The left-right dimension (long a subject of scholarly debate) appears to function as a repository of the historical memory of past partisan conflicts, encapsulating a rudimentary but nonetheless effective identification with the main parties and serving as an anchoring device in the absence of strong psychological identification with parties or institutionalized links to organized social interests.

This firm ideological anchoring continued to shut off the conservative Partido Popular from the moderate majority of voters even after the social-structural anchors of partisanship had weakened. The PP's prospects for electoral victory were thus a function of two factors: a decline in the popularity of the leader of the PSOE (which had become very much a personalistic, catch-all party), and a significant change in the public's perception of the PP's ideological stance. The popularity of Felipe González and the Partido Socialista did, in fact, erode prior to the 1993 elections. Indeed, in the face of persistent scandals, it appeared that the PSOE would be swept from power as early as 1993. However, the continuing strength of the ideological anchoring of electoral behavior, coupled with the PP's image as a right-wing party (placed at 8.2 on the left-right scale—far from the mean self-placement of voters at 4.7), drastically limited the interbloc shift of votes (to just 1.7 percent) and enabled the PSOE to remain in power. Similarly, following further erosion of the images of González and his party, this continuing ideological distance between the PP and the modal voter in 1996 allowed the PP to come to power with only the narrowest margin of victory. The PP was able to sweep to office with a sizable majority only in 2000, by which time its moderate behavior in office over the previous three years had convinced many voters that it was less conservative than it had been previously (shifting to 7.6 on the left-right scale), while many Spanish voters had themselves shifted from the center-left to the center (see Table 3.9).

Greece

Greece has emerged from this analysis as a truly exceptional case. Its population is more homogeneous than those of other southern European countries in terms of religion and the distribution of wealth, and in the absence of a significant regional cleavage. Lacking divisive social-structural cleavages, the bloc-anchoring barrier of Greece's party system is lower than those of the Spanish and Italian party systems. One obvious explanation of this finding is that inasmuch as the Greek population is socially homogeneous, it is unlikely that its electorate would be deeply divided and anchored by social cleavages. The Greek party system in the mid 1980s was, however, highly polarized on the left-right continuum. We contend that the answers to both of these puzzles—the absence of politically relevant social cleavages and the extent of ideological polarization in Greece—are the legacies of historical conflicts in interaction with strategic choices made by current political elites.

Twentieth-century Greek history has been marked by intense, destabilizing political conflict, including a period of profound social and political division (1916–17) during World War I, attempted coups in the interwar period, and the Civil War (1946–49). The ideological polarization of the electorate in the 1980s can be partially regarded as the scar tissue left over from past political fights. Those conflicts, however, almost invariably cross-cut lines of social cleavage, thereby reducing the political salience of those cleavages. The principal political cleavage in the first half of the twentieth century was an intraclass conflict between a traditionalist, monarchical right and a more democratic, modernizing republican force near the center of the political spectrum, both of which were supported by property-owning strata of Greek society. The working-class left was electorally insignificant, in part owing to the absence of the kind of class structure most commonly conducive to support for socialist, communist, and anarchist parties and movements, with the communist KKE receiving about 6–7 percent of the vote during the interwar period.

The most fundamental conflict of the early twentieth century was one that divided the Greek bourgeoisie into supporters of a strong monarchy, on the one hand, and those favoring a more limited form of constitutional monarchy or a liberal republic, on the other. Unlike the constitutional monarchies that had developed in most other parts of Europe following World War I, the Greek crown frequently intervened in partisan politics in a manner that violated the basic tenets of democracy and popular sovereignty (see Macridis 1981). The principal opponent of the monarchy during the interwar period was the Liberal Party under Eleftherios Venizelos, a nationalist modernizer and social reformer, who initially clashed with King Constantine I over whether Greece should enter World War I. Over the following twenty years, Greek politics was dominated by an unresolved struggle between liberal Venizelists and more conservative, monarchist anti-Venizelists. Although it to some degree involved economic issues, with the conservative landowning bourgeoisie supporting the monarchy, and more entrepreneurial sectors of the bourgeoisie and beneficiaries of Venizelos's land-reform policies (see Mavrogordatos 1983c) backing the Liberal Party, this struggle can by no means be regarded as "class conflict." Neither can it be regarded as analogous to the religious/anticlerical conflicts that divided the bourgeoisie in Italy, Portugal, or Spain in the nineteenth and early twentieth centuries. This period of unstable politics came to an end with King George II's proclamation of a dictatorship under General Ioannis Metaxas, who presided over an authoritarian regime from 1936 until the beginning of the Nazi occupation in 1941. The close association of the crown with the repressive Metaxas regime intensified and broadened hostility toward the monarchy.

In the course of World War II, the communist KKE grew enormously in political power owing to its participation in the anti-Nazi resistance movement. Following the war, the KKE-led leftist coalition adopted an antisystem stance, refusing to participate in the first postwar parliamentary elections in 1946, and leading an insurrection following restoration of the monarchy. This added a second ideological cleavage to the Greek political spectrum: in addition to the fading conflict between center and right over the monarchy, a civil war erupted between communists and anticommunists. This culminated in the trimodal and highly polarized distribution of Greeks on the left-right political spectrum, but it did not politicize or polarize society along class or religious lines. The communist rebellion was put down by the end of the 1940s, but it left an important political legacy in the form of a virulent anticommunism on the right and ostracism of the left from full participation in parliamentary and electoral politics (see Papayannakis 1981).

Thus, the most divisive conflicts that took place in Greece prior to the restoration of democracy in 1974 were highly polarizing, but they were essentially unrooted in fundamental class or religious cleavages. We contend that this is one of the factors that contributed to the relatively weak bloc-anchoring of the Greek electorate. Bloc-anchoring is also weak because of the manner in which Greece's contemporary political parties were founded. In creating Nea Demokratia and PASOK, Constantine Karamanlis and Andreas Papandreou either intentionally or unintentionally took steps that had the effect of blurring the traditional lines separating left from center from right. Karamanlis initiated this transformation of Greek party politics in two ways. First, he dissociated the right from the monarchy by convening a referendum on the monarchy and taking a neutral stand in that referendum. Given the unpopularity of the crown (whose meddling in partisan politics continued well into the 1960s and played a significant role in creating the conditions that led to the colonels' coup in 1967), this stance may have been electorally wise. But it also had the dual effects of laying to rest the monarchy/republic cleavage and redefining the right as a modern and fully democratic force (see Karakatsanis 1996). In defining Nea Demokratia's ideology and setting forth a set of programmatic principles, Karamanlis also moved the party away from the rigid and exclusionary traditionalism of the right and embraced the cause of modernization via a new "radical liberalism" (Loulis 1981a, esp. 81–82; Mavrogordatos 1981). In founding PASOK, Papandreou also blurred ideological cleavage lines. Even though his new party could be traced back to the Center Union (which his father had once headed), the initial ideological stance of the party was markedly leftist. But after initially staking out a "Marxist" and "socialist" position, the party moved back toward the center, eventually coming to power in 1981 as a party of the center-left.

Perhaps most important, both Karamanlis and Papandreou pursued relatively pragmatic catch-all strategies, focusing on their own prominent (indeed charismatic) personalities, while their political discourses polarized along ideological lines. As a result, in terms of the clienteles they hoped to attract, their organizational strategies, programs, campaign appeals, and ideological orientations, both of the electorally dominant parties in contemporary Greece intentionally eschewed traditional lines of social cleavage, although they still displayed a remarkable degree of ideological polarization.

This pattern underwent significant change following Papandreou's death in 1996. The rise of Costas Simitis to power has been accompanied by an increasing distancing from populist practices and rhetoric, as well as from the polarizing discourse so typical of his predecessor. In addition, the party's electoral appeals and programs have been characterized by a conscious adoption of moderate reformist ideas and principles. These ideas and principles became all the more dominant in the party's discourse as the country drew nearer to its goal of meeting criteria for entry into the European Monetary Union, which was widely expected to occur in January 2001. These features were especially prominent in the 2000 election campaign and underscore the party's desire to bring Greece closer into line with other EU countries.

The trend toward moderation and away from the polarizing logic of the past has also been discernible in Nea Demokratia since 1997, when Kostas Karamanlis (a nephew of the party's founder) assumed leadership. It was especially notable during the 2000 election campaign, when Karamanlis explicitly adopted a discourse identifying Nea Demokratia with the "middle ground" in Greek politics and placed a cohort of younger associates in positions of leadership in the party. Despite considerable grumbling from representatives of the older generation and the party's unreconstructed right wing, as well as from the rank and file ill at ease with the notion of the "middle ground," this trend seemed to persist even after the party lost its third straight election.

It remains to be seen whether this trend will persist, or whether it will prove to have been merely an astute electoral move designed to gain votes. If it crystallizes, it will contribute further to the moderation and pragmatism that have become salient features of Greek politics, beginning in the late 1990s, and will further enhance the political system's centripetal logic.

Some Concluding Reflections

It is clear that the social structure of a country has a considerable impact on the structure of partisanship that underpins democratic competition. To some extent, differences among these four southern European democracies, as well as changes over time within countries, can be accounted for by such social-structural factors. But we have also seen evidence that the relationship between social structure and social change, on the one hand, and the structure of partisan competition, on the other, is neither direct, deterministic, nor even merely reflective. We have seen that initial expectations concerning the likely outlines of party competition may be significantly divergent from those that actually emerge. Although the depth of the religious cleavage in Spain might have led one to expect that its post-Franco party system would feature a sizable Christian Democratic party as one of its key players, no such party actually came into existence. And despite the strength of religious sentiment in Portugal, politics there was dominated by parties of the left for more than a decade following the reestablishment of democracy, and partisanship is only weakly anchored in the religious cleavage. The pace of change in the social underpinnings of partisan competition may also depart substantially from what one might have predicted on the basis of social or cultural change per se. In contrast, for example, to the Netherlands, where continuous, incremental changes in partisanship over two decades can be seen to correspond roughly to the pace of secularization of Dutch society (van der Eijk and Niemöller 1992), the long-term secularization of Italian society did not produce significant change in the social bases of partisanship for over two decades: the religious cleavage separating parties of left and right remained largely intact throughout the 1970s and 1980s, and when change occurred, it did so abruptly. Finally, in some countries, the direction of change may be the opposite of what might have been predicted. In the case of Spain, a marked class polarization occurred between 1979 and 1982 that did not in any way have its origins in the mass-level characteristics of Spanish society. The same happened in the United States, where polarization increased along both class and religious lines, and, albeit to a lesser degree, in Britain, where class polarization increased somewhat between 1970 and 1987.

In our efforts to explain these anomalies, we have been drawn to the manner in which parties formulate their vote-mobilization strategies and present partisan alternatives to voters. The elite-driven collapse of the interclassist UCD and its replacement by the much more homogeneously middle-class AP as the principal party on the right of center in Spanish politics helps to account for the increased polarization that occurred in 1982. Similarly, the politicization of fundamentalist religion in the United States, the breakdown of the Democratic Party in the South, and the harsher policies toward the poor initiated by the Reagan administration help to explain the increased polarization in the United States, just as the breakdown of the "collectivist consensus" in Britain and its replacement by Thatcherite neoliberalism contributed to a slight increase in class polarization between the early 1970s and the late 1980s. And, in the case of Italy, we are led to wonder whether the religious basis of partisanship would have disappeared if the corruption and scandals of the early 1990s had not led to the destruction of the Christian Democratic party on the eve of the 1994 election. We conclude that these patterns of development of political parties in southern Europe can only be interpreted in light of the autonomous intermediary role played by political elites between social-structural factors and voting behavior.

When elites or party institutions evolve and adapt to changing circumstances (often in anticipation of an altered structure of electoral incentives), voters can respond to the possibility of change more readily. On the other hand, when partisan alignments are rigidly institutionalized, or when there are significant barriers to institutional change, cleavages may be frozen into patterns of voting until well past their period of high salience or even relevance to contemporary society. Differences between the Netherlands and Italy provide good examples. Given the absence of barriers to the entry of new parties inherent in the extremely proportional Dutch electoral law, partisan options presented to voters have changed incrementally and regularly over the past few decades. Accordingly, changes in voters' attitudinal predispositions (produced by *embourgeoisement,* secularization, or the emergence of postmaterial values) can be readily reflected in their electoral choices. In contrast, the Italian party system was thoroughly institutionalized along the lines initially established in the 1940s, some small-scale schisms from the PSI and PCI notwithstanding. Accordingly, value change could not be readily translated into electoral change until the early 1990s, when the parties themselves initiated processes of change (whether intentional, as in the case of the PCI, or not) that had the consequence of loosening their ties to the social structure. Thus, the partisan options presented to voters in 1994 were significantly different from those of previous elections. This "unfroze" the party system quite abruptly and made possible a radical realignment.

In short, this analysis of the anchors of partisanship has led to a reaffirmation of the role of party elites and institutions as autonomous actors within the changing social context of competitive politics.

4 Antiparty Politics and the Restructuring of the Italian Party System

Giacomo Sani and Paolo Segatti

In the course of two successive elections in the early 1990s, the Italian party system underwent a complete transformation. Throughout the first four decades of postwar competition, the electorate had displayed a very low level of volatility, change from one election to another was incremental and moderate, and governments displayed an extremely high level of continuity, in terms of both the parties and the individual politicians that formed the governing coalitions. The party system that emerged from the 1994 election was, however, totally different. Not one party remained unchanged. Some, anticipating a significant transformation of the political environment, had adapted by changing their names, symbols, and so on, in advance of that election. Others fragmented, and their leaders were redistributed among new political groupings. Still others disappeared from the political landscape altogether. At the same time, new protagonists appeared on the scene—most notably the Lega Nord and Forza Italia!—challenging the remnants of the old political class.[1]

This dramatic development raises several questions. As we saw in Chapter 3, one of the reasons why the Italian party system had been so stable from the early 1950s through the late 1980s was that it was well anchored in Italian society. Parties that had adopted mass-membership organizational structures had large bases of support. Levels of party identification were relatively high, certainly in comparison with other southern European polities. And the major parties were rooted in significant networks of secondary associations, especially trade union and religious organizations. How could such a well-anchored party system collapse with such rapidity? Does this represent complete discontinuity with the past? Was this outcome entirely unpredictable given our previous knowledge of the Italian electorate and Italian society? Was this dramatic development the product of causal factors particular to Italy, or was it the consequence of social trends (such as secularization, the erosion of class cleavages, etc.) found in a large number of Western democracies? And if it was the result of these broader social trends, can the Italian case be regarded as a harbinger of things to come in a number of established democracies?

We contend that this development can be attributed, at least in part, to certain distinguishing features of Italian political culture that had been present over the previous decades. As chapters 7 and 10 in *The Politics of Democratic Consolidation* indicate, public opinion in Italy has long been characterized by pervasive cynicism about parties and politicians. This stood as a paradoxical counterpoint to the fact that many Italians identified with parties and consistently supported them over several successive elections. Similarly, the consolidation of democracy in Italy, as manifested at the mass level in the high degree of democratic legitimacy, was juxtaposed with surprisingly widespread and intense dissatisfaction with the performance of Italy's democratic system. These long-standing negative sentiments about parties and politics were inflamed in the early 1990s by a series of short-term events (including illegal financing of political parties, alleged links with organized crime, and criminal indictments of prominent figures such as the former prime ministers Giulio Andreotti and Bettino Craxi) that galvanized the electorate and led to a precipitous decline in support for the existing parties. But these short-term factors would not have had such a devastating impact on the party system had it not been for the long-term weakening of the anchors of partisanship, which had enabled it to survive such crises in the past. It is not our intention in this chapter to recount the political scandals that provided the short-term stimulus for the collapse of the old order (see Della Porta 1992; Guarnieri 1992); neither shall we examine in detail the erosion of the organizational bases of partisanship (see Chapter 3 above and Morlino 1995). Our objective is to link these developments to the long-standing but previously neglected political-cultural origins of this change—the cynicism about and pervasive dissatisfaction with politics and politicians that had long been characteristics of Italian public opinion (see Morlino and Tarchi 1996 for a slightly different approach to this question).

To be sure, Italy was not unique with regard to the presence of such orientations among its electorate. Over the preceding two decades, social scientists in a number of democratic countries had uncovered evidence of a malaise affecting the relationship between the citizenry and the political system, and particularly between voters and parties.

Among other things, there appears to have been an erosion of the bond that once linked electors to political groups. Those who identified themselves with political parties have been progressively replaced by more independent voters who make up their minds more in terms of issues than of comprehensive worldviews (Dalton 1987). This is the result of deep social and cultural transformations, including an atomization of society that has weakened group or class linkages. Increased levels of education have modified citizens' expectations of the performance of the polity. Whereas parties could once count on the voters' deference, citizens seem more recently to prefer a direct relationship with political authorities through increased use of instruments of direct democracy such as the referendum (Inglehart 1990). Seen in this light, the crisis of participation that has affected parties and trade unions would seem attributable to a growing demand for new and more direct forms of involvement in politics, rather than to increasing apathy. Additional factors within the sphere of politics itself have also been regarded as significant causes of this phenomenon, such as the evolution of parties from mass to catch-all organizations (Mair 1992), as well as the prominent role played in political life by television (Sartori 1989).

There are, however, at least two peculiar aspects to the Italian confidence gap: it must in some respects be seen as a long-standing phenomenon, related to the way Italian democracy was consolidated after World War II. In addition, its alarming proportions raise questions about the extent to which persistent negative attitudes to politics can be important destabilizing factors.

Students of Italian politics have often noted the paradox of a strong party system operating in a political culture characterized by diffuse antiparty feelings (LaPalombara 1987). Seen from one vantage point, postwar Italian parties were a success story: they were able to quickly secure and maintain substantial electoral and organizational support. This was a particularly notable achievement if one considers how much Italian society was changing over the decades following World War II. At the same time, however, parties were often the target of criticism, and feelings of diffidence permeated popular as well as elite perceptions of the political class. In order to understand this apparent puzzle, we need to consider in some detail the two sides of the picture.

The Strength of Historical Parties

When democratic political life resumed in Italy after World War II, several political groups appeared on the scene. Some of these were newly born; others were reconstituted. They soon developed well-articulated organizational structures and quickly put down roots in the electorate. Seven of these parties—Democrazia Cristiana (DC); the Partito Comunista Italiano (PCI); the Partito Socialista Italiano (PSI); the Partito Socialista Democratico Italiano (PSDI); the Partito Repubblicano Italiano (PRI); the Partito Liberale Italiano (PLI); and the "neofascist" Movimento Sociale Italiano (MSI)—dominated the political scene from the late 1940s to the early 1990s. The success of these so-called historical parties, and particularly of the three major ones, the DC, PCI, and PS, in securing and retaining large and stable shares of the popular vote for over four decades was an impressive achievement. Indeed, as Maurizio Cotta (1992b) points out, in spite of widely divergent paths of political development, the electoral performance of the DC, PCI, and PS was not significantly different from that of the two major British parties: during the 1970s, these Italian parties received an average of 78.9 percent of the total vote, as compared with the 80.1 percent that went to the Conservative and Labour parties in Britain; and during the following decade, electoral support for the three largest Italian parties actually exceeded that of their two British counterparts by a margin of 74.7 percent versus 71.5 percent of the total vote.

The ability of Italian parties to secure broad and stable bases of support is even more remarkable in view of the persistently high levels of electoral participation, which exceeded 90 percent of eligible voters until the early 1980s and were only slightly lower thereafter. Parties were thus able, not only to preserve their shares of the vote, but to mobilize large segments of the citizenry time and again. New political groups occasionally emerged, but the historical parties effectively staved off challenges from them for over four decades.

The underpinnings of this successful performance were high rates of party membership and party identification. In the early 1960s, one voter out of six belonged to a party. By the late 1980s, membership rates had declined somewhat, but they were still remarkably high. The lack of fully comparable data on party identification makes it difficult to reach definite conclusions, but in general it appears that the extent of these psychological attachments to parties approximated those in several other Western democracies: Italy's levels of party identification in the late 1950s were similar to those recorded in 1961 in Britain; in the 1970s, they roughly equaled Germany's; and the 1980s, Italian voters' rates were higher than those of other southern European democracies. As late as the spring of 1990, approximately half of all Italian voters polled in a public opinion survey said that they felt "close" to a party.[2] Additionally, the linkage between parties and voters was reinforced by the phenomenon of subcultural identifications deeply rooted in the political traditions of the past (Sani 1974b; Parisi and Pasquino 1977).

Thus, a variety of relevant data indicate that, until recently, the relationship between parties and the electorate in Italy was not affected by particularly severe strains or tensions.

Mass Attitudes Toward Parties

As noted above, however, there is another side to the picture. The electorate's orientations toward specific parties and politicians contrast sharply with their images of parties in general. A considerable body of survey data spanning three decades shows that diffidence, lack of trust, and negative evaluations of parties were to be found side by side with positive orientations toward the major protagonists of political life. There were multiple manifestations of these seemingly contradictory aspects of Italian political culture: Italians complained that the party system was excessively fragmented while at the same time continuing to support a plethora of political parties; parties were accused of creating artificial conflicts, but they were also seen as instruments for the protection of various social groups; parties were considered indispensable for democracy and at the same time were accused of "being all alike."[3] Despite these inconsistencies, the bulk of the available evidence reveals that negative orientations toward parties and, more generally, toward the political sphere have been prevalent for decades. The negative orientations toward parties presented in Table 4.1 reflect a mix of attitudes that is, in part, common to other Western democracies, but they also reveal features peculiar to Italy's political culture.

Skepticism, cynicism, diffidence, and critical attitudes toward parties and politicians have been found in other democratic systems and appear to be compatible with strong parties (Verba, Nie, and Kim 1977). Antiparty opinions are apparently nurtured by a widely shared notion that links the behavior of parties to the unsatisfactory performance of the political system. In short, parties and politicians (especially governing parties and incumbent politicians) are often perceived, as they are in Italy, as being responsible for the malfunctioning of political institutions. Negative evaluations like these are somewhat similar to the confidence gap that has emerged in many Western democracies, beginning in the 1970s (Lipset and Schneider 1983).

There are four characteristics of antiparty attitudes, however, that

Table 4.1 Percentages of Italians Who Agree That . . .

	1972	1974	1976	1985–86	1990–91	1996
Parties create conflicts that don't exist	74%			55%	51%	
Parties are all alike				67	78	
Usually the persons we elect to parliament quickly lose contact with the voters		86			90	
Politicians are not very interested in what persons like me think		76		81	83	
Whoever gains power always tries to serve his personal interest			61	83		
People don't have much influence on what politicians do in office				80	76	
Parties are useless					22	31
Without political parties there can be no democracy					67	49
Parties are necessary to represent groups and social classes					63	49

Sources: Sani 1975; Four Nation Study; Mannheimer and Sani 1987; Morlino 1994; Bardi and Pasquino 1995; Sani and Segatti 1990; the Itanes-Cattaneo Survey of 1996.

set the Italian case apart from the others. First, Eurobarometer surveys over the past twenty years suggest that Italians are particularly dissatisfied with "the way democracy works in Italy." The "confidence gap" appears to be wider and deeper in Italy than elsewhere, and dissatisfaction progressively increased throughout this period: in 1973, only 27 percent of Italians said they were satisfied with the performance of the country's democratic system (the European average was 41 percent); by 1993, just 12 percent said they were satisfied with Italian democracy (the EU average was 43 percent [Weber 1983; Eurobarometer 1993]). Second, the perception that the political institutions were performing poorly emerged much earlier in Italy than in other democracies. Negative orientations of this sort were found as early as the 1950s.[4] Third, Italians have often singled out parties as the culprits but held relatively higher opinions of leading politicians. A survey conducted by Parisi, Cappello, Schadee, and Oppo in early 1990 (Gasperoni 1997), for example, revealed that voters' trust in the DC leaders Giulio Andreotti and Arnaldo Forlani was unrelated to their opinion of parties. Last, but not least, blaming parties for the malfunctioning of political institutions apparently does not necessarily imply a rejection of politics per se. It could be argued that feelings of dissatisfaction are to some extent a reasonable response to an objective reality, especially when politics fails for long time to solve societal problems. While this is certainly true, one might also argue that attitudes toward politics reflect frustration stemming from high expectations of politics and the perceived contrast between the reality of political life and "politics as it should be." Indeed, one of the keywords of public discourse in Italy has been a constant call for a "new way" of conducting political affairs (*un nuovo modo di fare politica*). We suspect that this attitude is a product of the influence on Italian political culture of the Catholic doctrine of the *bonum commune* and, in more recent times, of the socialist-communist belief system.

These orientations are not limited to specific segments of society; they can be found at approximately the same rates among a variety of social groups. As in other systems, negative attitudes toward parties appear to be somewhat more common among the less involved segments of the populace, but this does not mean that antiparty sentiments are necessarily linked to low cognitive competence, political alienation, and apathy. Strong criticisms of parties also come from relatively well informed citizens who keep in touch with political events. Indeed, it is among the more politically informed and active segments of the electorate that one often finds the angriest and most critical appraisals of the performance of the political system. This was as true in the 1950s as it was in the late 1980s (Di Palma 1970; Sani 1994a).

Survey data suggest that antiparty attitudes can be shaped by, or at least go together with, two rather different types of political disaffection. The first can properly be characterized as alienation or apathy. The second appears to be the product of frustration caused by the poor performance of political institutions, for which parties and partisan politics are blamed more than political leaders.

It should be stressed that in most cases, antiparty sentiments do not imply attitudes critical of democracy per se, or a denial of the role that parties should play in the working of democratic regimes. In the mid 1980s, for instance, less than the 10 percent of respondents in a national sample expressed a preference for a political regime without parties or with a single party (Calvi 1987). Other studies of the same period indicate that over two-thirds of those interviewed thought that democracy without political parties was impossible. The inconsistency between these attitudes and the pervasive suspicion of parties suggests, however, that the latter is indicative of a negative legitimation of democracy in Italy that represents more a rejection of undemocratic politics than a positive embrace of democratic institutions (Morlino and Montero 1995).

This brings us to the crux of the problem: how can one reconcile the stable and high levels of support received by traditional parties over four decades with the presence of strong and pervasive antiparty feelings? We believe that the answer to this question may be found in the pattern of party institutionalization dating from the early postwar years.

The Institutionalization of Parties and Antiparty Sentiments

There is widespread agreement that parties were the central actors in the Italian transition to democracy and in its consolidation.[5] Although Italian parties emerged from these processes with strong organizations, old sentiments of diffidence and cynicism about public authorities and politics was almost simultaneously transferred to the parties and politicians. As early as 1947, Piero Calamandrei, one of the fathers of the Italian constitution, noted that many Italians were convinced that an honest person should carefully avoid any contact with politicians because of their corruption (Calamandrei 1947). The link between the emergence of parties as powerful actors and the new stream of antipolitical feelings are to be found in the legacy of the fascist regime. When Fascism collapsed, it left behind a society different in several respects from that which preceded the breakdown of democracy in the early 1920s.

During Italy's first democratization process at the beginning of the twentieth century, attempts to build strong party organizations were hampered by certain characteristics of the social structure, as sociologists of that era noted. Roberto Michels and others have argued, for example, that the PSI was poorly centralized, bureaucratic, and undisciplined, and that Italy's weak industrial base limited its ability to attract substantial working-class electoral support (see Grassi 1990, 331–431). Instead, it incorporated into its ranks "two social classes that in all other countries have proven impervious to change, that is farmers and university professors." Michels's analysis is to some extent confirmed by the recent work of Stefano Bartolini (1993), who argues that the PSI of that period is a good example of a party that was successful at the polls but poorly organized and inadequately equipped to mobilize support along class lines, reflecting cleavages that had emerged in Italian society before World War I. It has often been noted that strong partisan attachments are more easily produced by political mobilization along the lines of either a predominant class cleavage or mutually reinforcing lines of social division. Italian society, in contrast, has been characterized by two important cross-cutting lines of division (religion and class) conducive to lower levels of polarization and weaker group identification (Lipset 1960; Verba, Nie, and Kim 1977).

After World War II, Italian mass parties more successfully conformed to Michels's criteria. They had stronger organizational structures and more stable bases of support. One is tempted to attribute this improved performance to the social changes that had occurred during the authoritarian period. The extent of the social-structural changes that had taken place by the beginning of the 1950s, however, was not impressive. As the data in Table 4.2 reveal, between 1921 and 1951, the urban middle class expanded from 16.3 to 26.5 percent of the economically active population. While the number of farm laborers declined by 10 percent as a share of the labor force, the industrial working class had expanded during these three decades by a modest 3 percent. Thus, the more notable change affected the middle class, a social stratum not usually suitable as a basis for strongly institutionalized parties, while the size of the industrial working class (upon which strong mass parties had traditionally been based) remained a relatively small segment of the labor force. Similarly, the cross-cutting nature of the cleavage structure also remained largely unaltered by the fascist interlude and the immediate postwar period. Hence, one might conclude that the "confining conditions" (to use Otto Kirchheimer's 1965 concept) for the development of strong partisanship had not substantially changed since Italy's previous democratic era.

But while the fascist interlude failed to substantially alter the social-structural context for the development of partisanship, it did have an

Table 4.2 Italian Social Structure, 1921 and 1951

Social Class	1921	1951
Bourgeoisie	1.7%	1.9%
Urban middle class	16.3	26.5
Small farmers	37.0	30.2
Working class (total)	45.0	41.2
(Farm laborers)	(21.8)	(11.8)
(Industrial workers)	(19.6)	(22.9)
(Service workers)	(3.5)	(6.5)

Source: Labini 1986, 20–21.

impact on the political, cultural, and institutional prerequisites for the emergence of strong parties after 1945. In the 1930s, Fascism extended and deepened the reach of the state over several public institutions (notably, e.g., local government and social security agencies).[6] The regime promoted a "top-down" form of authoritarian mobilization primarily by making the Fascist Party a type of compulsory mass party. For the first time, many Italians were mobilized at the national level and exposed to an ideology that played down the traditional social cleavages, emphasizing, instead, a new "political religion" that strongly linked nation and party (Gentile 1989; Pombeni 1985; Scoppola 1991). In the fascist ideology, partisanship was highly valued, but in the sense of loyalty to the *milizia della nazione* rather than in the pluralist sense of loyalty to a party. In other words, partisanship, understood as loyalty to the Fascist Party, was tantamount to loyalty to the nation itself, and disagreement with the party was seen as an assault on the nation.[7] It goes without saying that this conception of partisanship was antithetical to that of representing and advancing competing group interests in a pluralist democratic regime. In fact, Fascism constantly derided pluralist partisanship as a quintessential characteristic of parliamentary regimes. While it is impossible to ascertain to what extent the fascist idealization of party and devaluation of pluralist politics were shared by the masses, it is interesting to note that some aspects of this populist vision of partisanship reemerged in the postwar period, and that they are consistent with the paradox of strongly institutionalized parties, on the one hand, and widespread antiparty attitudes, on the other.

Shortly after the demise of the dictatorship in 1943, democratic parties were weak and unknown to many Italians. Nonetheless, they were able to build upon the mobilizations that accompanied the war and, in particular, the armed resistance movement that marked the transition to democracy (Pasquino 1990a; Bettinelli 1982). The PCI was especially successful in its organizational efforts thanks to the availability of personnel who had gained valuable experience in the resistance and to the traditional emphasis of communist doctrine on organization (Flores and Gallerano 1992; Poggi 1968; Cafagna 1993).

In the end, however, the most significant factors contributing to the strong institutionalization of parties were the mutually antagonistic perceptions held by political elites lining up on either side of the increasingly salient Cold War division between East and West (Morlino 1995). Those parties aligned with the Eastern Bloc (the PCI and, for a while, the PSI), with their limited legitimacy, continued their efforts in the late 1940s to expand and consolidate their mass organizations.

The organizational needs of the Christian Democrats were less pressing, given the preexisting network of support provided by the Church and a variety of Catholic associations. But in the early 1950s, DC leaders also embarked upon the creation of a genuine mass party that would be relatively autonomous from the Catholic hierarchy (Panebianco 1982; Kalyvas 1996).

At the mass level, the intense polarization induced by the Cold War had two important effects. First of all, polarization went together with a high degree of ideological fragmentation. The combination of polarization and fragmentation gave new strength to the populist vision of partisanship inherited from the recent authoritarian past. Accordingly, intense partisan feelings were accompanied by the belief that one's own political group was the genuine representative of the interests and values of all the people, while rival parties on the other side of the left-right cleavage were not regarded as fully legitimate competitors within the same body politic. Supporters of parties on either side of this division thus perceived one another as belonging to opposing camps, even though this antagonism was not rooted in sharply delineated social-structural differences. These perceptions (based in part on the polarization that arose out of the Cold War, and in part on the fascist conception of partisanship) impeded widespread acceptance of two central elements in democratic theory: (1) the notion that competition is the very essence of democracy, and (2) recognition that the winner of this competition is rightfully entitled to rule. Thus, the intense partisan attachments that arose out of the ideological polarization and the highly charged atmosphere of the early postwar years contained undesirable features.

The Cold War polarization also substantially affected the "freezing" of the party system. Many supporters of the Christian Democratic Party backed it more because they perceived it as a bulwark against communism than because they supported the DC's platform and ideological stands (Fegiz 1956; Barnes 1971). As late as the mid 1970s, fear of communism led a leading editorialist to urge moderate voters to keep casting their ballots for the DC even though they had "to hold their noses not to smell the stench of corruption." This had two implications. First, even though the fragmentation of the Italian party system presented voters with a multitude of options, the political alternatives that they faced were, de facto, significantly constrained by the political realities of the Cold War. Second, the expression of distrust toward parties was muted under these circumstances, given the need to maintain solid support for one's own party in the face of the threat posed by the opposition.[8] The partisan alignments frozen into place were thus significantly influenced by the Cold War.

It should be stressed that the key formative elements that largely determined the shape of the Italian party system and the nature of partisan orientations in Italy—the legacies of Fascism, war, and resistance, and the highly polarized competition among elites during the crucial first few years of party institutionalization—represent a clear predominance of the political over the social dimension. They resulted in partisanship patterns that were more intense and pervasive than Italy's social structure (characterized by cross-cutting class and religious cleavages) would have otherwise justified. In particular, the ideological polarization that accompanied the Cold War resulted in patterns of party institutionalization deeply rooted in the left-right cleavage. The salience of this dimension did not leave room for the surfacing of a number of other potential cleavages, most notably that based on the economic, cultural, and historical differences between the north and south of Italy.

Not only did this north-south cleavage have deep historical roots (Putnam 1993), but the wartime and immediate postwar experiences of the two regions were also substantially different. The south quickly fell under the military occupation of the Allies and thus did not undergo the mobilization associated with the resistance to the Nazi puppet Repubblica Sociale Italiana (the so-called Republic of Salò) in the north. The Allied Military Occupation also had a distinct influence over the social and political development of the south. The military occupation was accompanied, for example, by widespread corruption and black-marketeering, both of which tended to reinforce the particularism and familism that had characterized the south (Di Nolfo 1986; Scoppola 1991). The impact of these differences in wartime and postwar experiences was immediately apparent. In the referendum of 1946, southerners tended to favor preserving the monarchy, while more northern Italians voted for a republican regime. In that same year, a self-proclaimed antiparty movement, the Fronte dell'Uomo Qualunque (Common Man's Front), received massive support in the south (Setta 1975). Antifascist parties gained control in the south by the 1950s, but earlier experiences had a lasting influence. This was reflected in the persistent weakness of the PCI (Tarrow 1967) and in the prevalence of a premodern political style in which individuals were linked to politics primarily through personalistic and clientelistic networks (Cartocci 1990). This political tradition fostered a political culture in which party affiliation was often determined more by opportunism than by emotional, programmatic, or ideological motivation.

Eventually, this southern political style contaminated the entire Italian party system.

Finally, it should be noted that the institutionalization of parties was the product of an interactive learning process. At the beginning of the democratic transition, most of the new antifascist political elites did not conceive of parties as mass organizations. The notion of a party as an "organizational weapon" was initially embraced only by the left, not by the majority of moderate and left-of-the-center politicians, even after they had become fully aware of the mass character of the new democracy and of the role that parties would have to perform in the new institutional setting (Scoppola 1991; Moro 1979; De Luna 1982). Given the anxiety and fear stemming from the Cold War, however, these moderate elites were forced to change their minds.

In short, the way the partisan-political cleavage was implanted in Italian society during the early postwar period encouraged the development of strongly institutionalized parties. But it also gave them an ambiguous legitimation. This ambivalence reemerged at various junctures in the process of democratic consolidation.

Partitocrazia

Vis-à-vis other representative political institutions and citizens themselves, Italian political parties became very strong, going far beyond the role assigned to them by the constitution of 1948. For the parties in power, notably for DC, this implied the systematic blurring of the distinction between party organization and state institutions. The process went so far as to lead observers to conclude that public institutions had been transformed into a party structure at the service of a ruling class (Farnetti 1980). Opposition parties, notably the PCI, were forced to maintain a web of parallel organizations operating under tight party control, appearances of institutional autonomy notwithstanding. Popular evaluations of the political process were profoundly affected by this situation. The contrast between idealized expectations of parties, on the one hand, and the realities of partisan politics, on the other, inevitably produced a dim view of everyday politics and generated a good deal of cynicism.

Strategies devised by political elites to deal with this polarized political system had the same ambiguous effects. There being no prospect of an alternation in power at the national level, conflict was softened somewhat by blurring the partisan divisions in the policymaking process at the parliamentary level and in center-periphery relations (Di Palma 1977; Pizzorno 1993). Italy's failure to promote a comprehensive reform of local government provided considerable opportunities for party politicians, even for those who were denied access to the higher levels of government (Tarrow 1977; Rotelli 1991). Partisan conflict was also mitigated, beginning in the 1970s, in response to the protests of those years, by politicizing previously nonpolitical institutions such as school administrations and public health agencies. Both government and opposition parties claimed that this was conducive to "a more democratic society, and more efficient institutions," while it led de facto to an expansion in the reach and social penetration of politics, allowing parties and politicians to augment their roles and visibility.[9]

These strategies of co-optation and expansion of politics beyond the traditional arenas had two significant consequences. They reinforced the idea that the basic meaning of democratic representation was (in Hanna Pitkin's terminology) not "acting for," but "standing for" (Pitkin 1967). Thus, many Italians believed that an institution could only be considered democratic when every interest was proportionally represented within it. This, in turn, led both government and opposition parties to push for the "democratization" of a number of institutions previously considered nonpolitical.

The shortcomings and the unintended consequences of these co-optive strategies became clear in due course. Without any real prospect of parties' alternating in power, consensual democracy most often meant ineffective, slow-motion coalition government. With the expansion of politics into a wide range of social and economic institutions, moreover, opportunities for patronage and clientelism proliferated, and the potential for corruption increased. Given a high level of ideological polarization, these shortcomings remained hidden, or were regarded as an acceptable price to pay for coexistence, but when the ideological temperature began to cool down the high costs of allowing partisanship to permeate all spheres of society became more visible and objectionable. These perceptions became more common in the 1980s, and they interacted in an ultimately volatile manner with preexisting antiparty sentiments.

In sum, our argument is that the activation of antiparty feelings was linked to the processes by which parties became institutionalized in the early republican period and to the strategies adopted by political elites during the longer-term processes of democratic consolidation (which ended in the mid 1970s). Their relationship is, however, multidimensional. The early climate of ideological polarization and fragmentation promoted the development of emotionally charged bonds between many voters and their respective parties, characterized by a populist vision of partisanship. Other voters expressed disaffection toward parties because they were probably uneasy about the electoral choices made possible by the freezing of the party system in the 1950s. Strategies designed to soften the political conflict extended the reach of parties into a variety of institutions and augmented the visibility of politicians. The unanticipated consequence was that the notion that "parties had occupied the state," once a slogan endorsed by a few, became popular with the weakening of ideological conflict.

We have stressed this particular source of disaffection because it is critical for an understanding of Italian political culture. To be sure, there were other sources of political dissatisfaction and alienation related to processes of socioeconomic development common to other countries. These included the transformation of the social structure, higher levels of education, secularization, the decline of deferential attitudes toward elites, the increasing role of the mass media in political life, as well as a growing demand for "citizens' politics" (Inglehart 1990; Dalton 1987). A cultural shift in this direction became manifest in Italy from the 1970s. It did not, however, replace preexisting sentiments (Sani and Segatti 1990).

The Decomposition of the Italian Party System, 1991–1994

Until the end of the 1980s, popular support for the seven "historical parties" remained at high levels. In the parliamentary elections of 1987, the two major parties (the DC and the PCI) together garnered over 60 percent of the valid votes. When the strength of the third-place party, the PSI, is taken into consideration, the total reached 75 percent, almost the same level of support as in 1972. To be sure, during the 1980s, there were some indications that the political system was undergoing a process of change. There was an increase of electoral fragmentation as new political groups (most notably, the Greens) challenged the old protagonists, but their share of the popular vote remained quite modest. The net effect of the continued strength of the major parties and the inability of new parties to make serious inroads into their bases of support was that rates of electoral volatility between pairs of consecutive elections remained low,[10] while turnout levels, although somewhat lower than in previous decades, remained rather high.

The first signs that a major change might be imminent could be seen in the 1990 regional elections. In the northern third of the country, in particular, the recently formed regional leagues were able to attract support from sizable segments of the electorate at the expense of the traditional parties. In Lombardy, the Lega Lombarda came close to receiving one out of five votes cast. In other regions, the gains were less spectacular, but not insignificant by Italian standards: they reached 7.8 percent in the Veneto region, 6.1 percent in Liguria, and 5.1 percent in Piedmont. The leagues focused their attacks on the "Roman parties," accusing them of mismanagement, corruption, and excessive centralization. Demands for autonomy grounded on regional identities, coupled with a rejection of the traditional party system, met with a favorable response from the electorate.

The full magnitude of this new development became apparent in the 1992 parliamentary elections, in which the Northern League attracted 8.7 percent of all votes cast nationwide. Its 3.4 million votes represented a dramatic increase over the half million votes (1.3 percent of the total) it had received in the previous parliamentary election just five years earlier. Indeed, in some provinces, the Lega received the largest share of the vote, while in several others it challenged the Christian Democrats for the lead. In addition, other newcomers to the political scene, such as La Rete ("The Network"),[11] fared reasonably well too. As a result, the party system became even more fragmented than it had been in the past. More important, the shares of the popular vote accruing to the traditional parties declined to their lowest levels of the postwar period. The DC's vote fell below 30 percent, while the Partito Democratico della Sinistra (PDS)—the principal heir to the former PCI—was barely above the 16 percent mark, as can be seen in Table A.3 in the Appendix.

Italy's electoral geography had been rewritten. In past contests, there had been only relatively minor changes in the territorial distribution of the vote for the various political groups, and the traditional classification of certain regions as the "Industrial Triangle," the "Red Belt," the "White Area," and "the south"[12] maintained their validity well into the 1980s. In 1992, that pattern was shattered, and the country appeared to be divided into three new zones: the north, characterized by the advance of the leagues; the center, still largely favorable to leftist parties; and the south, in which support for governing parties, particularly the Christian Democrats and the PSI, was still relatively high. It should be noted that the differences among the three areas went beyond patterns of electoral behavior. They also involved major differences in levels of socioeconomic development (Sani 1993): the per capita income of the northern and central regions were 13 percent and 9 percent above the national average, while that of the south was 20 percent below the nationwide average. The three regions also manifested sharply divergent political styles. Fully 68.5 percent of southern voters, for example, cast preferential ballots for specific candidates (a reflection of continuing personalistic relationships in that less-developed region), while in the north and center only 43 percent and 36 percent did so.

A continuation of this trend could be seen in the series of local elections that followed the 1992 parliamentary contest. The electoral bases of the major historical parties continued to shrink, especially those of the Christian Democrats and the PSI. Public opinion polls carried out at the end of that year gave further indication that the erosion of these and other groups had reached massive proportions, giving rise to expectations that a major change might be imminent. Indeed, shortly thereafter a veritable electoral earthquake took place.

The first shock was the result of the referendum on the electoral law for the Senate held on April 18, 1993, in which voters were asked whether they favored modifying the proportional representation system in use since 1948. By a large majority, Italians voted in favor of changing the electoral law, thus opening the way for the adoption of a plurality, first-past-the-post system.[13] The second shock came in June, when municipal elections gave to the Lega control of several local governments. In the extremely important municipality of Milan, the list of candidates sponsored by the leagues received over 40 percent of the vote, and its candidate for mayor handily won a run-off election (with 57 percent of the vote) against a well-known leftist intellectual. Parties that had dominated the city's government in the past were devastated: the Christian Democrats received less than 10 percent of the vote, the former communists did not do much better, and the socialists were completely wiped out in the city that had once been their stronghold. The story was much the same in other communities, including major urban centers such as Turin and Catania. In a second round of local elections in November, the parties of the governing coalition were soundly defeated once again. In all major cities, the mayoral candidates of the traditional centrist parties failed even to make it to the second round. Their share of the vote fell to an all-time low, to the benefit of the MSI and the Lega Nord, which gained 10 percent and 15 percent respectively.

The final blow to the traditional centrist bloc came with the parliamentary election of March 1994. In the two months preceding the election, the PLI and PSDI disappeared from the scene altogether, while the PRI and PSI suffered deep splits that brought them to the brink of extinction. Many Christian Democrats attempted to limit future losses through a process of "renewal," which included a return to the name Partito Popolare Italiano, which the party bore in the prefascist period. This transformation ensured the survival of the party, but it was not without costs, insofar as it led to a schism in which a right-wing faction seceded and formed a rival Christian Democratic group, the Centro Cristiano Democratico (see Sani 1994c).

In part because of these changes and in part because of the constraints imposed by the new electoral law, the lineup of forces in the March 1994 campaign differed significantly from that of the past. After a fluid phase of negotiations, three electoral alliances emerged: a leftist bloc centered on the PDS; a center-right cartel in which the federalist Lega Nord and the centrist, "postfascist" MSI–Alleanza Nazionale, two rather incompatible partners, were linked by the media tycoon Silvio Berlusconi's newly created Forza Italia!; and the remnants of the old center parties, squeezed between the two major alliances (on the role of the media in the 1994 election, see Segatti 1994; Diamanti and Mannheimer 1994).

As preelection polls had anticipated, the returns constituted an electoral earthquake of a magnitude unprecedented in Italian history. The shift in votes among parties was huge: the volatility index score of 37.2 (measuring the net shift in votes) for the 1994 election was not only the highest in postwar Italian history but also one of the highest in European electoral history (Bartolini and D'Alimonte 1994, 447). At the individual level, electoral mobility was even higher—54 percent of voters changed parties in the proportional part of the ballot, as did 47 percent in the single-member-district portion of the vote for the Chamber of Deputies (Segatti 1997). The prevailing flow of votes was from the old center parties toward Berlusconi's new movement. Other prominent beneficiaries of this shift were Gianfranco Fini's Alleanza Nazionale, Umberto Bossi's Lega Nord, and, to a lesser extent, one or two parties of the left. At the same time, however, the interbloc shift (between parties of the left and parties of the right) was rather modest (see Chapter 3 above). In the end, the center-right coalition obtained a plurality of votes, as well as a large majority of the seats in the Chamber of Deputies and a near majority in the Senate. The left remained stable, with about a third of the vote, unable to expand its electoral base beyond its traditional bloc of supporters. The once-dominant center, however, suffered a humiliating defeat in the single-member-district round, and was spared from disappearing altogether only by picking up a modest number of the seats allocated through the proportional representation mechanism.

The transformation of the party system, heralded by the events of the previous two years, had reached its apex.

Antiparty Sentiments and the Crisis of the Party System

This brief summary of recent electoral trends, coupled with our earlier discussion of popular feelings toward parties, brings us to the central question of this chapter. Why was it only in the 1990s that popular attitudes of skepticism and cynicism toward politics in general, and political parties in particular, found an outlet in voting behavior in Italy?

Before discussing several possible answers to this question, let us review briefly those elements that had contributed to the structuring, or "freezing," of the Italian electoral market in previous decades. The most important of these factors were:

1. A stable configuration of the alternatives offered to the voters
2. The persistence of politicized and salient social cleavages
3. A set of stable alignments between organized social groups and political parties
4. High levels of party identification and/or relevance of the "subcultural" ("Red" vs. "White") dimension of voting
5. A definition of the space of competition largely shared by the mass and elite levels
6. Consistently high levels of political participation
7. A high degree of legitimacy enjoyed by traditional political elites

In sum, we could say that a frozen party system is characterized by a high level of stability in terms of main competitors, continuity of choice at the mass level, sociocultural underpinnings of partisan preferences, and regional patterns of support for the different groups.

Several interwoven developments contributed to the destabilization of this established order. The first involved changes in the international environment beginning in the late 1980s. For decades, the internal dynamics of Italian political life had been heavily constrained by the East-West conflict. From the onset of the Cold War, the PCI, Italy's second-largest political group, had been confined to a permanent opposition role at the national level because of its ties (real or presumed) with the communist regimes of eastern Europe. Even after its "break" with the Soviet Union and the inauguration of its "Eurocommunist" strategy, the PCI remained largely isolated, and the political system was thus deprived of the possibility of alternation in power. The collapse of the Berlin Wall and the demise of communist regimes in eastern Europe provoked an identity crisis within the PCI, leading to a split between, on the one hand, a majority faction that converted the bulk of the party into the PDS, which eventually joined the Socialist International) and, on the other hand, a radical minority that became Rifondazione Comunista, a group solidly rooted in the traditions of the past (see Chapter 8 below; Ignazi 1992). Given that the former PCI had entered into a traumatic transformation on the eve of these decisive elections, the electoral appeal of the second-largest of the traditional parties experienced a substantial (if temporary) decline.

The dramatic changes in the international environment that took place beginning in 1989 had other implications for Italian politics as well. With the disappearance of the communist threat, anticommunism was no longer a valuable weapon. The parties that had used it so effectively over the course of four decades (especially the Christian Democrats) could no longer evoke the specter of communism to rally the moderate segment of the electorate. Although the events of 1989 may have proved that the anticommunist parties had been right all along, their victory deprived them of their most powerful appeal to most voters. Released from the constraints previously imposed by the international environment, the dissatisfied electorate could turn to new and more palatable alternatives.

In the case of the DC, this problem was compounded by an additional factor: over the years, the process of secularization had been gradually eroding its base of popular support. The pool of practicing Catholics who had heavily contributed to the electoral base of the party was shrinking. Whereas over 70 percent of Italians attended religious services weekly in the late 1950s, by the mid 1980s, fewer than 30 percent did so. Moreover, the linkage between religion and politics had become weaker with the passage of time. By the end of the 1980s, it could no longer be taken for granted that a good Catholic would automatically cast a vote for the Christian Democrats. Although the DC continued into the 1990s to call upon Italian voters to maintain the "unity of Catholics," this traditional appeal no longer had the cogency of the past (Cartocci 1993). In the electoral turmoil of the two contests of 1992 and 1994, a sizable contingent of Catholic voters defected to other moderate groups such as the Alleanza Nazionale, Patto Segni, and Forza Italia! By the mid 1990s, the Partito Popolare Italiano was the only political group with a majority of devout Catholics in its ranks. The share of practicing Catholics in parties like Forza Italia! and Alleanza Nazionale was close to the average in the electorate as a whole (Diamanti 1997).

The multitude of scandals that came to light beginning in 1992 also had a devastating impact on the traditional parties and the old structure of partisan alignments. To skeptical voters, suspicious of and diffident about the world of politics, the revelation (amplified by the media) that high-ranking officials, up to and including former prime ministers, had been deeply mired in corruption could not but prove that they had been right all along. Even though these scandals primarily involved leaders of those parties traditionally in government, the delegitimatizing effect cast a shadow over some opposition parties as well, such that most of the traditional political class was effectively put on trial before the court of public opinion.

In this climate, it is hardly surprising that appeals by new political actors for a regeneration of politics would resonate positively with large segments of the electorate. The principal beneficiaries of this throw-the-bums-out atmosphere were the Lega (in the early phase, from 1992 through 1993) and, subsequently, Forza Italia! and the Alleanza Nazionale–MSI. But while all three exploited preexisting antiparty feelings, they did so in decidedly different ways, stressing quite divergent themes.

The *Leghe*

The history of the regional leagues (now federated under the label "Northern League") began with the appearance in the 1983 election of the Venetian League, whose initial program centered on the defense of the people and the language of Veneto, allegedly threatened by the excessive centralization of the political system. In the late 1980s, the leadership of the regional movement was taken over by the Lombard League and its leader, Umberto Bossi, who downplayed the themes of ethnic and linguistic distinctiveness somewhat and emphasized the threat to the prosperity of the north posed by a centralized and corrupt state. Accordingly, the league has based its appeals on the alleged differences between the "European" culture of the north, characterized by a market economy and a self-help ethic, and the "Mediterranean" culture of the south, permeated by clientelism and the expectation of never-ending handouts from politicians. Thus, over time, there has been a subtle shift from a cultural appeal involving the ethnic and linguistic traits of northerners to a standard refrain focusing on the drain of financial resources away from the productive northern regions to subsidize the south. In the past few years, this theme has been accompanied by a demand for a radical transformation of the state that would do away with the traditional unitary structure and replace it with a federal system, if not (as demanded by Umberto Bossi in May 1996) an independent northern state. Although the platform has changed somewhat over time, the territorial focus of the Lega's ideology, programs, and electoral base has remained constant (Biorcio 1991; Segatti 1992). Despite their efforts to implant the movement elsewhere, the Lega has been incapable of attracting significant electoral support outside of the north (Diamanti 1993).

Thus, the weakening of the traditional cleavages on which partisanship in Italy had previously been based—the social divisions of class and religion, and the political polarization of the Cold War—opened the door to other conflicts, which had always existed but had lain dormant, concealed and suppressed by the more salient social divisions of the postwar era. In the highly polarized climate of the early period of Italian democracy, the two major parties, in particular, had attracted substantial and durable bases of support through their respective appeals to the alliance among the workers of the north, the sharecroppers of the center, and the peasants of the south, on the one hand, and to Catholics in all areas of the country, on the other. Cultural differences rooted in local or regional identities lurked beneath the surface, occasionally finding expression as prejudices and stereotypes, but never activated as bases of political conflict except in the areas inhabited by linguistic minorities such as South Tyrol and Val d'Aosta.

In the 1990s, voters were much less constrained by the ideological barriers of the past, and they were presented with a fresh alternative couched in simple, direct, and sometimes uncouth language that departed from the stultifying jargon used by traditional politicians. The slogan "Roma ladrona, la Lega non perdona" ("Rome, big thief, the League does not forgive") and the attack on "Roman parties" successfully blended rediscovered geographical identities with protest against a corrupt political class, an inefficient bureaucracy, and an oppressive taxation system. Traditional parties—both those in government and those on the opposition benches—were portrayed by Bossi as bearing the major responsibility for the disastrous situation of the country. Party bureaucrats, with headquarters in Rome, were accused of siphoning off resources from the productive north to the advantage of the south. Clearly, preexisting antiparty feelings were the unifying element of this mix of attitudes which found a convenient outlet in support for the league.

Forza Italia!

The electoral appeals of Forza Italia! did not involve an outright rejection of parties but rather a call for a renewal of political life to be inaugurated by individuals drawn from all sectors of civil society and with no previous involvement in politics. Old parties were criticized for a pattern of recruitment based not on merit but on partisan grounds. Berlusconi and his collaborators contended that this, in turn, had given rise to rampant clientelism, corruption, and inefficiency, and had led to a degeneration of parties. Forza Italia! called for a "new Italian miracle," in which honest and competent men and women drawn from the professions and the business community would replace the old political class. Politics should be "deprofessionalized" and entrusted to people who, to use Berlusconi's oft-repeated phrase, "had successfully passed several tests in civil society." This appeal, as some sophisticated observers noted, clearly underestimated the need for specific skills and experiences relevant to the conduct of politics and the affairs of state. The rejection of professional politicians, however, was in line with the widespread desire for change, as well as with deep-rooted suspicion of parties and the elite. The strengthening of civil society in Italian politics also implied a reduction of the overweening role of the state in the economy, for which the traditional parties (as argued above) could legitimately be blamed. In brief, Forza Italia! based its appeals on the assertion that competent managers coming from the private sector could do a much better job at running the country as *l'azienda Italia* (the "Italian firm").

The Alleanza Nazionale

In contrast to both Forza Italia! and the Lega, the Alleanza Nazionale articulated points of view that tapped the more traditional elements of antiparty feelings. This is hardly surprising in view of the ideological heritage of the MSI (the backbone of AN) and the disproportionate concentration of its electoral base in those same southern regions that had given birth to the first Italian antiparty movement in the early postwar period. In its more radical form, the critique of parties articulated by some spokesmen of AN went beyond the charge that parties had become self-serving, degenerate organizations. AN candidates, in accordance with their party's platform ("Il programma della destra al governo"), also argued that partisan squabbles and the traditional parties' defense of narrow interests threatened the unity of the nation-state. In this view, parties had acquired a monopoly of the "representation function," and had become an artificial barrier between society and the state. The remedy suggested was to move away from party-based democracy through a robust injection of plebiscitarian and/or corporatist elements, such as the direct election of the head of government, the referendum as a regular decision-making instrument, and a greater role in political life for corporate bodies ("functional representation").

Tremors and Aftershocks

The electoral earthquake of 1994 virtually destroyed the old party system, as we have seen. It also led to patterns of government formation that were decidedly different from those that characterized the First Republic throughout its four decades of existence. In contrast with the center-left to center-right coalitions of this period (which always included the centrist DC and always excluded the principal parties occupying the left and right ends of the political continuum, the PCI and the MSI), and with the quasi-consociational practices of that period, especially the *lottizzazione,* which had given the DC, PCI, and PSI their own public television channels (see Marletti and Roncarola 2000), the Berlusconi government included the postfascist Alleanza, excluded the remnants of the DC, and adopted more majoritarian policies than had previously been embraced (attempting, for example, to dominate the public sector of television broadcasting completely).

The 1994 election did not, however, culminate in a stable new configuration of governing parties. Indeed, by the end of 1994, the Berlusconi government was already in serious trouble. The decision of Bossi's Lega to leave the governing coalition led to the collapse of the cabinet and a government crisis. It was succeeded by a "neutral" cabinet headed by Lamberto Dini, who had been Berlusconi's minister of finance, but who depended for parliamentary support on the Lega Nord and some parties that initially formed the opposition to Berlusconi's government. An attempt was made in February 1995 to form an all-party government (*governissimo*), with the objective of enacting a series of constitutional reforms, but after extensive negotiations this effort ended in failure. As a result, the president of the republic dissolved parliament and called early elections (which also represented a change from the past, when most parliaments sat for their full four-year terms despite repeated government crises).

The outcome of the 1996 election was yet another dramatic shift away from the practices of the First Republic. In 1994, victory went to a coalition that included the postfascist Alleanza Nazionale (heir of the MSI, which had been in opposition throughout the postwar period); in 1996, the largest party in the victorious center-left coalition (l'Ulivo) was the PDS, the largest remnant of the PCI. Italy had had the dubious privilege of being a democracy without alternation of major parties in power for half a century, but the 1994 and 1996 elections removed all traces of the "no alternation" stigma and brought the parties of the left to power for the first time. Perhaps the most emblematic sign of the changing times was the appointment of Giorgio Napolitano, a distinguished figure of the old PCI, as minister of the interior—a post traditionally considered the most sensitive in the Italian cabinet.

Another significant political development in 1996 was the Lega Nord's adoption of an openly secessionist stance. Previously, Bossi had claimed that the ultimate objective of his movement was to reform the strongly centralist structure of the Italian state in favor of some form of federalism. In 1996, however, the Lega Nord conducted its election campaign on the basis of an overtly secessionist manifesto. With this more radical orientation, the Lega actually increased its share of the vote, as can be seen in Appendix Table A.3.

Antiparty Sentiments and Political Change

It should be noted that the ultimate outcome of the 1996 election was much more affected by electoral alliances among parties and by the electoral law than by shifts in voter preferences. The structure of electoral competition did change dramatically. Competitiveness increased significantly, as reflected by a sharp decrease in the nationwide average margin of victory, from 17.7 percent to 10.9 percent. But these national-level figures are somewhat misleading. In the "Red Belt" and the south, changes were minimal. The major shift occurred in the north, where competitiveness increased dramatically. Whereas in 1994 almost three-fourths of the districts could be classified as "safe" (i.e., won by 15 percent or more), in 1996 almost half of these districts were "marginal," with the victor winning by 5 percent or less. It is important to note that these patterns of continuity and change perfectly reflect the evolution of electoral alliances. In the central and southern regions, the composition of the center-right coalition was basically the same in 1994 and 1996 (i.e., Forza Italia! and the Alleanza Nazionale). In the north, defection of the Lega from the alliance not only subtracted votes from the former center-right coalition, the Polo delle Libertà, but also changed the format of competition from that of a two-way to a three-way race in most districts. This benefited not only the Lega but also the parties of the center-left (Sani 1994b and 1996; Bartolini and D'Alimonte 1996). An additional element that should be taken into account is the restructuring of the pattern of electoral alliances with regard to parties near the center of the political spectrum. In 1994, the PPI—the surviving segment of the DC—and other remnants of the old centrist parties stood alone. In 1996, however, they allied themselves with the major coalitions of left or right. Given the large number of districts won or lost by a narrow margin, it is clear that the entry of these small but strategically important centrist parties and factions accounted for the margin of victory in many constituencies. Indeed, survey data indicate that voters' partisan preferences stabilized quite substantially between 1994 and 1996: the "floating" segment of the vote declined from 53.6 percent to 34.6 percent in the proportional part of the ballot during this period, while in the single-member-district vote, it declined from 46.6 percent to 10.6 percent of the total. Interbloc volatility (i.e., the net shift from parties of the left to the right, or vice versa) remained low, and most of the change in electoral outcomes derived from a restructuring of the center (Sani 1994c; Segatti 1997; Salvatore 1997; Cartocci 1997). Even parties without any territorial organizations (like Forza Italia!) were able to stabilize their electoral bases. Thus, despite a significant shift in parliamentary representation and the composition of government, there were substantial continuities at the mass level between the 1994 and 1996 elections.

Given the massive transformation of the party system and patterns of governance that resulted from the elections of 1994 and 1996, one might rightly wonder whether these tumultuous events were paralleled by any change in popular attitudes toward parties, politics, politicians, and democracy. A complete answer to this question is beyond the scope of this chapter. We can, however, reach some conclusions with a certain degree of confidence. There is no evidence of substantial changes in the political culture of the country. As in the past, Italian citizens continue to exhibit low political efficacy and a lack of trust. For example, despite the large turnover in the political class in the 1994 and 1996 elections,[14] the proportion of Italian voters interviewed in an Istituto Cattaneo survey in 1996 who agreed with the statement that "the persons we elect to parliament very quickly lose contact with the voters" was not significantly different from the 90 percent who endorsed that statement in 1990. Neither did political change and the alternation of parties in power contribute to increased trust in political institutions. Parliament is still invariably last

Table 4.3 Attitudes Toward Democracy, 1985, 1994, and 1996

	1985	1994	1996
Democracy is preferable to any other form of government	70.4%	77.5%	81.3%
Under some circumstances, a dictatorship is preferable to a democratic system	12.9	8.5	9.7
For people like me, one regime is the same as another	10.0	9.5	6.9
Don't know/No answer	6.7	4.5	2.1

Sources: For 1985, Four Nation Study; for 1994, Limes-Swg Survey; and for 1996, Itanes-Cattaneo Survey.

among those institutions ranked by survey respondents on that attitudinal dimension—especially in comparison with the police, the judiciary, and the Church. In 1996, as in 1985, a large number of Italians negatively evaluated political parties and their function in a democracy, although change is apparent in the data presented in Table 4.1.

Nonetheless, negative evaluations of parties and political institutions continue to coexist with high levels of support for democracy, and that support remains high despite the political turmoil of the mid 1990s, as can be seen in Table 4.3. These data suggest that democracy itself has not been put at risk by these dramatic events. The widespread antiparty orientations and populist attitudes, however, raise questions about the quality of Italy's democracy.

Some Concluding Observations

In the course of four years and three parliamentary elections, the Italian political system has been changed radically. This transition does not appear at the time of this writing to have reached closure, even if there were signs of electoral stabilization at the mass level in the 1996 election. Four central political issues still remain unsettled.

First of all, many among the political elite believe that long-term political stability requires additional modifications in the electoral system, beyond those enacted in 1993, as well as a more general constitutional reform.

Second, the more active role of prosecutors in the judiciary has given rise to unresolved conflict with the political class. Although exposure of widespread political corruption since 1992 has had many beneficial effects, this new kind of activism within the judiciary has unbalanced the relations among the constitutional powers. Politicians of all parties believe that some constitutional equilibrium must be restored, while many Italian citizens remain skeptical of politicians and supportive of prosecutorial activism.

Third, all the main coalitions remain internally divided. In the center-left camp, there has been an increasing conflict between Rifondazione Comunista (the "refounded," but unreformed, Communist party), which beginning in 1996 was part of the parliamentary majority but not represented in the cabinet, and the other parties in the Ulivo coalition. The conflict erupted in 1998 when RC decided to leave the parliamentary majority, causing the fall of the Prodi government. In both parties, one can observe a permanent tension between their identities as parties and as coalition members.

Last, but definitely not least, the relative success of the Lega in the northern regions in the 1996 election deepened a political division that could interfere with the consolidation of the new order, even if (as became apparent after 1998) Bossi's party has subsequently softened its secessionist stance.

Each of these factors could have a significant impact on the shape of the "political offer" that was the engine of political change in the early to mid 1990s.

Although these questions remain unresolved, some points are becoming clear. Antiparty sentiments in Italy persist. Based on the perceived gap between reality and the idealized notion of what a political party should be and how it should perform, they impose important constraints on the manner in which these issues may be resolved. Tensions deriving from this perceived gap are common elements of political culture, particularly in countries influenced by the Catholic doctrine of the *bonum commune,* but they were activated and reinforced in Italy by the fascist attempt to build a polity in which partisanship was to be developed side by side with the suppression of conflict and political competition. They were further exacerbated in the postwar period, when political elites faced with a highly polarized climate constructed a strong, well-anchored party system that was capable of delivering many "goods" to citizens (ideological worldviews, jobs, subcultural identities), except for the one most widely regarded as essential for guaranteeing the responsiveness of parties to voters: competition. There are no signs that the emerging political system will succeed in eliminating these mass-level negative feelings toward parties and politics. On the contrary, we anticipate that these attitudes might be further inflamed by continuing conflict with some sectors of the judiciary—a development that could delegitimize politics per se—as well by the plebiscitarian and populist orientation of many of the new protagonists on the Italian political scene.

At the same time, we conclude that antiparty sentiments themselves were insufficient as causes of the recent crisis of the Italian political system. As we have argued, parties have been able to coexist (not to mention thrive and remain stable over decades) side by side with negative feelings toward politics, politicians, and the parties themselves. Change occurred as the product of a combination of factors, some of which were peculiar to the Italian situation, while some are common to other democracies. The long-standing skepticism about parties and politics effectively primed public opinion, such that the discovery of a far-reaching web of political corruption by the judiciary and intense coverage by the media served as dramatic confirmation of what many voters thought they had known about politicians all along. This priming effect had such a massive impact, however, in part because old reference points and anchors of partisanship were weakening, while new alternatives were appearing. The causes of the party-system collapse of 1992–94 were thus multiple, and antiparty sentiments interacted with other factors to bring it about.

To what extent will these antiparty sentiments affect the evolution of the Italian party system in the future? In order to answer this question, it is necessary to take into account the social and cultural context in which the new parties are taking shape. As we have shown in this chapter (and elsewhere), this context is strikingly different from that of the immediate postwar period when the parties of the First Republic were established. The deep social cleavages that strongly stabilized partisanship in the past have substantially eroded. In addition, functions previously performed by party organizations appear to be fulfilled by other instruments, such as television, whose importance in linking candidates and voters was especially salient in the March 1994 election and is explored in detail in Chapter 5. This does not mean that parties are becoming unnecessary, but it does suggest that the conditions that so strongly influenced the shape of the old parties are not replicable today. Social cleavages and ideological polarization will not overshadow those aspects of political culture rooted in pervasive negative feelings toward parties, while the dominant position of television as a source of political information may amplify and broaden the reach of antiparty messages. In this context, it is likely that negative feelings toward parties and politics could have some impact on the reshaping of the Italian party system, although it is impossible to say what its effects may be. We can only cautiously suggest that the Italian paradox of the previous fifty years—of strong parties coexisting with a strong antiparty political culture—may no longer exist. We may now be faced with a situation characterized by an antiparty political culture and weak parties. The implications of this altered situation for the functioning of Italian democracy remain to be seen.

5 The New Campaign Politics in Southern Europe

Gianfranco Pasquino

Following their return to democracy, Greece, Italy, Portugal, and Spain have all held free, competitive, and meaningful parliamentary and local or regional elections, and some referenda. In Portugal, voters have also been called to the polls to elect the president of the republic directly five times already, in 1976, 1981, 1986, 1991, and 1996, choosing three different presidents. Owing to its semipresidential constitution, Portugal has also experienced a long phase of cohabitation between a socialist president and a social democratic prime minister. This cohabitation has had interesting implications for the way parties and leaders campaigned at election time. In addition, and most important, peaceful and orderly alternations in the government by different parties and coalitions have taken place in Greece, Portugal, and Spain, providing for significant changes in prime minister, in the governing personnel, and, of course, in policies.

It needs to be stressed that such an outcome—alternation of parties or coalitions in government—eluded Italy throughout the period now customarily called the First Republic, despite the fact that there is technically no Second Republic as yet, absent a dramatic constitutional rupture or incisive constitutional reform (although the latter may now be in the offing). In any case, the so-called First Republic dates roughly from 1946 to 1993, when a drastically revised electoral law, opposed by all major parties except the majority of the Partito Democratico della Sinistra (PDS), was drafted in the wake of a popular referendum. The two elections held under the new electoral law, in March 1994 and April 1996, produced the long-awaited and desired alternation in power of two very different, and highly diversified, coalitions. There is no doubt that these outcomes have to be seen, not just as episodic instances in a still incomplete transition to a new institutional and constitutional arrangement, but also as consequences of the emergence of a new campaign politics (Bartolini and D'Alimonte 1994 and 1997; Pasquino 1995a).

It is reasonable to expect that the styles of politics, and especially campaign politics, would undergo significant change in countries returning to democracy after a more (Portugal and Spain) or less (Greece) lengthy authoritarian experience, or a difficult political transition (Italy) from a party-dominated democratic regime to another, as yet undefined, democratic arrangement. It would not be surprising to find support in these countries for the equation, "new parties and new politicians = new campaign politics." Since the new parties and their politicians were obliged to appeal to new voters in a largely unknown and greatly changed political environment, the invention of new electoral techniques and tools had to be expected as a reasonable consequence. On the other hand, as a note of caution, not only does the repertoire of new electoral techniques and tools appear to be somewhat limited, but it is very much dependent on the nature of the political system, on the availability of those techniques and tools, and on the willingness of specific parties and politicians to use them. One is therefore justified in expecting, not astonishing breakthroughs of electoral imagination, but different mixtures of traditional and new techniques and tools in the different countries. The new, however, ought to prevail. As another note of caution, it must be added that the resort to new electoral techniques and tools does not necessarily imply that parties will lose their ties to specific social bases, or that politicians will deemphasize all specific social appeals. Both parties and politicians may, indeed, feel inclined to do so, but this outcome is by no means predetermined by their choice of new techniques and tools.

Whatever the new campaign politics is or has become in these southern European democracies, it may be useful to define the old campaign politics first. In order to do so in a manageable and convincing way, two perspectives are available. The first is to compare the way the political game is now being played in Greece, Portugal, and Spain and to identify the changes in the actors, the arenas, the issues, and the resources that occurred with the emergence of their respective democratic regimes. The second is to analyze closely the evolution of campaign politics in the case of a continuous democracy such as Italy. Exactly because Italy is now undergoing a complex transition, its case can be used as both a testing ground and a parameter for the evaluation of the changes that have taken place in the entire postwar period, and in an accelerated way in the past decade or so (see Parisi and Schadee 1995). In this chapter, I employ both perspectives.

I also seek to shed light on some aspects of the new campaign politics. Any attempt of this kind encounters formidable obstacles. All electoral campaigns take place within well-defined, and usually unique, institutional frameworks, and one must thus always take into account the structures of political opportunities available to the various political actors in their respective countries. In the case of transitions from authoritarian to democratic regimes, the change in the structure of political opportunities has understandably been dramatic, notwithstanding some underlying continuities worthy of exploration. Finally, there are always some elements of campaign politics that even experienced and shrewd observers cannot grasp, and at the national level never will. These include the electoral involvement of self-activating nonpolitical networks, professional organizations, informal groups playing a political communication role, and the reflected prestige enjoyed by well-known outsiders in politics. Unless they have explicitly publicized themselves, which they rarely seek to do, it is difficult to detect most of these participants and track their activities, and it is particularly hard to evaluate the impact of famous political outsiders such as Silvio Berlusconi on national electoral campaigns and their outcomes. These actors may nonetheless be highly significant, especially because the roots of the new campaign politics lie in the growing complexity of contemporary societies and political systems, and it is now reasonable to assume that most party organizations are no longer willing, and probably now unable, to manage all aspects of electoral campaigning.

The Old Campaign Politics

It is not easy to identify and summarize specific features of the old campaign politics (see Butler, Penniman, and Ranney 1981) common to all established democracies. On the whole, there is little doubt that the old campaign politics was fundamentally the product of party decisions, party organizations, and party activists. Obviously, the better structured and the more entrenched the party, the more pervasive its electoral campaign promised to be. The party was fully in charge of formulating and even communicating its electoral program. The mass media did have some ability to highlight certain aspects of the party program or of the candidates' personalities, but in the old campaign politics the extent of personalization of politics was limited—that is, the personal characteristics and qualities of the candidates were considered less important than their political positions. Moreover, most parties were producing their own flow of communications and easily counteracted political information independently disseminated by the mass media. It is also important to note that, at least up to the mid to late 1980s, television rarely played a dominant role in the political communication system. Finally, the electorates of established democracies continued to show a strong support for their parties and maintained a high level of identification with them. Most of the traits that characterized the old campaign politics were nicely captured and beautifully analyzed by Otto Kirchheimer (1966) in his discussion of the appearance of the catch-all party in Western democracies. It may be useful and revealing, therefore, to utilize Kirchheimer's analysis as a framework for the interpretation of the changes affecting campaign politics in southern Europe.

The Catch-All Syndrome

The best starting point for a comparative overview is a very simple assumption: in the old campaign politics, political parties practically dominated the political arena and the electoral process. If this simple characterization can be regarded as accurate, then the first obvious question involves the extent to which other actors have emerged in the new campaign politics and replaced political parties, or confined them to a relatively minor role. Relatedly, who are these new actors and what roles do they play? In the Preface to *The Politics of Democratic Consolidation* (Diamandouros and Gunther 1995, xi–xii), it was hypothesized that new democratic regimes may reflect more clearly various aspects of "modernity" than established democracies, because they have "leapfrogged" over development processes from an earlier era that left a lasting imprint on politics in older democratic systems. Accordingly, can we hypothesize that, because of the timing of their return to democracy, Greece, Portugal, and Spain entered directly into the era of the new campaign politics? And can one add that, because of its ongoing, protracted, and incomplete political transition, Italy, too, is experiencing in a rather dramatic way a sort of brand-new campaign politics? Is Italy making up for the time lost, and in which ways?

From many perspectives, Otto Kirchheimer's analysis of the emergence of the catch-all party most clearly identifies the issues we must address. Writing at the crossroads of the old politics and the new—during the early stages of the transformation of party politics in established democracies—Kirchheimer suggested that the transformation of class-mass or denominational mass parties into catch-all peoples' parties involved five changes: (1) the drastic reduction of the party's ideological baggage; (2) a further strengthening of top leadership groups; (3) the downgrading of the role of the individual party member; (4) a deemphasis of the *classe gardée* (protected class of loyal voters); and (5) the willingness of party leaders to secure access to a variety of interest groups. Taken together, these changes define *a contrario* the old campaign politics and describe key features of the new campaign politics. One important element in the catch-all thesis that has not been adequately explored (not even by Karl Dittrich, although he highlights this point) is Kirchheimer's (1966, 188) observation that "conversion to catch-all parties constitutes a competitive phenomenon. A party is apt to accommodate to its competitor's successful style because of hope of benefits or fear of losses on election day." Subsequent analyses and criticisms (e.g., Dittrich 1983) have succeeded neither in disproving nor in fundamentally modifying Kirchheimer's thesis,[1] which remains the best available starting point for our analysis of the new campaign politics.

Only one element is missing from Kirchheimer's analysis: the role of the media and, in particular, the role of television in politics. This is not surprising, because when Kirchheimer wrote, national evening news programs had just started in the United States. The political impact of television was very unclear and largely underestimated, both there and in Europe. Accordingly, Kirchheimer pointed to the persistent and rarely challenged ability of European political parties to control, if not to monopolize the processes of political communication. Writing three decades later, we are better able to assess the independent impact of television. Kirchheimer's framework nonetheless remains the most appropriate starting point for our discussion of the new campaign politics. In this overview, we need to ask to what extent the "new" has in fact replaced the "old" in the campaign politics of these southern European countries. Has the new politics been consolidated there or is it being counteracted by other developments?

Catch-All Campaign Politics

According to Kirchheimer, the first symptom of the transformation of politics is a drastic reduction in the party's ideological baggage. There is no need to elaborate on this point. Class-mass and denominational mass parties have not emerged in a viable way in the new democracies of southern Europe, with the possible exception of the Portuguese Communist Party. Perhaps the two most dramatic examples can be seen in Spain, where the Unión de Centro Democrático (UCD) emerged as the principal party of the center-right and never became

(Huneeus 1985) or wanted to be (Gunther, Sani, and Shabad 1986) a denominational mass party, and where the Partido Socialista Obrero Español (PSOE) jettisoned Marxism in a highly publicized way (Maravall 1981 and 1985). One might even add to these two important developments the decline of the communist parties of Greece and Spain as viable and relevant political actors well before the fall of the Berlin Wall. Even the Italian Communist Party, by far the most effective, the largest, and the least "communist" of these parties, felt rapidly obliged to change its name and logo, and to restructure its organization (although not very effectively). In any case, the new Partito Democratico Della Sinistra (PDS) underwent a schism and suffered heavy electoral losses before reacquiring some momentum. Nonetheless, in 1996, although constituting the major component of the governmental coalition, its electoral showing, 21.1, was still below that of 1953, 22.6.

All the other families of parties in southern Europe blend programmatic, populist, catch-all elements in their political-electoral appeals. Especially interesting, from this point of view, have been the transformation of PASOK in Greece and the Partido Popular in Spain. "For PASOK, the road to power essentially involved a long march from the left to the center of the spectrum, over seven years," that is between 1974 and 1981. Moreover, "in consequence of its electoral landslide, it may be safely assumed that the PASOK 'center of gravity' has actually coincided with the geometric center of the spectrum," so that "the centrality of PASOK in the notional Left-Right space has its counterpart in physical space: it is the remarkable homogeneity of its electoral support throughout the country" (Mavrogordatos 1983b, 41–42).

As to the Partido Popular (previously the Alianza Popular) in Spain, it has largely succeeded in shedding the image as well as the substance of its earlier identification with Francoism. Following conspicuous electoral defeats (Montero 1989), it has effectively and visibly moved toward the center of the political alignment, displacing the Centro Democrático y Social and winning most of its voters. It has successfully characterized itself as a viable and reassuring alternative to the socialist government, and, as such, it was rewarded by the voters with electoral advances in 1993 and 1996, coming to power with the latter victory. The transformation of the Partido Popular was the deliberate product and the desired consequence of the change of leadership from Manuel Fraga Iribarne to José María Aznar.

For its part, the Italian political experience shows the slow but irresistible transformation-disappearance of the two pillars of the postwar democratic regime: the class-mass (PCI) and the denominational (Democrazia Cristiana [DC]) parties, with the former undergoing a somewhat traumatic change of name, symbol, and policies in converting itself into the PDS and the latter experiencing a dramatic disintegration. Particularly noteworthy is the fact that one of the splinter groups that grew out of this disintegration, the Popolari, now forms part of a political coalition with the PDS.

Quite clearly, a different kind of campaign politics will be conducted by class-mass and denominational parties rather than by nonideological parties. The former parties will also differ substantially from the latter with regard to their ability to recruit and organize members, and to mobilize and sustain their activities. Among the parties surveyed in this chapter, only the Italian political parties of the First Republic seem really to deserve the label of mass parties from the point of view of their memberships and their territorial implantation. With regard to the PCI and its successors, the PDS and its unreconstructed communist rival, Rifondazione Comunista, there is a striking relationship between the growth and decline of membership and the parties' electoral fortunes. It should be noted that this relationship does not hold for the other Italian parties.

From the point of view of campaign politics, there is another important consequence deriving from the transformation into catch-all people's parties: the need for contemporary southern European parties to stress, not their limited and vague ideologies, but their programs, their policies, and their leadership in order to craft an attractive political profile. If one tentatively accepts the three-variable model utilized by the University of Michigan's Institute of Political Studies to predict the vote—as a function of party identification, issues, and candidates—then their relative weight, both as offered by the parties and as received by the voters in southern European democracies, has changed over time. While still relatively significant, party identification counts for much less than in the past. It remains a useful instrument for voters, but it cannot determine their votes all the time, in all elections, on all issues. The October 1995 Portuguese National Assembly elections, for example, provided "further evidence that a trend first noticed in the mid-1980s—the breakdown of party loyalties among an increasing proportion of the electorate—is continuing" (Corkill 1996, 406–7).

In general, "collective" issues can be seen to be declining in importance in electoral campaigns, while some specific issues have increased in significance. Electorates can be seen as including several distinct single-issue sectors, although these issue cleavages do not neatly divide voters into stable camps. This leads to the hotly debated problem of issue saliency and questions about what is salient in an electoral campaign. Although it remains difficult to evaluate the independent impact of issues on voting (as distinct from voters' party identification and the personalities of the candidates), several interesting examples deserve attention.

At least two Greek general elections, in October 1981 and June 1989, were fought primarily over issues. In October 1981, PASOK's "promise of 'Change' became the central theme and the single most effective battle cry of the campaign. Predictably, the promise of generic 'Change' proved irresistible. It could draw upon the quasi-universal dissatisfaction and even exasperation with the manifold limitations and failures of [Nea Demokratia's] policy. It could also be freely interpreted and thus attract the most diverse elements, as containing a solution to their own particular problems," George Mavrogordatos notes (1983b, 23–24). Michalis Spourdalakis offers a more critical interpretation:

> If political moderation crystallized by the simplistic slogan of *allaghi* [change] (which was the common denominator of almost all the parties participating in the election) was of great significance for the future development of Greek politics, it did not stand alone. The style and method of conducting the electoral campaign was the other significant characteristic of the 1981 elections which was to develop into a permanent trait of electoral competitions in the country. Here the common denominator of the parties' electoral tactics was the "commodification of the electoral antagonism." When politics are neither connected to their social base nor to concrete social projects in any structured, direct and conscious way, they are then bound to be confined to public relations, which in turn become subject to marketing techniques. (Spourdalakis 1988, 208)

Nikiforos Diamandouros's analysis of Greek postauthoritarian culture points to something more permanent in the electoral appeal of PASOK: a populist thread that "was not an exclusive preserve of the nonconservative forces" (Diamandouros 1994, 30) and that, quite understandably, fits nicely into the catch-all syndrome.

Some of the more negative implications of Spourdalakis's assessment were borne out by subsequent developments. In June 1989, after eight years of unscrupulous, pervasively clientelistic rule, PASOK itself became the target of a deeply felt issue, *katharsis*—that is, cleansing—of government and public administration:

> In the highly charged atmosphere created by the revelations of financial corruption, the programs of each of the parties played an even less

> important role than usual. Moreover, the "scandals" meant that attention was not primarily focused on PASOK's record in government but rather on the demands for Katharsis. In the event, the two dominant themes were the parties' opinions on the need for Katharsis and their varying perspectives on how to modernize Greece. (Featherstone 1990, 106)

The Portuguese general election of 1987 also deserves special attention because of its unexpected and extraordinary outcome—a victory by one party receiving an absolute majority of votes in a multiparty electoral contest run under a proportional system—and because it represents a significant turning point in the country's political evolution and democratic consolidation. The outgoing prime minister, Aníbal Cavaco Silva, leader of the Partido Social-Democrata (PSD), played an intelligent game. As described by Tom Gallagher:

> He ignored his competitors rather than attacking them systematically and made a pragmatic appeal to the electorate that can be summed up in the phrase: "I have governed and you are better off. Judge me by my results." There was no discussion of policies or ideas, and that struck a chord with those voters tired of sterile ideological debate that they found difficult to connect to ordinary realities. The PSD slogan, "Portugal cannot slow down," likewise captured the imagination of floating voters who were persuaded that necessary changes were afoot and that the country needed strong government after years of introspection and drift. (Gallagher 1988, 141–42)

When Cavaco subsequently "stunned his party by announcing that he would not be standing for reelection . . . the PSD was deprived of a major electoral asset" (Corkill 1996, 403) and lost the election.

In all likelihood, the optimistic picture of the country's future painted by Silvio Berlusconi in the Italian electoral campaign of 1994 was the most convincing factor in his propaganda, even more than his declared anticommunism. The promise of "one million jobs" appealed strongly to Italian voters, many of whom felt confidence in Berlusconi because he was the owner-chairman of a very successful enterprise, Fininvest, with its three major TV stations, and of a winning soccer team, Milan. No matter how misplaced and misleading the "one million jobs" promise was, it obliged the left to waste time trying to discredit Berlusconi, rather than presenting a positive, mobilizing, future-oriented vision of its own. It also forced leaders on the left to justify their roles as "professional politicians"—representatives of the political past and defenders of an inefficient state and its oppressive policies.

The personality of the candidate also appears to be a variable of growing importance. In the old campaign politics, voters were encouraged to trust their respective party organizations, to stick to their traditional party loyalties, and to vote as members of a particular social group. In the new campaign politics, parties ask for a programmatic vote by which the voters recognize the party's reliability and the candidate's competence in carrying out specific policies on one or more salient issues. In the old campaign politics, the party organization steered the electoral campaign machine and had charge of the recruitment and appointment of party personnel to governmental coalitions. In the new campaign politics, party leaders, a handful of the party's top candidates, and a few "experts" control the conduct of the campaign. Their roles are visible and prominent. The party organization is reduced to implementing policies designed elsewhere. Take, for instance, the case of the July 1987 general elections in Portugal:

> As before, the party machines in Lisbon imposed their choices on the provinces with rebellions only breaking out in a few district parties over an especially unpalatable choice. Except in the PSD, which nominated many candidates from its dynamic youth wing, there was little sign that talent was emerging from the local party grass-roots outside the hot-house atmosphere of Lisbon. The number of writers, columnists and celebrities who were placed high on party lists, having previously run for rival parties or having remained outside electoral politics, demonstrates the elitist and metropolitan character of politics right across the political spectrum. (Gallagher 1988, 140)

Again in Portugal, in October 1995, "the absence of real debate between the major parties ensured that personality rather than programme determined the outcome" (Corkill 1996, 404).

The personalization of electoral competition has emerged as a hotly debated issue in Italy. Recent proposals by a special parliamentary Committee for Constitutional Reforms would move the Italian system toward popular election of the president of the republic in a manner similar to French-style semipresidentialism. In the past, the Italian form of parliamentary government was not at all conducive to the personalization of politics. In contrast, personalization was inherent in the institutional mechanisms utilized in Greece and Spain from the very beginning, and this was certainly true of Portugal's semipresidential regime. Spain's constructive vote of no confidence, for example, allowed Felipe González to gain the limelight in 1981 and acquire public acceptability as a capable and responsible political leader. Indeed, the leadership factor played an extremely important role in the 1982 Spanish electoral campaign. One empirical study found that "53 per cent of [the] respondents who had voted for the UCD in 1979 shifted their support to another party in 1982 because of their rejection of the leadership style of the outgoing UCD government" (Gunther, Sani, and Shabad 1986, 417). In Greece, the head-on confrontation between Nea Demokratia and PASOK meant that Constantine Karamanlis and Andreas Papandreou were obliged to propel their personalities, their political biographies, and their governing capabilities to the forefront of the choices offered to voters. It must be added that both had already shown a very strong inclination to play the politics of personalization, which they did effectively and skillfully. The direct election of the president of the republic in Portugal allowed General Ramalho Eanes to personalize its politics both in 1976 and in 1981. In his turn, Mário Soares successfully exploited his toughly won popularity to defeat the candidate of the center-right in a very close presidential election in 1986, and Cavaco Silva succeeded in projecting his image as a capable prime minister and statesman both in 1987 and again in 1991. The lesson was learned by the opponents, and in October 1995, the Portuguese socialist leader António Guterres "projected a statesmanlike image in an attempt to capitalise on the PS's lead in the opinion polls" (Corkill 1996, 405). In Spain, the Partido Popular "had acquired a modern, youthful and attractive image" by March 1996 (Amodia 1996, 814).

The Italian transition has so far been characterized by the creation of a so-called government of professors, led by a former governor of the Bank of Italy, Carlo Azeglio Ciampi, who had never previously held elective office (Pasquino and Vassallo 1995), although it should be noted that in this first stage (April 1993–March 1994) half of the ministers were politicians. Similarly, following Berlusconi's government (April–December 1994), Lamberto Dini (Berlusconi's minister of the Treasury) formed a government characterized by the *International Herald Tribune* as consisting of "low-profile professionals," who felt encouraged to behave in an explicitly antipolitical or apolitical manner (Pasquino 1996). The two elections of the Italian transition, 1994 and 1996, have been won by newcomers: the entrepreneur Silvio Berlusconi and Romano Prodi, a professor of economics, better known as former chairman of the industrial state holding company IRI. Berlusconi's personality may have contributed to the victory of his coalition, especially since he was also a "political entrepreneur" (as defined by Joseph Schumpeter [1942]), as the founder and leader of a new political movement, Forza Italia! Prodi appeared only as the linchpin of a diversified and heterogeneous coalition, l'Ulivo ("The Olive Tree"). The common element favoring both Berlusconi and Prodi was that the antiparty, antipolitics wind continued blowing strongly in what were the first steps of the new campaign politics, as well as the first attempts to inaugurate a bipolar democratic competition. By 1996, however, Berlusconi was no longer a newcomer to politics.

The opening up of the parties to personalities recruited from outside their ranks leads directly to the second development foreseen by Kirchheimer: the further strengthening of top leadership groups. In the old campaign politics, what counted for many parties was the presentation of a unified and unifying party message or program and its decentralized diffusion and publicization by thousands of motivated party activists. In the new campaign politics, both the messages and the programs are somewhat diluted, becoming little more than catchwords or slogans. Political leadership is concentrated in the hands of one individual or a small group of party leaders. Moreover, there is usually an almost complete overlap between the roles of party and governmental or parliamentary leadership. The old campaign politics was meant to encourage society to acquire some representation in the palaces of power. The new campaign politics seems to be designed to allow the incumbents in those palaces to reach out to society in order to strengthen their power. At the center of the communication system, one only finds top leaders. Theirs is the power; theirs is the responsibility, if any; theirs are the successes or, less frequently, the failures. In fact, quite understandably, failures are attributed most of the time to factors outside of their control—to conspiracies of different kinds or just to unfavorable conditions. In the Italian case, the progressives, that is, the left, attributed their 1994 defeat to the overwhelming power of Silvio Berlusconi's TV stations and not to their spectacular inability to construct a broader, winning coalition or to their poor choice of electoral themes. Ironically, Berlusconi blamed his own 1996 defeat, not on his inability to master the coalition game, but on a newly approved regulation that prevented him from deploying his TV firepower.

The strengthening of top leadership groups is especially visible during electoral campaigns. As an obvious consequence, it also has a significant impact on the formation of governments. With the exception of the Italian First Republic, a very high degree of personalization has characterized politics in all the new southern European democracies. From the beginnings of their respective transitions to the present day, the Greek, Spanish, and Portuguese political systems provide many examples of leaders who have been willing and able to play up their personal qualities.

The duel between Karamanlis and Papandreou in 1974–81 both mobilized Greek voters and stabilized Greek democracy. In October 1981, Mavrogordatos writes,

> instead of a "charismatic duel," Greek voters were offered the reassuring and irresistible prospect of a "charismatic tandem." The personal authority and considerable constitutional powers of Karamanlis as President of the Republic represented the most visible and tangible guarantee for future normality and moderation, thereby defusing the disquieting and even anxiety-provoking aspects of a prospective PASOK victory at the polls. . . . Moreover, the prospect of President Karamanlis and Prime Minister Papandreou working together for the benefit of the country certainly fulfilled a deep-seated wish of the electorate, on the elemental but potent psychic level of charismatic identification. (Mavrogordatos 1983b, 20)

To a certain extent, a similar development took place in Spain. A (quasi) charismatic duel between Adolfo Suárez and Felipe González characterized the first few years of Spanish democracy. Following the decisive role played by King Juan Carlos in the attempted coup of February 1981, one might argue, the king and González came to constitute a new charismatic tandem, which reassured moderate voters and public opinion at large. Subsequently, Spanish politics in the 1980s and mid 1990s was dominated by the personality of González and by the attempt of the conservative opposition to identify a leader as popular and potentially as charismatic. While José María Aznar may never become this type of leader, he has at least succeeded in projecting an image reassuring enough to win the 1996 elections. Generally speaking, there is little doubt that González's personality and charismatic appeal made the difference in the October 1989 and, above all, in the June 1993 elections. In 1989, as one observer has noted, "Felipe González, seeing himself more as a statesman than a party leader in an electoral contest, kept his public appearances to a minimum" (Amodia 1990, 294). And in 1993, "González organized a campaign that would bring him victory against what appeared to be overwhelming odds. It was achieved by concentrating the whole operation around the leader's image. . . . The PSOE mounted the most highly personalized campaign since 1977. . . . Hence the presidentialist tone of Socialist strategy, a one-man campaign, an election turned into a plebiscite about Felipe González" (Amodia 1994, 184–85).

In Portugal, there was a peculiar personalization of politics from the very beginning of the transition, not only the obvious and overt personalization of party leadership by such figures as the socialist Mário Soares and the communist Alvaro Cunhal, but also the not-so-subtle personalization of politics by military leaders. Even though the Armed Forces Movement tried to resist this trend, some military officers became extremely popular and greatly influential. In the end, this resulted in the direct election of General Eanes to the presidency of the republic in 1976, in his active role in the formation of several governments, in his reelection in 1981, and, finally, in his briefly successful attempt to sponsor a political party, the Partido Renovador Democrático (PRD). "On the night of 6 October 1985, a feeling of disbelief spread through the Portuguese political system. The six-month-old Democratic Renewal party, with a long-list of neophyte candidates, running on a program based on little more than support for President Ramalho Eanes and the need to bring morality into parliamentary politics, had taken 18 per cent of the vote" (Bruneau and Macleod 1986, 203). However, the presidential aura could last only as long as the power of the office was wielded. The PRD's share of the vote declined very quickly, from 18.4 in 1985 to 4.9 in 1987, after Eanes was replaced as president by Mário Soares.

Nevertheless, Portuguese politics remained highly personalized, not only in the expected arena of presidential elections, but also in parliamentary elections. In the 1986 presidential contest, Soares won because his personality and his political career appeared more valuable, more appealing, and far superior in general to those of his opponent, the CDS leader Diogo Freitas do Amaral (backed by the PSD). In the general elections of 1987 and 1991, Cavaco Silva effectively exploited his position as incumbent prime minister, and "the scale of his victory" was in the first place "very much a personal endorsement especially from the young and a widening band of floating voters" (Gallagher 1988, 139). This was exceeded in the following election, in which Cavaco Silva "chose a high-risk strategy in strongly personalizing the campaign to its maximum. . . . Personification of the election" seemed the logical culmination of his "image-building efforts" over the preceding two years (Calder 1992, 168). An interesting parallel between Greece and Portugal had developed. The sharp and, perhaps, bitter competition between Cavaco Silva and Soares in the 1985 general elections and, by proxy (because Cavaco supported Freitas do Amaral) in the 1986 presidential elections was transformed into a substantially successful cooperation.

Borrowing Mavrogordatos's image, the (slightly less) charismatic duel in Portugal had also become a (slightly less) charismatic tandem.

"Rather than using his office to crusade in favor of socialism, as some had suspected, [Soares] settled for the role of a non-partisan, establishment figure and became known affectionately as Rei Mário (King Mário)" (Corkill 1991, 186). Moreover, "by opting for peaceful coexistence with the government, Soares ensured that Portugal's experiment in cohabitation was, in public perception, an unqualified success" (ibid., 187). In any case, Cavaco Silva himself "decided without consultation not to run a candidate in opposition to Soares in 1991. In so doing he recognized that the PSD had no one within its ranks of sufficient stature to be a credible alternative to the incumbent. The decision was rationalized on the grounds that the country required a sustained period of political stability and equilibrium" (Corkill 1991, 187–88).

The quasi-charismatic Portuguese tandem has provided for the reduction of party polarization, political stability, and government effectiveness. A more balanced assessment of the personalization of politics is offered in the conclusions to this chapter. Here, it suffices to stress that parties unable to rely on popular leaders have been at a distinct disadvantage in southern European politics. However, it must also be emphasized that the personalization of politics has been all the more effective when it has relied, not just on personalities, but also on the support of viable organizations (Pasquino 1990b and 1990c).

Kirchheimer points to another variable that is relevant to the increasing importance of personal political and party leadership: the downgrading of the role of the individual party member. The old campaign politics was largely based on the mobilization of party members and party activists, on their ability to disseminate and explain the positions of the party, and to reach and convince the voters, often through door-to-door campaigns. All of this presupposed an active party life, requiring the involvement, albeit in a subordinate way, of many (if not most) party members in deliberations over party policies, programs, alliances, and candidates. This did not necessarily amount to party democracy, although the process was characterized by a certain degree of debate, circulation of political ideas, and a fair amount of representation of different viewpoints. Party members were kept informed of important developments, receiving most of their political information directly from more or less democratically authorized party sources. In turn, party members constituted an important vehicle for the dissemination of ideas, opinions, positions, and platforms.

All this may have not yet disappeared in its entirety, but the concentration of power in the hands of party leaders has certainly produced some downgrading of the role of individual party members, as reflected in declining activism of party members and less than vigorous efforts to recruit new ones. "All Portuguese parties have experienced a decreased commitment on the part of their members. Disappointment with the results of political action, the availability of alternatives on a much greater scale than before, and the impact of the economic crisis have all undoubtedly contributed to this phenomenon" (Bruneau and Macleod 1986, 59). In October 1995, Portuguese party "leaders monopolized the campaign material and funds, reducing senior figures on the lists to street meetings and local visits" (Corkill 1991, 404).

Similarly, power in Greek political parties has "continued to flow downwards. This has been affected by the nature of state-civil relations and by the weakness of wider social structures. The parties have integrated their publics into a new legitimate political system, but as vehicles for debate and representation they are still relatively underdeveloped" (Featherstone 1990, 194–95). Spourdalakis goes further, strongly criticizing PASOK for having demoralized the rank and file and made the organization "a mere appendage to the government's legitimizing function" (Spourdalakis 1988, 258).

Spanish parties, aside from the PSOE and recently the Partido Popular, have been characterized by "factional infighting, frequent changes in leadership and party names, and even a willingness to cohabit with strange bedfellows"; the exceptional case of the PSOE is explained by "the strong discipline—sometimes described as Leninist—imposed on the party by Guerra and his acolytes . . . [which] left little room for dissident factions, and turned the party congresses held since 1979 into occasions for unanimity and enthusiastic applause" (Amodia 1994, 179). "The early years of Socialist government saw a decline in local branch activity to such an extent that one influential newspaper editor [José Luis Cebrián of *El País*] described the PSOE as simply 'a fabulous electoral machine and a political job centre'" (Gillespie 1990, 141).

The downgrading of party members is nowhere more visible and significant than in the political movement created by Silvio Berlusconi, Forza Italia! In fact, Forza Italia! has never had and does not really want party members. Berlusconi envisaged it rather as what might more appropriately be called a "political network": an aggregation of electoral committees sponsored, recognized, and, from time to time, dissolved from the top. The initial organizational network of Forza Italia! was provided by Publitalia, Berlusconi's company for the acquisition of advertising contracts. All efforts to go beyond Publitalia have failed (Maraffi 1995; Seisselberg 1996; McCarthy 1997). Despite repeated announcements, for example, no party convention has yet taken place at the time of writing (June 2000). This has not prevented Forza Italia! from suddenly emerging in second place among Italian political movements (Berlusconi abhors the word "party") in terms of votes and popular esteem, or retaining that position. Inasmuch as Forza Italia! consists of a parliamentary group and units associated with a business firm (now called Mediaset), reliable data on its political personnel can only be based on its representation in the Chamber of Deputies and the Senate. These data, presented in Table 5.1, indicate that Forza Italia! parliamentarians are mostly highly educated men in prestigious occupations, but with extremely limited political experience. The contrast with the parliamentarians of the Partito Democratico della Sinistra is striking, partly because of the PDS's roots in the old system. Forza Italia! is an exceptional case even when compared with the Northern League, whose parliamentarians have a socioeducational profile intermediate between those of FI and the PDS.

Table 5.1 Forza Italia!, Partito Democratico della Sinistra, and Northern League Parliamentarians Compared, 1994–1996

	Forza Italia!	PDS	League	Average
Pct. having served in three or more parliaments				
Chamber	2.6	8.2	1.7	8.9
Senate	2.1	10.2	0	9.5
Pct. female				
Chamber	10.0	19.9	10.0	11.3
Senate	2.1	15.9	0	8.3
Pct. college graduates				
Chamber	73.5	59.6	46.5	66.9
Senate	87.2	68.3	63.0	76.5
Pct. having previously served in party or elective office				
1994	7.7	43.7	22.2	32.9
1996	13.0	54.8	44.1	41.1
Pct. career politicians or trade unionists (Chamber only)				
1994	3.5 (4)	44.6 (57)	5.9 (7)	
1996	0.9 (1)	36.3 (53)	3.9 (2)	
Pct. entrepreneurs, managers, lawyers, professionals, university professors				
1994	66.1	23.4	51.6	
1996	72.6	32.1	50.0	

Source: Computed from Verzichelli 1997, 319, 326–27, 329–30, and 340.

The political inexperience of Forza Italia! parliamentarians has resulted in significant instances of political ineffectiveness, both in the government and in the opposition. This situation has been only slightly mitigated by the election of a seasoned former Christian Democrat as leader of the FI group in the Chamber of Deputies. Forza Italia!'s only organizational support, aside from that provided by Berlusconi and Mediaset, consists of a few ad hoc electoral committees created by parliamentary candidates relying on their own personal resources to finance their political activities, in pursuit of conspicuous rewards in terms of increased visibility. On the whole, it is now clear that Forza Italia! is not and never will be a traditional party based on membership, local structures, and an elected leadership.

The downgrading of party members in southern European political systems has been accompanied by several important changes. Most parties no longer look for energy and resources in their own ranks, but instead increasingly employ outside consultants and campaign staff. Paradoxically, they may wind up hiring people who would earlier have worked within the party in similar capacities, but whose qualities were inadequately put to use there, leading them to become freelance pollsters and political consultants. This shift from political craftsmen to professional managers is perhaps a distinguishing characteristic of the new campaign politics, whose consequences for both the nature of parties and the quality of democracy are as yet unforeseen. For example, the ups and downs of membership involvement and the financial resources available to fill the gaps left by declining membership dues and lack of militant enthusiasm may affect electoral outcomes. The personalization of politics and leadership cannot successfully address this problem.

Indeed, the reason why professional consultants and managers are hired is to go beyond the traditional borders of a specific class or denominational clientele. They must successfully deemphasize the *classe gardée* "in favor of recruiting voters among the population at large" (Kirchheimer 1966, 190). This is not an easy game to play; hence, party experts are shunned and professional consultants and managers are increasingly relied upon. This deemphasis of the *classe gardée* is notable with regard to most southern European parties, especially those focusing on the attainment of national office and control of governments. Mavrogordatos (1983b, 21) has highlighted the ability of PASOK in 1981 to "appeal to all the 'non-privileged' over their traditional party loyalties." Richard Gunther, Giacomo Sani, and Goldie Shabad have carefully analyzed how all Spanish parties crafted their electoral strategies. For conservative parties, "ideology posed no difficulty." Both the UCD and the AP "explicitly defined themselves as interclassist. The UCD behaved as a catch-all party *par excellence.*" However, "for the two major parties of the left, the PCE and the PSOE, the adoption of a broad target strategy required a redefinition of the notion of the working class." The PCE has by and large failed to complete this task successfully. In the case of the PSOE, the "inconsistency between the [PSOE's] catch-all electoral strategy and the party's exclusionary working-class ideology" provoked a crisis within the party in 1979, which was initially resolved through a high-risk blackmail strategy by Felipe González (who temporarily resigned as party leader) and the firm imposition of party discipline by Alfonso Guerra (Gunther, Sani, and Shabad, 1986, 183–90). The very fact that this transformation was attempted so early after the transition to democracy indicates that the catch-all constraints were already at work and were correctly perceived even by left-wing party leaders.

The perhaps inevitable downgrading of party members may not be a totally negative phenomenon, provided that voters are presented with other opportunities for political participation and influence. Nonetheless, this downgrading is and will continue to be a controversial issue in many political parties in southern European democracies.

The fourth dimension of the shift to catch-all politics identified and spelled out by Kirchheimer is also a contentious issue: the securing of access to a variety of interest groups. Instead of autonomously deciding which interest groups ought to be the focus of their attention and establishing long-term working relationships with them, political parties seem to have tried to present themselves as open to the demands of as many interest groups as possible. Transitions are usually dominated by political parties so that interest politics really emerges only once the democratic regime is reasonably consolidated (Schmitter 1995). In addition, southern European political systems have traditionally limited interest-group politics, which requires the ability of groups in society to organize independently of politics and, if necessary, to confront the power wielders. Nonetheless, there have been some significant signs of change in the four countries discussed here.

The Italian case has been most extensively analyzed from this perspective, and some distinguishing elements are therefore easily identified. For some time, the old campaign politics in Italy was characterized by the existence of close, almost symbiotic relationships (of either the *clientela* or the *parentela* variety, using LaPalombara 1964's terms) between certain parties and organized groups. For instance, the Ministry of Industry had its client groups in industrial associations, while Christian Democratic ministers, especially the minister of education, were clearly linked to Catholic organizations, such as those of Catholic elementary and junior high school teachers. Few associations or professional groups existed or played active political roles without previously establishing a good and preferably lasting relationship with a governing party (above all, with the DC). It took approximately thirty years for this situation to change (see Tarrow 1989). Most traditional associations, mainly those of industrial and agricultural interests, have succeeded in disengaging themselves from too close a relationship with political parties, while new groups have appeared that shun any intense, lasting relationship with parties. In return, parties have sought to establish different patterns of relationships with interest groups. Given that in the new electoral environment (where 75 percent of parliamentary seats are allocated in single-member constituencies) interest-group support may be necessary for victory, Italian parties have attempted, with great difficulty and limited success, to open themselves up to a wide array of associations, groups, and movements.

Political parties might want to "secure access to a variety of interest groups," as Kirchheimer indicated. However, now it is interest groups that decide whether, when, and with which resources they want to take advantage of the new situation. In Italy, many of them, especially Confindustria, the national business association, have decided not to deal preferentially with any political party. They regard such independence as less costly and as enhancing their bargaining abilities. Recently, even trade unions, although expressing a preference for the center-left l'Ulivo coalition, have declared that the Olive Tree government is a not a *governo amico* (government of friends).

It is difficult to provide as clear a picture for the other southern European countries. Increasingly, the working-class unions have detached themselves from left-wing parties, while business associations have developed a viable exchange-relationship only with conservative parties, especially when those parties are in government. On the whole, it appears that interest groups and professional associations play a rather limited political role, in part because they do not want to become involved, and in part because they lack the capability and the resources to do so. In Portugal, for instance, "few people join groups; those with the most obvious political implications, such as the unions and owners' associations, are split; and the Church is limited in its political role. There must undoubtedly be some other, more informal, means for groups to have access to government but it is not clear what these are" (Bruneau and Macleod 1986, 115). Philippe

Schmitter contends that, in Spain, Portugal, and Italy, these are "systems of interest intermediation that most resemble modern neocorporatism" (Schmitter 1995, 313). Schmitter also indicates, however, that "only in the cases of Spain and Italy is there any evidence that capitalist associations have tried independently to suborn parties and to influence the outcome of elections" (ibid., 314). Even this observation belongs, at least for Italy, to what now seems a distant past, difficult to revive. As for Greece, during its first term of office (1981–85), PASOK attempted to penetrate and politicize the trade unions, cooperatives, and the student movement, obliging Nea Demokratia to react with a similar attempt. Both parties utilized clientelistic practices vis-à-vis the administrative apparatus (Spanou 1996).

For a multiplicity of reasons, in none of the southern European democracies has there been a close and lasting relationship between parties and interest groups, as had characterized the First Italian Republic. Obviously, there remain significant political and social affinities between some parties and some interest groups, which are understandable products of the preferences of various groups for parties of the left or right. On the whole, too, the relationship of organized interests to organized parties in Greece, Portugal, and Spain has been an evolving one (see Linz 1981a; Fakiolas 1987). Indeed, this more flexible relationship has obliged political parties to frame their electoral appeals more broadly in order not to antagonize any potential supporters. And it has enabled political parties to govern without being fettered by inextricable ties and embarrassing promises.

It is safe to say that the new campaign politics in southern Europe has been characterized by the willingness of most or all political parties to show themselves available to accommodate inputs of different kinds from almost the entire spectrum of interest groups. It is not just a matter of receiving money, even though money remains very important in all electoral campaigns. Neither is it just a matter of shaping policies and writing amendments to bills, even though, of course, "special interest groups" are very interested in the substance of the policies. It is also a matter of providing candidacies and seats for representatives of specific interest groups in order to demonstrate the openness of the party organization, the legitimacy of those interests, and the governing potential of the party itself. Finally, and above all, it is a matter of drafting a catch-all party program that appeals to a wide variety of sectors. The breadth and generality of these appeals are illustrated by the various slogans utilized in past election campaigns: "Nothing but Spain Matters" (Alianza Popular, 1997); "Spain in Progress" (PSOE, 1989); "España en positivo" (PSOE, 1996);

"Change" (PASOK, 1981); "For Victory and New Progress" (PASOK, 1989); "Liberty-Creation-Social Protection" (Nea Demokratia, 1987); "Portugal for Everybody" (PS, 1987); "More Portugal" (PRD, 1987); "Portugal Cannot Slow Down" (PSD, 1987); "Razão e coração" (Reason and heart) (PS, 1995); "Pride in Being Portuguese" (PP, 1995).

All this having been said, it remains true that not even the emergence of what was called the "new politics" has completely disrupted the ability of political parties to control and run electoral campaigns effectively. Aside from a few exceptions, even while acquiring catch-all traits, only parties have the organizational, political, financial resources to sustain the protracted efforts required for electoral campaigns. Moreover, most changes from traditional campaign politics were introduced and monitored by the party organizations themselves, helping them to adapt successfully, especially when the party system was itself consolidated (see Katz 1987). When uncontrollable societal dynamics inevitably produced challenges, parties and party systems reacted in different ways, conditioned by their strengths as well as by the timing of those challenges. Driven by the political imperative to reach the voters in order to acquire or hold on to power in the face of altered conditions, these "competitive adjustments" were often very substantial and quickly implemented (see Gunther, Sani, and Shabad 1986, esp. chs. 3 and 4).

The most important of the challenges to the old party-dominated campaign politics emanated from the media. Almost from the very beginning of their democratic resurrection, the political systems of Greece, Portugal, and Spain clearly revealed important features of the new campaign politics. In part, the irruption of these new styles of campaigning into politics was the product of the reintroduction of competitive politics into societies in which television had become the principal medium of political communication. The impact of this medium was muted in other European democracies (including Italy, for some time) because established parties and other institutionalized political relationships could filter and reduce the impact of the majority of the challenges. Given its great impact on politics in southern Europe, we must devote considerable attention to the media in our exploration of the new campaign politics.

The Role of the Media

If there is a common denominator to campaign politics in the 1980s and 1990s, not only in southern Europe but in all democratic polities, it is the increasing role played by the media. In some cases, such as, for instance, the campaign run by the Italian TV impresario Silvio Berlusconi in the winter of 1993–94, the media are believed to have played a decisive role. While this may be an extreme example, one is safe in stating that the existing configuration of the media—their pluralism, their diffusion, their pervasiveness—is bound to have a significant impact upon the campaign politics of democratic systems. The impact of television is especially powerful.

Electoral politics in Italy and Spain have been most susceptible to the political influence of the media. Indeed, Berlusconi's extraordinary control over Italian television helped him to manufacture an electoral victory by himself allocating television coverage to parties and candidates, and through manipulation of political messages and images (Ricolfi 1994a). The increased political impact of television was due to occupation of the political space left empty by the declining roles previously played by several organizations such as the Church, the trade unions and traditional political parties. Specifically, the weakening of the old DC organizations, the disappearance of the Partito Socialista Italiano and minor centrist parties, and the frailty of the not yet (re)consolidated Partito Democratico della Sinistra, helped a new political figure like Berlusconi to capitalize on the "novelty-effect" of his candidacy and a completely new style of campaign politics. In this relative vacuum, Berlusconi in politics *was* the news, at least as presented by his own television broadcasts. The situation was exacerbated by the fact that he owned practically the entire private sector of TV broadcasting. He shrewdly used his media to bombard the voters even before the official start of the 1994 electoral campaign. In the end, he became prime minister in his first run for public office.

Spain is the other significant example. Television coverage is widely regarded as having been decisive in rescuing Felipe González from an expected defeat in 1993, enabling him to continue to serve for an additional three years as prime minister. In this case, television's political impact was not primarily because of biased coverage. Content analyses of broadcasts by all of Spain's major networks during the 1993 campaign reveals that, some marked partisan preferences by specific channels notwithstanding,[2] reasonably fair coverage was provided by each channel, and the aggregate impact of television-media bias is minimal, given that different channels exhibited modest biases in favor of different parties. Thus, "the effects of media bias on electoral behavior in Spain" were "relatively moderate, and . . . clearly interactive with other determinants of the vote, such as [the respondent's] initial ideological or partisan predisposition" (Gunther, Montero, and Wert 2000, 65).

Instead, the television "media effect" on politics was manifested in a substantial shift of votes toward the PSOE as the result of González's impressive performance in the second televised debate of the campaign. Confirming a journalist's assertion that this debate performance was decisive in shifting enough voters into the socialist camp to assure victory (Sinova 1993), an analysis of panel data from pre- and postelection interviews with a sample of Spanish voters revealed that just such a change took place, and was strongly associated with the respondent's perception of who had won that debate. The power of television was reaffirmed, in a negative way, in the 1996 election that brought the Partido Popular leader José María Aznar to power. Acknowledging González's impressive abilities to use television to his advantage, Aznar rejected "the offer of a head to head confrontation in front of the television cameras . . . , the PP preferring to run a prudent and moderate campaign" (Amodia 1996, 815). Had Aznar accepted the TV debate González insisted in asking for, the electoral outcome might have been different. "González personally had a crucial part in convincing most traditional Socialist voters that a vote for the PSOE was the only effective way of denying the PP an absolute majority. Interviewed at length three days before the election, on the same night as Aznar, comparisons between the two candidates could be drawn by a large television audience. There was no mistaking who was the consummate politician" (Gillespie 1996, 429–30). In Italy in 1996, on the basis of calculations similar to Aznar's, Romano Prodi accepted only one TV debate, rather than the three desired by his opponent, Berlusconi.

In Spain, the great political impact of television is a product of its complete dominance as a medium for political communication:

> In terms of actual viewing habits, surveys reveal that over 90 per cent of the population watch television every day, and 67 percent of our 1993 survey respondents said that they followed the news on television every day (with another 12 percent watching television news broadcasts three or four times a week). The number of viewing hours has increased steadily since the introduction of private television in 1990: by 1994, the average Spaniard was watching about three and one half hours of television per day. (Gunther, Montero, and Wert 2000, 58)

Even more significant, the increase in TV exposure has not been accompanied or in any way counterbalanced by an increase in the number of people reading newspapers. "Between the mid 1970s and 1994, the percentage of Spaniards over the age of 14 who read newspapers every day increased from 30–32 percent to 38 percent of those polled in media surveys" (ibid., 52).

Three different variables appear to be relevant to the impact of the media on electoral politics: first, whether the media are in a position to structure electoral and political competitions in a specific way; second, whether they compel the protagonists to behave in a certain way, therefore giving precise structural advantages through rewards and punishments to some political actors; and, third, whether the voters are actually and significantly influenced more by the medium, so to speak, than by the quality of the political actors participating in that portion of the electoral campaign that is televised. It must be added that the televised portions of the electoral campaign are usually growing by default—that is, because parties and politicians are no longer capable nor willing to employ grass-roots and door-to-door methods.

Compared with Italy and Spain, the role of the media (especially television) appears less significant in Greece and Portugal. To be sure, Portuguese politicians appreciated the political impact of the media, especially in light of the concern and preoccupation that grew out of coverage by the international press of the events of 1974–76. Indeed, "after the revolution, the media remained the focus of political controversy as successive governments forgot their leaders' earlier declarations about the sublime value of the freedom of the press and in turn attempted to control radio and television and to neutralize their critics in the widely circulated state-owned newspapers" (Bruneau and Macleod 1986, 165). Despite these efforts to acquire control of the media (recently a common feature of politics in eastern and central Europe), clear evidence is lacking concerning the impact of the Portuguese media on the new campaign politics, especially with regard to the extent to which political communication through the media has displaced other, more traditional channels.

With regard to Greece, several scholars have indicated that the traditional organization of mass political rallies, intended as a show of party strength, was reported, and to some extent distorted, by the television coverage given to them. Richard Clogg notes that "all the parties continued to place great emphasis on the size of their electoral rallies as a likely indicator of their performance at the polls" (Clogg 1987, 113). And George Mavrogordatos observes:

> To the benefit of PASOK, television primarily served as a sounding board for mass rallies. It magnified and projected their sensational effect throughout the country. It also magnified the personal appeal of Papandreou, both as a fiery orator in mystical communion with the

> crowd and as a moderate, articulate, and charming speaker addressing the viewers. Conversely, television also magnified the dismal lack of all these qualities on the part of the otherwise likable Rallis. (Mavrogordatos 1983b, 27)

Likewise, "to the benefit of the minor parties, television significantly increased the awareness of their existence, promoted their image, and especially that of their most attractive spokesmen: Ioannis Pesmazoglu (KODISO) and Leonidas Kyrkos (KKE-Esoterikou)" (ibid., 29). Subsequently, the importance of political rallies has been so reduced that in the three most recent Greek elections (1993, 1997, and 2000), "there has been a significant increase of the role of the media relative to that of rallies" (Diamandouros, personal communication; also see Dimitras 1994).

All this premised and duly taken into account, the way political parties and candidates campaign, and the way voters follow campaign politics in order to shape their opinions before voting must be regarded as much more complicated than could be captured by a direct and deterministic relationship between the media and the voters. Such effects must be subjected to careful scrutiny in light of empirical analysis. In particular, as the classic literature on political communication has revealed, it is extremely important to know whether voters discuss politics with relatives, friends, colleagues, and peers, whether they are linked into associational networks of different kinds, and how they receive political information from the communications media.

Fortunately, the Comparative National Elections Project (CNEP), a comparative cross-national survey, has undertaken public opinion polls in three of the four southern European democracies that included a number of items addressing these questions.[3] The first conclusion to be drawn from this survey is that Spaniards are significantly less involved in politics than are citizens of other southern European countries. As can be seen in Table 5.2, Spaniards tried much less of-

Table 5.2 Attempts to Influence the Political Views of Others

	Spain	Greece	Italy
Often	5.8% (84)	22.1% (264)	19.7% (493)
Sometimes	20.6 (297)	28.3 (338)	22.8 (570)
Rarely	23.8 (344)	19.8 (237)	18.5 (462)
Never	49.8 (720)	29.3 (350)	38.5 (963)
Don't know/No answer		0.6 (7)	0.6 (14)
Total	100.0 (1,445)	100.0 (1196)	100.0 (2,502)

Source: Comparative National Elections Project surveys of Greece, Italy, and Spain.

Table 5.3 Frequency with Which Respondents Followed Campaign Through Different Communications Media

	Every/Nearly Every Day	3 or 4 Times Per Week	1 or 2 Times Per Week	Less Frequently	Never
Television					
Greece	74.1% (716)	11.7% (113)	5.6% (54)	2.4% (23)	6.0% (58)
Italy	75.1 (1878)	17.2 (431)	5.0 (124)	0.4 (11)	2.0 (50)
Spain	59.3 (858)	13.5 (196)	8.6 (124)	5.5 (79)	8.0 (116)
Newspapers					
Greece	18.5 (179)	8.7 (84)	9.3 (90)	3.9 (38)	59.1 (571)
Italy	32.1 (803)	18.1 (452)	17.6 (441)	3.2 (81)	28.9 (722)
Spain	19.9 (288)	7.7 (111)	12.6 (183)	3.5 (51)	51.2 (741)
Radio					
Greece	14.9 (144)	6.5 (63)	4.7 (45)	3.6 (35)	69.2 (668)
Italy	2.4 (61)	0.1 (3)	0.1 (2)	0.0 (10)	97.3 (2434)
Spain	21.7 (314)	7.0 (101)	4.2 (61)	5.0 (73)	56.0 (823)

Source: Comparative National Election Project surveys.

Note: In Greece and Italy, this question was asked of all respondents. In the Italian survey, this question was asked after a "filter" question in which respondents were asked which newspaper they read most frequently, which television news broadcast they watched most frequently, and which radio news they followed most closely. Those who mentioned no paper or station are categorized as "never."

ten than Greeks or Italians did to persuade others to change their political views. Indeed, nearly half of the respondents in the Spanish survey said that they had never done so, and only about one out of every twenty said that they often did. Greeks and Italians were substantially more likely to be politically active in this manner.

The dominance of television as the principal medium of political communication in southern European democracies is clearly revealed in other data derived from these surveys. When asked how frequently they had followed news about the recently concluded election campaign through various communications media, the overwhelming majority of Greeks, Italians, and Spaniards revealed their heavy reliance on television for this kind of political information. As can be seen in Table 5.3, large majorities of survey respondents in all three countries said that they had watched television news broadcasts every day during the campaign. Nonetheless, some interesting national variations are apparent in these data. Italians were much more likely to have followed the campaign by reading newspapers than were Greeks or Spaniards. Over half of Italian respondents reported that they read about campaign politics in the newspapers at least three or four times a week, as compared with just over 27 percent of Greeks and Spaniards. Conversely, extraordinarily few Italians followed the 1996 campaign through radio news broadcasts, whereas radio was the second most preferred medium in Greece and Spain. And in Spain, as distinct from the other two countries, more voters listened to radio coverage of the campaign than read about it in the press.

The extremely low level of radio-news listenership during the campaign in Italy may partly be the result of the fact that (unlike in Greece and Spain) this question followed a "filter" question in which respondents were asked to name the radio news channel they most frequently listened to (which the extreme fragmentation of the radio broadcasting system in Italy makes difficult to answer),[4] but this finding accords with data from two other Italian surveys. Postelection polls conducted in 1994 and 1996 revealed that between 89 and 95 percent of Italians said that their principal source of political information was either television or newspapers, while only 5 to 10 percent preferred other media (including radio and magazines). Between these two, television was by far the preferred medium, with 73 percent in both polls selecting TV as their principal source of political information (Zucchini 1997, 103). All in all, these data suggest that, although all southern Europeans frequently follow political news through television broadcasts, the virtual absence of radio as a source of political news for Italians makes them more heavily dependent on television. And, as will be seen later, the political information produced by Italian TV was intrinsically highly biased.

Finally, it is interesting to examine responses to a question that was not asked of Italian voters. Greek and Spanish CNEP respondents were asked to select which of the various media was "most informative," "most credible," and "most influential." The results (presented in Table 5.4) reveal that, even though Spaniards most frequently selected television in each of these categories, they were far more willing to regard radio as an informative, credible, and influential medium, while Greek respondents were far more likely to regard none of these sources as "credible."

These data clearly reveal that an important element of the new campaign politics is characteristic of each of the three southern European electorates for which we have data: they all depend heavily on television as a source of information about politics, even though they vary significantly with regard to their use of the media in other respects. However, the predominance of a new campaign politics is not just a function of the strength of television as a political communication medium; it is also a function of the weakness of other, more traditional, channels for the flow of political information—especially political party organizations. In short, the impact of the new cam-

Table 5.4 Respondents' Evaluations of Each Source of Information

	Most Informative	Most Credible	Most Influential
Newspapers			
Greece	19.6% (234)	19.1% (228)	5.1% (61)
Spain	20.5 (295)	16.9 (241)	4.6 (66)
Magazines			
Greece	2.1 (25)	3.8 (45)	0.8 (10)
Spain	1.2 (17)	1.3 (19)	0.4 (6)
Radio			
Greece	5.5 (66)	7.5 (90)	1.7 (20)
Spain	26.6 (384)	27.0 (385)	6.8 (98)
Television			
Greece	62.1 (743)	38.6 (462)	82.6 (998)
Spain	44.6 (643)	33.0 (471)	83.1 (1193)
None			
Greece	4.8 (58)	25.3 (302)	4.6 (55)
Spain	2.2 (32)	16.6 (237)	2.4 (34)

Source: Comparative National Elections Project surveys of Greece, Italy, and Spain.

paign politics is partly dependent on the structure of political opportunities in each country.

The Structure of Political Opportunities

It took three decades for Italy to go beyond the old campaign politics and to embark on the new campaign politics. In sharp contrast, Greece, Portugal, and Spain were almost immediately thrust into the new campaign politics at the time of their return to democracy. As argued above, however, all four of these southern European electorates were quite similar with regard to the dominance of television as a source of political news. What explains the delayed embrace of the new campaign politics in Italy, then, is more closely related to the way in which its political environment opened the way to the displacement of the old by the new.

Two definitions of the structure of political opportunities can be provided. A strict definition would focus explicitly and exclusively on the institutional arrangements: the form of government, parliament, the electoral system, and the complex interactions among these sets of political institutions. For our purposes, however, this definition, although useful and necessary, is too narrow. I therefore offer a second definition, which also heavily involves these institutions, but adds to them the nature of the party systems and their dynamics, as well as the nature of the systems of organized interests (including the media) and their dynamics. The appearance of the new campaign politics is a joint product of features pertaining to institutional mechanisms and of developments in the political arena. All this said, it is important to keep in mind that the old campaign politics is not completely dead, and that the new campaign politics would not be viable without some traditional elements.

The Personalization of Politics

The personalization of politics is the product of two different sets of factors. The first derives from a regime's electoral mechanisms and institutional structures—above all, popular election (or something resembling it) of chief executives. The second is a response to the imperatives of the political role of the media, imposed upon willing and unwilling party organizations and party leaders alike. In the new southern European democracies, the media played a direct role in shaping the new campaign politics. Just by being there at the beginning of mass democratic politics,[5] the media in Greece, Portugal, and Spain presented substantial incentives for the personalization of politics. In Italy, where the political system had already been configured, and political parties were well entrenched, they interfered with, and ultimately (to some extent) disrupted the old campaign politics. The media acquired a political role only slowly, acquiring a fundamental momentum only when the party system collapsed in the period between 1992 and 1994. Unlike in the new democracies of Greece, Portugal, and Spain, organizational constraints on the politics of the media existed. Indeed, some of the media were party-controlled and some were government-controlled, especially before the 1976 reform of the public broadcasting system, RAI-TV.

As has already been indicated, some incentives toward the personalization of politics had been present in the Italian case for some time. Nonetheless, the constraints deriving from organized politics and from the nature of the institutional arrangements reduced and contained the new developments until the explosion of 1994 (Bentivegna 1995). Indeed, before 1994, it would have been very difficult to identify the leader of the majority and the leader of the opposition in Italian politics. There has always been, of course, a president of the Council of Ministers, but he was not necessarily the leader of the majority. Often he was not even the leader of the majority party of the governmental coalition. To be sure, there was the leader of the major opposition party, always a communist, but the other opposition forces were by no means willing to recognize and accept him as their leader—as *the* opposition leader. Even the specific label of opposition or minority leader was simply meaningless in the Italian context until 1994. Obviously, this nonrecognition hampered the personalization of politics.

The communists tried to highlight the importance of personalities in politics, while simultaneously eschewing the personalization of politics. This was not an easy game to play. In the late 1980s, they even created a shadow cabinet and designated a shadow prime minister. But this significant decision was accompanied by so many reservations that the overall experience ended in bitter disappointment. Following the 1994 electoral defeat, although he was not necessarily the leader of the center-left coalition, a candidate for the office of prime minister was identified in the person of Romano Prodi (former chairman of the state industrial holding company IRI), and a logo was designed for the coalition in the form of an olive tree. Thus, finally, the personalization of politics was not only accepted but even promoted and utilized for a specific partisan purpose: to offer the voters an alternative to Berlusconi.

It is widely acknowledged that one decisive element in the 1994 election was Berlusconi's successful effort to project a personality and a set of personal qualities that appealed to many voters. (The essence of this personal appeal was well summarized by Berlusconi in his famous statement: "I have always been successful in everything I have done. If I do not succeed in governing Italy, nobody will, and so much the worse for you.") It is also often asserted that Italians formulated their voting decisions largely in response to the personalities of the candidates for the office of prime minister. The extent to which the personal attractiveness of party leaders determined the voting decisions of Italians in 1994 and 1996 is a subject of some scholarly debate.[6] Whatever the outcome of this debate, it is not reasonable to conclude that the personal qualities of the candidates did not make any difference at all. Given the fact that the results of the Italian elections were very close, one can hypothesize that the personal qualities of the leaders of the two major coalitions did have an effect, perhaps even decisive, although for fewer voters than some scholars initially thought. This is most likely to have been the case in 1994, when the party system was undergoing a great deal of change and standing party loyalties either collapsed or became irrelevant because of the disappearance of the old party.

The Italian electoral system—the product of a popular referendum held in 1993—is complex. Three-fourths of the members of parliament are elected in single-member constituencies through a plurality system, and the remaining seats are allocated by proportional distribution among parties polling more than 4 percent of the votes at the national level. For the Chamber of Deputies, the voters cast two votes on two separate ballots: one for the candidate in the single-member constituency and the other for the preferred party list. Italian voters have become very competent in managing this complex electoral system. In single-member constituencies, they are perfectly aware that they must choose among candidates put up by coalitions, and this awareness has determined their decisions, especially in 1996. When it comes to voting for the 25 percent of the seats allocated by proportional representation, the voters know that they can support their favorite party and have indeed done so. This is very rational behavior. Since there is no direct popular election of the prime minister, and since the head of government will not be the leader of the majority party, Italian voters choose between the coalitions, indirectly accepting their candidates for the office of prime minister.

To what extent is the new campaign politics attributable to the irruption of the media into Italian politics in the 1990s, and how much does it owe to specific institutional arrangements? (Pasquino 1995b; Lancaster 1996). In addressing these questions, we must separate Italy from the other three southern European democracies. During a transition from authoritarianism to democracy, many citizens develop some identification with popular opposition leaders and will therefore reward some personalization of politics. This was the case in Italy, too, from the very beginning of the democratic experience in 1945, with the Christian Democrat Alcide De Gasperi, the communist Palmiro Togliatti, and the socialist Pietro Nenni exploiting and enhancing their great popularity as party leaders. Soon, however, Italian politics was, so to speak, depersonalized. This development was the joint product of the important roles played by powerful party organizations and, perhaps even more, of the nature of the Italian institutional system. A traditional multiparty parliamentary republic had been designed to prevent the appearance of a strong man, a new tyrant; with the goal of generating collaboration and not competition (let alone confrontation) among political parties (not among their leaders); and with the intention of giving birth to heterogeneous coalition governments. From this point of view, the Italian institutional system was successful in fostering stability, even stagnation, to the detriment of governability and, above all, of alternation (Massari 1996). The entire contemporary institutional debate in Italy, bitter and confused as it is, revolves around these two specific issues. How can one produce governability and introduce alternation? How can one create competition and avoid the personalization of politics not accompanied by transparent political accountability? (Fabbrini 1994 and 1997).

For several reasons, not only was the transition to democracy highly personalized in the cases of Greece, Portugal, and Spain (O'Donnell, Schmitter, and Whitehead 1986), but subsequent institutional arrangements have provided further incentives for the personalization of politics. These incentives were effectively utilized by political leaders whose names are positively associated with successful transitions and democratic consolidations. In contrast, central to the old campaign politics Italian-style was the party organization. Their varying organizational models notwithstanding—democratic centralism for the PCI; oligarchic, socially based factions for the DC; factions based on opinion and alliance options for the PSI—Italian parties were in firm control of all phases of campaign politics. They quickly superseded and absorbed the few remaining political notables and replaced them with an extensive network of party activists. Although never completely impermeable to outside personalities, Italian parties were nevertheless essentially staffed by part- or full-time party functionaries. These functionaries were not selected according to managerial criteria, vote-getting capabilities, or socially or professionally acquired prestige and popularity. They were either co-opted by the existing leadership or sponsored by outside organizations and selectively accepted by party leaders in the hope that they would eventually prove to be successful vote-getters. In most cases, but less so for the PCI, leaders and candidates were partly co-opted and partly sponsored from the outside. The first step was variably dependent on the nature of the parties, the quality of the candidates, the political circumstances, and the type of elections.

In Italy, politicians, especially candidates for elective office, became vote-getters through different processes. In some cases, they were simply the representatives of outside groups, with the electoral support of those groups. This process worked splendidly for the Christian Democrats, but less well for the other parties. Obviously, there was no need for specific campaign techniques in this case. Such techniques, particularly resort to the media, became important only when the candidate had no group identification or concentrated specialized support. For decades, however, both the processes of candidate selection and campaigning were party-controlled, if not party-dominated. The impact of the media began to be felt only with the elections of 1976. Several factors were responsible for the increased importance of the media: the lowering of the voting age to eighteen; the crisis of some political parties, mainly the Christian Democrats and the PSI; the relaxing of the ties between political parties and organized groups, especially trade unions and other socioeconomic groups; and the decision of the communists, and subsequently the Christian Democrats, to put up well-known independent personalities from other sectors of Italian society (the judiciary, academia, journalism, religious organizations, and even the Armed Forces) as candidates, some of whom were obviously more attractive to the media than the traditional members of the party apparatus simply because they were "new." At about the same time, some mayors were becoming particularly visible and newsworthy. Finally, two "opinion" newspapers—one, *Il Giornale,* appealing to moderate and conservative readers, and the other, *La Repubblica,* explicitly courting youthful and left-wing public opinion—were founded, at a time when the major Italian paper, *Il Corriere della Sera,* was taking a less progovernment posture; readership of dailies and weeklies was growing; and the national TV broadcasting system was being liberalized.

It is hard to assess how many votes were attracted by the independents, or *esterni* (the outsiders or unaffiliated), as the Christian Democrats dubbed those of their candidates who were not party members. Several of them became the new notables, with some important differences. Old notables were local candidates and leaders who were solidly in control of blocs of votes. The new notables rarely had local bases. Instead, they enjoyed and projected a national image, supposedly helping the party to improve its own image. Old notables were largely unknown to the national audience and often wanted to remain so. The new notables were eminently newsworthy. They either wrote columns in the papers or were written about. They were often TV guests and their political and parliamentary initiatives were widely reported. Unfortunately, the peculiar Italian electoral system of that time makes it exceedingly difficult to estimate the vote-getting capabilities of these independent candidates.

Perhaps there were nascent elements of the new campaign politics inherent in the piecemeal adjustments by Italian parties to the changing political situation. To some extent, independent candidates also personalized their politics, or had been chosen exactly in order to do what Italian parties were unwilling and unable to do. Shortly after 1976, the PSI personalized its politics by overemphasizing the role of its leader, Bettino Craxi. Always opposed to the personalization of politics for political and institutional reasons, the communists paradoxically were led by two charismatic personalities as secretary-general, Palmiro Togliatti (1945–64) and Enrico Berlinguer (1972–84). Even at the local level, several communist mayors (e.g., in Bologna, Turin, and Rome) more or less unwillingly and consciously personalized their politics. Nonetheless, at the national level, the PCI adamantly rejected and constantly criticized the personalization of politics.

The Christian Democrats always tried not to emphasize the specific and personal qualities of some of their officeholders. The DC was a party of many personal ambitions and factions, particularly after the disappearance from the political scene of its justly revered long-term leader, De Gasperi. Nonetheless, a significant personalization of politics was embodied in the leadership of Amintore Fanfani, Ciriaco De Mita, the indefatigable Giulio Andreotti, and especially Aldo Moro. The important point to be stressed is that for the DC, these developments were spontaneous, unplanned, and unforeseen, and the institutional system of shared responsibilities and limited personal power was not in itself conducive to the personalization of politics. On the contrary, it had been shaped in order to discourage this phenomenon. Electorally, it is impossible to say whether in Italy the personalization of politics could be considered rewarding. Institutionally, the lack of personalization was almost welcome, because it prevented the precise allocation of political responsibilities. Politically, personalization was rejected because it was supposed to antagonize indispensable coalition partners. From several points of view, then, the new campaign politics in Italy did not revolve around the personalization of politics. The only notable exception was the PSI's secretary, Bettino Craxi. In light of Craxi's criminal conviction and subsequent exile, and the disappearance of his party, the absence of this kind of personalization is not to be lamented.

Nonetheless, because of their own market imperatives, the Italian print media have recently promoted the personalization of politics, in part by celebrating political duels (see, e.g., Vespa 1995), extolling the virtues and chastising the vices of individual politicians, and stressing the simple quality of the leadership over the complexity of the party organizations. Thus, some personalization of politics has surfaced in spite of the intricacies of the Italian institutional arrangements. The lack of truly monocratic elective offices and of clear-cut competition between government and opposition has, however, hampered and delayed these processes. Finally, only recently have Italian interest groups transformed themselves into lobbies and tentatively entered the new campaign politics. Most of them remain content with influencing the party, parliamentary, governmental, and administrative policy-making process without resorting to flamboyant electoral campaign interventions and interferences.

From many points of view, then, there was very little in the way of a new campaign politics in the First Italian Republic. As long as parties dominated the electoral and political process and no alternation was possible, Italy manifested almost a "cartel-party syndrome" (in anticipation of the model advanced by Katz and Mair 1995), and the symptoms of anything resembling a new campaign politics were kept under control. Not even the new political actor of the 1980s, the Northern League, employed new techniques. On the contrary, it relied on traditional door-to-door (or pub-to-pub) canvassing, and on many small political rallies, at which some truly preposterous statements were advanced. The new campaign politics was liberated by the quasi disintegration of the old party system. It suddenly exploded during the transition to a new regime because of the appearance of the structural changes discussed above: the reform of the electoral system, the decline of the traditional parties, and, especially, the "taking to the field" of the TV tycoon Silvio Berlusconi.

Exploiting the advantage of the latecomer, Italy has probably surpassed all the other southern European countries in this respect and, to the bemusement of many inside and outside analysts and politicians, has entered upon an era of unbridled new campaign politics. The Italian political system is very easy prey for those who enjoy unregulated control of TV time. Moreover, Italian institutions, criticized and delegitimated as they have been, do not provide adequate checks and balances against the unfair advantages possessed by incumbents or by someone like Silvio Berlusconi, with his own television networks. In the interim, efforts to enhance the fairness of electoral competition have been limited to special legislation to create *par condicio* (equal conditions), providing for equal TV time during electoral campaigns. Its implementation remains widely controversial, perhaps ill-advised, and probably impossible.

The experience of the other three southern European countries discussed seems to be considerably different. First of all, none of the newly established party organizations in Greece, Portugal, or Spain is as well entrenched and encompassing as Italian party organizations were from 1945 to the mid 1980s (possible partial exceptions being the PSOE and PASOK [Gillespie 1989; Lyrintzis 1983b]). Thus, from the very beginning, southern European political parties had to look for new ways of disseminating their electoral and political messages, beyond the channels provided by their respective organizations. In the absence of a strong network of activists and political notables, two kinds of surrogates must be identified or created: a supportive network of social groups and professional associations, and a propaganda system capable of attracting the attention of the media and, perhaps above all, of television. And party leaders were particularly concerned with their use of the media for these purposes.

A second important factor differentiating Italy from the newly established southern European democracies is that in the latter, from the very beginning, most local notables were politically wiped out by the imperatives of electoral competition in the television era. Those who survived did so because of their national political stature. Some political notables, particularly in Greece, were capable of translating their positions of local renown and power into the acquisition of relatively safe seats (e.g., that held by George Mavros)—if and where such safe seats could be found. Some converted their social and political power into party power. But the old campaign politics, based as it was on the ability of the notables to acquire and deliver votes for their own election and consequently for the party, came to a sudden end. Instead, a handful of popular and powerful party leaders decide who will become a candidate and to whom safe seats will be allocated, perhaps exercising, according to their critics, excessive personal discretion in these processes. Party leaders also choose their teams, hiring and firing their ministers and reshuffling their governments on the basis of popularity as measured by surveys and public opinion polls. Apparently, for several reasons, the new southern European democracies did not fear (as Italy did) the creation of monocratic offices endowed with real and effective powers. Politics has therefore been personalized not only because of the existence of one visible and successful political leader, but above all because that visible leader will be the one to exercise real power.

Facilitating this development is the fact that the new southern European democracies were blessed with leaders who were attractive, experienced, capable, and already well known. Some of these drew their strength and appeal from their institutional roles (King Juan Carlos, Eanes, Karamanlis); others, from their party positions (Adolfo Suárez, Felipe González, Mario Soares, Andreas Papandreou, Aníbal Cavaco Silva, and, until his premature death, Francisco Sá Carneiro). The monocratic character of these offices is their most important characteristic, especially compared with the Italian case of powerless offices and timid leaders.

Bipolar Competition

The structure of electoral competition is also of considerable importance in understanding the new southern European democracies. All four countries adopted proportional representation systems (Lijphart

1994; Montero 1994), but, unlike Italy, Greece and Spain, and to some extent Portugal, adopted "corrected" or "reinforced" forms of PR, largely involving the election of deputies from districts significantly smaller than those of the Italian First Republic (and hence much less proportional in their distribution of seats).[7] The partial exception of Portugal notwithstanding, as a result of the disproportionality of these electoral systems (and their propensity to "manufacture" parliamentary majorities), a situation of bipolar competition has resulted. The voters have been offered the possibility of casting their votes, albeit indirectly, for a government and for its leader. Inevitably and consistently, the new campaign politics has revolved around and successfully exploited this possibility. We lack studies of the implications of these electoral systems for politics at the local level, but it is not far-fetched to hypothesize parochial considerations—the personalities and competence of local candidates—combining with their identification with a national party leader, especially if the leader is the prime minister or a credible candidate for that office.

Succinctly put, it is a matter of leaders against leaders, personalities versus personalities, the government against the opposition. All these bipolar competitions have led to and reinforced the personalization of politics, accelerated the circulation of political elites, and facilitated alternation in power. These developments further reinforce the new campaign politics.

Obviously, and unfortunately, all this is not enough to identify and define the new campaign politics. Resorting to some of the terms widely utilized in the analysis of social movements, one might want to inquire into the repertoires of the new campaign politics—that is, whether, in addition to the media, and especially television, new forms of electoral propaganda and political action have been deployed. The American case offers many examples of computerized campaign politics, mail and telephone propaganda, the emergence, expansion, and consolidation of political action committees, and so on. Unfortunately, not enough is known and reported about such developments in southern European democracies. In Italy, they are still of very limited importance. And I suspect this is even more so in the other political systems. Perhaps of greater importance are some forms of citizens' initiatives.

Conclusions: Institutions and Political Communication

Contrary to a widespread belief, the new campaign politics in southern Europe is not exclusively the product of the impact of political and electoral communication through television. It is, of course, true that the very existence of TV and its diffusion have made some of the tools and the techniques of the old campaign politics relatively obsolete, although still not totally useless. However, the impact of televised political communication has to be analyzed and assessed as an intervening variable between the information produced by the political protagonists and that filtered and received by the general public of voters. It is heuristic to hypothesize the existence of a relationship between, on the one hand, the choices made by parties and candidates and their definition of the issues and, on the other, the imperative to communicate all these components of the political message through television. Much more research is needed, focused explicitly on these relationships. In the absence of more detailed analysis, I have argued that the appearance of the new campaign politics in the recent southern European democracies, as well as in Italy, is essentially conditioned, if not substantially determined, by the interplay between the party system and the institutional arrangements.

At this point, then, the new campaign politics in southern Europe may seem neither particularly new nor especially striking when compared with campaign politics elsewhere among other consolidated European democracies. Insofar as there are peculiarities and variations, they are probably attributable to institutional and political factors—the form of government and the different versions of parliamentary government, the types of electoral systems, the nature and the dynamics of the party systems, the role of political personalities, the importance of directly elected offices—and even more specifically to their compounded effect. Of course, if there is no new model of democracy in southern Europe (Lijphart et al. 1988), why should one expect a completely new model of campaign politics? Nonetheless, all the peculiarities and variations remain extremely interesting and deserve considerable attention. In the best sense, they are the stuff of politics. To illuminate, to analyze, to understand, and to explain those peculiarities and differences means to go a long way toward understanding southern European politics, as well as the nature of contemporary democratic politics in general.

The transformation of European societies has significantly reduced, although not totally erased, almost all differences related to class origins, attachments, and perceptions. As a result, as foreseen and feared by Otto Kirchheimer, it has created the indispensable political space for catch-all politics. If political parties can no longer rely on their specific *classe gardée,* then they must frame their appeals with reference to other distinguishing factors. However, party programs, too, have acquired a distinct catch-all flavor. Most of them have, in fact, become mere slogans: easily communicated and vague enough to serve as guidelines for policy-making activities and, at the same time, to enable governments to sidestep political responsibility and accountability. The personalities of candidates have thus become the most important distinguishing factor for electorates that are neither highly mobilized nor highly informed. Almost by default, lacking other elements on which to base a sound political judgment, except their own left/right placement (Mavrogordatos 1983b; Gunther, Sani, and Shabad 1986; Bruneau and Macleod 1986), even interested and informed voters have been obliged to choose among personalities, their political biographies, and their electoral slogans. This choice is facilitated and, at the same time, made significant by the new institutional arrangements and by the dynamics of the party system. Political duels have quickly become the hallmark of southern European democracies. In general, the party system has adjusted to a bipolar pattern.

All this has produced a welcome rotation in government, or at least, on the part of the ins and the outs respectively, a reasonable expectation of and a desirable preoccupation with likely alternations. Following the results of the Spanish elections of March 1996, all these expectations have now been fulfilled. The new democracies of Spain, Portugal, and Greece were quickly blessed with what eluded Italy for almost fifty years, resulting in the degeneration of Italian politics. In the process, the fabric of their political systems has been revitalized. It remains to be seen whether the Italian transition will lead to a stable pattern of alternation among political players willing mutually to recognize their right to govern. Nevertheless, if democracy amounts to a self-correcting learning process, power holders, political actors, and voting citizens are all well advised to remain on the lookout. What is at stake in southern Europe is no longer the consolidation of the various democratic regimes but the quality of their democracies. And the new campaign politics contains as many threats, such as the possible manipulation of "private" television broadcasting, as promises, such as a more visible, better-monitored competition between closely scrutinized candidates.

In short, the new campaign politics in southern Europe is the product of the combined impact of the relative weakness of party organizations and the great pervasiveness of television. The imperatives of TV reporting have promoted the personalization of politics. In its turn, the personalization of politics has been facilitated and reproduced by some institutional arrangements. It has also been rewarded by those mechanisms and by the voters. In addition, alternation in office has created and maintained the conditions necessary to continue with the politics of personalization, which in any case cannot and will not be replaced either by reinvigorated political parties or a by a clash of programs and policies. All these factors have probably improved the new southern European democratic regimes. Some of these factors may even improve the quality of Italian democracy, although at the time of this writing that prediction seems somewhat premature.

6 In Search of the Center

Conservative Parties, Electoral Competition, and Political Legitimacy in Southern Europe's New Democracies

Takis S. Pappas

Who are southern Europe's conservatives, and what has been their role in the process of consolidating democracy in the region? Although of obvious importance, the study of conservative political forces has hitherto suffered from relative neglect. In part, this is a result of the fascination political scientists, especially in southern Europe, have always felt about the left rather than the right. This academic disinterest may also be the product of a certain notional bewilderment, since "conservative" politics is in no way as clear a category as "socialist" or "communist" politics. This lack of conceptual clarity is especially significant in southern Europe, where conservative parties have ranged from moderate to extreme, and from democratic to antidemocratic. Accordingly, in this region, the concept "conservative" has been both blurred and heavily burdened with negative connotations, despite the fact that southern European conservative parties have changed considerably and become loyal competitors in the current democratic regimes.

The lack of serious scholarly attention has left a number of intriguing questions unanswered. How heavily did the past weigh upon democratic conservatives, and how did they manage to overcome it and become instrumental in reinforcing democracy? What subsequently kept them in power, especially in overly politicized environments? How did they try to overcome the relative lack of appeal of conservative ideology in postauthoritarian politics? And, above all, what was the role of conservative parties in the consolidation of democratic regimes in southern Europe? Providing satisfactory answers to these questions requires a systematic analysis of conservative politics after the demise of authoritarian rule.

The purpose of this chapter is to examine the emergence of modern conservative parties in postauthoritarian southern Europe and see how they affected the development of stable democratic institutions in the region. The chapter makes two interrelated claims. The first is that the chief preference of all conservative democrats in the new regimes was to abandon far-right positions and move toward the center of the left-right continuum. The second claim concerns the actual outcome of such a move toward the center. Its success (or failure) depended upon the structure of political competition that emerged in each country with the advent of parliamentary politics, and, more particularly, on the strategies pursued by the moderate-conservative elites vis-à-vis the extreme right. Before venturing into such issues, however, it may be useful to begin with a short preview of the antecedents of modern conservatism in southern Europe and then draw a "topographic plan" of the main conservative forces that emerged in Greece, Italy, Portugal, and Spain after their respective transitions to democracy.

Conservatism in Southern Europe: From Past to Present

The origins of modern conservatism in southern Europe lie in the early decades of the twentieth century and largely coincide with the tortuous passage from precapitalist to capitalist economies, and from oligarchic to democratic politics in the region (see Malefakis 1992 and 1995). As new social forces entered politics after the end of World War I, it became evident that the oligarchic design prevalent since the nineteenth century was no longer viable. Confronted with crisis, at a time when the term "conservatism" was not yet burdened with the pejorative connotations it would later assume, southern Europe's leading conservatives found it necessary to propose an alternative political project, aiming at self-regeneration. The idea was to forge alliances between national bourgeoisies and what were then vaguely called the "respectable" middle classes or, with even less conceptual clarity, the "conservative classes" (Giner 1986, 13; see also Robinson 1979b, 511).

Eventually, that political venture turned sour. The main difficulty in any attempt to reform the old conservatism was its inability to pacify, let alone incorporate, the emerging masses by means of political initiative, social legislation, or ideological compromise. The conservative political parties, in particular, remained opportunistic coalitions of notables and office seekers. Everywhere in the region, personalities prevailed over political institutions, clienteles over party organizations, and selective patronage over generalized social policies. Traditionalist political elites used the state, either positively (e.g., by selective distribution of state benefits) or negatively (e.g., by selective repression of particular groups and the suppression of their demands), to keep society excluded from active politics. Once even those measures proved unsuccessful, and the efforts of the moderates seemed to fail, the reactionary segment of southern Europe's conservatism had no difficulty going "knocking at the barracks" for army support (Linz 1978, 30).

In the end, the coming of fascist or military dictatorships signaled the end of classic southern European conservatism. Italy was first, with Mussolini's March on Rome in October 1922. Only a few months later, in Spain, the Canovite political system was dismantled and replaced by the dictatorship of Miguel Primo de Rivera. Democracy was reinstituted in 1931, only to be abolished again five years later, when General Francisco Franco established his authoritarian rule. Portugal's fate was similar. The military governments that assumed power after the demise of democracy in 1926 paved the way for Antônio Salazar's Estado Novo, which lasted from 1933 until 1974. Greece had an early dictatorial experience in 1936 under Ioannis Metaxas. After World War II, Greek democracy enjoyed a new lease of life until the mid 1960s, when the country entered a period of protracted crisis. As in the rest of southern Europe, the conservative ultras in Greece finally put an end to pluralism by mounting a military coup in April 1967.

Everywhere in southern Europe the authoritarian experience invested "conservatism" with a pejorative meaning. For large social segments, conservative politics now simply became synonymous with "the right," which, in both everyday parlance and political sloganeering, carried distinctly derogatory, and even loathsome connotations. In reality, however, authoritarianism had already brought about the split of the conservative universe into two parts, the one extremist and reactionary, the other moderate and reformist. After the transition to democratic politics, these two parts would make strange allies as they pursued different political objectives. The extremist right would stand for a return to the undemocratic past; their reformist cousins, on the other hand, would now try to jettison that same reactionary past once and for all. That was an awkward predicament for the reformist conservatives and, to be sure, "a somewhat paradoxical state of affairs for a political ideology [such as conservatism] which values tradition as an essential symbolic element" (Cotarelo and López Nieto 1988, 80).

Before going any further, let us first draw a rudimentary map of the main political forces situated between the self-proclaimed socialist parties and the parties of the extreme right after the transition to parliamentary politics in each of these southern European countries. The electoral strength of southern European political conservatism in both its moderate and extremist variants from the time of the transition to democracy in each country to 2000 is shown in the Appendix.

In postauthoritarian Greece, the major vehicle of liberal conservatism has been Nea Demokratia (ND), which draws its political lineage from the interwar People's Party and political support from most quarters in society. Led by its charismatic founder, Constantine Karamanlis, this party managed the 1974 transition to democracy almost single-handedly and played a central role in the developments leading to democratic consolidation. Since its grave electoral defeat in 1981, and except for a short interval in 1990–93, when it held power again, ND has been the country's main opposition party. During these years, no party of the extreme right has openly threatened ND's predominance right-of-center. Only in the 1977 elections did a party of the authoritarian right, Ethnike Parataxis (the National Front), or EP, gain a respectable 7 percent of the vote. Before the next election, however, it was absorbed by ND.

In Spain, as in Greece, moderate conservatism has been represented at the national level by one major party—although not always the same one.[1] Until 1982, the predominant force in the political space to the right of the socialists was the Unión de Centro Democrático (UCD), an offshoot of moderate Francoism, which managed to steer the country firmly in a democratic direction. The UCD rapidly disintegrated as a result of incessant squabbling among its leaders, however, and was abruptly displaced by a party hitherto on the far right of the political spectrum, the Alianza Popular, or AP. With the disappearance of the UCD in 1983, and lacking serious opposition on the right-of-center,[2] the AP, renamed the Partido Popular, or PP, in 1989, moved successfully into the vacuum left by UCD and made the necessary ideological adjustments to appeal to moderate voters.

Ever since the 1974 transition to competitive politics in Portugal, moderate conservatism has been represented by two significant parties, which compete with one another for the same votes. To date, the Partido Social-Democrata (PSD, originally the Partido Popular Democrático, or PPD) and the Partido Popular (PP, originally the Centro Democrático y Social, or CDS) have shared the right-of-center between them. Both parties originated in the Estado Novo. The PSD was founded by a group of old regime mavericks, and the CDS was created by the young elite associated with Marcello Caetano. Both parties moved quickly to establish their democratic legitimacy, however, since, in postauthoritarian Portugal, this was the only way to power.[3]

Thanks to the system of extreme and polarized pluralism that existed in Italy until the mid 1990s, the political middle ground in that country has been more crowded with political parties than anywhere else in southern Europe. For the most part, Italian conservatism was until the 1990s dominated by Democrazia Cristiana (Christian Democracy), or DC. This party was able to remain in office for almost half a century by forming coalitions with minor parties, first of the center, and then of the noncommunist left and the nonauthoritarian right. A serious threat to the Christian Democrats and the democratic system came from the Movimento Sociale Italiano, or MSI, an antisystem party of former fascists founded in December 1946, which was unreconciled to democracy and advocated a return to the fascist past (see Ignazi 1989, 1994, and 1996). The precarious political balance that was maintained for so long in Italy, and that essentially guaranteed conservative rule, came to an abrupt end in the early 1990s. A new analytical framework for understanding Italian politics (especially its conservative variant) is needed in the wake of the collapse of the DC; the emergence of Forza Italia! (FI), founded in 1994 and led by the media magnate Silvio Berlusconi, as liberal conservative heir apparent; and the full integration of the neofascists into the political process in the guise of the Alleanza Nazionale (National Alliance), or AN.

The Quest for the Political Center in the New Southern European Democracies

The party systems that emerged in southern Europe after the transition to competitive politics developed along the familiar left/right dichotomy. A notable feature of these transitions was that, Portugal aside, moderate conservative political forces came to power after regime turnover and immediately assumed the task of building democracy. In this new political environment, the loudest demands in southern Europe were raised in the legitimacy-sensitive fields of political participation and social equality. Inevitably, then, ruling conservatives faced the double task of both appeasing social demands and incorporating their societies into the sphere of democratic politics. To this end, they sought both to build and institutionalize strong political party organizations and to deliver sufficient (and universal) social welfare benefits (see Pappas 1996). This required that conservative politicians (whether in office or out of it) both project a new, democratic image and convince voters that they had severed all associations with antidemocratic elements in their past. In political cultures replete with ideological symbolisms rooted in the cleavage between left and right, and where party identities are forged on the basis of symbolic legitimacy, it was a crucial matter for the old conservatives to appear in new clothes and speak with different voices than in the past (see Chapter 3 above). To put it simply, images mattered, and if the self-proclaimed reformist conservatives were to offset past debits with new credits, they had to search for new symbolic legitimacy.

Conservative leaders were thus faced with the dilemma of either holding onto their traditional niches on the right of the political spectrum (while elaborating a new set of conservative principles) or moving toward the center, which held out the prospect of democratic legitimacy and a larger pool of votes, albeit at the expense of ideological clarity. Of the two options, the latter was preferable. The transition to democratic politics had produced a diffuse radicalization throughout southern Europe, which, in the language of contemporary politics, tended to associate "the left with the future, with a rising historical force, [while linking] the right with a less valued past" (Laponce 1975, 17). Obviously, the new conservative democrats could not capitalize on their past, which would most likely have led them to electoral defeat and political marginalization. This is why all moderate conservative leaders in postauthoritarian southern Europe invariably encouraged and, indeed, actively pursued a centrist orientation.

The foregoing rationalization goes a long way toward explaining why the party systems that emerged in all the newly democratized polities in southern Europe developed strong centripetal drives—that is, competed for votes at the center. There were two main reasons for this. First, as numerous surveys revealed, the great majority of voters in all four countries located themselves near the middle of the left-right continuum (see Condomines and Barroso 1984, 425). Second, as Giovanni Sartori explains, "a center positioning is perceived by the non-extremized electorate as the *safe position*, the position that best secures the survival of existing democracy" (1976, 349). Such a stance was therefore most likely to enhance the democratic legitimacy and electoral acceptability of a conservative party. Given that both votes and democratic legitimacy were to be found at the center, it is hardly surprising that virtually all leaders of the right and center-right adopted centripetal tactics of political competition, while the electoral strategies adopted by the parties of the left sought to deprive conservative parties of democratic legitimacy. The latter often framed their attacks as opposing the putative heirs of the old authoritarian order, rather than the real, albeit imperfect, democrats that the moderate conservatives had actually come to be.

The centrist orientation adopted by the conservative democratic parties is reflected in their preference for the label "center," a term laden with positive connotations, as opposed to the word "right," which conjured up negative imagery. In Spain, for example, the principal party to the right of center called itself the Unión de Centro Democrático, which its founder, Adolfo Suárez, subsequently abandoned to found the Centro Democrático y Social. In Portugal, the Partido do Centro Democrático Social was the principal party of the right. Elsewhere, moderate conservative parties presented themselves as "Christian Democratic,"[4] "democratic," "liberal," "popular," or even "social democratic," as was the case with Portugal's PSD.[5] In no case did a significant southern European party adopt a rightist designation or voluntarily move to a position distinctly on the right.

Let us now briefly consider the political and ideological discourse developed by the leaders and the top elites of the parties already mentioned. Only the Christian Democrats in Italy found it relatively easy to dissociate themselves from the preceding undemocratic regime, given their participation in the resistance movement and their republican and antifascist stance following the war. Under the leadership of Alcide De Gasperi, the DC won the 1948 elections on a centrist political platform, advocating liberal reforms and social justice, and proclaiming the wish to overcome the legacies of the past (see Scoppola 1977). Moreover, as Italy at the time stood at the epicenter of the Cold War, it was the communist rather than the conservative political forces that had to prove their democratic credentials. The Italian situation was different from that which faced conservative democrats in the rest of southern Europe, as they negotiated their countries' transitions to democracy in the mid 1970s.

In the case of Greece, no one in the top leadership of Nea Demokratia has ever identified the party with the right. Even during the earliest years of its existence, ND was officially regarded as "a progressive party of the center . . . [even] leftist when dealing with social issues" (Evangelos Averoff, quoted in Loulis 1981a, 20). One of its leaders even speculated over whether ND "should be classified along with the socialist, social-democratic, or other democratic parties of Europe" (Papalegouras 1975, 14–16). With greater assurance, another party leader stated that "ND looks unafraid and without prejudice at non-Marxist socialism of the Western kind . . . and although ND is not, at least not until now, a socialist party, it does not hesitate to adopt and implement socialist measures when they seem useful"

(Kallias 1976, 18). In his opening speech at ND's first congress, in 1979, the party's leader, Karamanlis, classified ND as a "radical liberal" party, in an attempt, as he explained, to locate it somewhere between "traditional liberalism and democratic socialism" (1979, 1173–85). In reality, the ND leader was seeking to emphasize the "liberal" (read centrist) orientation of his party; the adjective "radical" was an extra reminder of the party's "progressiveness, its readiness to break with the past, and its occasional resort to social democratic politics" (Katsoudas 1987b, 99).

Democratic transition in Spain followed an evolutionary course, during which leading figures of the Franco regime played the dominant role in shaping postauthoritarian institutions. The absence of a clean break with Francoism made possible a certain symbiosis of a novel democratic political discourse with symbols, ideas, and men from the past (Malefakis 1982, 215–16). Nonetheless, the term "right" was imbued with the same sinister connotations in Spain as elsewhere throughout southern Europe: "The Spanish right's lack of legitimation . . . is so evident that even today [1988] the term 'right' is never used on its own, except in the political discourse of what we would call the 'extreme right.' In conservative circles, the term is always accompanied by that of 'Center'" (Cotarelo and López Nieto 1988, 81). Thus, "centrism" was as important for Spanish conservatives as it was for their counterparts in Greece and Portugal. Accordingly, the original objective of the Alianza Popular leader Manuel Fraga Iribarne was, in his words, to facilitate an alliance of the "center and center-right, and lay down the bases of a future party" whose center of gravity would be somewhere between left and right (Gunther, Sani, and Shabad 1986, 80). Fraga was, however, unable to steal the clothes of the UCD. It was this latter party that, having distanced itself more successfully from Francoism, came to be considered *the* center party in Spanish politics.

Because of the revolutionary character of the Portuguese transition, purely rightist parties, such as the Christian Democrats and the liberals, were either harassed or altogether banned from the political process in Portugal. In response, the moderate conservative parties displayed an even stronger centrist orientation than the Greek ND. In contrast to Karamanlis's rather shy use of the term "radical liberalism," for example, the PSD leader Francisco Sá Carneiro blatantly described his party as "a center-left party based on the ideals of European social democracy" (Frain 1991, 51). Making an appeal to voters scattered between the non-Marxist left and the center, the PSD adopted an ideology that may have been "very progressive in contrast to the past political identification of most of its members" (Bruneau and Macleod 1986, 78) but was the only politically feasible option in the highly radicalized context of Portugal's young democracy. The PSD even went so far as to apply for membership in the Socialist International—an effort defeated by a veto cast by the Portuguese socialists. As for Portugal's second conservative party, the CDS, its chances of representing the center as a "humanist," Christian Democratic party increased in direct proportion to the PSD's efforts to project a left-of-center image (Frain 1997, 79). In sum, the programs of both nonsocialist parties in Portugal "were more leftist than the party leaders, and the latter [were] more leftist than the party membership and voters" (Nogueira Pinto 1988, 196).

In any event, since politics is seldom the outcome of mere wishful thinking, neither self-labeling nor centrist ideological discourse was sufficient to secure the political center for southern Europe's conservative parties. That would depend on political battles yet to be waged during the process of democratic consolidation, whose outcome remained contingent upon the properties of each individual political system.

The Struggle for the Center: Constraints and Opportunities

The political center is an intermediate area in the space of electoral competition, lying somewhere between extreme left and extreme right and, for this reason, considered to be securely away from either extreme (Sartori 1976, 165; Daalder 1984, 94). Even if there is no center party (as most typically happens in situations of two-party competition—leading Maurice Duverger to assert that "the center does not exist in politics" (1964, 215 and passim), there may well exist in such political systems a *center tendency*.[6] This has most clearly been the case with southern Europe's new democracies.

All reformist conservatives in postauthoritarian southern Europe have adopted centripetal competitive strategies, both to maximize their share of the votes and to enhance their democratic legitimacy. The adoption of center-seeking competitive strategies by those conservatives who found themselves in power during and shortly after democratic transition had the added advantage of promoting political moderation and convergence, while at the same time it discouraged ideological polarization and divergence. In this respect, centripetal competitive strategies (which involved both electoral appeals and policies adopted while in government) were not only advantageous for the conservative parties themselves but also contributed to democratic consolidation.

Centripetal movement along the left-right dimension is not, however, unrestrained. The abandonment of a far-right position and image implies a clear break with the unreformed nostalgics of the past, which runs the risk of splitting conservatives into two antagonistic groups—one democratic, and the other reactionary and undemocratic. At the same time, the moderate conservatives' efforts to occupy the center were resisted by parties of the left or center-left, who also laid claim to that segment of the electorate. Thus, conservative parties were limited in their ability to move toward the center for fear of alienating voters and party activists on the right, as well as by the capacity of the left or center-left opposition to mount a successful challenge for centrist electoral support.

Of crucial importance for the success of the moderate conservatives' strategy is the existence of fault lines effectively separating them from their neighboring competitors on either left or right. Such fault lines are quite common in societies encumbered by highly ideologized politics where "the parties fight one another with ideological arguments and vie with one another in terms of ideological mentality" (Sartori 1976, 137). When such a fault line exists near the center of political competition, thus inhibiting trespassing between center-right and center-left, conservative centripetalism is severely constrained. Centripetalism is aided, however, when such fault lines are located toward the extremes of the political system, and especially (as in the case of postwar Italy) when they lie within the conservative bloc itself.

In short, the success or failure of these centripetal strategies all depended on the dynamics inherent in each country's structure of political competition. The rest of this chapter analyzes in detail the characteristics of the party system in each country, with particular emphasis on both the space and direction of political competition. Specifically, we shall test two propositions. The first is the hypothesis that the closer to the center conservative parties succeeded in positioning themselves, the better their prospects of winning and holding on to power. The second involves the extent to which a successful occupation of the center by liberal conservatives facilitated democratic consolidation in each country, as well as the quality of democracy itself.

Italy: Obsessive Centrism

During the four decades between the end of World War II and the end of the Cold War, Italian parliamentary politics was dominated by the conservative Democrazia Cristiana (DC). In the polarized party system that emerged after the transition to democracy in the mid 1940s, the DC succeeded in occupying the center, from which it excluded both the communist left and neofascist right for nearly five decades.

Indirectly succeeding the interwar Partito Popolare, Democrazia Cristiana was founded in September 1942 at the house of the Milanese steel magnate Enrico Falck. Its founders included a few former PP leaders (among them Alcide De Gasperi, who had been the last secretary-general of the PP) and some Catholic antifascists. They were soon joined by members of the Catholic Graduate Association, including the future party leaders Aldo Moro and Giulio Andreotti. What the DC's founders chiefly had in common was hatred of both fascism and communism, combined with an equally strong attachment to traditional values and the Catholic Church. The latter returned the courtesy by providing the newborn party with recognition, members, and sponsorship. In 1943, as the forces of resistance started gathering force, the Vatican abandoned its earlier ideas of supporting a solution similar to Francoism. Despite some misgivings, Pope Pius XII supported the nascent DC, helping to transform it from a mere "talking shop into a mass party" (Ginsborg 1990, 50). As a result, the Christian Democrats succeeded in retaining state power for more than forty years, striking deals with smaller parties of rightist, centrist, and even socialist persuasion. At the same time, the DC also made sure that the second largest national party, the communist PCI, remained excluded from power.

By and large, the essentials of contemporary Italian politics were forged during the five-year period beginning with the fall of fascism in the summer of 1943 and ending with the April 1948 general elections. Against a long legacy of intraparty conflict and mistrust, a grand coalition of the country's main antifascist forces—including Christian Democrats, socialists, and communists—was built in Italy during 1943–44. Its first initiative was to set up committees for national liberation to coordinate the transition to democratic politics. A further agreement stipulated that, after the war was over, a constituent assembly would be elected to draw up a new democratic constitution. Thus, one of the salient themes of Italy's democracy and its dominant conservative party—its antifascist temperament—emerged during the formative years of its democratic politics.

Italy was liberated from foreign occupation in April 1945. In June the following year, democratic elections served the dual functions of selecting representatives to the Constituent Assembly and adopting a republican form of government through a referendum (see Pasquino

1986a). The Christian Democrats emerged from that election as by far the largest party, with 35.2 percent of the national vote. They were followed by the socialists, who received 20.7 percent of the vote, and the communists, who obtained 19 percent. At the far right, the monarchist Fronte dell'Uomo Qualunque (the Common Man's Front) received a not insignificant 5.3 percent, thus presenting a visible threat to democratic legitimacy.

The tripartite antifascist coalition that had hitherto managed the transition to competitive politics broke up in May 1947 after the decision of De Gasperi to form a centrist government without parliamentary support from the left. The general election of 1948, pitting the DC against a popular front consisting of the socialist and communist parties, was fought in a climate of resentment and deep political polarization. With the Cold War already raging, the Christian Democrats, aided by the Catholic Church and the United States, were able to win a decisive victory and establish their hegemonic position in Italy's postwar politics. In the new political setting that emerged from the 1948 elections, the DC, standing for liberal democracy and economic reconstruction, and firmly opposing both communism and fascism, would become the major force representing moderate conservatism.

The Christian Democrats retained their hegemony in Italian politics until the early 1990s, because of two interrelated factors. The first is that Italy's electoral system of highly proportional representation allowed even the smallest parties to be represented in parliament, resulting in the fragmentation of Italy's political forces into too many parties, several of which were quite small. Most governments were therefore made up of weak and unstable interparty coalitions. The second important factor was that eligibility for inclusion in these government coalitions did not extend to the two extremes of the political competition space, the "antisystem" communists and neofascists, who were thus excluded from competition for the center.[7] As a self-declared "anticommunist and antifascist" force, as well as the largest party in any electoral contest until 1994, the DC was able to occupy the political center and dominate democratic politics by always serving as the major partner in successive coalition governments.

One important aspect of the Italian party system that has been underrated in the literature is that of the two fault lines separating the DC from the neofascist right and the left, the former cleavage was by far the deepest. Accordingly, when deciding whether to turn right or left in search of coalition partners, the DC always turned toward the left.[8] Moreover, it is important to note that the DC's successive "openings to the left," first to the socialist PSI and then to the communist PCI, were undertaken in direct response to renewed assertiveness by the extreme right in the political scene. Christian Democratic leaders knew that any attempt to cooperate with the neofascists at the national level was doomed to fail and would seriously undermine their party's democratic legitimacy. This basic calculus goes a long way to explaining the DC's behavior in searching for coalition partners on the left when centrist and moderate rightist parties proved insufficient for forming a government.

Opposition from an antisystem, nondemocratic right was a permanent feature of postwar Italian democracy. In the early postwar years, the far right of the political spectrum was occupied by both the monarchist Fronte dell'Uomo Qualunque and the neofascist MSI. The former party, born of the defeat of the monarchy in the referendum of 1946 and appealing predominantly to southern peasants, finally merged in 1972 with the MSI, which inherited most of its voters from the *qualunquista* movement but regarded itself as the heir to the prewar fascist legacy. The MSI was a party of the authoritarian right and stood for uncompromised nationalism, an assertive foreign policy, and the creation of a corporative worker state (Payne 1995, 504–5). Despite its small size, this party posed a continuing threat to Italian democratic politics in general and to the Christian Democrats in particular.

That the extreme right would be a significant minority in postwar Italian politics became evident as early as 1953, when a significant number of DC voters defected to the monarchists and the MSI. The monarchists increased their share of the national vote from 2.8 percent in 1948 to 6.9 percent, and the MSI from 2.0 to 5.8 percent. Although their combined power was somewhat reduced in the general elections of 1958, the parties of the extreme right still commanded a respectable 9.7 percent of the national vote. Meanwhile, the Christian Democrats were able to rule the country by forming successive coalition governments composed of the "systemic" center parties—that is, the social democrats, the republicans, and the liberals.

In 1960, a particularly traumatic episode showed that any move by the Christian Democrats to the extreme right was doomed to failure. In the spring of that year, in defiance of what was perhaps the major coalition-building convention in Italian politics, Fernando Tambroni, a second-rank DC politician, formed a government exclusively with the monarchists and the MSI. A few months later, the MSI provocatively decided to hold a party congress in left-dominated Genoa, resulting in violent street confrontations. This led to Tambroni's resignation and made it clear that the DC's only option was its "opening to the left."

Against this backdrop, between 1960 and 1962, the Christian Democrats and the socialists began exploring the possibility of a political alliance. This culminated in the first center-left coalition government, composed of social democrats, republicans, and, for the first time, socialists. This center-left coalition formula (initially implemented by the DC leader Amintore Fanfani) would persist until the mid 1970s, yielding a long series of short-lived and unstable governments. The only notable exception to this formula was the DC's renewed attempt to shift to the right in the aftermath of the 1972 general elections. Seeking to win back conservative DC voters whose defection had nearly doubled the MSI's share of the vote in 1968, to 8.7 percent, Giulio Andreotti tried to form a government of the center-right, including only the liberal and social democratic parties, but the experiment failed, making it evident that no government was possible without the socialists.

It soon turned out, however, that not even the socialists' help would suffice. Although from 1953 until the late 1970s, the DC's vote had displayed remarkable stability, ranging between 38.3 percent and 42.4 percent, the electoral support of its traditional coalition partners had declined. Given this situation, and as long as the door to the right remained firmly closed, the Christian Democrats were forced to drift further to the left. The communist leader Enrico Berlinguer had already, in 1973, advocated the need for a "historic compromise" between Italy's three major parties to cope with the country's problems. This initiative would have remained stillborn had the neofascist right not presented Italy's precarious democracy with yet another threat.

The repeated failures by MSI "to fit in with the system" led to the election in 1969 of Giorgio Almirante, a former official of the fascist Republic of Salò and proponent of extreme radicalism, as the new party leader. Rejecting the party's previous strategy of *insertimento* (systemic insertion), Almirante tried to halt the political isolation of MSI by pursuing a strategy of direct confrontation with all political opponents, with the ultimate objective of creating a broader party of the right that "could collect other political groups and independent opinion leaders" (Ignazi 1996, 697). This strategy met with some initial success: in the elections of 1972, the party nearly doubled its share of the vote. Widespread violence and terror by militant fascist groups led to an electoral setback in the regional elections of 1975, however, indicating that the strategy had backfired. The main victor was the communist left, while the DC vote declined. One year later, in the general elections of 1976, the Christian Democrats polled 38.7 percent of the vote and managed to remain the larger party. Still, the communist PCI had almost closed the gap, receiving 34.4 percent. All other parties performed poorly, making it impossible, for the first time since 1948, to form a centrist or center-right majority. In this situation, Berlinguer's continued call for a historic compromise could no longer be ignored. Between 1976 and 1979, communists were cautiously admitted to so-called "governments of national solidarity,"[9] thus eliminating one of Italy's two perennial political divisions, that between moderate conservatism and the communist left. This development left the extreme right as the only force outside formal democratic politics in Italy.

The grand coalition of the late 1970s could not be sustained for more than three years, and its demise further aggravated the shortcomings of Italy's postwar political system. Between 1979 and 1992, with the PCI back in opposition, the country tried to muddle through with weak governments based on the already precarious alliance of the DC with the PSI. The entire system seemed hamstrung. "The enduring but rather unproductive DC-PSI alliance is one element in the blocked Italian political system," one observer noted. "The other is the absence of any credible alternative" (Ginsborg 1990, 420).[10]

Developments since the early 1990s have radically altered the structure of Italian politics. The past decade must indeed be seen as "a watershed decade in Italian political development" (Bull and Rhodes 1997, 1; see also Morlino 1996; Newell and Bull 1997). The system of polarized pluralism described by Sartori, characterized by bilateral oppositions and the physical occupation of the center by a single party or alliance of parties, has now collapsed. And yet, the new Italian politics continues to display a high degree of centripetalism. As the fault lines of the postwar politics were destroyed, or simply rendered obsolete, most parties from both the left and the right of the political spectrum became eligible to contest the center and claim new democratic legitimacy. Nowhere was such a development more obvious than in the cases of the two hitherto antisystem parties, the communist PCI and the neofascist MSI. After the realignment of Italian politics, caused mainly by the disintegration of the old center, the majority in both these parties abandoned their previous extreme positions and opted for a centerward movement. Such centripetal tendencies are common in all consolidated democracies, and these recent Italian developments deserve further exploration.

Political change began in Italy with the split in 1991 of the PCI into the more moderate Partito Democratico della Sinistra (Democratic

Party of the Left), or PDS, and the unreformed breakaway Rifondazione Comunista (Communist Refoundation), or RC. On the other extreme of the political spectrum, the neofascist MSI, renamed the Alleanza Nazionale (AN), now led by the young and pragmatic Gianfranco Fini, sought new political legitimacy. As the fear of extremism subsided for the first time in postwar Italian politics, the traditional center could no longer claim to offer stability in an excessively polarized environment.

The general crisis of the party system hit the Christian Democrats hard, and in 1993, the DC disintegrated, seriously discredited by the *mani pulite* ("clean hands") investigation of corruption and illegal financing (Wertman 1995; Waters 1994). By early 1994, it had split into four main groups: the Partito Popolare Italiano (Italian Popular Party), led by the former DC secretary Mino Martinazzoli; the Patto Segni (Pact for National Renewal), under Mario Segni; the Centro Cristiano Democratico (Christian Democratic Center), under the twin leadership of Clemente Mastella and Pierferdinando Casini; and the Cristiano Sociali (Social Christians), led by Ermanno Corrieri. Other former DC members fled either right or left. To complete this picture of far-reaching change, the Socialist, Liberal, and Republican parties, all erstwhile DC allies in centrist coalition governments, also disintegrated. With the parties of the traditional center either gone or reduced to insignificance, that pivotal space of Italian politics was now up for grabs.

Given this novel structure of opportunities, new political formations arose: Berlusconi's fledgling Forza Italia! became the main contender for the highly contested center; the anticentralist Lega Nord had already made advances among the middle classes in northern Italy; and, last, but not least, projecting a new, more moderate image of conservatism, the Alleanza Nazionale was able to relegitimize itself as a prosystem party. These three parties contested the general elections of 1994 as a broad, although uncomfortable, right-of-center alliance (the so-called Freedom Alliance), and emerged victorious. Perhaps the most important consequence of this election was the dramatic growth in support for the AN, which received 13.5 percent of the national vote and rose to new importance and legitimacy in Italian politics.

In practice, however, the success of the Freedom Alliance proved short-lived. The increased centripetalism of Italian politics produced further developments in the political space previously occupied by the DC. Many traditional centrists, dissatisfied by the precarious nature of the center-right alliance, shifted their support to the center-left. The launching in early 1995 of the center-left coalition l'Ulivo ("The Olive Tree"), under the leadership of the former Christian Democrat Romano Prodi, provided many former supporters of the DC and its centrist allies with an attractive political option.[11] This shift to the center-left gave the Ulivo coalition a decisive victory in the 1996 elections.

It is, of course, too early for a definitive assessment of the state of Italian politics, let alone prognostications about its future. The new political environment is still in a flux, and more changes are certain to occur. One thing, however, stands out as a permanent reality. Although a major center party no longer exists in Italy, the predominant tendency is centripetal. And although the present system is essentially bipolar, this is unlikely to persist, given the intention of all main parties to occupy the center. Indeed, in the 1990s, all political battles seem to have taken place at the center of the political spectrum. And yet, any alliance, to capture the center, has to formally exclude the extreme right and the extreme left. Italy's already consolidated democracy is in need of a new consensus; and the only place to establish it is near the center of its political system.

Greece: Frustrated Centrism

The 1974 transition in Greece caused more than the demise of a seven-year-old military dictatorship. In essence, it brought to an end the political system established by the victors of the Civil War in the late 1940s. The major outcome of that conflict was the division of Greece into two mutually exclusive camps: on the conservative side stood the "nationally minded" Greeks; on the other, those who actually or allegedly identified with the left during the Civil War. Finding political expression in the postwar right, "nationally minded" Greeks established a system of "political apartheid" that broadly excluded the left from politics (Close 1993). When the military junta crumbled, Constantine Karamanlis, the old leader of the postwar right, was recalled to Greece from political exile, and, utilizing the vast amount of political experience and personal charisma he possessed, immediately set out to reestablish a democratic regime. Among Karamanlis's early concerns (as he stated on the occasion of the founding of Nea Demokratia) was the creation of a new liberal conservative party designed to introduce "a new political climate that could . . . lead away from the mentality and the habits of the past" (Karamanlis 1979–85, 1: 71–72). Such a move was necessary because, as had immediately become apparent, "the future prospects of the right urgently required a swift liquidation of [its authoritarian and royalist] legacy and a novel political project" (Mavrogordatos 1983b, 7).

In the mid 1970s, any association with the utterly discredited authoritarian past constituted a serious obstacle for the development of ND. Greek voters wanted more from their parties than a mere return to the status quo ante; above all they wanted new, untarnished images. Quite obviously, then, a modern conservative party simply could not pick up from where its predecessors had left off and also hope to represent the large segments of Greek society long subjected to exclusion. For this reason, Karamanlis sought to dissociate ND from its preauthoritarian ancestors and to acquire fresh democratic legitimacy by moving closer to the political center.[12] The carefully chosen name Nea Demokratia, for instance, was intended to emphasize both the "newness" and the democratic credentials of the party. In addition, Karamanlis carefully avoided references to his party's ancestry and controversial issues of the recent past. Symbolic gestures alone, however, would be insufficient to eliminate ND's links to the conservative camp's not-so-democratic past, particularly insofar as many of the party's political ideas and elites had their origins in the quasi-democratic postwar right and were not always in tune with the party leader's new priorities.

ND was the clear winner of the first general elections in November 1974. Still animated by the political euphoria of the sudden return to democracy, and well aware of Karamanlis's key role in that process, the Greek electorate gave the nascent ND a massive 54.4 percent of the national vote. Moreover, thanks to an electoral system tailor-made for the strongest party, ND's share of the vote translated into a much higher percentage of parliamentary seats—72 percent, or 216 out of 300 (see Vegleris 1981)—with the remainder distributed among the revamped centrist party, Center Union–New Forces (later renamed the Union of the Democratic Center, or EDIK), the newly founded socialist PASOK, and an alliance of the recently legalized communist parties. The antidemocratic right, under the leadership of the veteran politician Petros Garoufalias, was represented by the Ethnike Demokratike Enosis (National Democratic Union), or EDE, which campaigned for a return to the previous regime and the preservation of the monarchy. EDE performed miserably at the polls, however, receiving only 1 percent of the national vote and no seats at all.

During its first term in office, under the strong leadership of Karamanlis, ND organized a referendum that abolished the monarchy; adopted a new democratic constitution (despite the refusal of the opposition parties to vote for it); promoted the "de-juntification," or substantial purging, of the state administration; withdrew from the military command structure of NATO in protest over its perceived inability to prevent the occupation of northern Cyprus by Turkish military forces; and nationalized a number of businesses, a policy that its more conservative opponents quickly labeled "socialist." On the basis of this record, but also feeling that democracy had already been secured, Karamanlis decided to lead the country to the polls in 1977, well before the end of ND's first term in office. ND was once more the winner, but the election results were a real shock for the party. Despite the self-confidence and optimism of its leadership before the election, the party suffered an unexpected drop of 12.5 percent relative to its 1974 performance. The votes lost to ND were divided between the ascending socialist left and the authoritarian right, whose comeback was to plague liberal conservatism.

Increasingly dissatisfied with ND's reformist policies, the nostalgic fringe of the extreme right regrouped in the summer of 1977 into a new party, the Ethnike Parataxis (National Front), or EP, under the leadership of Stefanos Stefanopoulos, a long-time enemy of Karamanlis.[13] The seemingly unified political family of the right thus split into two irreconcilable factions: the liberal democrats, on the one hand, and the "[r]oyalist diehards, dictatorship nostalgics, religious fanatics and fascists" (Mavrogordatos 1983a, 75) of the EP, on the other, who campaigned mainly against ND for "having split the *ethnikofron* [nationally minded] camp" (Clogg 1987, 184). Generally speaking, whatever their many internal differences, the leaders of the EP all staunchly opposed further democratization, demanded amnesty for the imprisoned junta leaders, labeled Karamanlis "the grave-digger of the right," and invoked the threat of communism, which, they believed, was already at the gates, left wide open by the "ideologically disarmed" ND (see Katsoudas 1977). The EP's main electoral goal was to weaken Nea Demokratia to the point where it could claim to represent "purely nationalist" Greeks itself and oppose the "ulterior objectives of the extremist left." In 1977, the EP gained a respectable 6.8 percent of the national vote, much of which was at the expense of the ND.

Although it is certainly true that, as Richard Clogg asserts, "this resurgence in support for the far right was convincing evidence of Karamanlis's success after 1974 in seeking to distance ND from the authoritarian right," the 1977 electoral result was quite consequential for conservative politics in postauthoritarian Greece (Clogg 1987, 183). For the first time since the end of the Greek Civil War in 1949, the right appeared "deeply divided by a bitter internal struggle over its authentic representation" (Mavrogordatos 1983b, 6). Having broken the iron law of Karamanlist orthodoxy within broader conservatism, EP turned into a typical "blackmail party." As such, it sought to use its intimidation potential (Downs 1957, 127–32) to pull ND back to an ultraconservative stand and away from the political reformism toward which it had been edging. EP thus not only affected the direction and overall pattern of political competition; it also became instrumental in precipitating internal developments in ND, forcing that party to adapt its tactics to the new political environment. Squeezed between an unreformed right and the rapidly ascending socialists of PASOK in the aftermath of the 1977 elections, ND found itself confronted for the first time with a bilateral opposition. The dilemma thus facing ND was whether to steer toward the political center or try to recapture the voters on the extreme right that it had lost in the last election.

Not long after the 1977 general elections, Karamanlis charted a new policy aimed at winning centrist voters and distancing ND from the unreformed right-wingers. Matching his words with deeds, and hoping to infuse the party with new political and ideological vigor, in early 1978, Karamanlis brought Constantine Mitsotakis and Athanassios Kanellopoulos, two prominent figures from the traditional center, into ND. In the summer of 1978, and as the reactionary right seemed to be losing its initial momentum, a second and larger wave of former centrists joined forces with ND. For a brief time it looked as if Karamanlis's tactics stood a fair chance of succeeding, but the switch of top centrist figures to the right of the political spectrum was not quite matched at the level of the electorate. In municipal elections held concurrently with the ND's "broadening" to the center, most of the drifting centrists voted for leftist candidates. In contrast, many extreme-right candidates were elected with ND's tacit support—sometimes with impressive percentages.

Another important step away from the far right was taken in 1979, during the ND's First Congress. Overcoming the strong conservatism of many a congress delegate, Karamanlis imposed his liberal stand on the party. In his opening speech, in an attempt, as he himself explained, to locate it somewhere between "traditional liberalism and democratic socialism," he classified ND as a "radical liberal" party. To be sure, the ND leader was clearly seeking to emphasize the increasingly liberal character of his party, while the use of the label "radical" was meant to serve as a reminder of the party's "progressiveness, its readiness to break with the past, and its occasional resort to social democratic politics" (Katsoudas 1987b, 99). Even so, such a self-classification was both ambiguous and incongruent with current realities. It caused considerable confusion among ND's elites, cadres, and followers alike. It also facilitated the emergence of distinct internal tendencies concerning the ideological attributes and general orientation of the party. This clash set reformist conservatives who sought to open up the party to former centrist voters against hardline conservatives clamoring for a rapprochement with the far right.

The repercussions of this split in the conservative universe would make themselves felt time and again during ND's second term in office. As long as Karamanlis remained at the helm, however, he refused to give in, and remained adamantly committed to leading ND toward the political center. At a lower level within the party, however, an intense, if silent, war of positions had already begun. In 1980, after Karamanlis had left ND to become president of the Greek Republic, the traditionalist tendency of right-wing hardliners made a dynamic comeback, and, under the leadership of Evengelos Averoff, made a bid for the party leadership. The reformists' candidate against the traditionalist conservatives was George Rallis, scion of a distinguished political family, who was openly opposed to the reactionary right and determined to making a clean break with it.[14] Leading the moderates in ND, Rallis would follow the line suggested by Karamanlis and try to obliterate the old ultraconservative attributes within the party, replacing them with a liberal political discourse and modern organizational structures. In the end, it was the reformists who won the battle for succession in the party leadership, albeit by a very narrow margin.

Notwithstanding this development at the top, ND's chief dilemma concerning its centrist or rightist orientation and identity remained unresolved. With new elections set for October 1981, the matter acquired great urgency. This was especially so because EDIK's trouncing in the 1977 elections (the party's share of the popular vote had declined from 20.5 percent in the 1974 elections to 11.9 percent) created a vacuum in the political space previously occupied by the centrist party. ND and PASOK had moved swiftly to fill that vacuum. In doing so, each of them had to modify its ideological stance somewhat to make itself acceptable to the centrist voters they were wooing.[15] To win the undecided and temporarily drifting votes of the former center, both ND and PASOK attacked the positive image the other side was building for itself, and so further aggravated the country's already high ideological polarization. In this instance, it was PASOK that played its antiright cards most expertly. Taking advantage of the generalized themes that ND had employed to articulate its message of liberal conservatism, Andreas Papandreou astutely chose to ignore "liberalism" and stress "conservatism." From there, it was only a little step to equating conservatism with "reaction" and to evoking images of the postwar right. Given the derogatory connotations attached to "conservatism" during the early postauthoritarian years, ND was increasingly perceived as a deeply conservative party. Inversely, "progress" had been successfully claimed as a mission by PASOK, which quietly abandoned its early radicalism and emphasized its centrist lineage instead.[16] It was upon such perceptions that the main fault line in postauthoritarian Greece was constructed, effectively creating two irreconcilable camps, each dominated by one of the major parties.

It was in this ideologically charged setting that the 1981 elections were held. Faced with vicious antiright rhetoric from PASOK and openly disputed by the hardliners in his party, Rallis proved unable to hold the political center.[17] Blackmailed from within, ND eventually did a fatal volte-face toward the far right designed to reabsorb the EP breakaways. At first sight, it was a successful move: only a few weeks before voting day, and with a PASOK victory looming large, the EP leaders decided to withdraw from the contest, at the same time urging their followers to support ND, lest "social-Marxist" PASOK come to power. To seal the alliance, a number of former EP reactionaries (including its leader Spyros Theotokis) were placed prominently on the ND ticket.[18] Although it succeeded in recapturing the support of the far right, this move effectively alienated many a liberal voter and cost ND its share of the traditional center. Once PASOK emerged victorious from the electoral battle, ND realized that it had backed the wrong horse. Still worse, by allying itself with the extreme right, it had also destroyed the center-right image that Karamanlis had tried so hard to create.[19] Never again, since the elections of 1981, have conservatives on the far right considered creating a separate party to contest elections. Instead, they have preferred to remain sheltered within ND and, as a powerful, albeit not formally organized, bloc, to play tug-of-war with the party's more moderate majority. In this process, they have effectively frustrated ND's attempts to present a liberal image and recapture the center.

Following the 1981 election, victorious PASOK came to dominate the center, while ND drifted further to the right. The moderate Rallis was promptly replaced in the party leadership by the hardliner Evangelos Averoff, who completely abandoned ND's originally centrist orientation in favor of an ultraconservative one. Embracing the far right and employing scare-mongering tactics in his political confrontation with the center-left, the new leader essentially ceded the vital center space to PASOK.[20] After the unsatisfactory performance of ND in the elections for the European Parliament in 1984, the party leadership again changed hands. The new leader, Constantine Mitsotakis, assumed the task of bringing ND back to power. As long as ND proved unable to recapture the centrist constituency, however, this would remain a virtually unattainable goal, because, with electoral preference determined mainly by "position-voting related to party image" in Greece (Sartori 1976, 333; see also Pappas 1999), centrist voters could hardly be expected to vote for a party with an unappealing rightist image. No wonder then, that since 1981 (and with the sole exception of 1990–93, when a profound crisis in PASOK allowed it briefly to return to power), ND has remained in opposition, mainly as a result of its continuing failure to convince the electorate of its centrist credentials.

To be sure, during the period 1984–93, when Mitsotakis held the ND leadership, he pursued a centrist orientation for the party. At the ideological level, and breaking with its past reliance on state paternalism, ND now espoused a neoliberal project entailing massive privatizations in the economy and reduction of the bloated state apparatus. The move away from traditionalist hard-right positions became even more evident at the political level, where the search for ways to reduce PASOK's electoral appeal led ND to a gradual rapprochement with the left, including the communists. An early outcome of this initiative was the tacit support extended by the broader left to conservative candidates in the 1986 mayoralty races in the three largest Greek cities. Even more impressive was the coalition government formed by ND and the communists between July and November 1989 in order to "cleanse" public life of the problems generated by major scandals associated with PASOK's rule (see Pridham and Verney 1991). This was the first time in the postwar period (and only the second in modern Greek history) that communists had entered a government alongside conservatives, taking the key ministries of the interior and justice. Although stillborn, this short-lived coalition contributed a good deal to the reconciliation of the old Civil War enemies—as it would also contribute to the attenuation of the left/right cleavage in Greek politics.

Notwithstanding these developments, and chiefly because of PASOK's polarizing politics and aggressive "antiright" rhetoric, Greek voters have by and large never ceased to perceive ND as a rightist party, not a centrist one (see Pappas 1999, esp. ch. 7). This became particularly evident in the national elections of 1985, perhaps the most polarized elections in modern Greek history, in which the extreme right once again rallied massively behind ND against the perceived danger from the left.[21] In greater part, however, the loss of the center was simply the outcome of the continuous divisions between moderates and ultras within ND.

The rift between moderates and ultraconservatives has caused ND considerable internal discord. On two separate occasions, it has led moderate elements to leave ND and create separate parties. The first split occurred shortly after the 1985 elections, when Kostis Stefanopoulos, followed by nine ND deputies, abandoned the mother party to create the Demokratike Ananeosse (Democratic Renewal), or DIANA. Lacking both an inspiring leader and clear ideological message, however, DIANA was squeezed between the two larger parties and politically annihilated in the electoral campaigns of 1989–90. A far more serious split occurred in 1993, while ND was in power. The split was caused by a personal clash over the Macedonian issue between Prime Minister Mitsotakis and his foreign affairs minister, Antonis Samaras. The latter abruptly resigned and founded a new party, Politike Anoixe (Political Spring), or POLAN, which soon occupied the center-right space of the political spectrum, between PASOK and ND. Besides its nationalist rhetoric, the party tried to exploit rampant dissatisfaction with bad government and to capitalize on the youthfulness of its leader. The most immediate by-product of POLAN's defection, however, was the downfall of the ND government in September 1993.

During its years in power between 1990 and 1993, ND appeared determined to apply tough economic measures designed to help Greece converge with the other EU countries and meet the criteria for entry into the European Monetary Union (EMU). Despite its efforts, inflation remained high, the public deficit was out of control, and the public sector continued to expand. Both the lack of political determination and allegations of corruption cut short the government's initially ambitious privatization program. Overall, ND appeared to be "quite incapable of overcoming an image of generalized inefficiency, inertia, and sheer incompetence" (Mavrogordatos 1994, 315–16). Neither has the ND been able to alter perceptions of it as a purely conservative party, lacking both political flexibility and social sensitivity.

Following its electoral defeat in 1993, ND underwent two changes in party leadership while in opposition, which have, nonetheless, failed to improve its chances of recapturing office.[22] As in the past, ND was still faced with the dilemma of whether to move toward the center or remain on the right. Its electoral prospects were even dimmer in the mid to late 1990s, however, because of the decisive shift toward the center by PASOK, under the moderate and pragmatic leadership of Costas Simitis, who came to power following the death of Andreas Papandreou in 1996. The scope of PASOK's reorientation includes adoption of a neoliberal economic agenda, a clearly pro-European profile and adherence to EU imperatives, and much more moderate rhetoric. At the same time, ND—especially under the leadership of Costas Karamanlis, who assumed the party leadership in 1997—has also displayed a high degree of ideological moderation, wrapped up in modern political themes. This became clear in the 2000 election campaign, in which the main ND strategy was no less than to capture the "middle ground" in Greek politics. Although by a very thin margin ND lost that election to PASOK, this election campaign had the effect of helping to move the party toward the center, as perceived by many in the electorate. Its electoral defeat, however, suggested that many Greek voters still perceive a significant portion of the ND electorate and middle-level party elites as still sympathetic to the dictatorship or the monarchy, or as taking stances that encourage populism, extreme nationalism, or even racism, and to adopt positions diverging from the preferences of the majority of the Greek electorate.[23] Taken together, these initiatives continue to taint the party's public image by underlining its traditionalism and calling its democratic credentials into question.

Spain: Impulsive Centrism

Of the four southern European nations examined in this book, none bears the marks of moderation and restraint more strongly than Spain. The transition to democracy in that country may have been haunted by other demons, but its level of political polarization remained markedly low. As a result, particularly during the transition to democracy and shortly thereafter, almost all political forces in Spain displayed a remarkable degree of consensus and self-restraint. This moderation had a lasting impact on the basic character of Spanish partisan politics.

Spanish moderation was the product of several interrelated factors. For one, the weakness of the Spanish Communist Party allowed the socialists to adopt moderate positions and to dominate the center-left segment of the electorate from the very beginning of the democratic process. Similarly, Spanish political conservatism did not risk being outflanked on the right by electorally significant antisystem parties like the Italian MSI or the Greek EP. Spain's Fuerza Nueva succeeded in electing only one deputy to parliament (in 1979), and then it and other far-right groups virtually disappeared. The majority of Spanish conservatives, their Francoist origins notwithstanding, sought to avoid any direct association with the legacy, ideological themes, policies, and social ethos of the undemocratic past. Similarly, no conservative party was prepared to willingly place itself at the antidemocratic far end of the political spectrum, which would have left it unable to appeal successfully to the electorate. As a result, the ideological distance separating the parties on the left from those on the right was smaller in Spain than anywhere else in southern Europe (Maravall and Santamaría 1986, 99). This explains why social mobilization and, concomitantly, political polarization in Spain never reached levels comparable to those observed in Italy, Greece, or early postauthoritarian Portugal. Quite simply, this happened because the overwhelming bulk of Spaniards immediately after transition stood in the middle of the political spectrum (Gunther, Sani, and Shabad 1986, 55–57; Gunther 1986a, 30; Cotarelo and López Nieto 1988, 80). Spain, therefore, was different from both those countries where the left became exceptionally significant (Portugal, Italy), and those where the extreme right threatened to undermine democratic legitimacy (Italy, Greece). No wonder, then, that for the main political parties in postauthoritarian Spain, *centrismo* became the paramount political impulse.

Conservatives adopted a centrist stance in order to enhance their electoral appeal to the moderate majority of Spanish voters. Even before the collapse of Francoism, reformists within it were quick to advocate the need for a "civilized right" (José María Areilza) or to advance ideas such as "political development" (José Solís) and "liberalization" (Manuel Fraga Iribarne), which served to distinguish them from political fossils of the ultra-right such as Blas Piñar, Raimundo Fernández Cuesta, and José Antonio Girón. More than anyone else, it was Fraga who realized early enough that the surest way forward, and out of the fascist legacy, lay in the center. As he explained, "the center is neither conservative nor revolutionary, but reformist. It does not reject the established order, nor does it accept it unconditionally; the man in the center wishes to transform that order selectively . . . and progressively" (Fraga 1975, quoted in Amodia 1983, 6).

Eventually, however, it was the Unión de Centro Democrático that came to occupy the political center in the early democratic period. The UCD was a coalition of reformist elements that had emerged within the Franco regime in its final years and the moderate opposition to the dictatorship that (although organizationally weak and fragmented) proliferated in the early 1970s, when the regime was showing signs of decay. When Franco died, these groupings came out into the open searching for new roles.

In the course of 1976, many tiny political forces coalesced to create a competitive, center-oriented political party. Perhaps the most prominent reformist group in this new Partido Popular were the *tácitos,* who had been advocating the need for constitutional change since the beginning of the 1970s. In January 1977, the PP was transformed into the Centro Democrático, to which several other groups immediately adhered. Christian Democratic, liberal, and social democratic reformists were all to be found in these groups, along with "independent" politicians, most of whom had previously been associated with Franco's Movimiento Nacional who now emerged as converts to the new democracy.[24] Foremost among the latter was Adolfo Suárez, a "well-groomed member of the old Francoist elite" (Carr and Fusi 1979, 217) who had served the old regime first as director-general of the state-run television network and then as secretary-general of the Movimiento Nacional. Early in 1977, Suárez succeeded in bringing the disparate reformist groupings under a common political umbrella. Finally, in May that year, following the addition of twelve new small parties, the Centro Democrático was renamed the Unión de Centro Democrático (Union of the Democratic Center).[25] Under the leadership of the popular Suárez, the UCD was able to win the 1977 and 1979 elections comfortably.

After its first victory in 1977, the UCD made sincere efforts to develop a modern party organization. These included the dissolution of its constituent groups and the establishment of a unitary party organization with an executive committee and branches throughout the country. The project, however, fell short of its objectives in three crucial respects. First, no agreement could be reached among the party's leaders over the distribution of authority: Suárez's efforts to centralize and concentrate control of the party apparatus in his hands were fiercely resisted by the party's "barons," who saw themselves as coequal leaders of its constituent "political families." Second, the UCD did not develop special links to other organized interest groups, such as the Catholic Church or the main business associations. Indeed, it antagonized many of them in the course of making compromises with the left during negotiations over the new constitution (Gunther 1996, 45–46). It can reasonably be argued, therefore, that enactment of a new constitution in late 1978—itself an enormous accomplishment—"effectively marked the achievement of Suárez's political project, leaving him without a clear set of objectives" (Hopkin 1995, 232). Perhaps the UCD's gravest mistake was that it failed to construct and project an unambiguous ideology. To be sure, any party trying to gain the middle ground in politics is likely to neglect ideological precision (see Blondel 1978, 99–104). And the UCD tried to do more than that; it tried to accommodate all the ideological tendencies represented by the party's constituent parts. The result was "'an omnibus party,' whose vague, eclectic ideological predispositions were simply inherited from stands taken by the proto-parties who comprised the original coalition" (Gunther, Sani, and Shabad 1986, 104).

The UCD was eventually to die because it failed to remedy the diseases of its infancy, stemming from lack of intraparty cohesion, ideological soundness, and organizational rigor. After winning the 1979 elections, the party's fortunes began to decline dramatically. A series of political setbacks in 1979 and 1980 led Suárez to resign in January 1981.[26] His resignation brought about "the collapse of a model of party management which had emerged out of his initial dominance of the organization, and which depended on his continued dominance to function effectively" (Hopkin 1995, 232). Immediately afterward, the UCD abandoned the "presidential" structure that Suárez had sought to impose, and separated the posts of parliamentary leader (assumed by Leopoldo Calvo Sotelo) and party leader (which remained in the hands of men loyal to Suárez). Worse was yet to come. After a few months, the party split, much of its social democratic component going over to the socialists, while several conservative politicians moved toward the right-wing AP. Some Christian Democrats created their own party, the Popular Democratic Party, which later formed a coalition with the AP. The crowning blow came when Suárez himself abandoned the party he had founded and created a new centrist party, the Centro Democrático y Social (Social and Democratic Center), or CDS, whose future proved less bright than the UCD's. In the end, Calvo Sotelo failed to rescue the UCD from one of the worst defeats in electoral history. In the 1982 election, it barely managed to poll 6.9 percent of the national vote, thus allowing the AP to emerge as the second largest party in the Spanish party system (Marcus 1983, 281–86).

How did the UCD, with an eclectic ideology and a membership that included remnants of the previous regime, become so successful in the initial phase of Spanish democracy? The hypothesis can be sustained that the electoral success of the UCD would not have been possible had another party, the Alianza Popular, not existed on the right of the political spectrum. In the early post-Franco years, moderate centrist voters saw the AP as a threat to Spain's still-fragile democracy, and the UCD functioned as a "lightning rod" for antiright sentiment (Gunther, Sani, and Shabad 1986, 103). As long as the UCD existed, the AP was thus stymied by "negative party preference" on the part of an electorate that, knowing better what it disliked than what it liked, preferred the moderate UCD to the allegedly immoderate AP (Montero 1988, 160).

In many respects, this situation is comparable to the experience of the Italian DC. Several differences distinguish the two cases, however. To begin with, the space of competition in Spain was narrower than in Italy because of the smaller number of (relevant) parties. In addition, centripetal pulls in the Spanish system (but also the existence of Fuerza Nueva, a tiny party of ultra-right diehards) forced even the rightist AP to project a centrist image rather than attempt to tear up the system by developing centrifugal tendencies. As a result, the UCD was not held back by an antisystem party, as in Italy, while, at the same time, the boundary between the AP and the UCD remained porous, thus facilitating a relatively easy transfer of persons, ideas, and allegiances from one party to the other.

Be that as it may, the collapse of the UCD marked the drastic reconfiguration of the whole conservative space. Instead of being shared by two political parties, this area now became dominated by the AP, which had meanwhile successfully turned from a small elite group into a mass party. This party now set itself a new task—namely, to transform its rightist image into a more centrist one. Let us examine how the AP accomplished this task.

The AP was founded in October 1976 by Manuel Fraga Iribarne, heading a coalition of former Francoist ministers. Unlike the UCD, which united elites who opposed the continuation of Francoism, AP was a coalition of persons organically linked to the outgoing regime, mostly high-ranking Francoist officials.[27] On the whole, the circumstances surrounding the creation of this party were not different from those relating to the founding of the other main conservative parties in southern Europe. It originated from above, lacked a coherent ideology, and was short on democratic legitimacy. Even so, in the few months that elapsed between the breakdown of dictatorship and the creation of the UCD in the spring of 1977, the AP seemed poised to confront the socialist PSOE as the major force representing political conservatism. The emergence of the UCD, however, and its leaders' refusal to collaborate with the AP, effectively displaced the more conservative AP from the center and relocated it near the far right of the political spectrum, where it was to remain until the UCD's collapse.

That was hardly what Fraga had intended for his party. He had initially envisaged a "clearly democratic" party of the center-right that would be "open to all Spaniards who are not Marxist, not separatists, and not reactionary."[28] The AP's formative period can thus be seen as a "story of frustrated intentions and ambitions" (Gunther, Sani, and Shabad 1986, 78). Despite its noble intentions, the AP was immediately perceived by the Spanish public as "a party of the establishment" that stood for continuity with the previous regime (ibid., 5; Montero 1987, 10–14). In part, this was the result of Fraga's hasty decision to invite into the AP coalition such well-known antidemocrats as Gonzalo Fernández de la Mora and Enrique Thomás de Carranza, the leaders respectively of the diminutive National Spanish Union and the Social Popular Union parties.[29] As if those miscalculations were not enough, the nomination, in 1977, of Carlos Arias Navarro, the last Francoist prime minister, as an AP candidate for the Senate seemed to confirm that party's commitment to continuity and much closer association with the past than with the future. With election day approaching, over two-thirds of the voting public considered the AP to be a mere continuation of Francoism, and almost half questioned its democratic credentials (Montero 1988, 146). According to voters' perceptions, the AP was squarely placed on the far right of the political spectrum. Hence the poor results that it achieved in the first democratic elections of 1977—fourth place, with just 8.3 percent of the vote. This sense of continuity with the past would remain not just an unappealing characteristic but the AP's most serious and permanent liability.

In the two-year interval separating the first and the second national elections, the AP made an effort to improve its tarnished public image and thus increase its electoral share. Perhaps the most telling example of this was Fraga's decision to participate in the process of constitution-making, in spite of the internal split this caused in the party. During that time, and while the political environment in Spain was still fluid, the AP pursued a strategy of creating a *gran derecha,* a broader right, through the merging of several moderately conservative groupings left without a political roof after the 1977 elections. That process was greatly aided by the disintegration, in 1978, of the original AP coalition, which resulted from internal conflicts over the party's support for the constitution. Unwilling to endorse the new democratic constitution, several of the party ultras broke with AP, bringing about the dissolution of the party in November 1978. It was soon replaced by the Coalición Democrática (Democratic Coalition), or CD, a party composed of Fraga's adherents in the AP plus some minute conservative parties that had refused to cooperate with the UCD.

In the 1979 elections, the new coalition performed poorly, failing to attract the centrist majority of Spanish voters. As long as the UCD existed, and its leaders maintained intact the ideological barriers separating the two conservative parties, AP's centrist strategy could not pay off. Its electoral frustration in 1979 gave rise to another round of splits and internal squabbles. Ironically, however, it was that same electoral defeat that gave it new life. Shortly after the 1979 electoral setback, the AP convened its Third National Congress in an attempt to reconstruct the party's organization and ideology. With most of the founding fathers either voluntarily gone or purged from the party, the process of redefining the AP as a liberal conservative party committed to democratic legitimacy proved somewhat easier. The congress also placed important powers in Fraga's hands, eliminated many ideological inconsistencies rooted in the past, and developed a new electoral strategy centering on the concept of a "natural majority," to be established through electoral alliances with smaller centrist parties (Montero 1987, 15). More important, intense partisan activity and competent organization became a constant preoccupation of the party leadership.[30]

The elections of 1982 were a major watershed for Spanish politics, and the political system underwent dramatic changes. The socialist PSOE won an overwhelming majority, and the AP became the second largest party. Within the broader conservative camp, the majority of former UCD voters transferred their allegiance to the coalition headed by the AP, thus radically changing the country's electoral map (Sani 1986). The AP had triumphed, while the UCD was collapsing. As already indicated, the combined effect of these developments was the complete realignment of the conservative political landscape in Spain. With the disappearance of its main competitor on the center-right, the AP now directly confronted the ruling PSOE, with which it competed for votes and legitimacy (Montero 1986b). The AP thus emerged as the main opposition party in a political system that had become essentially bipolar. Regional nationalisms aside, there was now in Spain only one bold fault line of party competition, falling roughly midway between the AP and the socialist PSOE.[31]

As the main opposition party in the 1980s, the AP, much like the Greek ND during its years in opposition in the same period, failed to offer voters a positive ideological message, opting instead for negative tactics, such as demonizing the PSOE and opposing all reforms proposed by it. For the AP, as José Ramón Montero has put it, "radical condemnation of the socialist government proved to be a substitute for conservative policy formation" (Montero 1988, 151). Unable to make further inroads into the PSOE's base of support, the AP experienced disappointing electoral results in 1986, and again in 1989. By the end of the 1980s, the AP had failed in its bid to represent the entire center-right bloc and constitute a realistic alternative to the socialists. Intraparty dissent had never quite subsided, and Suárez's new party, the moderate Centro Democrático y Social, remained a force to be reckoned with. In that critical moment, Fraga made a last effort to "refound" the party and to invest it with a more centrist image. This process of "refounding" the AP consisted of three principal tasks, all of which were successfully carried out.

The first was to rename the Alianza Popular the Partido Popular (PP) in 1988. This was more than a rhetorical change. In part it reflected a commitment to complete the institutionalization of a well-organized and unified party in lieu of the shifting patterns of quasi-federal alliances and coalitions of the past, called by a different name in each election (Alianza Popular in 1977; Coalición Democrática in 1979; AP/PDP, or Grupo Popular, in 1982; Coalición Popular in 1986). In addition to stabilizing the party's identity, this was accompanied by a massive increase in its membership base: the AP had already become Spain's largest party (with 223,000 members in 1986); over the following decade, its membership would more than double, to more than 490,000 by 1996, greatly outstripping the next-largest party, the PSOE (with 365,000 members in that same year).[32] The name change was also intended to encourage identification with the mainstream of western Europe's moderate conservative parties.

Second, the older generation of party leaders were completely replaced in what was nothing less than a dramatic demographic turnover. The older cohort of party leaders, some of whom were still linked in the public's mind with Francoism, gave way to a much younger generation of political elites with no association with the former regime. In 1979, the AP's delegation in the Congress of Deputies had an average age of 57.4. In sharp contrast, the mean age of the PP Council of Ministers that took office on April 28, 2000, was 47.3, and the hypothetical "average" PP government minister would have been just 22 years old when Franco died. (Indeed, some of those who assumed important leadership positions in the party had been active in the anti-Franco opposition when they were university students.)[33] The most prominent symbol of this change was José María Aznar, who assumed leadership of the party at the age of 35; while he lacked the charismatic qualities of Felipe González, he was widely regarded as a youthful, honest, and efficient politician. It is important to note that although this demographic transformation helped to erase the association of the party's elite with the former authoritarian regime, it was accomplished without alienating the party's more traditional older supporters, as Manuel Fraga Iribarne's "dignified retirement" to the post of president of the government of his home region, Galicia, most clearly symbolized.

Third, the PP adopted a moderate political discourse and took ideological and policy stands designed to make the party more attractive to the large pool of centrist voters (Gangas Peiró 1995, 213–25; García-Guereta Rodríguez 1996, 7). The party and its leaders scrupulously avoided taking polarizing stands on such traditionally divisive issues as those associated with the religious cleavage and decentralization of the Spanish state. Indeed, it was accused of borrowing, if not altogether expropriating, several themes from the PSOE's platform, especially concerning individual rights and social welfare. This ideological and programmatic shift toward the center was accompanied by the absorption of voters and party activists who had earlier supported the UCD and the CDS. With the decomposition and electoral collapse of the CDS in the late 1980s and early 1990s, the PP became the only significant nationwide party to the right of the Socialist Party. In combination with the incorporation of several former CDS and UCD leaders into the PP, its appeal to moderate voters was enhanced substantially.

Having finally succeeded in dissociating itself in the public's eye from Francoism, the defeat of the socialists became the explicit aim of the new party leadership. The PP's sweeping victories in the regional and local elections of 1995 were the first signs of things to come. The following year, the PP won a plurality of seats in the Congress of Deputies (although it fell far short of a parliamentary majority) and toppled the PSOE from power, ending thirteen years of uninterrupted socialist rule (Gillespie 1996; Amodia 1996). Its lack of a parliamentary majority actually provided the "refounded" party with another opportunity to distance its image from the past: by reaching agreements on the formation of a minority PP government, "passively supported" in parliament by the PNV and CiU, the Spanish conservative party explicitly gave considerable power over the formulation of government to Basque and Catalan nationalists. In return for their parliamentary support, the Basques and Catalans secured more fiscal resources for their respective regional governments and, in the aggregate, greater autonomy from the Spanish state—something that would have been anathema to the Spanish-nationalist Franco regime.

Its moderation in government, the strong growth of the Spanish economy, and a leadership crisis and tactical errors by the PSOE (most notably, its electoral alliance with the communist-dominated Izquierda Unida) enabled the PP to substantially increase its share of the vote (to over 45 percent) in the 2000 elections (see Appendix Table A.5). This was not only an impressive electoral victory, but its outright majority of seats in the Cortes enabled the PP to form a single-party majority government, which was without precedent for a conservative party in Spain's democratic history. Overall, this triumph may be regarded as the culmination of the sustained effort by the party under its young leader to locate itself at what Aznar has described as "the reforming center" of the Spanish political spectrum.

Portugal: Gradual Centrism

Portugal's transition to democratic politics was substantially different from those of Spain and Greece, chiefly because of its revolutionary nature. Although Portuguese politics progressively converged with the politics of these other southern European countries, the story of democratization in this case is unique. In the aftermath of the coup that overthrew the old regime in April 1974, the major groups that emerged as potent political actors were the military, the communists, and, to a lesser extent, the socialists. Almost instantly, the revolutionary character of developments facilitated the emergence of a leftist popular movement, mainly drawing its strength from grain producers in the Alentejo area, industrial workers, and the urban poor. With the left growing stronger by the day, the Portuguese right found itself ill-prepared to face the new situation. Still bound by their legacy of *salazarismo,* the traditional conservative parties (liberals, progressives, and Christian Democrats) were in complete disarray, unable to influence the course of political change. There was a pressing need for the creation of a new force capable of representing Portugal's large conservative constituency, which had either supported the dictatorship or simply acquiesced in it, and now found itself without political spokesmen.[34] In this hostile environment, two conservative parties emerged in niches to the right of center.

As already noted, Portugal was the only country in southern Europe where the conservatives did *not* come to power immediately after the transition to democratic politics. Rather, they tried for a long time to survive in opposition by organizing solid, ideologically appealing political parties.[35] As in Spain, the conservative political space was split between two parties essentially competing for the same electoral constituency.[36] And, like everywhere else in the region, the challenge for the Portuguese conservatives was to move closer to the center of the emerging party system in order to claim their share of democratic credibility. In this case, however, that proved much more complicated than elsewhere, since both the revolutionary character of the transition and the ideological prominence enjoyed by the left had shifted the political spectrum sharply leftward.

In 1974, with three parties in Portugal calling themselves "communist," five "popular," four "democratic," and three "socialist" (Pimlott 1977, 37), none of the newly formed conservative parties could make any appeal to the past without endangering its (already questioned) legitimacy. To prove their democratic credentials, therefore, these parties had to use the language of the left, and occasionally its slogans and symbols. As one observer explained, "the bottom line is that parties on the right [should be] . . . capable of overcoming short-term symbolic disadvantages to ensure their long-term survival in the new political order" (Frain 1997, 77). In that rather absurd situation, "a right-distorted-to-the-left emerged out of the revolutionary transition" so that "party programs were to the left of the party leadership, and the party leaders were usually to the left of their membership bases and electorate" (ibid., 83). Given this background, "what [eventually] occurred [in Portugal] was not only a process of establishing democracy, but a process of a revolution tamed" (Maxwell 1995, 4). A good part of the credit for these two developments should go to the country's conservative forces. To understand why, we need to sort out the empirical record of developments.

The roots of the Partido Popular Democrático (Popular Democratic Party), or PPD, go back to the corporatist Estado Novo, and, more particularly, to Marcello Caetano's attempts at political liberalization in the late 1960s. The limited reformist plan that Caetano tried to implement included the holding of legislative elections in 1969, after which the formation of a "liberal wing" (*ala liberal*) in the Assembly, designed to further political reform, was made possible. When it became evident that in practice even this type of mild reform could not meaningfully be accommodated within the old regime, however, most members of the *ala liberal* resigned, thereafter remaining outside active politics. The revolutionary wave that shook Portugal in 1974–75 instantly marginalized these liberal conservatives, whose image was tarnished by allegations of collaboration with the authoritarian regime. It was against this backdrop that, in May 1974, three prominent members of the *ala liberal*, Francisco Sá Carneiro, Francisco Pinto Balsemão, and Joaquim Magalhães Mota, founded the PPD. Following its establishment, the party would incessantly try to dissociate itself from the old order and prove its democratic credentials by projecting a centrist image.

Indeed, just two days after the dramatic events of April 25, 1974, Sá Carneiro announced his intention to create a centrist party able to occupy the "empty space to the right of the [socialist] PS, in the center/center left" of the political spectrum (Frain 1991, 51). To overcome the difficulties posed by contemporary events, and especially to counter allegations of previous association with the authoritarian regime, the PPD founders projected a social democratic image for their party, in many ways reminiscent of Karamanlis's "radical liberalism." Accordingly, principles of social democracy found their way into the party platform in an attempt to "garner support from the majority of nonmarxist 'leftists' alienated by the radical rhetoric of the Socialists and the Communists at the time" (ibid., 78). To further validate its claim to the center-left, the Popular Democratic Party even sought admission to the Socialist International, but its application was vetoed by Portugal's Partido Socialista. After this debacle, the PPD became associated with the European Liberal, Democratic, and Reformist Group, on condition however that the word "liberal" would also be included in this group's political label. It is also noteworthy that during the early postauthoritarian period, the party was forced to make a number of tactical concessions, chief among which was its vote in 1976 in support of the new constitution, formally committing Portugal to a "transition to socialism," collectivization of the means of production, and nationalization of land. In October 1976, the PPD was renamed the Partido Social-Democrata (PSD).

Three eventful months after the founding of the PPD, in July 1974, Diogo Freitas do Amaral, a young law professor who had been Caetano's student and protégé, created another conservative party, the Partido do Centro Democrático Social (CDS). In contrast with the PPD, whose leaders had belonged to the moderate opposition to the old regime, most of the new party's founders were former collaborators with the Estado Novo and had accordingly been denied admission to the PPD. Arguing that the PPD had gone too far to the left, the CDS leaders described their own party as "Christian Democratic" and "humanist," representing the "real" center in Portuguese politics. As Freitas do Amaral distinguished the two formations of political conservatism: "[T]he CDS is a party of the center which says it is, and the PPD is a party of the center which says it is on the left" (Robinson 1979, 254). The CDS went on to attack the PPD, accusing it of complacency in the adoption of a socialist-inspired constitution, indifference to the economy's private sector, and neglect of social issues such as abortion and divorce. Despite all its attempts at projecting a centrist image, however, the CDS remained an easy target for its two main foes, the Partido Comunista Português (PCP) and Partido Socialista (PS), which labeled it a fascist party, and the media, which also insisted on identifying it with the old regime. As for the broad electorate, it considered the CDS "the most right-wing, conservative and Catholic" of Portugal's four major parties (Frain, 1997, 98). The CDS was the only party that voted against the new constitution.

Of Portugal's two conservative parties, it was the PSD that proved more successful in adopting centripetal strategies and, over time, occupying a good part of the center area in the party system (see Fernández Stock 1988). Once the revolutionary dynamic had subsided, the PSD became a governing party in two consecutive political coalitions, one with the rightist CDS (1979–82), and the other with the socialist PS (1983–85). Let it also be said, in this context, that the centripetal movement of the social democrats was significantly aided by the openly anticommunist stance of the PS, a fact that precluded the possibility of any kind of coalition exclusively involving parties of the left. With the major fault line in Portuguese politics thus falling between the communists and the socialists, coalition potential was limited to the political space lying between the center-left and the right. To be sure, maneuvers designed to occupy this space gave rise to acute conflicts and factionalism within the PSD, but these subsided considerably after its electoral victory in 1985.

By the end of the 1970s, Mário Soares's minority socialist government had already decisively shifted toward the center-right, and the PSD devised a strategy of bipolarization vis-à-vis the left. In 1979, along with the CDS and another small party, the Popular Monarchists, the PSD formed an electoral coalition called the Aliança Democrática (Democratic Alliance), or AD, which defined itself as a "moderate and reformist bloc." The AD managed to win the national elections of 1979, bringing to power a conservative government for the first time since the fall of the Caetano regime five years earlier. In October 1980, only ten months after first taking office, the AD won another national election, consolidating its position as the country's dominant political force. As the mainstay of this alliance, the PSD dominated the government and presided over the process of revising the 1976 constitution, but its initial optimism was cut short. In December 1980, the PSD's charismatic leader, Francisco Sá Carneiro, died in an airplane crash, and internal dissent and factionalism in the party followed. The election of a new leader, Francisco Pinto Balsemão, did not provide a satisfactory remedy, and he soon faced formidable challenges to his rule. Even worse, conflicts within the AD also increased, inasmuch as the minor partners, and especially the CDS, thought the situation opportune for asserting their own positions. To resolve the impasse, President Ramalho Eanes dissolved the Assembly in early 1983.

The 1983 general elections produced inconclusive results: the PS won first place, gaining 36 percent of the vote, and the PSD came second, with 27 percent, but neither of the two could govern alone. This made possible the formation of a centrist government, the Bloco Central, which included the two largest parties. The experiment proved most beneficial to the socialists. Many reasons other than past experience with minority governments prompted the PS to favor political cooperation. Chief among these were the deteriorating situation of the economy, which had made necessary the implementation of an economic austerity program, and Portugal's impending accession to European Community membership. Meanwhile, tensions inside the PSD mounted, as the various factions endlessly debated the party's position in the coalition. Unable to control the situation, Carlos Alberto de Mota Pinto resigned as leader of the party in December 1984. This further exacerbated intraparty tensions. At its Twelfth National Congress, held in May 1985, the PSD elected as its new leader Aníbal Cavaco Silva, a young professor of economics untainted by old political feuds. He would soon succeed in breathing new life into the disillusioned party. On 12 June of the same year, Portugal signed its Accession Treaty and became a member of the European Community. On the following day, the PSD formally withdrew from the Bloco Central and asked President Eanes to dismiss the government and call for early elections.

Under Cavaco's confident leadership, the PSD insisted on a strategy of contesting the elections on its own. This made it possible to attack the parties on both its left and its right. In pursuit of this strategy, it rejected the CDS's proposal to run on a joint ticket, and accused the PS of "inefficiency" and "conservatism." In the end, the gamble paid off. The PSD won the elections, although it failed to obtain a majority in the Assembly. Nevertheless, in the two years that followed, its minority government brought political stability and relative economic efficiency to Portugal. The new prime minister, in particular, offered the Portuguese people the image of a firm leader, who possessed personal integrity and was effective and capable in government. This explains the popular dissatisfaction that broke out, when a motion of censure in 1987 brought down the government headed by Cavaco Silva and provoked yet another electoral contest.

The 1987 election was the PSD's greatest triumph. As he had on previous occasions, Cavaco Silva rejected the option of forming coalitions with other parties before the election and pursued a clear centrist strategy. With the CDS thus effectively marginalized on the right, the PSD was able to move forcefully toward the center by employing leftist slogans and including leftist independents on its ticket. The party organization, too, long neglected and inefficient, grew in numbers, for the first time surpassing the 100,000-member mark in 1987 (Morlino 1995, 336–37). This strategy paid off handsomely, earning the PSD votes both right and left. The electoral result was a landslide for the PSD, which won 50.2 per cent of the national vote. This was the first absolute majority in the history of postauthoritarian Portugal and is especially noteworthy for a party originating on the right. Maintaining its momentum, and aided by its strong organization, the PSD went on to win the legislative elections of 1991, when it increased its electoral support to 50.4 per cent of the vote. Those were fruitful years for Portugal. Having firmly established itself as *the* center party, and enjoying an ample parliamentary majority, the PSD was generally credited with directing Portugal's economic reconstruction, integrating the country into the European Union, and consolidating its democracy.

The meteoric rise of the PSD and its dominance of Portuguese politics in the decade 1985–95 contrasted sharply with the decline of the CDS during the same period. Faced with an intensification of internal conflicts and a shrinking electoral base, which eventually fell below 5 percent, the party leadership remained undecided about which electoral strategy to follow. The most divisive issue was whether to retain a centrist platform—an option advocated by Freitas do Amaral and his followers—or switch to a rightist one. The results of the 1991 elections made it plain that centrism was not a viable option for the CDS and should, therefore, be abandoned (Frain 1997, 91–92). This led to the departure of the old party leadership. When a new leader, Manuel Monteiro, took over in 1992, he decided to steer the CDS clearly to the right and abandon the center to the PSD. Now described as representing the "democratic right, popular and nationalistic" (Frain 1997, 84), the party changed its name to the Partido Popular (People's Party), or PP. Its program advocated economic liberalism and mainly called for the reduction in the size and scope of state activity and support of private initiative. Perhaps more crucially, the PP diverged further from the PSD in connection to European integration, as it increasingly adopted positions opposed to the European Union.

After ten years in power, the PSD lost the 1995 legislative elections and returned to the opposition (Goldey 1997; Frain 1996). Its defeat was the combined result of deteriorating economic conditions, charges of corruption, and, last but not least, Cavaco Silva's decision to resign the leadership of the party only a few months before the election—a decision that effectively marked the end of the "Cavaco phenomenon." Lacking both the personal aura of his predecessor and his political ability, the new party leader, Fernando Nogueira, was unable to prevent the PSD's defeat.[37] The party lost votes both to its right and to its socialist left (Goldey 1997, 247). The CDS/PP, meanwhile, doubled its vote, vindicating its new conservative orientation.

To date, Portugal's conservative political universe remains divided between two political forces, the PSD and the PP. Both parties essentially compete for the same votes. To the extent, however, that in more recent years the PP has chosen to occupy the space on the right of the political spectrum, the PSD can credibly present itself as the sole party of the center. In this sense, the structure of party competition differs qualitatively in Portugal and Greece. In the former case, the existence of two parties emitting competing messages has produced a divide clearly demarcating the center from the right. The absence of such a situation in Greece implies that Nea Demokratia's programmatic centrism is to a great extent undermined by the existence of a strong right-wing faction within the party, pulling it away from the center. As a result, the line of demarcation between center and right remains blurred in Greece, commensurately weakening ND's capacity to appeal convincingly to centrist voters.

Conclusions

This chapter has sought to analyze the structure of conservative party competition in postauthoritarian southern Europe and examine how this has affected democratic politics in the region. My major argument has been that after the breakdown of authoritarianism, moderate conservative parties in Spain, Portugal, Italy, and Greece without exception pursued centripetal strategies designed to dissociate themselves from the antidemocratic (and hence illegitimate) right and sought to occupy positions at or near the political center. In a very real sense, then, both democratic consolidation and the nature of democratic politics in southern Europe are linked to the deliberate movement of the region's major conservative parties toward the center. It is now time to assess the success of such a strategy in each case, and also to examine the benefits of successful center placement for the conservative parties themselves.

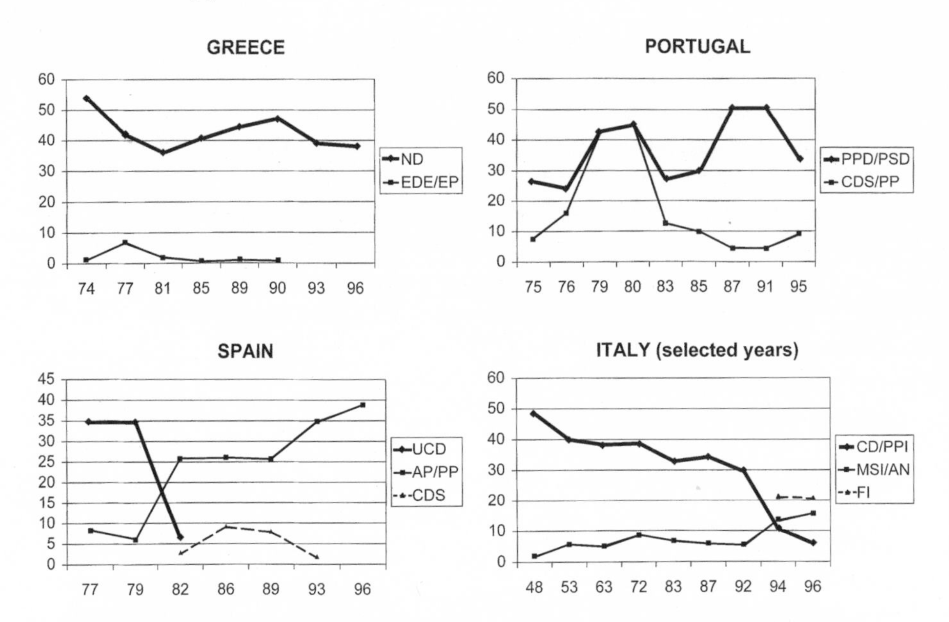

Fig. 6.1 Competition Between Parties of the Center-Right and Right or Extreme Right

As I have tried to show, centripetalism by moderate conservatives has, above all, depended on the mechanics and structure of political competition that developed in each country after the transition to democracy. The strategy succeeded when southern European conservatives managed both to move away from the antidemocratic far right of the political spectrum and to approach the legitimizing center. This, however, did not always happen. Quite often, the success of centripetal strategies hinged on the existence of opposition from the extreme right. Quite often, too, they were thwarted by the socialists, who progressively also converged on the center. By and large, however, the obstacles posed by the socialists were fewer, and their willingness to cooperate with the moderate conservatives grew stronger the more decisively the latter had broken with their unreformed kin on the far right. To gain a better understanding of the dynamics of this situation, we need to focus on the patterns of conflict between reformist and reactionary conservatives in postauthoritarian southern Europe. These are presented in summary in Figure 6.1.

To begin with some preliminary theoretical remarks, it is necessary to distinguish between cases where there is an extreme right-wing party and those where such a party is not available. When no such party exists, moderate conservatives are confronted with a unilateral opposition, which is to say that all external opposition is located to their left. This situation is best represented by the Spanish AP, after the collapse of the UCD, and the Greek ND, after it managed, in 1981, to absorb the extreme right. To begin with the AP first, after the socialists' electoral victory in 1982 and following the disintegration of the UCD, this party came to represent the quasi totality of Spain's conservative constituency. At first glance, such an arrangement seems to present few complications for conservatives, because all competition takes place only in one direction, toward the center. In reality, however, the picture is not that neat. In the absence of a party of its own, the nostalgic fringe of the authoritarian right finds shelter *within* the moderate conservative party and uses it as its primary means for fighting the left. For moderate conservatives, the inclusion of extreme rightist elements in their party has two negative consequences. It gives rise to serious internal tension, often leading to the development of irreconcilable intraparty factions, and also damages their capacity to upgrade the party image because of their apparent failure to break with the past. Fearing the loss of the extreme right-wing vote, the moderate conservative leadership strives to satisfy all intraparty tendencies, which inevitably results in the ideological overstretching of the party along the spectrum of political competition. When this happens, centripetal movement is either held back or altogether canceled. This is what happened with Nea Demokratia in Greece after it absorbed the EP in 1981. The consequences of that decision are still plaguing ND. The existence within its walls of moderate and "ultra" factions constantly fighting each other undermines ND's capacity to effectively compete with PASOK for the crucial center vote and, to a large extent, cancels its centripetal strategy.

When a party borders the moderate conservatives on the right, the latter are faced with bilateral opposition. In the democratic politics of the new southern Europe, this was the case with the DC, with ND before it absorbed the EP in 1981, and with the UCD throughout its short lifetime. It continues to be the case with the Portuguese PPD/PSD. How did the existence of such bilateral oppositions affect the moderate conservatives' capacity to pursue centripetal strategies? All in all, in such situations the moderates have two options: they can either open up a double front and attack both sides, or else they can resist on the right side and attack on the left. Resisting on both sides is not an option, because the moderates' opponents would then be likely to pursue a strategy of bipolarization, designed to squeeze them between competing extremes. Empirical evidence suggests that when the right-wing opposition is prosystem, moderate conservatives always opt for a strategy of bilateral opposition; conversely, when the right-wing opposition is antisystem, their choices are either a strategy of resistance or a strategy of gradual absorption (see Fig. 6.1 above).

To elaborate: if the right-wing opponent is a *prosystem* party, that is, a party abiding by the rules of the democratic game, the entire center-right political space is split between two conservative parties seeking to move toward the center and essentially compete for the same votes. This pattern mostly characterized Spanish politics before the disintegration of the UCD. It continues to be typical of Portuguese politics. In both cases, the party situated closer to the far right (in these cases, the AP/PP and the CDS/PP respectively) tries to move toward the center by simply outflanking its moderate conservative competitor. As a result, the latter is confronted with a bilateral opposition, involving the right-wingers on one side and the socialists on the other. An obvious by-product of such a pattern of opposition facing moderate conservatives is the emergence of internal dissension, factionalism, and even the splitting of the party. On the other hand, however, the existence of another party on the far right of the political spectrum works to the benefit of the moderate conservatives, because they are then able to claim for themselves more of the democratic legitimacy associated with the center.

The case is different when the party situated at the far right of the political spectrum is an *antisystem* party attempting to undermine the legitimacy of the democratic regime. Postwar Italy, where the DC was faced with the challenge of the neofascist MSI, and Greece between 1977 and 1981, when ND had to confront the unreformed EP, fall into this category. Whereas the DC opted for a strategy of resistance designed to meet the challenge emanating from the MSI, ND pursued a strategy of absorption aimed at the elimination of the extreme right through incorporation. Each of these strategies differentially affected the moderate conservatives' pursuit of centripetalism. What explains the different strategies adopted by the DC and ND vis-à-vis their opponents of the nondemocratic right? And how did each strategy affect the moderate conservative parties' centrist orientations?

As we have already seen, antifascism produced a very deep dividing line on the right of the political spectrum in postwar Italy, separating all democratic forces, including the DC, from the neofascist MSI. The existence of this fault line allowed the latter to use its small but dedicated membership to firmly occupy the far end of the political spectrum, which, as a result, remained beyond the realm of competition. Not faced with the danger of being outflanked by the antisystem MSI, the DC made no attempt to absorb it. Instead, successive DC leaderships were able to move decisively toward the center and gain both legitimacy and votes by presenting their party as the most stable foundation for democratic politics and Italy's main bulwark against fascism. For many Italians, caught as they were between the Scylla of the communist left and the Charybdis of the authoritarian right, the only choice was the more moderate Christian Democrats. The dilemma was best expressed by an influential conservative journalist who during the 1976 elections urged Italians to "hold your noses, and vote DC" (Montanelli 1976).

The case was different in early postauthoritarian Greece where, unlike in Italy, the fault line within broader conservatism separating reactionaries and democrats had not been so clearly drawn. Until 1981, and at least at the lower levels of the party, this situation permitted a relatively free movement of politicians, ideas, and voters between Nea Demokratia and the extreme right. It is the absence of a clear line of demarcation that best explains ND's decision to absorb the EP reactionaries just before the 1981 elections—a decision that spelled defeat for the party that year. Despite its declared intent to move toward the center, ND failed to establish uncontested democratic credentials. Its failure to reverse symbolic associations, to dissociate itself convincingly from the authoritarian past, prevented it from being accepted as a centrist, and hence wholly legitimate, party. In the final analysis, it was the socialist PASOK that proved more adept in occupying the political center. From there, to use a memorable phrase by Margaret Thatcher, it could "claim all the arguments of principle, while all that remained [for ND] were the arguments of accountancy."

Today, as in the early years of democratization, the quest of southern Europe's conservatives for the center is still imperative. Of the main parties representing conservative politics in the region, it is Spain's PP and Portugal's PSD that seem to have made the most convincing move toward the center. For the Greek ND, success in that direction still requires shaking off the rightist label that continues to plague it, and the reconfiguration of its identity in a manner more in tune with the centripetal logic of the country's party system. In Italy, after the collapse of the DC, the situation is still fluid, but most political battles are for the center. This persistence of a centripetal logic in current southern European politics is significant. If centripetalism benefits democratic consolidation, the inverse may also hold true: consolidated democracies such as those in southern Europe may tend to reinforce the centripetalism of political forces, especially conservative ones.

7 Mobilizers and Late Modernizers

Socialist Parties in the New Southern Europe

Hans-Jürgen Puhle

Over the past twenty-five years, the socialist or social democratic parties of southern Europe have made important contributions to the achievement of four historic objectives: democratization and the consolidation of democracy, Europeanization, modernization, and the creation of a modern welfare state. Of these, their contribution to democratization (to which they gave highest priority) has been their greatest success story. This is followed by their accomplishments on behalf of "Europeanization"—which includes opening their countries (some of which were somewhat isolated from the rest of Europe), making them more similar to the rest of western Europe, and helping to bring them into the European Union. Socialist or social democratic aspirations for income redistribution or welfare reform, in contrast, have often taken a back seat to policies focusing more on liberal reforms and basic economic, technological, and institutional modernization. This reflects their greater emphasis on democratic consolidation and the modernization of their societies than on the traditional objectives of socialism, even at the cost of undermining their once close relationships with allied trade unions. In the end, the socialist or social democratic (henceforth, simply "socialist") parties have contributed to a substantial transformation of southern European societies and political systems.

In turn, the altered political, social, and economic contexts that they helped to create contributed to a considerable change in the nature of these parties themselves. Socioeconomic modernity and consolidated democratic regimes jointly established a context within which a "centripetal logic" prevailed. This made it necessary for the socialist parties to flexibly adapt to the new style of the more fragmented, more personalized, less programmatic and less organized politics of the television age, as well as to address the perceived "crisis" of the catch-all party.

This chapter examines the nature and consequences of these two interactive processes—exploring the impact of party on society, and the impact of society on party—with regard to the Panellinio Sosialistico Kinema (Panhellenic Socialist Movement), or PASOK, in Greece; the Spanish Partido Socialista Obrero Español, or PSOE; and the Portuguese Partido Socialista, or PS, between the mid 1970s and the late 1990s. It pays particular attention to the trajectories of party building and party change, to the parties' general strategies and orientations, their capacities to build and preserve electoral coalitions, their positions within their respective party systems, and their relationships with organized social groups and with the state. Insofar as all three of these parties have held power in government, it also briefly examines the policies they have implemented, particularly with regard to the dilemmas they have faced in meeting the urgent requirements of political and economic consolidation and modernization, on the one hand, and the often limited potential for social reform, on the other. These tensions and cross-pressures are particularly important for socialist parties, given the extent to which the efficiency/equality cleavage has traditionally been linked to the very definition of socialism.[1] Although the trajectory and overall performance of the Partito Socialista Italiano (PSI) during and after the consolidation of Italian democracy following World War II is also dealt with in this chapter, diachronic analyses of the constellations of democratic consolidation would have required an extensive examination (much beyond the scope of this volume) of the greatly differing context within which the PSI evolved. Hence, the comparative analysis of the PSI has unavoidably had to be abbreviated.

The southern European socialist parties set out on these evolutionary processes with party legacies that were distinct but nonetheless included a number of common characteristics (constituting the core elements of a southern European "type"), and followed differing trajectories within different social and political contexts. In the end, however, the southern socialists arrived at the same level of democratic and party normalcy as their northern counterparts. This process of "convergence," however, is more complex than one might have anticipated: it did not consist simply of the southern European parties moving toward northern European socialist party models. To be sure, the southern European socialist parties underwent significant changes from the somewhat radical positions they had assumed when democracy was restored, and by the end of this process, they certainly differed from their earlier incarnations during previous democratic interludes. But the northern European parties have likewise evolved, in a manner that has brought them closer to the types of parties emerging in the south. Crises, economic, social, and cultural change, organizational fragmentation, and new campaign strategies and technologies, among other things, have flattened the classical differences between north and south and made the northerners more "southern," particularly insofar as the erstwhile builders of bureaucracies and well-organized machines had to adopt the more flexible and leader-centered strategies that the ad hoc mobilizers of the south had previously mastered.

This process of party adaptation and change is also particularly noteworthy insofar as the southern European parties have "leapfrogged" toward modernity: they arrived at the latest stage of the modern catch-all party without having to go through many of the earlier party types, transformations, and crises that the northerners had experienced. In part, this is because reemergence from clandestinity (the PSOE and PSI) or birth as new parties (the PS and PASOK) in the aftermath of authoritarian interludes left them unencumbered by the organizational, strategic, and ideological legacies inherited by the northern European socialist parties from an earlier era. But in part, the greater ease with which they adapted to the new style of party and campaign politics arose from a particularly southern political context of fragmentation, flexibility, structural underdevelopment, clientelism, and personalism. In general, the parties of the south have been more ad hoc mobilizers than builders of structures; as a result, they have been more flexible and better prepared to adjust to the new politics. This legacy helped the socialists of the south to become forerunners of a type of party that would emerge in the north as well, characterized by new styles of campaigning, looser and more flexible catch-all party organization, and reformulated moderate and centrist (or center-left) economic and social policy objectives.

This exploration of the nature and evolution of the socialist parties of southern Europe begins by examining the differing social, political, and historical contexts within which they emerged and initially evolved. In addition, it considers the legacies they inherited from their various incarnations in the preauthoritarian past.

Differing Contexts and Legacies

The most important of these contextual factors is one that differentiates between the socialist parties of the south at the time of their birth or rebirth and the party types adopted by their counterparts in the north during those same decades. In southern Europe, the socialist parties came to power or reached a maximum of influence in coalition governments after the "golden age" of European social democracy (1945–73) had allegedly ended, and a number of eminent prophets had categorically proclaimed no less than the "end of the social-democratic century."[2] These critics were referring to the established central European, Scandinavian, and Anglo-Saxon social democratic or labor parties, which had a long tradition as working-class movements. As summarized in Anthony Crosland's much quoted formula, these northern European parties were characterized in policy terms by political liberalism, a mixed economy, the welfare state, Keynesianism (although this was not adopted everywhere), and a commitment to greater social equality (Crosland 1956). The crises of the 1970s—particularly stagflation, technological, economic, and social-structural change, bureaucratic inefficiency, value change, and "electoral dilemmas"—interacted with the mistakes of political actors and a general fatigue in government to remove many northern European social democratic parties from power in the late 1970s or the early 1980s. They remained on the opposition benches for more than a decade and a half in Great Britain and Germany, but for shorter periods in the Scandinavian countries. The triumphant return of the British and German socialists to power in 1997–98 (not to mention the more complex French case) has shown that the "end of the social-democratic century" has by no means been the end of social democracy, it is also clear that the programs and priorities of Tony Blair's "New Labour" and Gerhard Schröder's "New Center" indicate that the "renewed" socialists of the European north have moved a long way from their parties' traditional positions.

The southern European socialist parties, in contrast, were out of government (or even out of the country) through most of the "golden age." They underwent a difficult phase of reorientation and arrived in power relatively late. All three enjoyed extended periods in government in the 1980s and 1990s (at a time when most northern socialist parties were in opposition); they have been less organized and much less closely tied to the working class than their northern counterparts (the more "northern" PSI notwithstanding); and, to varying degrees, they have pursued only part of the northerners' policy objectives—specifically, in Crosland's formula, political liberalism, a mixed economy, and a number of social and institutional reforms. They have had to adjust to their countries' particular developmental trajectories, priorities, and problems, and to find their positions within constellations that have been traditionally characterized by comparatively weak civil societies and relatively strong (although often inefficient and in many fields underinstitutionalized) states.

The Traditional Type of Southern European Socialist Party

Prior to the postwar Italian and what Samuel Huntington calls the "third wave" return to democracy, the socialist parties of Spain and Italy and their liberal/progressive forerunners in Greece and Portugal had had relatively short periods of parliamentary experience and long decades of exile or underground activities under repressive dictatorships. Previously, these parties had, moreover, exhibited features that distinguished them from their northern European counterparts. One of these distinguishing features was the weakness or fragmentation of working-class organizations and an "unorganic relationship" of the parties with "weak and ideologically fragmented labor unions."[3] In many respects, this was a by-product of the developmental backwardness that characterized the region. With the exception of some parts of Catalonia, the Basque provinces, and northern Italy, southern European countries were latecomers to industrialization. Except in these regions, premodern elements continued to prevail, retarding political modernization. These included traditional modes of production and labor regimes (with disproportionately large numbers of workers in the textile industry, agriculture, and services); a low degree of institutionalized societal pluralism; the persistence of extended family networks; locally and regionally based personalistic loyalties, clientelism, and *caciquismo,* linked with traditional state bureaucrats; and authoritarian, repressive, and often corporate traditions (particularly in the military) that strengthened the executive vis-à-vis the legislature and led to many dictatorial interludes. The formation of a strong and autonomous civil society was contained (with local exceptions), and politics remained "state-heavy," although the state and its bureaucracy were weak and inefficient. When the state belatedly modernized, the impetus came from above, as in Spain under Primo de Rivera and Franco, or in Italy under Fascism. Organized capitalism and neocorporatist arrangements were weak, and social welfare programs developed slowly (see Malefakis 1995; Puhle 1994). Under these circumstances, working-class political organizations were poorly developed. The southern European workers' parties secured parliamentary representation late and rarely participated in government (except in situations of crisis, as during the Spanish Second Republic and Civil War). And at the time when the southern European economies modernized, the socialist parties were excluded from power by authoritarian regimes. Before the 1970s, nowhere did southern European socialist parties have a chance to formulate policies during a significant reformist period. Fragmentation was another problem. In the two cases in which the southern European socialist parties had a working-class tradition (the PSOE and the PSI), challenges from strong competitors (anarchosyndicalists, communists, Basque nationalists, and, in Italy, Catholics) left the party unable to represent the whole class. Neither could these socialist parties rely on well-coordinated and hegemonic union movements, inasmuch as the unions were organized along ideological and party lines and had relatively low membership levels, except in Spain. And in Spain, by the 1930s, the unions had become stronger than the party, and hence often acted independently of the PSOE.

Another characteristic of southern European socialists was their relative unencumberedness by programmatic and organizational legacies of the kind that constrained their northern counterparts. The socialist parties of the south were traditionally less organized, institutionalized, and bureaucratized than those of the north. Membership, militancy, and autonomous party funding were considerably lower, the party machines smaller or almost nonexistent, and the parties' organizational structures much less deeply rooted and entrenched in the society and in all parts of the country. There has never been anything similar to the "tanker syndrome" of the massive social democratic organizations of the north; the southern European parties were more flexible and able to adapt to altered circumstances. Even in earlier periods they were much less mass parties than (sectorally often unstructured) parties aiming at tentative and selective mass mobilization.

(Re)birth, Transformation, and Democratic Consolidation

The socialist parties that emerged in southern Europe in the mid 1970s were, in many respects, different from their predecessors. Indeed, the Portuguese PS (founded in 1973, in Münstereifel, Germany) and PASOK in Greece (founded in 1974) were brand-new parties without any significant working-class traditions. And even though the Spanish PSOE had been founded in 1879—and, together with the socialist labor union Unión General de Trabajadores, or UGT (founded in 1888), had represented about one half of Spain's traditional labor movement until the end of the Civil War in 1939—it, too, could be regarded as a new party after its reorganization at its 1970 Toulouse congress, and after a young, hungry, and efficient executive around Felipe González and Alfonso Guerra had been installed at the party's last congress in exile, held in Suresnes, near Paris, in 1974. What remained as a legacy from earlier periods—besides an unequivocal commitment to democracy, an absence of theoretical debates, and some revolutionary rhetoric—was a tradition of factionalism along personalistic or clientelistic lines, occasionally camouflaged by programmatic differences that had survived more than three decades of exile, during which the socialist older generation increasingly lost contact with Spanish reality (see Mateos 1993).

In contrast, the Italian PSI was closer to the central European socialist party type. The party (founded in 1892) had been a well-organized mass party before 1922, although programmatically fragmented. Despite twenty years of fascism, it displayed much more continuity in the composition of its elite and in its mobilizational patterns than the PSOE. Its mass membership (more than half a million members) was the highest of all southern European socialist parties. The PSI's reorganization and programmatic reorientation did not begin until 1976, when a revolt of the younger generation made Bettino Craxi secretary-general at the party's Fortieth Congress. By that time, rent by factionalism (the famous *correnti*) and ideological debates, the PSI had clung to its postwar low point of 9.7 percent of the vote (compared to 34.4 percent for the PCI) in that year's general election (see Table 7.1). This triggered a move toward a more pragmatic realism in the early 1980s. By the time the predominant Christian Democrats conceded the premiership of the *pentapartito* coalition government to Craxi in 1983, the deconsolidation of the party system and the disappearance of the PSI in the early 1990s were not far off.[4]

With regard to the shifting electoral fortunes of these parties in the 1970s and 1980s, the Portuguese PS most closely resembles the Italian PSI in that it, too, failed to achieve an absolute majority or a hegemonic position until 1995. Nonetheless, in contrast with their Italian counterparts, the Portuguese socialists have almost always held a comfortable lead over their communist rivals (the PCP), and have occasionally attracted two or three times the communists' share of the vote. Also unlike the PSI, the PS was a frequent participant in cabinet formation from the very earliest days of Portuguese democracy. It played a key role in the Constitutional Assembly and led minority or coalition governments from mid 1976 to mid 1978, and from June 1983 to May 1985. In 1986, the party's leader, Mário Soares, was elected president of the republic in a tight run-off election against the conservative candidate, and in 1991, he was reelected with more than 70 percent of the vote, in spite of the fact that the government from 1985 to 1995 was led by the liberal Partido Social-Democrata (PSD). The socialists, falling just short of an absolute parliamentary majority, returned to government in 1995, and elected António Guterres prime minister. Another electoral triumph soon followed, when the socialist candidate for president of the republic, Jorge Sampaio, succeeded Soares in early 1996. In Greece and Spain, even though the PSOE and PASOK established themselves from the first elections on as the strongest forces of the left (with more than double or triple the electoral support of the communists), the socialist parties remained in the opposition through the transition and most of democratic consolidation. In 1981 and 1982, PASOK and the PSOE came to power with absolute parliamentary majorities. PASOK lost the 1989 elections, but returned to power in 1993. The PSOE continued in government until 1996, although progressive erosion of its share of the vote meant that its single-party minority government between 1993 and 1996 needed the support of the Catalan (and occasionally the Basque) nationalist parties.

All four of these socialist parties contributed to the establishment and consolidation of their respective democracies—albeit in different ways and at different stages of the transition and consolidation processes—however unprepared, weak, and structurally underdeveloped they may have been at the outset. They were new (with the exception of the PSI), inexperienced in politics, and not very disciplined, but, given the extent to which transitions and democratic consolidation processes privilege the roles played by parties, they soon found themselves in the center of crucial institution-building and legitimation processes (see Morlino 1995; Puhle 1997; Merkel and Puhle 1999). This was particularly significant for leftist parties that had never been allowed into politics (or even into "good society"), as in Portugal and Greece, or had been outlawed and persecuted for decades by fascist or semifascist dictatorships, as in Italy and Spain.

The PSI did not lead a government until the mid 1980s, by which time Italian democracy had already been consolidated, but the Italian socialists had contributed to the long and protracted consolidation of democracy at earlier stages. Particularly significant were the PSI's role in the *resistenza,* participation in the broad *arco constituzionale* before 1948, "opening" strategy in the late 1950s, and part in the *centro-sinistra* governments of the 1960s and 1970s.

The Portuguese socialists, and especially their leader, Mário Soares,

Table 7.1 Votes, Parliamentary Seats, and Membership of Southern European Socialist Parties

	PSOE			PASOK			PS			PSI*		
Year	Pct. Vote	Parl. Seats	Members (000s)	Pct. Vote	Parl. Seats	Members (000s)	Pct. Vote	Parl. Seats	Members (000s)	Pct. Vote	Parl. Seats	Members (000s)
1946										20.7	115	822
1948										31.0[b]	183	531
1953										12.7	75	780
1958										14.2	84	486
1963										13.8	87	492
1968										14.5[c]	91	
1972										9.6	61	560
1974				13.6	13				36			512
1975						8	37.9	116	82			539
1976			8				34.9	107	92	9.7	57	499
1977	29.3	118	150	25.3	93	27						483
1978			100						97			472
1979	30.5	121	101			65	27.3	74		9.8	62	484
1980						75	27.4[a]	74				510
1981			99	48.1	172	110			118			523
1981E				40.3								
1982	48.4	202	112			140						553
1983						200	36.1	101	135	11.4	73	558

1984E			153	40.6		220				11.2		572
1985			158	45.8	161		20.8	57				583
1986	44.6	184	168						41			593
1987			210			220	22.2	60	46	14.3	94	616
1987E	39.4						22.5					
1989 (June)	40.2	175	224	39.1	125				52			641[d]
1989 (Nov.)				40.7	128							
1989E	39.6			35.9			28.5			14.8		
1990			256	38.6	125	82			58			
1991			296			98	29.1	72	62			
1992			323						68	13.6	92	
1993	38.8	159	348	46.9	171	112			71			
1994						157			77	2.2	15	
1994E	30.7			37.6			34.8			1.8		
1995			373				43.9	112	84			
1996	37.5	141	383	41.5	162	156			93			
1999			360			220	44.0	115				
2000	34.7	125		43.8	158							

*PSI direct members

[a]1980: FRS

[b]In alliance with PCI

[c]In alliance with PSDI

[d]1988

E = election to European Parliament

were extremely important players in preventing democracy from being stillborn during the revolutionary period and in crafting democratic institutions and practices in the Constituent Assembly. They also played key roles in negotiating the extrication of the military from power and the decisive constitutional revisions of 1982, which made the Portuguese institutions completely democratic. The PSOE played an important role in the Spanish transition, as a central participant in negotiations that culminated in adoption of a democratic constitution backed by a broad consensus of both mass and elite opinion. In contrast, PASOK did not: the Greek transition unfolded under the premiership of Constantine Karamanlis, the leader of Nea Demokratia, and without interparty pacts. Nonetheless, after PASOK's rapid transformation into a catch-all party and abandonment, after 1977, of its semiloyal, anticapitalist and antisystem positions and Third World antidependency and national liberation rhetoric, it made an important contribution to the consolidation of democracy in Greece, comparable to the decisive, although less radical shift of the PSOE in 1979. It is important to note that, throughout the transition and the process of democratic consolidation, all four socialist parties gave priority to securing and stabilizing the new democratic institutions over whatever socialist programs and projects they may have had.

To what extent did the nature of the transition to democracy leave a lasting imprint on the nature of these parties or the democracies within which they functioned? Earlier studies of the so-called third wave of democratization have speculated about the extent to which a particular mode of transition (especially if "guided" from above by elites, culminating in a "pact," or taking the form of a revolutionary rupture) may confine or "freeze" political developments over the long term (see Karl and Schmitter 1991). In keeping with the argument set forth in Chapter 2 of this volume, the evidence regarding the southern European socialist parties reveals that, as long as the transition was completed (i.e., with the exception of Portugal prior to 1982) and democratic consolidation secured, subsequent political evolution does not appear to have been significantly influenced by the mode of transition over the long term. Neither the character and performance of the southern European socialist parties nor their policies have been shaped by whether or not a transition was negotiated. Only the Portuguese party system was significantly affected by the nature of the transition (with all parties temporarily shifted to the left as a response to the exigencies of the revolution, and with military officers continuing to play unusually prominent roles until the mid 1980s); but within a decade, Portuguese electoral politics had assumed a more "normal" configuration. But while the subsequent evolution of these parties does not appear to have been affected in a lasting manner by the nature of the transition to democracy (as will be seen in the party-by-party discussions below), it has been affected by the more salient features that characterize the nature of democracy in each country (as analyzed in detail in Chapter 2), especially whether it has taken on a more consensual or majoritarian form.

PASOK. This least traditional of southern European socialist parties evolved in 1974 out of a number of different centrist and leftist opposition groups. In Marxist terminology, PASOK is a "petit bourgeois" party, and it proclaims a populist ideology, but at least since 1977, it has displayed the typical mechanisms of a catch-all party, with a relatively stable, albeit faction-ridden professional elite. Michalis Spourdalakis has argued that the party evolved over a period of twenty years from a "cadre" party, to a "mass" party, to a "catch-all" party, to a "cartel" party, although I regard both the "cadre" and "cartel" characterizations as somewhat exaggerated (see Spourdalakis 1992 and 1996; and see also Katz and Mair 1995). More than any other of the parties examined here, PASOK has been seen as the party of one man: its founder and longtime leader, Andreas Papandreou, who framed the party's program and rhetoric, as well as its incomplete and (until the mid 1990s) underinstitutionalized structures, and dominated its odd decision-making processes until he became too ill to do so in the early 1990s. Papandreou also inspired the centralized and state-heavy bureaucratic clientelism that characterized PASOK rule and made Greece a *Parteienstaat* (party state) par excellence.[5]

Personalism, populism, clientelistic practices, and PASOK's initial Third World dependency and national liberation rhetoric are reflective of the context of Greek politics: relative socioeconomic and institutional underdevelopment, a long tradition of dependency, authoritarian rule, civil war, official anticommunism and exclusion of the left from power, state corporatism, a weak and fragmented civil society, and a peculiar "cultural dualism," with all its antagonistic and exclusionary mechanisms. The principal historical function of PASOK in the first two decades of the new democracy was to reverse these exclusionary practices, facilitating the integration of the left into politics and society. PASOK also served as a vehicle for the political empowerment of a heterogeneous coalition that included political and social have-nots, or "have-lesses"; progressive modernizers and professionals; and the mostly lower-class, antimodernist strata of what Nikiforos Diamandouros (1993 and 1994) has called the "underdog culture."

The price was centralism and the use of traditional (premodern) mechanisms to overcome the heterogeneity of the party's membership and elites. Analysts have usually distinguished between three groups or factions in PASOK (which, of course, have overlapped and changed over time): first, the left, consisting mostly of socialists, but also of ex-communists and more or less dogmatic Marxists, which dominated initially; second, the so-called *palaiokommatikoi* (former members of the populist Center Union party led in the 1960s by Georgios Papandreou, Andreas's father) or "conformists"; and third, the "technocrats," most of whom had been active in the student opposition against the Junta (see Spourdalakis 1988, esp. 67–68, and 1991, 163–64). Until the mid 1990s, it was basically "the three Ps"—Papandreou, populism, and patronage—that held these groups together, and the party's lack of programmatic clarity, numerous ideological and policy shifts, and slowness to modernize can all be traced to this heterogeneity.

The decisive shift of the party toward moderate reformism and catch-all electoral practices that began in 1977 was essentially produced by an alliance between the centrists ("conformists") and the technocrats, marginalizing the increasingly splintered historical left. In 1981, 53 percent of PASOK MPs had previously been active in the Center Union and its associated organizations, whereas 30 percent had belonged to one or another resistance organization; in the party's Central Committee, however, more newcomers and fewer centrists were to be found (Lyrintzis 1983a, 122). In 1994, of those delegates to the Third Party Congress who had previously been members of another party (about a quarter of all delegates), 47 percent said that they had been centrists, 38 percent had belonged to a party of the left, and only 6 percent had been members of Papandreou's Panhellenic Liberation Movement, PASOK's immediate predecessor.[6]

The Partido Socialista Obrero Español. In contrast to PASOK, the PSOE in Spain was able to modernize in a less encumbered way immediately after it took over the government in 1982, because it had completed significant reforms three years earlier. As Felipe González said to Javier Solana (later NATO secretary-general) during the Twenty-Eighth Party Congress, at which these reforms were formally proposed: "The country cannot wait until we mature. The country requires that we mature soon, and so we have to do it" (Juliá, Pradera, and Prieto 1996, 404; Juliá 1997, 537).

The PSOE entered the democratic era facing many of the same problems as PASOK. But its political evolution was also affected by the context of Spanish politics, including Spain's longer history of state-building than Greece, higher levels of institutionalization and professionalization, earlier industrialization, and "stronger" civil society. There was much less cultural dualism than in Greece, and clientelism (or *caciquismo*) was more fragmented, institutionally channeled, regionally differentiated, and had, in a peculiar way, been modernized and contained (see Puhle 1994; Linz 1977). The fact that the PSOE's elite, unlike that of PASOK, actively participated in negotiating and shaping the crucial pacts of the Spanish transition (as well as the more limited neocorporatist agreements of the early 1980s) helped to contain whatever intransigent or fundamentalist ideological features might have survived in the party. Also strengthening the hand of Felipe González in his efforts to moderate and modernize the party in 1979 was the fact that the party emerged from the founding elections of 1977 as the leading party of the opposition, only 5 percentage points behind the governing Unión de Centro Democrático (UCD). The palpable prospects of electoral victory reinforced the position of those favoring the conversion of a party that labeled itself (in the resolutions adopted at the Twenty-Seventh Party Congress in 1976) a "class party, and therefore of the masses, Marxist and democratic" into a center-left catch-all party. Indeed, in the elections of 1982, the PSOE even invaded the center-right and became, for a decade, Spain's undisputed center party, although with a somewhat leftist tinge.[7]

González's efforts to transform the PSOE into a centralized catch-all party with a moderate, reformist program first required that the heterogeneous clusters of socialist groups (the Socialist International counted twenty-three in 1976 [Juliá 1997, 474]) be unified, and that the divergent traditions of exile and underground resistance (the mentality of the "catacombs") and historical ideologies be overcome. The pragmatic alliance that had taken over the party in 1974 (which included dynamic young men from Seville, such as González, Guerra, Yáñez, and Galeote, and the Basque group around Redondo and Múgica, as well as some traditional labor leaders from French exile) managed to build a new centralized core organization of the party, to inspire the creation of (at least rudimentary) party structures all over the country and to organize the successful campaign of March 1977, after which the PSOE, as the strongest force of the opposition, almost automatically became the center of gravitation, adhesion, and integration for most of the smaller socialist (and, after 1982, even some communist) groups.[8] The party received some foreign assistance, basically from German and French sources (the impact of which has since been somewhat exaggerated in the literature).[9] What helped most, however, was the fact that the party had an undisputed and charismatic leader surrounded by a loyal team. González and his deputy Alfonso Guerra, who ran the party apparatus and in person controlled more than one-fourth of the votes at the party congresses (i.e., the bloc votes of the Andalusian delegation), managed to establish an almost absolute control of the executive. By the time of the party's Twenty-Ninth Congress in October 1981, the 99 percent voting majorities supporting the executive's proposals led some observers to speak of "democratic centralism" and draw unflattering parallels with North Korea.

Portugal's Partido Socialista. The trajectory of the Portuguese PS has been quite different from those of the Spanish and Greek socialist parties. Factors influencing the evolution of the party included (1) the particular constellation of socioeconomic development and state-society relations in Portugal; (2) the peculiar characteristics of a transition that started with a military coup, went through a short phase of social revolution with maximalist aspirations, and finally institutionalized parliamentary democracy by means of a number of protracted elite settlements; (3) the significant presence (particularly in the rural south) of an unreconstructed communist party (the PCP); and (4) the socialist party's own character as a new and heterogeneous catch-all party with little labor history and only shallow roots in Portuguese society.[10] To this we have to add (5) the fact that the party was in opposition for an entire decade (1985–95).

At the end of the authoritarian regime, Portugal was still an underdeveloped country, ranking last in western Europe with regard to most indicators. Most of the state bureaucracy was inefficient, the private sector of the economy lacked dynamism, industrial development was limited to the traditional enclaves around Lisbon/Setúbal and Porto, and agriculture—both in the minifundist north and latifundist south—remained comparatively unproductive. Civil society was weak, and although there were no significant linguistic or cultural cleavages as in Spain, there were clear urban/rural and north/south divides.

The organizational antecedents of the PS were liberal and republican, rather than socialist. This was particularly the case with the Resistència Republicana e Socialista (RRS) of 1953, which, led by Manuel Tito de Morais, Francisco Ramos da Costa, and the young Mário Soares (who had left the PCP in 1951), became the nucleus of a new socialist party, the Acção Socialista Portuguêsa (ASP) founded in April 1964 in Geneva with Soares as its secretary-general. It coordinated its domestic activities (under the leadership of Francisco Salgado Zenha) with other movements in opposition to the Salazar/Caetano regime. Externally, it concentrated on networking with and securing the support of the socialist and social democratic parties of the north (particularly Sweden, France, and Germany) and the Socialist International, of which the ASP became a member in 1972. The formal launching of the Partido Socialista in 1973 involved little more than a change of names.

The new party was dominated by urban professionals, intellectuals, and middle-class lawyers with a liberal, progressive, and republican background. It integrated Marxists, ex-Marxists, and non-Marxists, social democrats, former communists, and leftists of all kinds, progressive Catholics, as well as agnostics and freemasons, populists, pragmatic reformists, and some academic idealists with a maximalist revolutionary rhetoric (Soares 1976, 79; Bruneau and MacLeod 1986, 64–76). Given its heterogeneity, the party program could not be too specific: its 1973 Declaration of Principles subscribed to democratic pluralism and socialism, in the sense of collectivization of the means of production and distribution, economic planning, cooperativism, and workers' self-management. It further acknowledged Marxism as its "predominant theoretical inspiration," although Mário Soares hastened to add that the PS was not a Marxist party, and that Marxism was only one of its three principal inspirations, the other two being Christian humanism and cooperativism in the tradition of António Sérgio's "socialist humanism." Influenced by the revolution, the party's second Declaration of Principles (December 1974) strengthened its verbal commitment to Marxism. Thereafter, however, the party's declared orientation became more moderate:[11] in 1979, it embraced democratic socialism and a mixed economy; and in 1986 it underwent a full-fledged "Bad Godesberg" transformation, abolishing all Marxist rhetoric and deterministic assumptions, defining the PS as an "interclass party," and associating the democratic socialism of the twenty-first century with "the deepening of political democracy with a view to extending it to society as a whole."

We now turn our attention to a more detailed analysis of the processes through which these parties have transformed themselves over the course of the past two and a half decades.

Mobilization and Moderation: Toward the New Catch-All Parties

Beginning in the late 1970s, the socialist parties of the new southern European democracies transformed themselves into catch-all parties. They have subsequently experienced the same "crisis" of catch-all-ism that has characterized modern parties elsewhere: voting turnout has decreased and parties, in general, are held in low regard. Closely related to this transformation, party systems characterized by moderate levels of fragmentation ("two-parties plus"), lower levels of polarization, and centripetal dynamics of electoral competition have emerged in Greece, Portugal, and Spain.

The centripetal logic of democratic competition is of considerable importance as both a cause and a consequence of the transformation of the socialist parties. Parties were induced to move toward the center because that was where most of the voters were. In general, the spectacular electoral successes of the socialists can, to a high degree, be explained by the proximity between party placement on the left-right continuum and self-placement by the voters. The persistent salience of the left-right cleavage (as demonstrated in Chapter 3 of this volume) was of considerable importance in this process. Whether it represents a residual incarnation (or "memory") of earlier social cleavages, a more ideological and value-related divide, or a symbolic catch-all expression of the structure of competition, it has emerged as a significant "anchor" for partisan preferences among the electorates of all four southern European countries. This has greatly helped the socialist parties to retain the electoral support of their traditional constituencies (noncommunist workers, unionized wage earners, lower-middle-class service workers and bureaucrats, small shopkeepers, leftist professionals, and "underdogs") while at the same time moving toward the center in pursuit of votes from the "new middle classes" and the more affluent sectors of society. Indeed, the smashing electoral victories of PASOK in 1981, the PSOE in 1982, and the PS in 1995 posed a new strategic dilemma to the victorious governing parties: from which of these two wings of their enlarged and heterogeneous electorates would the greatest number of voters defect in harder times? Whether defections occurred gradually or more abruptly was, in large measure, a function of the presence or absence of a credible rival party to the right of center.

A third constituent element of the new catch-all character of the southern socialist parties is the importance of the party's leader and evaluations of his performance in office. As we saw in Chapter 5 above, a strong emphasis on the party's national leader is a central feature of the "new campaign politics" in the era of television, and personalism also happens to be a defining characteristic of the southern European socialist party type. But the electorate's focus on party leadership can cut both ways. As the electoral annihilation of Spain's Unión de Centro Democrático in 1982 indicated, unstable leadership and unrestrained factional rivalries can lead to massive repudiation at the polls (see Gunther 1986b; Hopkin 1995). This meant that in order for faction-ridden parties to be regarded as credible alternatives in government, they first had to establish party unity, contain factional conflict, and project an image of firm and convincing leadership. The socialist parties were by no means exceptions to this rule. Both PASOK and, especially, the PSOE successfully met this challenge prior to their electoral victories of 1981 and 1982. Conversely, the long years in opposition experienced by the Portuguese PS between 1985 and 1995 illustrate the price that may have to be paid for weak leadership and factional strife.

PASOK. The evolution of PASOK between 1974 and 1996 can be broken down into five distinct periods (for a somewhat different periodization, see Spourdalakis 1996 and 1998). The first phase (1974–77) saw a series of internal conflicts, schisms, and expulsions, which culminated in the consolidation of Andreas Papandreou's personal control of the "movement" and its emerging organization. Programmatically, the party was dominated during this period by radical demands for "substantial" democracy, populist rhetoric, and socialist promises in the anti-imperialist Third World national liberation mold along the lines set forth in the Declaration of Principles and Aims of September 3, 1974 (see Spourdalakis 1988, 288–96; Papandreou 1973).

In the second period (1977–81), PASOK became a unified and centralized party with a capable electoral machine, experienced an incomplete "Bad Godesberg" (by the end of which the level of ideological polarization was still higher than in the other southern European democracies at similar stages of their development), and set out on its ultimately successful "short march to power." The movement had become Greece's leading opposition party, with a quarter of the vote and strong catch-all overtones in the 1977 elections. It established a "peculiar pluralism," based on nearly autocratic rule, but adopted a moderate, reformist, partly technocratic image that gave credibility to the party's strategy of "change" (or *allaghi*—see Spourdalakis 1988, 131–223).

The third and fourth periods (1981–85 and 1985–89) are often treated as one, given that they span two uninterrupted terms in government. I prefer, however, to divide this decade into two periods, with a threshold in 1985 marking a qualitative shift with regard to the degree of clientelism, corruption, and scandals, as well as the beginning of the crisis of the catch-all party. Seen from a different perspective, this was accompanied by a shift from a historic period of "incorporation" (of formerly marginalized sectors into Greek political life) to "entrenchment" (see Diamandouros 1993). The party's 1981 election victory had been made possible, in part, by its absorption of voters previously supporting smaller parties, particularly the integration into PASOK of the followers of the centrist George Mavros (EDIK) and the leftist Manolis Glezos (EDA), and by the progressive marginalization of other small (mostly leftist) parties. In the end, PASOK had managed to mobilize the energies of a broad coalition that bridged the contradictions of the fragile traditional Venizelist modernizing alliance between the liberal entrepreneurial bourgeoisie and the populist petit bourgeois and peasant strata (which is also typical of anti-imperialist, nationalist, and populist movements of the Third World—see Mavrogordatos 1983c; Puhle 1986b), on the one hand, and sizable parts of the noncommunist working class and the unionized and leftist vote, on the other. In times of *desencanto* (disenchantment), the latter have usually been the first to break away.

PASOK's eight years in government in the 1980s were characterized by a lack of party institutionalization, an interpenetration of party and government, clientelistic practices, and increasing corruption scandals. The end of this period was marked by PASOK's loss of votes and electoral defeat in the three elections of 1989–90 (see Table 7.1), in large measure brought about by severe defections on the part of the better-educated, skilled wage earners, unionized workers, professionals, and in the urban centers. Although the party congress of September 1990 was badly organized and failed to resolve conflicts over many issues, it gave ample voice, for the first time, to Papandreou's critics. It also made it clear that dividing lines among groups with different historical backgrounds had been superseded by polarization along a new cleavage within the party, separating populists and modernizers.

The following period (1990–96) was characterized by efforts to revitalize the party's organizational structure (made necessary by the loss of government resources), to make it more "European,"[12] and to design more detailed and realistic policies, with the ultimate goal of modernizing Greek society. Some of these policies (particularly regarding the economy) would prove to be of considerable significance following the party's return to power in 1993. At the same time, however, the early 1990s were marked by the protracted illness of Papandreou, who complicated matters by refusing to step down even after he had been incapacitated, and by granting extraconstitutional influence to a *camarilla* of his family and friends. The result was a full-blown "succession crisis," which ended only with Papandreou's resignation and subsequent death in 1996 and the election of Costas Simitis first as prime minister and later that year as party leader. The beginning of the end of this phase had been signaled at the party's Third Congress (April 1994) and a subsequent conference clarifying institutional procedures.

The Partido Socialista Obrero Español. Since its de facto refounding in 1974, the PSOE has passed through six distinct stages. It is interesting to note that half of the thresholds separating these stages were marked by announcements or threats of resignation by the party's leader, Felipe González—in 1979 over the issue of "Marxism," in 1986 over NATO membership, and in 1990 in rhetorical solidarity with Alfonso Guerra—which preceded his actual resignation at the party congress of June 1997. The first phase began in 1974 and ended with the extraordinary congress of September 1979. This was a period when the party moved its headquarters from exile back to Spain, became legal, and laid the organizational, personal, and programmatic foundations of its subsequent success. The Twenty-Seventh PSOE Congress of December 1976 in Madrid, the first to be held in Spain since 1939, had a highly symbolic significance: even though it was still formally illegal and "underground," the party made it clear that it was back in Spanish politics. Another important event during this period was the founding election of the Spanish transition in 1977, which established the PSOE as the principal party of the left. This was followed by a determined effort over the following two years to absorb smaller socialist groups, centralize the party's organization, and modernize its program. During the second period (1979–82), with the governing Unión de Centro Democrático progressively disintegrating, the socialist PSOE consolidated its position as the only united catch-all party of the center. The PSOE was able to project an image of youth, credibility, moderation, and modernity, and to articulate demands for the change (*cambio*) desired by most Spaniards. And it was able to come to grips with the demands of campaign politics in the television age.

During these first two periods, the Spanish socialists had to resolve a number of problems before they could position themselves to win the 1982 elections. First, they had to work hard at the grass roots and establish the party throughout Spain, including those places that had never been socialist strongholds. Here it helped enormously that the PSOE (traditionally a "centralist" party) became the first statewide, nonregionalist political force to support demands for limited self-government rights of the regions, now reflected in the Estado de las Autonomías. Second, in order to demonstrate its unity, political realism, and moderation, it had to undergo a process of programmatic and ideological "modernization," as well as organizational reforms.

This was accomplished during a relatively short (but turbulent) time between the Twenty-Eighth Congress (which was suspended following González's resignation as secretary-general) in May 1979 and the extraordinary congress held just four months later. In the end, factionalism was marginalized, and the González team institutionalized its firm control over the party apparatus. This congress also did away with the party's self-characterization as a Marxist and democratic class and mass party (adopted in 1976), redefined it as a "democratic and federal mass party," and explicitly subscribed to ideological pluralism. In elections to the party executive committee, the traditional leftist *críticos* received no more than 7 percent of the vote, a share corresponding to the representation granted to the Izquierda Socialista, a minority faction "recognized" since 1983.[13] As the general elections of 1982 approached, the PSOE, in contrast to PASOK, was able to present itself as a unified, moderate, and modernized party asking for "a social pact for modernization," under a more honorable, more dynamic, and more determined leadership (Partido Socialista Obrero Español 1982 and 1984; Guerra 1984 and 1985). Its stability contrasted sharply with the unseemly images presented to voters by its principal rivals, the governing center-right UCD and the Partido Comunista de España (PCE), both of which were in the throes of divisive internal conflicts, defections, and schisms.

The third phase (1982–86/87) saw the PSOE in government with a comfortable majority of 202 out of 350 seats in the Congress of Deputies. This security in government, coupled with the fact that Spanish democracy had been consolidated, emboldened the González government to undertake a far-reaching program of economic readjustment, industrial reconstruction, and institutional modernization. Its victory became all the more complete when the PSOE gained control of most of Spain's big cities, as well as twelve of the seventeen autonomous community governments in the municipal and regional elections of 1983. One measure of the PSOE's success in mastering "catch-all" politics is that the party's electoral support in 1982 almost exactly matched the composition of the electorate at large. The PSOE attracted support from virtually all social strata in the 1982 elections, not only mobilizing some 2 million new voters but "borrowing" 1.2 million votes from the center-right UCD and about 1 million from the PCE. This made its constituency extremely heterogeneous. Accordingly, it was inevitable that when the socialist mobilization passed its peak and *desencanto* set in, the prolonged honeymoon of reformist unity came to a close, and the heterogeneous coalition began to crumble.

This gradual electoral decline began in 1986, with the loss of about 1.2 million votes compared with 1982. The majoritarian biases of Spanish electoral law, in combination with the perceived absence of any alternative (which resulted from continuing suspicion of the principal opposition party, the Alianza Popular), nonetheless enabled it to remain in power. But the processes of erosion had been set in motion. The catch-all party began to turn into what I would call a modified catch-all party, characterized by shrinking support (owing to rising abstention, *desencanto,* and negative views of parties), increasing fragmentation (with less party unity and more divergent patterns of campaigning), and the need to rely more on state or traditional (e.g., clientelistic) resources as a result of its decreased mobilizational potential (Puhle 1996 and 1997). Moreover, relations between the PSOE and its allied trade union, the UGT, began to deteriorate. Party/union relations were initially strained by the government's industrial reconversion program and relatively conservative monetary policies. But when it became clear in 1987 that the economic boom of 1985–88 was not creating the new jobs that had been promised in 1982 (800,000 new jobs, to be precise), and that social welfare benefits were not improving as expected, workers and students turned to the streets. Relations between the party and its erstwhile union ally became overtly conflictive, and the UGT leader Nicolás Redondo gave up his seat in parliament. In addition, in the 1987 local and regional elections, the party retained an absolute majority in only three Comunidades Autónomas (retaining its greatest strength in Andalusia, Extremadura, and Valencia), and lost over 5,000 municipal council seats.

Thus, the fourth period (1987–90) was characterized by the "breakup of the socialist family" (Gillespie 1990b). Increasing labor unrest culminated in the general strike of December 14, 1988, jointly organized by the UGT and the communist-led Comisiones Obreras. The politics of economic and social *pactos* had come to an end, as had the first wave of institutional reforms (marked by the resignation of the minister of education, José María Maravall in 1988). Although the party was still run by the González-Guerra alliance, differences between the two leaders (who themselves never voiced dissent in public) and their followers ultimately culminated in an intraparty cleavage between "liberals" (or modernizers [*renovadores*]) and *guerristas,* who took up the more traditional, eventually Keynesian, demands of the unions and often worked through old clientelistic networks (see Cazorla 1992). The *guerristas* also dominated important sectors of the central party apparatus and invested much energy in the preparation of a new long-range party program with a clear antitechnocratic and somewhat leftist tinge, the *Programa 2000* (Partido Socialista Obrero Español 1989; Guerra 1987). In January 1991, following almost a year of public debate over his brother's alleged corruption, Alfonso Guerra was replaced as deputy prime minister by Narcis Serra, but remained as second-in-command at party headquarters. A number of *guerristas* followed him out of the cabinet in March. Although the government thereby became more coherent and uniform, it also became even more "presidentialist" and isolated from the party.

During this period, the PSOE continued to lose support at the polls. The 1989 elections saw the defection of another million voters, or 4 percent of the total ballot, reducing its share to 40.2 percent, and it barely held onto a working majority in parliament (thanks largely to a boycott of the Cortes by the pro-ETA party, Herri Batasuna). Many of the young, urban middle-class voters who had been mobilized in 1982 left the socialist camp or abstained, as did many unionized and unemployed workers. The PSOE's voter base became incrementally older, less educated, and less urban, and more female, lower-class, and economically inactive. The significance of "leader voting" also slightly decreased.[14]

The fifth distinct period in the PSOE's development (1991–93/94) was one of open conflict along a diffuse left/right divide in the party, as the government went back to restrictive fiscal policies, budget cuts, stabilization programs, and devaluation in order to meet the European Union's criteria of convergence under the provisions of the Maastricht treaty. Alienation of the UGT, a decline in party unity, and a general sense of fatigue in government contributed to a loss of the party's absolute majority in the Congress of Deputies in 1993.[15] Although the party's share of the vote declined by only 1.4 percentage points, the 1993 election was a watershed in the sense that the conservative Partido Popular was finally able to overcome perceptions on the left that there was no acceptable alternative to the PSOE. The PP was finally able to obliterate the small Centro Democrático y Social (founded by Adolfo Suárez in 1982) and directly challenge the PSOE for votes at the center of the political spectrum. As a unified and renamed party, under the leadership of the youthful José María Aznar, it increased its share of the vote from 25.6 percent in 1989 to 34.8 percent in 1993. Where, in 1982, Alianza Popular had received only 9 percent of those on the center-left (vs. the PSOE's 40 percent share), by 1993, the PP had risen to 21 percent, while the PSOE's share declined to 27 percent (see Boix 1995, 49–52). Socioeconomic groups that had shifted to the PSOE in 1982 were also increasingly attracted to the revitalized Partido Popular: while the socialists retained stable support among the less-skilled strata of the urban working class (and actually increased their support in rural and agricultural areas, especially among agricultural laborers, temporary workers, retired people, and welfare recipients), there was dramatic erosion of support for the PSOE in the big cities and among the more dynamic service-oriented sectors, white-collar workers, and skilled workers.[16] This has led to a somewhat clearer class crystallization of the vote and represents a temporary setback for the PSOE's catch-all strategy. By the time of the 1994 European Parliament elections, the PP (which received 40.2 percent of the vote) even succeeded in reducing the socialist vote (30.7 percent) to what it had been before 1982.

In an effort to reduce the power of the *guerristas,* the modernizers (with their power base in the government) forged an alliance with several of the party's regional *barones,* who wished to rein in the emergence of statewide "tendencies" within the PSOE. Their victory at the Thirty-Third Party Congress in 1994 was a victory for Felipe González (for one last time), but it also reduced the power of the central party executive. Over the long term, this shift had the effect of increasing the power of the regional leaders and laying the foundations of a new institutionalization of influence and power within the party independent of the government.

During the sixth phase of the PSOE's evolution (1994–96), the *guerristas* became even more marginal. This final stage of the party's uninterrupted fourteen years in government did not, however, provide much of an opportunity for González to reconsolidate the party institutionally or personally. The prime minister had scant room for maneuver, given the constraints imposed on his minority government by his more conservative Catalan parliamentary ally, and pressures from the European Union and the international environment. González's leadership was also weakened by corruption and scandals involving high-ranking party and government officials dug up (and often exaggerated) by a sensationalist muckraking press.

Another modest decline in the PSOE's share of the vote in the 1996 election was enough to oust it from power, inaugurating a seventh distinct phase in the party's development. Loss of power provided an opportunity to initiate a process of party regeneration. Felipe González stepped down as party leader at the Thirty-Fourth Congress in June 1997. He did so in such a manner as to simultaneously strip his deputy Alfonso Guerra of every vestige of power, thus forcing the congress to make its own choice in replacing him.

Portugal's Partido Socialista. The PS in Portugal has been a moderate, center-left party almost from the beginning, although, as we saw above, the exigencies of the revolution pushed it rhetorically to the left, as manifested in the radicalization of its Declaration of Principles in December 1974. Even though that strong language was not rescinded until 1986, the party has consistently pushed for moderate policies and served as a strong force for democratization. Above all, it exercised considerable influence in the key institutional decisions of 1975–76, opposing establishment of a "unitary" labor union (which would have been dominated by hardline communists), defending individual liberties, pluralism, and the rule of law, and favoring the institutionalization of a representative government compatible with other western European governments. As Portugal's strongest party (with almost 38 percent of the vote in the Constituent Assembly elections of April 1975, and 35 percent in the parliamentary elections of 1976), its support was crucial in setting Portugal firmly on the road to democratic consolidation. In July 1976, after the turbulent revolutionary period ended, and with a democratic constitution ratified, the party's leader, Mário Soares, formed Portugal's first PS (minority) government.

The PS was a catch-all party from the very beginning. From the first elections until 1983, the party received substantial electoral support from an alliance that included the moderate working class of the north, the urban middle classes, lower-level professionals, white-collar urban workers, and small and medium rural proprietors in the Alentejo. The socialist party received support from at least 25 percent of each social class, with the strongest support coming from the lower middle and lower classes (Stock and Rother 1983; Lewis and Williams 1984, 132; Bruneau and MacLeod 1986, 67), and it received at least 20 percent of the vote in all parts of the country.[17]

But although the PS was successful from the start in advancing the cause of democracy and in establishing itself as an electorally successful catch-all party, its organizational capacities were limited, discipline was lower than in the PSOE or PASOK, and factional feuds weakened the party. Besides numerous personalistic loyalties, we can identify at least four groups with persistent and recognizable profiles: the *históricos,* the "moderates," the former members of the GIS (Socialist Intervention Group), and the "technocrats" divided the party elite through the late 1970s. In the early 1980s, the polarizing fight between Soares and the party secretariat led the factions to form two alliances: on one side were the *históricos* and moderates (most of them of the older generation) led by Soares, and on the other side were arrayed the (often younger) groups of technocrats and former members of the GIS. The Soares-led alliance dominated in the early 1980s, receiving about two-thirds of the vote at the 1981 and 1983 party congresses; the latter, younger group took control of the party apparatus in 1986, following Soares's election as president of the republic. While always a source of party weakness, the worst effects of factionalism were contained by three factors. The first was patronage and the need to work together to achieve the electoral victory necessary to make government patronage available to the various factions. The second was the able leadership of Mário Soares, a gifted populist orator who (although he faced more rivals within his party than Papandreou or González) knew how to impose his will on the party leadership (Janitschek 1974; Soares 1974 and 1976). Soares was able to establish centralism from above during the first half of the 1980s, but it remained a centralism with "tendencies." The third factor that helped to contain factionalism within the PS was outside competition. More than the PSOE or PASOK, the PS was dependent on decisions by outside actors (such as President Ramalho Eanes, when he fired Soares in 1978, and when he set up the rival Partido Renovador Democrático, or PRD, in the mid 1980s; or the PSD leaders Francisco Sá Carneiro and Aníbal Cavaco Silva, when they turned to the right in 1979 and 1985) and other organized groups, and the need to compromise with them (e.g., in securing crucial pacts with the military in 1975–76, and in forming coalition governments thereafter). Accordingly, until 1995, when they formed a single-party government for the first time, the Portuguese socialists' room for maneuver was more limited than that of their Greek or Spanish counterparts.

One significant difference between the PS and the Greek and Spanish socialist parties is that the PS emerged from the start as Portugal's largest party. A second significant difference is largely a product of Portugal's proportional electoral law, which led to a more fragmented parliamentary party system than in Greece or Spain (whose "proportional" representation electoral systems include "correctives" with highly majoritarian biases). This required the formation of multiparty coalition governments over the first decade of Portuguese democracy. The third distinctive feature is that in forging alliances with other parties to form governments, the Portuguese socialists found that the barrier between parties of the left and right (i.e., separating them from the liberal PSD) was more permeable than that dividing the communist left from the socialist left. The hardline Marxism-Leninism of the PCP made it completely unavailable as a potential coalition partner. Thus, the PS found itself engaged in a series of government coalitions with parties of the center and right over the first decade.

The first phase, whose most important developments have already been discussed, spanned the period between the founding of the party and formation of the first constitutional government in July 1976. Its most salient features were, obviously, the "first transition" (which toppled the Caetano regime) and the revolution; the Eanes-led countercoup, which initiated the "second transition" and efforts to establish a democratic regime; and the leading role played by the PS throughout this period.

The second phase (1976–79) was a period of protracted party consolidation in government. It ended when the PS lost the elections of December 1979, but the demise of the short "socialist era" had already begun when the Soares government (a coalition with the rightist Partido do Centro Democrático Social, or CDS, formed in January 1978) was dismissed just six months later by President Eanes, who, like most Portuguese, resented its austerity policies in times of recession. The increasing factionalization of the party's elite also became notable at this time. The most important acquisition was the incorporation of about fifty leftist intellectuals, technocrats, and members of GIS in 1978, among them Jorge Sampaio and António Guterres, who would lead the party in the 1990s. Another important development during this period was the adoption at the party's Third Congress in March 1979 of its program for the 1980s, *Dez anos para mudar Portugal,* drafted by the young "technocrat" António Guterres.

The third stage (1980–83) was a period of upheaval and open conflict within the party, which broke out after the PS lost the elections of December 1979 (an experience to be repeated in October 1980). This internal dissension was also triggered by an erratic move by Soares against swinging socialist electoral support behind President Eanes in 1980, in opposition to a position taken by the party's executive secretariat (which by odd circumstances was dominated by young former GIS members and technocrats). Even though he was no longer in government, and was opposed by a vast majority in the party, Soares won his war against the secretariat. His triumph culminated in the dismissal of the executive at the Fourth Party Congress of May 1981 and exclusion of its members (and their followers) from positions of party leadership for years. This victory effectively consolidated the undisputed leadership of Mário Soares, who could now even remove an influential and independent historic figure like Salgado Zenha from leadership of the party's parliamentary group. Factionalism was contained as long as Soares remained at the top. The Fifth Party Congress in October 1983 celebrated a reconciliation under conditions set down by the secretary general. In the general elections six months earlier, the party's new unity (which contrasted with the breakup of the

Aliança Democrática, or AD, the rightist governing coalition, consisting of the PSD, the conservative CDS, and the small Partido Popular Monarquico) helped to return the socialists to power with a vote similar to that of 1975. The new centrist coalition with the PSD, the Bloco Central, was the fruit of a silent rapprochement between the two parties that grew out of the negotiations over the constitutional reform of 1982 and was made possible by the death of the rightist PSD leader Sá Carneiro, who had been one of the architects of the conservative AD alliance.

The fourth phase in the development of the PS (1983–85) was marked by the complete domination of the party by Mário Soares and by the austerity policies of the Bloco Central government. It ended in May 1985 when the PSD under its new leader, Cavaco Silva, left the Bloco Central. The decision by Soares to abandon control of the party in order to run for presidency of the republic left the party effectively leaderless and culminated in the greatest electoral disaster of its history. The appearance of a new center-left party (the PRD, which looked slightly more leftist than the PS) under the leadership of the outgoing president, Eanes, served as a viable alternative for center-left voters dissatisfied with the socialists' liberal economic and social policies. Eanes's new party received 18.4 percent of the vote, about three-quarters of them from socialists.[18] Electoral support for the PS declined to 20.8 percent. The election of Mário Soares as president of the republic in 1986 (by a small margin, and with reluctant communist support against the conservative candidate Freitas do Amaral) was little consolation to the socialists, who were left divided and leaderless. A symbol of the party's division was that Soares was opposed in the first round of the presidential election by his former historic socialist ally Salgado Zenha.

The fifth stage (1986–95) lasted almost as long as the first four combined. It was a period of slow and (until 1989) delayed recovery, of personalistic rivalries, factionalism, weak and unsteady leadership, and further moderation. During this period, the governing PSD twice secured absolute parliamentary majorities, in 1987 and 1991, and imposed itself as a dominant party. The socialists' new leader, Vitor Constâncio, could neither unite the party nor take advantage of the breakdown of the PRD in the elections of 1987. Since Constâncio (a technocrat and member of the former secretariat) had been the candidate of the left, it was important for the cohesion and internal balance of the party for the Sixth Party Congress in June 1986 to ratify a moderate new social democratic program. The third Declaration of Principles officially abandoned all Marxist rhetoric, and subscribed to the concept of an interclass party and to pluralist democracy. The Portuguese socialists' "Bad Godesberg," coming several years later than the respective ideological reorientations of their Greek and Spanish friends (1977–79), did not give rise to an electoral backlash. Indeed, the policies previously adopted by the PS in government indicated to most voters that the party had already become a moderate catch-all party about a decade before the program ratified it de jure.

The party's slow recovery began in January 1989 with the election of Jorge Sampaio as party leader. Sampaio was helped in his efforts to modernize and reform the PS by the more or less united support of the former GIS faction and the technocrats, whereas the camps behind his rivals among the *históricos* (Alegre and Gama), the "moderates," and the unorganized *Soaristas* (including Soares's son João) were divided. An efficient former leader of the GIS with a moderate leftist reputation, who in the conflicts of the early 1980s had sided with the secretariat against Soares, Sampaio now beat the last of the *históricos*. With him a number of the younger technocrats of the late 1970s assumed positions of power within the party. These included the parliamentary leader António Guterres, who had been purged by Soares in 1983, and some members of an even younger generation. Signs of the party's electoral recovery could be seen in the local elections of December 1989, in which socialists (including Sampaio, who won the highly visible office of mayor of Lisbon) recovered control of a number of local strongholds, and in the general elections of 1991: despite another absolute majority for the PSD, support for the PS reached 30 percent, with most of its gain at the expense of communists (whose share of the vote declined to 8.8 percent) and the now extinct PRD.

Four years later, under António Guterres (who had assumed leadership of the party in 1992), the PS was returned to government with a comfortable plurality of 43.9 percent of the vote—only four seats short of a majority (a result to be repeated in 1999, when the party won even more seats). This was attributable, not only to the party's own achievements, its program of economic modernization, and its new and efficient campaign techniques,[19] but also to the impact of an economic recession, the wear of ten years in government, corruption, scandals, Cavaco Silva's erratic departure from his party's leadership, which left his successor Fernando Nogueira little time to take charge, and the usual disenchantment with political parties and politicians. With the socialists' return into government in October 1995, a sixth phase of the socialist trajectory has begun, which one day may be labeled as "regeneration in government."

Organizational Features of the Southern European Catch-All Parties

Among the distinctive features of the southern European socialist party type are relatively low levels of mass organization, weakly institutionalized structures of internal party governance, a high level of personalization of party leadership, and factionalism. As argued earlier in this chapter, the organizational underdevelopment of these parties was not necessarily disadvantageous. It made them more flexible and adaptable. Neither was personalization a drawback, since the emergence of television as the dominant medium of political communication favored campaigns that above all emphasized the leadership capabilities of the parties' top candidates. Factionalism would, however, present difficulties for these parties, particularly insofar as the low level of institutionalization of their central organs made it difficult to regulate and resolve conflict between factions.

For catch-all parties in the television age, mass membership is much less important than it was for the older mass parties based on class or religion. A party's elite, its organization, and the performance(s) of the party leader(s) in the media all count for more. Hence it has not been a major liability for the socialist parties in the new southern European democracies that their membership figures have, on the whole, remained relatively low: at the time of their greatest triumphs, in 1981–82, the Greek and Spanish socialist parties had just over 100,000 members apiece, and on forming its first single-party government in 1995, the Portuguese PS had even fewer.[20] Although party membership swelled when the socialists were in government, it remains clear that the strength of the party lay more in its capacity for ad hoc mobilization than in standing organizational strength. Thus, relatively low membership rates were not indicative of limited efficiency, particularly at a time when public financing of parties, providing between 60 and 90 percent of financial resources (del Castillo 1985; Puhle 1986a; Bruneau and MacLeod 1986, 30) was more important than members' dues.

The Spanish case reflects another significant departure from both the northern European model and from Spain's own history: PSOE members were more evenly distributed geographically in the post-Franco era than in periods before 1939.[21] And even though custom and the party's statutes required party members to affiliate with the socialist trade union, the UGT, only about half (in some regions, only about one-third) of them did so. Even among party members employed in traditionally unionized sectors of the economy, a surprisingly large number failed to adhere to this policy: 24 percent of skilled industrial and service workers, and 45 percent of agricultural workers, were not unionized in the early 1980s (Tezanos and Yañez 1981; Tezanos 1984, 61–75, and 1989). The party did not, in fact, need the unions as much as it had in its earlier history, because it had established an organizational presence throughout the country: by 1982, the number of local party branches (*agrupaciones*) had reached 3,000; after further increasing to 6,500 branches in 1985, it stabilized at around 4,000 *agrupaciones* nationwide after 1987. In addition, members no longer organized at the workplace, and an influx from the "new middle classes" and other nontraditional sectors, beginning in 1982, brought in recruits who were unlikely to have union ties. At the same time, however, employment by state agencies was increasing in importance as a vehicle for recruitment; in May 1984, for example, more than a quarter of the PSOE members were public servants,[22] and the share of the delegates to the national party congresses who held public office or were employed by the state rose from around 60 percent in 1981 and 1984 to about 70 percent in 1988 and 1990 (Maravall 1991, 15). Nonetheless, given the basic characteristics of "the new campaign politics" (see Chapter 5 above), the relative weakness of the party's mass membership base did not represent a serious liability. Two empirical studies have revealed that there was no direct causal relationship between membership density and electoral success per province (see Chapter 3 above; Puhle 1986a, 342). In addition, local elites were becoming much less significant as mobilizers of the vote than they had been in the Second Republic: indeed, in 1982, only 20 percent of voters (26 percent of PSOE voters) knew the name of the person leading the provincial list for which they had voted. Thus, the Spanish socialists could apparently afford to neglect the task of establishing ties with the associational life of civil society.

In terms of the structure of party organization and leadership, the PSOE can be regarded as highly centralized, at least between 1979 and 1997: González, Guerra, and their almost homogeneous executive committee held considerable powers and had the final say, not only with regard to key strategy and policy decisions, but also over the lists of candidates for all major elections, including regional elections and local elections in large towns. The delegates to party congresses and the members of the executive (at all levels) were elected from closed lists according to the winner-takes-all principle, and bloc-voting procedures were established and remained the rule until 1994 for national and regional congresses.[23] These procedures sharply constrained internal conflicts, although at the cost of strengthening oligarchical tendencies within the party. Even Felipe González warned in October 1986 against the tendency toward "oligarchization and intolerance" within the party (Maravall 1991, 15–16). Somewhat offsetting these markedly majoritarian and centralist procedures, votes on programmatic questions at party congresses were left to individual delegates. In addition, while "organized tendencies" were outlawed, minority "currents of opinion" were officially recognized and would receive 25 percent of the delegates if they were supported by 20 percent of the vote.

These characteristics were perhaps the unavoidable consequences of the new catch-all mechanisms of campaign politics, particularly the general tendencies toward personalized and leader-centered campaigns through the media, and the downplaying of programmatic issues and grass-roots mobilization by party militants and through rallies and meetings. Although these procedures and organizational features helped to make the PSOE an efficient electoral machine, until the mid 1990s, this came at the expense of restrictions on internal democracy and a lack of institutionalized party autonomy vis-à-vis socialist leaders in government. The centralizing mechanisms adopted in 1979, which had been successfully designed to streamline the party and to win elections, tended to stifle an independent party life once the PSOE was in government. Thus, one could assert (with some exaggeration) that the early modernization of the PSOE has been good for Spain, but less so for the PSOE.

The centralism, internal hierarchy, and oligarchization of the PSOE functioned well as long as the González-Guerra axis remained united. Once it broke under the pressures of the growing conflict between the government and the unions in the late 1980s, however, a new bipolar structure of factionalism emerged along the lines of a left/right cleavage (however unclearly perceived). The *guerristas* mobilized against the primacy of growth and modernization and demanded a greater emphasis on social policy. They received support from the traditional labor union subculture, from Izquierda Socialista sympathizers, and from the poorer and less developed regions of the country. The progovernment faction consisted of modernizers (*renovadores, Felipistas*), urban professional elites with social democratic or liberal traditions, members of the "new middle classes," and government employees. In the short run, the *guerristas* wielded much influence: they dominated the Thirty-Second Party Congress in 1991 and a number of regional federations, among them the powerful organization in Andalusia; they led three regional governments; and were supported by six or seven government ministers. The government technocrats, in contrast, had almost no influence in the party executive. Over the long run, however, the government faction prevailed. After Guerra and some of his followers had left the government, and relations between the two camps had become more antagonistic in 1991, González succeeded in replacing a number of *guerrista* regional leaders with his own allies at the Thirty-Third Party Congress in 1994, at which *guerrista* influence was contained: the bloc vote was abolished, and the position of the regional *barones* enhanced at the expense of the central party machine. *Guerristas* were excluded from the new government in 1993, and three years later only three of the party's seventeen regional federations (significantly, Asturias, Cantabria, and Galicia, all small ones) were dominated by a more or less *guerrista* majority. At the party's Thirty-Fourth Congress in June 1997, the *guerristas* were marginalized: they were given only two out of the thirty-three seats on the executive committee, although about a quarter of the 945 delegates were considered *guerristas.*[24]

In the course of this protracted struggle, the leaders of the party's powerful regional federations functioned as mediators, and occasionally joined forces with one or the other side (as at the Thirty-Third Congress, when the government faction forged an alliance with a number of regional leaders, most notably Joan Lerma from Valencia). This strategic maneuvering gave the *barones* considerable leverage, and eventually increased their power within the party. By the time of the Thirty-Fourth Congress in 1997, the *barones* were powerful enough to block all plans for party reform that would have implied their exclusion from the central party executive, as had been proposed by González. They also had a decisive say in the election of Joaquín Almunia to the party leadership after González's resignation. Thus, by the late 1990s, an autonomous party structure had emerged within the PSOE that was increasingly independent of the government, and that has established a balance of decision-making authority between the traditions of centralized leadership and the new power base in the regional federations.

This development was facilitated by Spain's constitutional structure as an Estado de las Autonomías, which, in the course of two decades of institutional development, established the regions as important political arenas and as a recruiting ground for strong political actors. Thus, the process of party building and institutionalization was substantially affected by the macrostructure of Spain's democracy itself. It would be interesting to see if moves toward state decentralization in Greece and Portugal will help to revitalize their socialist parties, as that process has in Spain.

While there are some important similarities between the Spanish and Greek socialist parties, PASOK was a party of a different type, its leader was stronger, and open factionalism was not permitted. For more than twenty years, PASOK has functioned as a "populist party" (Sotiropoulos 1996) that regards itself as a broad popular movement. In addition to establishing a local presence throughout the country, it has organized through its labor unions (PASKE), farmers' and trade cooperatives, professional and student (PASP) associations, women's and youth groups, and a number of advisory and patronage agencies, such as the Solidarity Bureau (a labor exchange for members). Throughout most of its history, however, the party's formal organizational structure did not matter much, because PASOK was a highly centralized, autocratically led party. As party congresses were rarely held (only four in twenty-two years), many of the members of the Central Committee and of the smaller Executive Bureau were appointed by the party leader, who also had decisive influence over the party's electoral lists once the preference vote was abolished in 1982. Papandreou thus became the ultimate source of legitimacy for almost everything in the party. The leader's charisma was not routinized, however, and intermediary institutions were not built. Decisions were usually made from the top down, and internal party democracy was not just minimal—as it was in the PSOE through most of the 1980s—it was nonexistent. Open criticism was not allowed, and until the beginning of the 1990s, dissenters were purged and expelled from the party by simple action of Papandreou's handpicked Disciplinary Council. This was the fate of leading party functionaries, cabinet members, and even one of the later contenders for the succession, Gerassimos Arsenis.

PASOK's organization and decision-making processes have, however, substantially changed since the party came to power in 1981. Its control of the government has enabled it to colonize government agencies and use them for partisan purposes in a system that might best be described as centralized "bureaucratic clientelism" (Lyrintzis 1993), employing the mechanisms of a "peculiar pluralism" (Spourdalakis 1991, 166, and 1988, 114–62) to integrate fragmented local and sectional interests and particularisms. This new clientelism is different from traditional clientelism in Greece, insofar as there has been a centralization of decision making concerning the more important decisions. Hence Michalis Spourdalakis's (1996) notion of a "centralized fragmentation" is well to the point. Paradoxically, this increase in power and resources did not redound to the benefit of the party and its institutionalization: indeed, as Papandreou and the party elite moved into government posts, the party and its parliamentary group were now run from the government, and its organization became even weaker than it had been before, leading many observers to regard PASOK as an "appendage to the government" (Spourdalakis 1988, 250; Sotiropoulos 1991, 108–14). Control of the government also failed to ameliorate the internal divisions within the party. Instead, the personalistic antagonisms, splits, crises, and purges that characterized PASOK's daily politics at the level below Papandreou now affected the government. Operating through the ministries, at least three party factions manipulated the bureaucracy, which was highly vulnerable to this kind of takeover because it had not been professionalized but was rather (as Nicos Mouzelis has argued) the type of weak bureaucracy typical of the semiperiphery. Staffed primarily by patronage, it was easily exploited by both PASOK and ND to satisfy the demands of their respective clienteles (see Mouzelis 1986; Sotiropoulos 1991). In 1984, 66 percent of the 140 members of PASOK's Central Committee were or had been occupying public office (excluding parliamentary mandates). In 1994, of the 811 delegates to the Third Party Congress, 41.4 percent were employed in the public sector. The public and private "petit bourgeois" sectors together added up to around 70 percent, but the public side was stronger.[25]

In contrast to the PSOE, where (despite the undisputed role of Felipe González) leadership was much more institutionalized, the *barones* of PASOK, apart from Papandreou's closest entourage, were relatively powerless. Lacking their own regional strongholds, they could only muster political influence if they had significant personal followings of their own and knew how to build coalitions within the clientelistic structures of the central party-bureaucratic complex. Papandreou's 1984 dismissal of Interior Minister Georgios Gennimatas, a fervent promoter of administrative and political decentralization, precluded the emergence of autonomous regional or local government bodies that might have served as power bases for the emergence of potential rivals or successors to the PASOK leader. This is one of the factors that later made the "succession crisis" so agonizing when it eventually occurred in the 1990s. The removal of Gennimatas from power shelved plans for decentralization that might have posed a challenge to the status quo of centralist clientelism for over a decade (see Sotiropoulos 1991, 100–104).

The party elite became convinced that party reform and institutionalization were necessary only after a series of electoral defeats in 1989 and 1990, and after Papandreou's health had begun to deteriorate. A slow process of party reform was initiated after the second and, particularly, third party congresses (in June 1990 and April 1994). Party headquarters were streamlined, the post of secretary-general was created, the disciplinary council was abolished, and criticisms were tolerated and more openly voiced. A reflection of this greater openness can be seen in 1990, when 40 percent of the party's new Central Committee voted against Papandreou, and in October 1994, when the party rebelled against the candidate lists proposed for the municipal elections. As long as Papandreou was in charge, however, these rebellions and protests served as a mere safety valve and did not change much. A more substantial institutionalization of the party began only with the formulation of rules governing the post-Papandreou succession in 1995 and 1996.

The organizational development of the Portuguese Partido Socialista has been characterized by less centralism (except in the early 1980s) and more open factionalism than in the other two parties. Like the PSOE and PASOK, however, the PS has remained somewhat underinstitutionalized, but this was not because it was run from the government. The party did achieve important organizational objectives: by 1983, it was represented in almost all of the country's municipalities. Only the founding of a women's organization came relatively late, in 1981. The establishment of a party machine profited from the technocratic skills of the many professionals in the headquarters and the *gabinete de estudos,* particularly former members of the GIS, and from generous public funding, which in the mid 1980s amounted to between 60 and 80 percent of the party's budget (Bruneau and MacLeod 1986, 30).

The party's decision-making processes were organized in a centralized, hierarchic way (see Partido Socialista 1992), but in a manner that respected the existing networks of "tendencies" and factions around historic leaders or small groups. These factional groups, all based in Lisbon, were more elitist and less clientelistic than those of the PSOE. In order to reduce the risks of stalemate, immobilism, or open feuds among factions, various mechanisms were debated to maintain the party's unity and strength vis-à-vis the outside. But they all revolved around the notion that the unity of the party could only be secured by strong leadership, whether it operated in Mário Soares's acerbic, even Bonapartist, fashion or through negotiation and integration, as preferred by Sampaio and Guterres. In the PS, institutionalization had its clear limitations.

Much of the southern European socialist parties' performance has also, however, been a function of their policies in government, particularly their efforts to modernize institutions and the economy and their social policies, which have deeply affected their relations with the unions.

Policies of Modernization

PASOK. During its first two decades, the Greek socialist party has done more for the democratization than for the modernization of the country. Its performance in government has been particularly mixed (see Tsoucalas 1986, 24–32; Petras 1987; Kalogeropoulou 1989; Lyrintzis 1993). Under Papandreou, modernization was largely postponed, with the important exception of Greece coming to terms (albeit reluctantly and despite eventual nationalist outbursts) with the consequences of its accession to the European Community in 1981 (see Verney 1990a; Veremis 1991). The socialist government paid much less attention to institution-building, checks and balances, accountability, and the establishment of transparent decision-making processes than it did to integration, inclusion, participation, and responsiveness, which played an important role in the process of democratic consolidation. The agenda for modernizing Greek society—which included professionalization, downsizing of the civil service and decentralization, efficiency-oriented banking and management reforms, educational reforms, deregulation and privatization, tax reforms, and measures designed to increase the productivity and competitiveness of small and medium-sized units of the huge self-employed sector (which included more than 40 percent of the labor force)—were primarily seen in the light of fragmented interest politics, corporatist status quo preservation, clientelistic reassurance, intraparty coalition-building, and interparty competition. This led some observers to conclude that notwithstanding the consolidation of democracy and subsequent "normalization," the PASOK-dominated Greek politics of the 1980s and early 1990s moved almost completely in the wrong direction (see Spanou 1996; Sotiropoulos 1991; Diamandouros 1997). At a minimum, it can be concluded that much time was irretrievably wasted. This failure to embrace modernization resulted from the fact that the party's heterogeneous core constituency included two strong groups with antimodernist biases: the self-employed (and the professional guilds) and those working in the public sector.

In line with the party's populistic logic, the economic and social policies of the Papandreou government were usually subordinated to the primacy of electoral politics. When PASOK came to power in 1981, the government adopted policies similar to those of the government of Prime Minister Pierre Mauroy (June 1981–July 1984) in France (and quite different from those of the PSOE): its Keynesian expansionary policies (increasing minimum wages and pensions, and providing incentives for investment) failed to stimulate production. Unlike in the rest of the European Community, Greek inflation rates were not brought down (they stood at 18.1 percent in 1985), but the trade deficit and unemployment rose. Some reluctant neoliberal adjustments from 1983 on lacked resolution, and reform of the fiscal system (to reduce tax evasion and increase revenues) was delayed by the imperatives of populistic and distributive priorities as the elections of 1985 approached. The party's reelection (albeit by a smaller margin than in 1981) put the socialist government in a position where it could, for a time, do what its economic experts thought fit: shift to austerity policies, devalue the drachma, end wage indexation, reduce labor costs, promote exports, and attract foreign capital (Tsoukalis 1991). While these measures succeeded in curbing inflation, they also triggered union protests and resistance, particularly in the strong public sector. Accordingly, they were abandoned. In November 1987, Papandreou (a former professor of economics) reverted to economic populism and distributive policies, provoking the resignation of his economics minister, Costas Simitis. Thus, the overall record of the PASOK governments of 1981–89 with respect to inflation, the public deficit, and the trade balance was one of failure. It was unable to secure the resources necessary to fund expanding social policies. Instead of catching up with the rest of western Europe in terms of economic competitiveness, Greece fell farther behind (see Maravall 1992, 24–34, and 1997, 152–77; Spourdalakis 1991).

Short-lived though PASOK's fruitless austerity policies were, they succeeded in alienating key sectors of the Greek electorate. PASOK supporters in the unions and on the left shifted their support to the communists, enabling the Kommounistiko Komma Elladas (KKE) to gain control over ten additional municipalities in the local elections of October 1986 (increasing its total to 53 out of 303). In the country's three biggest cities, Athens, Piraeus, and Thessaloníki, former PASOK supporters swung their votes to the conservative candidates for mayor, giving Nea Demokratia an important new power base for the national election in June 1989 (Kapetanyannis 1993). In that election, PASOK lost about 40 percent of the votes it had received in 1981. This was followed by two additional electoral defeats, in November 1989 and in April 1990 (Verney 1990b).

Aside from the unpopularity and ultimate failure of PASOK's economic policies, these setbacks were the result of a number of accumulated factors, including its overt abuse of patronage and state resources for clientelistic purposes, its lack of respect for democratic procedures and pluralism, Papandreou's illness and temporary absence from government, and the increasing conflicts within the party elite, which gave the impression of a partial vacuum in leadership and a lack of unity. Accusations of widespread corruption acquired salience and credibility through a series of scandals, such as the Koskotas scandal, which involved a number of high-ranking party officials and cabinet members and allegedly even the prime minister himself. Under these circumstances, the conservatives' call for *katharsis* (cleansing) was irresistible, even though ND was only able to form the first of a series of unstable governments by forging an unlikely coalition with its former enemies on the communist left. Although it succeeded in forming a single-party government in 1990, Nea Demokratia soon alienated many voters as a result of its disunity and of economic and social policies that drove the left back into the arms of PASOK. The negative image of the conservative party in the media, and court decisions that officially cleared Papandreou of the charges of corruption, helped return PASOK to power in 1993 (Dimitras 1994), after a low-key campaign displaying a new style that mixed the traditional populist techniques of mobilization with a new TV-dominated style of campaign politics. PASOK's parliamentary majority was inadvertently enlarged, too, as the result of electoral-law changes introduced by the ND government three years earlier.

After the 1993 election, the government seemed to be in better shape than the party. As PASOK's electoral program ("For the Present and Future Greece: Regeneration Everywhere") had indicated, the tone of the party's third term in government was more moderate and pragmatic, in some respects, even technocratic. On the whole, market-oriented policies of economic stability and growth, of curbing inflation (which was reduced to 8.3 percent in 1995), limiting the budget deficit, and cutting state expenditures prevailed over social policy concerns. Wage controls were tightened, real wages fell (even in the public sector), social expenditure was curtailed, and the party's pledge to reinstate the welfare state and maintain the principles of social solidarity became academic, at least for the time being, lacking adequate funding. Disenchantment and protest were not only voiced by the unions, by wage earners, and by pensioners, but also by farmers and lawyers who refused to be taxed. In September 1995, positive opinions of the government reached a record low of 14.2 percent,[26] and in the elections of September 1996, PASOK lost 5.4 percent of the vote compared to 1993.

It is not surprising that PASOK tried as long as seemed feasible to take full advantage of traditional mechanisms of Greek politics such as personalistic and clientelistic orientations, populistic, nationalistic, and "underdog" rhetoric, corporate interest intermediation and fragmentation, state patronage, and statism in general. The costs of this populist bias are obvious, however: PASOK's efforts to "colonize" the state at all levels, to channel its rule through government agencies, and to subvert traditional corporatist mechanisms have increased the role and influence of the state at the cost of the autonomy of civil society and democratic control. That the state was colonized and its institutions remained widely inefficient—"a Colossus with feet of clay" (Sotiropoulos 1993)—did not make it a "Prussian" agent of modernization either. Modernizing reforms have thus not only been significantly delayed but also made more difficult.

Clearly, PASOK does not bear sole responsibility for this state of affairs, because Nea Demokratia has used the same traditional clientelistic techniques. Although it may deserve credit for having been the first to break out of this traditional mold—which it did by choosing a leader in 1996 who has unequivocally endorsed a policy of institutionalization and modernization—PASOK will, however, also be remembered for having blocked reforms for almost a decade and a half.

Centralism and bureaucratic clientelism have certainly helped PASOK establish the image of a unified party, create loyalties, and win elections. Charismatic leadership, personalistic networks, and populist strategies have provided mechanisms of integration (although also of exclusion), mobilized support, and made the party capable of better adapting to the new politics in the television age and to the more recent crisis of catch-all parties. Failure to build organizational and clear decision-making structures of its own has, however, also had high costs for the party, which has remained essentially weak compared to government agencies and to the particularistic and clientelistic networks of Greek society.

The Partido Socialista Obrero Español. The Spanish socialist party's record reflects greater balance between democratization and modernization. The PSOE has unequivocally supported the process of democratization, and its behavior both in opposition and in office has been consistent with its democratic convictions and aspirations. But after 1982 (by which time the regime was largely consolidated), democratization was no longer a prime concern. The PSOE also gave great emphasis to Europeanization. Besides being internationalist by tradition, reinforced by its years in exile, the PSOE has been a European-minded party from the earliest stages of the transition, and the

Spanish socialists have worked, like all democratic forces in Spain (including the communists), for early accession to the European Community, in part in order to help secure democracy at home. As a party and in government, they have also taken their European responsibilities seriously (see Álvarez-Miranda 1995) and have never embraced a nationalism of the PASOK type. Also unlike in Greece, there has been no "lost decade" in Spain. Instead, Spanish socialist governments promptly and consistently adopted and implemented neoliberal economic policies, as well as structural reforms that had been postponed in the years of the transition to democracy. Under the PSOE, comprehensive economic and institutional modernization clearly took precedence over programs designed to extend the welfare state.

The PSOE government, in the words of Minister of Education José María Maravall, had three priorities: to consolidate the democratic system, to catch up with western Europe, and to introduce social democratic reforms of "social citizenship" (Maravall 1991, 20–21). All three of them were met, although in different degrees. The greatest success story involved the institutional and legal reforms of the PSOE's first term in office, directed at stabilizing, securing, and "rooting" democracy in Spain. Although it had been consolidated in a technical sense, Spanish democracy still needed much more anchoring in civil society and in widespread respect for new political institutions and the rule of law, especially since the socialists came to power only twenty months after an attempted military coup.[27] Civil and human rights were brought up to Western standards (through institutionalization of habeas corpus, legalization of conscientious objection and abortion, and provision for legal assistance), the autonomy of the judiciary was reaffirmed and secured financially, and Spain's backward and traditional educational system was substantially overhauled. Maravall's school and university reforms, which expanded compulsory education, increased enrollment, gave more autonomy to educational institutions, and asked for more professionalism and efficiency, were a particularly impressive step forward. The PSOE government also honored the constitutional consensus of 1978 in giving life and substance to the decentralized Estado de las Autonomías: the regional share of public expenditure grew from 3 percent in 1981 to 23.5 percent in 1991, and the range of policies entrusted to the Comunidades Autónomas has continued to expand, particularly with regard to health and education. In addition, many autonomy-minded (if only recently converted) socialist politicians in the regional governments, particularly in those parts of the country that previously lacked regionalist traditions and aspirations, have contributed much to the development of the new autonomous institutions and of new regional identities (Puhle 1998).

Another important achievement of the PSOE government was the success of its cautious and pragmatic but determined strategy to place the problematic Spanish military (which had not been as much discredited as the Greek colonels were after their abortive intervention in Cyprus) under the effective control of elected officials. This had to be combined with unprecedented organizational reforms aimed at more professionalization and a complete reorientation of the military's mission, which were competently carried out by Defense Minister Narcis Serra. Adjustment to NATO membership was complicated by the PSOE's call in the 1982 election campaign for a referendum on the subject of Spain's adherence to the alliance. The socialists subsequently decided that it was in Spain's interest to stay in NATO, but it required an enormous effort to convince the party rank and file (and later, the voters) of the wisdom of this. That Felipe González and his team managed to win the 1986 referendum (with 53 percent of the vote) against the overwhelming initial resistance of the party's rank and file may have given the socialist leaders the feeling that they could demand anything from the voters and get it. This optimism quickly vanished as a result of the parliamentary elections held three months later, when the PSOE's share of the vote declined by 4.3 percent. This was followed by electoral setbacks in the European elections of 1987 (when the PSOE received only 39.4 percent of the vote) and the general election of 1989.

Grosso modo, the Spanish economy went through five different phases between 1982 and 1996, creating serious constraints on social policies (see Lieberman 1995; Maravall 1993). "Catching-up with western Europe" and the exigencies of impending integration into the European Community also entailed structural, institutional, and especially economic modernization. To achieve this, the PSOE adopted policies designed to increase productivity and competitiveness; to encourage industrial restructuring (*reconversión industrial*); to offset the effects of deindustrialization; to attract capital by promoting solid growth, competitive interest rates, and low inflation; to deregulate the extensive state sector and make the remaining state agencies more efficient; to reduce the budget deficit; to liberalize markets (including the labor market); and to cut the costs of "unjustified" privileges and traditions. In its fourteen years in power, the PSOE was more liberal and less given to compromise with the welfare state's status quo than the Kohl government in Germany. On the whole, it followed a pragmatic, incrementalist strategy, although stopping short of some of the more dogmatic, "ruthless" measures of the Thatcher government in Britain, which less-developed Spain could not afford. The Spanish socialists' neoliberal economic policies were completely uninhibited by either traditional social democratic projects or the context of Spanish society. They were thus steadier than PASOK's.

Portugal's Partido Socialista. The Portuguese socialists did not have much of a chance to implement policies of their own until 1995, although they have been key agents of democratization from the beginning. Equally unmistakable were their European credentials: the PS and its predecessors, like the PSOE, but unlike PASOK, had been always internationalist and particularly European-minded (reinforced by their experience in exile), and they knew that they needed close relations with the rest of Europe in order to stabilize democracy and modernize the country. It was the Soares government that started negotiations with the European Community in 1977, and another Soares government that prepared Portugal for entry into the EC in January 1986. Although the country still remained far from "catching up with Europe" in the sense of modernizing, European integration implied high political costs in the short run, which the socialists were willing to pay. In order to meet the EC's accession criteria, to qualify for crucial IMF loans, and to attract more foreign investment, many sectors of the Portuguese economy had to be deregulated (including binding wage contracts, labor regulations, prices, and the banking and insurance sectors), and land reforms had to be reversed. In addition, after 1983, the socialist-led Bloco Central government had to devalue the currency and embark on a severe austerity policy in order to fight inflation and the budget deficit inherited from previous governments (particularly the conservative AD coalition).[28]

Except for the enactment of more liberal legislation on abortion, socialist policies of the 1970s and 1980s in Portugal, unlike in Spain, did not embark on major structural, legal, or administrative reforms. Steps to make the state bureaucracy more efficient and agriculture and industry more productive, to control the informal economy, to raise tax revenues, and to improve social services were postponed. So, too, were basic educational and welfare reforms, despite the fact that Portugal in the mid 1980s was a backward country, in which about 60 percent of the adult population had gone to school for less than four years, and only one-tenth of the unemployed were receiving benefits (Cravinho 1986, 113–14). But while the Portuguese socialists failed to adopt the modernization policies embraced by the PSOE, they also avoided erratic populist distributive policies of the kind often adopted by PASOK on the eve of general elections.

From 1985 until they returned to power a decade later, the Portuguese socialists' policies were confined to proposals made from the opposition benches, notwithstanding the fact the party actively joined in the interparty agreement with the PSD and CDS in 1989 to remove collectivist and state-interventionist clauses from the constitution. Since the socialists' programmatic reorientation of 1986, their programs have become more elaborate, more detailed, more reform-minded, and more technocratic (not unlike the PSOE's *Programa 2000*), and have broadly featured modernization, educational, administrative, and welfare reform, and European integration (see Partido Socialista 1995a, 1995b, and 1995c). The socialist minority governments of António Guterres after 1995 have made particular efforts to live up to these programmatic aspirations, with significant results in a number of important areas.

Social Policies and Party-Union Relations

What kinds of social policies can be implemented depends to a high degree on a government's general concept of modernization and on its economic, fiscal, and monetary policy priorities. Economic and social policies are closely intertwined, and both, in turn, affect relations between the governing party and various interest groups in the country. In the case of the southern European socialist governments, their policies have particularly affected relations with the labor unions to which they were considered to be close, whether or not specific ties to a socialist union traditionally existed. The latter was the case in Spain; in Greece and Portugal, the constellations of these forces have been different.

PASOK. As it has been stated above, the Greek socialist party had no particular working-class traditions, but it considered itself to be a broad popular movement that included working-class organizations or tried to exercise considerable influence among them. PASOK governments subordinated economic and social policies to the imperatives of electoral politics. Accordingly, expenditure on health, education, and pensions rose dramatically, and legal reforms were introduced (on education, see Tsoucalas and Panagiotopoulou 1992). The number of students doubled between 1981 and 1986, and the number of beneficiaries of public pensions went up by 5.4 percent per annum through the 1980s. The problem was that these benefits could not be financed without putting the state budget in deficit. Throughout the 1980s, public expenditure rose much faster than the revenues from taxes, and the social security deficit alone rose from 2.5 percent of GNP in 1980 to 9.3 percent in 1990. The total public debt reached 20 percent of GDP in 1989, as compared to 12.5 percent in 1983, and the pace of its growth accelerated in comparison with the seven previous years under conservative rule (see Maravall 1992, 34–48, and 1997, 177–97; Lyrintzis 1993; Thomadakis and Seremetis 1992). Electorally, these populist policies had an impact, mostly in favor of the socialists, but also against them on those rare occasions when austerity policies were adopted.

The relations between PASOK and the unions during the 1980s were, however, shaped much more by another strategy, which affected the whole range of relations among party, state, and society. PASOK's strategies of centralized bureaucratic clientelism went beyond conquering the state; they also aimed at colonizing all the important associations and interest groups in society, particularly the peak associations, and, of course, tight control of the media. These efforts bore striking similarities to the techniques of Latin American populist movements (like Peronism, the Vargas movement in Brazil, or the Mexican PRI). They were so successful in the 1980s that (until the early 1990s, when collective bargaining became more institutionalized and the labor unions began to slowly become more independent from state control) a state-corporatist mentality can be said to have prevailed over neocorporatist arrangements. As in all countries where populist techniques have been successful, the organizations of Greek civil society were still too weak to resist pressure from the state and from the parties in government, which Nea Demokratia had earlier exercised similarly to PASOK.

In Spain, two powerful labor organizations with historical links to the socialist and the communist parties (as well as a number of smaller and regional unions) compete for votes and representation in workshops, firms, and industries. In contrast, in Greece, the political parties, through their respective ancillary unions, have to compete for the majority within a single peak labor association in order to be able to determine the association's policies. Thus, it was important for any government to control the National Confederation of Greek Labor (GSEE), as well as the peak associations of farmers (PASEGES), of small business (GSEVE, which rated the highest scores of sympathy in all southern Europe),[29] and civil servants (ADEDY). Only the Federation of Greek Industry (SEB) managed to remain at a distance from party influence.

The socialist government waged a campaign to "democratize" the associations of the "popular" sectors by flooding them with new members and passing legislation that regulated the structure and the internal mechanisms of the interest groups in a uniform way, including the imposition of proportional representation as the compulsory system for all interest-group elections (effectively reproducing the results of the previous election, and abrogating the autonomy of the interest groups).[30] Unions and associations that did not comply with the new rules were subject to "intervention" by the not-very-independent courts (a Latin American practice), their elected executives were removed, and new provisional executives appointed. Most of these interventions focused on labor unions between 1981 and 1987, when labor conflict almost quadrupled as the unions fought against the government's short-lived austerity policy, as well as against attempted domination.[31] Particularly affected was the public sector: the share of PASOK representatives in the executive of the GSEE was increased from about one-third in 1977 to a clear majority as the result of several "interventions." But these ad hoc devices could not substitute for adequate institutionalization: in the end, they could simply be reversed once the socialists were out of government. The strategy of forcing the most important organizations of Greek society into PASOK's procrustean bed (Mavrogordatos 1988) eventually failed. In 1990, according to an informed estimate, the party was no longer in complete control of any of the more important peak associations. PASOK was strongest in the civil servants' association, it led the KKE by a small margin in the industrial labor unions, and it had a strong presence in the (Nea Demokratia-controlled) farmers' association, PASEGES; but it was weak in the small business organization, GSEVE, which was dominated by the KKE.[32]

Portugal's Partido Socialista. Like PASOK, the PS in Portugal had no traditional labor union "of its own." During the revolutionary years 1974–75, most Portuguese unions were controlled by the communists, who, jointly with the Movimento das Forças Armadas (MFA), launched a *carta aberta* ("open card") campaign in favor of "labor unity" (*unicidade*) under the tutelage of the PCP-led Intersindical (which became the CGTP-IN in 1977). Many socialist labor leaders sympathized with Intersindical, but in 1977 Soares and his collaborators began openly to fight communist aspirations to union hegemony, as did the Partido Popular Democrático (PPD), which later became the Partido Social-Democrata (PSD), when it founded its own union, TESIRESD, in late 1978. After bitter debates in both parties and without much consultation of "their" respective union leaders, the executives of the PS and the PSD decided in 1979 to set up a joint labor union federation, the União Geral dos Trabalhadores (UGT), whose executive board was composed by members of the PS and of the PSD in equal proportions. Within a few years, the Portuguese UGT was clearly dominated by the socialists, although it never became a socialist union in the sense of the Spanish UGT.[33] Despite notable gains in its share of organized labor (from about 14 percent in 1984 to 35 percent in 1989), it remained smaller than the dominant CGTP (60 as compared to 55 percent). The CGTP was strongest among industrial and agricultural workers, particularly metalworkers, and in public transport, whereas the UGT had its strongholds among bank employees and in other public and private services.[34] On the whole, the UGT does not seem to have been a particular asset of mobilization either for the Portuguese socialists or for the PSD. Like the CGTP, it eventually took part in tripartite bargaining, particularly between 1986 and 1992, but it also helped to organize demonstrations and strikes against the government's labor and social policies in 1988 and 1990.

The Partido Socialista Obrero Español. In contrast to their Portuguese and Greek counterparts, the Spanish socialists had a close traditional relationship with the Spanish socialist trade union, the Unión General de Trabajadores (UGT). Nonetheless, by the late 1980s, their economic and social policies had so alienated their labor allies that some observers have spoken of a "breakup of the socialist family." Despite the PSOE government's social and education policy achievements, by letting economic modernization take precedence over "social citizenship," the Spanish socialists embraced policies characterized by neoliberal economics and contained social reforms that might have been more appropriate for one of northern Europe's overdeveloped welfare states. In so doing, the PSOE took the risk of alienating its union allies and many other voters. When conflict broke out, they clearly thought that reforms could be viable even without trade union support, and, indeed, that their intended reforms would be weakened if they were negotiated with the unions (Maravall 1992, 43, and 1997, 191–99). Success proved them right: they could afford to antagonize the unions, at least for a time, and their term in office probably would not have been prolonged if they had returned to more populist rhetoric and redistribution policies à la PASOK.

The economic and social policies of the PSOE government have been characterized by Carles Boix as a new type of social democratic supply-side strategy cum redistribution within a noncorporatist political system with weak labor unions and a dependent central bank (Boix 1996 and 1998a). This policy mix departed from standard neoliberalism in several ways. It combined tight monetary policies with expansionary fiscal policies. Between 1982 and 1995, inflation was brought down from 14.6 to 4.9 percent, and exports of goods and services increased from 18.4 to 24.1 percent of GDP, but the standing public debt grew from 13 percent to 33.4 percent of GDP between 1982 and 1991. Also in contrast to standard neoliberalism, the Spanish state sector maintained an activist stance: more than $9 billion of public funds went into the reconversion of uncompetitive firms (about one-third of Spanish industry); the share of GDP devoted to public expenditure rose by 11.2 percent (with 5.3 percent going to supply-side intervention and 5.9 percent to social policies). The rate of increase in wages (.8 percent between 1983 and 1995) was below the EC average, and owing to capital-intensive industrial restructuring and some steps toward liberalizing the extremely rigid labor market, unemployment remained high (Maravall and Fraile 1998). Some of these policies were initiated in Spain's last act of corporatist concertation (and the only socioeconomic pact the socialist government concluded), the Acuerdo Económico y Social (AES) of October 1984.[35] On the other hand, and very much in contrast to Thatcherite Britain, the same legislative package aimed at securing the participation of organized labor by further institutionalizing labor relations and increasing unemployment benefits, although not to the extent agreed upon and expected by the unions. Union expectations continued to be disappointed even after Economics Minister Miguel Boyer had left the government in 1985. General wage agreements were either avoided or postponed, and in the boom years 1987–88, when company profits quadrupled in Spain, the new minister, Carlos Solchaga, insisted that employers restrict wage increases to 4 percent, in an effort to combat inflation. In the 1986 union elections, because of its perceived proximity to the government, the UGT lost many of the gains it had achieved since 1982. Eventually even those branch associations that had tried to remain loyal to the government (in public service and the metal and chemical industries) began to turn away.

The burden of the economic transition was borne disproportionately by the unemployed (particularly the long-term unemployed, women, and young people) and the underemployed in unskilled and part-time low-paying occupations, many of whom had to rely on the typical southern European cushion of extended family networks and the underground economy. Unemployment reached a peak of 24.1 percent in 1994, driving the average unemployment rate for the fourteen years of PSOE government to 19.9 percent, in contrast to the European average of 9.4 percent (Maravall and Fraile 1998).

More typical social democratic and indeed "modernizing" features can be found in other sectors of the PSOE's social policy, particularly with regard to the rise and improved administration of contributive pensions (1985), the extension of noncontributive benefits and compensatory programs for needy low-income groups (1990), and the national health service (1986). The number of beneficiaries went up, although in the long run often at the cost of the quality of service or of reduced benefits per capita. Public expenditure on pensions, unemployment benefits, health, and education rose by 57.6 percent between 1982 and 1989, as compared to only 39.7 percent between 1975 and 1982; the share of public social expenditure increased by about 3 percent of GDP from 1982 to 1989, but still remained far below the EC average (17.8 percent, as compared with 25 percent). And in contrast to Greece, the Spanish socialists managed to generate increased tax revenues to pay for these services (from 30.2 percent of the GNP in 1980 to 38.4 percent in 1990), particularly by making income tax collection more efficient and raising the share paid by high-income taxpayers. Expenditures continued to rise more than public revenues, however, averaging 8.3 percent per year as opposed to 7.1 percent (Gunther 1996b; Maravall 1993 and 1997; Maravall and Fraile 1998).

Overall, the imperatives of economic modernization and stabilization (including those resulting from increasing Europeanization) often took precedence over the development of social policies, preventing the PSOE from achieving the ideal social democratic equilibrium between economic efficiency and social equity. In the end, however, the socialists' modernization policies achieved impressive results, particularly during their first two terms in government. The long years of socialist rule have given Spanish politics and society continuing stability and sufficient time to address many of the structural problems that were postponed during the transition or papered over by tactical compromise. Indeed, the end of the era of socioeconomic pacts and a return to more conflictual modes of interest intermediation may be regarded as a sign of "normalization." Despite measurable disappointments, voters in 1986 and 1989 approved the performance of the PSOE to the extent of reelecting it to continue to implement its policies (see Partido Socialista Obrero Español 1986 and 1989b; Guerra and Tezanos 1992). Nonetheless, the long continuity of the PSOE in government aggravated conflicts with unions, made it difficult for the party to serve as a mediator between the government and the unions and other disappointed groups, and weakened its resolve to fully implement its strong initial mandate (Maravall 1992, 45), leading to a slowdown in the pace of reforms since the late 1980s. A mandate for "change" cannot be stretched over decades.

By the end of the 1980s, it had already become clear that cyclical *desencanto* had turned into a lasting structural disenchantment. In the words of Maravall, "a silent electorate supported an isolated party" (Maravall 1992, 50; Jiménez 1995). The most notable erosion of long-term support for the party was the estrangement between the party and the UGT, from which the PSOE did not recover as long as it was in government. After the UGT chief Nicolás Redondo denounced the government's version of a market economy as leading to "greater unemployment, greater inequality, and greater poverty" in 1985, labor activities were directed more against the state than against private employers.[36] Renewed mobilization helped to reverse the decline in union membership, beginning in 1985, although the share of unionized workers in Spain (between 10 and 15 percent of the labor force in the late 1980s and early 1990s) remained the lowest in Europe.[37] Open conflict between the unions and the government reached its climax when, on December 14, 1988, all Spanish unions and many other professional organizations organized a massive, statewide general strike denouncing the deficiencies of the government's social policies, in particular, its failure adequately to address the problems of unemployment and job insecurity.

The impact of the strike, in which about 8 million workers participated, can hardly be overestimated. The immediate reaction of the government was to quickly begin implementation of a number of social policy programs that had been postponed, particularly with regard to unemployment compensation and to the extension of pension schemes and of the health service (see Camiller 1992, 256). Nonetheless, widespread discontent cost the party another million votes in the 1989 elections, much of it to the benefit of the Communist Party, whose flamboyant and erratic but orthodox new leader, Julio Anguita, skillfully advanced the "class option" in the course of the campaign. An additional consequence of the December 1988 strike was that it initiated increased cooperation among the labor unions. This collaboration has continued, resulting in a more vigorous defense of the unions' core constituencies against the challenges of advancing structural change, on the one hand, and, on the other, in a far-reaching pact in April 1997 between unions and employers regarding further labor market deregulation.[38] Finally, the split between the governing party and the unions promoted and intensified a new factionalism within the PSOE, and added a new line of conflict to the older divide between pragmatists and the left.

Nonetheless, these increased conflicts made it clear that there was life in the party independent of the government—that the party was back, and that it aspired to be more than an appendage of the government. Thus, despite its problems and the "breakup of the socialist family," the mid 1990s marked the beginning of a new era for the PSOE.

Renewal in Government and Opposition

In the mid 1990s, the socialist parties in the new democracies of southern Europe seem to have reached a significant threshold. Although the Partito Socialista Italiano practically disappeared after the 1994 elections, and was effectively replaced by the reformed ex-communist Partito Democratico della Sinistra, Democratici della Sinistra, and other groups, the Greek, Portuguese, and Spanish socialist parties experienced the beginnings of a major renewal. Its principal feature was that all three parties committed themselves to modernization of the state and society and simultaneously began to modernize and institutionalize their own structures—a course embarked on by the PSOE fifteen years earlier. Even the Spanish socialists were now forced to turn their attention to rebuilding and extending party structures, which had been neglected during the PSOE's long period in government. Party reform was necessary for all three parties—for PASOK, in order to overcome the agonizing succession crisis after Papandreou's departure and retain its share of the electorate; for the PS, in order to take advantage of the PSD's fatigue in government by unifying and mounting a successful campaign; and for the PSOE, in order to contain the new factionalism, reverse its long-term loss of votes, and fully adapt both to its role in opposition and the new age of modified catch-all parties, after its traditional alliance with the UGT had weakened.

The contexts within which this reform unfolded were different in each case. The Spanish socialists, despite having undertaken significant reform in the aftermath of the extraordinary congress of 1979, undertook this latest round of reorganization from the opposition benches, having lost the elections of 1996. The Portuguese PS initiated reform in opposition, but after its 1995 election victory, it had to continue with these efforts while in government—a situation that is usually not conducive to innovation or restructuring. In the case of PASOK, renewal was complicated not only by its incumbency in government but also by traditional constraints. The most visible feature of party renewal in all three cases has been a change in top leadership posts, as well as in the executive committees, where it was combined with some generational turnover, particularly in Portugal and Spain. It would be difficult, however, to think of the new party leaders as of a "new" political generation: Costas Simitis and Joaquín Almunia were among the founding fathers of their parties, and even António Guterres, although he was not deeply involved in the longer prehistory of the PS, has certainly been a key player in the party since the late 1970s.

It should also be noted that renewal and party reforms are still far from complete. Indeed, in the case of PASOK, they have just begun, although partial reforms significantly contributed to the party's victory in the 1996 elections: adoption of procedural rules to handle the post-Papandreou succession, and the orderly and timely takeover of party and government leadership by Simitis helped to improve the party's image. So, too, did the new leader's record of honesty and noninvolvement in the scandals of the 1980s, his pragmatic priorities, his ability to build coalitions among the party elite, and his strong campaign performance.[39]

The resources (and challenges) of government incumbency may help to overcome the conservatism that has characterized PASOK in the past. Under Papandreou, the party relied on traditional techniques, which impeded structural change, as well as societal modernization. Indeed, Papandreou's emblematic occasional statement that "there are no institutions, only the people" is strikingly reminiscent of Margaret Thatcher's famous remark that "there is no such thing as society"; both statements are anti-institutional, antistructure, ideological, populist, and conservative. With the "normalization of Greek politics" in the mid 1990s (see Diamandouros 1997, esp. 33–37), PASOK may have passed its most turbulent times, despite the many problems remaining on the agenda. But in order to carry out the new program of modernization and reforms called for by Simitis credibly and efficiently, it will be necessary for PASOK to stop being a functionally conservative party. In the end, it will not be enough to Europeanize and perform well in government; substantial party reforms may be required to break up the paralyzing structures of bureaucratic clientelism and make PASOK a modern party, social democratic or not.

So far, PASOK has undergone gradual reform in the post-Papandreou era. These changes have been facilitated by the performance of the first four years of the Simitis government, characterized by steady progress toward modernizing the state and society. The elections of April 2000 further contributed to party reform by strengthening the two major parties, reinforcing the centripetal logic of party competition, and giving the center-right opposition party a final push toward its democratic "civilianization." Moreover, PASOK's victory and increased share of the total vote (43.8 as compared to ND's 42.7 percent), which ran counter to the typical pattern in which electoral support for incumbent parties tends to decline, have stabilized Simitis's position and weakened (if not silenced) his more traditional erstwhile rivals. Thus, in the new century, the resistance to party reform has clearly become more marginal.

The Portuguese Partido Socialista somewhat earlier made significant progress toward reform and institutionalization aimed at overcoming the strong personalistic tradition of the party and its factions. Until the early 1990s, the PS essentially functioned as a patronage machine of the old type, but although it was embedded in various forms of clientelism, it never built up a system of centralized bureaucratic clientelism the way PASOK did. Initially, the PS had been led by a strong populist leader with a personalistic leadership style, and it remained relatively fluid, open, and weakly organized by reason both of its heterogeneous composition and catch-all character and of a high degree of factionalism and internal instability. When it was in government, it always had to compromise and was checked by a strong coalition partner. But in the mid 1980s, when its opposition status removed these constraints, and the election of Soares as president of the republic relaxed his grip on the party, a leadership vacuum precluded the needed party reforms and prevented its institutionalization. Since the centralizing reforms under the inspiring leadership of Sampaio and Guterres in the early and mid 1990s, however, and the overhauling and streamlining of the party apparatus on the eve of the 1995 election campaign, this has changed. The stability in government of the PS (whose security in office was slightly improved by the 1999 elections), the stagnation and electoral losses of its rivals, the undisputed leadership of Guterres, and the fact that most of the party elite hold government posts have, conversely, created new problems, of a kind long familiar to its Greek and Spanish friends, for the party. Leonardo Morlino has stated that, until the mid 1990s, the PSD was the only Portuguese party that had successfully institutionalized itself (Morlino 1995, 346–47). Since the mid 1990s, the PS has been the second party to do so, and the process has even continued while the party has been in government, as occurred earlier in the case of the PSD.

In the case of the Spanish socialists, party reform had a different focus. Both because of its heritage and the efforts of the 1970s, the PSOE was more institutionalized than the PS, and party/state relations in Spain differed from those in Greece. In the case of the PSOE, centralized leadership and patronage were moderated by an increasing need to balance the various regional interests within the party. In contrast to PASOK's centralized bureaucratic clientelism, the PSOE could afford to work much less through the state bureaucracy, and its clientelistic mechanisms were more institutionalized, group-related, and, in the 1990s, even more pluralistic, in the sense that there were several regional-based clientelistic networks to be accounted for. In line with the southern European tradition of the strong state, Spain became a party state par excellence during the long rule of the socialists, but it could never be governed arbitrarily as the personal fief of its leader, as Greece was in Andreas Papandreou's heyday. Besides being less populistic, the Spanish socialists had to respect the greater professional independence of the civil service and the judiciary, the rights and interests guaranteed by the autonomy statutes of the regions, and many traditional allegiances and strongholds in society that were not socialist.

Party reforms, in the Spanish case, have essentially addressed the issue of the autonomy of the party vis-à-vis the socialist government; they have mostly been reforms of already existing institutions and mechanisms, and they were propelled by the dynamics of factional strife. These reforms began in earnest in 1996, when the party was voted out of government after fourteen years and faced a difficult, and in the end futile, struggle to regain power. This has given the PSOE at least a chance to regenerate and try to "put its house in order," as many had wanted it to do for some time. The loss of control over the central government (at the regional level there are still some socialist administrations) has, indeed, triggered and accelerated a number of major changes in the party's organization and personnel, the most conspicuous of which was the handing over of party leadership from González to Joaquín Almunia at the Thirty-Fourth Congress in June 1997. Renewal had already begun during the agonizing and scandal-ridden last two years of the socialist government, even if it remained contained. A first convincing sign of the party's elites' desire to reduce oligarchical structures, dependency on the government, factional strife, and stalemate appeared at the Thirty-Third Party Congress in 1994, when the bloc vote was abolished, the mechanisms of closed lists and "winner-takes-all" were questioned, and alternative strategies were debated. These and other changes were intended to revitalize participation and debate within the party and to restore closer ties between the leaders and the grass roots, and between the party and society.

This serious effort to reform the party was stimulated by a number of developments. The electoral advances of the Partido Popular under José María Aznar represented such an erosion of electoral support as to make it clear that the PSOE could no longer afford to antagonize or neglect crucial social sectors and interests as before. In addition, the government faction's efforts to defend itself against the *guerristas* and increasing criticism following the split in the "socialist family" had seriously weakened the party executive. More than anything else, the government faction's need for support and its alliance with a number of influential regional leaders and federations helped to reestablish the party, its congresses, and its committees as central arenas for decision making, with an autonomous structure, independent of the government.

At the same time, however, the extent of possible reform was limited by the vested interests of the regional *barones*, who, through their alliances with the government faction, had managed to establish themselves as powerful actors at the national level. Thus, at the Thirty-Fourth Party Congress in 1997, the principle of closed lists was upheld, and Felipe González failed to secure approval of his proposal to reduce the size of the party's executive committee from thirty-six to twenty-three members at the cost of the regional leaders. Of the thirty-three members of the new executive (whose election was negotiated between the regional federations and the outgoing national executive), seven were regional *barones*. The Thirty-Fourth Congress did, however, approve two momentous decisions. One called for constitutional reforms that would develop the Spanish Estado de las Autonomías into a full-fledged federal system. The second institutionalized primary elections (in which all party members would be encouraged to participate) for the nomination of candidates for prime minister "and other high office" (like that of mayor or president of a Comunidad Autónoma). The second was a remarkable decision that was (perhaps prematurely) praised as an antioligarchic move that could help not only to democratize the party but also to increase participation, to bridge the widened gap between the political parties and citizens (see Solé Tura 1998), and, one might add, to cope with the crisis of the catch-all party. For a time, it appeared to have dramatically enhanced the quality of democracy within the party: the fact that a new and widely respected party leader, Joaquín Almunia (who was seen by many as a temporary stand-in for González), was defeated as the party's candidate for prime minister by a relative outsider, the Catalan socialist José Borrell,[40] who received 54.8 percent of the vote, winning in all regions except the Basque country, Castille-La Mancha, and Andalusia, clearly indicated that there was an alternative to the oligarchical practices of the past. Another round of primary elections in June 1998 (in anticipation of forthcoming regional and local elections) produced more surprises, particularly the ouster of the machine candidate Joaquín Leguina as candidate for mayor of Madrid by the former foreign minister Fernando Morán, who was backed by the *críticos* and *guerristas*. This populistic institutional novelty at least temporarily enhanced the vitality of grass-roots participation in party affairs, and gave the PSOE's renewal and reform efforts more credibility among the public at large than the various programmatic efforts that have been made.[41] Thus, despite highly publicized trials implicating high-ranking former socialist government officials in the atrocities of the "dirty war" against Basque separatism (leading to the conviction of former Interior Minister José Barrionuevo and others), as well as vigorous anti-PSOE campaigns in the conservative or opportunistic media, popular support for the party seemed to recover, as reflected in public opinion polls conducted in mid 1998, and in the regional elections of 1999.[42]

In the general elections of March 2000, however, the PSOE, against all the odds (and opinion-poll predictions), experienced its greatest electoral disaster since 1979: the party lost 1.6 million votes (falling to 7.8 million) and its share declined from 37.6 to 34.7 percent, whereas the governing PP garnered a total of 10.2 million votes (i.e., more than the PSOE had received in 1982) and, with 45.2 percent of the vote, almost 6 percentage points more than in 1996, won an absolute majority in parliament. The socialists lost almost everywhere, especially in Catalonia, Valencia, Galicia, Murcia, the Canary Islands, and the Baleares. This resounding defeat, which subsequently triggered the resignation of Joaquín Almunia as party leader, as well as of the entire executive committee, was the product of many causes. First, the PP benefited from a booming economy, declining rates of unemployment, particularly good relations with both employers and unions, and a relatively unproblematic performance in government. A number of structural weaknesses and severe mistakes of the PSOE itself also contributed to the disaster. After the resignation of José Borrell (the winner of the primaries who was brought down by the party machine), the party's leadership remained undecided and weak, the processes of reform and regeneration went into stalemate, and the party's *barones* blocked decisions. In addition, the PSOE committed major strategic errors in first making an erratic move toward the center and then forging an unconvincing and inefficient alliance with the unattractive communist Izquierda Unida (IU). This alliance led to a massive collapse of support for the socialists among voters of the center-left, ending the "structural majority" that the PSOE had enjoyed among those voters since 1982.

Party reforms would have to be relaunched and reinvigorated at the party congress scheduled for July 2000. And in terms of its electoral prospects, the PSOE may have an even longer way to go before it can confidently look toward a return to government. For all of the contributions the party made to stabilize democracy, to modernize the economy and the state, to expand welfare, and to join and "catch up" with Europe, it will by and large be remembered at the end of the century for the deficiencies and limitations of its last years in government, in a wider context of rising disenchantment, where most people thought that "all parties are the same" (increasing from 13 percent in 1980 to 63 percent in 1992 [Maravall 1997, 200–244]), when conflicts increased and resources shrank, solutions became more difficult, political imagination scarcer, and the catch-all parties had entered crisis. By the end of the century, however, it was clear that the PSOE has become a "normal" modern party, like the PS and (to a lesser extent) PASOK, in that it has now begun to display more of the general features of a modernized catch-all party in advanced Western democracies than those of its particular southern European legacy.

Toward More Convergence

The preceding analysis provides scant support for the notion of a "new southern European socialism." Much of it is not new, and what is new may not be particularly southern European. To be sure, as noted earlier, these parties shared some commonalities in terms of their relative underinstitutionalization (with personalistic networks prevailing over bureaucratic organization), flexibility, and their tendencies to be ad hoc mobilizers rather than builders of structures. These common core similarities notwithstanding, we have also seen that these parties had distinctive features initially and followed different developmental trajectories in accordance with their differing economic, social, cultural, and political contexts, as well as their peculiar institutional and political legacies. The performance, the politics, and policies of the socialist parties, notably in government, have also been conditioned by specific mixes of legacies and structures, limited opportunities for action, and concrete decisions. As we have seen, the outcomes have been mixed. But while the parties retain certain distinguishing characteristics, they have also exhibited similarities (particularly their ability to "leapfrog" over earlier organizational forms to more clearly take on modern forms and practices), and they have tended to converge, not only with their southern European socialist sister parties, but also with those of northern Europe. Thus the distinctive lines of the initial southern common core of characteristics have been blurred, and, in a way, the southern European socialist parties have become less "southern."

These parties have embraced policies calling for less regulation, freer markets, and more efficiency and competition. This implies, among other things, a substantial redefinition of the relationship between the state and the agents of civil society, between government and the traditional clientelistic or corporate interests, between the parties and the labor unions. In turn, these reforms have led to significant changes in the character and role of the socialist parties themselves. The parties and their politics and policies have become more moderate and more mixed, no matter what their particular historical trajectories were. But while they converged on these policy commitments, the socialist parties also evolved in differing ways, in response to the distinctive social and political contexts within which they developed.

We also see variation with regard to the pursuit of the four historic objectives identified at the beginning of this chapter: democratization, Europeanization, modernization of the state and society, and welfare state development. In every case, the socialist parties' record was outstanding on democratization and Europeanization. They differed, however, in the extent to which they were willing and able to modernize the state and the economy, and to extend the welfare state. The PSOE presents us with the most impressive record in this regard, in large part because it governed alone from 1982 until the mid 1990s. The PS accomplished the least, in part because it did not have much of a chance to implement these reforms prior to its formation of a single-party government in 1995. In the case of PASOK, it took more than a decade of changing priorities and populistic meandering before the party elite succeeded in setting a steady reformist course. It should be noted that the meaning of "modernization" or "welfare state building and reform" in a specific case has been dependent on context, and hence differed from country to country. Although all three countries were latecomers to the mechanisms of the welfare state, the extent of development of social policies has varied more or less in accord with the country's level of socioeconomic development. And the manner in which "modernization" effectively redefined the role of the state also varied: although "modernization" everywhere included efforts to make state structures and bureaucracies more professional, efficient, and responsive, to reduce the traditional state-heaviness of the southern European countries and to strengthen civil society, we can also find socialist policies of modernization that have "brought the state back in" by improving the efficiency of tax collection and regulating labor relations (generally against union resistance). Modernization also involved a stricter professionalization, routinization, and control of the civil service (even in Greece after 1995), and the reorganization of the state bureaucracy and the judiciary, even if such reforms were often still partly overshadowed by personalistic and clientelistic legacies and corruption.

The modernizing reforms, which in some cases were achieved in close cooperation with big business interests (as in Spain), have loosened the ties that might have existed between the socialist parties and some of the labor unions. They have also changed the traditional patterns of state-society relations and, under the increasing pressures of European integration (particularly following Maastricht), have made them more "European." All southern European socialist parties have responded positively and productively to the European challenge, with only PASOK facing some initial difficulties.

Among the four "historic" objectives, the principal concern of the southern European socialist parties has been the consolidation, stabilization, societal "rooting" and, if and when possible, the extension of democracy. They all stressed the "primacy of politics," in which politico-institutional reforms were put first, and economic and social reforms were postponed. This has led some critics to observe that democracy may have been reestablished at the cost of social democracy. It was only when democracy was consolidated and the socialists were in a position to define government policies (in its pure version only in Greece and Spain) that they turned their attention to defining what particular brand of social-democratic reformism they would embrace. Here again, such decisions reflected a mix of some older ideas and conceptions, drawn from established models of social democratic (and occasionally even conservative) reformism in northern Europe or elsewhere, and the need to respond to the particular situations of their respective countries.

With regard to the transformation of the parties themselves, we have seen strict convergence on one central tendency: this has involved deradicalization, an adjustment to the centripetal logic of the new political system, policy moderation, and a rapid transformation into catch-all parties. No matter how radical the parties may have been in the beginning, and irrespective of the different paths the transitions and democratic consolidations may have taken, it has been the logic of the new democratic game at its most advanced stage (i.e., inclusive mass democracy in the television age) that has finally framed and shaped the parties. Here the PSOE learned a bit faster than PASOK, and both learned much faster than the Portuguese PS. Although the Greek and the Spanish socialists both adopted moderate programs in the late 1970s, in the case of PASOK, Papandreou's meandering course and populist rhetoric led to more relapses. And the difficulties of the PS had less to do with its relatively late adjustment to explicit programmatic and ideological moderation than with its open factionalism, its undisciplined elites, and its first leader's erratic moves.

In the new game of democratic politics, centralized, undisputed, and convincing leadership and adoption of the mechanisms of the catch-all party and of the new campaign politics, were prerequisites for electoral success (see Harmel et al. 1995; and Pasquino 1990b). In a way, strong leadership also became an additional source of legitimation in times of *desencanto* and in response to calls for a "change." The Greek and the Spanish socialists managed to establish the required degree of centralism and stable leadership earlier, more convincingly, and more consistently than the Portuguese. The styles of the Greek and Spanish leaders varied, however, particularly once the parties came to power and their leaders tended to run the party from the government: whereas PASOK under Papandreou was more personalistic (almost "Ottoman"), Felipe González projected a more institutionalized leadership style. In all three cases, it took almost two decades before the party elites were convinced that a more autonomous party structure was necessary and institutional reforms were initiated. Party reforms appear to be more quickly implemented when the party is not in government, as illustrated by the PS before 1995 and the PSOE after 1996.

Another prerequisite for success in the new centripetal political systems was movement toward the political center. For parties in multiparty systems, however, this creates a strategic dilemma: while socialist parties must move to the center to compete with parties of the center-right or right for the lion's share of the votes, they must also strive to retain support from voters on the left. Thus, to offset the party's policy moderation and appeals to the center, it often helped to cultivate leftist memories—to preserve the historical notion of a socialist party being a party primarily of the underprivileged and the "have-less"—to keep the respective elites, currents, or even factions within the party. As the experience of the "break-up of the socialist family" in Spain indicates, the loss of traditional ties to the unions and to associational life more generally can culminate in serious electoral setbacks. Here, of course, credibility often depends on the specific degree, mode, focus, and contents of the political moderation the socialists display when they are in government. On the other hand, the close socialist victories in the Portuguese and Greek elections of 1999 and 2000 and the unexpected defeat of the Spanish socialists in the election of March 2000 seem to bear a clear message: at the end of the twentieth century, socialists tend to lose elections whenever they seem to appear to be more convincing and credible modernizers. And they lose even more when they think they can go back to the archaic (and nostalgic) tradition of proclaiming a "unity of action of the left" (as the ill-advised PSOE campaign of 2000 did).

In the end, we can see signs of convergence among the socialist parties of Europe, both north and south, and even with the center-right catch-all parties in these regions. "Convergence" has resulted from several factors. In part, it is a response to the pressures of governing in an increasingly integrated Europe. More important, it is a product of the centripetal logic of the democratic game of politics in the television age. The southern socialists have converged toward their northern counterparts as the exceptional characteristics of their polities and societies have faded, and as they have "normalized" their politics within full-fledged modern democracies. But at the same time that the southerners have converted to catch-all parties within centripetal democratic systems, their northern friends have moved from the classic catch-all party to a modified, more loosely coupled and fragmented, less organized and institutionalized catch-all party. Accordingly, they could no longer make efficient use of their traditional structures and had to develop better mechanisms for ad hoc mobilization, which has brought them closer to the southerners. We can find similar symptoms of a "crisis" of catch-all parties in both the south and the north, as reflected in declining voter turnout, *desencanto,* shifting social bases of partisanship, and new competitive structures that are less entrenched, less organized, more personalized, and more focused on the short term. In this context, the southerners seem to have a comparative advantage, because their parties have always had a greater ability for ad hoc mobilization, have been more personalistic, lack heavy bureaucracies, and have been more flexible. But the parties of the north have learned fast, as can be seen in the recent transformation of socialist parties in Britain, France, and Germany. In a way, they have become more "southern." The gap between north and south has narrowed.

8 Four Actors in Search of a Role

The Southern European Communist Parties

Anna Bosco, in collaboration with Carlos Gaspar

The failed attempt to reform Russian communism, the eastern European revolutions of 1989, and the collapse of the USSR severely tested all communist parties during the past decade. Still, the collapse of communism in eastern Europe has not been the most difficult challenge faced by the Partito Comunista Italiano (PCI), the Partido Comunista de España (PCE), the Partido Comunista Português (PCP), and the Kommounistiko Komma Elladas (Greek Communist Party, or KKE) since they regained legality, the PCI in the mid 1940s and the others in the 1970s.

In fact, all four parties' greatest challenges have been, first, to establish themselves and to achieve legitimacy in the context of consolidated democratic regimes, and, second, to find suitable political roles within their respective systems. That is, they have had to undergo a process of democratic integration, moving from their erstwhile anti-system stances and consequent political marginalization to full inclusion in the political game, and even to participation in governing coalitions. Second, they had to adapt to societies in rapid transformation, a development that has entailed considerable change in their electoral support, in terms both of class and of social values. In this sense, the collapse of "real socialism" helped to accelerate a process of internal transformation that had, in part, already been set in motion, and that affected, among other things, ideology, strategy, organization, and the social composition of party support. Without that process, these parties' response to the more visible challenge coming from eastern Europe would probably have been different. As we shall see, these varying objectives were interrelated. The role each communist party plays in the party system depends largely on the extent of its democratic integration. At the same time, both its political role and its degree of integration influence the ways in which a party recruits its voters.

We begin this chapter by examining the processes of democratic integration followed by the four communist parties since the transition to democracy. The PCI, the PCE, the PCP, and the KKE had been the main political enemies of their respective authoritarian regimes. Once those authoritarian systems disappeared, the four parties had to gain acceptance as loyal democratic political forces in order to play a political role in the new regime. Democratic integration was especially complicated for communist parties. Long regarded as antisystem political forces, they now had unequivocally to accept democracy and the rules of the democratic game. And, once they had adopted a democratic stance, they had to undergo a gradual legitimation in the eyes of the other political parties. We argue that the timing and trajectory adopted by each party in pursuit of democratic integration depended on a distinct set of constraints and opportunities, as well as on its ability to overcome and exploit them. Indeed, not all of these parties chose at the outset to abandon their antisystem identity and opt for a more democratic one. The parties' varying strategic choices, we argue, are best explained by their individual histories, the form the transition took in each country, and the political context within which each party had to operate.

As we shall see, however, the communists' democratic credibility did not depend solely on their adoption of a democratic stance: acceptance of the PCI, the PCE, the PCP, and the KKE as legitimate democratic parties was directly affected by the electoral and competitive strategies of the other political forces as well. Moreover, even the securing of democratic credibility did not mean that the communist parties could expect to join a government coalition over the short term: this measure of acceptance was also dependent on other constraints and opportunities of the political game in each country.

The second section of this chapter focuses on the adaptation of the four communist parties to social and political environments that had been greatly transformed over the previous twenty years. In order to enhance their appeal to potential supporters, the parties changed their organizational structures and became more flexible and adaptable. In the end, the social bases of these parties came to include higher percentages of younger voters and more supporters from the middle and upper classes, broadening their electoral appeal beyond the traditional boundaries of their respective *classes gardées*.

In the third section of this chapter, we examine the communist parties within the context of their party systems. As we shall see, advances in democratic integration and varying circumstances in interparty competition altered the four parties' positions within their respective party systems, as well as the political roles they have played over the past two decades. The conclusions drawn from this analysis are summarized in a final section.

Looking for a Place in a Consolidating Democracy

By the mid 1990s—following the disappearance of the communist parties' so-called external "source of legitimation,"[1] their internal transformations, and adaptation to altered social environments and to their respective regimes—the PCI, the PCE, the PCP, and the KKE had all become proregime forces. No longer could they be regarded as antiregime organizations, defined by Leonardo Morlino as "a party that wishes to change the regime and does not accept the norms and structures of authority of the current regime."[2] The existence of well-organized antiregime parties with strong electoral support indicates that the process of democratic consolidation is not yet complete, because large numbers of voters and a substantial section of the national political elite do not regard the current regime as legitimate. Thus, the transformation of these parties into clearly proregime forces significantly broadened the scope of democratic consensus. This was important, not only for the consolidation of democracy,[3] but also from the point of view of the other parties and of the party systems themselves. Indeed, their recognition as proregime forces was a necessary step toward their much-sought-after inclusion in the political game, particularly given their initial isolation as a result of having been outlawed for decades. It is hardly surprising, therefore, that, despite differences in individual strategies, each party advanced its candidacy as a partner in government as a means of becoming integrated into its country's democratic regime. This was not an easy objective to attain, however. Several factors slowed down the political integration of the communist parties, on occasion transforming the process into an obstacle course.

Two concepts can enhance our understanding of the difficulties encountered by the PCI, the PCE, the PCP, and the KKE in their quest for a role in government. The first is *party adaptation*, which entails a change in one or more sectors of party life—such as ideology, political strategy, or organization—in response to an event perceived as a strong challenge to the party. Various studies have suggested that parties are conservative organizations that do not initiate change without a significant jolt from the outside (see Panebianco 1982; Harmel and

Janda 1992 and 1994). This may include electoral defeat, a major international development, or the birth of a new party competing for the same electoral space. Alternatively, it can take the form of an opportunity, such as an electoral crisis facing a main competitor, that is seized upon and exploited. The crucial point is that such external stimuli must be perceived by the party elite as events that require party adaptation. Quite often, it is the main opposition group within the party that perceives the challenge, while the ruling elite denies its very existence. In such cases, internal conflict may change the dominant coalition heading the party. As several studies have underscored, party adaptation tends to be more profound and widespread when it is accompanied by a shift in the party's internal distribution of power in which incumbent leaders are replaced and a new dominant coalition is established (see Panebianco 1982; Bosco 1993; Harmel et al. 1995).

The political integration of antiregime forces always requires a certain amount of adaptation designed to establish their credentials as loyal democrats. Such changes, however, usually take the form of a reaction to challenges that precipitate a crisis within the organization rather than that of a shift in accordance with a long-term plan for party development. Furthermore, the decision to introduce changes—or not to do so—may give rise to conflict between the leadership and internal opposition groups, leading to prolonged paralysis of party life and rendering adaptation dependent on the outcome of that conflict. Even when adaptation has been initiated, it may produce unanticipated outcomes or take longer than originally expected, which may, in turn, result in additional internal problems. In short, party adaptation, although necessary for the integration of antiregime parties, may generate periods of uncertainty and conflict that will complicate and prolong the process of integration.

The second key concept is the *inner party system.* According to Morlino, where antiregime forces exist, proregime political forces tend to form "inner party systems" from which antiregime parties are excluded. In these systems, the elites of proregime parties collaborate and redefine the terms of reciprocal competition so as to "reduce the electoral appeal of actors who are not clearly proregime" and to "marginalize and isolate them from decision-making and the management of resources" (Morlino 1986, 229). The "inner system" is created when the leaders of the proregime parties refuse to form coalitions with the antiregime party because of its ideological distance from the others. The patterns of competition characterizing such systems are different from those of systems lacking antiregime actors.

By prolonging the exclusion of antiregime parties, the actors in the inner system ensure their continued control of numerous resources in a number of ways. To begin with, participation in government allows proregime elites to gain a firm foothold in the state administration, to fill the most influential jobs, and to act as gatekeepers vis-à-vis important interest groups (Morlino 1991). Lacking the legitimacy accorded to governing parties, "outsiders" are effectively prevented from competing for large sections of the electorate. Indeed, many voters would never support them, simply because, whether correctly or not, they are perceived as antiregime (Cotta 1990, 64). At the same time, proregime parties as a whole enjoy an electoral advantage simply by reason of belonging to the inner system. In practical terms, this means that communist parties wishing to play a role in government must first gain legitimacy as proregime forces and break into the inner system. This, in turn, constitutes a prior condition for success in appealing to segments of the electorate heretofore denied them, and in playing a role in the political game on an equal footing with the other parties.

Obtaining democratic legitimacy, however, entails two dimensions—one subjective and the other objective (Sartori 1974, 213; Morlino 1980, 172). The first dimension requires that the antiregime party shift its position, accept the key institutions of the regime "as the only legitimate framework for political contestation" (Gunther, Puhle, and Diamandouros 1995, 7), include these changes in official documents (statutes, party programs, etc.), respect the rules of the democratic game, and behave accordingly. The second dimension requires that these changes be perceived and recognized by the other parties and, hence, by the electorate itself. We can conceptualize the two dimensions as thresholds that an antiregime party must cross successively before it can enter the inner system and engage in electoral competition on a more equal footing.

Whether a party has crossed the first threshold can be ascertained from examining party documents and programs and the public speeches prepared by party officials. Whatever forms it takes, such change is not "silent" or "covert," because the mass media and the leadership of proregime parties will comment upon it and discuss it at length. Ascertaining whether doubts concerning a party's loyalty to democracy have been eliminated—that is, whether the "objective threshold" has been crossed—is a more complex task. Some have suggested that a useful criterion would be the party's coalition potential or its capacity to be included in a governing coalition (Morlino 1980, 172, and 1986, 219). The problem with this suggestion is that participation in government can only be evaluated post facto. We must, therefore, search for less rigid indicators of acceptance, such as (1) participation in coalition governments at the local level; (2) success in forming electoral alliances at the national level with parties belonging to the inner system; and (3) explicit acknowledgment of a party's newfound democratic loyalty by proregime parties or by important institutional actors.

The key point is that successful crossing of the subjective threshold does not, on its own, ensure that the objective threshold will also be crossed. An erstwhile antiregime party may accept the regime without necessarily being accepted by it (Sartori 1974, 213). A long time may pass before both thresholds are crossed, because exclusionary inner party systems often develop specific competitive rewards that are not lightly relinquished by proregime parties. Indeed, crossing the objective threshold entails termination of the inner system by proregime forces, which, in turn, requires that proregime parties overhaul and redefine their competitive strategies, relinquishing their competitive rewards. Not surprisingly, this process can last for years.

We can now reformulate the questions on democratic integration raised at the beginning of this chapter. First, when and how did the PCI, the PCE, the PCP, and the KKE accept democracy? Second, when and how were they recognized as proregime actors? Third, is this transformation explainable by the integration strategy adopted by the parties or was it the outcome of successive phases in party adaptation? Fourth, how did each party overcome the obstacles posed by the existence of an exclusionary system?

At the moment of democratic transition, the PCI, the PCE, the PCP, and the KKE all had the same objective: to escape the isolation imposed upon them by authoritarian regimes that had considered them their main enemies and to achieve integration into the new political system as potential coalition partners and participants in governance. Although this was a goal common to all, both the way it was pursued and the degree of success achieved varied from party to party.

The Partido Comunista de España. In Spain, democratic consolidation was achieved smoothly via elite settlement, following intensive negotiations and agreements in which the leaders of the main political groups all took part (Burton and Higley 1987; Gunther 1992). The PCE substantively contributed to this outcome, and underwent considerable adaptation, both of which rendered more credible its acceptance of democratic institutions. In the mid 1970s, the PCE had three central objectives: legalization; acceptance as a moderate, democratic political force; and putting the Spanish Civil War behind it. Painful memories of the Civil War and the resulting isolation into which the PCE was plunged during the Franco era had already encouraged the party to recast its ideology in the mold of Eurocommunism.[4] This was accompanied by other significant changes: in July 1976, the traditional communist cells were replaced by territorial branches (*agrupaciones*); in April 1977, the Spanish monarchy and the national flag were recognized; and in April 1978, at the party's Ninth Congress, Leninism was abandoned. The search for alliances accompanying this strategy aimed at the creation of a government of "democratic concentration"—that is, a cabinet formed by the Unión de Centro Democrático (UCD) and Partido Socialista Obrero Español (PSOE) with the external support of the PCE, the only party, according to its leader, Santiago Carrillo, that could guarantee the consolidation of democracy and offer a progressive solution to the country's economic problems.

The PCE's efforts to forge a moderate image were successful. During Easter Week 1977, the party was legalized, and the policy of *consenso* allowed the communists to play an important role at crucial moments of regime instauration, such as in drafting the constitution and the Moncloa pacts. Thus, the PCE was able to play a significant political role in Spain's democratization—far greater than might have been expected from the meager 9.2 percent of the vote it won in the first general election of June 1977. In addition, and thanks to a process of elite settlement that involved the communist leaders in face-to-face negotiations and official agreements with the other parties, the PCE was quickly recognized as a proregime force—so much so that Carrillo emerged as one of the leaders most involved in the democratization process. Hence, not only was the PCE recognized as a proregime party from the very beginning of the instauration, but it also had no difficulty in simultaneously crossing both the subjective and objective thresholds of democratic acceptance.

On the other hand, the leadership's integration strategy did not achieve all its objectives. First, electoral performance remained low and disappointing (10.8 percent in 1979 versus 9.2 percent in 1977)—falling far behind the "Italian dream" of a left under communist hegemony. Second, the PCE was allowed no role in government. Once the constitution had been approved, in October 1978, and *consenso* was over, the communists were left out of the decision-making process. Effectively isolated by the UCD, which was heading for an irreversible crisis, the PCE proved unable to bring about a collaborative arrangement with the PSOE, which was intent on replacing the UCD in office and took care not to become involved in a government of "democratic concentration." This explains why the pact between the PCE and the PSOE signed after the municipal elections of 1979, which allowed them to take over thousands of municipalities, was confined to the local level and did not lead to subsequent agreements. Third, between the end of 1980 and mid 1982, the PCE had to confront a complex internal crisis resulting variously from Carrillo's decision to transform the party's ideology and organization; disappointment over the party's electoral performance; and the difficulties encountered in merging the party that had operated in exile with that of the interior, which brought generational conflict out into the open. Carrillo's strategy faced twofold opposition. On the one hand, the pro-Soviet wing of the PCE, most of whose members belonged to the Catalan Communist Party (PSUC), rejected Eurocommunism. On the other, the *renovador* (reformist) wing clamored for greater internal democracy, as well as for more autonomy for regional parties. The party was rocked by conflict, internal splits, and a general demobilization (Gunther 1986d; Mujal-León 1986). The cumulative impact of these problems became fully visible in the results of the 1982 elections (see Appendix Table A.5).

The Partido Comunista Português. Contrary to their expectations, neither in Spain nor in Portugal did the communists play a leading role in overthrowing the authoritarian regime. In Portugal, however, the transition via *ruptura* and the subsequent phase of popular mobilization allowed the PCP much greater room for maneuver than it could ever have dreamed of (see Linz 1981b). In the months following the coup d'état, the party, supported by a crucial section of the Movimento das Forças Armadas (MFA), pursued a successful strategy of "institutional occupation" (Barreto 1987, 123–24). The result was participation in all six provisional governments, solid representation in a large number of local administrations, control of the unitary trade union confederation, and influence on several sectors of the media. The role of the party was further enhanced by the acceleration, after March 1975, of the occupation of the large estates in the southern part of the country and by the start of nationalizations.

The PCP leadership, which in 1974–75 witnessed the realization of most of the "national democratic revolution" it had envisaged in its 1965 program, felt that the situation was ripe for a socialist democracy. It could not admit that Portugal might be ruled by a "bourgeois" democratic regime of the Western kind, as envisaged by Mário Soares's socialist party. For Álvaro Cunhal, the PCP leader, the choice was between dictatorship and socialism. On the other hand, the rejection of liberal democracy by the communists transformed the transition into a confrontation between rival projects for the future of the regime. This development deeply divided both the civil elites and the armed forces. It came to an end on 25 November 1975 with the defeat of the PCP and its radical military allies.

Once the revolutionary period was over, the PCP did not accept the consolidation of the liberal democratic regime. It began, rather, to defend the "conquests" of the revolution from the attempts of the "reactionaries" to return to the status quo ante. According to the party—which regarded the constitution as "the main legal obstacle to any form of coup d'état" (Partido Comunista Português 1979, 39)—only by defending the economic (agrarian reform and nationalizations) and institutional gains (political role of the armed forces, semipresidential form of government) of April 25 that had already been enshrined in the constitution could the country advance along the path toward socialism. It was this thinking that led the PCP to oppose the constitutional revisions of 1982 and 1989, as well as Portugal's entry in the European Community, as developments that would alter the heritage of the revolution.

The PCP thus supported the new regime, but only because it saw it as a starting point for its transformation along socialist lines. Accordingly, it refused to follow the other political parties in seeking to transform the regime into a liberal democracy of the classic type, with the military firmly under civilian control and the extensive public sector erected during the revolution dismantled (see Maxwell and Monje 1991). Unlike the PCE, the PCP chose a strategy of adaptation to democracy designed to allow it to acquire legitimacy and to carve out a political role for itself without modifying its identity as a revolutionary, Marxist-Leninist force. To this end, Cunhal continued to seek an agreement with the Partido Socialista (PS) to form a left-wing government that, in his eyes, would constitute a "democratic alternative." The communists, however, failed to achieve their goal. In fact, the PCP's decision not to modify its identity led to the setting up of an inner system from which the communists were excluded. As a result, the "democratic alternative" did not come about even when the PS and the PCP obtained an absolute majority of seats in 1976 and 1983. The existence of an inner system also explains why the socialists opted for minority cabinets in 1976–77 and formed coalitions with the right-wing Partido do Centro Democrático Social (CDS) in 1978 and the center-right Partido Social-Democrata (PSD) in 1983–85.

As Appendix Table A.3 shows, however, until 1983, the PCP maintained a good electoral record. The new Partido Renovador Democrático (PRD), sponsored by General Ramalho Eanes, the president of the republic, was perceived by Álvaro Cunhal as likely to facilitate breaking through the "no-man's-land" that had been created around the communists. In the October 1985 elections, the PRD got 17.9 percent of the vote. Most of these came from supporters of the PS, which slumped from 36.1 percent to 20.8 percent of the vote. This development lent a new equilibrium to relations within the left, as the PCP, with 15.5 percent of the vote, now found itself only 5.3 percentage points behind the PS. It also gave a majority of seats to a possible alliance involving the PS, the PRD, and the PCP.

The expectations of the communist leaders, who had seen the PRD as a potential ally capable of forcing the socialists into an agreement to govern the country that would also include the PCP, were disappointed. The strategies and objectives of the three parties remained too far apart. The motion of censure against Aníbal Cavaco Silva's minority government presented by the PRD in the spring of 1987 was intended to set up a new PRD-PS cabinet, with external support from the PCP. The move, however, failed. The negotiations between the *renovadores* and the socialists never got under way, and parliament was dissolved. New elections in July 1987 introduced a radical change in the party system and forced the PCP to confront the definitive failure of its strategy of integration into the existing democratic regime.

The Partito Comunista Italiano. Two features distinguish the history of the PCI from that of the other communist parties in southern Europe. First, the sociopolitical setting of the transition and of the instauration of democracy, and, second, the size of the party, which, from 1953 on, was established as the second party in Italy, with percentages varying between a fifth and a third of the electorate. In the markedly polarized climate of the Cold War, the exclusion of the communists from government in 1947 and their electoral defeat in 1948 produced a frozen "inner system" in the Italian party system that isolated the PCI as an antiregime force, and prevented its reentry into government. Given the specific historical conjuncture in which the Italian party system was molded and the competitive logic it engendered, changing this situation was to take far longer in Italy than in other southern European countries (see Morlino 1982; Pasquino 1986). As Maurizio Cotta puts it, the *conventio ad excludendum* vis-à-vis the PCI helped the regime achieve an initial level of democratic consolidation by the beginning of the 1950s (Cotta 1990, 62). This, however, was a consolidation "under limiting conditions," because the party believed not to accept democratic values, institutions, and rules was not a minor group but a major political force, with an efficient organization, whose electoral support continued to grow from 1946 until 1976 (Cotta 1990, 59). This makes the Italian case unique among those examined here, since the achievement of full consolidation depended on the PCI's capacity to transform itself into a proregime force. This was not a predicament faced by the PCE, because it was immediately accepted as a democratic party, and the small size of the KKE and the shrinking electoral support of the PCP prevented them from becoming serious obstacles on the road to democratic consolidation.

The PCI's strategy of democratic integration can be summarized in three points. First, as many scholars have pointed out, the mode of democratic consolidation in Italy conforms to the elite convergence model (see Burton, Gunther, and Higley 1992; Cotta 1992a). According to this model, the antiregime and semiloyal political forces, having been defeated by a victorious coalition that continues to win elections and to control the government, are forced to relinquish their antisystem identity step by step in the hope of broadening their electoral support and, eventually, gaining office. This is the line of development followed by the PCI, which, starting with its 1947 vote in support of the constitution, tried to establish its credentials as a loyal democratic force by modifying and attenuating its policies and ideology over a period of time. The search for legitimation proceeded via a series of *svolte,* or turning points, which led the PCI further and further away from Moscow and heightened its acceptance of the rules and institutions of the democratic regime. From this point of view, it can be argued that by 1975–76, public support for Eurocommunism, explicit acceptance of NATO, and recognition of the "historically universal value of democracy" in a statement by the party's leader, Enrico Berlinguer, had made the PCI a subjectively proregime force. In other words, the party had crossed the first of the two thresholds to democratic acceptance (Pasquino 1988, 8).

The second element in the PCI's integration strategy was its readiness to join other political forces in coalition governments. Although the party was excluded from power at the national level, it took part in numerous governments at the municipal, provincial, and regional levels. This was especially the case after 1975, when PCI and PSI governed together in many local administrations (see Pridham 1988). Like the PCP, the PCI's commitment to forming alliances was a kind of cleavage-bridging mechanism (see Sani 1976, 1), designed to dissipate any doubts about its loyalty to democracy. Unlike the PCP, however, the leaders of the PCI combined their proposals for government alliances with "turning points" that modified the party's identity. In the mid 1970s, the *compromesso storico*—the strategy articulated by Berlinguer after the 1973 military coup in Chile with an eye to bringing about a historical compromise with the Democrazia Cristiana (DC) and the Catholics—and the simultaneous development of Eurocommunism allowed the PCI to join the parliamentary majority by supporting two Christian Democratic cabinets (see Hellman 1988; Flores and Gallerano 1992). The success of this initiative, which lasted from July 1976 to January 1979, proved limited, however. To be sure, the support it extended to the governments of "national solidarity" and the role it played in combating terrorism undoubtedly allowed the PCI to reinforce its credibility as a democratic party (see Guidorossi 1984, 109–27). At the same time, the refusal to allow the party full access to the cabinet meant that its explicit legitimation was once again postponed. Disappointment with this turn of events marked the beginning of a phase of demobilization among the rank and file that was explicitly reflected in the June 1979 elections, when, as seen in Appendix Table A.2, the party lost votes for the first time in thirty years. The "democratic alternative," that is, an alliance with the socialists and the smaller lay parties intended to detach the DC from government, which Berlinguer inaugurated in 1980 in an attempt to brush off the failure of the "historic compromise," proved no more successful. The "alternative" was stillborn because the socialists turned their backs on the PCI and embarked on a new period of center-left governments with the DC and other minor allies, once again excluding the PCI from the inner system (see Merkel 1987).

The third element in the PCI's integration strategy was its decision to take advantage of opportunities in parliament, whose polycentric nature allowed the opposition to play an important role in decision making (Cotta 1990). Thanks to a consensual institutional culture, which considered parliament an arena for mediation between government and opposition, the PCI was able to take part, along with the parties in the government majority, in the law-making process and in the election of incumbents to some of Italy's highest offices, such as those of the president of the republic, the presidents of the two houses, and so on. This process was given a boost by the 1971 reform of the parliament's standing orders, which increased the influence of the parliamentary groups over the organization of parliamentary business and led to a sort of "parliamentary integration" of the communists that helped to make up for their exclusion from the government.[5]

In a nutshell, the PCI attenuated its positions so as to cross the subjective threshold of democratic acceptance and declared that the time was now ripe for it to enter government in alliance with other political forces. This behavior corresponds to the elite convergence model of consolidation. It is important to stress, however, that elite convergence does not imply that a party's transformation into a proregime force will receive immediate recognition, as was the case with the PCE. The PCI in fact remained "suspended" between the subjective and objective thresholds of democratic acceptance, and in the decade following the end of "national solidarity," the parties of the inner system continued, more or less explicitly, to use the *conventio ad excludendum* to ensure their own electoral and governmental strength.[6] In practical terms, this meant that the PCI's integration strategy had failed, even though, in the first half of the 1980s, the party did not fully realize this. Accordingly, the 1979 electoral decline and the 1983 stalemate were interpreted as an adjustment after the huge advance of 1976. Indeed, even as late as 1986, the documents of its Twenty-Second Congress credited the PCI with substantially holding on to its electoral support (Partito Comunista Italiano 1986, 70). Like the PCE and the PCP, the PCI only became aware of the failure of its strategy after a new electoral defeat, in 1987.

The Kommounistiko Komma Elladas. The KKE is the only one of the four parties whose transformation into a proregime force enabled it to join two coalition governments, one of them with the right-wing Nea Demokratia party (July–October 1989). Participation in a coalition government, however, is not the KKE's only interesting feature. On the one hand, its transformation into a proregime force is a good example of elite convergence. The party relinquished its more radical features in order to broaden its electoral appeal. The whole process unfolded extremely rapidly, with a mere two years between its decision to change policy and its inclusion in the government. On the other, unlike the PCE and the PCI, the KKE was an orthodox communist party, with close links to the Soviet Union, more similar to the PCP in its ideological stances. For this reason, even after the end of the long period of illegality (1947–74) that followed the Civil War, the Greek communists were not regarded as a legitimate force, and remained confined to a sort of political ghetto (Diamandouros 1991, 26). In addition, the KKE had to deal with political and institutional constraints that were absent in the other cases. To begin with, it had to make room for itself in a rather crowded political space, competing with a socialist party whose positions were, initially, quite radical, as well as with a Eurocommunist group, the KKE-Esoterikou (KKE-Interior), or KKE-Es, which had split off from the KKE a few months after the colonels' coup of April 1967.[7] At the same time, the communists were also penalized by a "reinforced" proportional electoral system that underrepresented their votes in terms of seats, while granting the two main parties the chance to form single-party governments. This provided institutional underpinning for the exclusion of the KKE from the inner system.[8] Thanks to all these constraints, the KKE has played a modest role in the party system, and it has had to resign itself to being a secondary option as a potential partner for the other parties.

The chances of an orthodox communist party that moderates its radical aims rapidly with an eye to gaining legitimacy and a role in government depend greatly on its strategy for democratic integration. In the case of the KKE, this can be divided into two phases. In the first, which coincided with the Nea Demokratia governments of 1974–81 and the first PASOK cabinet of 1981–85, the Greek communists maintained their antiregime ideology and policies intact. Following the restoration of democracy, the KKE's main objective was to establish its hegemony over the KKE-Es by reasserting its control over communist identity (Achimastos 1990, 376–77, 457–59). This goal was achieved quite early, initially in 1977 and finally in 1981, when the KKE-Es failed to win a single seat, while the KKE vote rose to 10.9 percent (see Appendix Table A.1). Having established control over the communist political space, the KKE tried to break out of its isolation by offering to join the socialists in government, but without in anyway modifying its identity. Thus, following PASOK's victory under Andreas Papandreou in the 1981 elections, the communists more than once unsuccessfully proposed the creation of a left-wing "democratic government" coalition.

The conditions for changing the KKE's strategy matured after PASOK's second electoral victory in 1985. Indeed, from 1987 on, opinion polls revealed that the socialists were losing ground, thereby giving the parties on their left a strong chance to increase their electoral support. This trend gained momentum when PASOK leaders were besmirched by scandals in 1988. Realizing that, on its own, the KKE was unable to attract the voters who were deserting PASOK, the communist leaders went in search of a coalition partner, exactly as the PCP had done with the PRD. Their most natural ally was the KKE-Es, which in 1987 had relinquished its communist identity and become the Ellenike Aristera (Greek Left), or E. Ar., hoping to unite the traditional and the new left movements (Verney 1987b). However, a coalition with the E. Ar. would have obliged the KKE to abandon the more radical aspects of its program, such as the dictatorship of the proletariat and the demand that Greece leave the European Community, and, with these, its former strategy of democratic integration. In the December

1988 declaration announcing the establishment of the alliance, the KKE formally accepted Greece's membership in the EC and the democratic road to socialism. Thus was born the Synaspismos tes Aristeras kai tes Proodou (Coalition of the Left and Progress), or SYN, which included not only the KKE and the E. Ar. but some former socialists and other left-wing elements as well (Pridham and Verney 1991, 51).

It was, therefore, the concrete prospect of increasing its vote within a stabilized democracy that made the KKE decide to modify its identity and cross the subjective threshold of democratic acceptance. It is worth noting that the other parties acknowledged this change at once. The signing of the agreement was immediately followed by a meeting of the leaders of the opposition—the ND, KKE, E. Ar., and Demokratike Ananeosse (Democratic Renewal), or DIANA—that was accorded major attention by the press, in which the democratic loyalty of the KKE and, thereby, the legitimacy of the Synaspismos were recognized. Concrete proof of that shift was the parties' decision to introduce an electoral reform geared toward a more proportional system. The new law was passed partly because the KKE/SYN had already been accepted by the two principal parties as a possible government partner. Consequently, when the June 1989 elections, held under the new electoral law, failed to give either PASOK or ND an overall majority, and a single-party government became impossible, the two major parties courted Synaspismos as a partner in a coalition government (see Perifanaki 1990; Achimastos and Papathanassiou 1990).

Contrary to PASOK's expectations that the reform of the electoral law would lead to an alliance with the communist left, the first coalition government since 1974 brought together the Nea Demokratia and SYN. The new government was formed to ensure the prosecution of socialist leaders, envisaged under a complex law concerning the accountability of cabinet ministers. Such prosecution would become legally impossible if parliament were dissolved, so the new government was formally designated an interim arrangement, destined to last only until new elections were held in the fall. The inclusion of the KKE in this coalition government, in which it held two vital ministries (those of Justice and the Interior), did not merely mean that its legitimation was now complete, and that it had crossed at one go both the subjective and objective thresholds of democratic acceptance. It also signaled the end of the rift created by the Greek Civil War (see Featherstone 1990; Verney 1990b and 1991).

Democratic Consolidation and Party Adaptation

Our examination of the integration strategies pursued by the PCI, the PCE, the PCP, and the KKE leads to the following general observations. First, the communists' opposition to the authoritarian regimes in southern Europe and their contribution to the instauration of their democratic successors were not enough to ensure these parties' integration into the new political systems. Put differently, the crucial role played by the PCI in the World War II resistance movement and in founding the new republic, the credentials the PCE won for its struggle against Francoism and its responsible behavior during the instauration phase, and the opposition of the outlawed PCP and KKE to their respective authoritarian regimes were not enough to place these parties on the same footing with the other political forces. For each of them, therefore, the advent of democracy posed the problem of legitimation and of political integration into the new regime.

Second, not every party adopted a strategy geared to gaining recognition as a proregime force from the start. On this point the PCI and the PCE differed from the PCP and the KKE. The PCP's strategy for integration precluded any change in ideology or program. The party did not modify its image or its political message even when it had a chance to capture the socialist voters disappointed by the "central bloc" cabinet formed by the PS and the PSD from 1983 to 1985. Indeed, it was in order to avoid becoming Eurocommunist that the PCP chose to support President Eanes's PRD in 1985. In fact, Álvaro Cunhal had intended the alliance with the *renovadores* to achieve a sort of division of "electoral labor," which would assign to the PRD the task of winning over the middle-class voters who had abandoned the PS, while allowing the PCP to represent workers and farm laborers. Faced with the opportunity created by the likelihood of a notable fall in the socialist vote, the PCP chose a course of action that was diametrically opposed to that of the KKE, which adapted its position in order to form Synaspismos. It is also true, however, that back in 1974, the transformation of the KKE into a proregime force was not one of the Greek communists' objectives. This came about only fifteen years later. The historical and political contexts in which the parties operated and the forms the transition took explain the differences in their initial choices.

Third, the process of legitimation involving the communist parties was influenced by the form consolidation took. Where an elite settlement occurred, involving the reciprocal recognition of all actors taking part in negotiations and agreements, the parties that crossed the subjective threshold of democratic acceptance had no difficulty in crossing the objective one as well. The PCE demonstrated its loyalty as a democratic party by undergoing a profound process of ideological and organizational adaptation, which soon resulted in its being accepted as a proregime party. When democratic consolidation took the form of elite convergence, however, or when there was no initial settlement, several outcomes became possible. In this regard, the comparison between the PCI and the KKE is illuminating. In Greece, the KKE modified a few points in its program and was immediately accepted as a proregime force by the other political actors—so much so that, in its first experience as a government party, it was given control of two crucial ministries. In Italy, on the other hand, the far more radical changes undertaken by the PCI did not achieve as much. Doubts continued to be raised concerning its democratic credibility, while the role assigned to the communists during the period of national solidarity was to defend the castle, but from "outside the walls."

This comparison highlights the importance of "competitive contingencies" or constraints and opportunities of the political game. In Greece, the political situation in the second half of the 1980s was such that, for different reasons, both PASOK and ND considered an alliance with the communists a lesser evil. In Italy, on the other hand, even as late as the mid 1980s, an alliance with the PCI was regarded as too costly by large sectors of the PSI, and certainly as less advantageous than participation with the DC in the inner system. That system's preservation was further encouraged by the existence in Italy of a larger number of parties and a more proportional electoral system than in Greece.

Fourth, all four parties changed their integration strategies over a period of time. In each case, this was because of changes in electoral resources and opportunities, proving that, quite independently of their degree of adherence to the democratic regime, all parties were already "tied tightly to the win and loss column provided by the total electoral market" (Schlesinger 1984, 383). Thus, the KKE became proregime when it saw that it could absorb part of PASOK's voter base, whereas the other three parties decided to change when they began to lose votes. Throughout the 1980s, the PCI, the PCE, and the PCP had to reckon with the implications of electoral defeat. In each case, defeat served to highlight the failure of these parties' strategies of democratic integration and to underscore their continued political isolation—a situation from which they had unsuccessfully tried to escape by opting for a moderate political message and/or by seeking to form alliances with the socialists.

In 1982, the PCE's share of the popular vote slumped from 10.8 percent to 4 percent. This decline of almost 60 percent was all the more dramatic because the defectors transferred their support en masse to the PSOE. On the other hand, the overall majority obtained by the PSOE eliminated any prospect of a left-wing alliance and relegated the communists to the sidelines. In 1987, the PCI had to admit that the "substantial electoral hold" that it had thought it possessed until the previous year no longer existed. A net loss of 3.3 percent, together with notable gains for the anticommunist PSI, which increased its share of the vote by 2.9 percent, diminished the credibility of the "democratic alternative" and revealed that the PCI was still isolated and far from achieving a place in government.[9] That same year, the PCP was badly defeated, with its share of the vote falling from 15.5 percent to 12.1 percent, putting an end to its prospects of playing a determining role in the political game. In fact, the left-wing majority was swept away in 1987. The PSD achieved an absolute majority, the PRD's support fell from 17.9 percent to 4.9 percent of the vote, and the PS, with 22.2 percent, once again became the major opposition force in competition with the PSD for the moderate vote. As a result, the PCP returned to its splendid isolation.

The opportunity for the KKE to increase its electoral strength and the defeat of the PCI, the PCE, and the PCP at the polls induced all four parties to rethink their integration strategies and to change them. These changes occurred before the collapse of the Berlin Wall complicated matters further. Let us see how this came about.

The Partido Comunista de España. Santiago Carrillo's resignation after the PCE's 1982 defeat did not spare the party a violent internal argument over responsibility for the electoral results and the prospects for the future. The clash between the former party leader and the young Gerardo Iglesias, to whom Carrillo had handed over the post, was not just a succession struggle. It was primarily a dispute over the model of a communist party most suitable to the political and social realities of a rapidly growing country such as Spain in the 1980s. Iglesias felt that the party should change both its internal structure and its relations with society. He argued that it was necessary to loosen the party's "democratic centralism" and to reduce the role of ideology, transforming the PCE into a "lay" party, based upon its political program. The communists' inability to broaden their electoral base on their own also led him to believe that it was necessary to move beyond the party's special relationship with the trade unions and the working class, and to forge new bonds with such new social movements as pacifism, the ecologists, and feminism (see Iglesias 1984). To this end, in

1984, the party launched its policy of "social and political convergence," designed to make the PCE attractive to a broad range of progressive forces (parties, movements, independents). Whereas Iglesias championed the need to adapt the party, and to abandon or diminish the significance of important elements of traditional communist identity, Carrillo's supporters continued to fight for a class-based party, with strong links to workers' organizations, and a structure based on the ever-valid principles of "democratic centralism." According to Carrillo, the PCE should not seek support in new social areas but should fully reoccupy its own, communist, electoral space.[10]

The confrontation ended in 1985 with Iglesias's victory and the splitting of the PCE. In early 1986, at the beginning of an election year, Ignacio Gallego, the leader of the pro-Soviet wing of the PCE, who could not even accept Eurocommunism, and the group loyal to Santiago Carrillo founded separate communist parties, respectively known as the Partido Comunista de los Pueblos de España (PCPE) and the Mesa para la Unidad Comunista. Following the exit of the internal opposition, Iglesias was able to proceed with his reform project. In April 1986, the Izquierda Unida (United Left), or IU, was born. Besides the PCE, which, given its resources, formed the backbone of the movement, it included Gallego's PCPE, a group of former socialists who had founded the PASOC (Partido de Acción Socialista), a substantial group of independents, and a few small parties with limited followings. Only Carrillo's communists refused to join the alliance.[11]

The new coalition was, by all accounts, a potent factor for change, affecting both the PCE's role within the party system and the very identity of the communist party. Indeed, in terms of competition, the establishment of the IU reversed the negative electoral trend identified with the PCE. In the June 1986 elections, the coalition's share of the vote moved slightly beyond that of 1982. In 1989, however, the IU doubled its vote, and increased both its percentage and its seats in parliament (see Appendix Table A.5). The coalition's greater electoral weight was subsequently confirmed in the 1991 and 1995 municipal elections, the 1994 European elections, and the 1993 and 1996 general elections. These results demonstrated that the IU had succeeded in attracting voters from outside the traditional communist base. In other words, by setting up Izquierda Unida, the PCE had offered an attractive alternative to sections of the electorate that were dissatisfied with the PSOE in government but would never vote for a communist party *tout court.*

At the same time, the IU's electoral advance inevitably set in motion a process of institutionalization of the coalition, which lessened the importance of the PCE and forced the party to modify its organization and identity. Initially, the IU was an alliance, in which the visibility and individuality of each component was assured by a rigid system of "quotas" (each party had a fixed number of representatives in the collective presidency) and the principle of unanimity, linked to veto power, in all decision making. Furthermore, even though the coalition partners did not use their separate logos in elections, the coalition's leader was the secretary of the communist party. Thus, the PCE maintained an important source of identification, especially after a new leader, Julio Anguita, replaced Iglesias both as head of the party (in 1988) and of Izquierda Unida (in 1989).[12] In short, the IU was, at first, merely the sum of its political parts, among which the PCE played a predominant role.

All this changed after the elections of 29 October 1989. The alliance's impressive results signaled a "point of no return" for the PCE and its allies, inasmuch as it became obvious that Izquierda Unida was capable of guaranteeing sustained electoral growth. Two weeks later, moreover, the Berlin Wall came crashing down, and the PCI in Italy decided to change its name, becoming the Partito Democratico della Sinistra (Democratic Party of the Left), or PDS, confirming to all, and especially to the PCE, that it was worth investing in a progressive alliance to veil the communist presence. Since the "lesson" of these two events was that Izquierda Unida was a winning choice that would be costly to abandon, the crucial issue debated within the PCE and the IU in the following years was the consolidation of the coalition.

However, both the PCE and its allies split on the issue of how Izquierda Unida should be institutionalized. Even before the Wall collapsed, a group of "modernizers," which included many who had worked with Iglesias, suggested that the alliance should be transformed into a "new kind" of party—along the lines of the new left—and that the PCE should be disbanded (see Berga 1991; Sartorius 1992). On the other hand, the orthodox wing of the PCE, led by the powerful Andalusian federation, was suspicious of any change in the status quo and refused to modify the structure of the coalition. In contrast to what happened in the early 1980s, the struggle ended in a compromise, arrived at in 1991–92, that reflected the respective strength of the two groups. The PCE abolished democratic centralism, strengthened its federal bias, and restricted its role in the coalition to a few well-defined functions (such as stimulating debate and drafting the theoretical framework, training militants, and maintaining a presence in social movements and trade unions). Although its influence was reduced, the PCE survived as a party. By the same to-ken, the IU became more cohesive than a mere alliance, although it did not become a party. The system of "quotas" was abolished, and elections for the governing bodies took place with opposing lists of candidates. Unanimity gave way to majorities and minorities in decision making, and internal currents were allowed to form and were granted financial resources and freedom of expression in public. Finally, the coalition's statutes stated that only Izquierda Unida, via its governing bodies, had the right to establish links with society. All these changes produced similar results. The IU became more autonomous of its component groups, replacing a distinctively vertical principle of organization, based on parties and groups, with a horizontal one, which facilitated the coalescence of splinter groups from various parties around issues (see Bosco 1993, 248–308).

In a nutshell, Iglesias's decision to create a progressive cartel in which parties and social movements could coexist, gain electoral representation, and, after a while, merge into a homogeneous political force was the direct result of careful rethinking of the reasons why the PCE's postauthoritarian integration strategy had failed. To be sure, that strategy had helped the party become legal. But it had not given it entry into government and had led to a grave internal crisis that went beyond the loss of votes. The IU was created before the fall of the Berlin Wall. The new challenge from eastern Europe was used by the progressive elements within the coalition to give greater impetus to the consolidation process by demanding the dissolution of the PCE and the abandonment of the party's communist identity. This, however, was a stillborn demand, since the PCE had been a proregime party for some time, and its presence was not considered an obstacle to the IU's electoral growth.

The Partido Comunista Português. The PCP's electoral defeat in 1987 brought forward, for the first time since 1974, an internal opposition calling for a debate on Álvaro Cunhal's political choices. Unlike the PCE, however, the organizational constraints and political culture of the monolithic Portuguese party led to the emergence of a weak and fragmented opposition, composed mainly of communist intellectuals. Despite their relative weakness, these "critics" managed to get the party to discuss its strategy of adaptation to democracy. Indeed, the opposition felt that the electoral results had proved that the PCP's strategy of trying to form a coalition government with the PS without abandoning its revolutionary outlook had been a definite failure. Since an alliance with the PRD and the PS was no longer possible, the party was, once again, confined to a ghetto, from which it would be able to emerge only after a thorough process of renewal.

A number of milestones underpinned this transformation. First, the PCP had to decide, once and for all, to accept democracy and EC membership. According to the "critics," the 1987 elections proved that democracy in Portugal had been consolidated. This meant that the PCP had to accept the democratic regime without "mental reservations," that is, without believing that, sooner or later, it would be possible to "revive" the revolutionary process it had "suspended" in 1975.[13] To accept democracy also meant accepting the European Community, which Portugal had joined in 1986. The search for support among new social groups was the second milestone of this change. The PCP had to admit that Portuguese society had developed and modernized since 1974. Economic development had caused new social forces to emerge, had brought about the diversification of the working class, and had reduced the number of agricultural laborers. The communists could thus no longer afford to be regarded as representatives of the urban and rural proletariat alone. The third milestone was the democratization of the party organization, still trapped within the plaster cast of "democratic centralism." Basically, the opposition wanted the party leadership to take account of the transformations that had already occurred in the democratic regime and in Portuguese society, and to modernize the party—just as the Eurocommunists had done in the mid 1970s.

The leadership, which was in complete control of the party machine, rejected all demands except those concerning the acceptance of democracy and of the EC. In 1988, the PCP's Twelfth Congress adopted a new party program, which replaced that of 1965. In the new document, the April revolution was for the first time described as *inacabada,* or unfinished, and the objective of a "democratic and national revolution" was replaced by that of an "advanced democracy on the brink of the twenty-first century." The new program also recognized that "democracy has an intrinsic value" that was not merely instrumental, and it included a long series of guarantees for the defense of the democratic regime (Partido Comunista Português 1989, 243–45).

Put otherwise, in 1988, the PCP made public its formal acceptance of democracy, thereby crossing the subjective threshold of its transformation into a proregime party. The PCP's new attitude toward the regime was reflected in the manner in which it dealt with the second revision of the constitution. Although it voted en bloc against the 1989 constitutional revision as a whole, the party gave its approval to numerous individual changes to the text. In so doing, it assumed responsibility for 90 percent of the new constitution (Magalhães 1989, 101).

The changes undergone by the PCP after its 1987 defeat were thus considerable, although not as far-reaching as the opposition had demanded. The leadership refused to modify the identity of the party, even after the fall of the Berlin Wall. After having praised the "good government" of the Soviet Union for decades, the PCP now began to condemn the errors and aberrations of the "socialist model" as it had developed in eastern Europe, but it still held fast to its communist ideology and insisted on its image as a proletarian, Marxist-Leninist party, organized along the lines of "democratic centralism" (see Gaspar and Rato 1992, 157–87, 251–307).

Although circumscribed, this change, reminiscent of the equally restricted one adopted by the KKE, bore fruit. After the Twelfth Congress, there were several signs that the process of recognizing the PCP's democratic credibility had begun. In 1989, Jorge Sampaio, the secretary of the PS, ran for the presidency of the Lisbon Municipal Chamber (i.e., the office of mayor) in alliance with the communists. This "Por Lisboa" coalition managed to wrest control of the city administration from the conservatives for the first time in ten years, a success repeated in 1993. It was of vital importance for the PCP, not only because the party was thus able to take office in the country's largest municipality, but also because Lisbon became a showcase for the kind of left-wing alliance that the communists had always aspired to. Another indication of the PCP's growing legitimation dates to Álvaro Cunhal's eightieth birthday, when Mário Soares, the president of the republic, expressed his good wishes to the aging communist leader in one of the main daily newspapers. In a long article recognizing the democratic contributions of the PCP, Soares wrote, among other things: "Besides, with the disappearance of the Soviet Union, . . . the communists today are a party like any other, and there is no reason for exclusions, particular suspicions, or discrimination" (*Diario de Noticias,* November 10, 1993). This explicit legitimation of the PCP as a democratic force was significant both because its source was the highest institutional authority in the country and because Soares himself had been largely responsible for setting up the inner system that excluded the PCP.

The Partito Comunista Italiano. Defeat in 1987 made it abundantly clear to the Italian communists as well that their strategy for democratic integration had failed. The exclusionary system was still in place, and the PCI could no longer be sure of increasing its vote, or even of preserving its grass-roots support. As in the case of the PCE, it was a new PCI leadership that proposed an abrupt about-face. Achille Occhetto, who was made assistant secretary in June 1987 and secretary-general a year later,[14] immediately took certain decisions designed to (in his words) transform "the role [of the PCI] in Italian politics" (Pasquino 1988, 321). Culminating at the PCI's Eighteenth Congress in March 1989, these entailed the modification of central components of the party's strategy of adaptation to democracy, including deradicalization of its ideological stance. In addition, the "consociational" model of democracy was officially dropped, along with the PCI's demand for a role in government. Despite opposition from the party's orthodox wing, the PCI redefined itself as "a modern, reformist party," shelved all reference to the October Revolution and to the fathers of the communist movement (except Marx), and reiterated its identification with other European left-wing parties. It also reasserted its full adherence to democracy, now referred to not as "*a* path *to* socialism" but "*the* path *of* socialism," to underscore the fact that socialist conquests are only possible in a democratic setting. Furthermore, the party centered its political program on the entirely new concept of citizens and their rights. The traditional communist program was modified by the introduction of new principles, including some feminist concerns, rejection of violence, and defense of the environment. Finally, the party's internal organization was profoundly transformed by the adoption of a new statute that put an end to democratic centralism, and made possible the de facto formation of internal factions (see Prospero 1990; Curi 1991).

In this manner, the "democratic alternative" was preserved, but the communist leaders lent it new credibility by making radical changes in the party's institutional strategy. As early as November 1987, Occhetto declared that the PCI would renounce the consociational mechanisms that had bedeviled the Italian political system in the past and opted, instead, for a clear distinction between majority and opposition. This decision introduced an important transformation in the party's institutional culture and gave rise to additional changes. In June 1989, the PCI formed a shadow cabinet on the British model. Most important, between 1987 and 1991, it renounced the system of proportional representation in favor of the majority system. In so doing, it paved the way for an alternation in government decided by the will of the electorate rather than by the political parties (see Fabbrini 1990; Pasquino 1988). In short, the 1987 electoral defeat opened the way to important changes in the PCI's mode of adaptation to the inner system set up at the end of World War II. As a result, even before the collapse of "real socialism," Italian communists had already undergone considerable change. This being the case, Occhetto's proposal, a mere three days after the initial breaching of the Berlin Wall, to accelerate change further by relinquishing the PCI's communist identity and transforming it into a new political entity nonetheless surprised the party and led to a heated debate between supporters and opponents of change that was played out over a period of fifteen months and in two successive congresses (the Nineteenth, in March 1990, and the Twentieth, in January 1991 [see Ignazi 1992; Baccetti 1997]).

Of the four parties examined here, the PCI was the only one that faced up to the challenge of eastern Europe by renouncing its identity and constructing a completely new one. Yet it was the one that least needed the change, because it had already undergone a long series of "rifts" and "turning points" that had led it to sever its ties with Moscow and to accept the rules and institutions of the democratic game. Why then did it undertake such a radical about-face? For one thing, as Occhetto himself asserted (to the Central Committee in November 1989), the failure of the various models of "real socialism" forced the party to shed "once and for all an old ideological skin," which in practice had already been replaced (Partito Comunista Italiano 1990, 7). A further explanation can be found in the fifteen years separating the transformation of the PCI into a proregime force, during the mid 1970s, and its legitimation as a loyal democratic force—a process still incomplete on the eve of the fall of the Berlin Wall. The decision to abandon the PCI's communist identity was inspired by the desire to unblock the Italian party system. Occhetto himself explicitly acknowledged this, on November 14, 1989, when, addressing the party's Direzione (executive committee), he affirmed that the purpose of the about-face was to "remove all alibis" and "make alternation possible" (Occhetto 1994, 189). By radically changing its ideology, the PCI tried to gain "in the field" the legitimation that the members of the inner system had not yet fully conceded to it. Thus, the PCI's leadership turned the collapse of "real socialism" into a resource to be exploited in their efforts to reposition the party within the national party system. Their objective was to found a new party inspired by the socialist ideals of freedom and equality, to join the Socialist International, to attract all the progressive forces of the country (Greens, radicals, progressive Catholics), and, above all, to launch a new phase in Italian politics by setting up, together with the socialists, the "democratic alternative" that until then had remained a theoretical option.

These changes began with Occhetto's statements on November 12, 1989, and ended in early 1991, when the Partito Democratico della Sinistra (Democratic Party of the Left), or PDS, was born during the

PCI's Twentieth Congress. The symbol of the PDS was an oak with roots reaching down into the old emblem of Italian communists—the red flag with a hammer and sickle, reproduced in small size. The foundations for the new party were successfully laid despite lacerating tensions within the PCI and a rift with its orthodox wing, which went off to found its own, more leftist party, the Rifondazione Comunista (Communist Refoundation), or RC.

In the Italian case, therefore, it was the absence of unequivocal and explicit legitimation by the proregime parties that forced the PCI to introduce profound changes unnecessary in the other cases. After it had become a subjectively proregime force in the mid 1970s, the PCI did not receive political recognition for its transformation. Thus, its decision to relinquish its communist identity was the key to crossing, once and for all, the objective threshold of democratic acceptance. In so doing, it brought to an end to a fifteen-year long period of "suspension."

The Kommounistiko Komma Elladas. It is useful to examine the transformation of the Greek communist party by comparing it with the PCE. Both parties formed coalitions in which they were the main actors. Unlike Izquierda Unida, however, Synaspismos was very short-lived. A mere two and a half years after it was set up, in 1991, the KKE left the alliance and went back to its old ideology and policies. This became evident at its Fourteenth Extraordinary Congress (December 1991), when the party leaders confirmed that the KKE was based on Marxist-Leninist principles and proletarian internationalism. Following the departure of the more traditional communists, Synaspismos subsequently transformed itself from a coalition into a party in June 1992. These developments are best understood when placed in their proper context (Dimitras 1990; Pridham and Verney 1991).

In June 1989, although it had only recently been created, Synaspismos entered government for the first time. But sharing the government with the Nea Demokratia did not pay off in electoral terms. Indeed, in the November 1989 election, the KKE and its allies lost votes, mainly to the socialists—their share of the vote falling from 13.1 percent to 11 percent. Since neither PASOK nor ND won an overall majority, however, a new coalition government was formed, this time consisting of three parties (PASOK, ND, and Synaspismos). In April 1990, when the third election in less than a year was held, Synaspismos lost more votes, slipping to 10.3 percent. In the aggregate, from June 1989 to April 1990, the KKE and its allies lost over a quarter of their grassroots support (see Appendix Table A.1). Thus, unlike Izquierda Unida, Synaspismos was unable to retain the votes gained in the June

1989 election despite its participation in the government. As a result, traditional communists came to conclude that the coalition was not worth maintaining, and, above all, not worth sacrificing the KKE's identity for. This rift between those favoring a renewal of the KKE and those who tenaciously held to traditional communist dogma was widened by debate over current developments in Gorbachev's USSR—an issue that had already produced a split in the party well before 1989 (Spourdalakis 1990; Smith 1993).

Izquierda Unida also experienced a painful internal debate (which ended only in December 1994) over developments in eastern Europe, but it did not split in two. There are three possible reasons for this. First, the same dominant coalition headed both the IU and the PCE, whereas in Greece the KKE and the SYN were headed by two different sets of leaders. At the KKE's Thirteenth Congress, held in February 1991, the orthodox wing won by a hair's breadth and elected a conservative, Aleka Papariga, to the post of party secretary (see Doukas 1991). The president of Synaspismos, however, was a progressive member of the KKE's Politburo, Maria Damanaki, who was elected with the support of proponents of party change. It was she who decided—much like the modernizers in the IU—to transform the coalition into an autonomous political party with an independent political position. Second, along with electoral defeat, the KKE had simultaneously to face the challenge emanating from eastern Europe. This prevented the party from reaching a compromise on its internal debate, as Izquierda Unida had done. Whereas PCE hardliners realized that the communist party's political survival could be guaranteed only through Izquierda Unida, their Greek counterparts were able to leave Synaspismos without too much regret, particularly given the electoral setbacks of 1989–90 and their belief that they could retain their own identity and still play a dominant role to the left of PASOK without the reformists.[15]

Finally, the coalition's demise was made easier by the nature of the adaptation and of the subsequent legitimation of the KKE/SYN. In Greece, adaptation was not the result of electoral defeat but, rather, the outcome of the leadership's calculations concerning future electoral success. This made adaptation in Greece more fragile and less deeply felt than in Spain, where debate over creating and, subsequently, over strengthening Izquierda Unida absorbed the PCE for almost a decade, producing considerable inner tensions, but, in the end, reaffirming the party's commitment to the coalition. The "easy" legitimation attained by the KKE, in contrast, allowed it to cross the objective threshold without delay or problems, but at the cost of rendering stillborn the process of ideological and organizational overhaul. Paradoxically, the rapid acceptance of the communists by the other political forces allowed the conservatives in the KKE to avoid the many problems posed by ideological transformation and led them to consider Synaspismos in purely instrumental terms. Under such circumstances, the rift with the progressive group, which had assigned the task of modernizing the party to Synaspismos, became inevitable.

Looking for a Place in Society

So far, we have seen how the communist parties of southern Europe adapted to the consolidation of their respective democratic regimes. We shall now focus on their capacity to adapt to social change. The structure of social stratification in each of our countries has profoundly changed over the past twenty years, albeit not at the same pace. The working class, that is, agricultural laborers and industrial workers, has shrunk; new sections of the middle class have emerged; education has become far more widespread; and increasing incomes and free time, coupled with changes in values and needs ever more closely aligned to the postmaterialist model, have redefined the characteristics of the social base from which the four parties draw their members and voters. Let us begin by assessing the extent to which social change has led these parties to distance themselves from the traditional model of a communist party, centered internally and organizationally on "democratic centralism" and externally and electorally on the class cleavage.

The Internal Dimension: Organization

Communist parties have traditionally been organized in accord with the Leninist model. This entails a huge apparatus of full-time party functionaries and adherence to the principles of the fundamental "law" of democratic centralism, which prohibits factions: "the ban on faction . . . is . . . the master rule of the rules of the game," Ronald Tiersky asserts (1985, 66). Thus, one indicator of the transformation of the southern European communist parties is the extent to which they allow for the existence of recognized factions inside the party and, especially, its leadership groups. On this point, the PCP and the KKE differ from the PCI and the PCE.

The PCP and the KKE still base their internal organization on democratic centralism and base recruitment to leadership positions on loyalty to the incumbent leaders: indeed, career advancement is possible only if one conforms to the positions of the party leadership. Organized factions are neither allowed nor tolerated. Quite often, even a mere tendency to support political lines other than those of the dominant coalition is inadmissible (see Panebianco 1982, 87). In Portugal, an opposition group asked that Cunhal accept democracy in the aftermath of the PCP's electoral defeat in 1987, and it raised its voice again following the eastern European upheaval of 1989–91. But that group was weak and fragmented, because the party's internal rules did not allow it to organize and gain access to resources. Indeed, it was easy for the leadership to eliminate critics, either by forcing them to resign or simply by expelling them. Things were not much different in the KKE, where the same dominant coalition that had organized the party's entry into Synaspismos quickly and easily withdrew from that alliance and expelled any member who favored remaining within the coalition. In both cases, the rigid structure of the organization was linked to the past history of the incumbent leaders. By the time of the Portuguese revolution, for example, the PCP's leaders had already been in charge of the party for three or four decades. Most of this time had been spent underground, subject to the iron rules of secrecy and discipline, and in the absence of internal debate. Some analysts maintain that this experience of clandestinity explains the extraordinary cohesion of the PCP leaders, as well as their peculiar inhibition against dissent and differences of opinion (Pereira 1990). Leadership stability was also preserved by a policy of gradual and controlled replacement that did not change until the end of the 1980s. It was only after 1988 that the older leaders were replaced by members in their forties who had joined the party between the mid 1960s and 1974, and who had, subsequently, risen rapidly to the top, thanks to the party's expansion in the revolutionary period. It is worth stressing that the generational turnover did not lead to any political rift. This was partly because the "funnel-shaped" structure of recruitment ensured that no member of the opposition would be promoted, and partly because Cunhal (who had led the party since 1940, as secretary-general since 1961) kept a tight control over the whole process. It was only in December 1992, that, at the age of 79 and with the turnover completed, he relinquished his office to a successor, Carlos Carvalhas, while retaining control over the PCP by occupying the new post of president of the party's National Council.

The KKE was also led (until 1987) by a coalition of rather elderly men who had emerged in the 1940s, at the time of the resistance and the Civil War. The cohesion of the Greek leadership arose not only from past experience but also from the 1968 split, which took the Eurocommunists out of the party, led to the founding of the KKE-Es, and enhanced the KKE's ideological homogeneity. The secretary-general, Harilaos Florakis, two years older than Cunhal, had been in office since 1973. Only in 1987 did a few younger members join the older leaders. Not surprisingly, their political views were not too different from those of the older cohort: indeed, one of these, Aleka Papariga, was soon to become the leader of the orthodox wing of the party. Nonetheless, there was somewhat more generational difference within the KKE leadership than in the PCP, differentiating the generation of the 1940s, which became active during the resistance and the Civil War, from the "generation of the Polytechnic," which came into the party after the 1967 military coup d'état. In the second half of the 1980s, when Gorbachev's reforms received the support of the Polytechnic generation, the generational cleavage became a political one and disrupted the unity of the KKE leadership (see Smith 1992).

The PCE and the PCI proved to be more adaptable. The Spanish party was less influenced by the Leninist organizational matrix. Thus, although the rules of democratic centralism were faithfully reproduced in the party statutes until 1991, adherence to these rules was more formal than effective, and their nonapplication was tacitly recognized, to the extent that, in 1988, the Control and Guarantees Committee described democratic centralism as "a cluster of ineffectual principles."[16] In the PCI, democratic centralism was slowly abandoned over a decade. In the 1979 party statute, it was referred to as a "method rather than a principle." In 1989, the Eighteenth Congress did away with democratic centralism, granting members rights that implicitly opened the way to the formation of factions, a practice explicitly recognized in 1991 after the birth of the Partito Democratico della Sinistra.

To be sure, differing political positions reflected in more or less organized tendencies had always existed within the leaderships of the two parties. One need only point to the *gerardistas* and the *carrillistas* in the PCE, or to the traditional distinction between center, right, and left in the PCI. Nonetheless, it was only in the late 1980s, when the two parties were decisively transformed, that these tendencies began to clash and organize themselves as factions. In Spain, the group supporting renewal (which included members of both the PCE and the Partido de Acción Socialista, along with independents and others) demanded that the PCE be disbanded, and set up an organized faction, Nueva Izquierda, to defend its program. This forced the leadership, in May 1992, to allow the existence of factions within the coalition, although not within the PCE. Factions were also formally recognized in the constitution of the PDS (Ignazi 1992, 96–99).

It is not possible to write about communist organization without referring to the parties' capacity to recruit and retain members. As can be seen in Table 8.1, all four of these southern European communist parties experienced declines in membership during the 1980s, some variations notwithstanding. The two parties that underwent the most extensive adaptation and changed their political line most radically, the PDS and IU, were able to stabilize their membership levels by the mid 1990s. In contrast, parties that restricted their processes of adaptation and continued to adhere to the classic model of organization

Table 8.1 Membership in the Italian, Portuguese, and Spanish Communist Parties

	Italy		Portugal	Spain	
Year	PCI/PDS	RC	PCP	PCE/IU	PSUC/IC
1974 (July)			14,593		
1975			112,000		
1976	1,814,317		115,346		
1977	1,814,154		142,512	191,607	29,850
1978	1,790,450		157,569	156,184	24,852
1979	1,759,295		164,713		
1980	1,751,323		187,018		21,807
1981	1,714,052			132,069	
1982	1,673,751				6,645
1983	1,635,264		200,753	82,877	6,241
1984	1,619,940				7,014
1985	1,595,668			67,808	6,533
1986	1,551,576				4,031
1987	1,508,140			62,342	
1988	1,462,281		199,275		
1989	1,421,230				
1990	1,319,905				10,788
1991	989,708	112,278		40/55,000	
1992	769,944	119,094	163,506	57,303	10,000
1993	690,414	121,055			
1994	700,000	120,000		52,711	10,000
1996			140,000		

Sources: For Italy 1976–90, official data published in *L'Unità,* January 31, 1991; 1991–93, Organization Department of the PDS; 1994, *L'Unità,* February 9, 1995; RC, *Politica in Italia.* Edizione 1995 (Bologna: Il Mulino, 1995). For Spain 1977–85, official data published by the PCE; 1987, *El País,* February 19, 1988; for 1991, first figure is official PCE figure, second figure is more realistic estimate provided by Nueva Izquierda; IU data from IU presidency; PSUC and IC data provided by the organization department of the PSUC/IC. For Portugal, official data published by the PCP.

continued to suffer declining memberships. The Portuguese party's inflated official data (which include individuals who had not renewed their membership cards) conceal a substantial decline in the 1980s, most likely to about 58,000 dues-paying members by 1992 (Bosco 1993, 375–79). And in the case of Greece, reliable estimates show that the KKE dropped from 100,000 members in the mid 1980s to 25,000 five years later (Kapetanyannis 1987, 166; Vasileiou 1991).

The External Dimension: The Search for New Voters

To what extent has the composition of the communist parties' electoral support changed over time in accord with the transformation of social structures in southern Europe? Lack of strictly comparable data makes a response to this question somewhat difficult, but analysis of the social makeup of these four communist voter bases will facilitate an understanding of the extent to which these parties were able to adapt to the profound transformations of these societies over the past few decades.

The Partito Comunista Italiano and Partito Democratico della Sinistra. During the 1970s and 1980s, voters supporting the PCI progressively came to resemble the Italian population as a whole. As the survey data presented in Table 8.2 indicate, between 1968 and 1987, the traditional overrepresentation of workers in the PCI's electoral base had been significantly reduced, as had the underrepresentation of other occupational categories. Particularly noteworthy is the increase, during the 1970s, in the number of white-collar employees, teachers, and technicians who voted for the PCI. These figures underscore the success of the PCI in attracting electoral support from the middle classes, culminating in a major electoral advance in 1976 (see Corbetta et al. 1988, 391–95). The increasing similarity between communist and other voters is confirmed by the former's mean position on the left-right self-placement scale. From the late 1970s to the end of the following decade, PCI voters shifted toward the center-left of the spectrum, moving from a mean position of 1.7 on a ten-point scale in 1978 to 2.8 in 1987. During that same period, the mean position of the Italian electorate as a whole remained almost the same, shifting from 4.5 to 4.8 (Mannheimer 1990, 55).

Since the birth of the Partito Democratico della Sinistra, there has been an increasing convergence between PDS voters and the national electorate. Some dissimilarities in the categories shown in tables 8.2 and 8.3 notwithstanding, data collected in 1994 indicate that the overrepresentation of workers has declined further, while white-collar

Table 8.2 Occupations of PCI Voters, 1968–1987 (%)

	1968	1978–79	1987
Employers, executives, and professionals	−4.4%	−3.7%	−2.7%
Shopkeepers, artisans	−4.7	−5.6	−2.6
Employees, teachers, and technicians	−11.4	−2.5	−2.5
Industrial workers	+17.5	+14.5	+8.5
Farmers	−3.1	−2.8	−3.0

Source: Mannheimer 1990, 56.

Note: The table shows the differences between the PCI voters and the whole electorate.

Table 8.3 Occupations of PDS Voters, 1994 (%)

	PDS Voters	Difference from the Italian electorate*
Employers and professionals	1.3%	−0.9%
Shopkeepers	9.8	−1.8
Executives and employees	22.3	+5.6
Industrial workers	25.8	+7.4
Students	6.0	−0.4
Housewives	12.0	−7.7
Pensioners	18.1	−1.5
Unemployed	4.7	−0.7

Source: Gabriele Calvi and Andrea Vannucci, *L'elettore sconosciuto: Analisi socioculturale e segmentazione degli orientamenti politici nel 1994* (Bologna: Il Mulino, 1995), 24.

*The differences between PDS voters and the entire electorate, by occupation.

workers are, for the first time, overrepresented. The PCI/PDS has been able to attract the white-collar and managerial classes in huge numbers, while retaining its solid base among industrial workers.

One facet of the electoral base of the PCI/PDS, however, shows some erosion. As can be seen in Table 8.4, the PDS in 1994, like the PCI in the 1980s, seemed unable to attract the young. When one notes that in 1975, 48 percent of those who voted communist were under thirty, whereas those over fifty were a mere 19.7 percent of its voters, it becomes obvious that the party's electoral base has aged (Sani 1981, 115).

The Partido Comunista de España and Izquierda Unida. The PCE is the party that best adapted to changes in the social structure. Thanks to the establishment of Izquierda Unida, it managed to attract a relatively young, educated, urban middle-class voter base. A comparison of PCE voters' in 1979 with those of the IU in 1993 bears out this point. The PCE always had large numbers of young voters. In 1979, 36 per-

Table 8.4 Changes in the Age of PCI/PDS Voters, 1975–1994 (%)

Age Groups	1975	1987	1994*	Party Voters in Age Group, 1994
18–25	+13.3%	−2.9%	−4.0%	10.4%
26–35	+0.9	+2.2	−1.2	18.4
36–45	−2.4	−0.2	+5.3	22.5
46–55	−3.9	+3.6	+0.3	15.8
56–65	−4.7	−0.2	−0.9	13.7
66+	−3.1	−3.0	+0.7	19.3

Sources: 1975 and 1987, Mannheimer 1990, 57; 1994, CIRM exit poll of March 27/28, 1994, based on a sample of 20,613 interviews.

*For 1994, the age groups are 18/24, 25/34, 35/44, etc. The table shows the differences between PDS voters and the whole electorate, by age groups, and, for 1994, the composition by age of the party electorate as well. The signs + and − respectively show overrepresentation and underrepresentation of PCI voters compared with the national electorate.

Table 8.5 Age Distribution of PCP Voters, 1991, and IU Voters, 1993 (%)

	Partido Comunista Português		Izquierda Unida	
Age Groups	PCP Voters	Difference from Portuguese Electorate	IU Voters	Difference from Spanish Electorate
18–24	8.6%	−6.1%	23.1%	+7.3%
25–34	16.4	−2.7	27.9	+7.5
35–44	26.2	+8.6	19.4	+1.7
45–54	11.6	−3.8	14.1	−0.7
55–64			9.3	−5.7
65+			6.4	−9.9
55+	37.2	+4.1		

Sources: For Portugal, Bacalhau 1994, 177; for Spain, Centro de Investigaciones Sociológicas, *Estudio n. 2061, postelectoral,* June 1993 (5,001 interviews); for the comparison with the whole electorate, CIS, *Estudio n. 2108, postelectoral,* June 1994 (2,500 interviews).

cent of its voters were under thirty (as compared with only 25 percent for the PSOE). Another third (34.5 percent) were between thirty and forty-nine, and the remaining 29.4 percent were older (Linz et al. 1981, 446). Fifteen years later (see Table 8.5), Izquierda Unida supporters were still very young on average. IU voters are also highly educated, as revealed in a June 1993 poll (CIS survey #2061): university graduates, 11 percent of the Spanish population, make up 19.8 percent of the IU's electoral support.

Lastly, even an examination of the occupations of Izquierda Unida

Table 8.6 IU Voters by Occupation, 1993 (%)

	IU Voters	Difference from Spanish Electorate
Executives and professionals	3.2%	+0.3%
Technicians and mid-level officials	9.5	+4.5
Small employers	4.2	−2.2
Farmers	0.3	−1.0
Employees*	14.3	+3.2
Workers	15.6	+4.6
Pensioners	7.7	−9.7
Unemployed	12.7	+2.1
Students	12.7	+5.2
Housewives	13.3	−8.8
Others	6.4	+1.7

Source: CIS, *Estudio n. 2061, postelectoral,* June 1993 (5,001 interviews).

*Employees = clerical workers or white-collar employees.

voters shows how adaptable the coalition has been. As can be seen in Table 8.6, in 1993, technicians, white-collar workers, professionals, and managers were overrepresented among IU voters. Put otherwise, between 1979 and 1993, the relationship between voters working in industry and in the service sector had been inverted: 32.3 percent and 18.9 percent respectively in 1979, compared with 15.6 percent and 31.2 percent in 1993. Like the PDS, the IU was not particularly attractive to those detached from the production process, such as pensioners and housewives, although these categories were more numerous in the Italian party than in the Spanish coalition. Finally, as with the PCI/PDS, the political attitudes of PCE/IU voters have become more moderate (moving from a mean position on the ten-point left-right continuum of 2.3 in 1982 to 2.9 in 1993) and are now closer to those of the average voter (whose mean position was 4.8 in 1994).[17]

All these data confirm the enhanced capacity of the IU, compared to the PCE, to attract broad-based electoral support that does not only reflect class cleavage. Furthermore, recent studies have shown that the IU is more successful in attracting the votes of the postmaterialists. José Ramón Montero and Mariano Torcal (1992 and 1994) have calculated that 39 percent of those who voted for the coalition can be called postmaterialists, as against 19 percent for the PSOE and 13 percent for the PP.

The Partido Comunista Português. The PCP proved to be less adaptable to social change than the PCI and the PCE/IU. Its electoral performance improved until 1979, remained unchanged from 1980 to

1983, and then went into a steady decline; the party lost 51 percent of its voters between 1983 and 1991. A quick glance at interparty flows reveals that this loss was from a stagnant electoral base, without vote transfers from other parties. That said, it is important to understand the characteristics of this shrinking electoral base.

In Portugal, the popular mobilization of the revolutionary period and the political role played by the PCP in promoting nationalizations and agrarian reform helped bring about the party's solid electoral and organizational entrenchment in the industrial districts of Lisbon and Setúbal, and in the great latifundia areas of Alentejo and Ribatejo. The loyalties thus created allowed the party to construct a solid base of support—the "red zone"—that in subsequent years was to decline only very slowly. Data for 1983, the high point in the PCP's electoral performance, prove that its electoral support was based on class cleavages. Almost 44 percent of the communist vote was made up of agricultural laborers and industrial workers, both skilled and unskilled. The national average for the same categories was 20 percent. Conversely, middle-class employees, and upper-middle-class entrepreneurs and managers were underrepresented (by 4 percent [Bacalhau 1989, 252]).

In the 1980s, there were profound changes in the social and productive structure of the country. Massive urbanization and the transfer of large numbers into the service sector reduced the PCP's privileged electoral reservoir of agricultural and industrial laborers. In 1981, these sectors represented 43 percent of the Portuguese active population. By 1992, this figure had been reduced to 28.7 percent. Conversely, the middle and upper middle classes, made up of the self-employed, professionals, technicians, managers, and entrepreneurs, grew at a bewildering pace, jumping from 19.5 percent to 37.5 percent of the working population, while the number of white-collar workers remained steady (Almeida et al. 1994, 326). In short, these changes resulted in an increase in the very occupational groups that the PCP had traditionally found difficult to attract.

During the early 1980s, the communist leaders were well aware that the party's weak points were the middle classes and the young. To attract these groups, they devised two similar strategies: rather than reformulating their political message, they sought in the Partido Renovador Democrático a political ally likely to appeal to voters the PCP could not attract on its own. As we have already seen, this strategy required the PRD to win over middle-class voters who were leaving the Partido Socialista during the 1985 elections. But the PRD fell apart within two years. The same strategy was used to attract the young. This time, the PCP organized a Green party—the Partido Ecologista "Os Verdes"—which, from 1987 on, became its ally in the Coligação Democrática Unitária (Unitary Democratic Coalition), or CDU. This proved to be another failure. The number of young voters remained limited, and the PCP's extremely tight control over Os Verdes created a split in the new party and revealed its artificial nature (Stock 1991).

The crisis that hit the PCP after its 1987 defeat was a reaction to the party's inability to adjust to the transformation of Portuguese society. It is, therefore, hardly surprising that, in the ensuing debate, this inability emerged as the internal opposition's main theme. The critics were forced out, however, and the issue of how to reach out to the middle classes was shelved. In 1992, the new party program added a few lines on the role of the middle classes, but, as Luis Sá, a leading member of the PCP, put it in a 1994 interview, "the effort the party made to attract the middle classes was not great enough, nor wide-ranging enough, nor as effective as it should have been. . . . Thus the PCP continues to lose industrial workers and agricultural laborers and does not overcome the challenge [posed by] the development of a service sector and the depopulation of the Alentejo."

In the first half of the 1990s, most of the PCP's electoral support came from workers in the Lisbon industrial belt and from rural laborers in the Alentejo (Bacalhau 1994, 116). As Table 8.7 shows, the self-employed were still underrepresented. On the other hand, the unemployed, housewives, and pensioners made up almost half the PCP's electoral support. As for age groups (see Table 8.5), the PCP continues to have trouble recruiting the young, but is well represented among those aged between thirty-five and forty-four—who were aged between sixteen and twenty-five in 1974 and have stayed faithful to the left—and those over fifty-five. Lastly, the political attitudes of communist voters did not approximate those of the average voter. If any-

Table 8.7 PCP Voters by Occupation, 1994 (%)

	PCP Voters	Difference from Portuguese Electorate
Self-employed	6.0	−7.0
Dependent workers	41.0	+3.0
Unemployed	9.0	+3.0
Pensioners	28.0	+7.0
Students	7.0	+3.0
Housewives	11.0	−1.0
Others	1.0	−2.0

Source: Villaverde Cabral 1995, 181.

thing, the distance became greater, unlike in Spain and Italy. From 1986 to 1991, the mean position of Portugal's communist voters on the left-right continuum remained unchanged at 2.7, while the Portuguese electorate consolidated its center-right position, moving from 5.3 to 5.7 (Bacalhau 1989, 253, and 1994, 58 and 136).

The Kommounistiko Komma Elladas/Synaspismos. The available information on the KKE's social makeup is scant. Many observers have noted the difference between the KKE and the KKE-Es, which always attracted very young voters from the urban middle class and did best among those under twenty-five. The KKE's electoral base is more balanced. Although its best results are in cities, it also has a solid base in rural areas. As for age, data for the 1985 elections indicate that its best results were among the young—those aged between eighteen and thirty-four—and among those between sixty-five and sixty-nine (Varvaroussis 1988; also Kapetanyannis 1987; Featherstone 1987). It also has strong working-class support, although this is hard to quantify (Achimastos 1990, 353–57).

Right up to the end of the 1980s, the KKE's electoral support was centered in the working class, while the KKE-Es voters were mainly of middle-class origin (see Table 8.8). From the point of view of adaptation to social change, therefore, the creation of the Synaspismos was an astute move, since it allowed the KKE to attract support from the upper middle classes—a feat it could not pull off on its own. A study of the votes cast in the municipalities of the huge Athens B electoral district during the three elections of 1989–90 bears out this interpretation. In June 1989, the newly formed Synaspismos achieved its best results in districts with a relatively young, highly educated population, usually with well-paid jobs in the service sector. These were modern, dynamic voters and, for that very reason, quite volatile. This volatility accounts for their loss to Synaspismos between November 1989 and April 1990. On the other hand, the coalition lost fewer votes in dis-

Table 8.8 Communist Parties' Electoral Support by Social Class, 1987–1990 (%)

	1987		1990
	KKE	KKE-Es	Synaspismos
Upper	11.3%	28.1%	18.2%
Middle	40.5	50.0	48.7
Lower	48.2	21.9	33.1

Source: Vasileiou 1991, 24.

tricts where the voters were mostly working-class (Manolopoulos and Niarchos 1991).

The capacity of Synaspismos to appeal to different voters from those who traditionally supported the KKE emerges quite clearly from an examination of the political attitudes of its electoral base. The mean self-positioning of communist voters (KKE + KKE-Es and SYN) shifted from 2.1 in May 1985 to 3.1 in October 1989, whereas the attitudes of the Greek electorate as a whole stayed firmly anchored midway along the left-right continuum, moving from 5.4 to 5.6 (Voulgaris 1990, 153–54). Hence, in less than five years, largely because of the formation of the coalition, the supporters of the communist left in Greece underwent a process of moderation unequaled in southern Europe. Synaspismos did not consolidate, however, and once the communists left, it is quite likely that the two parties' respective shares of the vote approximated what the KKE and the KKE-Es individual shares had been earlier.

In adapting to democratic consolidation, the PCI and the PCE were thus the two parties that underwent the most drastic changes. This adaptation increased their capacity to adjust to social change and to secure bases of support throughout the electorate. In so doing, they were able in the early 1990s to reverse the declining trend from which they had been suffering. Conversely, the PCP and the KKE, which sought to combine adaptation and readaptation to democracy with as little modification in their identities as possible, found it very difficult to keep pace with social change. In both cases, ideology has continued to weigh heavily upon the parties, in the process compromising their chances of electoral success and forcing them to seek refuge in their traditional voter bases.

Looking for a Place in the Party System

To what extent did the communist parties' adaptation to democratic consolidation and their subsequent organizational, ideological, and strategic transformations enable them to reposition themselves within their respective party systems? Let us begin to answer this question by examining the political trajectory of the Partido Comunista de España. As we have seen, the PCE had already been legitimated as a proregime force by the second post-Franco general election in 1979. Yet the party was unable to achieve its objective of entering a coalition government. The PCE's inability to join the government was due, therefore, to contingencies of competition rather than to the existence of an inner system created to marginalize the communists in the political game. To understand how these contingencies of competition arose and evolved over time, we need to distinguish among three phases, characterized by differing competitive contingencies that excluded the communists from government.

In the first phase (1977–81), Spain had a moderate multiparty system and the PSOE was still in opposition. The legitimation of the PCE provoked an intense debate within the ranks of the socialists over the type of relationship to maintain with the communists. After the April 1979 local elections, the PCE and the PSOE held power jointly in many municipalities, and part of the socialist leadership envisaged a similar alliance at the national level. However, two convulsive socialist congresses, held in May and September 1979, secured the victory of those supporting the strategy of moderation (abandonment of Marxism) and of independence (rejection of alliances) chosen by Felipe González. This development constituted a defeat for the left wing of the party, which favored an agreement with the PCE. Carrillo's proposal for a government of "democratic concentration" was never realized. Despite the PSOE's decision to block a left-wing coalition for the time being, the electoral strength of the socialist and communist parties after the 1979 elections (30.5 percent and 10.8 percent respectively) seemed to leave such a possibility open for the future.

The 1982 elections inaugurated the second political phase, which was to last until the eve of the 1993 elections. The PSOE's absolute majority in parliament established a predominant-party system that, with a few changes, was to endure even beyond the 1986 and 1989 elections. These parliamentary majorities eliminated the likelihood of a government agreement with the communists. Instead, the PCE/IU became a minor force in the opposition, trailing the right-wing AP/PP, which, throughout this period, held on to a stable support of roughly 25–26 percent of the vote.

This static party-system configuration conceals the effects of significant electoral shifts within the left, however, which increasingly converted the IU into a redoubtable competitor. Following the debacle of 1982, communist electoral support stabilized substantially, while, at the same time, the number of socialist voters abandoning the governing party to vote for the PCE/IU rose from virtually none in 1982 to 2.5 percent in 1986, and to 8.7 percent in 1989. By the end of the 1980s, over a third of the IU's voters (35 percent in 1986 and 36 percent in 1989) had abandoned the governing socialist party. This progressively transformed the composition of the IU's voter base, as described above. The decade following the 1982 elections thus witnessed a gradual but continuous readjustment within the ranks of the left, while the IU steadily closed the gap with the "decreasingly predominant" PSOE (see Sani 1986, 10, 13; CIS surveys #1543 [1986] and #1842 [1989]).

Three factors ensured the continuation of this competitive relationship: the governing difficulties experienced by the PSOE, the reorganization of the PCE, and the stability of the vote for the right. As the difficulties of the socialist government increased—involving economic restructuring and crisis, high unemployment, and corruption charges—and conflict between the PSOE government and the trade unions multiplied (culminating in the general strike of December 14, 1988), the number of discontented voters who shifted to the IU increased. This was both because these voters agreed with the issue positions of the IU, which often sided with the unions, and out of a desire to "punish" the PSOE with a *voto de castigo* (punitive vote). Improvement in the IU's electoral fortunes was also facilitated by the fact that the PCE had successfully addressed the severe crisis of the early 1980s. The establishment of the IU and the subsequent consolidation of its organization, program, and leadership—with the party's leader, Julio Anguita, rapidly acquiring popular appeal—were essential in transforming the PCE and its allies into the preferred choice of discontented socialist voters. The stability of the balance of power between the PSOE and the AP/PP constituted the third element necessary for the continued maintenance of these competitive relations.

A third phase, characterized by an electoral takeoff by the conservative Partido Popular, began with the elections of June 6, 1993. The party received 34.8 percent of the vote, just 4 percentage points behind the PSOE, which obtained 38.8 percent and 159 seats. The end of absolute majorities and the new balance of power between the PSOE and the PP proved that the predominant-party system was giving way to a bipolar one, in which the PP already constituted a governing alternative (see Vallés 1994; Wert et al. 1993). This transformation allowed the PSOE to mobilize the whole left wing to prevent the right from gaining power. Hence, despite widespread discontent over how the socialists had governed, the *voto en contra* (against the PP) prevailed over the *voto de castigo* (against the PSOE) [Arango and Díez 1993].

This development halted the flow of votes from the PSOE to the IU: in 1993, for the first time since 1982, the electoral loyalty of IU voters declined (from 91 percent to 78 percent), and the number of IU voters who shifted to the PSOE increased from 3.4 percent to 14.2 percent. At the same time, the number of socialist voters who transferred their vote to the IU fell from 8.7 percent to 4.9 percent (CIS survey #2061 [1993]). The net effect was that the IU received the same number of votes (9.6 percent of the total) as in 1989 and eighteen parliamentary seats, despite earlier optimistic expectations of continued electoral gains. Izquierda Unida's performance was further damaged both by its electoral message—which attempted to identify the PSOE with the PP and the neoliberal right, thereby undermining prospects for an alliance with the PSOE—and by a heart attack suffered by Julio Anguita in the midst of the election campaign.

The PSOE's loss of its parliamentary majority forced it, however, to seek an agreement with other political forces. In the end, an agreement was reached with the Catalan party Convergència i Unió (CiU) and the Partido Nacionalista Vasco (PNV), but, for the first time, the IU was also asked to take part in the formal consultations for the formation of a government. These discussions did not produce an agreement, in part because the only groups that really wanted it were the modernizing current of the IU, the Nueva Izquierda faction, and the left wing of the PSOE, Izquierda Socialista, while the leadership of the PSOE opposed it. Yet the very fact that these talks were held, and that Izquierda Unida was, at least in principle, considered as a possible government partner meant that the IU was, for future purposes, endowed with a coalition potential that it had not possessed before. The end of the predominant-party system gave the IU, which by 1993 had become the third-largest group in the Congress of Deputies, more political weight than it had had in the past. Its enhanced role in the party system became clear after its success in the 1994 European elections, when its share of the vote rose to 13.4 percent, compared to 6.2 percent in 1989, giving it nine as opposed to four seats in the European Parliament. Similar improvements were registered in the 1994 Basque and Andalusian elections and in the 1995 elections for the Catalan parliament (in which the Iniciativa per Catalunya, the IU's Catalan partner, increased its share from 6.5 percent to 9.7 percent of the vote and from seven to eleven seats) and for municipal governments and those of the other autonomous regions.

The IU leadership moved quickly to take advantage of its enhanced political position. After the European elections, Anguita launched the slogan that the coalition must "overtake" the PSOE. In the Andalusian regional parliament, where its twenty seats had made it the decisive partner for any coalition, Izquierda Unida refused to join the socialists in government and instead reached an agreement with the PP that gave it the position of speaker of the house. Outflanking the PSOE on the left by claiming that the socialist party was no longer distinguishable from the PP did not, however, prove a winning strategy. Notwithstanding its previous electoral gains, support for the IU rose less than forecast in the March 1996 general elections, and it obtained only a disappointing 10.6 percent of the votes and twenty-one seats. As in 1993, a polarized electoral campaign against the conservative PP allowed González to mobilize left-wing voters. Concerned with the antisocialist stance of the IU leadership, many IU voters chose to support the PSOE as a means of defeating the right. The IU's strategy led the coalition to a resounding defeat in Andalusia, where early regional elections were held simultaneously with the national ones. The IU slumped from 19.2 percent to 14.1 percent of the votes, retaining only thirteen of its twenty seats, while the PSOE rose from 38.6 percent to 43.8 percent of the votes (Wert 1996).

The elections produced a new political situation. To be sure, the PP was for the first time in power, albeit without an overall majority of votes (it received 38.8 percent). The PSOE, on the other hand, was back in opposition, but with its electoral base almost intact (37.5 percent, as opposed to 38.8 percent in 1993). This turn of events triggered a lively debate within the IU. Albeit with different emphases, the modernizers in Nueva Izquierda, the Iniciativa per Catalunya, and the Madrid federation, as well as members of Anguita's entourage, all pointed out the necessity for a dialogue with the PSOE. Following an initial phase of uncertainty, during which Nueva Izquierda changed its status from a faction to a political party within the IU coalition, the leaders of the PSOE and IU held two meetings in July 1996. These culminated in the decision to appoint a commission made up of representatives from the two parties to institutionalize the dialogue between the IU and the PSOE.

It is important to stress that the formation of a PP cabinet has meant that the leadership of left-wing opposition to the government has passed to the PSOE. Consequently, for the first time since its establishment, the IU has lost the advantageous position that gave it most of the *voto de castigo* cast against the PSOE.

The next general elections, held on March 12, 2000, showed that in the new political situation it has become virtually impossible for the coalition to defend its electoral base and compete for new votes. The PP received 45.2 percent of the valid vote and the absolute majority of seats, while the PSOE remained an opposition party with a reduced electoral base (34.7 percent). IU lost over half of its electoral support, obtaining 5.5 percent of the votes and eight deputies, as opposed to 10.6 percent and twenty-one seats in 1996. These results not only reversed the positive electoral trend of the coalition but represented a defeat that seemed to take the communist left back to the electoral collapse of the early 1980s.

Paradoxically, Izquierda Unida's electoral debacle smashed the first government agreement signed by the PSOE and the communist left since 1977. According to the agreement, in case of electoral success, the two left forces would have formed a joint executive on the basis of a shared political agenda. Such a pact was not enough, however, to mobilize the electorate of the left, a large part of which decided to abstain. First of all, the agreement had been hurriedly reached about a month before the elections, too late to persuade the potential voters that it was a strategic choice and not a political expedient to stop the foreseeable electoral decline of the left. Furthermore, the agreement had been signed on behalf of Izquierda Unida by Francisco Frutos, secretary-general of the PCE. Frutos, who had temporarily replaced Julio Anguita, incapacitated by a heart operation, had a hard time overturning Anguita's antisocialist strategy, which Frutos himself had strongly supported in the recent past. Third, in 2000, IU had lost the pluralistic image conveyed in the previous elections, inasmuch as the party of the modernizers, the Partido Democrático de la Nueva Izquierda, had been expelled from the coalition by Anguita and his supporters in 1997. Finally, the 2000 defeat had been preceded by the electoral slump of the coalition in the 1999 municipal and European elections, when IU received only 5.7 percent of the European vote (losing five deputies out of nine) and 6.5 percent of the local vote. In the aftermath of the 1999 defeat, the coalition rejected Anguita's resignation, thus missing the opportunity to promote a much-needed process of change before the national election. Such a change has now become unavoidable if IU wants to survive in the Spanish party system.

Portugal. The status of the Partido Comunista Português within the Portuguese party system is quite different. In examining how interparty competition and the ways in which the PCP was excluded have evolved in that country from 1976 until the present, it is, again, useful to distinguish among three specific phases. During the first decade of the new Portuguese democracy (1976–85), proregime political forces set up an inner party system that excluded the PCP from government. This was a period of high political instability. No legislature completed its full term, and there were nine governments in as many years. Further complicating this picture were serious economic problems and continuous debate over the revision of the constitution. Despite these difficulties, the PS, the PSD, and the CDS redefined their competitive strategies to isolate the PCP and exclude it from decision making. As a result, the PS ignored the absolute left-wing majority of seats it gained together with the PCP in the 1976 and 1983 elections, opting instead to form minority cabinet or coalition governments with the CDS or the PSD. Furthermore, the PS, the PSD, and the CDS reached an agreement to revise the constitution in which they made no concessions to the communists. The political marginalization of the PCP did not, however, lead to its electoral marginalization. Until the 1983 elections, the party kept expanding, and it had the most loyal followers in the whole political system. Thus, the PCP's isolation did not result in a loss of votes to the socialist party. According to Mário Bacalhau, in 1983, the PCP retained the support of 89 percent of its 1976 voters, only 6 percent of whom crossed over to the PS (Bacalhau 1989, 246). The radical attitudes of PCP voters and their persistent diffidence vis-à-vis Mário Soares, who was responsible for the anticommunist offensive during the transition, curbed electoral volatility in the left block. On the other hand, the fact that there was hardly any transfer of votes from the PCP to the PS reinforced the minority position of the PS and forced it to join politically unhomogeneous coalitions.

In the second phase, 1985–87, the birth of the Partido Renovador Democrático modified the Portuguese four-party format, triggering a crisis of the inner party system. Characterized as it was by a strong antiparty appeal, it was difficult for the PRD to align wholeheartedly with the parties that had shared government responsibility since 1976. The PCP's leadership had hoped that the PRD would help the communists to emerge from their isolation, but in reality, the arrival of the PRD had contradictory consequences. On the one hand, the PS, the PCP, and the PRD formed an opposition that held an absolute majority of seats in parliament and rejected various bills proposed by Cavaco Silva's minority government. The influence of the PCP increased commensurately, as it became a necessary ally for the PS and the PRD. In so doing, it also helped weaken the inner system. On the other hand, with its wavering strategy and deep internal cleavages, the PRD was unable to transform the agreements that linked the opposition parties into a government alliance. It therefore frustrated the PCP's hopes of a government made up of socialists and *renovadores* with external support from the communists. In short, the PRD's difficulties prevented a crisis of the inner system from coming to a head and, from 1987 on, contributed to the redefinition of that system.

In the most recent period (1987 to the present), the absolute parliamentary majority secured by the PSD in the 1987 elections transformed the Portuguese party system into a predominant-party one. In an attempt to reabsorb the electoral support of the two smaller parties, the PSD and the PS both competed for centrist votes, dismissing any form of agreement with either the CDS or the PCP. In this new scenario, the PS tried to reconstruct the inner system in two ways. First, in the discussion of a second revision of the constitution that began after the 1987 election, it demanded that a constructive vote of no confidence be introduced into the constitution. This would have allowed the socialist party to form a minority government without having to bargain for the support of the PCP, since an alternative government could only be set up in the improbable circumstances of an agreement among the PSD, the CDS, and the PCP. In other words, the PS leadership was in search of a mechanism that would make a socialist minority government independent of PCP pressures and demands. The PSD took great care not to concede such an advantage to its principal rival, and the proposal was not approved (see Magalhães 1989, 74–75; Martins 1988, 115–26). Yet it was a sign of the PS's desire to reconstitute the inner system with new characteristics.

The socialist strategy was to compete for votes in the center, while at the same time drawing communist votes. This strategy received a boost from the "unfreezing" of communist electoral support that began in 1985, when many PCP voters backed the PRD in the hope that it would be a reliable ally for their party. At the next elections, however, only a very small share of the vote that had fled to the *renovadores* came back, and the PCP retained only 74 percent of its 1985 voters, while 13.2 percent abstained and another 8.4 percent shifted to the PS (Lima and Fraga 1985 and 1987). Further deterioration was apparent in the 1991 elections, in which the PCP retained a mere 60 percent of its 1987 voters, while the remaining 40 percent moved off in various directions. For the first time, the number of voters who went over to the PS (20.5 percent) was higher than those who abstained (14 percent) (Lima 1991). Naturally, the weakening of the traditional loyalty of communist voters provided the socialists with an incentive to maintain the inner system.

What, then were the consequences of the PCP's democratic legitimation? The most obvious outcome of the progressive acceptance of the communists as a proregime actor was the split in the PS over the strategy the party should adopt toward the PCP. On the one hand, the party secretary, António Guterres—elected in 1992—insisted that the party should compete for PSD votes. In so doing, he refused to contemplate any form of alliance with the PCP. The surveys carried out for the party confirmed that this centripetal strategy would be electorally rewarding. Guterres decided that the party would go it alone at the 1995 general election, and, if it failed to win an absolute majority, would form a minority government.

Other prominent members of the PS, such as the then head of state, Mário Soares, and the mayor of Lisbon, Jorge Sampaio, were not averse to an agreement with the PCP. These sectors of the socialist party were aware of the communist electoral persistence. This had been proved in the December 1993 local elections, when the PCP kept the same number of votes as in 1989 (12.8 percent), while the PS, with 36.1 percent, was unable to get an absolute majority. These sectors of the PS saw the municipal elections as a sign that a left coalition was necessary if they were to defeat the center-right. This position was further confirmed in the 1994 European elections, when the PCP's share of the vote held steady at 11.2 percent.

The parliamentary election of October 1, 1995, returned the socialist party to power after a decade of Cavaco Silva governments. The PS received 43.9 percent of valid ballots, and was just four seats short of an absolute majority in the 230-seat National Assembly. This enabled Guterres to form a minority government, which could enact its legislation with the backing or abstention of either the PCP or the CDS/PP, each of which held fifteen seats, and did not force the socialists to enter into an overall "legislative agreement" with the communists. As Appendix Table A.4 indicates, the PCP obtained 8.6 percent of the valid votes and lost two seats. But it managed to increase its number of votes, and data concerning interparty vote shifts reveal that the PCP had returned to higher levels of voter loyalty, retaining 82 percent of its 1991 voters and losing only 7.3 percent to the PS. In addition, the PCP was able to attract votes from "the abstention party," first-time voters, and former PSD voters, more than offsetting defections by former supporters and helping to reverse the party's electoral fortunes (Lima 1995). These gains were consolidated in subsequent elections. In the January 1996 presidential election, the PCP played a crucial role in ensuring a first-round victory of the socialist candidate, Jorge Sampaio, against the former prime minister, Cavaco Silva. The withdrawal of the PCP candidate a week before the election made it possible to rally communist voters behind Jorge Sampaio, giving him 53.8 percent of the vote.

A PS minority government and a president of the republic well disposed toward the PCP seemed to offer to the communists the opportunity to play more than a marginal role in the Portuguese political system. This new role did not materialize, however, as the PCP continued to behave as an extreme opposition party, voting against the budget bills introduced by Guterres in 1996, 1997, and 1998, opposing the 1997 constitutional reform, and rejecting Portugal's adherence to the European Monetary Union (Cunha 1997; Bosco 1998). Unexpectedly, these opposition policies seemed to pay off in the election of October 10, 1999, as the party improved its vote share to 9 percent (although the number of votes it received actually declined), and increased its parliamentary representation by two seats, to seventeen, making it the third largest party in parliament (see Appendix Table A.4). Furthermore, the interparty vote shifts showed that the PCP was increasing its voter loyalty as well as its ability to attract new votes, both from first-time voters and former socialist voters, the latter accounting for 6.2 percent of the PCP's electoral support in 1999 (Lima 1999). For the communist party, the most important outcome of the election was that the PS, with 44 percent of valid votes, was one seat short of an absolute majority, opening up another opportunity for the PCP to play a relevant role in the political system. To do so, however, the communist leadership must change its political strategy and resume the aborted processes of party change that began at the end of the 1980s.

Greece. The road to political integration followed by the KKE was almost ideal-typical. First, the party accepted the democratic regime; then, within a very short time, it was accepted as a democratic competitor by the proregime forces, and, equally rapidly, it participated in two coalition governments. No other southern European communist party experienced such a smooth road to political integration or was so quickly admitted to participation in a coalition government.

The KKE story underscores the significance of "competition contingencies," that is, the constraints and opportunities relating to interparty competition that so significantly affect the timespan needed for a party to gain recognition as a proregime force and to be included in government. A second crucial explanatory factor was the KKE's participation in Synaspismos. This alliance with other political forces, some more moderate than the communists, allowed the KKE to project a more moderate image and gave greater visibility and credibility to the transformation of the KKE, which facilitated its access to power. The fact that the PCE and PDS also set up left-wing coalitions in Spain and Italy, albeit of a somewhat different kind, points to the importance of this option, not only from a strictly political viewpoint, but also as a way of conveying the idea of change to the electorate.

The subsequent breakdown of this alliance, however, carried considerable costs for both parties. In 1993, the KKE and the remainder of Synaspismos presented separate lists of candidates in a highly polarized election. The party system retained its strongly bipolar structure, with Nea Demokratia and PASOK once again occupying center stage. PASOK's victory brought Andreas Papandreou, now aged seventy-four, back to power. All the parties to the left of PASOK lost votes because of the electoral law and the structure of competition. The KKE, which had reverted to the fundamental principles of Marxism-Leninism, mobilized its traditional electoral support and made use of its strong ideological appeal and organizational resources to counter the growth of Synaspismos. It achieved that narrow goal but paid a considerable price: its electoral performance slipped to 4.5 percent of the vote and nine seats. Synaspismos, on the other hand, which, under the leadership of Maria Damanaki had emerged as a full-fledged party, sought to attract those members of the KKE who had not accepted the party's decision to leave the coalition. The gamble, however, did not pay off. Squeezed between KKE and PASOK, Synaspismos found itself relegated to the uncomfortable position occupied for years by the KKE-Es. It missed by a hair the minimum 3 percent threshold required for entering parliament, and was denied representation (see Appendix Table A.1). This defeat led to a change at the top: at an extraordinary congress held in late 1993, Maria Damanaki resigned and was replaced by Nikos Kostantopoulos (see Dimitras 1994; Mavrogordatos 1994). In the 1994 European elections, when competition was less polarized, both Synaspismos and the KKE increased their shares of the vote, rising to 6.3 percent and two seats each. Nevertheless, these results were lower than their combined total in the 1989 European elections, when the coalition had won 14.3 percent of the votes (Dimitras 1994b). In the 1996 general elections, Synaspismos reentered parliament, having obtained 5.1 percent of the vote and ten seats, while the KKE saw its electoral support rise to 5.6 percent and the number of its seats to eleven. Finally, in the 2000 elections, the KKE maintained almost the same percentage of votes (5.5 and eleven seats), while Synaspismos's share of the popular vote and of parliamentary seats decreased to 3.2 percent and six respectively.

In the end, the KKE had once again become the largest party to the left of PASOK and held on to its communist identity, although it paid a high price for this. Not only did the breakup of the broader Synaspismos coalition reverse many of the gains that won the KKE inclusion in two governments in 1989, but the party has lost nearly half of its electoral support since 1985, and a new leftist party has emerged with almost equal electoral strength.

Italy. Achille Occhetto's aim in radically transforming the PCI and founding a new political party was to "remove all possible alibis" from parties that still invoked the communist threat in order to maintain their electoral support. The PDS was created to put an end to this, to cross the objective threshold of democratic acceptance, and to play a role in government. What the communist leaders failed to anticipate was that the birth of the PDS would coincide with a much broader political transformation, considered by many to be a transition to a new democratic regime (Pasquino 1994; Caciagli et al. 1994). The collapse of "real socialism," the *mani pulite* ("clean hands") judicial inquiries into political corruption and links between the Mafia and politics, and the 1993 electoral law reform radically changed Italy's political system, and especially its party system. Thus, in contrast to the PCE, the PCP, and the KKE, which became proregime forces and were integrated into *preexisting* political systems, the PDS gained legitimation and was integrated into a *new* party system, in which both the parties and their competitive interactions had all changed. Let us examine how these international, judicial, and institutional factors helped transform both the Italian party system and the PDS's position within it.

The collapse of communism in eastern Europe led to the decline of the communist/anticommunist cleavage and weakened the electoral appeal and rewards of the parties that had installed the inner system. This became evident in the 1992 elections, the first after the fall of the Berlin Wall, when the DC and the PSI together lost 5.3 percent of their vote relative to 1987, while the Lega Nord, an outsider party, forcefully affirmed its presence, increasing its share of the vote from 1.3 percent to 8.7 percent. As Appendix Table A.3 shows, even though the PCI's leadership had responded to the collapse of eastern European communism by creating the PDS, the new party's share fell to 16.1 percent, ten percentage points lower than that of the former PCI. At the same time, Rifondazione Comunista won 5.6 percent of the votes and thirty-five seats, signaling that a solid neocommunist group had emerged to the left of the PDS. Taken together, the PDS and RC results were 6.6 percent below the combined vote share of the PCI and the tiny Democrazia Proletaria (which later joined RC) in 1987 (see Daniels 1992; Magna 1992).

The *mani pulite* inquiry, initiated in 1992, was devastating for the PSI and the DC, as well as for the small parties allied to them. The result was a redefinition of political options, because the DC and PSI splintered and disappeared as such from the party system.[18] The *mani pulite* inquiry hardly touched the PDS, however, and had no effect whatsoever on the Movimento Sociale Italiano (MSI), the other party excluded from the inner system. Paradoxically, the *mani pulite* inquiry allowed these two parties to translate their protracted marginalization from government into an important political resource. The electoral consequences of the magistrates' inquiries became evident in the 1993 municipal elections, which decimated the DC, the PSI, and the small centrist parties. The result was an acceleration of the fragmentation and transformation of the old parties, radically changing the Italian political scene.

Finally, the adoption of a new law for local elections and of new laws for the Chamber of Deputies and the Senate signaled the passage, however incomplete, from proportionality to quasi majoritarianism. This led parties to redefine their competitive strategies to profit from the opportunities offered by new rules of the game favoring the formation of broad electoral coalitions.[19] In short, the integration of the PDS took place at a moment of transition resulting from profound changes in the international, electoral, and judicial environments, and affecting the parties, their competition strategies, and the party system as a whole (Morlino 1998, 327–31).

At first, and much as had happened in the case of the PCE and the PCP, the prospect of accepting the PDS as a proregime force produced a split in the socialist party over the strategy to be adopted vis-à-vis the former communists. Claudio Martelli, second in command in the PSI, went against Bettino Craxi's line by suggesting a government alliance with the PDS. The suggestion, made in the fall and winter 1992, arrived too late, however. Faced with judicial inquiries that were about to directly involve the PSI leadership, both Craxi and Martelli himself were forced to resign.

Soon thereafter, as with the KKE, the PDS's legitimation led to participation in government. On April 28, 1993, three members of the PDS were included in the cabinet of Carlo Ciampi, a former governor of the Bank of Italy. This experience in power did not last long. The three ministers resigned the day after assuming office when the Chamber of Deputies failed to pass the authorization necessary for the *mani pulite* judges to proceed with their investigation of Craxi. This very short tenure in office notwithstanding, the granting of three portfolios (Finance, Parliamentary Relations, and University) to the PDS marked the end of the *conventio ad excludendum* and the complete integration of the party born from the transformation of the PCI.

In fact, the PDS was soon to become the central pivot for one of the poles around which the Italian party system was regrouping. As early as the municipal elections of June and November–December 1993, the PDS proved its extraordinary capacity to coalesce with other groups. The new electoral law provided for the direct election of mayors by means of either a plurality or a run-off majority system, depending on the size of the municipality. The PDS astutely exploited the new opportunities thus created to negotiate agreements and set up alliances of differing compositions, reflecting the local state of affairs. Some coalitions included Rifondazione, while others excluded that party and included more moderate groups, such as the progressive Catholics. The results above all signaled the success of the PDS, which, together with its allies, won power in such important cities as Catania, Genoa, Naples, Rome, Trieste, Turin, and Venice. The PDS's pivotal role on the center-left was consolidated in the 1994 general elections, when it put together a coalition of eight parties, known as "The Progressives" (*i progressisti*), which included not only the RC and the Greens, but also Catholic, socialist, and small lay groups.[20]

The Progressives' performance in the 1994 general election, however, fell short of their earlier success in the previous municipal elections. The very coalition-building capacity demonstrated by the PDS in the local elections triggered the creation of a right-wing coalition centered on the television magnate Silvio Berlusconi and his movement, Forza Italia! (which managed to incorporate parties as diverse as the Lega Nord and the MSI). The Progressives won 33.8 percent and 38.7 percent of the seats respectively in the Chamber of Deputies and the Senate, whereas Forza Italia! and its allies made off with the absolute majority of seats in the Chamber (58.1 percent), but not in the Senate (49.5 percent). This brought to power a center-right government led by Berlusconi (see Bartolini and D'Alimonte 1995).

This electoral disappointment indicated that the Progressives were positioned too far to the left to win in a centripetal party system. Furthermore, they were a heterogeneous electoral coalition, with little internal cohesion. This was partly because the new electoral law for the Chamber of Deputies allocates a quarter of the seats on the basis of proportional representation, via an ad hoc vote, thus giving smaller parties a strong incentive to defend their individual identities. Consequently, divisions among the eight parties that emerged during the talks to set up the coalition were confirmed later, when the formation of a unitary parliamentary group under the Progressive banner proved impossible, and a federal one had to be settled for.

Besides, by presenting itself as an electoral coalition, divided by internal quarreling, the alliance did not encourage the development of party identification among voters. Indeed, in single-member-district elections, the Progressives were unable even to hold on to the votes of all those who had voted for the coalition's individual parties on the proportional-representation ballot. The contrast with Izquierda Unida's experience suggests that the Progressives should have presented themselves as more than an electoral alliance: the more the IU institutionalized itself and moved away from the electoral cartel formula, the more votes it attracted, partly because, in so doing, it diluted the influence of the PCE within the coalition.

Another problem for the Progressives was the absence of an authoritative leader who could act as guarantor for the whole coalition vis-à-vis the electorate, as the Izquierda Unida's Julio Anguita had done in Spain. In Italy, although lacking a leader like Anguita, the left nonetheless had to face an electoral campaign strongly personalized by Silvio Berlusconi. Indeed, the Progressives declared they would choose the incumbent prime minister, Carlo Ciampi, as the next premier. In the absence of a unifying leading figure, Achille Occhetto, the PDS's party secretary, became the coalition's most visible leader. When the right was once again successful in the European elections, and the PDS slipped from a 20.4 percent share of the vote in the national elections to 19.1 percent, Occhetto resigned, and was replaced by Massimo D'Alema.

By the time of the April 1996 election, the two main problems of the left-wing alliance had been resolved. In February 1995, Romano Prodi, a highly respected economist and former president of the IRI state holding company, offered to lead a center-left coalition. This opened the way for an alliance between the PDS and the left-wing of the Partito Popolare Italiano (PPI), made up of former representatives of the DC. In March, Prodi was accepted as candidate for prime minister by a varied set of political forces. In addition to the PDS and the PPI (which had by then split into two parties, one of which supported the rival center-right coalition), the alliance included the socialist, liberal, social-Christian, and Green groups.

The decision of the PDS leadership to form an alliance with the center and to support a leader external to the party met its first crucial test in the regional and local elections of April 1995. The new center-left coalition campaigned with a different composition in different parts of the country. In eight regions, it excluded the Rifondazione Comunista, while in four others both the RC and the PPI were included. The coalition, which adopted the olive tree (l'Ulivo) as its name and symbol, won the presidency in 9 out of 15 regions, and was victorious in 56 out of 76 provinces, and 205 out of 282 municipalities. The results showed that, at a local level, D'Alema had made the right choices with regard to overcoming the problems that had plagued the 1994 progressive alliance.[21]

In July, the Partito Democratico della Sinistra held a special "thematic Congress," whose aim was to modify the party's ideology and to complete the transformation initiated in 1991. The PDS explicitly assumed a social democratic and laborist identity and declared itself in favor of a more limited role for the state, a move regarded as a liberal turning point. The Congress also renewed the party's support for the Ulivo coalition and formally appointed Romano Prodi as its candidate for prime minister and Walter Veltroni, editor of the newspaper *L'Unità* and number two in the party, as its candidate for deputy prime minister. Finally, in December the political program of the Ulivo coalition was made public. Thus, in the two years following the 1994 election, the left-wing coalition had undergone a thorough transformation. With a new composition, a new leader and program, and a new symbol, the alliance set up by the PDS was well prepared for the approaching electoral competition. The electoral coalition was further strengthened by Prime Minister Lamberto Dini's decision to form a new party (Rinnovamento Italiano) and join l'Ulivo, which allowed the alliance to present an image of moderation and competence, to attract centrist voters, and to reassure the business sector.

In the April 1996 general election, l'Ulivo gained 284 out of 630 seats in the Chamber of Deputies and 157 out of 315 in the Senate (D'Alimonte and Bartolini 1997). This placed it well ahead of the right-wing Polo delle Libertà, led by Berlusconi, which obtained 246 seats in the Chamber and 116 in the Senate. Both the Ulivo coalition and Rifondazione took advantage of the electoral law by concluding pacts under the terms of which they would not field candidates in competition with each other. Rifondazione Comunista, with 8.6 percent of the votes and 35 seats in the Chamber, not only increased its electoral base by almost 40 percent, but also won the opportunity to influence the center-left government, because given l'Ulivo's lack of a parliamentary majority, Prodi needed the support of other parties. While ensuring that the government received a vote of confidence in its initial appearance before the Chamber, the RC leader, Fausto Bertinotti, made it clear that, in the future, RC support would depend on the government's policies.

The Prodi cabinet marked the return of the PDS to government for the first time since its very brief 1993 participation in the Ciampi cabinet. In the cabinet sworn in on May 18, nine out of twenty portfolios were given to the PDS. Its secretary-general, Massimo D'Alema, did not join the government, but Veltroni was appointed deputy prime minister, and the party gained control of such important ministries as Interior, Finance, Industry and Tourism, and Education and Research.

The Prodi government remained in office until October 1998,

when Rifondazione Comunista, whose 35 deputies and 20 senators were essential to the survival of the cabinet, decided to vote against the draft of the budget bill.[22] This caused the ouster of the Ulivo government by a vote of no confidence. It also led to a split in RC itself, inasmuch as its president, Armando Cossutta, refused to withdraw support from Prodi and formed his own group, the Partito dei Comunisti Italiani (Party of the Italian Communists), or PDCI. The Prodi cabinet was replaced by a new one headed by D'Alema. The new government included two new parties: Cossutta's PDCI, which obtained the important Ministry of Justice, and a new centrist party, the Unione Democratica per la Repubblica (Democratic Union for the Republic), or UDR. The latter group, which brought together deputies from several existing parties, had been set up by Francesco Cossiga, a former president of the republic, after the 1996 election. D'Alema, who was the first member of a former communist party ever to become prime minister in a western European country, turned over direction of the party to Veltroni, who, in turn, left the government. The PDS had previously changed its name, in February 1998, becoming the Democratici della Sinistra (Democrats of the Left), or DS, and replaced the hammer and sickle with the rose of European socialism as its symbol. In addition, the new party drew together four lay and socialist political groups (mostly members of l'Ulivo) and adopted a federation-like model of organization with the goal of becoming more unitary over time. The processes of change begun in the Italian left in 1989 have not yet come to an end (Hellman 1998; Massari and Parker 1999).

The preceding analysis suggests that the transformation of these four southern European communist parties into proregime forces allowed them to play important roles within their respective party systems, bringing to an end a long isolation inaugurated after the installation of new democratic regimes.

Concluding Remarks

At the beginning of the chapter, we asked three questions. Have communist parties been integrated into the democratic regimes set up in Italy in the 1940s and in Greece, Portugal, and Spain in the mid 1970s? Have the communist parties been able to adjust to the social changes in each country? And, lastly, in what way has their position in the party system changed? By examining the process of integration followed by the PCI, the PCE, the PCP, and the KKE, we have sought to understand the consequences, if any, of democratic consolidation for the communist parties of southern Europe.

Our analysis indicates that the answer to the first question is clearly affirmative. It also suggests that democratic consolidation has led them to undertake a series of more or less profound changes that helped them emerge from the isolation that was the inevitable outcome of their antiregime stance and join the political fray. At the same time, these changes affected the relative position of the communist parties within their respective party systems. The particular role played by the PCI, the PCE, the PCP, and the KKE within these systems varied, however, depending on the mode of their transformation into proregime forces and on the circumstances of interparty competition in each country. Finally, their ability to broaden their electoral appeal beyond the traditional class cleavage depended on the image projected, on the proposals made, and, lastly, on the changes introduced by each of the four parties, as well as on their positions within the party system. This said, the main lesson to emerge from this study of the processes of democratic integration is that, in adjusting to the environment created by democratic consolidation, the PCI, the PCE, the PCP, and the KKE followed different paths.

If we imagine an ideal type for the process of democratic integration of antiregime parties, we can envisage a path that proceeds in neat stages. First, the party accepts the democratic regime. Next, its new attitude is reflected in a transformation of the inner system recognizing this new proregime identity. Finally, the party manages to play a significant political role, possibly in government, within the new democratic regime. A closer look at the various trajectories followed by the communist parties of southern Europe suggests, however, that the process of democratic integration is not at all straightforward (see Roth 1963) and that each case diverged from the ideal type.

To begin with, the decision to transform themselves into proregime parties was not part of the integration strategy adopted at the end of the authoritarian period. Some of the parties held on to their traditional identity for a long while and only gradually realized that entry into the inner system would require its modification. Quite often, a change in the resources or opportunities offered by the electoral arena forces parties to initiate a phase of adaptation that can lead to inner conflict and, hence, can have a destabilizing effect on party organization. Thus, the PCP and the KKE signaled their formal acceptance of the liberal democratic regime only some fifteen years after the end of authoritarian rule, when an electoral challenge had modified relations on the left and, in particular, relations with the socialists. In Portugal, the majority made up of the PS, the PRD, and the

PCP disintegrated, while in Greece, the shrinking of PASOK's electoral support seemed to indicate growth opportunities for the extreme left.

Secondly, acceptance of democracy does not automatically confer recognition of a party as a proregime force. The PCI's integration experience proves that a party can be "blocked" for a long time, half way between the subjective and objective thresholds of democratic acceptance. Indeed, the radical change of the party—dissolution of the PCI and creation of the PDS—is largely explained by its fifteen-year exclusion from power after 1975–76. That none of the other parties was forced to relinquish its communist identity was owing to the fact that none saw its democratic credentials rejected for so long.

Finally, recognition as a proregime actor does not mean that a communist party can expect to be included in the government soon. This depends on the contingencies of the political game; on the capacity of the parties to exploit them; and, possibly, on new phases of party adaptation. To become a proregime force merely guarantees an opportunity—shared equally with the other parties—to appeal to a range of voters and take part in decisions that, until then, have been the exclusive preserve of the inner-system parties. Thus, the PCE, which had been recognized as a proregime actor from the very beginning of democratic instauration, has yet not been granted a role in government. The absolute majority of seats achieved by the PSOE in 1982 and confirmed in successive elections led the PCE/IU to compete for discontented socialist voters. Having to do so, however, meant that the party adopted a line of strong opposition to the government that made impossible any agreement with the PSOE.

Hence, the four parties encountered different obstacles, which had different effects on their integration. In the case of the more orthodox parties, such as the PCP and the KKE, the main obstacle was their inability to adapt. In the case of the PCP, change was rather limited and came too late to allow the party to recover votes. For this very reason, an internal conflict ensued that had destabilizing effects on such a monolithic organization. In the case of the KKE, where a timely adaptation was decided from above, it was, paradoxically, the very absence of internal dissent and discussion over the creation of Synaspismos that made this change so fragile. With the PCI, the main obstacle was the inner system. Overcoming it required successive phases of party adaptation. Finally, the PCE proved quite able to adapt, and its rapid acceptance as a proregime force served as a sign that, in Spain, there was no inner system to be overcome. Thus, the main obstacle in the way of the Spanish party's integration proved to be the competitive contingencies that, for over a decade, froze the party system around the PSOE.

The preceding comparison helps clarify one further point. The inner party systems work well in certain institutional settings characterized by either a limited number of parties and an electoral law that ensures an alternation between parties that win an absolute majority of seats, or, conversely, a proportional representation system and a large number of parties, which make possible the formation of various kinds of coalitions, while securing the exclusion of the antiregime force. The inner systems of Greece and Italy exemplify these two extremes. In Portugal, on the other hand, the institutional setting did not help the inner system. This was partly because the electoral law did not facilitate the creation of artificial majorities, forcing the major parties to form either minority or coalition governments most of the time. Also, it was partly because the small number of parties did not allow for the formation of a broad range of coalitions.

At this point, it should be easier to understand how inner systems can be transformed and fall apart when, for some reason, the institutional incentives described above no longer exist. In Greece, a new and more proportional electoral law prevented PASOK and ND from winning the usual absolute majority, and precipitated the crisis of the inner system. The KKE quickly adapted to the new situation by setting up Synaspismos. In Italy, the end of the international cleavage, the outbreak of the *mani pulite* investigations, and the new electoral law completely transformed the political scene, making it impossible, henceforth, to form the old coalitions centered on the DC. Here, again, by shedding their former identity, and by creating the PDS, the leaders of the communist party were able to adapt to the crisis of the inner system and win the long-sought integration.

In Portugal, despite the absence of strong institutional incentives for its preservation, the inner system did not enter a period of crisis until 1985. The entry of a new party onto the scene produced the first signs of transformation. This led to the formation of an unusual opposition majority, which gave the PCP a chance to leave the sidelines to which it had been relegated. However, unlike the PCI and the KKE, the PCP was not ready to make the best of this crisis of the inner system. From 1983 to 1985, when it was clear that the PS would lose votes, the PCP did not seize the opportunity to start a process of adaptation that would have allowed it to increase its vote and to play a different role vis-à-vis the PS and the PRD. On the contrary, the communist leadership waited until 1988, after the disastrous 1987 electoral results, to adapt to democracy. As we have seen, however, these changes were meager and have not allowed the PCP to play a relevant political role under either Cavaco Silva's majority governments (1987–95) or the minority cabinets of Guterres (1995 to the present).

To conclude, the PCI, the PCE, the PCP, and the KKE have followed separate routes to democratic integration. These different paths explain the differing positions occupied by each neo- and postcommunist party within its party system. Similarly, the manner in which each party is coping with social change is explained by the different trajectory traveled on the way to democratic integration, and by the role played by each party within its own party system. Hence, the analysis of the way in which the communist parties of southern Europe adapted to democratic consolidation suggests that dissimilarities may be more important than similarities. In other words, membership in the same ideological family and adoption of the same form of party organization in the same international context have been less influential than the political circumstances of each country and the individual history of each party.

9 Conclusion

Richard Gunther and P. Nikiforos Diamandouros

The basic characteristics of southern European politics at the end of the twentieth century differ greatly from those that prevailed during previous democratic and semidemocratic interludes in the region. Historically, all four of the countries under examination in this volume lacked traditions of democratic stability. And yet, by the 1990s, consolidated democratic regimes had unquestionably been established throughout the region. Until recently, significant antisystem parties were to be found in each country on both left and right, but, in the course of the past few decades, these either declined in electoral support to near irrelevance (in Greece and Portugal) or transformed themselves into trustworthy democratic competitors. The polarization and endemic instability that had characterized pre-Salazar Portugal, pre-Franco Spain, and post–Civil War Greece has been replaced by stable, centripetal political systems allowing for alternation in government between two moderate parties in all three countries. Finally, the "polarized pluralism" that characterized Italian politics during the first four postwar decades has given way to a markedly different democratic system, despite the continuing high level of fragmentation of the party system. In the aggregate, it can be said that politics in southern Europe has come to resemble the style of institutionalized partisan conflict to be found in previously established democracies of western Europe. In short, the politics of the southern European "semi-periphery" has shed its "aberrant" character, has ceased to be distinctive, and has converged with the "normal" politics of modern democracies.

From one perspective, this development could be seen as rather banal and lacking theoretical significance. In terms of the timing of their socioeconomic development, southern European societies were laggards or—in Alexander Gerschenkron's terminology—"late developers." Following bursts of extremely rapid growth, they have approximated western European social-structural characteristics and levels of affluence. It is, therefore, not surprising that their political parties and patterns of mass-level political behavior have changed accordingly. Thus constructed, a socioeconomic determinist argument would imply, for example, that as social change transforms society and the lifestyles of individual citizens, so, too, more moderate political parties should become dominant and polarization, at least on class issues, should decline.

More detailed analysis of change in partisan politics in these countries shows, however, that a simplistic socioeconomic determinist model is inadequate to account for the mixed patterns we have observed. Such a model overlooks the important and autonomous role of politics in generating change. Put otherwise, it overlooks the key role of political elites in analyzing the evolving environment within which they function and in formulating responses in terms of their parties' programmatic "offerings" to the electorate, their organizational structures, their mobilization strategies, and the images of their candidates and leaders. It also fails to take into consideration the role of political elites in crafting key political institutions (especially those structuring legislative relations, the balance of political authority between center and periphery, and the translation of votes into parliamentary seats) and consolidating a new democratic regime. We contend that these political decisions play crucial, independent roles in structuring political relations in democratic regimes, and that the uneven patterns of change we have observed in southern Europe cannot be exclusively or even mainly accounted for by a simplistic socioeconomic reductionist model. Our empirical studies of southern European democracies thus provide powerful corroboration of an argument made by Giovanni Sartori over two decades ago (Sartori 1976).

Without doubt, mass-level factors (especially cultural, economic, and social-structural factors) are of considerable importance in explaining these changes. Political elites formulate strategies and adjust their patterns of behavior in accordance with their perceptions of the preferences of voters and the needs of their respective societies. Thus, economic development and social change greatly affect the manner in which elites calculate political advantages to be secured through alternative courses of action. But these social changes do not in themselves bring about political transformations of the kinds analyzed in this book. Indeed, on occasion, elites may opt for courses of action that are inconsistent with the incentives seemingly presented by an objective social reality. For example, in accord with the *embourgeoisement* hypothesis, implicit in a socioeconomically reductionist interpretation, most major political parties in southern Europe have moved toward more moderate positions. This is certainly true of the conservative and socialist parties in the region, as well as of the Spanish and Italian communist parties. It is not true, however, of the Portuguese Communist Party and the Greek KKE, which, until surprisingly recently, maintained radical stands and refused to formally repudiate past practices and views, even after they had accepted the democratic rules of the game. One significant partisan group, moreover, the Northern League, shifted away from a relatively moderate position within a governing coalition to a more radical, proindependence stand that poses new challenges to the Italian political system. These differing trajectories were produced by choices made by political elites and supported by mass actors, which countered the incentives that others perceived as inherent in a new social and political environment.

The basic nature and timing of change, moreover, were neither unilinear nor in lockstep with changes in the social structure, even though, over the very long term, these social transformations appear to underpin a general convergence among parties. The patterns of alignment between parties and segments of society in Spain, for example, became more polarized in 1982. This development was inconsistent with the relatively consistent trends toward greater *embourgeoisement* and secularism in Spanish society. Rather, it was the outcome of the collapse of the centrist, interclassist Unión de Centro Democrático (UCD), an event whose origins were to be found entirely at the elite level of that party (see Gunther 1986b). In the Italian case, the timing and pace of change were completely out of keeping with the steady, incremental transformation of Italian society. Despite the fact that aggregate levels of religious sentiment had declined greatly between the 1960s and mid 1980s, religiosity remained the strongest predictor of the vote and weakened only slightly throughout this period. Then, despite the fact that the secularization process had run its course by the mid 1980s and aggregate indicators of religious practice had remained roughly constant after 1985, the religious cleavage abruptly disappeared as a barrier separating left from right in 1994. The radical transformation of the Italian party system that began in that year was, on the one hand, triggered by events restricted to the elite level of party politics—specifically, the corruption scandals unearthed by the *mani pulite* investigations—and, on the other, by the considerable reconfiguring of the "political offering" to voters resulting, above all, from the breakup of Democrazia Cristiana. In describing these patterns of change, Chapter 3 in this volume (inter alia) appropriately uses the analogy of an earthquake: just as pressures build up along tectonic plates, social change may introduce tensions into old patterns of alignment. As Walter Dean Burnham (1970) notes, however, political change often occurs abruptly, and with occasionally devastating impact, just as the earth rapidly shifts along a previously stable fault line. The stimulus for this change, at least in the Italian case, was the discrediting of the former dominant elites and their hasty efforts to create more credible organizational frameworks for their candidacies.

With regard to Italy, this abrupt change was also manifested in the principal modes of conducting electoral campaigns. All of the social-structural and technological prerequisites for a "new campaign politics" had been in place for decades. Indeed, as a product of the "economic miracle" of the 1950s, Italian society had modernized much earlier than its neighbors. In addition, widespread access to television was available at an earlier stage in Italy than in Spain, Portugal, or Greece, and Italians had become even more dependent than Spaniards on television as a source of political information. Nonetheless, the "new campaign politics" was fully apparent in Spain from the very first democratic elections, but was absent from Italian campaigns until 1994. Comparatively speaking, parties were weakly developed as organizations in Spain. They implemented "catch-all" electoral strategies (largely eschewing institutional links to organized interests), depended primarily on television in reaching voters, and prominently featured the quasi-charismatic personal qualities of national-level party leaders—especially Adolfo Suárez and Felipe González in the first two elections. In Italy, in contrast, mass party organizations remained very strong (indeed Democrazia Cristiana's membership peaked in 1990), ties to organized interest were highly visible and institutionalized, and the personalities of national party leaders were downplayed, even in the case of Enrico Berlinguer of the Partito Comunista Italiano (PCI), where a potentially charismatic figure actually led the party. It was only in 1994 that the nature of campaign politics changed. And when it occurred, change was abrupt and radical. Mass organizational bases for political parties are only substantial in the cases of the Partito Democratico della Sinistra (PDS) and Rifondazione Comunista, which largely inherited these structures from the former PCI. The principal party of the right—Forza Italia!—does not even have an institutionalized base of party activists. The new Italian parties have adopted broad catch-all strategies, interest groups have distanced themselves from parties, and the Church has largely been neutralized by the scattering of former Christian Democrats among parties in both the conservative and left-of-center coalitions. Television has clearly become the dominant medium of campaign communication. Indeed, in all of democratic history there is nothing to compare with Silvio Berlusconi's use of his massive television empire as a springboard to power at the national level. In addition, partisan politics has become highly personalistic. In contrast with the "boardroom politics" of decidedly uncharismatic faction leaders, such as Giulio Andreotti, party politics is now dominated by the almost larger-than-life figures of Umberto Bossi, Romano Prodi, Silvio Berlusconi, and Gianfranco Fini. This change has been both profound and abrupt. And it became manifest in the same manner and through the same process as the dissolution of the old structure of partisan alignments. "The new campaign politics was liberated by the quasi disintegration of the old party system. It suddenly exploded during the transition to a new regime," Gianfranco Pasquino observes (p. 218 above). Accordingly, Pasquino argues, one cannot adequately account for the emergence of a "new campaign politics" exclusively on the basis of social-structural change or technological advances, such as the development of television as the dominant communications medium. Conscious decisions by political elites interact with an evolving environment to produce these changes.

The adequacy of a simple socioeconomic reductionist model is further undercut by the fact that the institutionalization of politics significantly constrains political development in a "path dependent" manner. Once in place, institutional rules, organizational structures, and behavioral norms tend to stabilize certain patterns of behavior and fix them over time, even continuing into periods when the social-structural or environmental circumstances that gave them their defining characteristics have disappeared or significantly changed. For over four decades, for example, the Italian political system retained important traits inherited from the late 1940s. Founded in the aftermath of World War II, and at the outbreak of the Cold War, the party system institutionalized and perpetuated the polarization along religious lines and between left and right that characterized that era. These developments were the product of a conscious strategy on the part of the founders of Democrazia Cristiana to mobilize the infrastructure of the Catholic Church as a bulwark against a perceived communist threat. As the long-term product of this decision, the religious factor remained the principal anchor of the left-right division in Italian society until 1994.

Clientelistic relationships that allowed local notables to play a dominant role in rural areas were another characteristic of the immediate postwar period that was also frozen into the structure of Italian politics. A premodern feature stemming from a time when Italy was far from affluent, economically developed, or socially "modern," this organized expression of particularism took on new forms over time, as clientelistic networks linked associational interest groups to parties, adding another basis to the formation of factions within the governing parties. These varieties of institutionalized particularism remained important features of Italian parties until the 1990s, even though, by then, the dysfunctionality of these relationships—especially when they shaded over into cronyism and outright corruption—had become apparent. In the end, public revulsion over these practices brought the old party system down. The tenacity of these patterns of alignment and party-organizational features, however, remains impressive. It should also be noted that this same argument can help to explain similar developments in two other countries. As in Italy, democratic parties were established in Japan in the immediate postwar period, when its society was also largely agrarian and traditionalist. Japanese parties, like their Italian counterparts, institutionalized factionalism and local clientelistic networks within the fabric of the major parties, to the extent that the elite-recruitment process has been largely dominated by factional politics. To a somewhat lesser extent, the major Greek parties were also characterized by clientelism. In this case, it was not the circumstances prevailing at the time when the new parties were born in the mid 1970s that imparted this premodern feature to Greek parties. Rather, it was the fact that the authoritarian interlude was so brief that the new parties were founded by old politicians with roots in the traditional politics that preceded the colonels' seizure of power in 1967. As in Italy, clientelism in Japan and Greece paved the way for cronyism and corruption, but (to date, at least) it has had less devastating political consequences for the relevant elites and their political organizations.

If path dependency, or "freezing," helps to explain why "old campaign politics" dominated by traditional cleavage parties characterized Italian partisan politics for nearly five decades, "leapfrogging," another concept introduced earlier in this volume, helps to account for the very different patterns of politics in Spain, Portugal, and Greece. Italian parties were founded at a time when the mass-organization model for parties was still dominant, when Italian society was relatively underdeveloped, and when television had not yet been developed for mass use. Conversely, when party organization began in earnest in the mid 1970s, Spain was a relatively modern, urbanized, affluent society, in which television had secured a dominant position. Portugal and Greece were somewhat less developed socioeconomically, but their parties were created in a context that was greatly different from the environment of poverty that had characterized postwar Italy, and access to television was widespread in both countries. Parties were thus in a position to "leapfrog" over developmental stages that had characterized the evolution of political parties in early-developing countries.

Unlike in Italy, where the "old campaign politics" was institutionalized early on and for decades stifled the emergence of its "new" counterpart, in Spain, Portugal, and Greece, all of the defining features of modern campaign politics were fully apparent from the very beginning. Unlike under the Italian first republic, when "boardroom politics" led to the recruitment of gray and decidedly uncharismatic characters to the top positions of national leadership, the powerful personalities and leadership abilities of Mário Soares, Adolfo Suárez, Felipe González, Constantine Karamanlis, and Andreas Papandreou were amply apparent and heavily stressed from the very first democratic elections. Unlike in Italy, where parties had high levels of mass membership and close ties to equally well institutionalized secondary associations, parties in Greece, Portugal, and Spain never developed the levels of affiliation that characterized the previously established parties of central and northern Europe, including Italy. They also either eschewed the development of close linkages with allied secondary associations or, as in the case of the Spanish socialists (who had inherited a powerful trade union ally from the pre-Franco era), found them incompatible with the catch-all politics they had adopted as their dominant mechanism for electoral mobilization. As Hans-Jürgen Puhle persuasively argues in this volume, low levels of affiliation and the lack of close ties to other social groups have, in the aggregate, left the major parties of southern Europe relatively "unencumbered" in comparison with their northern European counterparts, and therefore more flexible and adaptable to the exigencies of "the new campaign politics" than many of northern Europe's established political parties, afflicted with the "tanker syndrome." This unencumberedness, combined with the fact that these parties were founded in modern social contexts, in the age of television, and in the wake of authoritarian interludes during which party politics was completely suspended, has allowed southern European political parties to leapfrog to the status of modern catch-all parties more readily than their more encumbered northern counterparts. This conclusion stands in sharp contrast with assertions that primordial characteristics of southern European societies (especially their political cultures) continue to determine the basic nature and evolution of politics in the region (see, e.g., Wiarda 1989).

The research agenda of this project has focused on two powerful and interrelated forces that have transformed southern Europe: socioeconomic modernization and democratization. *The Politics of Democratic Consolidation,* the volume preceding this one, primarily analyzed the processes of democratization and democratic consolidation. Subsequent volumes will more fully explore the various dimensions of modernization relating to economic and cultural change, and to the state and public policy. This book, which deals primarily with the structure of governance and of political parties and the dynamics of electoral competition, has uncovered clear evidence that parties and politics are affected by these two processes. This relationship, however, is recursive: the direction of causality flows both ways—partisan politics is both affected by and itself influences these two transformative processes.

The relationship between democratization and parties was most extensively first explored in *The Politics of Democratic Consolidation* in Leonardo Morlino's "Political Parties and Democratic Consolidation in Southern Europe." Parties and party leaders were found to be functionally privileged by the democratization process, and, in sharp contrast to many post-Soviet transitions, played a positive, if not decisive, role in the consolidation of democratic systems in all four of the countries discussed. In this volume, we have seen evidence that democratic consolidation, in turn, has profoundly influenced the strategies, calculations, and behavior of party elites. In contrast with polities in the throes of transition and with unconsolidated, unstable democracies, the context of a consolidated democracy establishes a centripetal and self-reinforcing dynamic. Acceptance of a single, unambiguous set of "rules of the game" and acknowledgment of the legitimacy of the established institutions of democracy channels conflicting demands through structures specifically designed to regulate, if not resolve, conflict. The absence of consensus that these are indeed the only appropriate venues for the expression of conflict can, on the other hand, encourage the articulation of demands (e.g., in the streets or through armed clashes) in a manner not conducive to the dialogue and mutual concessions implicit in democracy. This often leads to polarization, and may result in instability, destabilization, deconsolidation, and potential breakdown. Widespread agreement on the rules of the game—including explicit guarantees of civil and political liberties—also lessens suspicions among contending elites and gives them confidence that, even if they lose one round, they will still be around to fight again in the future (see Burton et al. 1992, 30–31). These institutionalized procedures also impose clear norms on the expression of conflict, including an explicit prohibition of violence. Taken together, these characteristics of consolidated democracies lessen the stakes inherent in a given conflict, avoid dynamic processes that can lead to polarization (e.g., the dialectic of rocks, clubs, and tear gas that sometimes characterizes street mobilizations), and improve the chances that a compromise solution will emerge. They can also set in place a centripetal dynamic in which elites are encouraged to moderate their rhetoric and behavior, because, in a stable, consolidated democracy, that is the most likely way to win. Finally, civility breeds civility: cordial and mutually respectful interactions among elites can be self-perpetuating over time. In short, democratic consolidation establishes a context that encourages political moderation. It is not accidental that the overwhelming majority of parties studied in this volume, irrespective of how radical or even "antisystem" their stands may have been at the onset of the transition, subsequently moderated both the style and the content of their politics, either in the interest of consolidating democracy (e.g., the Spanish Communist Party) or in order to adjust to, and benefit from, the opportunities offered through participation in the politics and processes of a consolidated regime.

The relationship between socioeconomic modernization and parties also flows in both directions. Moderate catch-all parties are much more likely to emerge and thrive in modern, affluent societies than in less socioeconomically advanced contexts—typically characterized by an inegalitarian distribution of wealth. Insofar as modernization facilitates the expansion of the comfortable middle strata, and insofar as political elites perceive those middle strata as preferring moderation to radicalism (see Goldthorpe et al. 1969; Dahl 1966), a powerful centripetal dynamic of electoral competition is set in place. As we have seen in this volume and elsewhere (e.g. Gunther, Sani, and Shabad 1986), most party elites in the new democracies of southern Europe adopted moderate, catch-all strategies of electoral competition and party development largely because they thought those strategies were most likely to be successful in the context of newly affluent and modern societies.

Once in government, however, it was necessary for party elites to adopt policies regarding the modernization of their economies, societies, and even their parties. All had inherited inefficient parastate industries, uncompetitive business practices, and corporatist labor restrictions from their respective predecessor authoritarian regimes. Throughout the early and tenuous years of democracy, they all postponed the painful and potentially polarizing steps necessary to restructure, but by the mid 1980s, when stiff competition and demands for deregulation from their new European Community partners loomed large, it became clear that reforms were necessary. The responses of the governing elites of Greece, Portugal, and Spain to these challenges were very much affected by (and, in turn, influenced) the political variables that have been the central concern of this book. In the case of Spain, the governments formed by the Partido Socialista Obrero Español in the 1980s were emboldened to promptly adopt restructuring policies. This was so because, by the time the PSOE came to power in 1982, Spanish democracy had been consolidated, and because the parliamentary majority the party enjoyed and the absence of a credible alternative in government (owing, in turn, to the nature of partisan competition in Spain's specific macroinstitutional context) gave it the security it needed to implement unpopular policies. In short, democratic consolidation and overwhelming electoral success were prerequisites for the adoption of bold modernizing policies. (In contrast, the preceding UCD governments had lacked a parliamentary majority and functioned in a political context that was decidedly unconsolidated.) But implementation of those modernizing policies, in turn, had a dramatic impact on the nature of the PSOE itself. One of the most aggrieved sectors of Spanish society was organized labor, particularly in heavy industries that were the target of government restructuring. Adoption of neoliberal monetary policies, efforts to liberalize the labor market, and the closing of inefficient firms in the parastate sector alienated the party's traditional trade union ally and led to "the breakup of the socialist family." Paradoxically, this loss of a once-valued institutional linkage helped "modernize" the party by pushing it even closer to the catch-all ideal type. In the case of Greece, by way of contrast, the populism of Andreas Papandreou (who thoroughly dominated party politics and government for most of the 1980s), coupled with the clientelism that permeated both PASOK and Nea Demokratia until the early 1990s, deterred both major parties from modernizing reforms. Modernization policies were only embraced in earnest after Papandreou had passed from the scene and a new generation of modernizing elites, led by Costas Simitis, succeeded in gaining control of PASOK in the mid 1990s. In short, parties, modernization and democratic consolidation are all closely intertwined.

In the end, all four of these countries have shed the structures and practices of traditional political parties. Moderate catch-all parties, with comparatively "light" organizational frameworks and a propensity to focus their election campaigns on the leadership capacities of their national leaders have come to predominate. In this sense, a notable convergence has occurred, not only among these four southern European countries, but also with the established parties of northern Europe. But this convergence has been neither unidirectional nor as simple as it seems. First, it is not characterized by the "lagging" south "catching up" with the more advanced north: to be sure, northern and southern political parties have converged toward one another, but in many respects, the parties of the south leapfrogged toward modern forms more readily and quickly than their northern counterparts. Second, while the southern European political parties may have become more alike, the same cannot be said of many other key features of their political systems. There is no "southern European model" of politics, except insofar as there has been a decided shift toward a majoritarian alternation in power between two major parties or blocs: this pattern had always characterized Greece and Spain, but it emerged in Portugal only in the mid 1980s, and in Italy only in the mid 1990s. Instead, the four countries have evolved in markedly different directions—some featuring political decentralization, others remaining highly centralized; some have evolved toward "two-plus" party systems, while Italy's party system has become even more fragmented than ever.

All four of these southern European democracies have consolidated, but the transition to the politics of democratic persistence has not meant stagnation. These systems have continued to develop in accordance with their own internal dynamics and not toward greater homogenization in the oft-cited process of "globalization." Although they have all become centripetal modern democracies, politics in each of these countries has evolved along different trajectories, from different starting points, culminating in different democratic political systems. In short, these southern European democracies have become typically European and vary among themselves about as much as western European democracies do in general.

Appendix

Table A.1 Percentage of Votes and Number (and %) of Parliamentary Seats Won by Major Parties in National Elections in Greece, 1974–1996

	Left				Right		
	KKE	KKE-Es/SYN	PASOK	Center Union	ND	EDE	Other
1974	9.5%		13.6%	20.4%	54.4%	1.1%	1.1%
	8		15	61	216	0	0
	(2.7%)		(5.0%)	(20.3%)	(72.0%)	(0)	(0)
1977	9.4	2.7%	25.3	12.0	41.8	6.8	2.0
	11	2	93	16	171	5	2
	(3.7)	(0.7)	(31.0)	(5.3)	(57.0)	(1.7)	(0.7)
1981	10.9	1.3	48.1	1.5	35.9	1.7	0.6
	12	0	172	0	115	0	0
	(4.0)	(0)	(57.3)	(0)	(38.3)	(0)	(0)
1985	9.9	1.8	45.8		40.8	0.6	1.1
	12	1	161		126	0	0
	(4.0)	(0.3)	(53.7)		(42.0)	(0)	(0)
1989		13.1	39.1		44.3		3.5
June		28	125		145		2
		(9.3)	(41.7)		(48.3)		(0.7)
1989		11.0	40.7		46.2		2.2
Nov.		21	128		148		3
		(7.0)	(42.7)		(49.3)		(1.0)
1990		10.3	38.6		46.9		4.2
		19	123		150		8
		(6.3)	(41.0)		(50.0)		(2.7)
1993	4.5	2.9	46.9		39.3		6.4
	9	—	170		111		10
	(3.0)	—	(56.7)		(37.0)		(3.3)
1996	5.6	5.1	41.5		38.1		9.7
	11	10	162		108		9
	(3.7)	(3.3)	(54.0)		(36.0)		(3.0)
2000	5.5	3.2	43.8		42.7		4.8
	11	6	158		125		0
	(3.7)	(2.0)	(52.7)		(41.7)		(0)

Sources: For 1974–96, Diamandouros 1998, 184–86; for 2000, http://www-public.vz.uni-duesseldorf.de.

Note: The KKE-Esoterikou ran in coalition with the KKE in 1989 and 1990. Synaspismos includes the KKE-Es in 1993 and 1996.

Table A.2 Percentage of Votes and Number (and %) of Parliamentary Seats Won by Major Parties in National Elections in Italy, 1946–1983

	Left					Right				
	Other Left	PCI	PSI	PSDI	PRI	DC	PLI	Mon.	MSI	Other
1946		18.9%	20.7%	—	4.4%	35.2%	6.8%	2.8%	5.3%*	5.9%
		104	115	—	23	207	41	16	30	20
		(18.7)	(20.7)	—	(4.1)	(37.2)	(7.4)	(2.9)	(5.4)	(3.6)
1948		31.0		7.1%	2.5	48.5	3.8	2.8	2.0	2.4
		183		33	9	305	19	14	6	5
		(31.9)		(5.7)	(1.6)	(53.1)	(3.3)	(2.4)	(1.0)	(0.9)
1953		22.6	12.7	4.5	1.6	40.1	3.0	6.9	5.8	2.8
		143	75	19	5	263	13	40	29	3
		(24.2)	(12.7)	(3.2)	(0.8)	(44.6)	(2.4)	(6.8)	(4.9)	(.5)
1958		22.7	14.2	4.6	1.4	42.4	3.5	4.8	4.8	1.7
		140	84	22	6	273	17	25	24	5
		(23.5)	(14.1)	(3.7)	(1.0)	(45.8)	(2.9)	(4.2)	(4.0)	(0.8)
1963		25.3	13.8	6.1	1.4	38.3	7.0	1.7	5.1	1.3
		166	87	33	6	260	39	8	27	4
		(26.3)	(13.8)	(5.2)	(1.0)	(41.3)	(6.2)	(1.3)	(4.3)	(0.6)

1968	4.4%	26.9	14.5		2.0	39.1	5.8	1.3	4.5	1.5
	23	177	91		9	266	31	6	24	3
	(3.7)	(28.1)	(14.4)		(1.4)	(42.2)	(4.9)	(1.0)	(3.8)	(.6)
1972	1.9	27.2	9.6	5.2	2.9	38.8	3.9		8.7	1.8
	0	179	61	29	15	266	20		56	4
	(0)	(36.0)	(9.7)	(4.6)	(2.2)	(42.4)	(3.3)		(8.9)	(0.5)
1976	1.5	34.4	9.7	3.4	3.1	38.8	1.3		6.1	1.7
	6	227	57	15	14	263	5		35	8
	(1.0)	(36.0)	(9.0)	(2.4)	(2.2)	(41.7)	(0.8)		(5.6)	(1.3)
1979	1.4	30.4	9.8	3.8	3.0	38.3	1.9		5.3	6.1
	6	201	62	20	16	262	9		30	24
	(1.0)	(31.9)	(9.8)	(3.2)	(2.5)	(41.6)	(1.4)		(4.8)	(3.8)
1983	1.5	29.9	11.4	4.1	5.1	32.9	2.9		6.8	5.4
	7	198	73	23	29	225	16		42	17
	(1.1)	(31.4)	(11.6)	(3.7)	(4.6)	(35.7)	(2.5)		(6.7)	(2.7)

Source: Toniolo 1990.

Note: In 1946, * indicates vote for the short-lived Fronte dell'Uomo Qualunque (Common Man's Front). The PCI and PSI fielded a joint list of candidates in 1948; the PSI and PSDI fielded a joint list in 1968. "Other Left" includes the PSIUP and Democrazia Proletaria in 1976–83.

Table A.3 Percentage of Votes and Number (and %) of Parliamentary Seats Won by Major Parties in National Elections in Italy, 1987–1996

	Left					Right				
	Other Left	PCI	PSI	PSDI	PRI	DC	PLI	Lega	MSI	Other
1987	1.7%	26.6%	14.3%	2.9%	3.7%	34.3%	2.1%	1.3%	5.9%	7.2%
	8	177	94	17	21	234	11	2	35	31
	(1.3)	(28.1)	(14.9)	(2.7)	(3.3)	(37.1)	(1.7)	(0.3)	(5.6)	(4.9)
	RC	PDS	PSI	PSDI	PRI	DC	PLI	Lega[a]	MSI	Other
1992	5.6	16.1	13.6	2.7	4.4	29.7	2.8	8.7	5.4	11.0
	35	107	92	16	27	206	17	55	34	41
	(5.6)	(17.0)	(14.6)	(2.5)	(4.3)	(32.7)	(2.7)	(8.7)	(5.4)	(6.5)
	RC	PDS	AD	PSI	PPI	Patto Segni	FI	Lega	AN	Other
1994[b]	6.0	20.4	1.2	2.2	11.1	4.7	21.0	8.4	13.5	11.5
	39	109	18	14	33	13	99	117	109	79
	(6.2)	(17.3)	(2.9)	(2.2)	(5.2)	(2.1)	(15.7)	(18.6)	(17.3)	(12.5)
	RC	PDS	PPI	Lista Dini		CCD/UDC[c]	FI	Lega	AN	Other
1996[b]	8.6	21.1	6.8	4.3		5.8	21.0	10.1	15.7	6.6
	35	171	75	26		30	123	59	93	18
	(5.5)	(27.1)	(11.9)	(4.1)		(4.8)	(19.5)	(9.4)	(14.8)	(2.9)

Sources: Toniolo 1990; Sani 1992; Bartolini and D'Alimonte 1994; Ignazi 1997.

[a]Includes Lega Autonóma Veneta in 1992.

[b]The percentage of the vote refers to those cast for the proportional representation segment of the ballot, while the number and percentage of seats refers to the total number of seats in the Camera dei Deputati through both the proportional and single-member segments of the ballot.

[c]UDC ran with PPI in 1994.

Table A.4 Percentage of Votes and Number (and %) of Parliamentary Seats Won by Major Parties in National Elections in Portugal, 1975–1999

	Left				Right		
	PCP	UDP/MDP	PS	PRD	PSD	Aliança Democratica	CDS
1975	12.5%	4.9%	37.9%		26.4%		7.6%
	30	6	116		81		16
	(12.0)	(2.4)	(46.4)		(32.4)		(6.4)
1976	14.4	1.7	34.9		24.4		16.0
	40	1	107		73		42
	(15.2)	(0.4)	(40.7)		(27.3)		(16.0)
1979	18.8	2.2	27.3			45.3	
	47	1	74			128	
	(18.8)	(0.4)	(29.6)			(51.2)	
1980	16.8	1.4	27.4			47.6	
	41	1	74			134	
	(16.4)	(0.4)	(29.6)			(53.6)	
1983	18.1	0.9	36.1		27.4		12.4
	44	0	101		75		30
	(17.6)	(0)	(40.4)		(30.0)		(12.0)
1985	15.5	1.3	20.8	17.9%	29.9		10.0
	38	0	57	55	88		22
	(15.2)	(0)	(22.8)	(18.0)	(35.2)		(8.8)
1987	12.1	0.9	22.2	4.9	50.2		4.4
	31	0	60	7	148		4
	(12.4)	(0)	(24.0)	(2.8)	(59.2)		(1.6)
1991	8.8	0.1	29.1	0.6	50.6		4.4
	17	0	72	0	135		5
	(7.4)	(0)	(31.3)	(0)	(58.7)		(2.2)
1995	8.6	0.6	43.9	0.2	34.0		9.1
	15	0	111	0	85		15
	(6.5)	(0)	(48.3)	(0)	(40.0)		(6.5)
1999	9.0	2.5	44.0		32.3		8.4
	17	2	115		81		15
	(7.4)	(0.9)	(50.0)		(35.2)		(6.5)

Source: Comissão Nacional de Eleições.

Note: The PSD and CDS joined to form the Aliança Democrática in the 1979 and 1980 elections.

Table A.5 Percentage of Votes and Number (and %) of Parliamentary Seats Won by Major Parties in National Elections in Spain, 1977–1996

	Nationwide Parties					Regional Parties		
	Left			Right				
	PCE/IU	PSOE/PSP	UCD/CDS	AP/PP	Other	PDC/CiU	PNV	Other
1977	9.2%	28.9/4.4%	34.0%	8.0%	7.8%	2.8%	1.7%	3.2%
	20	118/6	165	16	0	11	8	6
	(5.7)	(35.4)	(47.1)	(4.6)	0	(3.1)	(2.3)	(1.7)
1979	10.8	30.5	35.1	6.1	6.8	2.7	1.7	6.3
	23	121	168	9	1	8	7	13
	(6.6)	(34.6)	(48.0)	(2.6)	(0.3)	(2.3)	(2.0)	(3.7)
1982	4.0	48.4	6.5/2.9	26.5	2.5	3.7	1.9	3.6
	4	202	12/2	106	0	12	8	4
	(1.1)	(57.7)	(3.4/.6)	(30.3)	(0)	(3.4)	(2.3)	(1.1)
1986	4.5	44.6	9.2	26.3	3.7	5.1	1.6	5.0
	7	184	19	105	0	18	6	11
	(2.0)	(52.6)	(5.4)	(30.0)	(0)	(5.1)	(1.7)	(3.1)

1989	9.1	39.9	7.9	25.9	5.5	5.1	1.2	5.4
	17	175	14	107	0	18	5	14
	(4.9)	(50.0)	(4.0)	(30.6)	(0)	(5.1)	(1.4)	(4.0)
1993	9.6	38.8	1.8	34.8	3.8	4.9	1.2	5.1
	18	159	0	141	0	17	5	10
	(5.1)	(45.4)	(0)	(40.3)	(0)	(4.9)	(1.4)	(2.9)
1996	10.6	37.5	—	38.8	1.8	4.6	1.3	5.4
	21	141	—	156	0	16	5	11
	(6.0)	(40.3)	—	(44.6)	(0)	(4.6)	(1.4)	(3.1)
2000	5.5	34.7	—	45.2	1.8	4.3	1.6	6.9
	8	125	—	183	0	15	7	12
	(2.3)	(35.7)	—	(52.3)	(0)	(4.3)	(2.0)	(3.4)

Sources: For 1977, Gunther, Sani, and Shabad 1986 and Ministerio de la Governación, *Elecciones Generales 1977: Resultados Congreso por Provincia,* 1979–96; for 1979–96, Ministerio del Interior, *Elecciones Generales 1979;* for 2000, Junta Electoral Central, *Boletín Oficial del Estado,* April 4, 2000.

Notes

Chapter 2. Democracy, Southern European Style

1. A survey conducted in 1978, for example, asked respondents which prime minister had provided the best government for Portugal. Marcelo Caetano was preferred by 28 percent of those polled, and all of Portugal's democratic prime ministers combined were mentioned by a total of only 21 percent. The runner-up to Caetano was Mário Soares, with 9 percent. Data from Bruneau 1981, 14–15.

2. Excerpt from a statement by the PSOE constitutional *ponente* Gregorio Peces-Barba, published in *El Socialista,* May 7, 1978, II and III.

3. In actual practice, most candidates for prime minister in Spain will make great efforts to secure the support of other parties (usually by offering policy-relevant "side payments" during negotiations preceding the investiture) in an effort to come to office with majority support on the first ballot.

4. For discussions of the powers of the Spanish executive, see Donaghy and Newton 1987; Zaldívar and Castells 1992; Colomer 1995; Lancaster 1996.

5. The Basques, for example, successfully negotiated the reestablishment of the *conciertos económicos*—a medieval procedure whereby the four Basque provinces collect all taxes, then negotiate with the Spanish government an annual sum as reimbursement for services rendered within the region by the central government. For other regions, the process is the reverse: the central government collects most taxes, then negotiates with the regions over the amount that they will receive as payment for performing services previously transferred from the Spanish state administration.

6. Indeed, the UCD government of Leopoldo Calvo Sotelo secured the support of the PSOE in 1981 for passage of legislation (the Ley Orgánica para la Armonización del Proceso Autonómico, or LOAPA) that would have moved Spain in this direction. It was vigorously opposed by the Basque and Catalan nationalist parties, and most of its controversial provisions were ruled unconstitutional by the Spanish Constitutional Court.

7. Dissatisfaction with the way the simpler versions of proportional representation had operated stemmed, inter alia, from the fact that whereas 45.8 percent

of the popular vote obtained PASOK a comfortable majority of 161 seats in parliament in the 1985 election under reinforced proportional representation, 46.2 percent and 46.9 percent shares in the November 1989 and April 1990 elections gave Nea Demokratia only 148 and 150 seats respectively. See Clogg 1987.

8. See Clogg 1987; Featherstone 1987; Penniman 1981; Mavrogordatos 1983a and 1983b; Lyrintzis 1984; Pridham and Verney 1991; Nicolacopoulos 1989.

9. The Greek system's strict majoritarianism notwithstanding, two instances from the very recent past suggest that the logic of consensualism may be making a timid entry into Greek political practice. The first of these concerns proposed amendments to the constitution. In both the last parliament before the 1996 elections and in the one issuing from them, the two major parties exhibited a remarkable tendency to extend bipartisan support to the overwhelming number of proposed amendments. Initial indications suggest that the spirit of consensualism has persisted in the parliament brought forward by the 2000 elections. This revisionary parliament will determine both the scope and the nature of the amendment process. Even more significant, the same trend was also observed in a small but qualitatively important number of ordinary legislative proposals that received bipartisan support in the 1998 sessions of parliament. It is too early to tell whether this embryonic experiment in consensualism constitutes a harbinger of things to come or a temporary departure from established patterns. If it persists, it may well mark an important evolution of the Greek political system toward a style of government allowing for a limited degree of consensualism in carefully circumscribed areas perceived as meriting broader legitimacy. See Alivizatos 1990.

10. On the roots of the Greek centralist tradition, see Petropulos 1968. See also Verney 1994; Verney and Papageorgiou 1992.

11. For authoritative accounts of the founding and evolution of PASOK, see Spourdalakis 1988 and 1998, n. 1; Sotiropoulos 1996. On Nea Demokratia, see Pappas 1998.

12. For studies of polarization as a feature of the Greek political system, see Mavrogordatos 1984; Seferiadis 1986; Kalyvas 1997; Featherstone 1990; Papadopoulos 1989; Pridham and Verney 1991; Sotiropoulos 1995.

13. For assessments of the impact of international factors on the evolution of domestic Greek politics in the years following EC accession (1981), which also contain solid bibliographies relating to this general topic, see Kasakos and Ioakimidis 1994; Psomiades and Thomakakis 1993; Featherstone and Yfantis 1996; Tsinisizelis 1996; Verney 1987a and 1990a; Tsingos 1994.

14. The emergence of breakaway parties drawing their support primarily, if not exclusively, from those adherents of the underdog coalition most adversely affected by the policies of restructuring and rationalization of the market and the state pursued by their reformist rivals has yet to receive adequate attention. While failing to destabilize the party system, these developments have imparted a new dimension to it and have underscored the significance of the protest vote generated by its evolution. In the 1996 election, POLAN got only 2.9 percent of the popular vote, and was thus excluded from parliament, entry to which requires a minimum of 3 percent. The party did not contest the 2000 elections. DIKKI, on the other hand, which was founded in 1995 and occupies virtually the same location in the left-right spectrum as PASOK, won a handsome 4.4 percent in the 1996

elections and became the fifth party in the current parliament. In 2000, the party received 2.69 percent of the popular vote and was excluded from parliament.

15. Local government in Italy also had an integrative effect, albeit less relevant than the parliamentary one. While the left was excluded from power at the national level, its presence in local government, particularly its nearly constant rule of the so-called red areas, gave it stable positions of power and solidly acquired interests.

16. In 1974, there was one referendum; in 1978, two; in 1981, five; in 1985, one; in 1987, five; in 1989, one; in 1990, three; in 1993, eight; in 1995, twelve; in 1997, seven; in 1999, one; in 2000, seven. Among the most important and hotly debated of these referenda were the 1974 vote on legalization of divorce and the 1985 referendum on salaries. In 1990, 1997, and 2000, seventeen referenda were declared invalid because voter participation did not surpass the minimum threshold of 50 percent plus one.

17. In Senate elections, each voter has one vote, and the candidate receiving a plurality through the first segment is the winner. A party that elects a senator through the single member/majority segment of the ballot, however, has all votes that were cast for its victorious candidate subtracted from the total of its votes for its proportional list in the second segment of the election. At the regional level, the remaining votes are the basis for calculating (according to the d'Hondt system) the proportion due to each party list present in the electoral district, or *circoscrizione*.

The procedure for the Chamber of Deputies is similar, except that each voter casts two votes—one for the single-member district and another for the proportional party list at the *circoscrizione* level—and that in calculating vote shares for party lists in the second, proportional representation segment, all the votes (plus one) for the *second-place* candidate in the single-member segment are subtracted from the votes of the party that won the seat in the single-member round before allocating seats on a proportional basis (using the Hare system). In addition, unlike in the Senate elections, independent candidacies are not permitted, and more than one party list can support the candidate in the single-member constituency. Also, in addition to the majoritarian biases inherent in all single-member district systems, a 4-percent minimum nationwide vote is established by law as a prerequisite for receiving representation through the proportional representation segment for the Chamber of Deputies. For the Senate, there is no legal threshold, but since the allocation of proportional representation seats is calculated at the regional level, there is a de facto threshold of about 10 percent (actually, it can be either much lower or much higher) of votes cast for proportional representation seats. In the aggregate, the rules for the Lower Chamber may be considered as slightly more proportional than those for the Senate. In fact, the aforementioned differences interact to shape two different subsystems. These differences are largely the result of the fact that the Senate is close to the previous law, minus the ten words repealed by the referendum, while for the Lower Chamber a more proportional mix was elaborated.

18. That coalition included Forza Italia!, MSI-AN, the Northern League, and two smaller groups, the Centro Cristiano Democratico and the Unione di Centro Democratico.

19. Even under the Berlusconi cabinet, 52.3 percent of governmental legislative activity was made up of decree-laws. For an analysis of the role of such decrees, see Cazzola and Morisi 1981.

Chapter 3. The Anchors of Partisanship: A Comparative Analysis of Voting Behavior in Four Southern European Democracies

The authors wish to express their gratitude to Spain's Comisión Interministerial de Ciencia y Tecnología, whose financial support made possible their 1993 electoral survey, and the Centro de Estudios Avanzados en Ciencias Sociales of the Fundación Juan March, whose travel support made it possible for them to meet frequently to undertake this extensive analysis. They also wish to thank Laura Morales and Pablo Oñate for their assistance in various stages of this research, Janet Box-Steffensmeier, for her extraordinarily helpful methodological advice, and Paul Beck, Peter Mair, and Hans Daalder, for their insightful comments on earlier drafts of the manuscript.

1. Important contributions to this debate include Inglehart 1990; Dalton, Flanagan, and Beck 1984; Bartolini and Mair 1990; Franklin, Mackie, Valen, et al. 1992; Budge and Farlie 1983; Mair 1997; Crewe and Denver 1985; Pennings and Lane 1998.

2. This analysis follows in the footsteps of Rose 1974 and Franklin, Mackie, Valen, et al. 1992. It uses a somewhat different methodology (Probit analysis, instead of "tree analysis" and OLS regression), but its conclusions are (reassuringly) consistent with those of these earlier studies.

3. The Four Nation Study was undertaken in the spring of 1985. It involved 2,000 interviews in Portugal, 2,498 in Spain, 2,074 in Italy, and 1,998 in Greece. We wish to express our appreciation for the use of these data to the coordinators of the study, Giacomo Sani and Julián Santamaría, as well as to the other principal investigators, Mario Bacalhau, Maria José Stock, Rosa Conde, Ubaldo Martínez, Giovanna Guidorossi, Renato Mannheimer, Franco Mattei, Leonardo Morlino, Giuliano Urbani, Maria Weber, George Th. Mavrogordatos, Ilias Nicolacopoulos, and Constantinos Tsoucalas. One of the authors of this chapter (Montero) was a member of the Spanish team. It should be noted at this point that we have weighted the Greek sample to partly offset some unrepresentative features of that survey. (Weighting instructions will be provided to readers on request.) The 1993 Spanish data (n = 1,448) are from the Comparative National Elections Project (CNEP) survey under the direction of José Ramón Montero, Richard Gunther, José María Maravall, and Ludolfo Paramio. Analysis of voting behavior in the 1979 Spanish election was based upon DATA's 1979 postelection study (n = 5,439), under the direction of Richard Gunther, Giacomo Sani, and Goldie Shabad. Our 1982 data are from the postelection survey (n = 5,463) conducted by DATA, S.A., under the direction of Richard Gunther, Juan Linz, José Ramón Montero, Hans-Jürgen Puhle, Giacomo Sani, and Goldie Shabad. The Greek data (n = 1,196) from the 1996 election are from the CNEP survey conducted by Ilias Nicolacopoulos and Nikiforos Diamandouros. The Italian data from 1996 (n = 2,502) were collected by the Cattaneo Institute's Committee for the Study of the Political Transition, whose members include Paolo Bellucci, Roberto Cartocci,

Piergiorgio Corbetta, Ilvo Diamanti, Aldo Di Virgilio, Marco Maraffi, Arturo Parisi, Gianfranco Pasquino, Hans Schadee, and Paolo Segatti. Data for Austria, Britain, West Germany, and the United States in the 1970s were from the Eight Nation Political Action Study under the direction of Mark Abrams, Alan Marsh, Klaus Allerbeck, Max Kaase, Hans Klingemann, Leopold Rosenmayr, Anself Eder, Inga Findl, Kathleen Stoffl, Elfie Urbas, Samuel Barnes, Ronald Inglehart, M. Kent Jennings, Barbara Farah, Giovanni Sartori, Alberto Marradi, Giacomo Sani, Pertti Pesonen, David Matheson, and Risto Saenkiaho. Sample sizes for those surveys were as follows: Great Britain, 1,483; West Germany, 2,307; Austria, 1,585; United States, 1,719; Italy, 1,779; and Finland, 1,224. The Netherlands and Switzerland were excluded from this analysis because the fragmentation of their party systems made Probit analysis (which requires large samples in order to produce statistically significant findings) impossible. Data from the 1987 British election were from the British General Election Study, 1987 (n = 3,826), conducted by Social and Community Planning Research under the direction of A. F. Heath, R. M. Jowell, and J. K. Curtice. And data for the 1992 U.S. presidential election (n = 1,295) are from the CNEP survey conducted by Paul Allen Beck, Russell Dalton, and Robert Huckfeldt.

4. This is confirmed by an examination of individual-level survey data. A post-election survey undertaken by the Centro de Investigaciones Sociológicas in March 2000 (#2384) revealed that 15 percent of those who had voted for the PSOE and 12 percent of those who had supported Izquierda Unida in 1996 cast ballots for the Partido Popular in the first election of the new millennium.

5. For Spain, see Malefakis 1970; Payne 1973, 60 and 119–23; Vicens-Vives 1967, 43–57; and Brenan 1969, 131–69. For Portugal, see Bermeo 1986.

6. The literature on the role of religion in politics in southern Europe is so extensive that it cannot be cited here, except to present one representative study for each country. For Spain, see Montero and Calvo 1999; for Portugal, see de França 1984; for Italy, see Segatti, 1999; and for Greece, see Prodromou 1994.

7. In 1990, 43 percent of Spaniards claimed to attend religious services once a month or more. For 1975, see Vázquez Rabanal 1976; for 1981 and 1990, the European Values Study World Values Surveys, 1981–82 and 1990–91; and for 1985, the Four Nation Study (see n. 3 above).

8. Of respondents in the Four Nation survey, 33 percent of Portuguese, 28 percent of Spaniards, 27 percent of Italians, and 13 percent of Greeks claimed that they attended religious services once a week or more.

9. In this regard, Spaniards were very close to the European Community mean of 65 percent (*Eurobarometer*, #32 [1989]).

10. A small sample of this enormous scholarly literature includes Fuchs and Klingemann 1989; Inglehart and Klingemann 1976; Sani and Sartori 1980; and Huber and Inglehart 1995. With regard to studies of the four southern European countries, representative works include Bacalhau 1990 and Montero 1994; for Italy, see Mannheimer and Sani 1987; and for Greece, Mavrogordatos 1984.

11. This nearly tripolar distribution pattern fits well with the three political families (left, right, and center) analyzed by Mavrogordatos (1983b and 1984). See also Kalyvas 1997.

12. See Barnes, McDonough, and Pina 1985, 700, and 1986, 73–74; Mannheimer and Sani 1987, 116–17; van der Eijk et al. 1992, 419.

13. Examples of the extremely extensive literature on this subject include, on Spain, Astudillo 1997; on Portugal, Stoleroff 1992; for Greece, Kristsontonis 1992; and for Italy, Braun 1996.

14. For three different perspectives on this weakness, see Pérez Díaz 1987; Maravall 1981; Gillespie 1989.

15. It should also be noted that steps were taken to make Spain more comparable with the other cases by eliminating from the sample all residents of the Basque and Catalan regions, within which linguistic and cultural differences have given rise to the emergence of two distinctly different party systems. This step was necessary given our primary analytical focus on competition between parties of the left and right, since the dynamics of partisan competition in these two regions are entirely different from the rest of Spain, with center-right regional-nationalist parties virtually displacing nationwide center to center-right parties from these regional party systems, and with Basque and Catalan national identification overlapping with the class and religious cleavages. "Spain" in this analysis is thus a hypothetical construct that differs from reality insofar as it is devoid of the regional nationalist cleavages that have had such a marked impact on the dynamics of Spanish politics. Not to have taken this corrective step would have seriously confounded our analysis of the class, religious, and left-right variables for Spain.

16. Probit is analogous to ordinary-least-squares multiple regression techniques, except that it was designed specifically for dichotomous variables with skewed distributions, such as vote for a particular party in a multiparty system (see McKelvey and Zavoina 1975). Specifically, since OLS regression techniques assume an interval-level dependent variable with a normal distribution (assumptions that are invalid in the case of dichotomous voting decisions), it would have "the undesirable effect of causing regression analysis to severely underestimate the relative impact of certain variables" (McKelvey and Zavoina 1975, 119). Probit was specifically designed to sidestep this problem.

17. McKelvey and Zavoina 1975, 112. It should be noted that ever since King 1986, standardized measures such as R^2 have fallen out of favor. Indeed, there are some pitfalls in the use of such measures. One of them was identified in McKelvey and Zavoina 1975 itself: care must be taken to assure that the results of the analysis are statistically significant. This has been done in all of the following tables, where the Chi-square level of significance for all equations was at the .001 level, unless otherwise noted (with the superscript following the R^2 representing the level of significance). This step having been taken, these data can be regarded as reasonable estimates of the percentage of variance explained. For critiques of Gary King's challenge to the use of R^2, see Lewis-Beck and Skalaban 1991; Luskin 1991. Gary King (1991) has subsequently acknowledged that his original criticism went too far.

18. It should be noted that these interviewers' evaluations were used in this analysis only after they were very rigorously analyzed and corroborated with other measures (such as through cross-tabulations against self-reporting of income and occupational status). It should also be noted that whenever there was excessive colinearity among these economic variables, the weaker of the variables was elim-

inated from the equation (this usually resulted in a strengthening of the Chi-square measure of reliability of the equation, and often of the R^2 as well).

19. Although the 1981 survey of Greece lacked the occupational status variable, its weakness as a determinant of the vote was confirmed by the analysis of the 1996 data, which included occupational status and the aforementioned interviewer's evaluation of the quality of the respondent's housing and neighborhood.

20. Between 1956 and 1984, the class polarization of the U.S. electorate reportedly (Miller and Lockerbie 1992) increased, a trend that continued until 1992 according to our findings. Franklin 1992 (in ibid.) reports no decrease in class voting in Britain between 1974 and 1983, whereas we found evidence of a slight increase between 1970 and 1987. See also Nieuwbeerta 1995; Evans 1999.

21. In the British case, the variable was Anglican or other (i.e., other Protestant, Catholic, Jewish, or nonbeliever).

22. See Anthony Mughan, "Belgium," Ole Borre, "Denmark," Cees van der Eijk and Kees Niemöller, "Netherlands," Clive Bean, "New Zealand," Henry Valen, "Norway," and Maria Oskarson, "Sweden," in Franklin et al. 1992.

23. Indeed, Mussolini himself once complained in a conversation with a friend:

> If you could imagine the effort it has taken me to search for a possible equilibrium in which I could avoid the collision of antagonistic powers that touched each other side by side, jealous, distrustful one of the other, government, party, monarchy, Vatican, army *militizia,* prefects, provincial party leaders, ministers, the head of the Confederazioni, and the giant monopolistic interests, etc., you will understand they are the indigestions of totalitarianism, in which I did not succeed in melting that "estate" that I had to accept in 1922 without reservations. A pathological connecting tissue linking the traditional and circumstantial deficiencies of this great, small Italian people, which twenty years of tenacious therapy has succeeded in modifying only on the surface. (Translated from Aquarone 1964, 302)

See also Pasquino 1986, 58; Farnetti 1978.

24. Bellucci, Maraffi, and Segatti 1998, 25, concurs with this interpretation, concluding that the realignment of 1994–96 "was determined more by the decomposition and restructuring of the political offering and the new rules of the game than by new mass orientations. Leadership was an important factor in the realignment."

Chapter 4. Antiparty Politics and the Restructuring of the Italian Party System

1. In some respects, the crisis that unfolded in the early 1990s resembles other turning points in the history of Italy, such as the demise of the historical right and the coming to power of the left in 1876, and the crisis of participation that exploded at the turn of the century.

2. This survey was conducted by Arturo Parisi and Stefania Cappello (University of Bologna), Hans Schadee (University of Trento), and Anna Oppo (University of Cagliari).

3. See, e.g., Guidorossi 1984; Sani 1990; Mannheimer and Sani 1987; Fabbris 1977; Calvi 1987; Morlino 1984.

4. In later periods, negative evaluations of the public administration remained at the same level or increased. A 1986 Doxa study reported, for example, that such negative assessments had increased to 53 percent, from 35 percent in 1967. Di Palma 1970.

5. See, e.g., Hine 1990; Pasquino 1990a; Cotta 1992a; Morlino 1992.

6. It is important to stress, however, that under Fascism the systemic interpenetration between party and the public sector was not followed by significant changes in recruitment criteria, except, perhaps, in some new agencies created by the fascist regime and at the level of local government. The widespread politicization of bureaucratic careers in the public sector from the mid 1950s on can thus be considered a "democratic improvement." See Maraffi 1990.

7. In practice, however, the Fascist Party never realized this ambitious role, and the regime centered on the charismatic figure of Il Duce, Mussolini, rather than becoming a party government, as the "leftist" fascist faction would have liked. On the nature of the relationship between the Fascist Party, government, and the state in the early formative period of the fascist regime, see De Felice 1968.

8. Silvio Lanaro (1992) calls this syndrome of distrust the syndrome of the *apoti* (literally, those who do not drink). This metaphor captures the attitude of those who voted for the DC or some other government party but stood clear of the ideologies disseminated by those parties.

9. At that time, a large segment of public opinion agreed with this claim. In 1977, 63.6 percent of Italian citizens agreed that expanding democracy in various social institutions was a viable strategy for solving various institutional problems. This point of view was, however, more widespread among leftist voters. See Guidorossi 1975.

10. The volatility rate between 1983 and 1987 was 7.6, and between 1983 and 1979, it was 7.2. Some scholars have argued, however, that although aggregate volatility rates remained stable, there was an increasing mobility at the individual level. See Biorcio and Natale 1987.

11. La Rete, which asserts that Italian politics must be rebuilt on an entirely new moral basis, is a party founded at the beginning of the 1990s by leftist Christian Democrats, including the mayor of Palermo, and a group of well-known intellectuals.

12. Italian students of political geography long ago adopted these four labels to indicate distinct patterns of electoral support and styles of political behavior. The "Industrial Triangle" includes the northwestern industrial provinces around Turin, Milan, and Genoa, where support for the major parties was balanced; the "Red Belt" and the "White Area" consist of the central and northeastern regions, in which the communist and the Christian Democratic parties respectively were able to secure large majorities of the vote. "The south" is characterized by a balanced distribution of the vote among the major parties, accompanied by premodern forms of political behavior.

13. According to the reform eventually enacted in August 1993, 75 percent of the seats in both houses were to be allocated to candidates receiving pluralities

of the votes in single-member districts. The remaining 25 percent of the seats were to be assigned to party lists, according to an extremely complicated process. For discussions of the characteristics of the new system, see D'Alimonte and Chiaramonte 1993; Pappalardo 1994; Sani 1994b; Morlino 1995.

14. In 1994, about 70 percent of those elected to the Chamber of Deputies had no previous parliamentary experience. In 1996, the turnover fell to about 40 percent, which was nonetheless higher than in the elections of previous decades. See Verzichelli 1994 and 1997.

Chapter 5. The New Campaign Politics in Southern Europe

1. A recent attempt to design a new party model, the so-called "cartel party . . . in which colluding parties become agents of the state and employ the resources of the state to ensure their own collective survival," does not appear convincing either. In any case, there is no evidence that cartel parties have tried to devise anything new and significant in terms of electoral techniques and campaign politics. Indeed, if their goal is to achieve "a shrinkage in the degree to which electoral outcomes can determine government actions," cartel parties ought to be very reluctant to implement new techniques. Any kind of innovation may easily become disruptive of the equilibria so painfully achieved. In fact, so-called cartel parties do not innovate at all; they only try to protect their niches with the help of state power. "Democracy becomes a means of achieving social stability rather than social change, and elections become 'dignified' parts of the constitution." All quotations from Katz and Mair 1995.

2. One observer noted that in the October 1989 elections "even the Madrid daily *El País,* usually not unsympathetic to the Socialist cause, felt the need to denounce the biased coverage, describing Spanish television as 'a gigantic propaganda apparatus in the hands of the government'" (Amodia 1990, 295).

3. The Comparative National Elections Project (CNEP) consists of surveys containing a common core of questionnaire items regarding the sources of information about politics used by voters during the course of election campaigns: from secondary associations to which they belong; through conversations with friends, neighbors, co-workers, and family members; and via direct unmediated communications from the media. These common questionnaire items have been administered in Bulgaria, Chile, Germany, Great Britain, Greece, Italy, Japan, Spain, the United Kingdom, the United States, and Uruguay. See Chapter 3, n. 3, above.

4. Whereas Spain has large nationwide networks, Italian radio is highly fragmented into a large number of independent broadcasting stations, so the "filter" question (asking respondents to name their preferred radio station) may have excluded too many respondents from the follow-up question (Marletti and Roncarolo 2000).

5. See Roldán 1985; Pimlott and Seaton 1983; Katsoudas 1987; Bruneau and Macleod 1986.

6. On the negative side of this argument is Francesco Zucchini (1997, 120), who points out that only 5.6 percent of respondents in 1994 mentioned "party leader" as the principal reason for voting as they did (as compared with "party,"

"electoral coalition," and "spatial positioning." On the other side, Gunther and Montero (in this volume) found that the respondent's attitude toward the party leader "explained" about 10 percent of variance in vote choice for the seven largest parties in the 1996 election, and was much more important as a determinant of vote choice among parties within each left-right bloc.

7. See Vegleris 1981; Clogg 1987; Gunther 1989; Caciagli 1994; Bruneau and Macleod 1986.

Chapter 6. In Search of the Center: Conservative Parties, Electoral Competition, and Political Legitimacy in Southern Europe's New Democracies

1. Since it is mainly concerned with national politics, this chapter does not deal with such right-wing nationalist parties as the Partido Nationalista Vasco and the Convergència i Unió, the Catalan Nationalist Union.

2. In 1982, Adolfo Suárez, a former UCD prime minister, founded the Centro Democrático y Social (CDS). This party performed modestly in the elections of 1986 and 1989, but in 1993 it failed to elect a single deputy.

3. A party of the nondemocratic, ultraconservative right, the Partido Democrático Cristão (Christian Democratic Party), which appeared in Portuguese politics as early as 1974, was later banned from electoral competition, allegedly for trying to subvert democracy.

4. After the disintegration of DC in 1993, one of the splinter parties that came out of it was the Centro Cristiano Democratico, which later became part of the center-right coalition Polo delle Libertà.

5. Referring more particularly to Spain, Cotarelo and López Nieto remark that "from the point of view of the right, Social Democracy became something of an indefinable political attitude, charged with a vague enthusiasm for 'social issues' and steeped above all in moderation. In other words, it was moderation as a program, precisely the aspect in which the right with its past tradition of intolerance found itself in need of relegitimation" (1988, n. 6).

6. "A center 'tendency' always exists; what may not exist is a center party" (Sartori 1976, 131 and 202).

7. Following Sartori (1976, 133), I define as "anti-system" any party whose ideology "undermines the legitimacy of the regime it opposes," thus threatening the whole political system with a severe legitimacy crisis.

8. It should be noted, however, that a certain degree of cooperation between the DC and the MSI did take place at the municipal administration level, especially in the south.

9. The communists did not receive any ministries, but were consulted about major political decisions. In exchange, they promised to support the government and not cause its downfall.

10. "In 1987 the pattern of actors still resembled that of the early elections of 1948–53" (D'Alimonte and Bartolini 1997, 112).

11. The centrist orientation of l'Ulivo is indicated by its chief components: (1) the PDS-European Left; (2) the Popolari, drawing their political lineage directly from the DC; (3) the Dini List, a small group based around Lamberto Dini,

a conservative centrist; (4) various heirs of the old PSI; (4) the Pattisti of Mario Segni; (5) the Italian Democratic Movement, led by Sergio Berlinguer; and (6) the Greens. It is noteworthy that the communist RC was not included in the coalition because of the strong objections raised by most of its constituent parts. On the other hand, the RC also regarded l'Ulivo as excessively centrist.

12. ND has a long and distinct party lineage. It is the fourth successive manifestation of political conservatism in Greece, following the interwar Laïkon Komma (People's Party), and the postwar Hellenikos Synagermos (Greek Rally) and Ethnike Rizospastike Enosis (National Radical Union).

13. The enmity between the two men had its origin in the decision of King Paul, after the death of Papagos in 1955, to violate the seniority line, and handpick young Karamanlis as prime minister instead of supporting the more obvious candidacy of Stefanopoulos.

14. The following excerpt from a speech by Rallis, delivered at a regional congress of ND in 1981, is quite characteristic of his views:

> We [in ND] stand opposite to the [supporters of the] pro-juntist right, who hypocritically claim to have the same origin as ourselves. To them I reply that Cain and Abel were brothers, too, until the one killed the other. Likewise, the gap between us and those who killed democracy . . . cannot be bridged. Because today, as in the past, all their discourse and action is directed against democracy. . . . [They still stand for] the historically *passé* system of persecution, imprisonment, and exile for the communists. (Rallis 1983, 8)

15. Eventually, the former EDIK space was occupied more by PASOK than by ND. See Mavrogordatos 1983b; Featherstone and Katsoudas 1985.

16. Perhaps the greatest success during the 1981 campaign was the addition to the PASOK electoral ticket of the former EDIK leader George Mavros. For the ideological development of PASOK, see Spourdalakis 1988.

17. Rallis (1983, 278) writes in his autobiographical account for that period, "I am supposed to lead ND to electoral victory while being challenged by my political opponent [Papandreou] and, at the same time, attacked from behind and all other sides [within ND]."

18. The reactionary eight was, nonetheless, represented in that election by a resuscitated political formation, the Komma Proodeftikon (Party of the Progressives), or KP, headed by Spyros Markezinis. In the polarizing elections of 1981, the KP secured a poor 1.7 percent of the vote, since most erstwhile EP supporters had been absorbed by ND in its fight against the menace from the left.

19. According to nationwide opinion polls, already by 1980, 73.2 percent of the voters considered ND to be a purely "right-wing" party, and only 19.4 percent thought of it as a "liberal" (i.e., centrist) one. See Loulis 1995, 35–36.

20. To the degree that opinion polls accurately reflect political climates, in March 1983, ND was preferred by 82.1 percent of "rightist" and 73.3 percent of the "center-right" voters; only 6.8 percent of the "centrist" voters would vote for it. In contrast, PASOK seemed to be the top option for 62.5 percent of "centrist" and 81.5 percent of "center-left" voters (Loulis 1981b, 63). These findings are congruent with the data provided by *Eurobarometer,* #19 (Spring 1983), where 34.8 percent of the ND electorate was found to be located at the very far right of the po-

litical spectrum (position 10 on a ten-point scale), as reported by Papadopoulos 1989, 63.

21. The standard bearer of the far right in the party spectrum, the Ethnike Politike Enosis (National Political Union), or EPEN, campaigned for the release of the former dictator George Papadopoulos from prison and won a negligible 0.6 percent of the vote in the 1985 elections.

22. The first of those changes in party leadership took place in the aftermath of the 1993 electoral defeat, when Mitsotakis resigned and was replaced by the more populist Miltiades Evert. The same scenario was repeated after ND's more recent defeat as the polls in 1996, after which Evert was succeeded by Costas Karamanlis, the young and inexperienced nephew of the party founder.

23. See the results of a nationwide opinion poll centered around the profile of the center-right in contemporary Greece, conducted by Project Research Consulting on behalf of the Centre of Political Research and Information (Athens) in March 1997.

24. The process of consolidating the UCD as a party is described in detail in Gunther, Sani, and Shabad 1986, esp. 92–104. As those authors write, "The key factor in the UCD's success was its ability to bring together the moderate opposition to *Franquismo* and the reformists who held official posts within the regime itself" (92).

25. According to Cotarelo and López Nieto 1988, 81, the UCD was "the result of the fusion of 48 pre-existing parties."

26. Of these the most important were the electoral losses in the Basque and Catalan regional elections, the negative outcome of the Andalusian referendum, and a censure motion in 1980 against the government.

27. At the local level, the party elite was composed of notables with extensive personal networks who had played crucial roles under the old regime, toward which they still felt a certain ideological affinity. Indicative of this continuity with the authoritarian regime are the many positive references to the dictator's name made by Carlos Arias Navarro, a former prime minister under Franco, in a television appearance as an AP candidate for the Senate during the first democratic elections. See Gunther, Sani, and Shabad 1986, 84–92.

28. Interview with Manuel Fraga Iribarne, quoted in Gunther, Sani, and Shabad 1986, 81.

29. An analysis (including both political and financial considerations) of Fraga's decision to include Francoist ultras in the coalition forming AP is to be found in Gunther, Sani, and Shabad, 83–88.

30. In 1982, membership stood at 100,000, and in 1987 it reached 222,000 (Cotarelo and López Nieto 1988, 88). Displaying extraordinary activism for a conservative party, the AP called no fewer than eleven party congresses from its foundation in 1976 until 1993. For details on the party's organizational growth, see López Nieto 1998, 254–69.

31. It is worth comparing this development with the situation in Spain's early transition years when, according to Linz, the Spanish political system displayed the characteristics of polarized multipartyism (with its consequent emphasis on the bilateral nature of opposition that was exerted on the UCD). See Linz 1980.

32. Data from Gunther, Batella, and Montero forthcoming. The author is

grateful to Richard Gunther and José Ramón Montero for supplying much of the information concerning the evolution of the PP after 1988.

33. Examples include Education Minister Pilar del Castillo and her husband, Guillermo de Gortázar (PP secretary in charge of the ideological training of new party militants), who had been members of the "red flag" faction of the Communist Party in the anti-Franquist opposition.

34. That constituency included small landholders of the agrarian northern regions; owners of big farming estates and petty industrialists in the central and southern regions; the traditionalist middle classes and churchgoers everywhere; and big financial and industrial interests.

35. The early transition period was particularly hard for both conservative parties, because their leftist opponents did not hesitate to ransack their local party offices, beat or otherwise harass their candidates, sabotage their rallies, and destroy their electoral propaganda materials.

36. Voters' opinions on a number of issues amply confirm that there was very little to distinguish between these two parties. See Bruneau and Macleod 1986, 95–96.

37. After electoral defeat in 1995, Nogueira resigned the party leadership and was promptly replaced by liberal Marcelo Rebelo de Sousa.

Chapter 7. Mobilizers and Late Modernizers: Socialist Parties in the New Southern Europe

1. For more detailed, systematic, and comparative evaluations of the policies, achievements, and dilemmas of the southern European socialists, see Maravall 1992, 1995, and 1997; Bresser, Maravall, and Przeworski 1993. I am grateful to Nikiforos Diamandouros and Richard Gunther for their critical and constructive comments and their patience as editors.

2. Dahrendorf 1980 and 1989. See also Bell 1973; Panitch 1985; Przeworski and Sprague 1986; Scharpf 1987; Merkel 1993; Kitschelt 1994.

3. Merkel 1993, 67. See also Merkel 1992; Keman 1988; Hine 1986. And for the term "third wave," see Huntington 1991.

4. For the development of the PSI, see Merkel 1985 and 1987; Di Scala 1988; Pasquino 1986b; Hine 1989; Cazzola 1985.

5. See Featherstone 1990. On PASOK, see Spourdalakis 1988 and 1991; Diamandouros 1991 and 1997; Sotiropoulos 1991, 1995, and 1996; Lyrintzis 1984a, 1984b, 1987, and 1993; Mavrogordatos 1983b; Featherstone and Katsoudas 1987; Clogg 1987; Kariotis 1992; Tzannatos 1986.

6. Data derived from Project Research Consulting, "Research on Political Culture" (MS, Athens, 1994), based on interviews with 811 delegates to the congress.

7. On the PSOE, see Serfaty 1984; Puhle 1986; Maravall 1991; Sastrústegui 1992; Craig 1993 and 1995; Gunther 1986b; Gunther, Sani, and Shabad 1986; Gillespie 1989, 1990b and 1992; Merkel 1989; Tezanos 1983 and 1989; Román 1987; Juliá 1988 and 1997; Boix 1995; Amodia 1994; González and Guerra 1977; Guerra et al 1986. For the socialists in Catalonia, see Colomé 1989, 1991, and 1992.

8. Until the summer of 1978, not only the Valencian and the (now unified)

Catalan socialist parties (earlier Reagrupment, Congrès, Federació), but also Tierno Galván's small but influential and prestigious Partido Socialista Popular (PSP) joined forces with the PSOE.

9. A number of authors have stated, for example, that the help of the German Social Democrats for the PSOE channeled through the office of the Friedrich Ebert-Stiftung in Madrid amounted to about 27 million DM between 1976 and 1980, a sum that has never been substantiated by any evidence. Cf. Juliá 1997, 471; Misse 1996, 603–4; Powell 1994, 113. According to our calculations and estimates for the five years in question, a sum of about 15–17 million DM might be more realistic. See Koniecki 1996.

10. See Chapter 2 of this volume. And see also Linz and Stepan 1996, 116–29; Maxwell 1986 and 1995; Maxwell and Haltzel 1990; Bruneau and MacLeod 1986; Opello 1985; Graham and Wheeler 1983; Graham and Makler 1979; Braga de Macedo and Serfaty 1981; Graham 1992; Gladdish 1990; Bermeo 1986; Barreto 1987; Sänger 1994.

11. This ideological moderation was facilitated by the walkout of a number of syndicalist, cooperativist, Trotskyite, and otherwise leftist groups in 1977. See Partido Socialista 1973, 1975, and 1979. And see also Stock and Rother 1983; Bruneau and MacLeod 1986, 26–37 and 64–76; Robinson 1991–92 and 1993; Gallagher 1979; Sänger 1994, 113–16, 199–205, 408–21.

12. In 1990, PASOK became a member of the Socialist International; in 1992, it was among the founding members of the European Socialist Party.

13. Izquierda Socialista's share of the PSOE's rank and file was somewhat higher; in the early 1980s, it could muster between 15 and 20 percent of these. See Puhle 1986a; Gillespie 1992 and 1989, 376–419. For the programmatic debates and the party congresses, see Guerra 1977; Partido Socialista Obrero Español 1979 and 1981; Bustelo et al. 1976; González 1976; Guerra 1979 and 1986; García Santesmases 1985.

14. For studies of these election results, see Boix 1996; del Castillo and Sani 1986; Sastrústegui 1992, 37–39; Amodia 1990; Montero 1992; Justel 1992.

15. On the 1993 elections, see Wert, Toharia, and López Pintor 1993; Lancaster 1994; del Castillo 1994; Boix 1995. For 1996, see Gillespie 1996b; Amodia 1996.

16. Chhibber and Torcal 1997 argues that this realignment of social groups was a direct response to economic policies adopted by the PSOE governments, and by the stands taken by the leaders of other parties toward those policies. See also Chapter 3 of this volume.

17. The particular strongholds of the PS were the Algarve, the north coast, and the centre-south (Lisbon, Santarem, and Setúbal, except in 1980), whereas its support was least in the northern interior (Bragança, Viseu, Vila Real) and in Evora (except in 1976). In 1983, the PS made gains in the north and the center of the country, but lost in the Alentejo.

18. Thomas Bruneau and Alex Macleod (1986, 203–10) estimate that, of the PRD voters in 1985, 73 percent had previously voted for the PS, 18 percent for the communist Aliança Povo Unido, and 6 percent for the PSD. Mário Bacalhau sets these figures at 57 percent, 10 percent, and 8 percent respectively, with 20 percent being newly mobilized voters and 3 percent shifting from the CDS (Ba-

calhau 1994, 56). In 1987, the PRD lost over three-quarters of its voters (its share declining from 18.4 to 4.9 percent, and then to 0.6 percent in 1991), most of whom (particularly the young) switched to the PSD (Gallagher 1988, 142–45).

19. The PS mounted a very well organized, coordinated, and centralized campaign, combining a flexible, moderate, and open technocratic approach with sentimental appeals for compassion, "change," and a "new majority," adopting a red heart as its symbol, rather than a rose or a fist, and the slogan "Razão e coração" (Reason and heart).

20. For membership figures, see Table 7.1. The data provided by parties have to be interpreted with caution, however, as it is often unclear whether actual dues-paying members or "alleged members" are being counted. The revised data published by the Portuguese PS in 1998 give much lower figures for years before 1983 than did earlier estimates. I am grateful to Michalis Spourdalakis, to the International Department of the PS, and to Reinhard Naumann for providing me with the most recent figures.

21. See Tezanos 1983, 89–134, and 1985; Puhle 1986a, 326–32; Tezanos et al. 1981; Partido Socialista Obrero Español 1984, 48.

22. Gillespie 1989, 429. This trend was to continue: although the socialists had pledged before to make no more than 4,000 political appointments, they made more than 25,000 between 1984 and 1987 alone. See Kraus and Merkel 1993.

23. It should be noted that a quota of 25 percent for women on the executive committee was set by the Thirty-First Party Congress in 1988; it was increased to 40 percent at the Thirty-Fourth Congress nine years later.

24. The two *guerristas* were Caballero and Vázquez; one seat went to the traditional Izquierda Socialista (Ana Noguera). The *guerristas* also failed to install their candidate, Carmen Hermosín, in Alfonso Guerra's place as deputy secretary-general.

25. The remaining 10.8 percent of the delegates to that congress were employed in the private sector, 8.5 percent were pensioners, 20.4 percent self-employed, and 3.6 percent workers (Sotiropoulos 1992, 102; Lyrintzis 1986, 118–19; Sotiropoulos 1991, 107; and Project Research Consulting 1994).

26. Data from MRB and Tases surveys, in the Athens newspaper *Kathemerine*, September 10, 1995; also see Spourdalakis 1996.

27. On the consolidation of democracy in Spain, see Linz and Montero 1986; Gunther, Diamandouros, and Puhle 1995; Linz and Stepan 1996; Cotarelo 1992; Pérez Díaz 1987 and 1993; Pérez Yruela and Giner 1988.

28. The center-right PSD, whose erratic economic policy at the time followed rather narrowly defined interests, was part of the Bloco Central as well as of the AD coalition. Maravall 1995, 163, and 1993, 113; Dornbusch, Eckaus and Taylor 1979; Murteira 1979; Baklanoff 1992–93; Bermeo 1990.

29. In 1985, on a scale of 1 to 10, the national averages of sympathy for organized interests in Greece were 7.8 for the GSEE, 7.9 for PASEGES, and 7.5 for the interests of small business, but only 3.3 for the industrialists (SEV). In all other southern European countries, the averages were much more balanced between labor and industry (both around 4.5). Data from the Four Nation Study, cited in Chapter 3, n. 3, above.

30. Greek labor unions were regulated by Law 1264/82 and the agricultural

cooperatives by Law 1257/82, stipulating a one man–one vote principle for this sensitive sector, as Law 1712 did even for big business. Under Law 1746, the Chambers of Commerce and Industry were merged with those of Trades and Crafts. Law 1361/82 regulating the professional associations of agriculture was defended by the then minister of agriculture, Costas Simitis, on the grounds that the organization of farmers was not the exclusive affair of the farmers but an affair of the state because thereby "the course of society is affected." The law gave PASOK control (55 percent in 1983) and the KKE an enormous overrepresentation (41 percent) in PASEGES. See Mavrogordatos 1988 and 1993.

31. In 1987 12.3 million working hours were lost to strikes, as compared to 3.5 million in 1981 and 6.5 million in 1982 (Maravall 1992, 42).

32. Estimates of party strength in national peak associations for 1990 are: PASEGES—ND 50 percent, PASOK 41, KKE 9; GSEE—ND 18 percent, PASOK 39, KKE 38; ADEDY—ND 35 percent, PASOK 41, KKE 16; GSEVE—ND 30, PASOK 12, KKE 58 (Mavrogordatos 1993, table 2).

33. At the UGT's Third Congress in Braga in March 1984, 733 of the 1,148 delegates represented the PS, or "socialist tendency"; 255 the official "social democratic tendency," TSD, which was recognized by the PSD; and 160 the traditional, but marginalized, TESIRESD. See the figures in *Expresso Revista,* April 7, 1984; Schmitter 1995; Barreto and Naumann 1998; Sänger 1994.

34. In 1989, of the 1 million organized workers (28.6 percent of the labor force, much closer to the Greek than to the Spanish rate), 550,000 belonged to the CGTP (215 unions in 1983, of which 153 were local groups), 350,000 to the UGT (49 unions), and 100,000 to independent unions. See Schmitter 1995, 294 and 300; Visser 1990, 173–74; and for 1984, Chilcote 1993.

35. The Acuerdo Económico y Social ended a phase of corporatist concertation that had begun with the Pactos de la Moncloa of 1977 (formally a pact between the political parties), which fulfilled an important function during the transition. Additional pacts had been concluded by the former UCD governments in 1979 (AMI) and 1981 (ANE). From the mid 1980s to the mid 1990s, pacts became less viable for several reasons, among them the lack of sufficient centralization and a broad base of support from the unions and the increasing conflict between the government and employers, on the one hand, and the unions, on the other.

36. *ABC,* May 10, 1985; Camiller 1994;. See also Gillespie 1990b and 1992; Astudillo 1997.

37. UGT membership increased steadily from almost 415,000 in 1985 to 655,000 in 1989 and 820,000 in 1994; CCOO membership rose from 427,000 in 1985 to 527,000 in 1989 and 787,000 in 1994. The CCOO benefited in 1985 from its opposition to the PSOE government. See Jordana 1996; and, for comparative data, Table 3.11 in this volume.

38. The April 1997 pact—which was hailed by *El País* as "probably the most important social agreement signed in Spain over the past 15 years" and contained measures to lower labor market rigidities in order to reduce unemployment and temporary work—was signed by the UGT, the CCOO, and the employers' organizations CEOE and CEPYME. See *European Industrial Relations Review,* no. 280 (May 1997). On the problems of labor "unity," see Richards and García de Polavieja 1997.

39. It should be noted that PASOK secured a comfortable electoral victory in 1996, despite a decline in its share of the popular vote, because of a loss of electoral support by ND, combined with the powerful majoritarian biases of the electoral system in underrepresenting smaller parties, such as the communist KKE (which obtained 5.6 percent of the vote), the Left Coalition Synaspismos (with 5.1 percent), and Dikki, which had split from PASOK (with 4.4 percent).

40. José Borrell later resigned in response to allegations of corruption by his staff.

41. See, e.g., Obiols 1987; Reventós 1993; Guerra 1994 and 1997.

42. See *El País,* May 10, 1998, 15; May 28, 1998, 20; and August 28, 1998, 13.

Chapter 8. Four Actors in Search of a Role: The Southern European Communist Parties

The authors wish to thank P. Nikiforos Diamandouros, Richard Gunther, Manuel Lucena, Leonardo Morlino, and Ioannis Voulgaris for their careful reading of and comments on an earlier version of this chapter.

1. Angelo Panebianco (1982) uses the phrase "source of legitimation" for extranational sponsors (i.e., the Comintern and the USSR) of communist parties. We use it here to refer to the socialist regimes of eastern Europe and the international communist movement.

2. See Morlino 1980, 169. This is a somewhat more demanding definition than Giovanni Sartori's "antisystem party" (which focuses mainly on the principles, ideology, and message the party transmits to the mass level) or Juan Linz's "disloyal" party (which concentrates mainly on behavior and activities). See Sartori 1976, 133–34; Linz 1978, 27–31.

3. See Morlino 1986, 219; Burton, Gunther, and Higley 1992, 7–8; Gunther, Puhle, and Diamandouros 1995, 13–14; Cotta 1990, 57–59.

4. Embracing Eurocommunism entailed renouncing armed insurrection and the dictatorship of the proletariat, choosing a democratic and parliamentary path to socialism, and rejecting the international proletarian movement in favor of strategic autonomy. See Carrillo 1977; Mujal-León 1983.

5. On the role played by the PCI in parliament, see Di Palma 1977; Fabbrini 1990, 753–77. It has been calculated that "three-fourths of Italian legislation produced between 1948 and 1971 was passed with the consent of the communists" (Cazzola 1974, 99).

6. Thus, even after the PCI's Eighteenth Congress, the PSI leader Bettino Craxi regarded its changes as "a face-lifting operation." See Hellman 1993.

7. The two parties, which remained separate from then on (even though they did form an alliance for the 1974 elections), diverged on several points. Fundamentally, the birth of the KKE-Es marked the exit of moderate Eurocommunists from the KKE. This helped make the KKE homogeneous, compact, and orthodox. It also squeezed the KKE-Es between the KKE and PASOK, with few card-carrying members and few voters. See Kapetanyannis 1979 and 1987; Papayannakis 1981, 13; Varvarousis 1988.

8. As George Mavrogordatos (1984) put it, the Greek political system, with its tripolar structure, was encouraged to function as a bipolar system, with PASOK

and ND alternating in government and the communist pole pushed to the sidelines.

9. Thanks to the prestige its leader, Bettino Craxi, had acquired in three years as premier, the PSI won the biggest increase in votes since 1946, both in percentage terms and in terms of an expansion of its electoral base (which increased by 30 percent).

10. Carrillo expounded his ideas very clearly in a letter he wrote to the party leadership, which was published in *Mundo Obrero* on 25 April 1985.

11. The front formed by the PCE to support the "no" camp in the 12 March 1986 referendum on joining NATO, was reorganized as a coalition for the June general election. On the birth of the IU, see Mujal-León 1986.

12. Julio Anguita had been elected mayor of Cordoba in 1983 with an absolute majority of votes—the only such case in the history of the PCE. In 1984, Anguita founded Convocatoria por Andalucía (CA), a heterogeneous coalition of parties and movements that, in line with the Iglesias project, was a local anticipation of the Izquierda Unida. This was also crowned with success, since the IU-CA doubled its vote between 1982 (8.4 percent) and 1986 (17.6 percent). Anguita's charisma—a quality Iglesias seemed to lack—did not go unnoticed, and the leader rose to the top posts in the PCE and IU.

13. In a November 1991 interview, Zita Seabra, one of the leaders of the internal opposition, explained the attitude of the PCP toward the democratic regime until 1987 very clearly: "The party had an ambiguous political line. Namely, it asserted that the revolution was ongoing and, at the same time, that it was not by playing the electoral game that we would achieve power. . . . But for us it was clear that there would never be an armed revolution or a coup d'état in Portugal and that the revolution had ended ten years before. We felt the PCP ought to adapt to democratic consolidation [because] there was no other way by which to achieve power if not via the elections."

14. Achille Occhetto took over from Alessandro Natta, who had become the PCI's secretary-general after Berlinguer's sudden death in 1984.

15. It should also be stressed that the KKE was more concerned with retaining control over its traditional voters than with the expansion of its electoral base. The goal of class purity was more important for the KKE than for the PCE.

16. "Informe de la Comisión Central de Garantías y Control," *Mundo Obrero,* February 18, 1988, 36–41. As early as 1978, the PCE recognized the secrecy of the ballot for all internal elections, and the official list of candidates was regularly accompanied by a second list made up of the candidates excluded from the official one, so that they, too, could receive votes.

17. See Centro de Investigaciones Sociológicas surveys #2061 (1993) and #2108 (1994); and Montero and Torcal 1990.

18. The PSI split into five different groups, and the DC in six. See Di Virgilio 1994.

19. The new electoral law is described in chapters 2 and 4 of this volume. For more detailed descriptions, see D'Alimonte and Chiaramonte, 1994; Fusaro 1995.

20. The progressive alliance was made up of the PDS and the RC (ex PCI); the PSI and the Rinascita Socialista (ex PSI); the Alleanza Democratica (ex PSI and small lay parties); the Greens; and La Rete and the Cristiano Sociali (ex DC).

21. The Ulivo coalition was made up of the PDS, the PPI, the Patto Segni, the Alleanza Democratica, the Socialisti Italiani, the Pri, La Rete, the Greens, the Liberali, the Laburisti, the PSDI, and Cristiano Sociali. On the local and regional elections, see Di Virgilio 1996; Gilbert 1996.

22. The RC had also voted against the budget bill in October 1997, leading Prodi to resign, albeit only for a few days.

References

Achimastos, Myron. 1990. "L'idéologie politique du parti communiste grec (1974–1985): Limites et dynamiques de l'efficacité idéologique communiste dans la société grecque." Ph.D. diss., Université de Paris VII.

Achimastos, Myron, and Ioanna Papathanassiou. 1990. "Les élections du 18 juin 1989 en Grèce: Note sur la répartition des voix communistes." *Communisme* 22–23: 168–78.

Agüero, Felipe. 1995. *Soldiers, Civilians, and Democracy: Post-Franco Spain in Comparative Perspective.* Baltimore: Johns Hopkins University Press, 1995.

Alivizatos, Nicos C. 1979. *Les institutions politiques de la Grèce à travers les crises, 1922–1974.* Paris: Librairie générale de Droit et de Jurisprudence.

———. 1990. "The Difficulties of 'Rationalization' in a Polarized Political System: The Greek Chamber of Deputies." In Liebert and Cotta 1990.

Almeida, João Ferreira de, António Firmino da Costa, and Fernando Luis Machado. 1994. "Recomposição socioprofissional e novos protagonismos." In António Reis, ed., *Portugal 20 anos de democracia.* Lisbon: Circulo de Leitores.

Álvarez-Miranda Navarro, Berta. 1995. *Los partidos políticos en Grecia, Portugal y España ante la Comunidad Europea: Explicación comparada del consenso europeísta español.* Madrid: Instituto Juan March de Estudios e Investigaciones.

Amodia, José. 1983. "Union of the Democratic Center." In David S. Bell, ed., *Democratic Politics in Spain: Spanish Politics After Franco.* London: Frances Pinter.

———. 1990. "Personalities and Slogans: The Spanish Election of October 1989." *West European Politics* 13, 2: 293–98.

———. 1994. "A Victory Against All the Odds: The Declining Fortunes of the Spanish Socialist Party." In Richard Gillespie, ed., *Mediterranean Politics,* vol. 1. London: Frances Pinter.

———. 1996. "Spain at the Polls: The General Election of 3 March 1996." *West European Politics* 19: 813–19.

Aquarone, Alberto. 1964. *L'organizzazione dello stato totalitario.* Turin: Giulio Einaudi.

Arango, Joaquín, and Migual Díez. 1993. "6-J: El sentido de una elección." *Claves de Razón Práctica* 36: 10–18.

Astudillo, Javier. 1997. "Los recursos del socialismo: Las cambiantes relaciones entre el PSOE y la UGT, 1982–1993." Ph.D. diss., Instituto Juan March de Estudios e Investigaciones, Madrid.
Bacalhau, Mário. 1989. "Mobilidade e transferência de voto através das sondagens." In Mário Baptista Coelho, ed., *Portugal: O sistema político e constitucional, 1974–1987.* Lisbon: Instituto de Ciências Sociais.
———. 1990. "Transition of the Political System and Political Attitudes in Portugal." *International Journal of Public Opinion Research* 2: 141–54.
———. 1994. *Atitudes, opinões e comportamentos políticos dos Portugueses, 1973–1993.* Lisbon: Edições Heptagono.
Baccetti, Carlo. 1997. *Il PDS: Verso un nuovo modello di partito?* Bologna: Il Mulino.
Baklanoff, Eric N. 1992–93. "Portugal and the EC Single Market: The Challenge of Structural Reform and Convergence." *Portuguese Studies Review* 2: 77–90.
Bardi, Luciano, and Gianfranco Pasquino. 1995. "Politicizzati e alienati." In Arturo Parisi and Hans Schadee, eds., *Sulla soglia del cambiamento.* Bologna: Il Mulino.
Barnes, Samuel H. 1971. "Modelli spaziali e l'identificazione partitica dell'elettore italiano." *Rivista italiana di scienza politica* 1: 123–43.
———. 1974. "Italy: Religion and Class in Electoral Behavior." In Rose 1974.
Barnes, Samuel, Peter McDonough, and Antonio López Pina. 1985. "The Development of Partisanship in New Democracies: The Case of Spain." *American Journal of Political Science* 29: 695–720.
———. 1986. "Volatile Parties and Stable Voters." *Government and Opposition* 21: 56–75.
Barreto, António. 1987. *Anatomia de uma revolução: A reforma agraria em Portugal.* Lisbon: Europa-América.
Barreto, José, and Reinhard Naumann. 1998. "Portugal: Industrial Relations Under Democracy." In Ferner and Hyman 1998.
Bartolini, Stefano. 1986. "La volatilità elettorale." *Rivista italiana di scienza politica* 16: 363–400.
———. 1993. "I primi movimenti socialisti in Europa: Consolidamento organizzativo e mobilitazione politica." *Rivista italiana di scienza politica* 23: 217–81.
Bartolini, Stefano, and Roberto D'Alimonte. 1994. "La competizione maggioritaria: Le origini elettorali del parlamento diviso." *Rivista italiana di scienza politica* 24: 634.
———, eds. 1995. *Maggioritario ma non troppo: Le elezioni politiche del 1994.* Bologna: Il Mulino.
———. 1996. "Come perdere una maggioranza: La competizione nei collegi uninominali." *Rivista italiana di scienza politica* 26: 655–702.
———, eds. 1997. *Maggioritario per caso.* Bologna: Il Mulino.
Bartolini, Stefano, and Peter Mair, eds. 1984. *Party Politics in Contemporary Western Europe.* London: Frank Cass.
———. 1990. *Identity, Competition and Electoral Availability.* Cambridge: Cambridge University Press.
Bell, Daniel. 1973. *The Coming of Post-Industrial Society.* New York: Basic Books.
Bellucci, Paolo, Marco Maraffi, and Paolo Segatti. 1998. "Continuity and Change

in Italian Electoral Behavior." Paper presented at the Convegno internazionale, Democrazie, transizione, politica, scelte elettorali, Istituto Cattaneo, Bologna, July 1.

Bentivegna, Sara. 1995. "Attori e strategie comunicative nella campagna elettorale." In Pasquino 1995b.

Berga, Juan B. 1991. "Izquierda Unida como propuesta." *Nuestra Bandera* 151: 55–58.

Bermeo, Nancy Gina. 1986. *The Revolution Within the Revolution: Workers' Control in Portugal.* Princeton, N.J.: Princeton University Press.

———. 1990. "The Politics of Public Enterprise in Portugal, Spain and Greece." In Ezra Suleiman and John Waterbury, eds., *The Political Economy of Public Sector Reform and Privatization.* Boulder, Colo.: Westview Press.

Bettinelli, Ernesto. 1982. *Alle origini della democrazia dei partiti.* Milan: Edizioni di comunità.

Biorcio, Roberto. 1991. "La lega come attore politico." In Mannheimer 1991.

Biorcio, Roberto, and Paolo Natale. 1987. "La mobilità elettorale degli anni ottanta." *Rivista italiana di scienza politica* 19: 385–430.

Blondel, Jean. 1978. *Political Parties.* London: Wildwood House.

Boix, Carles. 1995. *Building a Socialdemocratic Strategy in Southern Europe: Economic Policy Under the Gonzalez Government, 1982–1993.* Working Paper 1995/69. Madrid: Centro de Estudios Avanzados en Ciencias Sociales, Instituto Juan March de Estudios e Investigaciones.

———. 1996. *Partidos políticos, crecimiento e igualdad.* Madrid: Alianza.

———. 1998a. *Political Parties, Growth and Equality: Conservative and Social Democratic Strategies in the World Economy.* New York: Cambridge University Press.

———. 1998b. *Partisan Governments and Macroeconomic Policies in OECD Economies.* Working Paper 1998/122. Madrid: Centro de Estudios Avanzados en Ciencias Sociales, Instituto Juan March de Estudios e Investigaciones.

Bosco, Anna. 1993. "Il partito assediato: PCE e PCP tra crisi e mutamento." Ph.D. diss., Università di Firenze.

———. 1998. "Eppur si muove: La lenta trasformazione del Partito Comunista Portoghese." *Studi politici* 2: 43–85.

Braga de Macedo, Jorge, and Simon Serfaty, eds. 1981. *Portugal Since the Revolution: Economic and Political Perspectives.* Boulder, Colo.: Westview Press.

Braun, Michael. 1996. "The Confederated Trade Unions and the Dini Government: 'The Grand Return to Noe-Corporatism'?" In Caciagli and Kertzer 1996.

Brenan, Gerald. 1969. *The Spanish Labyrinth: An Account of the Social and Political Background of the Civil War.* Cambridge: Cambridge University Press.

Bresser Pereira, Luiz Carlos, José María Maravall, and Adam Przeworski. 1993. *Economic Reforms in New Democracies.* Cambridge: Cambridge University Press.

Bruneau, Thomas C. 1981. "Patterns of Politics in Portugal Since the April Revolution." In Braga de Macedo and Serfaty 1981.

———. 1991–92. "Defense Modernization and the Armed Forces in Portugal." *Portuguese Studies Review,* Fall–Winter, 28–43.

———, ed. 1997. *Political Parties and Democracy in Portugal: Organizations, Elections, and Public Opinion.* Boulder, Colo.: Westview Press.

Bruneau, Thomas, and Alex MacLeod. 1986. *Politics in Contemporary Portugal: Parties and the Consolidation of Democracy.* Boulder, Colo.: Lynne Rienner.
Budge, Ian, Ivor Crewe, and Dennis Farlie, eds. 1976. *Party Identification and Beyond: Representations of Voting and Party Competition.* New York: Wiley.
Budge, Ian, and Dennis Farlie. 1983. *Explaining and Predicting Elections.* London: Allen & Unwin.
Bull, Martin, and Martin Rhodes. 1997. "Between Crisis and Transition: Italian Politics in the 1990s." *West European Politics* 20, 1: 1–13.
Burnham, Walter Dean. 1970. *Critical Elections and the Mainsprings of American Politics.* New York: Norton.
Burton, Michael, Richard Gunther, and John Higley. 1992. "Introduction: Elite Transformations and Democratic Regimes." In Higley and Gunther 1992.
Burton, Michael, and John Higley. 1987. "Elite Settlements." *American Sociological Review* 52: 295–307.
Bustelo, Francisco, et al. 1976. *Partido Socialista Obrero Español.* Barcelona: Avance.
Butler, David, Howard R. Penniman, and Austin Ranney, eds. 1981. *Democracy at the Polls: A Comparative Study of Competitive National Elections.* Washington, D.C.: American Enterprise Institute.
Caciagli, Mario. 1994. "Spagna: proporzionale con effetti maggioritari." In Oreste Massari and Gianfranco Pasquino, eds., *Rappresentare e governare.* Bologna: Il Mulino.
Caciagli, Mario, Franco Cazzola, Leonardo Morlino, and Stefano Passigli, eds. 1994. *L'Italia fra crisi e transizione.* Bari: Laterza.
Caciagli, Mario, and David I. Kertzer, eds. 1996. *Italian Politics: The Stalled Transition.* Boulder, Colo.: Westview Press.
Caciagli, Mario, and Alberto Spreafico, eds. 1990. *Vent'anni di elezioni in Italia, 1961–1987.* Padua: Liviana.
Cafagna, Luciano. 1993. *La grande slavina.* Venice: Marsilio.
Calamandrei, Piero. 1947. "Patologia della corruzione parlamentare." *Il Ponte* 10: 829–75.
Calder, Carlos. 1992. "An Orange Sweep: The Portuguese General Elections of 1991." *West European Politics* 15, 2: 167–70.
Calvi, Gabriele. 1987. *Indagine sociale italiana.* Milan: Franco Angeli.
Camiller, Patrick. 1992. "Spain: The Survival of Socialism?" In Perry Anderson and Patrick Camiller, eds., *Mapping the West European Left.* London: Verso.
Campbell, Angus, Phillip Converse, Warren Miller, and Donald Stokes. 1960. *The American Voter.* New York: Wiley.
Capo Giol, Jordi. 1990. *La legislación estatal en la España democrática.* Madrid: Centro de Estudios Constitucionales.
Carr, Raymond, and Juan Pablo Fusi Aizpurua. 1979. *Spain: Dictatorship to Democracy.* London: George Allen & Unwin.
Carrillo, Santiago. 1977. *"Eurocomunismo" y Estado.* Barcelona: Grijalbo.
Cartocci, Roberto. 1990. *Elettori in Italia.* Bologna: Il Mulino.
———. 1993. *Tra la lega e la chiesa.* Bologna: Il Mulino.
———. 1997. "Indizi di un inverno precoce: Il voto proporzionale tra equlibrio e continuità." *Rivista italiana di scienza politica* 26: 609–54.
Cazorla Pérez, José. 1992. *Del clientelismo tradicional al clientelismo de partido: Evolu-*

ción y características. ICPS Working Paper 55. Barcelona: Institut de Ciències Polítiques i Socials.

Cazzola, Franco. 1972. "Consenso e opposizione nel parlamento italiano: Il ruolo del PCI dalla I alla IV legislatura." *Rivista italiana di scienza politica* 2: 71–96.

———. 1974. *Governo e opposizione nel parlamento italiano: Dal centrismo al centro-sinistra, il sistema della crisi.* Milan: Giuffrè.

———. 1985. "Struttura e potere del Partito Socialista Italiano." In Gianfranco Pasquino, ed., *Il sistema politico italiano.* Rome: Laterza.

Cazzola, Franco, and Massimo Morisi. 1981. "La decisione urgente: Usi e funzioni del decreto legge nel sistema politico italiano." *Rivista italiana di scienza politica* 11: 447–82.

Chhibber, Pradeep, and Mariano Torcal. 1997. "Elite Strategy, Social Cleavages, and Party Systems in a New Democracy: Spain." *Comparative Political Studies* 30: 27–54.

Chilcote, Ronald H. 1993. "Portugal: From Popular Power to Bourgeois Democracy." In James Kurth and James Petras, eds., *Mediterranean Paradoxes: Politics and Social Structures in Southern Europe.* Providence, R.I.: Berg.

Clogg, Richard, ed. 1983. *Greece in the 1980s.* London: Macmillan.

———. 1987. *Parties and Elections in Greece: The Search for Legitimacy.* Durham, N.C.: Duke University Press.

———, ed. 1993. *Greece, 1981–89: The Populist Decade.* New York: St. Martin's Press.

Close, David H. 1993. "The Legacy." In id., ed., *The Greek Civil War, 1943–1950: Studies of Polarization.* New York: Routledge.

Colomé, Gabriel. 1989. *El Partit dels Socialistes de Catalunya: Estructura, funcionament i electorat, 1978–1984.* Barcelona: Edicions 62.

———. 1991. "The 'Partit dels Socialistes de Catalunya.'" In Maravall et al. 1991.

———. 1992. "The PSC: Mass Party or Catch-All Party?" In Merkel et al. 1992.

Colomer, Josep M. 1995. "España y Portugal: Regímenes de liderazgo de partido." In id., ed., *La política en Europa.* Barcelona: Ariel.

Condomines, Jonas, and José D. Barroso. 1984. "La dimension gauche-droite et la competition entre partis politiques en Europe du Sud." *Il Politico* 49, 3: 405–38.

Converse, Philip. 1969. "Of Time and Partisan Stability." *Comparative Political Studies* 2: 139–71.

Corbetta, Piergiorgio, Arturo M. L. Parisi, and Hans M. A. Schadee. 1988. *Elezioni in Italia: Struttura e tipologia delle consultazioni politiche.* Bologna: Il Mulino.

Corkill, David. 1991. "The Portuguese Presidential Election of 13 January 1991." *West European Politics* 14, 4: 185–92.

———. 1996. "Portugal Votes for Change and Stability: The Election of 1995." *West European Politics* 19, 2: 403–9.

Cotarelo, Ramón, ed. 1992. *Transición política y consolidación democrática.* Madrid: Centro de Investigaciones Sociológicas.

Cotarelo, Ramón, and Lourdes López Nieto. 1988. "Spanish Conservatism, 1976–87." *West European Politics* 11, 2: 80–95.

Cotta, Maurizio. 1990. "The 'Centrality' of Parliament in a Protracted Democratic Consolidation: the Italian Case." In Liebert and Cotta 1990.

———. 1992a. "Elite Unification and Democratic Consolidation in Italy: A Historical Overview." In Higley and Gunther 1992.

———. 1992b. "Continuità e discontinuità nei sistemi partitici europei." In Mauro Calise, ed., *Come cambiano i partiti.* Bologna: Il Mulino.

Craig, Patricia. 1993. "The Spanish Socialist Workers' Party: Organization and Ideology in a Contemporary Social Democratic Party." Ph.D. diss., Yale University.

———. 1995. *Political Mediation. Traditional Parties and New Social Movements: Lessons from the Spanish Socialist Workers' Party.* Working Paper 1995/67. Madrid: Centro de Estudios Avanzados en Ciencias Sociales, Instituto Juan March de Estudios e Investigaciones.

Cravinho, João. 1986. "The Portuguese Economy." In Maxwell 1986.

Crewe, Ivor. 1976. "Party Identification Theory and Political Change in Britain." In Budge, Crewe, and Farlie 1976.

Crewe, Ivor, and David Denver, eds. 1985. *Electoral Change in Western Democracies: Patterns and Sources of Electoral Volatility.* London: Croom Helm.

Crosland, Anthony R. 1956. *The Future of Socialism.* London: Jonathan Cape.

Cunha, Carlos. 1997. "The Portuguese Communist Party." In Bruneau 1997.

Curi, Umberto. 1991. "La genesi del partito democratico della sinistra." In Umberto Curi and Paolo Flores d'Arcais, eds., *L'albero e la foresta: Il partito democratico della sinistra nel sistema politico italiano.* Milan: Franco Angeli.

Daalder, Hans. 1984. "In Search of the Center of European Party Systems." *American Political Science Review* 78: 92–109.

Daalder, Hans, and Peter Mair, eds. 1983. *Western European Party Systems.* Beverly Hills, Calif.: Sage Publications.

Dahl, Robert A. 1966. "Some Explanations." In Dahl, *Political Oppositions in Western Democracies.* New Haven, Conn.: Yale University Press.

Dahrendorf, Ralf. 1980. "The End of Social-Democratic Consensus." In *Life Chances: Approaches to Social and Political Theory.* London: Weidenfeld & Nicolson.

———. 1989. "Tertium Non Datur: A Comment on the Andrew Shonfield Lectures." *Government and Opposition* 2: 131–41.

D'Alimonte, Roberto. 1998. "The Italian Transition Between Parties and Coalitions." Paper presented at the Convegno internazionale, Democrazie transizione politica scelte elettorali, Istituto Cattaneo, Bologna, July 1.

D'Alimonte, Roberto, and Stefano Bartolini. 1997. "'Electoral Transition' and Party System Change in Italy." *West European Politics* 20, 1: 110–34.

D'Alimonte, Roberto, and Alessandro Chiaramonte. 1993. "Il nuovo sistema elettorale italiano: Quali opportunità?" *Rivista italiana di scienza politica* 22: 513–47.

Dalton, Russell J. 1988. *Citizen Politics in Western Democracies: Public Opinion and Political Parties in the United States, Great Britain, West Germany, and France.* Chatham, N.J.: Chatham House.

Dalton, Russell J., Paul Allen Beck and Scott C. Flanagan. 1984. "Electoral Change in Advanced Industrial Democracies." In Dalton, Flanagan and Beck 1984.

Dalton, Russell J., Scott C. Flanagan, and Paul Allen Beck, eds. 1984. *Electoral Change in Advanced Industrial Democracies: Realignment or Dealignment?* Princeton, N.J.: Princeton University Press.

De Felice, Renzo. 1968. *Mussolini: Il fascista. L'organizzazione dello stato fascista, 1925–29.* Torino: Einaudi.

Del Castillo, Pilar, ed. 1985. *La financiación de partidos y candidatos en las democracias occidentales.* Madrid: CIS–Siglo XXI.

———, ed. 1994. *Comportamiento electoral y político.* Madrid: CIS.

Del Castillo, Pilar, and Giacomo Sani. 1986. "Las elecciones de 1986: Continuidad sin consolidación." In Linz and Montero 1986.

Della Porta, Donnatella. 1992. *Lo scambio occulto: Casi di corruzione politica in Italia.* Bologna: Il Mulino.

De Luna, Giovanni. 1982. *Storia del partito d'azione.* Milan: Feltrinelli.

Diamandouros, P. Nikiforos. 1983. "Greek Political Culture in Transition: Historical Origins, Evolution, Current Trends." In Clogg 1983.

———. 1984. "Transition to, and Consolidation of, Democratic Politics in Greece, 1974–83: A Tentative Assessment." In Pridham 1984.

———. 1986. "Regime Change and the Prospects for Democracy in Greece." In O'Donnell, Schmitter, and Whitehead 1986.

———. 1991. "PASOK and State-Society Relations in Post-Authoritarian Greece, 1974–1986." In Vryonis 1991.

———. 1993. "Politics and Culture in Greece, 1974–91: An Interpretation." In Clogg 1993.

———. 1994. *Cultural Dualism and Political Change in Postauthoritarian Greece.* Madrid: Centro de Estudios Avanzados en Ciencias Sociales, Instituto Juan March de Estudios e Investigaciones.

———. 1997. "Greek Politics and Society in the 1990s." In Graham T. Allison and Kalypso Nicolaidis, eds., *The Greek Paradox: Promise vs. Performance.* Cambridge, Mass.: MIT Press.

———. 1998. "The Political System in Postauthoritarian Greece, 1974–1996." In Ignazi and Ysmal 1998.

Diamandouros, P. Nikiforos, and Richard Gunther. 1995. "Preface." In Gunther, Diamandouros, and Puhle 1995.

Diamanti, Ilvo. 1993. *La lega.* Rome: Donzelli.

———. 1994. "La politica come marketing." *Micromega* 2: 60–77.

———. 1997. "Identità cattolica e comportamento di voto: U'Unità non e' più una virtù." In Parisi and Corbetta 1997.

Diamanti, Ilvo, and Renato Mannheimer. 1994. *Milano a Roma.* Rome: Donzelli.

Dimitras, Panayote. 1990. "The Difficulty of 'Throwing the Rascals Out' in 'A Vast Madhouse': The Triple Greek Elections of 1989–1990." *Greek Opinion* 5: 6–21.

———. 1994a. "The Greek Parliamentary Elections of October 1993." *Electoral Studies* 13: 235–39.

———. 1994b. "Greece: Notes on the 1994 Elections to the European Parliament." *Electoral Studies* 13: 343–46.

Di Nolfo, Ennio. 1986. *Le paure e le speranze degli Italiani.* Milan: Mondadori.

Di Palma, Giuseppe. 1970. *Apathy and Participation: Mass Politics in Western Societies.* New York: Free Press.

———. 1977. *Surviving Without Governing: The Italian Parties in Parliament.* Berkeley: University of California Press.

———. 1980. "Founding Coalitions in Southern Europe: Legitimacy and Hegemony." *Government and Opposition* 15 (Spring): 162–89.

Di Scala, Spencer M. 1988. *Renewing Italian Socialism: Nenni to Craxi.* Oxford: Oxford University Press.

Di Virgilio, Aldo. 1994. "Dai partiti ai poli: La politica delle alleanze." *Rivista italiana di scienza politica* 24: 493–547.

———. 1996. "Le elezioni regionali e amministrative: Bipolarizzazione con riserva." In Caciagli and Kertzer 1996.

Dittrich, Karl. 1983. "Testing the Catch-All Thesis: Some Difficulties and Possibilities." In Daalder and Mair 1983.

Donaghy, Peter J., and Michael T. Newton. 1987. *Spain: A Guide to Political and Economic Institutions.* New York: Cambridge University Press.

Dornbusch, Ruediger, Richard S. Eckaus, and Lance Taylor. 1979. "Analysis and Projection of Macroeconomic Conditions in Portugal." In Graham and Makler 1979.

Doukas, George. 1991. "The Thirteenth Congress of the KKE: Defeat of the Renovators." *Journal of Communist Studies* 7: 393–98.

Downs, Anthony. 1957. *An Economic Theory of Democracy.* New York: Harper.

Duverger, Maurice. 1964 [1951]. *Political Parties: Their Organization and Activities in the Modern State.* London: Methuen.

Ebbinghaus, Bernhard, and Jelle Visser. 1999. "When Labour Institutions Matter: Union Growth and Decline in Western Europe, 1950–90." *European Sociological Review* 15: 135–58.

EIU [Economist Intelligence Unit]. 1998a. *Country Profile: Italy, 1997–98.* London: EIU.

———. 1998b. *Country Profile: Spain, 1997–98.* London: EIU.

———. 1998c. *Country Profile: Portugal, 1997–98.* London: EIU.

———. 1998d. *Country Profile: Greece, 1997–98.* London: EIU.

Evans, Geoffrey, ed. 1999. *The End of Class Politics? Class Voting in Comparative Context.* Oxford: Oxford University Press.

Fabbrini, Sergio. 1990. "Le strategie istituzionali del Pci." *Il Mulino* 39: 753–77.

———. 1994. *Quale democrazia: L'Italia e gli altri.* Rome: Laterza.

———. 1997. *Le regole della democrazia.* Rome: Laterza.

Fabbris, Guido. 1977. *Il comportamento politico degli italiani.* Milan: Franco Angeli.

Fakiolas, Rossetos. 1987. "Interest Groups: An Overview." In Featherstone and Katsoudas 1987.

Farneti, Paolo. 1978. "Social Conflict, Parliamentary Fragmentation, Institutional Shift and the Rise of Fascism: Italy." In Juan J. Linz and Alfred Stepan, eds., *The Breakdown of Democratic Regimes.* Baltimore: Johns Hopkins University Press.

———. 1980. "La coalizione monopolistica." *Biblioteca della liberta,* April–September, 77–78.

Featherstone, Kevin. 1987. "Elections and Voting Behaviour." In Featherstone and Katsoudas 1987.

———. 1990. "The 'Party-State' in Greece and the Fall of Papandreou." *West European Politics* 13, 1 (1990): 101–15.

Featherstone, Kevin, and Dimitris Katsoudas. 1985. "Change and Continuity in Greek Voting Behaviour." *European Journal of Political Research* 13: 27–40.

———, eds. 1987. *Political Change in Greece Before and After the Colonels.* London: Croom Helm.

Featherstone, Kevin, and Kostas Yfantis, eds. 1996. *Greece in a Changing Europe: Between European Integration and Balkan Disintegration?* Manchester: Manchester University Press.

Fegiz, Pierpaolo Luzzatto. 1956. *Il volto sconosciuto dell'Italia.* Milan: Giuffre.

Fernández Stock, Maria José. 1988. "El centrismo político y los partidos del poder en Portugal." *Revista de Estudios Políticos* 60–61: 139–72. *See also under* Stock

Ferner, Anthony, and Richard Hyman, eds. 1992. *Industrial Relations in the New Europe.* London: Blackwell.

———, eds. 1998. *Changing Industrial Relations in Europe.* 2d ed. Malden, Mass.: Blackwell.

Flores, Marcello, and Nicola Gallerano. 1992. *Sul Pci: Un'interpretazione storica.* Bologna: Il Mulino.

Fraga Iribarne, Manuel. 1975. "Teoría del Centro." In *Legitimidad y representatión.* Madrid: Grijalbo.

Frain, Maritheresa. 1991. "The Emergence of Political Parties on the Right and the Consolidation of Democracy in Post-Authoritarian Regimes: The PPD/PSD in Portugal, 1974–1987." Ph.D. diss., Georgetown University.

———. 1995. "Relações entre o presidente e o primeiro-ministro em Portugal, 1985–1995." *Analise Social* 30: 653–78.

———. 1996. "Portugal's Legislative and Presidential Elections: 'A New Socialist Majority.'" *South European Society and Politics* 1, 1: 115–20.

———. 1997. "The Right in Portugal: The PSD and the CDS/PP." In Bruneau 1997.

De França, Luis. 1984. *Comportamento religioso da população portuguesa.* Lisbon: Moraes / Instituto de Estudos para o Desenvolvimiento.

Franklin, Mark, Tom Mackie, Henry Valen, et al. 1992. *Electoral Change: Responses to Evolving Social and Attitudinal Structures in Western Countries.* New York: Cambridge University Press.

Freitas do Amaral, Diogo. 1991. "The Constitution and Governance." In Maxwell and Monje 1991.

Fuchs, Dieter, and Hans-Dieter Klingemann. 1989. "The Left-Right Schema." In M. Kent Jennings, Jan van Deth, et al., *Continuities in Political Action: A Longitudinal Study of Political Orientations in Three Western Democracies.* Berlin: Walter de Gruyter.

Gallagher, Michael. 1991. "Proportionality, Disproportionality and Electoral Systems." *Electoral Studies* 10, 1 (March): 33–51.

Gallagher, Tom. 1979. "Portugal's Struggle for Democracy: The Role of the Socialist Party." *West European Politics* 2: 198–217.

———. 1988. "Goodbye to Revolution: The Portuguese Election of July 1987." *West European Politics* 11, 1: 139–45.

Gangas Peiró, Pilar. 1995. "El desarrollo organizativo de los partidos políticos españoles de implantación nacional." Ph.D. diss., Instituto Juan March de Estudios e Investigaciones, Madrid.

García-Guereta Rodríguez, Elena. 1996. "The Spanish 'Partido Popular': A Case Study of Intra-Party Power Distribution Through a Period of Party Change." Paper presented at the ECPR Joint Sessions of Workshops, Oslo, 29 March–3 April.

García Santesmases, Antonio. 1985. "Evolución ideológica del socialismo en la España actual." *Sistema* 68: 61–78.

Gaspar, Carlos, and Vasco Rato. 1992. *Rumo à memória: Crónicas da crise comunista.* Lisbon: Quetzal Editores.

Gasperoni, Giancarlo. 1997. *ITANES 1990–1996: Italian National Election Studies.* Results of the Nationwide Voter Sample Surveys Conducted by the Istituto Cattaneo in 1990, 1992, 1994, and 1996. Bologna: Istituto Carlo Cattaneo.

Gentile, Emilio. 1989. *Storia del partito fascista, 1919–1922: Movimento e milizia.* Rome: Laterza.

Gibson, Heather, ed. 2000. *Economic Transformation, Democratization and Integration into the European Union: The Case of Southern Europe.* London: Macmillan.

Gilbert, Mark. 1996. "L'ulivo e la quercia." In Caciagli and Kertzer 1996.

Gillespie, Richard. 1989. *The Spanish Socialist Party: A History of Factionalism.* Oxford: Clarendon Press.

———. 1990a. "Regime Consolidation in Spain: Party, State and Society." In Pridham 1990.

———. 1990b. "The Break-Up of the 'Socialist Family': Party-Union Relations in Spain, 1982–1989." *West European Politics* 13: 47–61.

———. 1992. *Factionalism in the Spanish Socialist Party.* ICPS Working Paper 59. Barcelona: Institut de Ciències Polítiques i Socials.

———. 1996. "The Spanish General Election of 1996." *Electoral Studies* 15, 3: 425–32.

Giner, Salvador. 1986. "Political Economy, Legitimation, and the State in Southern Europe." In O'Donnell, Schmitter, and Whitehead 1986.

Ginsborg, Paul. 1990. *A History of Contemporary Italy, Society and Politics, 1943–1988.* London: Penguin Books.

Gladdish, Ken. 1990. "Portugal: An Open Verdict." In Pridham 1990.

Goldey, D. B. 1997. "The Portuguese General Election of October 1995 and Presidential Election of January 1996." *Electoral Studies* 16, 2: 245–54.

Goldthorpe, John H., et al. 1969. *The Affluent Worker in the Class Structure.* Cambridge: Cambridge University Press.

González, Felipe. 1976. "La unidad de los socialistas." *Sistema* 15: 45–51.

González, Felipe, and Alfonso Guerra. 1977. *Partido Socialista Obrero Español.* Bilbao: Ediciones Albia.

Graham, Lawrence. 1992. "Redefining the Portuguese Transition to Democracy." In Higley and Gunther 1992.

———. 1993. *The Portuguese Military and the State: Rethinking Transitions in Europe and Latin America.* Boulder, Colo.: Westview Press.

Graham, Lawrence S., and Harry M. Makler, eds. 1979. *Contemporary Portugal: The Revolution and Its Antecedents.* Austin: University of Texas Press.

Graham, Lawrence S., and Douglas L.Wheeler, eds. 1983. *In Search of Modern Por-*

tugal: The Revolution and Its Consequences. Madison: University of Wisconsin Press.

Grassi, Fabio. 1990. "Modelli e struttura del socialismo italiano." In Quagliarello Gaetano, ed., *Il partito nella bella epoque.* Milan: Giuffrè, 1990.

Guarnieri, Carlo. 1992. *Magistratura e sistema politica.* Bologna: Il Mulino.

Guerra, Alfonso, ed. 1977. *XXVII Congreso del Partido Socialista Obrero Español.* Barcelona: PSOE.

———, ed. 1979. *Este viejo y nuevo partido.* Madrid: Fundación Pablo Iglesias.

———. 1984. *Felipe González: De Suresnes a la Moncloa.* Madrid: Novatex.

———. 1985. "El socialismo y la España vertebrada." *Sistema* 68–69: 5–18.

———. 1994. "El futuro del Estado." *Sistema* 118–19: 11–22.

———. 1997. *La democracia herida.* Madrid: Espasa-Calpe.

Guerra, Alfonso, et al. 1986. *El futuro del socialismo.* Madrid: Sistema.

———, eds. 1987. *Nuevos horizontes teóricos para el socialismo.* Madrid: Sistema.

Guerra, Alfonso, and José Félix Tezanos, eds. 1992. *La década del cambio: Diez años de gobierno socialista, 1982–1992.* Madrid: Sistema.

Guidorossi, Giovanna. 1984. *Gli italiani e la politica: Valori, opinioni, atteggiamenti dal dopoguerra a oggi.* Milan: Franco Angeli.

Gunther, Richard. 1986a. "El realineamiento del sistema de partidos de 1982." In Linz and Montero 1986.

———. 1986b. "El colapso de UCD." In Linz and Montero 1986.

———. 1986c. "Los partidos comunistas de España." In Linz and Montero 1986.

———. 1986d. "The Spanish Socialist Party: From Clandestine Opposition to Party of Government." In Stanley G. Payne, ed., *The Politics of Democratic Spain.* Chicago: Council on Foreign Relations.

———. 1988. "Spain and Portugal." In Gerald A. Dorfman and Peter J. Duignan eds., *Politics in Western Europe.* Stanford, Calif.: Hoover Institution Press.

———. 1989. "Electoral Laws, Party Systems, and Elites: The Case of Spain." *American Political Science Review* 83 (September): 836–58.

———. 1992. "Spain: The Very Model of the Modern Elite Settlement." In Higley and Gunther 1992.

———. 1996a. *Spanish Public Policy: From Dictatorship to Democracy.* Working Paper 1996/84. Madrid: Centro de Estudios Avanzados en Ciencias Sociales, Instituto Juan March de Estudios e Investigaciones.

———. 1996b. "The Impact of Regime Change on Public Policy: The Case of Spain." *Journal of Public Policy* 16: 157–201.

Gunther, Richard, José Ramón Montero, and Joan Botella. Forthcoming. *Democracy in Modern Spain.* New Haven, Conn.: Yale University Press.

Gunther, Richard, P. Nikiforos Diamandouros, and Hans-Jürgen Puhle, eds. 1995. *The Politics of Democratic Consolidation: Southern Europe in Comparative Perspective.* Baltimore: Johns Hopkins University Press.

Gunther, Richard, José Ramón Montero, and José Ignacio Wert. 2000. "The Media and Politics in Spain: From Dictatorship to Democracy." In Gunther and Mughan 2000.

Gunther, Richard, and Anthony Mughan, eds. 2000. *Democracy and the Media: A Comparative Perspective.* New York: Cambridge University Press.

Gunther, Richard, Hans-Jürgen Puhle, and P. Nikiforos Diamandouros. 1995. "Introduction." In Gunther, Diamandouros, and Puhle 1995.

Gunther, Richard, Giacomo Sani, and Goldie Shabad. 1986. *Spain After Franco: The Making of a Competitive Party System.* Berkeley: University of California Press.

Haltzel, Michael, ed. 1990. *Portugal: Ancient Country, Young Democracy.* Washington, D.C.: Wilson Center Press.

Harmel, Robert, Uk Heo, Alexander Tan, and Kenneth Janda. 1995. "Performance, Leadership, Factions and Party Change: An Empirical Analysis." *West European Politics* 18: 1–33.

Harmel, Robert, and Kenneth Janda. 1992. "Environment, Performance, and Leadership as Factors in Party Change." Paper presented at ECPR Joint Sessions, University of Limerick, March 30–April 4.

———. 1994. "An Integrated Theory of Party Goals and Party Change." *Journal of Theoretical Politics* 6: 259–87.

Hellman, Stephen. 1988. *Italian Communism in Transition: The Rise and Fall of the Historic Compromise in Turin, 1975–1980.* New York: Oxford University Press.

———. 1993. "The Left and the Decomposition of the Party System in Italy." In Ralph Miliband and Leo Panitch, eds., *Real Problems, False Solutions: Socialist Register, 1993.* London: Merlin Press.

———. 1998. "The Italian Left in the Era of the Euro." *Italian Politics and Society* 49: 4–20.

Higley, John, and Richard Gunther. 1992. *Elites and Democratic Consolidation in Latin America and Southern Europe.* New York: Cambridge University Press.

Hine, David. 1986. "Leaders and Followers: Democracy and Manageability in the Social Democratic Parties of Western Europe." In William E. Paterson and Alistair H. Thomas, eds., *The Future of Social Democracy: Problems and Prospects of Social-Democratic Parties in Western Europe.* Oxford: Oxford University Press.

———. 1989. "The Italian Socialist Party." In Tom Gallagher and Allan M. Williams, eds., *Southern European Socialism: Parties, Elections and the Challenge of Government.* Manchester: Manchester University Press.

———. 1990. "The Consolidation of Democracy in Post-War Italy." In Pridham 1990.

Hoover, Greg. 1989. "Intranational Inequality: A Cross-National Dataset." *Social Forces* 67: 1008–26.

Hopkin, Jonathan. 1995. "Party Development and Party Collapse: The Case of Unión de Centro Democrático in Post-Franco Spain." Ph.D. diss., European University Institute, Florence.

Huber, John, and Ronald Inglehart. 1995. "Expert Interpretations of Party Spaces and Party Locations in Forty-Two Societies." *Party Politics* 1: 73–111.

Huneeus, Carlos. 1985. *La Unión de Centro Democrático y la transición a la democracia en España.* Madrid: Centro de Investigaciones Sociológicas.

Huntington, Samuel P. 1991. *The Third Wave: Democratization in the Late Twentieth Century.* Norman: University of Oklahoma Press.

Iglesias, Gerardo. 1984. "Por la renovación y el fortalecimiento del PCE." In *Documentos Políticos aprobados por el XI Congreso del PCE.* Madrid: Mundo Obrero.

Ignazi, Piero. 1989. *Il polo escluso: Profilo del Movimento Sociale Italiano.* Bologna: Il Mulino.

———. 1992. *Dal Pci al Pds.* Bologna: Il Mulino.
———. 1994. *Postfascisti: Dal MSI al AN.* Bologna: Il Mulino.
———. 1996. "From Neo-Fascists to Post-Fascists? The Transformation of the MSI into AN." *West European Politics* 19, 4: 693–714.
———. 1997. "Italy." *European Journal of Political Research* 32 (1997): 417–18.
Ignazi, Piero, and C. Ysmal, eds. 1998. *The Organization of Political Parties in Southern Europe.* Westport, Conn.: Greenwood Press.
Inglehart, Ronald. 1990. *Culture Shift in Advanced Industrial Society.* Princeton, N.J.: Princeton University Press.
Inglehart, Ronald, and Hans-Dieter Klingemann. 1976. "Party Identification, Ideological Preference and the Left-Right Dimension Among Western Mass Publics." In Budge, Crewe, and Farlie 1976.
Janitschek, Hans. 1984. *Mário Soares: Portrait of a Hero.* London: Weidenfeld & Nicholson.
Jiménez, Fernando. 1995. *Detrás del escándalo político.* Barcelona: Tusquets.
Jordana, Jacint. 1995. "Trade Union Membership in Spain, 1977–1994." Labour Studies Working Papers, Centre for Comparative Labour Studies, University of Warwick, August.
———. 1996. "Reconsidering Union Membership in Spain, 1977–1994: Halting Decline in a Context of Democratic Consolidation." *Industrial Relations Journal* 27 (September): 211–24.
Juliá, Santos, ed. 1988. *La desavenencia: Partido, sindicatos y huelga general.* Madrid: El País-Aguilar.
———. 1997. *Los socialistas en la política española, 1879–1982.* Madrid: Taurus.
Juliá, Santos, Javier Pradera, and Joaquín Prieto, eds. 1996. *Memoria de la transición.* Madrid: Taurus.
Justel, Manuel. 1992. *El líder como factor de explicación de voto.* ICPS Working Paper 51. Barcelona: Institut de Ciències Polítiques i Socials.
Kalyvas, Stathis. 1996. *The Rise of Christian Democracy in Europe.* Ithaca, N.Y.: Cornell University Press.
———. 1997. "Polarization in Greek Politics: PASOK's First Four Years, 1981–1985." *Journal of the Hellenic Diaspora* 32, 1 (June): 83–104.
Kallias, Constantine M. 1976. *He ideologia tes Neas Demokratias* (The Ideology of [the] New Democracy [Party]). Athens: N.p.
Kalogeropoulou, Eftalia. 1989. "Election Promises and Government Performance in Greece: PASOK's Fulfillment of Its 1981 Election Pledges." *European Journal of Political Research* 17: 289–311.
Kapetanyannis, Vasilis. 1993. "The Left in the 1980s: Too Little, Too Late." In Clogg 1993.
———. 1979. "The Making of Greek Eurocommunism." *Political Quarterly* 50: 445–60.
———. 1987. "The Communists." In Featherstone and Katsoudas 1987.
Karakatsanis, Neovi M. 1996. "Negotiated Transition . . . Successful Outcome: The Processes of Democratic Consolidation in Greece." Ph.D. diss., Ohio State University.
Karamanlis, Constantine. 1979–85. *Hoi logoi tou K. Karamanle* (The Speeches of K. Karamanlis). Athens: N.p.

Kariotis, Theodore C., ed. 1992. *The Greek Socialist Experiment.* New York: Pella.

Karl, Terry. 1990. "Dilemmas of Democratization in Latin America." *Comparative Politics* 23, 1: 1–22.

Karl, Terry L., and Philippe C. Schmitter. 1991. "Modes of Transition in Latin America, Southern and Eastern Europe." *International Journal of Social Science* 128: 269–84.

Kasakos, Panos, and P. C. Ioakimidis, eds. 1994. *Greece and EC Membership Evaluated.* London: Pinter.

Katsoudas, Dimitrios K. 1977. "O choros tes extremistikes dexias" (The Chorus of the Far Right). *Epikentra,* October, 15–19.

———. 1987a. "The Media—The State and Broadcasting." In Featherstone and Katsoudas 1987.

———. 1987b. "The Conservative Movement and New Democracy: From Past to Present." In Featherstone and Katsoudas 1987.

Katz, Richard S., ed. 1987. *Party Governments: European and American Experiences.* New York: De Gruyter.

Katz, Richard S., Peter Mair, et al. 1992. "The Membership of Political Parties in European Democracies, 1960s–1990." *European Journal of Political Research* 22: 329–45.

———. 1995. "Changing Models of Party Organization and Party Democracy: The Emergency of the Cartel Party." *Party Politics* 1, 1: 5–28.

Keman, Hans. 1988. *The Development of Surplus Welfare: Social Democratic Politics and Policies in Advanced Capitalist Democracies (1965–1984).* Leiden: University of Leiden.

King, Gary. 1986. "How Not to Lie with Statistics: Avoiding Common Mistakes in Quantitative Political Science." *American Journal of Political Science* 30: 666–87.

———. 1991. "'Truth' Is Stranger than Prediction, More Questionable than Causal Inference." *American Journal of Political Science* 35: 1047–53.

Kirchheimer, Otto. 1965. "Confining Conditions and Revolutionary Breakthrough." *American Political Science Review* 59, 4 (December): 964–74.

———. 1966. "The Transformation of the Western European Party Systems." In Joseph LaPalombara and Myron Weiner, eds., *Political Parties and Political Development.* Princeton, N.J.: Princeton University Press.

Kitschelt, Herbert. 1994. *The Transformation of European Social Democracy.* Cambridge: Cambridge University Press.

Koniecki, Dieter, ed. 1996. *20 años de la Fundación Friedrich Ebert en España.* Madrid: Fundación Friedrich Ebert.

Kraus, Peter A., and Wolfgang Merkel. 1993. "Die Linksparteien." In Walther L. Bernecker and Carlos Collado Seidel, eds., *Spanien nach Franco.* Munich: Oldenbourg.

Kristsontonis, Nicol. 1992. "Greece: From State Authoritarianism to Modernization." In Ferner and Hyman 1992.

Kuznets, Simon Smith. 1979. *Growth, Population and Income Distribution: Selected Essays.* New York: Norton.

Laakso, Markku, and Rein Taagepera. 1979. "'Effective' Number of Parties: A Measure with Application to West Europe." *Comparative Political Studies* 12, 1: 3–27.

Labini, Paolo Sylos. 1986. *Le classi sociali negli anni ottanta.* Bari: Laterza.

Lanaro, Silvio. 1992. *Storia dell'Italia repubblicana.* Venice: Marsilio.

Lancaster, Thomas D. 1994. "A New Phase for Spanish Democracy? The General Election of June 1993." *West European Politics* 17: 183–90.

———. 1996. "Executive-Legislative Relations in Southern Europe." *South European Society and Politics* 1: 186–205.

LaPalombara, Joseph. 1964. *Interest Groups in Italian Politics.* Princeton, N.J.: Princeton University Press.

———. 1987. *Democracy, Italian Style.* New Haven, Conn.: Yale University Press.

Laponce, J. A. 1975. "Spatial Archetypes and Political Perceptions." *American Political Science Review* 69, 1: 11–20.

Lewis, J. R., and A. M. Williams. 1984. "Social Cleavages and Electoral Performance: The Social Bases of Portuguese Political Parties, 1976–1983." In Pridham 1984.

Lewis-Beck, Michael S., and Andrew Skalaban. 1991. "The R-Squared: Some Straight Talk." *Political Analysis* 2: 153–72.

Lieberman, Sima. 1995. *Growth and Crisis in the Spanish Economy, 1940–93.* London: Routledge.

Liebert, Ulrike, and Maurizio Cotta, eds. 1990. *Parliament and Democratic Consolidation in Southern Europe.* London: Pinter.

Lijphart, Arend. 1984. *Democracies: Patterns of Majoritarian and Consensus Government in Twenty-One Countries.* New Haven, Conn.: Yale University Press.

———. 1994. *Electoral Systems and Party Systems: A Study of Twenty-Seven Democracies, 1945–1990.* Oxford: Oxford University Press.

Lijphart, Arend, Thomas Bruneau, P. Nikiforos Diamandouros, and Richard Gunther. 1988. "A Mediterranean Model of Democracy? The Southern European Democracies in Comparative Perspective." *West European Politics* 11: 7–25.

Lima, José A. 1991. "Aníbal de estimação." *Expresso Revista,* October 12, 7–12.

———. 1995. "Eleições 95: Um mar de rosas." *Expresso Revista,* October 7, 28–40.

———. 1999. "Vitória eleitoral, derrota política." *Expresso Revista,* October 16. Published at www.expresso.pt.

Lima, José A., and Luís Fraga. 1985. "A revolução de 6 de Outubro." *Expresso Revista,* October 12, 13–18.

———. 1987. "A maioria impossível." *Expresso Revista,* July 25, 34–38.

Linz, Juan J. 1977. *Tradición y modernización en España.* Granada: Universidad de Granada.

———. 1978. *The Breakdown of Democratic Regimes: Crisis, Breakdown, and Reequilibration.* 4 vols. Baltimore: Johns Hopkins University Press.

———. 1980. "The New Spanish Party System." In Rose 1980.

———. 1981a. "A Century of Politics and Interests in Spain." In Suzanne Berger, ed., *Organizing Interests in Western Europe.* Cambridge: Cambridge University Press.

———. 1981b. "Some Comparative Thoughts on the Transition to Democracy in Portugal and Spain." In Braga de Macedo and Serfaty 1981.

———. 1982. "The Legacy of Franco and Democracy." In Horst Baier, Hans Mathias Kepplinger, and Kurt Reumann, eds., *Öffentliche Meinung und sozialer Wandel.* Oppladen: Westdeutscher Verlag.

———. 1990. "Reflexiones Sobre la Sociedad Española." In Salvador Giner, ed., *España: Sociedad y política.* Madrid: Espasa-Calpe.

———. 1993. "Innovative Leadership in the Transition to Democracy in Spain." In Gabriel Sheffer, ed., *Innovative Leadership in International Politics.* Albany: State University of New York Press.

Linz, Juan J., Manuel Gómez-Reino, Francisco Andrés Orizo, and Darío Vila Carro. 1981. *Informe sociológico sobre el cambio político en España, 1975–1981.* Madrid: Fundación FOESSA.

Linz, Juan J., and José Ramón Montero, eds. 1986. *Crisis y cambio: Electores y partidos en la España de los años ochenta.* Madrid: Centro de Estudios Constitucionales.

Linz, Juan J., and Alfred Stepan. 1996. *Problems of Democratic Transition and Consolidation.* Baltimore: Johns Hopkins University Press.

Linz, Juan J., Alfred Stepan, and Richard Gunther. 1995. "Democratic Transition and Consolidation in Southern Europe, with Reflections on Latin America and Eastern Europe." In Gunther, Diamandouros, and Puhle 1995.

Lipset, Seymour M. 1960. *Political Man: The Social Bases of Politics.* New York: Doubleday.

Lipset, Seymour Martin, and Stein Rokkan, eds. 1967. *Party Systems and Voter Alignments.* New York: Free Press.

Lipset, Seymour Martin, and William Schneider. 1983. *The Confidence Gap: Business, Labor and Government in the Public Mind.* New York: Free Press.

López Nieto, Lourdes. 1998. "The Organizational Dynamics of AP/PP." In Ignazi and Ysmal 1998.

Loulis, J. C. 1981a. "New Democracy: The New Face of Conservatism." In Penniman 1981.

———. 1981b. "The Greek Conservative Movement in Transition: From Paternalism to Neo-Liberalism." In *The New Liberalism: The Future of Non-Collectivist Institutions in Europe and the U.S.* International Symposium. Athens: Centre for Political Research and Information.

———. 1995. *He krise tes politikes sten Hellada: Ekloges, koine gnome, politikes exelixeis, 1980–1995* (The Crisis of Politics in Greece: Elections, Public Opinion, Political Developments, 1980–1995). Athens: I. Sideris.

Luskin Robert. 1991. "Abusus Non Tollit Usum: Standardized Coefficients, Correlations, and R^2s." *American Journal of Political Science* 35: 1030–44.

Lyrintzis, Christos. 1983a. "The Rise of PASOK: The Greek Election of 1981." *West European Politics* 5: 99–118.

———. 1983b. "Between Socialism and Populism: The Rise of the Panhellenic Socialist Movement." Ph.D. diss., London School of Economics and Political Science.

———. 1984. "Political Parties in Post-Junta Greece: A Case of 'Bureaucratic Clientelism'"? In Pridham 1984.

———. 1986. "The Rise of PASOK and the Emergence of a New Political Personnel." In Tzannatos 1986.

———. 1987. "The Power of Populism: The Greek Case." *European Journal of Political Research* 15: 667–86.

———. 1993. "PASOK in Power: From 'Change' to Disenchantment." In Clogg 1993.

Lyrintzis, Christos, and Ilias Nicolacopoulos, eds. 1990. *Ekloges kai kommata ste dekaetia tou '80: Exeleixeis kai prooptikes tou politikou systematos* (Elections and Parties in the Decade of the 1980s: Evolution and Perspectives of the Political System). Athens: Themelio.

Mackie, Tom, Renato Mannheimer, and Giacomo Sani. 1992. "Italy." In Franklin, Mackie, Valen, et al. 1992.

Mackie, Thomas T., and Richard Rose. 1991. *The International Almanac of Electoral History.* 3d ed. London: Macmillan.

Macridis, Roy C. 1981. "Elections and Political Modernization in Greece." In Penniman 1981.

Magalhães, José. 1989. *Dicionário da revisão constitucional.* Lisbon: Europa-América.

Magna, Nino. 1992. "Dal Pci al Pds: Geografia di un declino." *Politica ed Economia* 12: 21–24.

Mair, Peter. 1992. "La trasformazione del partito di massa in Europa." In M. Calise, ed., *Come cambiano i partiti.* Bologna: Il Mulino.

———. 1997. *Party System Change: Approaches and Interpretations.* Oxford: Clarendon Press.

Malefakis, Edward. 1970. *Agrarian Reform and Peasant Revolution in Spain: Origins of the Civil War.* New Haven, Conn.: Yale University Press.

———. 1982. "Spain and Its Francoist Heritage." In John H. Herz, ed., *From Dictatorship to Democracy: Coping with the Legacies of Authoritarianism and Totalitarianism.* Westport, Conn.: Greenwood Press.

———. 1992. *Southern Europe in the Nineteenth and Twentieth Centuries: An Historical Overview.* Working Paper 1992/35. Madrid: Centro de Estudios Avanzados en Ciencias Sociales, Instituto Juan March de Estudios e Investigaciones.

———. 1995. "The Political and Socioeconomic Contours of Southern European History." In Gunther, Diamandouros, and Puhle 1995.

Mannheimer, Renato, ed. 1990. "Vecchi e nuovi caratteri del voto comunista." In Caciagli and Spreafico 1990.

———. 1991. *La Lega Lombarda.* Milan: Feltrinelli.

Mannheimer, Renato, and Giacomo Sani. 1987. *Il mercato elettorale: Identikit dell'elettore italiano.* Bologna: Il Mulino.

Maraffi, Marco. 1990. *Politica ed economia in Italia.* Bologna: Il Mulino.

———. 1995. "Forza Italia." In Gianfranco Pasquino, ed., *La politica italiana: Dizionario critico, 1945–1995.* Rome: Laterza.

Maravall, José María. 1978. *Dictatorship and Political Dissent: Workers and Students in Franco's Spain.* London: Tavistock.

———. 1981. *La política de la transición.* Madrid: Taurus.

———. 1985. "The Socialist Alternative: The Policies and Electorate of the PSOE." In Penniman 1985.

———. 1991. "From Opposition to Government: The Politics and Policies of the PSOE." In Maravall et al. 1991.

———. 1992. *What Is Left? Social Democratic Policies in Southern Europe.* Working Paper 1992/36. Madrid: Centro de Estudios Avanzados en Ciencias Sociales, Instituto Juan March de Estudios e Investigaciones.
———. 1993. "Politics and Policy: Economic Reforms in Southern Europe." In Bresser Pereira, Maravall, and Przeworski 1993.
———. 1995. *Los resultados de la democracia.* Madrid: Alianza.
———. 1997. *Regimes, Politics and Markets: Democratization and Economic Change in Southern and Eastern Europe.* Oxford: Oxford University Press.
Maravall, José María, et al. 1991. *Socialist Parties in Europe.* Barcelona: Institut de Ciències Polítiques i Socials.
Maravall, José María, and Marta Fraile. 1998. *The Politics of Unemployment. The Spanish Experience in Comparative Perspective.* Working Paper 1998/124. Madrid: Centro de Estudios Avanzados en Ciencias Sociales, Instituto Juan March de Estudios e Investigaciones.
Maravall, José María, and Julián Santamaría. 1986. "Political Change in Spain and the Prospects for Democracy." In O'Donnell, Schmitter, and Whitehead 1986.
Marcus, Jonathan. 1983. "The Triumph of Spanish Socialism: The 1982 Election." *West European Politics* 6, 3: 281–86.
Marletti, Carlo, and Franca Roncarolo. 2000. "The Media, Political Communication and Change in Italian Democracy." In Gunther and Mughan 2000.
Martins, Guilherme D'Oliveira, et al. 1988. *A revisão constitucional e a moção de censura construtiva.* Lisbon: Fundação Friedrich Ebert.
Massari, Oreste. 1996. "Italy's Postwar Transition in Contemporary Perspective." In Geoffrey Pridham and Paul G. Lewis, eds., *Stabilising Fragile Democracies.* New York: Routledge.
Massari, Oreste, and Simon Parker. 1999. "Le due sinistre tra rotture e ricomposizioni." In D. Hine and S. Vassalo, eds., *Politica in Italia: Edizione 1999.* Bologna: Il Mulino.
Mateos, Abdón. 1993. *El PSOE contra Franco: Continuidad y renovación del socialismo español, 1953–1974.* Madrid: Ed. Pablo Iglesias.
Maurer, Lynn M. 1995. "Legislative-Executive Relations in a Newly Consolidated Democracy: The Case of Spain." Ph.D. diss., Ohio State University.
Mavrogordatos, George Th. 1981. "The Greek Party System: Old Wine in New Bottles?" Paper presented at the meeting of the Spanish Political Science Association, Madrid, May 26–29.
———. 1983a. "The Emerging Party System." In Clogg 1983.
———. 1983b. *The Rise of the Green Sun: The Greek Election of 1981.* London: King's College, Centre for Contemporary Greek Studies.
———. 1983c. *Stillborn Republic: Social Coalitions and Party Strategies in Greece, 1922–1936.* Berkeley: University of California Press.
———. 1984. "The Greek Party System: A Case of 'Limited Polarized Pluralism'"? *West European Politics* 7, 4: 156–69.
———. 1988. *Metaxy Pityokampte kai Prokrouste: Oi epangelmatikes organoseis ste semerine Ellada* (Between Pityocamptes and Procrustes: Professional Associations in Today's Greece). Athens: Odysseas.
———. 1990. "Koinonikes proypotheseis ton symmachikon kyverneseon" (Social

Preconditions of Coalition Governments). In Lyrintzis and Nicolacopoulos 1990.
———. 1993. "Civil Society Under Populism." In Clogg 1993.
———. 1994. "Greece." *European Journal of Political Research* 26: 313–18.
Maxwell, Kenneth, ed. 1986. *Portugal in the 1980s: Dilemmas of Democratic Consolidation.* New York: Greenwood Press.
———, ed. 1991. *Portuguese Defense and Foreign Policy Since Democratization.* Camões Center Special Report No. 3. Columbia University.
———. 1995. *The Making of Portuguese Democracy.* Cambridge: Cambridge University Press.
Maxwell, Kenneth, and Michael H. Haltzel, eds. 1990. *Portugal: Ancient Country, Young Democracy.* Washington, D.C.: Wilson Center Press.
Maxwell Kenneth, and Scott Monje, eds. 1991. *Portugal: The Constitution and the Consolidation of Democracy, 1976-1989.* Camões Center Special Report No. 2. Columbia University.
McCarthy, P. 1997. "Forza Italia: I vecchi problemi rimangono." In Roberto D'Alimonte and David Nelken, eds., *Politica in Italia.* Bologna: Il Mulino.
McKelvey, Richard D., and William Zavoina. 1975. "A Statistical Model for the Analysis of Ordinal Level Dependent Variables." *Journal of Mathematical Sociology* 4: 103–20.
Medeiros Ferreira, José. *O comportamento politico dos militares: Forças armadas e regimes politicos em Portugal no sec XX.* Lisbon: Imprensa Universitaria, 1992.
Menapace, Lidia. 1974. *La Democrazia Cristiana: Natura, structtura e organizzazione.* Milan: Mazzota.
Merkel, Wolfgang. 1985. *Die Sozialistische Partei Italiens: Zwischen Oppositionssozialismus und Staatspartei.* Bochum: Brockmeyer.
———. 1987. *Prima e dopo Craxi: Le trasformazioni del PSI.* Padua: Liviana.
———. 1989. "Sozialdemokratische Politik in einer postkeynesianischen Ära? Das Beispiel der sozialistischen Regierung Spaniens, 1982–1988." *Politische Vierteljahresschrift* 30: 629–54.
———. 1992. "After the Golden Age: Is Social Democracy Doomed to Decline?" In Christiane Lemke and Gary Marks, eds., *The Crisis of Socialism in Europe.* Durham, N.C.: Duke University Press.
———. 1993. *Ende der Sozialdemokratie? Machtressourcen und Regierungspolitik im westeuropäischen Vergleich.* Frankfurt: Campus Verlag.
———, et al. 1992. *Socialist Parties in Europe II.* Barcelona: Institut de Ciències Polítiques i Socials.
Merkel, Wolfgang, and Hans-Jürgen Puhle. 1999. *Von der Diktatur zur Demokratie: Transformationen, Erfolgsbedingungen, Entwicklungspfade.* Opladen: Westdeutscher Verlag.
Mershon, Carol, and Gianfranco Pasquino, eds. 1995. *Italian Politics: Ending the First Republic.* Boulder, Colo.: Westview Press.
Meynaud, Jean. 1965. *Les forces politiques en Grèce.* Lausanne: Etudes de Science Politique.
Miller, Arthur, and Brad Lockerbie. 1992. "United States of America." In Franklin, Mackie, Valen, et al. 1992.

Misse, Andreu. 1996. "La financiación de los partidos políticos." In Juliá, Pradera, and Prieto 1996.

Montanelli, Indro. 1976. "Turatevi il naso, e votate DC." *Il Giornale,* June 20.

Montero, José R. 1981. "Partidos y participación política: Algunas notas sobre la afiliación política en la etapa inicial de la transición española." In *Revista de Estudios Políticos* 23: 33–72.

———. 1986a. "Iglesia, secularización y comportamiento político en España." *Revista Española de Investigaciones Sociológicas* 34: 131–59.

———. 1986b. "El sub-triunfo de la derecha: Los apoyos electorales de AP-PDP." In Linz and Montero 1986.

———. 1987. "Los fracasos políticos y electorales de la derecha española: Alianza Popular, 1976–1986." *Revista Española de Investigaciones Sociológicas* 39: 7–44.

———. 1988. "More than Conservative, Less than Neoconservative: Alianza Popular in Spain." In Brian Girvin, ed., *The Transformation of Contemporary Conservatism.* London: Sage.

———. 1989. "Los fracasos políticos y electorales de la derecha española: Alianza Popular, 1976–1987." In José Félix Tezanos, Ramón Cotarelo and Andrés de Blas, eds., *La transición democrática española.* Madrid: Sistema, 1989.

———. 1992. *Sobre la democracia en España: Legitimidad, apoyos institucionales y significados.* Working Paper 1992/39. Madrid: Centro de Estudios Avanzados en Ciencias Sociales, Instituto Juan March de Estudios e Investigaciones.

———. 1993. "Las dimensiones de la secularización: Religiosidad y preferencias políticas en España." In Rafael Díaz-Salazar and Salvador Giner, eds., *Religión y sociedad en España.* Madrid: Centro de Investigaciones Sociologicas.

———. 1994. "Sobre las preferencias electorales en España: Fragmentación y polarización, 1977–1993." In Del Castillo 1994.

———. 1997. "Secularization and Cleavage Decline: Religiosity and Electoral Behavior in Spain." Paper presented to the ECPR Joint Session of Workshops, Bern, February–March.

Montero, José Ramón, and Herman Calvo. 1999. *Tracing Cleavage Decline: Religiosity, Parties and Electoral Behavior in Spain.* Madrid: Instituto Juan March de Estudios e Investigaciones.

Montero, José Ramón, and Mariano Torcal. 1990. "La cultura política de los españoles: Pautas de continuidad y cambio. *Sistema* 99: 39–74.

———. 1992. "Política y cambio cultural en España: Una nota sobre la dimensión postmaterialista." *Revista Internacional de Sociologia* 87: 61–100.

———. 1994. *Value Change, Generational Replacement and Politics in Spain.* Working Paper 1994/56. Madrid: Centro de Estudios Avanzados en Ciencias Sociales, Instituto Juan March de Estudios e Investigaciones.

Morán, María Luz. 1989. "Un intento de análisis de la 'clase parlamentaria' española: Elementos de renovación y permanencia." *Revista Española de Investigaciones Sociológicas* 4: 61–84.

Morisi, Massimo. 1991. "Il parlamento tra partiti e interessi." In Leonardo Morlino, ed., *Costruire la democrazia: Gruppi e partiti in Italia.* Bologna: Il Mulino, 1991.

Morlino, Leonardo. 1980. *Come cambiano i regimi politici.* Milan: Franco Angeli.

———. 1982. "Del Fascismo a una democracia débil: El cambio de régimen en

Italia, 1939–1948." In Julián Santamaria, ed., *Transición a la democracia en el Sur de Europa y América Latina.* Madrid: Centro de Investigaciones Sociológicas.

———. 1984. "The Changing Relationship Between Parties and Society in Italy." In Bartolini and Mair 1984.

———. 1986. "Consolidamento democratico: definizione e modelli." *Rivista italiana di scienza politica* 16: 197–238.

———, ed. 1991. *Costruire la democrazia: Gruppi e partiti in Italia.* Bologna: Il Mulino.

———. 1992. "Partiti e consolidamento democratico nel Sud Europa." In M. Calise, ed., *Come cambiano i partiti.* Bologna: Il Mulino.

———. 1995. "Political Parties and Democratic Consolidation in Southern Europe." In Gunther, Diamandouros, and Puhle 1995.

———. 1996. "Crisis of Parties and Change of Party System in Italy." *Party Politics* 3, 1: 5–30.

———. 1998. *Democracy Between Consolidation and Crisis: Parties, Groups and Citizens in Southern Europe.* Oxford: Oxford University Press.

Morlino, Leonardo, and José R. Montero. 1995. "Democracy and Legitimacy in Southern Europe." In Gunther, Diamandouros, and Puhle 1995.

Morlino, Leonardo, and Marco Tarchi. 1996. "The Dissatisfied Society: The Roots of Political Change in Italy." *European Journal of Political Research* 30: 41–63.

———. 1996. "Crisis of Parties and Change of Party System in Italy." *Party Politics* 2, 1: 5–30.

Moro, Roberto. 1979. "I movimenti intelletuali cattolici." In Roberto Ruffili, ed., *Cultura politica e partiti nell'età della costituente.* Bologna: Il Mulino.

Mouzelis, Nicos. 1986. *Politics in the Semi-Periphery: Early Parliamentarism and Late Industrialisation in the Balkans and in Latin America.* London: Macmillan.

Mujal-León, Eusebio. 1983. *Communism and Political Change in Spain.* Bloomington: Indiana University Press.

———. 1986. "Decline and Fall of Spanish Communism." *Problems of Communism* 2: 1–27.

Murteira, Mário. 1979. "The Present Economic Situation: Its Origins and Prospects." In Graham and Makler 1979.

Newell, James L., and Martin Bull. 1997. "Party Organisations and Alliances in Italy in the 1990s: A Revolution of Sorts." *West European Politics* 20, 1: 81–109.

Nicolacopoulos, Ilias. 1989. "A Brief Review of Greek Electoral Systems." *Focus on the News* (Athens News Agency), 21 April.

Niemi, Richard G., G. Bingham Powell, Jr., Harold W. Stanley, and C. Lawrence Evans. 1985. "Testing the Converse Partisanship Model with New Electorates." *Comparative Political Studies* 18: 300–322.

Nieuwbeerta, Paul. 1995. *The Democratic Class Struggle in Twenty Countries, 1945–1990.* Amsterdam: Thesis Publishers.

Nogueira Pinto, Jaime. 1988. "La derecha y el 25 de abril. Ideología, estrategia y evolución política." *Revista de Estudios Políticos* 60–61 (April–September): 185–205.

Obiols, Raimon *Los futuros imperfectos.* Barcelona: Plaza & Janes.

Occhetto, Achille. 1994. *Il sentimento e la ragione.* Milan: Rizzoli.

O'Donnell, Guillermo, Philippe C. Schmitter, and Laurence Whitehead, eds. 1986. *Transitions from Authoritarian Rule: Prospects for Democracy.* 4 vols. Baltimore: Johns Hopkins University Press.

OECD [Organization for Economic Cooperation and Development]. 1977–93. *National Accounts.* Vol. 2. Paris: OECD.

———. 1990. *OECD Economic Outlook, Historical Series, 1960–1988.* Paris: OECD.

Opello, Walter. 1985. *Portugal's Political Development: A Comparative Approach.* Boulder, Colo.: Westview Press.

———. 1991. *Portugal: From Monarchy to Pluralist Democracy.* Boulder, Colo.: Westview Press.

Panebianco, Angelo. 1982. *Modelli di partito: Organizzazione e potere nei partiti politici.* Bologna: Il Mulino.

Panitch, Leo. 1985. "The Impasse of Social Democratic Politics." *Socialist Register* 22: 50–97.

Papacosma, S. Victor. 1988. *Politics and Culture in Greece.* Ann Arbor: University of Michigan Center for Political Studies.

Papadopoulos, Yannis. 1989. "Parties, the State and Society in Greece: Continuity Within Change." *West European Politics* 12, 2: 54–71.

Papalegouras, Panages. 1975. "Ideologikes theseis tes 'Neas Demokratias'" (Ideological Positions of "New Democracy"). *Nea Politike* 3 (December): 14–16.

Papandreou, Andreas. 1973. *Democracy at Gunpoint: The Greek Front.* London: Penguin Books.

Papayannakis, Michalis. 1981. "The Crisis in the Greek Left." In Penniman 1981.

Pappalardo, Alessandro. 1994. "La nuova legge elettorale in parlamento: Chi, come e perchè?" *Rivista italiana di scienza politica* 24: 287–310.

Pappas, Takis S. 1996. *Grand Designs, Narrow Choices: Conservatives and Democracy in Southern Europe.* Working Paper SPS No. 7. Florence: European University Institute.

———. 1999. *Making Party Democracy in Greece.* London: Macmillan.

Parisi, Arturo, and Piergiorgio Corbetta, eds. 1997. *A domanda risponde.* Bologna: Il Mulino.

Parisi, Arturo, and Gianfranco Pasquino. 1977. "Relazioni partiti-elettori e tipi di voto." In Arturo Parisi and Gianfranco Pasquino, eds., *Continuità e mutamento elettorale in Italia.* Bologna: Il Mulino.

Parisi, Arturo, and M. A. Hans Schadee, eds. 1995. *Sulla soglia del cambiamento: Elettori e partiti alla fine della prima Repubblica.* Bologna: Il Mulino.

Partido Comunista Português. 1979. *IX Congresso—Partido Comunista Português.* Lisbon: Edições Avante!

———. 1989. *XII Congresso do Partido Comunista Português.* Lisbon: Edições Avante!

Partido Socialista [Portugal]. 1973. *Declaração de princípios e programa do Partido Socialista.* Lisbon: Textos Portugal Socialista.

———. 1975. *Declaração de principios, programa e estatutos do Partido Socialista aprovado no congresso do PS em Dezembro de 1974.* Lisbon: Partido Socialista.

———. 1979. *Dez anos para mudar Portugal.* Lisbon: Partido Socialista.

———. 1992. *Estatutos do Partido Socialista.* Lisbon: Partido Socialista.

———. 1995a. *Programa Eleitoral de Governo do PS e da nova maioria.* Lisbon: Partido Socialista.

———. 1995b. *Estados gerais para uma nova maioria: Contrato de legislatura.* Lisbon: Partido Socialista.

———. 1995c. *Programa do XIII governo constitucional.* Lisbon: Partido Socialista.

Partido Socialista Obrero Español. 1979. *28 Congreso PSOE, Memoria.* Madrid.

———. 1981. *29 Congreso PSOE, Memoria.* Madrid.

———. 1982. *Por el cambio: Programa electoral del PSOE.* Madrid: PSOE.

———. 1984. *PSOE: Comisión ejecutiva federal, Memoria de gestión 1981–1984, XXX Congreso del PSOE.* Madrid: PSOE.

———. 1986. *Programa 1986/90, para seguir avanzando por el buen camino.* Madrid: PSOE.

———. 1989a. *Manifiesto del Programa 2000.* Madrid: Ed. Pablo Iglesias.

———. 1989b. *Programa electoral 1989: España en progreso.* Madrid: PSOE.

Partito Comunista Italiano. 1986. *Documenti per il congresso.* Roma: L'Unità.

———. 1990. *Il comitato centrale della svolta: Documenti per il congresso straordinario del PCI.* Vol. 1. Roma: L'Unità.

Pasquino, Gianfranco. 1986a. "The Demise of the First Fascist Regime and Italy's Transition to Democracy, 1943–1948." In O'Donnell, Schmitter, and Whitehead 1986.

———. 1986b. "Modernity and Reforms: The PSI Between Political Entrepreneurs and Gamblers." *West European Politics* 9: 120–41.

———, ed. 1988. *La lenta marcia nelle istituzioni: I passi del Pci.* Bologna: Il Mulino.

———. 1990a. "Party Elites and Democratic Consolidation." In Pridham 1990.

———. 1990b. "Political Leadership in Southern Europe." *West European Politics* 12: 118–30.

———. 1990c. "Liderazgo y comunicación política." *Psicología Política* (January): 65–85.

———. 1994. *Shaping a Better Republic? The Italian Case in a Comparative Perspective.* Working Paper 1994/62. Madrid: Centro de Estudios Avanzados en Ciencias Sociales, Instituto Juan March de Estudios e Investigaciones.

———. 1995a. "Executive-Legislative Relations in Southern Europe." In Gunther, Diamandouros, and Puhle 1995.

———, ed. 1995b. *L'alternanza inattesa: Le elezioni del 27 marzo 1994 e le loro conseguenze.* Soveria Manelli (Catanzaro): Rubbettino.

———. 1996. "The Government of Lamberto Dini." In Caciagli and Kertzer 1996.

———. 1998. "New Government, Old Party Politics." *South European Society and Politics* 3: 124–33.

Pasquino, Gianfranco, and Salvatore Vassallo. 1995. "The Government of Carlo Azeglio Ciampi." In Mershon and Pasquino 1995.

Patterson, Thomas E. 1993. *Out of Order: How the Decline of the Political Parties and the Growing Power of the News Media Undermine the American Way of Electing Presidents.* New York: Knopf.

Payne, Stanley G. 1973. *A History of Spain and Portugal.* Madison: University of Wisconsin Press.

———. 1984. *Spanish Catholicism: An Historical Overview.* Madison: University of Wisconsin Press.

———. 1995. *A History of Fascism, 1914–1945.* Madison: University of Wisconsin Press.

PCI. *See* Partito Comunista Italiano
PCP. *See* Partido Comunista Português
Penn World Tables. http://pwt.econ.upenn.edu/
Penniman, Howard R., ed. 1981. *Greece at the Polls: The National Elections of 1974 and 1977.* Washington, D.C.: American Enterprise Institute.
———. 1985. *Spain at the Polls, 1977, 1979, and 1982.* Washington, D.C.: American Enterprise Institute.
Pennings, Paul, and Jan-Erik Lane, eds. *Comparing Party System Change.* London: Routledge.
Pereira, José Pacheco. 1990. "A clandestinidade: Componente da cultura comunista." *Risco* 14: 89–99.
Pérez Díaz, Victor. 1987. *El retorno de la sociedad civil.* Madrid: Instituto de Estudios Económicos.
———. 1993. *La primacía de la sociedad civil.* Madrid: Alianza.
Pérez Yruela, Manuel, and Salvador Giner, eds. 1988. *El corporatismo en España.* Barcelona: Ariel.
Perifanaki, Virginia. 1990. "Il nuovo sistema elettorale e il voto di preferenza in Grecia." *Il Politico* 55: 143–66.
Petras, James. 1987. "The Contradictions of Greek Socialism: PASOK in Power." *New Left Review* 163: 3–25.
Petropulos, John A. 1968. *Politics and Statecraft in the Kingdom of Greece, 1833–43.* Princeton, N.J.: Princeton University Press.
Pimlott, Ben. 1977. "Parties and Voters in the Portuguese Revolution: The Elections of 1975 and 1976." *Parliamentary Affairs* 30, 1: 35–58.
Pimlott, Ben, and Jean Seaton. 1983. "Political Power and the Portuguese Media." In Graham and Wheeler 1983.
Pitkin, Hanna. 1967. *The Concept of Political Representation.* Berkeley: University of California Press.
Pizzorno, Alessandro. 1993. "Le difficoltà del consociativismo." In id., *Le radici della politica assoluta.* Milan: Feltrinelli.
Podolny, Joel. 1993. "The Role of Juan Carlos I in the Consolidation of the Parliamentary Monarchy." In Richard Gunther, ed., *Politics, Society, and Democracy: The Case of Spain.* Boulder, Colo.: Westview Press.
Poggi, Gianfranco, ed. 1968. *L'organizzazione partitica del Pci e dalla Dc.* Bologna: Il Mulino.
Pombeni, Paolo. 1985. *Introduzione alla storia dei partiti politici.* Bologna: Il Mulino.
Porch, Douglas. 1977. *The Portuguese Armed Forces and the Revolution.* Stanford, Calif.: Hoover Institution Press.
Powell, Charles T. 1994. "La dimensión exterior de la transición." *Revista del Centro de Estudios Constitucionales* 18: 79–116.
Powell, G. Bingham. 1970. *Social Fragmentation and Political Hostility: An Austrian Case.* Stanford, Calif.: Stanford University Press.
Pridham, Geoffrey, ed. 1984. *The New Mediterranean Democracies: Regime Transitions in Spain, Greece and Portugal.* London: Frank Cass.
———. 1988. *Political Parties and Coalitional Behaviour in Italy.* London: Routledge.
———, ed. 1990. *Securing Democracy: Political Parties and Democratic Consolidation in Southern Europe.* London: Routledge.

Pridham, Geoffrey, and Susannah Verney. 1991. "The Coalition of 1989–90 in Greece." *West European Politics* 14: 42–49.

Prodromou, Elizabeth. 1994. "Religion and Politics in Greece: Church-State Under PASOK." Ph.D. diss., MIT.

Project Research Consulting. 1994. "Research on Political Culture."

Prospero, Michele. 1990. *Il nuovo inizio: Dal PCI di Berlinguer al Partito Democratico della Sinistra.* Chieti: Métis.

Przeworski, Adam, and John Sprague. 1986. *Paper Stones: A History of Electoral Socialism.* Chicago: Chicago University Press.

PS. *See* Partido Socialista (Portugal)

PSOE. *See* Partido Socialista Obrero Español

Psomiades, Harry J., and Stavros B. Thomadakis, eds. 1993. *Greece, the New Europe, and the Changing International Order.* New York: Pella Press.

Puhle, Hans-Jürgen Puhle. 1986a. "El PSOE: Un partido predominante y heterogéneo." In Linz and Montero 1986.

———. 1986b. "Was ist Populismus?" In Helmut Dubiel, ed., *Populismus und Aufklärung.* Frankfurt: Suhrkamp.

———. 1994. "Probleme der spanischen Modernisierung im 19. und 20. Jahrhundert." *Jahrbuch für Geschichte von Staat, Wirtschaft und Gesellschaft Lateinamerikas* 31: 305–28.

———. 1996. "Was kommt nach den 'Volksparteien'? Gegenwärtige Krisenwahrnehmungen im historischen Kontext." In Manfred Hettling and Paul Nolte, eds., *Nation und Gesellschaft in Deutschland.* Munich: Verlag C. H. Beck.

———. 1997. "Politische Parteien und demokratische Konsolidierung." In Wolfgang Merkel and Eberhard Sandschneider, eds., *Systemwechsel 3: Parteien im Transformationsprozess.* Opladen: Leske & Budrich.

———. 1998. "Das Baskenland zwischen Separatismus und Integration." In Franz-Josef Hutter et al., eds., *Das gemeinsame Haus Europa: Menschenrechte zwischen Atlantik und Ural.* Baden-Baden: Nomos.

Putnam, Robert D. 1993. *Making Democracy Work: Civic Traditions in Modern Italy.* Princeton, N.J.: Princeton University Press.

Rallis, Georgios. 1983. *Hores efthynes* (Hours of Responsibility). Athens: Evroekdotike.

Reventós, Joan. 1993. *Renovación socialista.* Barcelona: Hacer.

Richards, Andrew, and Javier García de Polavieja. 1997. *Trade Unions, Unemployment and Working-Class Fragmentation in Spain.* Working Paper 1997/112. Madrid: Centro de Estudios Avanzados en Ciencias Sociales, Instituto Juan March de Estudios e Investigaciones.

Ricolfi, Luca. 1994a. "Elezioni e media: Quanti voti ha spostato la Tv." *Il Mulino* 43, 356: 1031–46.

———. 1994b. "Il voto proporzionale: Il nuovo spazio politico italiano." In Bartolini and D'Alimonte 1994.

Robinson, Richard. 1979a. *Contemporary Portugal.* London: George Allen & Unwin.

———. 1979b. "Political Conservatism: The Spanish Case, 1875–1977." *Journal of Contemporary History* 14 (October): 561–80.

———. 1991–92. "The Evolution of the Portuguese Socialist Party, 1973–1986,

in International Perspective." *Portuguese Studies Review* 1: 6–26.
———. 1993. "The Individual and the State in Contemporary Portugal." *Portuguese Studies Review* 2: 86–98.
Roldán Ros, Juan. 1985. "The Media and the Elections." In Penniman 1985.
Román Marugán, Paloma. 1987. *El Partido Socialista Obrero Español en la transición española: Organización e ideología, 1975–1982.* Madrid: Depto. de Ciencia Política y de la Administración.
Rose, Richard, ed. 1974. *Comparative Electoral Behavior.* New York: Free Press.
———, ed. 1980. *Electoral Participation: A Comparative Analysis.* Beverly Hills, Calif.: Sage.
Rotelli, Ettore. 1991. *Il martello e l'incudine.* Bologna: Il Mulino.
Roth, Guenther. 1963. *The Social Democrats in Imperial Germany.* Totowa, N.J.: Bedminster Press.
Salvatore, Vassallo. 1997. "Struttura della competizione e risultato elettorale." In Parisi and Corbetta 1997.
Sänger, Ralf. 1994. *Portugals langer Weg nach "Europa."* Frankfurt: Lang.
Sani, Giacomo. 1974a. "A Test of the Least-Distance Model of Voting Choice, Italy 1972." *Comparative Political Studies* 7: 193–208.
———. 1974b. "Determinants of Party Preference in Italy: Toward the Integration of Complementary Models." *Comparative Political Studies* 18: 315–29.
———. 1975. "L'immagine dei partiti nell'elettorato." In Mario Caciagli and Alberto Spreafico, eds., *Un sistema politico alla prova.* Bologna: Il Mulino.
———. 1976. "Mass Constraints on Political Realignments: Perceptions of Anti-System Parties in Italy." *British Journal of Political Science* 6: 1–32.
———. 1981. "La composizione degli elettorati comunista e democristiano." In Alberto Martinelli and Gianfranco Pasquino, eds., *La politica nell'Italia che cambia.* Milan: Feltrinelli.
———. 1986. "Los desplazamientos del electorado: Anatomía del cambio." In Linz and Montero 1986.
———. 1991. "Church Attendance and the Vote for the DC: Evidence from the 1980s." *Italian Politics and Society,* 13–18.
———. 1992. "1992: La destrutturazione del mercato elettorale." *Rivista italiana di scienza politica* 22: 540.
———. 1993. "Le Italie del cinque aprile." *Polis* 7, 2: 207–28.
———. 1994a. "Modelli di cittadino e comportamento di massa." In Renato Mannheimer and Giacomo Sani, eds., *La rivoluzione elettorale.* Milan: Anabasi.
———. 1994b. "Dai voti ai seggi." In Renato Mannheimer and Ilvo Diamanti, eds., *Milano a Roma.* Rome: Donzelli, 1994.
———. 1994c. "Una vigilia di incertezze." In Bartolini and D'Alimonte 1994.
———. 1996. "La competizione nei collegi uninominali nelle elezioni del 1994 e del 1996." *Quaderni di scienza politica* 3: 185–94.
Sani, Giacomo, and Giovanni Sartori. 1980. "Polarización, fragmentación y competición en las democracias occidentales." *Revista del Departamento de Derecho Político* 7: 7–38.
Sani, Giacomo, and Paolo Segatti. 1990. "Mutamento culturale e politica di massa." In Cesareo Vincenzo, ed., *La cultura dell'Italia contemporanea.* Turin: Edizioni Fondazione Giovanni Agnelli.

Sartori, Giovanni. 1974. "Rivisitando il 'pluralismo polarizzato.'" In Fabio L. Cavazza and Stephen R. Graubard, eds., *Il caso italiano*. Milan: Garzanti.

———. 1976. *Parties and Party Systems: A Framework for Analysis*. Cambridge: Cambridge University Press.

———. 1989. "Videopolitica." *Rivista italiana di scienza politica* 2: 185–97.

Sartorius, Nicolás. 1992. *Un nuevo proyecto político: Contribución al debate en la izquierda*. Madrid: El País / Aguilar.

Sassoon, Donald. 1986. *Contemporary Italy: Politics, Economy, and Society Since 1945*. London: Longman.

———. 1988. *Contemporary Italy: Economy, Society, and Politics Since 1945*. 2d ed. London: Longman.

Sastrústegui, Miguel. 1992. "PSOE: A New Catch-All Party." In Merkel et al.

Scharpf, Fritz. 1987. *Sozialdemokratische Krisenpolitik in Westeuropa*. Frankfurt: Campus Verlag.

Schlesinger, Joseph A. 1984. "On the Theory of Party Organization." *Journal of Politics* 46: 369–400.

Schmitter, Philippe. 1995. "Organized Interests and Democratic Consolidation in Southern Europe." In Gunther, Diamandouros, and Puhle 1995.

Schumpeter, Joseph. 1942. *Capitalism, Socialism and Democracy*. New York: Harper.

Sciolla, Loredana. 1986. "Dimensioni della secolarizzazione." *Rassegna italiana di sociologia* 1: 5–36.

Scoppola, Pietro. 1977. *La proposta politica di De Gasperi*. Bologna: Il Mulino.

———. 1991. *La repubblica dei partiti*. Bologna: Il Mulino.

Seferiadis, Seraphim. 1986. "Polarization and Nonproportionality: The Greek Party System in the Postwar Era." *Comparative Politics* 19, 1 (October): 69–93.

Segatti, Paolo. 1992. "L'offerta politica e i candidati della Lega." *Polis* 2: 257–96

———. 1994. "I programmi elettorali e il ruolo dei mass media nelle elezioni del marzo 1994." In Bartolini and D'Alimonte 1994.

———. 1997. "Un centro instabile ma non troppo." In Parisi and Corbetta 1997.

———. 1999. "Religione e territorio nel voto alla DC, 1948–1992." *Polis* 1: 45–65.

Seisselberg, J. 1996. "Conditions of Success and Political Problems of a 'Media-Mediated Personality-Party': The Case of Forza Italia." *West European Politics* 19, 4: 715–43.

Serfaty, Meir. 1984. "Spain's Socialists: A New Center Party?" *Current History* 83: 164–84.

Setta, Sandro. 1975. *L'uomo qualunque, 1945–1948*. Bari: Laterza.

Share, Donald. 1989. *Dilemmas of Social Democracy: The Spanish Socialist Workers Party in the 1980s*. Westport, Conn.: Greenwood Press.

Sinova, Justino. 1993. *Un millón de votos*. Madrid: Ediciones Temas de Hoy.

Smith, Ole. 1992. "The Impact of Gorbachev on the Greek Communists." In *The Southeast European Yearbook, 1991*. Athens: Hellenic Foundation for Defense and Foreign Policy.

———. 1993. "The Greek Communist Party in the Post-Gorbachev Era." In David S. Bell, ed., *Western European Communists and the Collapse of Communism*. Providence, R.I.: Berg.

Soares, Mário. 1974. *Portugal amordaçado*. Lisbon: Arcádio.

———. 1976. *Portugal: que revolução? Dialogo com Dominique Pouchin.* Lisbon: Perspectivas & Realidades.

Solé Tura, Jordi. 1998. "El entusiasmo y el vértigo." *El País,* March 27, 18.

Sotiropoulos, Dimitri A. 1991. "State and Party: The Greek State Bureaucracy and the Panhellenic Socialist Movement (PASOK), 1981–1989." Ph.D. diss., Yale Univerity.

———. 1993. "A Colossus with Feet of Clay: The State in Post-Authoritarian Greece." In Psomiades and Thomadakis 1993.

———. 1995. *The Remains of Authoritarianism: Bureaucracy and Civil Society in Post-Authoritarian Greece.* Madrid: Centro de Estudios Avanzados en Ciencias Sociales, Instituto Juan March de Estudios e Investigaciones.

———. 1996. *Populism and Bureaucracy: The Case of Greece Under PASOK, 1981–89.* Notre Dame, Ind.: Notre Dame University Press.

Spanou, Calliope. 1996. "Penelope's Suitors: Administrative Modernisation and Party Competition in Greece." *West European Politics* 19: 97–124.

Spourdalakis, Michalis. 1988. *The Rise of the Greek Socialist Party.* London: Routledge.

———. 1990. "The Greek Left in Centre Stage." *Canadian Dimension* 2: 39–43.

———. 1991. "PASOK in the 1990s: Structure, Ideology, Political Strategy." In Maravall et al. 1991.

———. 1992. "A Petty-Bourgeois Party with a Populist Ideology and Catch-All Party Structure: PASOK." In Merkel et al. 1992.

———. 1996. "PASOK's Second Chance." Department of Political Science, University of Athens.

———. 1998. "PASOK: The Telling Story of a Unique Organizational Structure." In Ignazi and Ysmal 1998.

Stock, Maria José. 1991. "The Portuguese Greens: Growing Pains or Compromised Future?" Paper presented to the ECPR Joint Workshops, University of Essex, March. *See also under* Fernández Stock

Stock, Maria José, and Bernd Rother. 1983. "PS: a trajectória de um partido." *Expresso Revista* 14: 37–44.

———. 1992. "Between Corporatism and Class Struggle: The Portuguese Labour Movement and the Cavaco Silva Governments." *West European Politics* 15: 118–50.

Tarrow, Sidney. 1967. *Peasant Communism in Southern Italy.* New Haven, Conn.: Yale University Press.

———. 1977. *Between Center and Periphery: Grassroots Politicians in Italy.* New Haven, Conn.: Yale University Press.

———. 1989. *Democracy and Disorder: Protest and Politics in Italy, 1965–1975.* Oxford: Oxford University Press.

———. 1990. "Maintaining Hegemony in Italy: 'The Softer They Rise, The Slower They Fall.'" In T. J. Pempel, ed., *Uncommon Democracies: The One-Party Dominant Regimes.* Ithaca, N.Y.: Cornell University Press.

———. 1995. "Mass Mobilization and Regime Change: Pacts, Reform and Popular Power in Italy, 1918–1922, and Spain, 1975–1978." In Gunther, Diamandouros, and Puhle 1995.

Tezanos, José Félix. 1983. *Sociología del socialismo español.* Madrid: Tecnos.

———. 1984. “Sociología del sindicalismo español.” *Claridad* 1: 61–75.

———. 1985. “Continuidad y cambio en el socialismo español: El PSOE durante la transición democrática.” *Sistema* 6: 19–60.

———. 1989. “Continuidad y cambio en el socialismo español: El PSOE durante la transición democrática.” In José Félix Tezanos, Ramón Cotarelo and Andrés de Blas, eds., *La transición democrática española.* Madrid: Sistema.

———, et al. 1981. *Las perspectivas de crecimiento de la afiliación al PSOE.* Madrid: PSOE.

Tezanos, José Félix, and José Antonio Gómez Yáñez. 1981. *Estudio sociológico de participación: Encuesta a los afiliados del PSOE.* Madrid.

Thomadakis, Stavros B., and Dimitris B. Seremetis. 1992. “Fiscal Management, Social Agenda, and Structural Deficits.” In Kariotis 1992.

Tiersky, Ronald. 1985. *Ordinary Stalinism: Democratic Centralism and the Question of Communist Political Development.* Boston: George Allen & Unwin.

Toniolo, Dario. 1990. “Appendice statistica.” In Caciagli and Spreafico 1990.

Tsakloglou, Panagiotes. 1993. “Changes in Inequality in Greece in the 1970s and 1980s.” Discussion Paper 1993/5. Athens: Department of International and Economic Studies, Athens University of Economics and Business.

Tsingos, Basilios Evangelos. 1994. “Underwriting Democracy, Not Exporting It: The European Community and Greece.” Ph.D. diss., Magdalen College, University of Oxford.

Tsinisizelis, Michael. 1996. “Greece.” In Dietrich Rometsch and Wolfgang Wessels, eds., *The European Union and Member States: Towards Institutional Fusion?* Manchester: Manchester University Press.

Tsoucalas, Constantine. 1986. “Radical Reformism in a ‘Pre-Welfare Society’: The Antinomies of Democratic Socialism in Greece.” In Tzannatos 1986.

Tsoucalas, Constantine, and Roy Panagiotopoulou. 1992. “Education in Socialist Greece: Between Modernization and Democratization.” In Kariotis 1992.

Tsoukalis, Loukas. 1991. “The Austerity Programme: Causes, Reactions and Prospects.” In Vryonis 1991.

Tzannatos, Zafiris, ed. 1986. *Socialism in Greece: The First Four Years.* Aldershot, Hants: Gower.

Vallès, Josep M. 1994. “The Spanish General Election of 1993.” *Electoral Studies* 13: 87–91.

Van der Eijk, Cees, Mark Franklin, Tom Mackie, and Henry Valen. 1992. “Cleavages, Conflict Resolution and Democracy.” In Franklin, Mackie, Valen, et al. 1992.

Van der Eijk, Cees, and Kees Niemöller. 1992. “Netherlands.” In Franklin, Mackie, Valen, et al. 1992.

Varvaroussis, Stérios. 1988. “Le parti communiste grec de l’intérieur.” *Communisme,* 17: 88–100.

Vasileiou, Konstantinos. 1991. “Profile of the Left.” *Anti,* June 28.

Vázquez Rabanal, Alfredo. 1976. “La situación religiosa en España.” In *FOESSA: Estudios sociológicos sobre la situación social de España, 1975.* Madrid: Editorial Euramérica.

Vegleris, Phaedo. 1981. “Greek Electoral Law.” In Penniman 1981.

Verba, Sidney, Norman Nie, and J. Kim. 1977. *Participation and Political Equality: A Seven Nation Comparison.* Cambridge: Cambridge University Press.

Veremis, Thanos. 1991. " Greece and NATO." In Vryonis 1991.
Verney, Susannah. 1987a. "Greece in the European Community." In Featherstone and Katsoudas 1987.
———. 1987b. "The Spring of the Greek Left: Two Party Congresses." *Journal of Communist Studies* 3: 166–70.
———. 1990a. "To Be or Not to Be in the European Community: The Party Debate and Democratic Consolidation in Greece." In Pridham 1990.
———. 1990b. "Between Coalition and One-Party Government: The Greek Elections of November 1989 and April 1990." *West European Politics* 13: 131–38.
———. 1994. "Central State-Local Government Relations." In Panos Kasakos and P. K. Ioakimidis, eds., *Greece and European Community Membership Evaluated.* London: Pinter.
Verney Susannah, and Fouli Papageorgiou. 1992. "Prefectoral Councils in Greece: Decentralization in the European Union Context." *Regional Politics and Regional Policy* 2, 1–2 (Spring–Summer): 109–38.
Verzichelli, Luca. 1994. "Gli eletti." In Bartolini and D'Alimonte 1994.
———. 1997. "La classe politica della transizione." In Bartolini and D'Alimonte 1994.
Vespa, Bruno. 1995. *Il duello: Chi vincerà nello scontro finale.* Milan: Mondadori.
Vicens-Vives, Jaime. 1967. *Approaches to the History of Spain.* Berkeley: University of California Press.
Villaverde Cabral, Manuel. 1995. "Grupos de simpatia partidária em Portugal: Perfil sociográfico e atitudes sociais." *Análise Social* 30: 175–205.
Voulgaris, Ioannis. 1990. "Allaghes sto eklogiko soma tes aristeras kai kommatikos antagonismos, 1985–1989" (Changes in the Electorate of the Left and Party Competition, 1985–1989). In Lyrintzis and Nicolacopoulos 1990.
Vryonis, Speros, Jr., ed. 1991. *Greece on the Road to Democracy: From the Junta to PASOK, 1974–1986.* New Rochelle, N.Y.: A. D. Caratzas.
Waters, Sarah. 1994. "'*Tangentopoli*' and the Emergence of a New Political Order in Italy." *West European Politics* 17, 1 (January): 169–82.
Weaver, R. Kent, and Bert A. Rockman, eds. 1993. *Do Institutions Matter? Government Capabilities in the United States and Abroad.* Washington, D.C.: Brookings Institution.
Weber, Maria. 1983. *Italia: Un paese europeo?* Milan: F. Angeli.
Wert, José Ignacio. 1996. "Las elecciones legislativas del 3-M: Paisaje después de la batalla." *Claves de Razón Práctica* 61: 36–44.
Wert, José Ignacio, Juan José Toharia, and Rafael López Pintor. 1993. "El regreso de la política: Una primera interpretación de las elecciones del 6-J." *Claves de Razón Práctica* 34: 32–42.
Wertman, Douglas. 1995. "The Last Year of the Christian Democratic Party." In Mershon and Pasquino 1995.
Wiarda, Howard. 1989. *The Transition to Democracy in Spain and Portugal.* Washington, D.C.: American Enterprise Institute.
Zaldívar, Carlos Alonso, and Manuel Castells. 1992. *España: Fin de siglo.* Madrid: Alianza.
Zucchini, Francesco. 1997. "La decisione di voto: I tempi, l'oggetto, i modi." In Parisi and Corbetta 1997.

Contributors

Anna Bosco is an assistant professor of political science at the University of Trieste and Assistant Editor for Italy of the journal *South European Society and Politics*. She is the author of *Comunisti: Trasformazioni di partito in Italia, Spagna e Portogallo* (Communists: Party Change in Italy, Spain and Portugal).

Risa A. Brooks completed her dissertation in political science at the University of California, San Diego, and is a postdoctoral fellow at the Center for International Security and Cooperation at Stanford University.

Thomas C. Bruneau is a professor of national security affairs at the Naval Postgraduate School in Monterey, California. He is also the director for Latin America at the Center for Civil-Military Relations. In addition to his many joint publications with Mário Bacalhau, his most recent publication on Iberia is *Political Parties and Democracy in Portugal*.

P. Nikiforos Diamandouros is a professor of political science at the University of Athens, co-chair of the Social Science Research Council's Subcommittee on Southern Europe, and the national Ombudsman of Greece. His recent publications include "Democratization in Southeastern Europe: Theoretical Considerations and Evolving Trends," "Southern Europe: A Third Wave Success Story," and *The Origins of State-Building in Modern Greece, 1821–1828* (in Greek).

Richard Gunther is a professor of political science and Executive Director of International Studies at the Ohio State University and co-chair of the Social Science Research Council's Subcommittee on

Southern Europe. His principal publications include *Public Policy in a No-Party State, Spain After Franco* (with Giacomo Sani and Goldie Shabad), *Elites and Democratic Consolidation in Latin America and Southern Europe* (with John Higley), *Politics, Society and Democracy: The Case of Spain,* and *Democracy and the Media* (with Anthony Mughan).

Arend Lijphart is a research professor emeritus of political science at the University of California, San Diego. His principal publications include *The Politics of Accommodation, Democracy in Plural Societies, Democracies, Power-Sharing in South Africa, Electoral Systems and Party Systems,* and *Patterns of Democracy.*

José R. Montero is a professor of political science at the Universidad Autónoma de Madrid and at the Centro de Estudios Avanzados en Ciencias Sociales, Instituto Juan March, Madrid. He is a member of the Standing Committee for the Social Sciences, European Science Foundation, and has served as director of the Economics and Social Science Program of the Comisión Interministerial de Ciencia y Tecnología and as deputy director of the Centro de Investigaciones Sociológicas. He has published extensively on parties, political culture, voting behavior, and electoral systems.

Leonardo Morlino is a professor of political science at the University of Florence, chair of the Italian Political Science Association (1999–2002), and director of the Research Center on Southern Europe. His main publications include *Como cambian los regímenes, Democracy Between Consolidation and Crisis, Parties, Groups and Citizens in Southern Europe,* and *Democrazie e democratizzazioni.*

Takis S. Pappas teaches politics at College Year in Athens. He is the author of *Making Party Democracy in Greece* and *Eastern Europe's Wheels of Change: Departures from Communism in Comparative Perspective.*

Gianfranco Pasquino is a professor of political science at the University of Bologna and adjunct professor of politics at the Bologna Center of the Johns Hopkins University. For 2001 he is Fellow of Christchurch at Oxford. His most recent publications are *Capire l'Europa* and *La Transizione a parole.* He is co-editor of and contributor to the 2000 edition of the yearbook *Politics in Italy.*

Hans-Jürgen Puhle is a professor of political science at the Goethe University of Frankfurt am Main. His principal publications include

Politische Agrarbewegungen in kapitalistischen Industrigesellschaften, Revolution und Reformen in Lateinamerika, Bürger in der Gesellschaft der Neuzeit, Bauern im Widerstand, Von der Arbeiterbewegung zum modernen Sozialstaat, Staaten, Nationen und Regionen in Europa, and *Von der Diktatur zur Demokratie.*

Giacomo Sani is a professor of political science at the University of Pavia and professor emeritus at Ohio State University. His principal publications include *Spain After Franco* (with Richard Gunther and Goldie Shabad), *Il mercato elettorale* (with Renato Mannheimer), and *La rivoluzzione elettorale* (with Renato Mannheimer).

Paolo Segatti is an associate professor of political science at the University of Trieste. His research and publications have analyzed Italian political culture and voting behavior and the transformation of the Italian political system. Among his most recent publications (with Marco Maraffi and Paolo Bellucci) is *PCI, PDS, DS.*

Index